Counseling Across the Lifespan

*This book is dedicated to our respective families,
for helping us understand firsthand the importance of
development across the lifespan.*

Counseling Across the Lifespan

Prevention and Treatment

Edited by

Cindy L. Juntunen
University of North Dakota

Donald R. Atkinson
University of California, Santa Barbara

Sage Publications
International Educational and Professional Publisher
Thousand Oaks ▪ London ▪ New Delhi

For information:

Sage Publications, Inc.
2455 Teller Road
Thousand Oaks, California 91320
E-mail: order@sagepub.com

Sage Publications Ltd.
6 Bonhill Street
London EC2A 4PU
United Kingdom

Sage Publications India Pvt. Ltd.
M-32 Market
Greater Kailash I
New Delhi 110 048 India

Printed in the United States of America

Library of Congress Cataloging-in-Publication Data

Counseling across the lifespan: Prevention and treatment / edited by
Cindy L. Juntunen and Donald R. Atkinson.
    p. cm.
Includes bibliographical references and index.
  ISBN 0-7619-2395-0 (cloth: alk. paper)
  1. Counseling. 2. Developmental psychology. I. Juntunen, Cindy Lee.
II. Atkinson, Donald R.
  BF637.C6 C633 2001
  361´.06—dc21   2001002251

        03   04   05   10   9   8   7   6   5   4   3   2

Acquiring Editor:	Nancy S. Hale
Editorial Assistant:	Vonessa Vondera
Production Editor:	Diane S. Foster
Editorial Assistant:	Kathryn Journey
Copy Editor:	Barbara Coster
Typesetter/Designer:	Marion Warren
Proofreader:	Joyce Kuhn
Indexer:	Rachel Rice
Cover Designer:	Jane Quaney

CONTENTS

PREFACE

A s academics with a combined 37 years of university teaching experience, we have felt a growing frustration with the increasing emphasis placed in counselor and counseling psychology training programs on diagnosing and treating psychopathology. We document in Chapter 1 a number of historical reasons for this trend, including changing economic conditions, the privatization of psychological services, and trainee enchantment with the intricacies of treating a debilitating mental disorder. The result has been that counselor and counseling psychology training programs now routinely offer an assessment course that covers *Diagnostic and Statistical Manual of Mental Disorders (DSM)* and courses in counseling theories and techniques that focus almost exclusively on treatment strategies for *DSM* diagnoses. Lost in the process is attention to treating the life adjustment problems experienced by the average person. Methods for preventing these problems and for promoting healthy development receive even less attention.

However, the reality is that everyone faces life adjustment problems, although only a relatively small minority of individuals qualify for *DSM* diagnoses. Most mental health practitioners (even those trained as clinical social workers and clinical psychologists) spend the majority of their time working with clients who have normal life adjustment problems such as schooling difficulties, relationship problems, career choices and changes, parenting concerns, and meaning-of-life issues. Furthermore, the managed care movement of the 1990s, with the goal of reducing the excessive treatment costs associated with fully developed mental illness, has placed a premium on the prevention of mental health problems.

This book was born out of our concern that counselors, counseling psychologists, social workers, and other mental health practitioners are not being adequately trained to deal with the life adjustment problems that almost everyone experiences in the course of their lifetime. We are concerned that implicit in the current emphasis on pathology and psychotherapy is the assumption that direct service providers need not be trained in the strategies of preventing mental illness, that if service providers understand the nature and treatment of mental illness, they will be able to develop effective strategies for preventing pathology. We take issue with this assumption, and we believe that counselors, counseling psychologists, and other mental health practitioners need a strong foundation in normal human development and problem prevention strategies in order to meet the mental health needs of the 21st century.

This book is designed for use in courses that cover counseling theories, techniques, and issues. For example, it might be used as the primary text in an introduction to counseling class to acquaint students with the important role that preventive counseling strategies can play in their future careers as counselors. It might be used in a counseling and psychotherapy techniques course to supplement an existing text on psychotherapy theory and techniques. Or it might be used as a required reading in a practicum course in which students are confronted with the reality of having to design preventive and treatment interventions for developmental concerns.

After an introduction that identifies the need for a developmental, preventive emphasis, the book is organized by developmental stages across a person's lifespan. Chapters within each lifespan stage identify a specific concern associated with that stage of human development. Although some of the concerns are relevant to more than one life stage, we have placed them in the life stage where they initially develop or can best be prevented. Each chapter documents the prevalence of the concern and how it can lead to serious mental health problems. Prevention theory and techniques are discussed, and an example of at least one successful prevention program is provided. Explicit examples of counseling interventions are woven throughout the chapters, providing readers with an array of strategies that can be applied with clients in a variety of situations. Vignettes to stimulate further thinking about how to design prevention programs are included in each chapter along with additional resources to aid mental health practitioners in implementing prevention programs.

The topics in the book include issues that many or most people are likely to encounter such as making decisions about relationships, choosing behaviors that will affect health, and making transitions in education and vocational settings. Also included are issues such as abuse and violence, which some may not consider developmental in nature. However, as the authors of these chapters demonstrate, the high prevalence of violence has an impact on a large proportion of our population, either directly or indirectly, and its presence in the life of a client does not assume pathology or mental illness on the part of the client. Therefore, preventive and treatment strategies for violence-related issues are included in recognition of the increasing likelihood that clients will present these concerns as primary.

We believe this book fills a void in counselor, counseling psychology, social work, and other mental health practitioner training programs created by the overemphasis on pathology and psychotherapy. That void often becomes apparent when student practitioners meet clients who have real concerns that are not readily explained by a *DSM* diagnosis. Such clients are often best served by a counselor who can think in terms of prevention and promotion of personal strengths rather than remediation of an illness. We hope the book will enhance the ability of counselors to meet client needs and contribute to a resurgence of interest in preventive counseling as a means of reducing both mental health suffering and costs.

—Cindy L. Juntunen
—Donald R. Atkinson

PART I

Introduction

CHAPTER 1

Counseling in the 21st Century

A Mental Health Profession Comes of Age

Donald R. Atkinson

Over the course of the 20th century, counseling grew from an educator role that supplemented vocational guidance to a full-blown profession in its own right. The foundation of the profession, laid in the first decade of the last century, included a heavy commitment to preventing problems, promoting development, and resolving concerns for "normal" (nonpsychotic) people of all ages. Although the two major professional organizations that represent counselors have continued to acknowledge the important role of prevention, professional interest in prevention and development has waned since the mid-1970s (Conyne, 2000). Now the counseling profession has an opportunity to capitalize on current societal interest in prevention for both mental and physical health care, provided that counselors are willing and able to reembrace their philosophical foundations.

The purpose of this chapter is to review the history of counselor education and counseling psychology and document their shared foundation in prevention and development. This historical perspective helps explain why counselors are so well suited to seize the initiative in the mental health movement toward greater emphasis on prevention. The chapter also examines why prevention has played a secondary role to remediation in mental health policy and practice and provides evidence that the time is right for counselors to reembrace prevention as a primary professional role.

EMERGENCE OF COUNSELING AS A PROFESSION

The emergence and maturation of counseling as a profession occurred in two stages over the course of the 20th century, with roughly the first 50 years being a role development stage and the last 50 years a profession development stage. Most historical accounts of counseling trace the roots of the profession to the educational guidance, vocational guidance, and mental health movements of the early 1900s (Aubrey, 1986; Gladding, 1996; Whitely, 1980).

The First Half-Century: A Period of Role Development

The conception of the educational guidance movement is usually attributed to Jesse B. Davis, a principal in the Grand Rapids, Michigan, school system, who instituted weekly guidance lessons in English classes in 1907 with the goal of building character and preventing problems. Frank Parsons, often referred to as the father of guidance, is credited with establishing vocational guidance when he founded Boston's Vocational Bureau in 1908 (Aubrey, 1986). The birth of the mental health movement is usually associated with the publication of *A Mind That Found Itself* by Clifford Beers in 1908.

Although the mental health movement of the early 1900s provided counseling with a foundation in prevention, most of the professional activities that would lead to the development of a counseling profession occurred within the vocational guidance track. The first national professional organization to represent counselors, vocational or otherwise, was the National Vocational Guidance Association (NVGA), founded in 1913. The first professional journal for counselors was *National Vocational Guidance Bulletin,* which was published by the NVGA and began appearing on a regular basis in 1921. Two major historical events prior to 1940 also contributed significantly to the growth of vocational guidance. Both World War I and the Great Depression created an increased need for vocational guidance, the former to place (mostly) men in the rapidly expanding roles within the military and the latter to match unemployed workers with the jobs that were available.

Although historical events in the United States prior to 1940 gave impetus to vocational guidance, the seeds of counseling as a unique role and a profession were germinating during this time. According to Aubrey (1986),

> although the formal recognition of counseling did not occur until after almost three decades of vocational guidance, this acknowledgment was long overdue. Even a cursory reading of such early guidance leaders as Parsons (1909), Bloomfield (1915), or Kitson (1915) reveals traces of what later was to be called counseling. Furthermore, counseling as a psychological process is apparent in much of the legacy of the early mental health movement, the work of G. Stanley Hall and his disciples in the child-study movement, the introduction of psycho-

analysis to the United States in 1909 by Freud's lectures at Clark University, and in the application of psychometrics during and following World War I. (p. 7)

The extension of counseling beyond the vocational arena into other aspects of human development was given a major boost with the publication of *Counseling and Psychotherapy* by Carl Rogers in 1942. The impact of Rogers and this book on the development of the counseling profession can hardly be overstated. For the first time, the conditions for both remediating personal problems and facilitating personal development were combined under one rubric. Rogers is also credited with formally recognizing for the first time that "problems of adjustment in one aspect of living have effects on other aspects of life, and of the complexity of the processes of counseling concerning any type of individual adjustment" (Super, 1984, p. 18). Furthermore, by setting forth core conditions for remediating problems and promoting development, Rogers challenged the long years and rigid standards of training required by psychoanalytic theory to become an agent of therapeutic change. For the first time, it became evident that school counselors, college counselors, vocational counselors, rehabilitation counselors, social workers, and other mental health workers could provide the conditions needed to facilitate client attitudinal and behavioral change without the lengthy training traditionally required of psychiatrists. According to Aubrey (1986), the widespread acceptance of Rogers's theory and philosophy in the 1940s led directly to a major shift from guidance to counseling as the primary function of counselors in schools and other settings.

The return to the United States of military personnel following the end of World War II was another event that contributed significantly to the development of counseling as a profession. Immediately following the war, the federal government pumped large sums of money into the Veterans Administration (VA) in order to address the physical, psychological, and vocational needs of returning veterans as well as to meet the need in the United States for more highly trained and educated white-collar and professional workers. In a move that had major ramifications for the professionalization of counseling, the VA established the position of "counseling psychologist" to address the psychological and vocational needs of veterans. Numerous veterans enrolled in college upon returning home, supported by VA funds and the GI bill. Federal money was also made available to help colleges hire psychologists to address the educational, psychological, and vocational needs of these returning veterans. Many of these psychologists identified themselves as counseling psychologists (Gelso & Fretz, 1992).

Thus, by the end of the first half of the 20th century the majority of counselors were working in educational settings (kindergarten through college) and VA hospitals. For the most part, counselors in the late 1940s shared a common interest in preventing problems and promoting career and personal development. Although some counselors at that point in time provided treatment to children and young adults experiencing psychological problems, few of them would have claimed that they were primarily treating individuals who were psychologically dysfunctional.

The Second Half-Century: A Period of Professional Development

Two professional organizations were established in 1952 that would pull together various counseling specialties while bifurcating counseling as a profession on the important issue of minimal training for professional competence. The American Personnel and Guidance Association (APGA) was formed that year when the National Vocational Guidance Association (NVGA) merged with several other associations, each of which was given divisional status in the new organization. The four divisions that comprised the APGA in 1952 were the NVGA, the National Association of Guidance Supervisors and Counselor Trainers, the American College Personnel Association, and the Student Personnel Association for Teacher Education (Gladding, 1996).

During the last half of the 20th century, the organization that began as the APGA underwent two name changes that reflected an increased commitment to counseling as a profession. In 1983, the APGA changed its name to the American Association for Counseling and Development (AACD), and in 1992 the name was changed again to the American Counseling Association (ACA). These name changes came after considerable soul-searching and debate on the part of the membership. According to Gladding (1996), "there was a growing awareness among its leaders that the words *personnel* and *guidance* no longer described the work of its members" (p. 18) and that "the new name (American Counseling Association) better reflected the membership and mission of the organization" (p. 19).

The name changes also reflected a gradual evolution from a primarily vocational and educational counseling focus to a broad array of counseling professions. By the end of the 20th century, the four original divisions of the APGA had expanded to 17 ACA divisions and included newer divisions for marriage and family counselors, mental health counselors, and college counselors in addition to the older divisions for vocational counselors, school counselors, and rehabilitation counselors. As the APGA evolved into a more comprehensive professional organization for counselors, it became actively involved in promoting credentials for professional counselors. During the 1970s, the APGA accepted master's degree training as the standard for professional competence and began lobbying for state licensure of master's-level counselors. Virginia became the first state to license counselors in 1976. As of 1999, 45 states plus the District of Columbia licensed professional counselors.

The second half of the 20th century also witnessed the professionalization of counseling as a specialization within the already established discipline of psychology. In 1952, the same year that the APGA was formed, Division 17 of the American Psychological Association changed its name from Counseling and Guidance to Counseling Psychology, reflecting a desire on the part of members to identify as counselors and psychologists while deemphasizing guidance as a professional activity. Because the American Psychological Association (APA), as the parent organization, had established the doctoral degree as the minimal level of training for unsupervised service providers, a doctoral degree in psychology was (and continues to be) required for membership in Division 17 (counseling psychologists who hold a terminal master's degree may join the organization as associates).

Most counseling psychologists in the 1950s worked in higher education (Sampler, 1980). Due to the expansion of insurance coverage to include some mental health treatments in the 1960s, cutbacks in federal support for public mental health services in the 1970s, and privatization of psychology in the 1980s, however, counseling psychologists increasingly looked to settings outside higher education for employment opportunities. Responding to the demands of students, many counselor training programs housed in departments other than psychology made efforts to ensure that their graduates could be licensed as psychologists (Gelso & Fretz, 1992). These efforts included changing the title of their department or degree, or both, to include counseling psychology, changing their curriculum to meet APA accreditation requirements, and lobbying state psychology licensing boards to ensure that their graduates could sit for the psychology licensing examination.

Thus, by the 1990s, many counselors and counseling psychologists were licensed to provide psychotherapy in private practice. The result was a shift in focus for many professional counselors from preventing problems and promoting development to remediation of problems. A number of studies had already found that there was little difference between the professional activities of counseling psychologists and clinical psychologists (Fitzgerald & Osipow, 1986; Goldschmitt, Tipton, & Wiggins, 1981; Osipow, Cohen, Jenkins, & Dostal, 1979; Tipton, 1983; Watkins, Lopez, Campbell, & Himmell, 1986). Gelso and Fretz (1992) reviewed some of these studies and concluded that "there is consistent evidence that far more time is being spent [by counseling psychologists] on remedial, therapeutic activities than on the preventive and developmental/educational activities that have long been identified as major themes in the profession" (p. 5).

PREVENTION AND FOCUS ON NORMAL DEVELOPMENT
STILL ASSOCIATED WITH THE COUNSELING PROFESSION

Although increasing numbers of counseling and counseling psychology practitioners are licensed for private practice, and although surveys indicate that they spend most of their time on remediation of client problems, the counseling profession continues to identify with prevention and development. Recently, Gladding (1996) examined definitions of counseling offered by both the ACA and Division 17 of the APA and identified the following common points:

1. Counseling is a profession (p. 6).
2. Counseling deals with personal, social, vocational, empowerment, and educational concerns (p. 7).
3. Counseling is conducted with persons who are considered to function within the "normal range" (p. 7).
4. Counseling is theory based and takes place in a structured setting (p. 8).
5. Counseling is a process in which clients learn how to make decisions and formulate new ways of behaving, feeling, and thinking (p. 8).
6. Counseling encompasses various subspecialties (p. 8).

Drawing on the professional literature, Gelso and Fretz (1992) identified three roles and five unifying themes of counseling psychology; these roles and themes also can be found throughout ACA publications describing professional counseling. The three roles they identified are prevention, remediation, and development. The five unifying themes they identified are these:

1. The focus on intact, as opposed to severely disturbed, personalities (p. 7)
2. The focus on people's assets and strengths and on positive mental health, *regardless* of the degree of disturbance (p. 8)
3. An emphasis on relatively brief interventions (p. 8)
4. An emphasis on person-environment interactions rather than an exclusive focus on either the person or the environment (p. 9)
5. An emphasis on educational and career development of individuals and on educational and vocational environments (p. 9)

Thus, both counselors and counseling psychologists continue to be trained to focus on prevention and treatment of normal life adjustment concerns. Before discussing how this focus places counseling in an excellent position to address the mental and physical health needs of society in the foreseeable future, we briefly examine how prevention differs from treatment and how preventive counseling, remedial counseling, and psychotherapy differ from each other.

DISTINGUISHING PREVENTION AND TREATMENT INTERVENTIONS

According to Albee and Ryan-Finn (1993), the historical antecedents of prevention can be found in the methods of public health in the early part of the

20th century and of treatment in the rise of psychotherapy in the latter part of the 19th century. Albee and Ryan-Finn credit Clifford Beers and the public health and psychiatry faculty at Johns Hopkins University for initiating the mental hygiene movement in the first decade of the 20th century and for drawing attention to the need for preventive programs. They attribute the foundation for mental health treatment to the work of Sigmund Freud and the psychotherapy movement.

Mental health prevention and treatment programs ostensibly have very different goals and target very different populations. The goal of prevention is the deterrence of anticipated mental health problems and the maintenance and enhancement of normal social and psychological development. Normally functioning people or people at risk are targets for prevention programs (Conyne, 1997). Parent training programs, designed to increase knowledge about child-rearing practices and enhance child-rearing skills, are an example of a preventive approach to mental health problems. The goal of treatment, on the other hand, is the amelioration of existing mental health problems; people who are already experiencing the problem are targeted for treatment. Alcohol abuse programs, designed to eliminate problem drinking, are an example of a treatment approach to a mental health problem.

Although it is quite easy in the abstract to distinguish prevention from treatment, it is often difficult to make this distinction in practice. Treatment of one type of problem behavior may actually prevent another type of problem. For example, smoking cessation programs are aimed at stopping smoking behavior, but they also have the effect of preventing health problems. Furthermore, some programs designed to prevent future problems are offered in concert with treatment for past problems. Child abuse prevention programs, for example, often combine prevention with treatment of child abuse victims and survivors. Thus, Conyne (1994) suggests that prevention exists on a continuum with treatment. To better understand this continuum, it is useful to further distinguish between *primary, secondary,* and *tertiary* prevention programs. Durlak (1995) defines primary prevention as "intervention with normal populations to preclude the occurrence of problems" (p. 2), secondary prevention as "intervention during the early development of difficulties" (p. 3), and tertiary prevention as intervention designed "to reduce the prevalence of established disorders or problems" (p. 3). Thus, tertiary prevention, which is intended to reduce the prevalence and long-term effects of established problems, overlaps considerably with remediative and rehabilitative treatment interventions.

Other characteristics serve to distinguish types of prevention programs. Durlak (1995) points out that some prevention programs are person centered and some are environment centered. Person-centered prevention programs involve direct intervention with individuals and typically include skill-building or competency-building activities. A drug abuse education program for elementary school students that teaches them how to say no to drugs is an example of a person-centered prevention program. Environment-centered programs focus on changing the environment, with the goal of having an indirect effect on individuals. Providing escorts after dark on a university campus for students walking to and from their residence halls or their sources of transportation is an example of an environment-centered prevention program.

Durlak (1995) also identifies three categories of prevention programs based on the types of people they target. Some prevention programs are designed for application to everyone in a given population; this type of intervention is sometimes referred to as a *universal preventive intervention*. Providing drug abuse education for all seventh-grade students in a school district is an example of a universal prevention program. Another type of program (*selective preventive intervention*) is intended only for those individuals considered to be at risk for a particular problem. Providing a special language and reading program for students whose parents neither read nor write English is an example of a selective prevention program aimed at an at-risk population. The third type of preventive program (*indicated preventive intervention*) targets individuals who manifest behaviors that are precursory to some dysfunctional behavior. A program to redirect a second grader's aggressive tendencies with the goal of avoiding evolution into conduct disorder is an example of indicated prevention.

With this overview of mental health prevention and treatment intervention programs as a background, we next examine how prevention and treatment are manifested in counseling.

PREVENTIVE COUNSELING, REMEDIAL COUNSELING, AND PSYCHOTHERAPY

Conyne (1997) defines preventive counseling as "the programmatic, before-the-fact application of comprehensive counseling methods with healthy or at-risk groups to enhance competencies and avert dysfunction" (p. 260) and distinguishes it from remedial counseling, which "is applied after the fact to correct already occurring dysfunction within an individual, group, or family system" (p. 260). Ten defining qualities of preventive counseling were presented in Conyne (1994):

1. It is before the fact.
2. It focuses on healthy people or people at risk.
3. It is used to reduce incidence.
4. It is group- and population-based.
5. It is used to reduce risk factors and to increase protective factors.
6. It is ecological and systemic.
7. It is culturally sensitive and valid.

8. It is concerned with social justice and is intended to include minority-group representation.

9. It is collaborative.

10. It is empowering. (pp. 3-4)

On the basis of a survey of graduate students in counseling and other helping professions over a 9-year period, Conyne (1997) also identifies 10 preventive counseling skills clusters. Although some of the 10 skills clusters overlap with skills needed for remedial counseling, several are somewhat unique to preventive counseling. These include a primary prevention perspective, social marketing skills, collaboration skills, and organization and setting dynamics skills. For a discussion of these and the other six skills clusters, the reader is referred to Conyne (1997).

The remedial function of counseling is often mistakenly viewed as psychotherapy. Notwithstanding a few authors who have argued that counseling and psychotherapy are indistinguishable, counselors and counseling psychologists generally agree that remedial counseling and psychotherapy can be conceptualized as distinctly different across a number of criteria. These criteria include type of problem, etiology of the problem, role of the client, role of the helper, and treatment process (Gelso & Fretz, 1992; Gladding, 1996; Super, 1984).

In terms of type of problem, remedial counseling focuses on life adjustment and subclinical problems experienced by many otherwise "normal" people; psychotherapy focuses on *DSM-IV*-diagnosable psychopathology experienced by a relatively small percentage of the population. Problems addressed in remedial counseling are often of an interpersonal nature, involving conflicts with other people, institutions, or some aspect of the environment. Problems addressed in psychotherapy focus on internal, intrapsychic conflicts. In remedial counseling, clients are actively involved in determining the goal of treatment; in psychotherapy, typically they are not. The helper role in counseling treatment is that of facilitator, someone who helps the client marshal resources to resolve the problem. The helper role in psychotherapy is that of an expert who assesses, diagnoses, and treats the problem (Gelso & Fretz, 1992; Gladding, 1996). These differences in goal setting and helper role are not trivial, as anyone who has experienced both traditional counseling and traditional psychotherapy can readily attest.

Admittedly, the cost-containment exigencies of managed care have tended to blur other distinctions between remedial counseling and psychotherapy in recent years, particularly with regard to length of treatment and treatment setting. Traditionally, psychotherapy has involved a long-term relationship (often 20 or more sessions), whereas remedial counseling has involved a short-term relationship (fewer than 12 sessions). However, managed care has forced psychotherapists to rely increasingly on "brief" psychotherapy to treat their clients, and treatment plans in excess of 6 sessions are often routinely disapproved. Also, historically, a significant proportion of psychotherapy has taken place in inpatient settings like residential treatment facilities, whereas remedial counseling has usually taken place in outpatient settings like educational facilities and community agencies. However, efforts by managed care companies to reduce the costs associated with inpatient treatment have greatly reduced the provision of psychotherapy in residential treatment facilities. Interestingly, these changes brought about by the managed care industry's efforts to contain treatment costs has moved psychotherapy in the direction of remedial counseling, rather than vice versa, suggesting that remedial counseling (or brief psychotherapy) is the more cost efficient of the two forms of treatment. As indicated by Cummings, Budman, and Thomas (1998), some evidence exists to suggest that these cost savings associated with short-term treatment can be made without loss of treatment effectiveness: "In over 20 years of research, Cummings and his colleagues found that if psychotherapists were trained in short-term as well as long-term therapies, 85% of patients responded to therapy in under 15 sessions (with a mean of 8.6)" (p. 462).

What remedial counseling and psychotherapy have in common, however, is that they are both forms of remediative treatment; that is, they both involve the remediation of existing client problems. As will become evident in the next section, both remedial counseling and psychotherapy often compete with preventive counseling for scarce resources.

PREVENTION AND TREATMENT INTERVENTIONS COMPETE FOR MENTAL HEALTH FUNDING

Conflicting views about the etiology of mental illness have created an unfortunate tension among policymakers between the proponents of prevention programs and the proponents of treatment programs. In general, liberal politicians see poverty as the cause of social ills and are therefore responsive to prevention programs, whereas political conservatives tend to blame individuals for their problems and to oppose prevention programs that are seen as reflecting a policy of social change. Proponents of prevention programs often argue that the best use of scarce mental health resources is to alleviate the social and environmental conditions associated with mental health problems. For example, as support for their position, they point to the numerous epidemiological studies that have shown very poor people at the highest risk for mental disorders. Proponents of treatment programs typically attribute mental illness to physical and organic causes and argue that remediation of existing problems should be a priority for scarce resources.

Albee and Ryan-Finn (1993) point out that a strong prevention philosophy emerged in the mental health field in the 1960s and early 1970s following publication of the final report of the Joint Commission on Mental Illness and Health. Publication of the final volume of that report in 1960

> led President Kennedy to propose, for the first time in American history, the use of federal funds for the development of an effective system of intervention in the field of mental disorders. Included in his message to Congress was the urgent request for funding for efforts at prevention and community interventions. . . . President Johnson's War on Poverty encouraged a social psychiatry that had as its goal the reduction of the miserable living conditions that apparently spawned high rates of mental disorders, alcoholism, and drug use. The Commission on Mental Health appointed by President Carter included in its final report a proposal for major increases in prevention efforts. With the election of Ronald Reagan in 1980, all these efforts came to an abrupt halt. (Albee & Ryan-Finn, 1993, p. 116)

However, in 1990, President George H. W. Bush's administration initiated Healthy People 2000, once again bringing attention to the role of prevention in physical and mental health. As part of Healthy People 2000, the U.S. Department of Health and Human Services (HHS) developed "healthy objectives" for the nation that were to be achieved by the year 2000. The Healthy People initiative was expanded upon during President Bill Clinton's administration: A total of 467 objectives were identified in 28 health-related areas as part of Healthy People 2010. The prevention focus of the initiative is reflected in the introduction by HHS Secretary Donna Shalala to Healthy People 2010:

> [Healthy People 2010] represents an opportunity for individuals to make healthy lifestyle choices for themselves and their families. It challenges clinicians to put prevention into their practices. It requires communities and businesses to support health-promoting policies in schools, worksites, and other settings. (U.S. Department of Health and Human Services, 2000, p. i)

Mental illness was included as 1 of 10 Leading Health Indicators in Healthy People 2010. Furthermore, all the other nine indicators included environmental and lifestyle factors (e.g., physical activity, substance abuse, environmental quality) that could be addressed through preventive counseling interventions.

Healthy People 2010 notwithstanding, a bias exists among mental health service providers, as well as policy makers, that favors treatment programs over preventive programs. According to Albee and Ryan-Finn (1993), financial incentives have historically made treatment programs more attractive than prevention programs between both physical and mental health practitioners:

Our medical system, as well as our psychotherapeutic delivery system, gains extensive personal and monetary rewards for engaging in and espousing individual treatment. Because of the high cost incurred during such treatment, however, there is little money available for prevention and little acceptance of a prevention philosophy by mainstream medicine and psychology. (p. 116)

This may explain why counseling practitioners, counselor educators, and counseling researchers seem so enamored with remedial counseling (and psychotherapy) and give so little attention to prevention by comparison. This bias among practitioners was noted by Gelso and Fretz (1992), who observed that counseling psychologists devote more time to remediation than to prevention or development (p. 6). The preference among counseling practitioners for remediation over prevention is not surprising, given a similar bias in counselor training programs. A recent survey suggests that counselor educators support the philosophy of primary prevention, but that training in prevention gets short shrift in counselor training programs because counselor educators do not perceive a societal demand for prevention (Kleist & White, 1997). A similar effect occurs in counseling research; after reviewing school counseling outcome research published between 1988 and 1995, Whiston and Sexton (1998) concluded that "the large number of studies in the responsive services area might also suggest that researchers, and potentially counselors, may be more interested in remediating problems rather than focusing on developmental or preventive programs" (p. 76). The dynamics of tenure review at most major universities may help account for researcher prioritization of treatment research over prevention research. As Holden and Black (1999) point out, longitudinal prevention research is both time consuming and expensive and therefore not the kind of research that nontenured university faculty are likely to pursue. Thus, the university system of granting tenure based on research published within the first 6 years of a professor's career provides an incentive for counseling and psychology professors to establish a record of short-term treatment research rather than long-term prevention research.

To garner support for primary prevention programs, advocates must demonstrate that they are effective at preventing problems. Although much more research has been done on problem remediation than on problem prevention, a recent meta-analysis of 177 primary prevention programs did provide evidence that programs designed to prevent behavioral and social problems in children and adolescents were effective (Durlak & Wells, 1997).

Part of the difficulty in garnering support for programs aimed at primary prevention of social ills is the difficulty in proving not only that they are effective, but that they are cost-effective as well. It is much easier to demonstrate the cost-effectiveness of remedial interventions; the costs of interventions that are effective in eliminating a problem can be compared to determine which is most cost-effective. Determining cost-effectiveness for prevention programs involves not only determining how much the prevention program costs but also estimating the savings obtained by eliminating future remediation expenses. Without long-term, longitudinal studies that follow up on individuals who have either received or not received a prevention intervention, there is no sure way to prove that prevention programs are producing cost savings by eliminating the need for subsequent treatment programs.

Cohen (1998) provided an example of how the monetary value of "saving" youths at risk of dropping out of school, committing crimes, abusing drugs, and engaging in other forms of delinquency might be appraised in terms of potential benefits and savings. He estimated the potential benefits associated with saving a high-risk youth by estimating the lifetime costs associated with the typical high-school dropout, career criminal, and drug abuser. Based primarily on lost wages, work productivity, and fringe benefits, he estimated that the typical cost of dropping out of school is between $243,000 and $388,000 per person. In estimating the costs associated with a heavy drug user, Cohen included costs associated with the manufacture and sale of drugs, drug rehabilitation, decreased work ability, medical treatment, drug overdose, crime committed by drug users, and criminal justice system involvement. The total cost associated with heavy drug use was determined to be between $370,000 and $970,000. In accounting for the costs associated with a career criminal, Cohen included costs to the victim and criminal justice system as well as lost wages during the time of incarceration. Estimates of costs for the career criminal ranged from $1.3 million to $1.5 million. On the basis of these figures and the costs of typical prevention programs, Cohen estimated that

> a [high school] graduation incentive program would need a success rate of at least 3 to 5% to be cost-beneficial. Delinquent supervision, which costs about $10,000 per participant, would need only about a 1 in 1,000 success rate to recover the benefits of saving one youth from becoming a career criminal. (p. 30)

Thus, school dropout and delinquency prevention programs only need to save a small percentage of juveniles from dropping out of school or from entering a career of crime in order to be cost-effective.

Although the United States is considered by most of the world to be a privileged nation, one in which the majority of citizens live in relative affluence, numerous social concerns afflict large portions of the U.S. population that could be addressed by primary prevention programs. The public became increasingly aware of the need for primary prevention programs in our schools during the late 1990s as the result of the highly publicized tragic shootings involving students in Jonesboro, Arkansas, Springfield, Oregon, Littleton, Colorado, and elsewhere (Barovick et al., 1999). School violence and many other social problems afflicting large portions of the United States could be addressed through preventive counseling. The following are just a few examples (figures taken from the 1999 edition of *Statistical Abstract of the United States* [U.S. Bureau of the Census, 1999], unless otherwise noted):

▶ 12.8% of the babies born in 1997 were born to teenage mothers.

▶ Although the number of adolescents giving birth have stabilized at about 500,000 per year, the number of out-of-wedlock births for adolescents is increasing (Solomon & Liefeld, 1998).

▶ 48,266 new cases of AIDS were reported in 1998.

▶ More than 870,000 divorces or marriage annulments occurred in 1997.

▶ Almost 1 in 20 (4.9%) students in Grades 10 to 12 dropped out of school in 1997; among Hispanic students, the rate was 7.3%.

▶ 2,700,369 children were the subject of a child abuse or neglect report in 1997; 889,665 cases of child abuse were substantiated that year.

▶ Approximately one third of all girls experience some from of sexual harassment before seventh grade; four out of five experience it before they graduate from high school (American Association of University Women, 1993).

▶ Almost a million (929,166) clients used substance abuse treatment services in 1995.

▶ 1,758,000 delinquency offenses were disposed in juvenile courts in 1996.

Some of these problems are the result of lifestyle choices on the part of individuals. Others are the result of antisocial behavior on the part of perpetrators. What these and many other social problems confronting U.S. society share in common is that they are preventable. Clearly, preventive and remedial counseling can and should play an important role in preventing and remediating these social problems.

COUNSELING AS A MEANS OF PREVENTING PHYSICAL HEALTH PROBLEMS

Although the counseling profession has traditionally focused on the prevention and treatment of mental health problems, recently counselors have recognized their role in the prevention of physical health problems. As explained by Lewis, Sperry, and Carlson (1993), this new role for counselors is a spin-off of changes that have taken place in the physical health care system.

A century ago, infectious diseases were the leading causes of death. Now, although diseases such as tuberculosis, measles, poliomyelitis, influenza, and pneumonia are still present, they can be treated through medical means that are at our disposal. In contrast, illnesses and disabilities related to life-styles show few signs of abatement. . . . The afflictions that affect the largest number of people today are of the type that are more likely to be affected by behavioral interventions than by strict reliance on traditional medicine. And behavioral interventions are clearly in the counselor's bailiwick! (p. 5)

Physical health practitioners have been aware for some time that many of the serious health problems confronting the United States are the result of dysfunctional lifestyle choices and are therefore preventable. According to Cummings (1977), more than 69% of visits to medical doctors in the 1960s and early 1970s involved physical symptoms that had an emotional rather than an organic etiology. McGinnis and Foege (1993) reviewed government records and published medical reports "to identify and quantify the major external (nongenetic) factors that contribute to death in the United States" (p. 2207). Although death certificates normally cite the primary pathophysiological conditions (e.g., heart disease, cancer, cerebrovascular disease) found at the time of death, these medical conditions are often not the actual or root cause of the condition leading to death. In their analysis of the approximately 2,148,000 deaths reported in 1990, McGinnis and Foege determined that about half were the result of external factors and that many of the external factors were a function of lifestyle choices. As can be seen in Table 1.1, the three leading external causes of death were found to be tobacco use, dietary factors and activity patterns, and alcohol consumption, accounting for approximately 800,000 deaths in 1990 (or approximately 37% of all deaths that year). Furthermore, McGinnis and Foege speculated that "although immunizations and infection control measures already prevent as many as 135 million infections and 63,000 deaths annually in the United States, a substantial fraction of the infections and deaths that do occur are also preventable" (p. 2209), as are illnesses and deaths due to toxic agents. Thus, even the deaths due to microbial and toxic agents may be preventable if people modify their lifestyle.

Promoting health and preventing illness, disability, and premature death through lifestyle changes is the single overarching purpose of Healthy People 2010. According to *Healthy People: Understanding and Improving Health* (U.S. Department of Health and Human Services, 2000), "individual behaviors and environmental factors are responsible for about 70 percent of all premature deaths in the United States" (p. 19). Despite our affluence and sophisticated health care system, women in 18 other countries and men in 24 countries (including Cuba, Costa Rica, and Ireland) have longer life expectancy at birth than their counterparts in the United States. The report cites the following Leading Health Indicators from 1997 as evidence that U.S. citizens are engag-

TABLE 1.1   Actual Cause of Death in the United States in 1990

	Deaths	
Cause	Estimated No.	Percentage of Total Deaths
Tobacco	400,000	19
Diet/activity patterns	300,000	14
Alcohol	100,000	5
Microbial agents	90,000	4
Toxic agents	60,000	3
Firearms	35,000	2
Sexual behavior	30,000	1
Motor vehicles	25,000	1
Illicit use of drugs	20,000	<1
Total	**1,060,000**	**50**

Source: Data compiled from *Journal of the American Medical Association,* 1993, Vol. 270, pp. 2207-2212.

ing in unhealthy and violent lifestyles that contribute to disease, disabilities, and early death:

▸ Only 15 percent of adults engaged in the recommended amount of physical activity (p. 27).

▸ Approximately 11% of children 6 to 19 years of age and 23% of adults age 20 and older were overweight and obese (p. 29).

▸ 36% of adolescents and 24% of adults were current smokers (p. 31).

▸ For adults, 16% had engaged in binge drinking and 6% had used illicit drugs in the 30 days prior to being surveyed (p. 33).

▸ Up to 15% of adolescents and 77% of unmarried adults were sexually active but failed to use condoms (p. 35).

Physical inactivity, obesity, smoking, substance abuse, and unprotected sex all involve behaviors that could be altered with appropriate preventive counseling. Although mental health workers may find it difficult to document the cost-effectiveness of programs designed to prevent social ills like drug abuse and school violence, substantial evidence already exists that behavioral health interventions are cost-effective in reducing physical health care costs. In a series of studies conducted in the 1960s and 1970s, Cummings (1967) and his associates documented that "medical utilization typically is reduced by 62% over 5 years following the application of behavioral interventions, and that the reduction in costs substantially exceeds the cost of providing the behavioral health service" (p. 5). A more recent experimental study reported by Cummings produced similar results. The Hawaii Medicaid Study randomly assigned 36,000 Medicaid eligibles on the island of Oahu to experimental and control groups and tracked their medical utilization over 7 years. According to Cummings, "the cost of creating the behavioral health care system was recovered by medical-surgical savings within 18 months, and the significant reduction in medical utilization continued thereafter with no additional behavioral health care required to maintain the cost savings" (p. 12).

Lewis et al. (1993) suggest that counselors can augment the work of medical practitioners by helping people adopt and maintain healthy lifestyles. They define health counseling as "an action-oriented process through which a helper enables a client to make life-style changes that lead in the direction of optimal health" (p. 5). These authors encourage counselors in a variety of settings (e.g., schools, human services agencies, health care organizations, private practice) to embrace a holistic, biopsychological perspective in an effort to promote physical health as well as interpersonal and social competence and psychological and emotional well-being. As we will see in the next section, there is more reason now than ever for counselors to do so.

MANAGED CARE AND THE CURRENT FOCUS ON PREVENTION AND SHORT-TERM TREATMENT

Although the election of Bill Clinton to the presidency in 1992 helped create a climate that was somewhat more responsive to prevention programs than had existed in the two previous administrations, arguably one of the most powerful actuating forces for prevention programs in health care in the 1990s was the emergence and rapid growth of health maintenance organizations (HMOs). The impetus for the emergence of HMOs as the predominant insurance model in the health care system was the desire to contain rapidly escalating health care costs that were inherent in the fee-for-service insurance model. Insurance providers were particularly motivated to reverse the escalating costs of mental health care. According to Hersch (1995), between 1980 and 1995, "mental health care costs doubled as a percentage of the overall health care dollar, whereas overall health care costs doubled as a percentage of GNP" (p. 17). At the same time, however, there was a growing awareness that behavioral health interventions can be used to reduce physical health care costs as well as mental health care costs.

HMOs have stressed prevention programs that have the potential for holding down treatment costs for both physical and mental health problems. In particular, HMOs have endorsed psychoeducational activities and materials as a means of promoting healthy lifestyles. The rationale for HMOs to emphasize prevention, and the impact it is likely to have on mental health service provision in the future, has been clearly stated by Cummings (1995):

> There is a growing body of evidence that indicates preventive services in the form of psychoeducational groups reduce the demand for both psychotherapy and inappropriate medical-surgical utilization. These psychoeducational groups range from stress management, parenting programs, and smoking cessation, to programs designed to improve compliance with medical regimens in hypertensives, diabetics, and other chronic diseases where noncompliance is rampant. . . . It is very likely, as a result of empirical findings, that only 25% of the psychotherapy of the future will be individual. It is anticipated that another 25% will be group therapy, whereas half of the psychological interventions will be preventive services in the form of structured psychoeducational programs involving small group participation. (p. 14)

Although mental health service providers who were trained in the medical model and committed to psychotherapy as treatment have been traumatized by the change to managed care (Hersch, 1995), counselors may well have benefited from the managed care emphasis on prevention and brief treatments. Recognizing the psychological/behavioral bases of physical health problems and the cost-containment benefits of prevention, many employers in both the private and public sectors have instituted employee assistance programs and psychoeducational training run by counselors. According to Foos, Ottens, and Hill (1991),

> large corporations such as McDonnell Douglas Corporation and Adolph Coors Company increasingly are making programs such as fitness training, stress management, drug and alcohol prevention, and smoking cessation available to their employees. From a practical standpoint, employers will encourage employee participation in order to increase worker productivity, reduce lost work days, and reduce general medical costs. . . . There is increasing evidence that broad-based mental health programs such as those provided by McDonnell Douglas and by Adolph Coors can be exceptionally cost-effective. (p. 333)

Thus, despite a long-standing bias in favor of treatment, events of the 1990s suggest a revived interest in prevention by policy makers and mental health practitioners. We believe the trend toward greater emphasis on prevention will continue well into the 21st century.

TIME FOR COUNSELORS TO REEMBRACE PREVENTION

Counseling has progressed a long way since the early days of the 20th century. However, some of the gains made by counselors in the past 30 years have de-emphasized the preventive and developmental foci that defined the profession during its formative years. In particular, the licensing and insurance reimbursement movements of the 1970s and 1980s, although allowing counselors and counseling psychologists to provide direct service to clients in a variety of settings for a variety of problems, have caused the profession to emphasize treatment (remediative counseling and psychotherapy) over prevention.

However, as suggested by Romano and Hage (2000), "the changing demographics of the U.S. population, the escalating cost of health care, and the complex relationships between the social, emotional, and physical dimensions of the human condition are exceptionally strong reasons for implementing a prevention-focused agenda in counseling" (p. 750). It is the thesis of this book that by reembracing our prevention and development roots, counselors will be ideally positioned to provide the mental health services demanded by cost-conscious HMOs and accountability-conscious policy makers as we enter the 21st century. Furthermore, the application of preventive and remedial counseling to the promotion of physical health care represents a relatively new, challenging, and potentially rewarding direction for counselors of the future.

In this chapter, we have focused on two (prevention and remediation) of the three roles that define counseling. In the next chapter, we focus on the third role and discuss theories of development with the goal of identifying tasks and concerns that most of us confront as we move through life. We believe that preventive and remedial counseling strategies designed to address specific client concerns are best understood within a developmental context, that the tasks undertaken in each of the various life stages create unique concerns that must be addressed by unique preventive and remedial counseling strategies.

CHAPTER 2

Development, Developmental Concerns, and Counseling

Cindy L. Juntunen

D evelopment can be defined as "systematic and successive changes over time" (Lerner, 1996, p. 781). These changes occur throughout the lifespan and across various domains of human experience—emotional, cognitive, physical, social, and moral. The significance of human development is sometimes overlooked in mental health training, lost in the emphasis of preparing counselors to work with clients who require remediative interventions for mental health disorders. However, counseling and counseling psychology have long considered development and developmental concerns central to the mission of the counseling profession.

The American Counseling Association (1995) is self-described as "an educational, scientific, and professional organization whose members are dedicated to the enhancement of human development throughout the lifespan." Similarly, counseling psychology is formally described as a specialty that "focuses on personal and interpersonal functioning across the lifespan and on emotional, vocational, educational, health-related, developmental and organizational concerns" (American Psychological Association Commission for the Recognition of Specialties and Proficiencies in Professional Psychology, 1999).

The purpose of this chapter is to describe how counselors can work effectively with client concerns that are developmental in nature. Developmental concerns are difficulties or stressors related to the changes people encounter throughout their life rather than concerns related to mental illness or pathology. Developmental concerns can be addressed with counseling strategies from any theoretical perspective, as we demonstrate in this book. Within this chapter, we present some general developmental guidelines in order to provide structure for understanding the developmental concerns presented in the following chapters.

Numerous theories have been developed to better describe and understand human development. The field of human development is substantial, and summarizing the myriad existing theories and philosophies is beyond the scope of this chapter. Instead, we present several major characteristics of various developmental theories, emphasizing the application of these characteristics for planning preventive counseling interventions. Following an introduction to those characteristics, we discuss implications for counseling and introduce the catalyst model (Cummings, 1995) of counseling as an example of integrating several developmental tenets into work with clients. The chapter closes with a discussion of the flexibility of developmental stages and a summary.

INTRODUCTION TO DEVELOPMENTAL PRINCIPLES

In the following chapters of this book, you will find suggestions for ways you can help clients address developmental concerns. This section provides an overview of assumptions and beliefs of developmental psychology that will help place those suggestions, and your own interventions, in the context of development. Four assumptions are considered: (1) Development is a process of change over time, (2) development occurs across the lifespan, (3) development requires an interaction between the individual and the environment, and (4) development takes place within a rich context.

HUMAN DEVELOPMENT IS A PROCESS OF CHANGE OVER TIME

People are constantly changing and being changed, often in "enduring and irreversible ways." (Grusec & Lytton, 1988, p. 3). Such change is inevitable, occurring in conjunction with maturing bodies, dynamic environments (Grusec & Lytton, 1988), and evolving relationships with others.

That people change may appear so obvious as to go unmentioned. However, recognizing that change is normative, even essential, is necessary to approach counseling work with developmental concerns. Change will occur in the presence of varying personal and environmental factors, many of which are discussed below. These variables can serve as protective factors (those aspects that are likely to facilitate successful transitions through change) or risk factors (aspects of a person or situation that might increase vulnerability to negative change). Many of the issues that clients bring to counseling (e.g., relationship concerns, parenting questions, career indecision, and health decisions) are a function of lifespan change that can be anticipated. Often, early intervention or prevention programs for these concerns can save significant resources in time, emotional energy, and money. Educating people, especially young people, that humans will change over time and encounter these developmental crisis points can itself be a preventive intervention.

Sometimes, change will be less anticipated, perhaps occurring because of an interaction between an individual's developmental stage and existing risk factors. Examples of these types of developmental concerns are school behavior problems, adolescent violence and suicidality, divorce, and career dissatisfaction. Risk factors for any of these concerns might exist in the environment or within the context of the individual's personal experience. Prevention programs can be utilized to minimize the impact of environmental risk factors, and early intervention with an individual can help to reduce the impact of personal risk factors.

The process by which developmental change occurs is as important as the fact that it does occur. Most contemporary developmental theorists acknowledge that development occurs throughout the lifespan and involves an interaction between individuals and their environment (Lerner, 1996). Lifespan change and the relationship with the environment will be more fully explored to address the process of development.

DEVELOPMENT OCCURS ACROSS THE LIFESPAN

Early developmental theorists such as Sigmund Freud and Jean Piaget focused their attention on development as a phenomenon of childhood and adolescence. The developmental work of Freud (1905), Piaget (1926), and others emphasized the idea that the major tasks of development are completed during the early years. Freud's (1905) theory of development stresses that the important developmental transitions are made prior to adolescence, as the child works through psychosexual stages in which gratification or the lack of gratification triggers developmental growth or delay. Mahler, Pine, and Bergman (1975) studied the relationship between infants and parents and proposed that the groundwork for adult development is established by about the age of 3 years. The primary tasks in this model are to (a) separate from the caregiver, (b) individuate, and (c) recognize that the caregiver remains available (through object constancy). This recognition then allows the child to move independently, knowing that help can be obtained.

According to Piaget (1926), children's intellectual development occurs as the child learns from and affects the environment. Children are viewed as explorers and scientists, developing logical tools as they learn to construct ideas of how things work. The child then uses the processes of assimilation and accommodation to make sense of the information they are gathering to form cognitive schemes. Gottfredson (1981) also attended to the environment and the developing child, with an emphasis on cognitive and future career development. Gottfredson introduced the importance of gender and power in childhood development. In the four stages of development outlined in her model, children are first orientated to size and power, then sex roles, social class, and eventually to a sense of self by about the age of 14.

Clearly, these models emphasize the growth and development of children and preadolescents. Early development was assumed to lay the foundation for adult life, reflected in terms such as *the formative years,* and direct attention was seldom paid to actual adult transitions. Following World War II, however, increasing interest was focused on the issue of adult development, or development across the lifespan (Lerner, 1983).

Erik Erikson (1963) proposed an early and widely recognized model of lifespan development, describing eight stages of psychosocial development from birth through death. Each stage contains a primary task, or crisis, with an accompanying preferred resolution. As individuals move through these stages and crises are resolved, they become increasingly prepared to interact with a wider social world. In the early stages of development, the child is moving from the encapsulated world of self and caregiver toward autonomy and a sense of competence. In adult development, the individual is interacting with the entire human world in intimate and more broad, social ways (Erikson, 1963). Eventually, adults may begin to see themselves as contributing to society and the next generation and appreciate the life that has been lived, if developmental crises have been successfully resolved.

Erikson (1963) comments directly on the importance of adult development when describing the seventh stage, generativity versus stagnation, which occurs during middle adulthood:

> The section on generativity would of necessity be the central one, for this term encompasses the evolutionary development which has made man the teaching and instituting as well as the learning animal. The fashionable insistence on dramatizing the dependence of children on adults often blinds us to the dependence of the older generation on the younger one. (p. 266)

Models of moral development have also considered adulthood an important period of development. Kohlberg (1971) proposed that moral development occurs across six stages, two of which occur during adolescence and adulthood. Briefly, Kohlberg's model of moral development suggests that children's moral reasoning develops by focusing on issues of punishment (Stage 1), satisfying own needs (Stage 2), altruism and approval from others (Stage 3), and eventually authority and maintenance of the social order (Stage 4). As individuals mature, they are more likely to develop a sense of right and wrong that is personal and separate from the group. During the final two stages, adolescents and adults develop a general sense that there are different values and begin to seek consensus (Stage 5) and eventually develop their own abstract and comprehensive ethical principles (Stage 6).

Building on the work of both Erikson and Kohlberg, Jane Loevinger (1976) proposed that six stages of ego development occur during adulthood. In this model, the ego is viewed as the principal organizing processor of the personality and the moderator of values, morals, goals, and cognition. In the first stage of Loevinger's model, Conformist, the adult adheres to external social rules. Through a process of realizing that one's actions affect others (Conscientious-Conformist) and recognizing the complexity of the world (Conscientious), the individual begins to develop respect for individuality (Individualistic) and a higher tolerance of ambiguity (Authonomous). Eventually, inner conflicts are resolved in the Integrated stage. Within each of the six stages, the individual needs to develop in the areas of character development (standards and goals), interpersonal styles (patterns of relating to others), conscious preoccupations (important things on the person's mind), and cognitive style (the person's characteristic way of thinking). Loevinger's stages of ego development have received some empirical support related to the use of the Sentence Completion Test, which she designed to measure ego development (Aiken, 1998).

Some developmental theorists focus on the transitions that humans must make to successfully navigate changing demands and expectations. Daniel Levinson (1978) focused on the transitions between different stages of development during adulthood, suggesting that adult development consists of building a life that consists of both a sociocultural (or external) side and a personal (or internal) side. Adults move through stages lasting several years and then enter a transition period, during which they prepare for the next stage. Levinson's model first proposed the *midlife crisis* concept, which has since been widely debated. Briefly, Levinson's model suggests that the Early Adult Transition (ages 17 to 22) forms a basis for living in the adult world. Between the ages of 22 and 28, individuals Enter the Adult World and test out preliminary connections to adult life. The Age 30 Transition (30 to 33) allows for a revision of life structure to provide more satisfaction as settling down is approached. The Settling-Down stage itself (ages 33 to 40) involves establishing oneself in employment and in society. This is then followed by the Midlife Transition (45 to 50), during which life is reevaluated and one's relationship to the external world is addressed. Middle Adulthood (ages 50 to 55), the Age 50 Transition, and Culmination of Middle Adulthood mirror the Early Adulthood and Settling-Down stages. Finally, the Late Adult Transition (ages 60 to 65) is assumed to include changing abilities and a sense of mortality.

It is important to note that most of these models of development were based on the experience of White, middle-class populations, primarily male. In fact, Levinson's model was based on interviews with 40 men, 10 in each of four occupational groups (Aiken, 1998). Developmental theories have been criticized for the limited validation of their relevance for women and populations of color. However, as the following two sections demonstrate, recent theories more appropriately consider environmental and contextual factors.

DEVELOPMENT REQUIRES AN INTERACTION BETWEEN THE INDIVIDUAL AND THE ENVIRONMENT

Piaget (1926), as mentioned above, saw the developing child as an explorer in the world, gaining logic as new experiences were encountered and described. In this view of development, children change and grow from their own efforts to master the environment (Cole & Cole, 1993). Although the environment is acknowledged as a source of developmental influence, it is not necessarily an active partner in the process. Contemporary developmental theories contain a growing recognition that development occurs as a result of the individual and the environment interacting with each other.

Bronfenbrenner (1979) pointed out a discrepancy in what was said about development and what was implemented in the research and practice of developmental psychology in the late 1970s. He stated, "To assert that human development is a product of interaction between the growing human organism and its environment is to state what is almost a commonplace in behavioral science" (p. 16). However, he pointed out, this principle, though widely believed, was seldom implemented in research or practice in psychology. Instead, almost all the work done in the field focused on the individual and gave at best cursory attention to the environment in which the individual existed (Bronfenbrenner, 1979).

Contemporary human development researchers do tend toward greater attention on the relationship between the individual and the environment of the individual (Lerner, 1996). This approach is not universal. But Lerner contends that even researchers who are continuing to look at biological or genetic factors in development are increasingly noting the possible influence of the contextual environmental system in which individuals exist (Lerner, 1996). Emphasizing the relationship between the individual and the environment, or context, diminishes the importance of the "nature-nurture" debate that divided developmental psychology for decades. In the interaction between individual and environment, genetic factors (nature) serve as part of the context that is provided by the individual. Therefore, both nature and nurture are important—both are part of the interaction necessary for development.

The relationship between the changing individual and the environment is a two-way interaction. As the individual changes, so does the environment. Children, for example, are active members and contributors to the systems in which they live. Children often develop in an environment dominated by parents and other caregivers. As the children change, these adult caregivers seldom remain static. The caregivers learn how to respond to the child's mood or behavior in different ways, essentially shaping part of their adult development and the environment of the child.

This emphasis on the two-way interaction of development was recently reinforced by Shanahan, Valsiner and Gottlieb (1997). Describing developmental concepts that are relevant across disciplines, they proposed the following description of the structure of development: "Development occurs in systems that are structured both hierarchically and horizontally, and relationships within these systems are bi-directional" (p. 37). In other words, people develop within systems that are organized in a vertical and lateral fashion. For example, an adult human is a system experiencing biological, emotional, social, and cultural events. As employees, individuals may be part of a system that includes society, workplace, boss, and people they supervise. This is one vertical hierarchy in which individuals exist. They will also be interacting with co-workers and peers, in relationships that are more likely to be horizontal. The individual will both influence and be influenced by the other members of this system (bidirectional). The relationships between the person and varying levels of the environment shape and foster (or hinder) development. Furthermore, as they develop and change, the environment is changed by their actions.

This interaction between individuals and their environment can also be applicable to the system of humans and the social environment more broadly. Understanding the nature of the individual-environment interaction is essential for developing successful preventive and educative counseling interventions. Counselors are in a unique position to affect the environment positively when they design interventions that foster positive development. Preventive programs can be used to change the environments of family, school, work, society, and so forth. Positive changes in these multiple levels of the environments will foster positive development by individuals. Then, as increasing numbers of individuals navigate developmental crises successfully, the social environment will become more supportive of healthy development. In this manner, preventive and educative strategies can produce a self-sustaining cycle of increased healthy development. However, to create change in the environment, several contextual factors must be considered.

CONTEXTUAL FACTORS CONTRIBUTE TO THE
PERSON-ENVIRONMENT INTERACTION

The human environment is shaped by the influence of many contextual factors: individual differences (including genetic factors), family relationships
and support, community resources, social and political policies and changes,
and economic resources and opportunities (Lapan, 1999). Each of these contextual factors has an impact on the environment, the individual, and the
interaction of the two.

One important contextual factor that has been too frequently overlooked is
that of culture. The contextual factor of culture is pervasive and important,
having a major impact on development. When culture has been considered in
development, it is often identified as a risk factor, accompanied by the assumption that members of minority groups will have delays in "normal" development. In response to developmental theories that compared African American
children unfavorably, John Ogbu (1985) suggested that Black children be considered in light of a cultural ecological theory of development, which requires
that the development of children, of all individuals, be considered in light of
the social group in which they live. Children are born into a social situation,
and they are brought up to survive and, we hope, thrive within that particular
social system (LeVine, 1977). It is crucial to consider cultural ecology when
talking about development for minority group individuals in a given society. In
the United States, the norm for successful development has been established by
middle-class majority culture norms, which may not be appropriate for non-
majority group members.

However, even such a cultural ecological developmental theory may not be
sufficient for understanding development. Bronfenbrenner (1985), in response
to Ogbu's suggestions, states that we also need to recognize that social systems
are dynamic systems. Being born into a social system does not mean growing
up in a static social system—in fact, many people move in and out of different
social situations, and the social environment itself changes.

The change in the social environment within developmental psychology itself is apparent when one considers the attention paid, only recently, to gender
and development. Gilligan (1982), in a groundbreaking study of women's development, criticized the assumptions of Developmental Theory, which were
based almost exclusively on the study of boys and men. With an emphasis
on moral development, Gilligan pointed out that the basic assumptions of Developmental Theory are not as relevant for women. Girls and women were
much more likely to emphasize relationships and caring over the traditional
male values of justice and law (Gilligan, 1982). Similarly, Miller (1994) argues
that traditional models of development, which emphasize individuation and
separation, have actually served to pathologize women. When the need for

interdependence and connected relationships is not recognized as part of "normal" development, women seem to be developing in an inferior or delayed manner. It can be argued that such gender differences and biases would have not been acknowledged or recognized if societal change did not occur. The interaction between social change for women and developmental theorists is allowing Developmental Theory itself to develop.

The dynamic nature of the social environment is apparent when one considers the importance of sociopolitical contextual factors. Political elections, changes in legal precedent, and policy decisions all have an impact on the social environment, often in ways that differentially affect people of different cultural backgrounds. Economic conditions may change in response to or as contributors to political change, having a domino effect on community resources, family resources, and the relationships within family and community. The interaction of all of these potential changes results in a constantly evolving environment, one that is simultaneously interacting with the developing individual residing therein.

Clearly, many factors can contribute to human development, and the relative importance of these factors may not be completely clear. However, counselors who are cognizant of contextual factors are better able to respond proactively to both groups and individuals, helping prevent or minimize the effects of difficult developmental transitions that can occur throughout the life cycle.

IMPLICATIONS FOR COUNSELING

People develop by making changes in relationship to their environment and life events, each change building on past experience to further the development of the individual. Many of these changes are positive, leading to healthy or optimal development. Others can have negative consequences, resulting in mental, physical, or social health concerns. Counselors can affect social mental health issues by fostering positive human development and educating clients about ways to prevent mental health concerns.

Developmental concerns are events or difficulties that create opportunities for change, both negative and positive, in a client's life. Developmental tasks, or crises (Erikson, 1963), are encountered by individuals throughout the lifespan. The resolution of such tasks, whether successful or unsuccessful, provides individuals with a foundation for responding to the next developmental event and moving forward into the next developmental stage (Erikson, 1963).

Developmental concerns occur across the various domains of human experience. Cognitive, emotional, physical, moral, and social functioning all develop and change as developmental tasks are encountered, and these aspects may be differently affected by individual developmental experiences. Cognitive change might occur without accompanying emotional change; physical and social development might surpass moral development. The relationship between developmental tasks and developmental domains provides a complex series of change events through which most individuals travel, sometimes faltering as they prepare for yet another change.

Developmental Theory offers insight into the nature of developmental concerns and provides an alternative conceptualization of client concerns. Rather than emphasizing mental illness or pathology, developmental constructs allow us to look at client issues as a function of developmental delays or blocks (Ivey & Rigazio-DiGilio, 1991). Developmental Theory also recognizes the individual's strengths and protective factors, as well as vulnerability to developmental delay (Kenny, 1996). Consistent with the traditional professional identity of counseling, this framework is health oriented rather than illness oriented and is inclusive of preventive strategies as well as remediative treatments. If we assume that certain types of developmental crises exist, or are likely to occur for specific groups or individuals, then appropriate prevention and early intervention programs can promote successful resolution of those crises, inhibiting the development of mental health problems. Developmental Theory therefore provides an important framework for addressing client concerns from preventive, educative, and early intervention perspectives.

As outlined earlier in this chapter, contemporary Developmental Theory seems fairly consistent on several important tenets: (a) Development is a process of cumulative change that occurs across the lifespan and is affected by risk and protective factors, (b) development occurs as humans interact with their environment, and (c) a variety of contextual factors contribute to the individual and to the environment, adding complexity to the interaction. These characteristics of development have clear implications for counselors working with clients who have developmental concerns. As humans move through life and encounter developmental transitions, they will sometimes be unable to move forward without help. Some developmental tasks or transitions are expected; others arrive without warning. Such transitions may be upsetting or joyous, accompanied by dread or relief, chronic or acute. Many developmental transitions are almost universal; others are more or less likely to be experienced depending on risk factors specific to a person or an environment. When delays occur, the continuity of development can be interrupted. In any event, clients will somehow need to navigate these transitions and crises in order to move on to further development.

Development, and developmental delay, occurs as a function of the interaction between the individual and contextual factors that make up the environment. Contextual factors themselves may serve to protect or put at risk the development of a given individual. The counselor serves (at least) three critical purposes for helping clients work with developmental concerns: (1) to prepare people for potential upcoming developmental concerns so that harm can be prevented, (2) to help individuals access resources within their environment that can support positive change, and (3) to offer secondary prevention and treatment services to mediate the effect of developmental concerns that are not prevented.

THE CATALYST MODEL

Cummings (1995) suggested that "to succeed as a prime provider [in the managed care environment] will require a fundamental and even pervasive shift in values from the traditional approach, which is referred to as the dyadic model, to the time-effective approaches, which are referred to here as the catalyst model" (p. 12). He went on to identify a number of "paradigm shifts" that psychotherapists can make to provide effective, time-managed counseling. Some of these paradigm shifts (discussed below) are consistent with many developmental tenets and correspond well to work with developmental concerns.

Paradigm Shift 1
Dyadic model: Few clients are seen, but for lengthy courses of treatment, usually individually.
Catalyst model: Many clients are seen, for brief episodes of treatment, very often in nontraditional modes.

Paradigm Shift 2
Dyadic model: Treatment is continuous, often weekly or even more frequently.
Catalyst model: Treatment is brief and intermittent throughout the life cycle.

Paradigm Shift 3
Dyadic model: The therapist is the vehicle for change, and emphasis is on treating psychopathology. The aim is a "cure" in some form.
Catalyst model: The therapist is merely a catalyst for the client to change, and the emphasis is on restoring the inevitable drive to grow that has gone awry.

Paradigm Shift 5
Dyadic model: Therapy continues until healing occurs and the client is terminated as "cured" to some degree.
Catalyst model: Therapy is yeast for growth outside therapy, and formal treatment is only interrupted. The client has recourse to therapy as needed throughout the life cycle.

Paradigm Shift 6
Dyadic model: Individual and group psychotherapy in the office are the main modalities by which healing takes place.
Catalyst model: Every healing resource in the community is mobilized, often as a better approach than office practice. Rather than disdaining support groups or

self-help programs, the practitioner cooperates with and offers consultation to these resources. (p. 13)

The catalyst model should sound familiar to counselors. Counselors have been providing brief treatment in nontraditional modes, facilitating client growth, and mobilizing community resources throughout clients' lifespans for at least the past half century. The catalyst model is also consistent with the use of a flexible, contextual developmental approach. The catalyst model emphasizes seeing the client throughout the lifespan, using flexible intervention strategies to serve as a catalyst for client growth. Furthermore, the counselor is encouraged to mobilize community resources, thus initiating contact with the context of the client as well as the individual client. The catalyst model and a theory emphasizing individual-context relationships are more likely than the traditional psychotherapy model and theory to prepare counselors to see the client as part of a system, recognizing the various risk and protective factors contributing to the client's social environment.

By recognizing the importance of *interaction* with the environment, counselors can approach developmental concerns from a preventive and educative stance and move beyond the psychopathology approach to working with individual clients. In this way, counselors foster the cycle of positive human development and positive environmental change, becoming agents of change at the social as well as individual level.

DEVELOPMENT AS A PROCESS OF STAGES

The remaining chapters of this book identify a set of critical and frequent issues that clients might present across the lifespan. To adequately organize the information, we've chosen to divide the chapters into sections corresponding to five life stages: childhood, adolescence, young adult, midlife, and older adult. These stages are consistent with much of the organization of the developmental literature, because many developmental models assume that growth occurs in stages. However, such models have been criticized because they are often assumed to restrict development to occurring within certain age ranges.

Baltes (1983) suggested that development is better viewed as multidirectional and multidimensional rather than a forward-moving, inevitable process. Certainly, forward growth is part of development; however, it is a single part and not the whole of development. Developmental changes may occur only in later life, may begin in earlier life but not continue throughout the lifespan, or may stop and start at points without apparent continuity (Baltes, 1983). Awareness of the continuity, or discontinuity, of development can provide the counselor with valuable information when helping clients work on developmental concerns. Rather than assuming that age is the primary predictor of developmental issues, it is important to attend to individuals' developmental history, their environmental situation, new opportunities for change that are affecting their current situation, and other contextual factors that may be relevant for the current concern.

With this caveat in mind, it is important to note that the developmental concerns presented in this book have the potential to occur at various places throughout the lifespan. The structure provided by this text does not preclude recognition of the fact that these developmental issues could arise in other stages. Recognizing that the individual client will also have an individual developmental history is an important precursor to addressing developmental concerns.

SUMMARY

The process of development creates several opportunities for humans to change, be it for the better or for the worse. As individuals and groups move through developmental transitions, various crisis points will be encountered. The counselor who is prepared for such crisis points can offer help through prevention and treatment strategies designed to foster the individual's ability to move through that crisis and emerge with a stronger foundation for future change. The remaining chapters of this book are designed to provide you with the tools you need to offer that kind of help. Remembering the key characteristics of development and applying those to decisions about client intervention will provide you with a context for developing interventions and treatment plans. Using preventive strategies will enable you to create change opportunities for clients in individual and group situations, limiting their future losses and increasing their potential for positive development.

PART II

Childhood

The definition and recognition of childhood has varied across time and cultures. Until the early part of the 17th century in Europe, children were largely viewed as miniature adults. Frequently, children assumed adult work roles and other responsibilities by the age of 10 years (Aiken, 1998). By the late 19th century, child welfare groups had developed to improve the living conditions and treatment of children, particularly in Europe and North America (Aiken, 1998). As these changes occurred, childhood became a stage of development distinct from any others. With influence from Freud, Piaget, and other developmental theorists, childhood became a highly studied stage of development, often assumed to include all the key developmental events.

During the earliest stages of development, children encounter conflicts related to their relationships with and dependence on others. Erikson (1963) suggested that the primary tasks of children involved developing a sense of trust, autonomy, initiative, and industry. As children grow, they begin to see themselves as separate from their caregivers but still need to feel that they can depend on the significant adults in their lives. If dependable caregivers are available, the child can grow toward independence with a sense of trust in the world.

Children also learn about relationships as they grow, although the need for establishing relationships and interdependence may be more salient for girls than for boys (Gilligan, 1982). Throughout childhood development, children form relationships with their parents, caregivers, siblings, and teachers, in homes, schools, and other institutions. Learning to navigate these relationships can be difficult as well as rewarding. In addition to mastering these developmental tasks, many children are exposed to a variety of potential risk factors that will affect their interactions with others.

Within the United States, the risks and opportunities that affect children vary considerably. Although it might be argued that children in the United States are relatively secure, there are indications that significant risk factors also exist for millions of U.S. children. In 1995, more than 14 million children (20.8% of the population) lived below the poverty level. Of these, 5 million were preschool children younger than 6 years of age (Lewit, Terman, & Behrman, 1997). In 1993, the National Commission on Children said of children living in poverty, "The harshness of their lives and their tenuous hold on tomorrow cannot be countenanced by a wealthy nation, a caring people or a prudent society" (Lewit et al., 1997, p. 1). Yet it is unlikely that the number of children living in poverty will decrease in the near future. Only limited research has been completed since passage of the Personal Responsibility and Work Opportunity Reconciliation Act of 1996, which formalized welfare reform in the United States. However, some early investigations of the impact of welfare reform suggest that children in families leaving welfare support may be at increased risk for poverty. In a study of 5,200 individuals and families who had left the welfare roles since 1996, the Children's Defense Fund (2000) found that more than half the working parents interviewed were earning less than $7 per hour. Furthermore, 58% of those working had family incomes below the poverty line. One third to one half of the families did not receive adequate health insurance, child care, or food stamps.

In 1996, the U.S. federal government spent $12.7 billion on child welfare services, with almost $7 billion allocated to out-of-home placement for children (Green, Boots, & Tumlin, 1997). In 1997, almost 3 million children (or 4.2% of the children's population) were involved in a report of child abuse; 889,665 reports were substantiated (Child Welfare League of America, 1997).

The issue of violence and aggression by children is also gaining increased attention. During the 1996-1997 school year, 57% of all public schools, and 45% of the public elementary schools, in the United States reported at least one incident of violence. The National Center for Education Statistics (1998) announced that for every 100,000 public school students, the following incidents were reported:

▶ 26 attacks or fights with a weapon

▶ 17 robberies

▶ 10 rapes

▶ 444 attacks or fights without a weapon

▶ 274 incidents of theft or larceny

▶ 234 incidents of vandalism

Poverty, removal from the family home, parental employment, and violence are just a few of the many factors that are likely to have an impact on childhood development. Because all of these can contribute to lifetime difficulties, it is essential that we focus energy on preventive programs that can eliminate some of these risk factors and minimize the impact of others.

In Chapter 3, Stephanie San Miguel Bauman addresses both the risk and protective factors that are likely to support the development of resilience in children. Discussing the construct of resilience as successful adaptation in the face of challenges, the author briefly describes the research relevant to this area of study and provides a description of the resilient child. She then discusses the importance of attending to the various environments of the child's world and presents implications for counseling practice in the promotion of resilience.

In Chapter 4, Elizabeth Vera and Michael D. Gaubatz discuss the emotional and social competencies essential for healthy development in school-age children. Specifically, they discuss factors that influence children's development of perspective-taking ability, conflict resolution skills, and communication skills. Family, peer, and cultural influences on social competency are discussed prior to the presentation of a case example that brings together the various components of social competency development.

Chapters 3 and 4 consider children within their family system as well as other environments. It is fairly normative for children to encounter significant disruptions in their family lives at one or more points in development. In Chapter 5, Merith Cosden and Maria Gutierrez note that as many as one half of all children are predicted to experience divorce in their families in the next decade. The authors discuss some of the factors such as demographic variables, family conflict, parenting, and discipline styles that are likely to affect adaptation to divorce among children. They then present the implications for preventive interventions and for working with divorce issues through family, individual, and group counseling.

Within Chapters 3, 4, and 5, a broad array of issues related to overall adaptation, peer relationships, and family relationships are presented. The authors demonstrate several ways that primary and secondary preventive strategies can foster positive development that provides a foundation for a lifetime of developmental transition.

CHAPTER 3

Fostering Resilience in Children

Stephanie San Miguel Bauman

Today's children live and grow in environments filled with harm and risk. For instance, one fourth of children in the United States live in poverty and one third deal with poor health. Physical, educational, and social problems exist and affect all developmental phases from the fetal period to adolescence (Simeonsson, 1994). Risk factors, "biological or psychosocial hazards that increase the likelihood of a negative developmental outcome" (Werner & Smith, 1992, p. 3), abound. Some stem from direct threats, whereas others consist of lack of opportunities (Garbarino, 1990). Specific risk factors include characteristics of children themselves as well as circumstances in their families, schools, and communities that may impede their growth and adjustment (Morrison, Furlong, & Morrison, 1997). Simeonsson (1994) concludes,

> It is clear that the scope of problems is extensive, spanning the range from mild to extreme expressions and encompassing the acute problems of intentional injury and violence and the endemic problems of school failure and delinquency. It is also clear that current services are unable to address the full extent of the problems and disorders of children and youth. (p. 4)

Beginning in the late 1950s and making significant strides in the 1970s and 1980s, researchers in the area of developmental psychopathology assessed children at different times during their development to clarify the nature of risk factors that contribute to emotional and social maladjustment. The most influential literature in the area includes work by Rutter (1979), Garmezy, Masten, and Tellegan (1984), and Werner and Smith (1982). Of particular interest were children considered to be at high risk due to neonatal stress, poverty, neglect, abuse, physical handicaps, war, parental schizophrenia, parental depression, parental alcoholism, and parental criminality. The resultant body of research found that, although some children in the longitudinal projects developed various problems, typically more than half became healthy, competent young adults (Benard, 1991; Werner & Smith, 1992). Thus, the phenomenon of resilience was discovered.

Resilience is "manifested competence in the context of significant challenges to adaptation" (Masten & Coatsworth, 1998, p. 206) or "successful adaptation following exposure to biological and psychosocial risk factors and/or stressful life events" (Werner, 1990, p. 98). Werner and Smith (1992) estimate that one third of children who are considered at risk are resilient. Currently, U.S. and European researchers from disciplines such as psychology, psychiatry, pediatric medicine, education, and sociology are interested in the identification of protective factors that enable individuals to circumvent risk factors and demonstrate resilience. Protective factors modify, ameliorate, or buffer an individual's reaction to a situation that ordinarily leads to maladaptive outcomes (Werner & Smith, 1992). Protective factors and resilience research build on the earlier research that documented the resiliency of people who were at risk in childhood. They also reflect an increased interest in the transactional-ecological model of human development in which the human personality is considered a self-righting mechanism that actively adapts to its environment on an ongoing basis (Benard, 1991; Werner, 1990).

In a review of the research on protective factors and resilience, Werner (1990) found a small number of studies that explored protective factors in infants and young children who were exposed to biological issues that affect individuals. Concerns included perinatal complications, congenital heart defects, cerebral palsy, Down's syndrome, and sensory deficits. A larger number of studies investigated resilient children affected by caregiving issues in their immediate families such as parents at risk for child abuse, parents with mental illness, and parents with alcoholism. The greatest number of studies on resilience focused on individual resilience under conditions of chronic poverty. At present, an increasing number of investigations exist of protective factors in the lives of children who have been abandoned or orphaned and refugee children or children from war-torn countries, all of whom have experienced upheavals of their social context. Studies that address the interplay between multiple risks and protective factors at the level of the individual child, the immediate family, and the broader social context are still limited in number.

The study of risk, resilience, and protective factors is intriguing, with implications for practice (Gordon, 1995). In fact, research on risk factors began to inform prevention efforts in the 1980s (Benard, 1991). Resiliency research not only offers hope based on scientific evidence but guides institutions such as schools in their efforts to look at strengths and to promote resiliency

(Henderson & Milstein, 1996). Mental health practitioners can also use research findings to help resilient children remain resilient and to enhance resilience in nonresilient people. Benard (1991) explains, "If we can determine the personal and environmental sources of social competence and wellness, we can better plan preventative interventions focused on creating and enhancing the personal and environmental attributes that serve as the key to healthy development" (p. 2). To this end, this chapter discusses the resilient child and competence-enhancing family, school, and community contexts. I also explore the implications for counselors who strive to foster resilience in children.

THE RESILIENT CHILD

What does resilience look like in a child? Benard (1991) observed that the process of development in the resilient child is, quite simply, the process of healthy human development. In other words, resilient children succeed with the major developmental tasks expected for persons of their age and gender in the context of the children's culture, society, and time (Masten & Braswell, 1991; Masten & Coatsworth, 1998). A brief consideration of the tasks commonly associated with different developmental periods by theories of human development is helpful at this juncture. Psychosocial tasks often identified for infancy include smooth eating and sleeping patterns, attachment to caregivers, and differentiation of self from the environment. Developmental tasks for the toddler and preschooler include some self-care such as independent toileting, language, self-control and compliance, and the formation of gender identity. By the time the resilient child reaches preschool, the child combines autonomy with the ability to seek support when needed (Werner, 1990). As children enter school, they are expected not only to control their behavior and comply with directions from parents but also to control their behavior in the school context. Developmental tasks commonly identified for the age period of middle childhood include school adjustment as reflected in attendance and appropriate conduct, academic achievement, getting along with peers, and rule-governed conduct as demonstrated by following societal rules for moral behavior and prosocial conduct (Masten & Braswell, 1991; Masten & Coatsworth, 1998).

Werner (1990) proposes an androgynous model of competence for the middle childhood years rather than one based on attributes traditionally stereotyped by gender. Girls who are resilient tend to display autonomy and independence. Resilient boys tend to be emotionally expressive, socially perceptive, and nurturant. In other words, these resilient youngsters are both caring and risk taking. Instead of limiting themselves to rigid, narrowly sex-typed behavior, they possess a broad spectrum of flexible coping skills.

The following specific attributes have been consistently identified as descriptors of the resilient child: social competence, problem-solving skills, autonomy, and sense of purpose and future (Benard, 1991). Each of these attributes encompasses a variety of behaviors, abilities, or attributes and will be discussed briefly. Although these descriptors have been associated with resilience, they have yet to be established as causal influences (Masten & Coatsworth, 1998).

Social competence refers to prosocial behavior such as responsiveness, flexibility, empathy, caring, communication skills, and a sense of humor. Social competence helps children form positive relationships from an early age with others. Indeed, infants with good coping abilities under conditions of risk tend to have temperamental characteristics that draw positive attention from others. For example, they tend to be active, alert, responsive, and sociable (Werner, 1990) or to be described as appealing and easygoing (Masten & Coatsworth, 1998).

Problem-solving skills include the ability to think abstractly, reflectively, and flexibly. Problem solving also includes the ability to try different solutions for both cognitive and social problems (Benard, 1991). A number of studies of resilient children have found positive associations between individual resilience and intelligence and central nervous system integrity. A reasonable explanation is that children who are better able to understand events around them are better positioned to figure out coping strategies in the face of adversity. There is little evidence, however, that high intelligence in itself leads to more effective coping. Reflecting on the importance of problem solving in preschool children, Werner (1990) asserts, "From repeated experiences in successfully overcoming frustrating situations, either on their own initiative or with the help of others, they derive in childhood a sense of self-efficacy and confidence that leads to a strong belief that they are able to influence their environment positively" (p. 105).

Autonomy is "a sense of one's own identity and an ability to act independently and exert some control over one's environment" (Benard, 1991, p. 4). In his psychosocial stage development theory, Erik Erikson (1963) conceptualized the development of autonomy as initially faced from 1 to 3 years of age. Resilience research also documents the importance of autonomy at other developmental periods; resilient children during middle childhood are characterized by a sense of competence and self-efficacy (Werner, 1990).

The resilient child's *sense of purpose and future* includes a number of attributes. In terms of the present, they possess healthy expectancies, goal directedness, success orientation, achievement motivation, educational aspirations, persistence, hardiness, and a sense of coherence. Complementing a belief in a bright future, the child also displays hopefulness, a sense of anticipation, and a sense of a compelling future (Benard, 1991).

The work of the Search Institute (Benson, 1993, 1996) reflects efforts to list specific factors that promote resilience. In the Search Institute's work, internal or personal assets for an adolescent include educational commitment and a sense of caring about school. External assets such as caring behaviors on the part of family, neighborhood, and school are also considered. Some of the Search Institute's assets are precise (e.g., a B grade average or better in school; 6 or more hours per week in artistic pursuits and sport or organized club activities; and 1 or more hours per week in religious activity). This specificity, however, meets with some criticism. Detailed lists of development assets are faulted for not having a consistent basis in the larger body of resilience research literature, being inattentive to social context and subject to misapplication (Howard, Dryden, & Johnson, 1999).

Resilience is not static; it changes as the child develops or as the context changes. A person may cope effectively with adversity at one point and then struggle under other difficulties at another time (Rutter, 1987). It is expected, however, that a resilient child has the capability to perform competently in the future and is likely to continue to be less susceptible to future stressors (Werner, 1990). Luthar and Zigler (1991) have raised the important and interesting question of whether children who attain competence under adversity experience psychological distress. Specifically, they caution that children may appear competent on behavioral indices (e.g., lack of externalizing symptoms such as acting out and aggressive behavior) yet struggle with psychological difficulties of an internalizing nature (e.g., depression or anxiety). Counselors should be mindful of this possibility when working with outwardly resilient children.

Although the qualities associated with resilience in children have been evident in children of various racial, ethnic, and socioeconomic backgrounds (Gordon, 1995, 1996), Masten and Coatsworth (1998) observe, "Deciding whether a child is competent can be difficult when a child lives in a cultural or community context that differs markedly from the larger society in which the community or cultural group is embedded" (p. 207). Attention must be paid to social context (Howard et al., 1999). Coll et al. (1996) present an integrative model for the study of developmental competencies in young children. This model places critical aspects of the environment at the center of its framework. It asserts that in order to understand the developmental process in children of color, one must attend to the unique ecological circumstances these children encounter. For instance, one unique ecological circumstance is racism. Racism leads to widespread and systematic assumptions about the inherent superior status of certain races and to discrimination against other races. In educational settings, past racism was reflected in school segregation and other legal barriers that restricted minority children from educational institutions that were accessible to White children. At present, more subtle forms of racism exist, including low educator expectations and attitudes, biased curriculum, and tracking and socializing into limited employment prospects. This integrative model poses the challenge of identifying the alternative competencies in children of color that might be missed by traditional assessment strategies. These alternative competencies would fall not only in the realms of established behavioral competencies but also would include the child's ability to deal with racism, discrimination, and social and psychological segregation.

The Environment of the Resilient Child

As evident from the discussion of the resilient child who is culturally diverse, resilience includes not only personal but also environmental factors (Gordon, 1996). Resilience can be discouraged or promoted by the child's environment, given that children live and grow in a habitat that includes family, friends, neighborhood, school, the physical environment, and social geography and climate (e.g., laws, institutions, and values) (Garbarino, 1990; Masten & Coatsworth, 1998). On the basis of a review of diverse studies of protective factors, Werner (1990) identified two kinds of protective factors in addition to dispositional characteristics of the child: (1) affectional ties and socialization practices within the family that facilitate trust, autonomy, and initiative, and (2) external support systems (e.g., friends and school) that reinforce competence and foster a set of values. Similarly, Benard (1991) identified a triad of protective factors in the contexts of family, school, and community: caring and support, high expectations, and participation. A closer look at the family, school, and community of the resilient child is in order.

The Family of the Resilient Child

The quality of the resilient child's immediate caregiving environment is an important protective factor, particularly in the aspects of caring and support, high expectations, and encouragement of the child's participation in family life (Benard, 1991). Most children who are considered resilient have had the chance to form a close bond with at least one person (not necessarily the mother or father) who provided them with stable care and adequate and appropriate attention during the first year of their life (Werner, 1990). Recent investigations of the family environment agree with this assertion. Research also suggests that a caring and supportive familial relationship continues to be essential throughout childhood (Benard, 1991). Parents and family members such as grandparents and older siblings can provide stable care, adequate and appropriate attention, and positive models of identification (Werner, 1990).

High expectations and participation in family life are closely aligned. The development of resilience is facilitated by families that set high expectations for their children's behavior from an early age. High expectations are reflected in authoritative parenting that is warm and caring, that establishes a clearly defined family structure, and that consistently sets and enforces limits (Masten & Coatsworth, 1998; Werner, 1990). Some expectations may relate directly to a child's participation in and assumption of family responsibilities such as being assigned chores (e.g., cleaning) or given responsibilities (e.g., care of siblings) (Werner & Smith, 1982). It is thought that meeting high expectations in the area of familial responsibilities provides a way for children to gain a sense of their worth and ability as a contributing member of their family.

School and the Resilient Child

Outside the family, school is perhaps the institution with the most potential for providing the environment and conditions that nurture resiliency in children (Henderson & Milstein, 1996). Weissberg, Caplan, and Harwood (1991) argue that "the educational system offers the most efficient and systematic means available to promote the psychological, social, and physical health of school-age children" (p. 835). Accordingly, the literature on the impact of the school on the outcome for children from high-risk environments proliferated during the 1980s (Benard, 1991). In a review of studies about the impact of school environment on resiliency, Gordon (1995) identified the following positive influences: fostering social unity and support, establishing reasonably high academic standards on students, and giving students responsibility. Thus, parallels are seen between protective factors in the family context and protective factors in the school context: Caring and support, high expectations, and participation and involvement remain important (Benard, 1991).

The level of caring and support within the school is a predictor of positive outcomes for children. This caring can come not only from school personnel but also from peers and friends. For example, in the Kauai Longitudinal Study (Werner & Smith, 1992), teachers and school were among the most commonly encountered protective factors for children as they successfully overcome poverty, perinatal stress, parental psychopathology, and family dysfunctions. Teachers and school staff foster resilience by investing energy into bonding with, caring for, and supporting at-risk youths (Henderson & Milstein, 1996).

High rates of academic success are seen in schools that establish high expectations for their students and provide support to meet those expectations. To foster resilience in the school context, it is also important to provide students with opportunities for participation, a meaningful environment, and responsibility. The opposite of involvement is alienation or a lack of bonding to the school. Research shows that lack of bonding to school is a risk factor in alcohol and substance abuse, delinquency, teen pregnancy, school failure, depression, suicide, and school violence (Benard, 1991; Morrison et al., 1997).

Community and the Resilient Child

A community not only directly influences its children but also indirectly affects them through its influence on families and schools. Given Maslow's

(1987) hierarchy of human needs, in which physiological needs and safety needs are paramount, perhaps the greatest protection a community could offer children would be in the form of basic resources. These resources would support healthy development through the provision of health care, child care, housing, education, job training, employment, and recreation (Benard, 1991). If families are connected to neighborhood and community resources that can help them meet basic needs, then they may be better empowered and positioned to assume responsibilities for themselves and their neighborhood (Wandersman & Nation, 1998).

A community that fosters resilience supports its family and schools, has high expectations and clear goals for its families and schools, and facilitates active participation and involvement in the life and work of the community. Neighborhoods, for example, can provide an environment in which children can be exposed to positive influences such as community or religious leaders (Garbarino, 1995; Wandersman & Nation, 1998). Communities with cohesive and organized social networks also show lower rates of crime, delinquency, and child abuse (Wandersman & Nation, 1998). The importance of linkages between families and schools and schools and communities must be appreciated. Benard (1991) reflects, "It is only at this intersystem level—and only through intersystem collaboration within our communities—that we can build a broad enough, intense enough network of protection for all children and families" (pp. 19-20).

IMPLICATIONS FOR COUNSELORS

Assessment of Risk and Protective Factors

To foster resilience in children, a counselor must first gather information about the children and their context. Drawing on a framework used in developmental psychopathology, a practitioner can evaluate risk status by exploring whether a child is meeting developmental challenges. Although there are some instruments available to assess development in infants and preschoolers such as the Denver Developmental Screening Test (Frankenburg, Dodd, & Fandal, 1973), assessment tools that effectively measure developmental tasks for older children are less common (Masten & Braswell, 1991). To offset this constraint, the developmental assessment process draws information from multiple measures, including direct testing, naturalistic observation, and interviews. Multiple perspectives of child, parent(s), teachers, and helping professionals are sought, based on the assumption that behavior always has a context (Vernon, 1993). The fundamental question is whether the child is succeeding with the major developmental tasks that face a person who is the child's age and gender and who is from the same culture and society (Masten & Coatsworth, 1998).

Once the counselor ascertains the child's level of success with major developmental tasks, the identification of risk and protective factors proceeds by asking the following questions:

1. What factors place the child at risk? Recall that some risk factors identified in the research literature include child temperament, child health concerns, neglect, abuse, parental alcoholism, parental mental illness, racism, discrimination, social and psychological segregation, poverty, and war.

2. What protective factors exist for the child as an individual? Does the child display social competence, problem-solving skills, autonomy, or a sense of purpose and future?

3. What protective factors does the family provide? Is the family context characterized by caring and support, high expectations, or opportunities for participation and involvement?

4. What protective factors does the child's school provide? Is the school context characterized by caring and support, high expectations, or opportunities for participation and involvement?

5. What protective factors does the child's community provide? Is the community context characterized by caring and support, high expectations, or opportunities for participation and involvement?

Throughout the assessment process, counselors are advised to attend to the number, frequency, duration, and intensity of risk and protective factors (Benard, 1991).

Rak and Patterson (1996) offer an alternate diagnostic strategy for counselors to assess resilience in children aged 6 to 12 and adolescents. Their 25-item resilience questionnaire looks at the variables of temperament, family environment and interactions, self-understanding, self-esteem, previous history of stress response, and influences on the child that engender optimism and a positive attitude about service to others and the community. The questionnaire is designed as an agenda for an initial assessment interview with the child or adolescent client. When necessary, significant caregiver input is secured about early childhood.

Rutter (1987) cautions that the search for processes that protect people from risk differs from the search for factors that will simply make children feel good. In fact, sometimes protection resides in the successful engagement with risk rather than the avoidance of it, just as immunization entails exposure to and successful coping with a limited dose of an infectious agent. Consequently, protection may consist of exposure to psychosocial stressors and adversity, successful coping, and the subsequent adaptive changes. Werner (1990) also agrees that graduated challenges may enhance children's competence and well-being.

Prevention and Promotion Strategies

Prevention and promotion are complementary processes. An activity or service that facilitates a child's development, adaptation, or functioning will also prevent maladaptation, delay, or disorder (Simeonsson, 1994). For example, prevention of illness, school failure, disorder, and distress is a complementary process to the promotion of health, learning, well-being, and actualization. In the realm of risk and resilience, the aim of prevention is to obtain a favorable balance between stressful life events and protective factors by decreasing exposure to risk factors and stressful life events and increasing the number of available protective factors. If the balance shifts from vulnerability to resilience, then adaptation is possible. If stressful life events outweigh the protective factors, then even a resilient child can develop problems (Werner, 1990).

How can a counselor decrease risk factors and increase protective factors? The counseling profession's discussion of how to foster resilience is nascent and lacks specificity (Rak & Patterson, 1996). In the developmental psychopathology literature, however, strategies geared at fostering resilience in children are categorized in different ways. One way is to group them according to whether they focus on risk, resources, or process (Masten & Coatsworth, 1998). In order to provide guidance to counselors, the following sections define these strategies. In addition, examples demonstrate how practitioners might employ risk-focused, resource-focused, or process-focused strategies with children who are at risk due to poverty.

Risk-Focused Strategies

Risk-focused strategies eliminate or prevent risk factors (Masten & Coatsworth, 1998). For example, prenatal care, routine well-child checkups, and free and reduced lunch programs attempt to avert health concerns of children reared in poverty. This is crucial, because the prevalence of threats to children's health such as learning disorders, emotional and behavioral problems, and vision and speech impairments appears greater among children of low socioeconomic status (Simeonsson & Gray, 1994). Another example of a risk-focused strategy is a housing program to prevent homelessness or substandard living conditions. A counselor's contribution to these risk-focused strategies might include establishing or coordinating a prevention program that includes health and housing services. A counselor might also identify children in need of such services and refer their families to helpful programs and agencies.

Resource-Focused Strategies

Resource-focused strategies reduce the impact of risks or stressors that already have occurred by improving access to existing resources or by adding previously unavailable resources (Masten & Coatsworth, 1998). Availability of toys and materials and exposure to a variety of stimuli appear to facilitate good health and development for all children (Bradley et al., 1994). Thus, one resource-focused strategy for children living in poverty is the provision of toys, books, and other educational materials that parents can use with their children (Seitz & Provence, 1990). Provision of mentors is another resource-focused strategy. Staff members in schools, community centers, and youth centers are all potential role models and guides for the children they serve. Mentors may also be provided through organizations such as Big Brothers and Big Sisters (Rak & Patterson, 1996).

Resource-focused strategies require that counselors be familiar with a wide variety of agencies and services to which they can refer children and families. Potential resources include local volunteer organizations (e.g., church groups or counseling hotlines), government agencies and services (e.g., Bureau of Employment Security and the Department of Human Services), national nonprofit organizations (e.g., Alcoholics Anonymous, March of Dimes Foundation, and the National Association for the Advancement of Colored People), and school district services (e.g., school nurses, school counselors, and school psychologists). Some ways to identify pertinent resources are canvassing telephone books, attending meetings of professional organizations, talking with colleagues, and interviewing various service providers (Baker, 2000).

Process-Focused Strategies

In contrast to risk-focused strategies or resource-focused strategies, process-focused strategies address adaptational systems that appear linked to competence. Attachment, self-efficacy, and self-regulation are among the most important adaptational systems (Masten & Coatsworth, 1998). Poverty inhibits some of these adaptational systems in parents because it creates stresses and frustrations that limit a parent's ability to provide stimulating and nurturing care. Poverty also decreases the availability of emotional, financial, and practical support (McAdoo, 1988). Thus, one important process-focused prevention strategy consists of parent education, which provides information about child development and general caretaking. It fosters connections between parents and informal and formal support services. Assistance in a parent's decision-making process in the areas of educational and career concerns may also be provided. Notably, mental health practitioners such as clinical social workers and psychologists already have contributed to process-oriented strategies in high-profile, high-caliber prevention programs geared toward families of low socioeconomic status such as the Yale Child Welfare Program (Seitz & Provence, 1990). Furthermore, due to their professional training, counselors currently provide process-oriented assistance through counseling and consultation activities.

In a discussion of guidance and counseling with children at risk, Rak and Patterson (1996) provide process-focused suggestions that likely are applicable to the more specific population of children raised in poverty. They recommend age-appropriate guidance groups to teach resiliency skills such as problem solving. They also promote techniques that develop transferable skills to enhance self-concept. These techniques include role play that improves self-expression, conflict resolution that ameliorates interpersonal struggles at home and in school, creative imagery, and bibliotherapy.

Additional Considerations

As previously mentioned, the categorization of prevention strategies as risk focused, resource focused or process focused is one of a variety ways to approach strategies geared at fostering resilience in children. Counselors also decrease risk factors and increase protective factors when they employ strategies with varied levels of action and multiple foci. For instance, action may be taken on a small or large scale (Benard, 1991). The scope of primary prevention is wide and is reflected in efforts of a universal nature that are designed to promote well-being in the population at large (Gordon, 1983). A school safety assembly involving all students, a community-sponsored celebration of diversity on the Martin Luther King, Jr. holiday, and a new student orientation program at a middle school are examples of this kind of primary prevention. In contrast, some prevention efforts may take place through the efforts of one person or in the form of a targeted opportunity. Examples of such secondary prevention measures include an anger management group for students considered at risk for aggression; a career fair for girls interested in science, math, and engineering; and the assignment of a peer counselor or foster grandparent to a socially isolated child.

In addition, a strategy may aim to effect change in the child or to effect change in the context in which the child develops and changes. For example, one-on-one tutoring, participation in a friendship group, and bereavement counseling aim to change individual child capabilities. On an individual level, successful coping may take different forms, including the children's own actions in physically removing themselves from the adverse situation, their cognitive appraisal of the situation, or emotionally distancing themselves from the harmful situation (Rutter, 1987).

An alternative to changing the child is changing the context. Treatment for a parent's alcoholism is targeted at a change in context. Other examples of efforts to change context include teacher in-service training on building a positive school environment and the formation of partnerships between schools and community groups to promote literacy. Strategies to increase resilience may also strive for a best fit between children and their context. Garbarino (1990) defines opportunities for development as "relationships in which children find material, emotional, and social encouragement compatible with their needs and capacities as they exist at a specific point in their developing lives" (p. 79). A child's environment can inhibit his or her developmental competencies when a discrepancy exists between the expectations, goals, and values of the environment and those of the child and family. In contrast, a child's environment can promote developmental competencies when there is congruence between the expectations, goals, and values (Coll et al., 1996). Ultimately, a dual focus on promoting competent young people and creating competence-enhancing environments is advised (Weissberg et al., 1991).

Prevention efforts informed by research on resilience are still in their formative stages, but increasing examples of the application of this framework are available. Educators, for instance, continue to pursue an understanding of how schools can help their students evolve into competent learners, workers, and citizens (Henderson & Milstein, 1996). Translating risk and resilience concepts into an educationally based paradigm, Morrison et al. (1997) outline a comprehensive response to school violence through the creation of a safe school environment. Drug and alcohol abuse prevention has also been approached from the perspective of fostering resilience in at-risk children and their environments (e.g., Benard, 1993a, 1993b; Hawkins, Catalano, & Miller, 1992; Hawkins, Lishner, Catalano, & Howard, 1985). Recent examples of applications of resilience theory and research include efforts to assist children who have witnessed community homicide (Levy & Wall, 2000) and to help homeless students (Reed-Victor & Pelco, 1999).

As evident from the examples of different prevention and promotion strategies, prevention practice has expanded beyond short-term, individual-focused interventions to include long-term, comprehensive, environment-focused approaches that enhance protective factors in families, schools, and communities (Benard, 1991). Concomitantly, counselors have recognized the need for enhanced counseling services that not only offer individual and group counseling but also offer prevention programs for children at risk (Stafford, 1999). Consequently, mental health professionals now have the opportunity to establish multidisciplinary, multicomponent prevention programs to foster resilience. Counselors also have the option of coordinating their own intervention services such as individual counseling with others' prevention efforts that are geared toward the family or are based in the school or community (Weissberg et al., 1991). Strategic questions that may assist the practitioner who strives to foster resilience in children at risk include the following:

1. What risk-focused, resource-focused, or process-focused options are possible?

2. How can action be taken on a small scale? On a large scale?
3. What strategies will promote competence in the individual child? What strategies will create a competence-enhancing environment?

SUMMARY

Counselors know all too well that today's children live and grow in environments filled with harm and risk. They recognize that current mental health services only partially address the wide range and intensity of problems. Yet, supported by research findings from the area of developmental psychopathology, mental health practitioners also appreciate the self-righting tendencies of children toward normal development except under the most persistent negative conditions (Werner, 1990).

Counselors who strive to foster resilience in children must learn about individual children and their context. They must be able to identify the risk factors that are present. They must also explore the resilience factors that exist, that could be enhanced, or that could be provided. By utilizing their knowledge and skills as independent practitioners, as collaborators with other helping professionals, or as leaders in comprehensive prevention efforts, counselors may make important contributions to reducing risk and fostering resilience. Undoubtedly, it is imperative that counselors consider children valuable resources who are, in themselves, resourceful. As Benard (1991) reminds us, the alternative is to view children as problems, to hold low expectations, and to deny them opportunities for meaningful participation and contribution to family, school, and community life.

VIGNETTE

Paul is a 7-year-old Asian American boy who lives with his aunt in the Pacific Northwest. Although money is often in short supply, his aunt makes sure to provide for his basic needs. Paul and his aunt are not and have never been particularly close. He finds her very strict and intimidating. He seldom sees his parents, who both struggle with alcohol and substance abuse. He does, however, look forward to regular visits from his paternal grandfather, who takes him fishing and encourages him in his studies. Paul's teachers describe him as somewhat anxious but well behaved, well liked by his peers, and bright. In fact, he was recently recognized as the student of the month at a recent school assembly. Though often commenting on how Paul has "pulled himself up by his bootstraps," his teachers still worry about whether he will continue to do well, because he comes from a neighborhood known for its gang activity.

1. Is Paul succeeding with the major developmental tasks that face a person his age and his gender in his culture, society, and time?

2. What factors place Paul at risk?

3. What protective factors exist for Paul as an individual?

4. What protective factors do his family, his school, and his community provide?

5. What protective factors could be enhanced or could be provided to Paul or to his family, school, and/or community?

6. Identify one or two specific actions a counselor might take to reduce risk and foster resilience for Paul.

ADDITIONAL RESOURCES

Print Resources

Benard, B. (1991). *Fostering resiliency in kids: Protective factors in the family, school and community.* Portland, OR: Northwest Regional Laboratory.

Henderson, N., & Milstein, M. M. (1996). *Resiliency in schools: Making it happen for students and educators.* Thousand Oaks, CA: Corwin.

Masten, A. S., & Coatsworth, J. D. (1998). The development of competence in favorable and unfavorable environments. *American Psychologist, 53,* 205-220.

Morrison, G. M., Furlong, M. J., & Morrison, R. L. (1997). The safe school: Moving beyond crime prevention to school empowerment. In A. P. Goldstein & J. Close (Eds.), *School violence intervention: A practical handbook* (pp. 236-264). New York: Guilford.

Rak, C. F., & Patterson, L. E. (1996). Promoting resilience in children at risk. *Journal of Counseling and Development, 74,* 368-373.

Vernon, A. (1993). *Developmental assessment and intervention with children and adolescents.* Alexandria, VA: American Counseling Association.

Internet Resources

Children, Youth and Families Education and Research Network: http://www.cyfernet. org

National Network for Family Resiliency: http://www.nnfr.org

Resiliency in Action: http://www.resiliency.com

ResilienceNet: http://resilnet.uiuc.edu

CHAPTER 4

Promoting Social Competencies in School-Aged Children

Elizabeth Vera
Michael D. Gaubatz

Physical and cognitive changes occur during childhood that have dramatic implications for the rest of one's life. Social and emotional developmental changes also occur in which children develop, among other things, social competence—a range of interpersonal skills that allow them to integrate their feelings, thoughts, and actions to achieve social and interpersonal goals (Caplan et al., 1992; Catalano, Berglund, Ryan, Lonczak, & Hawkins, 1998). Social competence not only has meaningful importance for counselors and child development professionals but is a key factor in the prevention of childhood psychosocial problems such as delinquency and drug use (Catalano et al., 1998; Chung & Elias, 1996; Durlak, 1980) and in the treatment of behavioral and emotional problems such as oppositional defiance, conduct disorder, depression, and anxiety.

This chapter explores the component and integrated skills of social competence, including such skills as encoding and interpreting relevant social cues, generating effective solutions to interpersonal problems (e.g., conflict resolution), anticipating consequences to one's actions, and translating social decisions into effective action (Elias, Gara, Schuyler, Branden-Muller, & Sayette, 1994). As a consensus of research suggests, emotional development and social competence are inextricably linked and mutually influenced (Berk, 2000; Newman & Newman, 1998). Because both social and emotional development are also influenced by family, peer, and cultural experiences, this chapter examines the acquisition of social competence skills against a background of emotional and relational contexts. Beginning with an outline of major models and components of social competence development, we explore the influences of family, peer, and cultural contexts on social competence and briefly discuss the research evaluating the effectiveness of various social competence intervention programs. Finally, we present a case study, accompanied by case discussion questions, that demonstrate key facets of promoting social competence in children.

PERSON-ENVIRONMENT INTERACTION
AND SOCIAL COMPETENCE DEVELOPMENT

By definition, understanding social competence development involves considering children within their environmental contexts. Because children's social interactions typically involve their families, peers, and community members, it is impossible to talk about the development of social competencies acontextually. Children's social competencies are influenced not only by individual traits like temperament and intelligence but also by the family interaction patterns to which they are exposed, the peer pressures they experience at various stages of their lives, and larger cultural factors such as the social construction of gender and ethnic socialization norms. Although these factors are known to affect children's acquisition of social competencies, a key question remains unanswered in social competencies research: What is the mechanism by which such intrapersonal and contextual factors influence development?

Developmental "outcome" is often measured in social competence research by counting the number of friends children have or by indexing children's involvement in such peer activities as sports, clubs, and organizations (Chung & Elias, 1996). The relationship between such measures and actual skill development, however, is unclear. Although social competencies can influence the number of social interactions a child may have, factors having little to do with the child's skills may affect the child's opportunities to engage in such activities. Many children, for example, live in neighborhoods and attend schools without sports or are unable to play outside with peers because their parks and streets are unsafe. In such circumstances, children's limited opportunities in the environment, not their lack of social competency skills, may restrict their social involvement.

Social interaction and the development of social skills, however, are bidirectionally related: If children have limited opportunities to engage in social interactions, they may acquire limited social competence. If a child is raised without siblings or sibling contact, for example, the child's preschool social world may be limited to interactions with adults. The effects of such an up-bringing on the child's experience in school may then depend on several things. In some circumstances, the caregivers or parents may seek out ways to encourage the child's social development by finding peers in play groups or by spending a lot of time interacting with the child. In such a situation, the child may become socially skilled and in fact may benefit from the exposure to more competent "playmates," as theorists like Vygotsky (1978) might expect. Alternatively, if children were forced to spend a lot of time alone, they may become more comfortable engaging in solitary play and may have difficulty incorporating peers into their social world in the future. As Asher, Hymel, and Renshaw (1984) found, children who are withdrawn and prefer participation in isolated activities, even when other children are present, tend to form negative views of their social competence. Such self-perceptions in turn discourage them from seeking out experiences that might enhance their social competency skills.

It is impossible to predict children's social development based on their family structure (e.g., being an only child versus having siblings), socioeconomic status (e.g., being raised in a poor or wealthy community with varying qualities of organized activities for children), or other demographic characteristics (see Bronfenbrenner, 1986). The interpenetration between environmental contexts and the development of social competence can be quite complex.

SOCIAL SKILLS AND SOCIAL COMPETENCE

Social competence can refer to many specific sets of skills. Three of the most common are perspective-taking ability, conflict resolution skills, and communication skills. Selman's (1980) work on perspective-taking development in children and adolescents established the relationship of perspective taking to the development of empathy. Perspective-taking ability can be thought of as a child's ability to understand what others may be thinking or feeling and to understand that the child's own perspective may differ from another's (Berk, 2000). This concept appears to be critical to the development of other social skills; children who are unaware of the feelings and needs of others often are difficult to be around and may be rejected by peers.

Conflict resolution skills are a related set of social skills. The ability to respond to conflict in ways that promote collaborative problem solving (e.g., the use of negotiation strategies and compromise) is thought to be highly adaptive and may be an indication of a child's moral development (Berk, 2000; Killen & Nucci, 1995). Conflict resolution skills may be thought of as interpersonal problem-solving skills that emphasize the mutuality of one's own and other persons' needs. Children who attempt to impose their own preferences on peers or adults may lack the skills needed to manage normal conflicts that occur within all relationships. Conflict resolution abilities also may be critical to violence prevention and to the maintenance of friendships (Guiliano, 1994).

Communication skills are also a critical component of social competence. Being able to express oneself in respectful and assertive ways is related both to getting one's own needs met and to respecting the needs of others. Whereas passive forms of communication can be detrimental to getting one's needs met, aggressive forms of communication can be detrimental to respecting the needs of others and have been associated with the development of violent behavior in youth (Farrington, 1992; Guiliano, 1994; Loeber & Stouthamer-Loeber, 1998). Understanding how children learn to communicate their feelings, thoughts, and needs therefore has important implications for the competencies they gain, or fail to gain, later in life.

Perspective-taking abilities, communication skills, and conflict resolution skills are not only interrelated, however; they are influenced in similar ways by the environmental contexts in which children develop. Understanding the potential influences of family, peer groups, and culture is an important part of articulating social competency development.

Family Influences on Social Competencies

Some of the first social interactions children experience are with their primary caregivers. As early as during infancy, children learn how to form attachments to their parents and other caregivers that directly influence their formation of relationships later in life. In fact, some writers have argued that the process of becoming ready for friendships may begin in infancy (e.g., Newman & Newman, 1998). Generally speaking, parents and other primary caretakers influence the social development of their children in two key ways. The first is through social learning and the process of imitation: Young children often imitate their caretakers as they learn about ways of interacting with people or solving problems. If caretakers are dismissive of the needs of others or impose their needs on others, their children may learn to do the same. In this regard, discipline or parenting styles often become a major source of information for children (Newman & Newman, 1998). Children exposed to violent discipline, for example, may be more likely to become aggressive in their communication styles and conflict resolution efforts (Baumrind, 1967). However, cultural differences have influenced the effectiveness of various parenting styles (Deater-Deckard & Dodge, 1997; Kelly, Power, & Wimbush, 1992), and authoritarian discipline does not always have a negative effect on the social skills of the child.

Another way that parents and caregivers influence children's social development is through the quality of attachments they establish with them. Bowlby (1982) argues that the affectional bond between children and their parents, in particular their mothers, is critical in providing them with a secure base from which to form other relationships. In support of this view, research has suggested that children's social adjustment is strongly correlated with various indices of parent-child attachment (Rice, 1990; Sroufe & Fleeson, 1986). It is also possible, however, that poor parent-child relationships may cause children to initiate greater contact with peers, possibly to compensate for needs unmet by the family (Schneider & Younger, 1996). As Quintana and Lapsley (1987) noted, the many dimensions of parent-child attachment may have differential importance, for particular children, on various aspects of their development. Although a relationship between quality of attachment and social competence may exist, it may not be a unidirectional relationship for all children.

Peer Influences on Social Competencies

As toddlers, children are in the process of developing their first social relationships. They develop friendships with siblings and day-care peers through play or structured preschool programs. In each of these social contexts, children are active agents in the formation of their relationships. Why, then, are some children more successful in their early friendships and able to develop relationships with ease, whereas other children are socially awkward and find it difficult to develop friendships? One way that peers influence social development is through the establishment of peer norms, which shape the behaviors in which children engage to gain and maintain social acceptance.

Peer groups develop norms, or rules of acceptance and rejection (Newman & Newman, 1998). Research has suggested that adults and parents begin to lose some of the influence they have on children by middle childhood, and some research has suggested that the pressures children experience to conform to peer group norms may peak as early as the fifth or sixth grade (Gavin & Furman, 1989). This phenomenon obviously can become problematic if children's peer norms support antisocial behaviors such as teasing, bullying, or even delinquency. Even at young ages, therefore, it is important to pay attention to the friends children acquire, because these peers not only provide a major context for subsequent social competency development but also shape the behaviors children engage in to gain and maintain social acceptance.

Peer acceptance or rejection is a powerful influence on the development of children's social skills. Peer rejection is a potent predictor of feelings of loneliness and when coupled with self-blaming attributions (e.g., blaming oneself for a lack of social acceptance) may result in feelings of hopelessness and a future lack of initiation in friend-seeking behavior (Crick & Ladd, 1993; Renshaw & Brown, 1993). Peer interactions, then, can be positive as well as negative in their effects on children's development of social competence.

Cultural Influences on Social Competencies

Research has suggested that children's cultural context is critically connected to their social development (Bronfenbrenner, 1986; Lind, Huo, & Tyler, 1994; Turner, Norman, & Zunz, 1995). Most of this research has focused on children's gender and ethnic group socialization. Lind et al. (1994), for example, found that both gender and ethnicity influenced adolescents' preferences for resolution styles such as persuasion and negotiation. Although gender differences manifested in children's preferences for particular conflict resolution strategies, their research suggested that children did not differ as to whether they thought fairness was an important criterion in such situations. Lind et al.'s research focused on children's gender-specific attitudes, but Turner et al. (1995) investigated the extent to which social competency and resilience programming might be differentially effective for boys and girls. Their recommendation of the use of separate, gender-specific interventions was based on two observations: Girls appeared to be in greater need of interventions that taught assertive communication skills. In contrast, boys appeared to experience fewer problems with assertive communication but greater problems with the escalation of conflicts into violent or aggressive confrontations (Guiliano, 1994). Such gender differences, which have been supported by Vera et al. (2000), suggest that differences in boys' and girls' communication and socialization styles make them vulnerable to different social competency concerns.

Research has made an equally compelling case for the need to consider ethnic and racial group differences in understanding children's social competency skills (Dumas, Rollock, Prinz, Hops, & Blechman, 1999). In cultures that promote a deferential respect for adult authority, assertive communication between children and adults (such as is often promoted in social competency interventions) may be seen as inappropriate. Conversely, in collectivist cultures that value group over individual needs, children may engage in culturally appropriate self-sacrificing behavior with their peers that may be seen in Western cultures as passive.

There is growing consensus (see Dumas et al., 1999) that such cultural differences should be considered when developing programming to promote children's social competence. Perhaps the most effective way to incorporate cultural considerations into social competence programming is by initiating extensive preintervention contact with cultural groups targeted for intervention, using strategies such as focus groups, the development of informal relationships, and familiarization with the community (see Dumas et al., 1999; Lerner, 1995; Reiss & Price, 1995). As Bronfenbrenner (1986) observed, generalizations about children based on their ethnicity, race, social class, or gender often ironically become less accurate, and more stereotypical, as an observer strives toward greater "etic" objectivity. An accurate understanding of contextual influences arguably comes only from genuinely community-embedded, culturally responsive approaches to program development (and data gathering) that generate authentic knowledge about the child's social norms and needs.

INTERVENTIONS: PROMOTING SOCIAL COMPETENCE IN CHILDREN

Because they play a key role in the prevention and treatment of childhood problems, a growing number of programs have been developed to promote social competencies in children. Prevention and competency promotion outcome research has not yet reached consensus about the best ways to promote specific social competencies (e.g., conflict resolution, initiating or joining activities), but most research suggests that interventions aimed at promoting such competencies, as a whole, are in fact beneficial (Catalano et al., 1998).

One program developed by Johnson, Johnson, Dudley, and Acikgoz (1994) appeared to successfully promote perspective-taking, conflict resolution, and communication skills among primarily Caucasian elementary school children. During a 3-month period, fifth- and sixth-grade research participants were trained in a 14-hour school-based program to practice integrative negotiation and perspective-reversal procedures. Although the negotiation component of Johnson et al.'s program focused on teaching students to negotiate mutually satisfying solutions to social problems, their "reversal" procedure focused on helping students view problems from multiple perspectives (Johnson et al., 1994). The negotiation model that guided the program consisted of six steps: (1) identifying and describing one's own needs, (2) describing one's own feelings, (3) explaining the reasons underlying one's wants and feelings, (4) reversing perspectives, (5) brainstorming at least three potential mutually beneficial agreements, and (6) reaching a tentative agreement. The authors' teaching methods included cooperative learning exercises, role playing, drill and review exercises, and small group discussions. The program's effects on participants, compared to control group students, showed significant gains in their understanding of conflict resolution strategies and in their ability to apply negotiation procedures to actual conflicts.

Another successful model of social competency intervention, the PACT program (Positive Adolescent Choices Training), was developed by Hammond and Yung (1991). Used with primarily African American middle school students, Hammond and Yung's program consisted of 20 hours of weekly programming in which children were taught communication, conflict resolution, and negotiation skills. Methods used in the program included teaching students how to give negative feedback (e.g., how to express displeasure or criticism calmly), how to receive negative feedback (e.g., how to react appropriately to another person's anger or criticism), and negotiation skills (e.g., identifying problems, potential solutions, and generating compromises). Compared to a nonprogram control group, PACT participants showed significantly lower levels of subsequent violent and aggressive behaviors as indicated by juvenile court records over a 3-year period. Significantly, the program appeared to curb many of the childhood legal problems that have been argued to result from ineffective or poorly developed social skills (Hammond & Yung, 1993).

These two programs together typify curriculum-based approaches to the promotion of social competency. They also illustrate direct-service interventions that counselors can use to promote social skill building. Although they appear to be effective in building the skills of individual participants, these programs do not directly address contextual issues, including family issues, peer norms, and community issues, that are influential in the development of social competency in children. Systems-based, or contextually oriented, programs, on the other hand, aim directly at changing the contextual influences on children's social behavior (Guerra, Tolan, & Hammond, 1994).

One such "contextual" program was developed by Hawkins, Catalano, and Morrison (1989), who designed an intervention to change children's peer norms by increasing their opportunities to develop prosocial bonds with family members, school systems, and peers. Hawkins et al.'s program taught participants' teachers specific classroom management techniques to support their appropriate behavior and interpersonal attachments in the classroom and included a family-based component designed to improve the family management and conflict resolution skills of the participants' parents. Hawkins et al.'s program then addressed peer-focused social skills on an individual level but only after addressing these systemic variables, anticipating that such skills would be supported within the participants' peer and family contexts. Research evaluating the program found significantly lower levels of problematic behavior among participants both at school (as measured by reduced suspensions and aggressive acts in Grades 1 through 4) and at home, compared to a control group of nonparticipating children.

Critical writing by Kumpfer and Alvarado (1998) and Reese, Vera, Simon, and Ikeda (2000) supports Hawkins et al.'s (1989) explicit emphasis on family, peer, and cultural contexts. In essence, programs that include family and peer contexts in their scope of interventions are better able to enhance the "protective factors" available to children. As research has long suggested (e.g., Masten & Coatsworth, 1998; Patterson, 1980), children who are raised by nurturing parents or caregivers and given opportunities for social and emotional growth are more likely to develop a broad spectrum of social competencies. Programs that focus exclusively on promoting skills in individual children without simultaneously promoting these larger contextual influences among their family members and peers may be implementing only "half a solution" (see Kumpfer, 1996). Social competency promotion programs should therefore be designed to intervene holistically, and systemically, in the larger developmental contexts of the child. In such contextually focused programs, counselors may be providing less direct service and more consultation or psychoeducational services to parents and teachers.

CASE EXAMPLE

Social competencies intersect both the "internalizing" and "externalizing" emotional and behavioral concerns with which many children struggle. Kristen, an 11-year-old Caucasian girl experiencing anxiety and occasional bouts of dysphoric mood, exemplified the first of these: Social skill deficits contributed to Kristen's social isolation and negative peer interactions, problems that in turn amplified her anxiety and low self-confidence at school.

In addition to anxiety and occasional dysphoria, Kristen displayed social inattention and frequent academic disengagement that led her to miss school a total of 14 days during the previous year, a pattern that amplified with the onset of the new academic year. Kristen's fifth-grade (current) teacher reported that her achievement was below that of the previous year and had recently declined markedly. According to the teacher, Kristen often embraced new topics but fell behind over time as her poor homework and frequent absences caught up with her. The teacher reported Kristen had few friends "and often seems lonely and a little bit scared . . . when she's not lost in class." With her parents' consent, Kristen was referred to a social competency group formed 6 weeks into the fall semester.

Individual and Group Social Competency Interventions

During an initial session with the school counselor, Kristen said that she experienced frequent anxiety related to social interactions with other girls in her class. Because her best friend transferred to another school the previous year, she felt she had "no friends left at all." Kristen also reported that she believed other girls were "making fun of [her] in class," although she could never clearly make out what they were saying. Rarely interacting with her classmates, Kristen spent much of her recess time playing alone or with girls from the fourth-grade class who shared the playground with her group.

Although Kristen came from a family with comfortable resources, her parents appeared to inconsistently provide the emotional support and opportunities for social growth that researchers have suggested may be critical to children's development of social competencies (e.g., Masten & Coatsworth, 1998; Patterson, 1980). In a teacher-parent conference attended by the counselor the previous year, Kristen's mother was alternately detached and stridently judgmental in her views about Kristen. Kristen's previous teacher reported that whereas Kristen's father occasionally contacted her and expressed optimism about reengaging Kristen in her academic work (e.g., homework, etc.), "he never really seemed to follow through—ever." Kristen's extended family members, both maternal and paternal, lived in a distant state and maintained little contact with her parents.

Because Kristen displayed microskills deficits such as poor interpersonal greetings, poor eye contact, and verbal nonresponsiveness in addition to the macroskill and metacognitive issues that were the focus of the social competencies group, Kristen saw the school counselor in individual sessions concurrent with her group participation. In weekly sessions, Kristen and the counselor used didactic strategies, role playing, and homework assignments to address Kristen's social skills and the cognitions she experienced during stressful interactions (including confrontations) with her peers. Kristen and the counselor also identified strategies to enhance Kristen's resilience against feelings of anxiety and sadness, including narrative therapy and solution-focused strategies that made use of Kristen's own language systems to marshal resources she already was using effectively (DeShazer, 1985; White & Epston, 1990). Kristen was asked, for instance, to identify strategies she used effectively in the past, or imagined future, to "put worry in the trash can." Using drawings, games, and conversational walks on the school grounds, Kristen and the counselor integrated competency-based perspectives into Kristen's view of and narratives about herself. In one particularly fecund session, Kristen integrated the perspective of her cat when identifying strengths (e.g., kindness, sense of humor) on which she could build in her interactions with her classmates, reporting that "these are good things Tiger already knows about me."

With the cooperation of her primary teacher, Kristen's classroom seating assignment was changed so she would be sitting behind rather than in front of the classmates she believed were talking and laughing about her. Kristen's teacher also collaborated with Kristen and the counselor to promote Kristen's social competency gains and to develop behavioral strategies to help Kristen more effectively self-manage her academic work. Kristen's parents were enlisted in this effort to increase the consistency of the modifications and, through family consultation sessions with the counselor, to view Kristen's academic efforts through a competency-based prism that heightened their recognition of her strengths and efforts to change. According to Kristen's mother, these sessions had the additional effect of increasing the interactions Kristen and her family had around "happy things."

In the social competencies group, Kristen learned to recognize other students' feelings and to more effectively articulate her own. She also learned conversational skills and social-cognitive problem-solving strategies that contributed to her improved social interactions and improved self-view academically and interpersonally.

Meeting in 1½-hour weekly sessions over the course of 10 weeks, Kristen's group consisted of seven members and targeted three primary social competencies: perspective-taking skills, communication skills, and conflict resolution skills. The group addressed perspective-taking competencies and communication skills through skills-acquisition techniques such as modeling, behavioral rehearsal, and homework. Conflict resolution skills were addressed in the group using a metacognitive model designed to improve members' use of such problem-solving strategies as problem recognition and formulation, generation of alternative solutions, and solution selection and evaluation strategies (see D'Zurilla & Goldfried, 1971).

Participants were asked to identify behavioral choices in detailed past or imagined future confrontations with classmates and to explore the potential effectiveness of each alternative in light of precepts learned in the group. Specific skills were modeled by facilitators or group members and rehearsed during group sessions and in homework assignments (e.g., invite a peer into an activity, reflectively listen to a peer's story). Group members' parents and caregivers also participated in two psychoeducational sessions in which they were taught to reinforce the prosocial skills students learned in the group.

The beginning sessions of Kristen's group established a cognitive/attitudinal set in which the learning of social competencies was viewed as parallel to learning a new game in which members were expected to make individually varying progress across a wide variety of skill sets (see Walco & Varni, 1991). Group rules, including taking turns, boundaries of appropriate feedback, and a "team" view of the group as a whole, were also established in these early sessions. Later group sessions addressed specific competencies (e.g., conversational skills, verbal complimenting, joining activities, extending invitations) through modeling and processing activities, followed by discussions organized around reflective questions. Time near the end of each session was used to review important skills or strategies that group members learned during the session. Homework, including opportunities to practice specific new competencies, was assigned for intervening weeks.

After the termination of the group, follow-up individual sessions were scheduled to reinforce positive changes in Kristen's interpersonal and academic behaviors and to reinforce Kristen's "re-storyings" of her growing competencies through solution-oriented questioning (e.g., "What did you do well this week?" "What good things would your teacher/classmates/cat tell me about you?"). By the end of the fall semester, Kristen's social and academic engagement and her school attendance had increased markedly, and she described herself as having "lots of friends." According to her teacher, her parents, and her own self-report, these improvements were maintained throughout the year.

SUMMARY

Counselors can play an important role in promoting the development of social competencies in children through a variety of approaches. By engaging in traditional, direct service (i.e., counseling, therapy), as is described in Kristen's case, counselors can help children develop specific competencies while attending to the unique individual, cultural, and familial factors of the child. Alternatively, through the development and implementation of programs focused on environmental or contextual influences on social competency promotion (e.g., programs for parents, teachers), counselors can encourage the development of such competencies indirectly as consultants or psychoeducators.

Clearly, the development of social competencies is important to the well-being and mental health of children. Not only do such competencies facilitate the establishment of healthy relationships with family members and peers, but they also are involved in preventing the development of problematic behaviors (e.g., violence) and psychological disorders (e.g., depression). This chapter has presented an overview of some of the skills, mechanisms, and contextual influences involved in social competency development and has described various programs and approaches to social competency promotion. Counselors who embrace a developmental approach to working with children will need to attend to many aspects of their functioning, yet given the importance of social competencies to school, peer, and family experiences, we must continue our efforts to understand the ways we can best promote social development.

VIGNETTE

Whereas Kristen exemplified the "internalizing" symptoms many children experience (and to which social competency concerns often contribute), Miguel exemplifies childhood "externalizing" concerns. An otherwise well-adjusted sixth grader, Miguel has displayed oppositionality toward peers and authority figures who have restricted his opportunities for healthy reciprocal social interactions. In turn, Miguel's lack of positive interactions has contributed to his recent pattern of irritable, angry, and occasionally hyperactive behaviors.

The fifth child in a Mexican American family of six boys, Miguel was described by his teacher as "the ignored one in the family." Miguel's mother and father both work as food service employees; his mother also works as a hotel maid during the evenings. Miguel's family lives in a public housing project in an impoverished residential/industrial section of Chicago, and he attends school in the same neighborhood.

Although Miguel has done well in his academic work in the past, he recently has become increasingly oppositional toward his teacher and his parents and has gotten into several small fights with classmates outside his school. During his interactions with the counselor, he presented with appropriate eye contact and a warm smile and generally showed a high level of intelligence and conversational competence. According to his teacher, Miguel's recent problems appear rooted in several recent, brief, but quickly escalating social conflicts that have compromised his relationships with his classmates and heightened his vulnerability to frustration in other areas of his life.

———

1. Miguel's microlevel social skills are solid, but he appears to suffer from metacognitive and macrolevel social skill deficits. With particular attention to Miguel's inner-city school setting, how might you design a small-group intervention to focus on these issues (considering group size, member selection and screening, scheduling, and parental and teacher consent, among other variables)? How would you acquire knowledge about Miguel's community? What activities, with what goals, would you have in mind for the first few sessions of the group?

2. How would you know if the group intervention wasn't working with Miguel? How would you handle oppositionality or aggressive behaviors (including aggressive verbal behaviors) if they emerged in the group?

3. What strategies or approaches might you use with Miguel in individual sessions if these were indicated? What would you do if you felt family systems issues were contributing to Miguel's oppositionality?

ADDITIONAL RESOURCES

Print Resources

Cowen, E. L., Hightower, A. D., Pedro-Carroll, J., Work, W. C., Wyman, P. A., & Haffy, W. G. (1996). *School-based prevention for children at risk: The primary mental health project.* Washington, DC: American Psychological Association.

Hammond, W. R., & Yung, B. R. (1995). *PACT: Positive Adolescent Choices Training: A model for violence prevention groups with African American youth.* Champaign, IL: Research Press. Available: http://www.researchpress. com

King, C., & Kirschenbaum, D. (1992). *Helping young children develop social skills: The social growth program.* Pacific Grove, CA: Brooks/Cole.

Khalsa, S. (1996). *Group exercises for enhancing social skills and self-esteem.* Sarasota, FL: Professional Resource Press.

LeCroy, C. W. (1994). Social skills training. In C. W. LeCroy (Ed.), *Handbook of child and adolescent treatment manuals* (pp. 126-169). New York: Lexington Books.

Videotape

Hammond, W. R., & Gipson, V. (1995). *Dealing with Anger: Givin' It, Takin' It, Workin' It Out: A violence prevention program for African American youth.* Champaign, IL: Research Press. Available: http://www.researchpress.com

Internet Resource

TeenCentral.Net: http://www.teencentral.net
   Sponsored by the American School Counselor Association, this Web site helps teens cope with issues like fitting in and family and peer problems.

CHAPTER 5

Prevention and Treatment of Behavior Problems for Children of Divorce

Merith Cosden
Maria Gutierrez

On March 24, 1998, in Jonesboro, Arkansas, 13-year-old Mitchell Johnson and 11-year-old Drew Golden brought firearms to school and killed four classmates and one teacher. The country was shocked that such young children could be responsible for these murders. Various articles tried to make sense of their actions. An article in *Time* magazine (Labi, 1998) offered this explanation: "The amiable goofy kid [Mitchell Johnson] was upset by the 1994 divorce of his parents. . . . Close friends and young relatives had watched his behavior deteriorate" (pp. 28-37). One of Mitchell's relatives was quoted as saying, "Since they [Mitchell's parents] split, he's gone downhill." The article implies that their divorce was the cause of Mitchell's deteriorating behavior, which eventually led to the violent school shootings.

It is estimated that one third to one half of all children in the next decade will experience a divorce in their family (Grynch & Fincham, 1992). In many ways, the prevalence of divorce has reduced its social stigma. Children are not ostracized from play groups, nor are adults excluded from their social circle because they have gone through a divorce. The myth of the "broken home" has been replaced by research that shows that children of divorce, as a group, experience similar levels of adjustment problems to those of children who have not experienced divorce (Amato & Keith, 1991; Burroughs, Wagner, & Johnson, 1997). Nevertheless, as evidenced by the *Time* article, the media still portray divorce as a contributing factor to adolescent behavior problems and criminal activity. In reality, the impact of divorce on children varies. To understand how divorce can affect child adjustment, specific risk and protective factors need to be examined (Pedro-Carroll & Alpert-Gillis, 1997).

A divorce officially occurs when legal papers are signed. However, these papers typically reflect the culmination of a lengthy process of family conflict and spousal separation. For children, the events that precede the divorce and how the family responds during and after the separation have a greater impact on adjustment than the divorce itself (Brown, Portes, & Christensen, 1989; Emery & Forehand, 1993). In a 10-year longitudinal study of children of divorce, Wallerstein et al. (e.g., Wallerstein & Blakeslee, 1989) found that children varied both in their immediate and long-term adjustment to divorce. In addition, immediate and long-term adjustment problems were often not related; that is, some children had a difficult reaction immediately after a divorce but few adjustment problems over time, whereas others didn't evidence problems until many years later.

A number of factors have been associated with child adjustment problems to divorce. For example, certain demographic characteristics of the child (gender) and the family (socioeconomic status) are related to child behavior problems. Most of the factors associated with child outcomes, however, reflect ongoing family processes. These include (a) interparental conflict, (b) parent-child relationships, (c) changes in disciplinary practices, and (d) perceptions of social support.

DEMOGRAPHIC VARIABLES

Two major demographic variables have been linked to risk status for children going through a divorce: (1) Sex is a risk factor, with boys demonstrating more behavior problems than girls after a divorce, particularly when there are high levels of marital conflict at home (Brown et al., 1989), and (2) changes in economic status and ensuing disruptions in normal activities are likely to have a detrimental impact on children after a divorce. Specifically, children are more likely to have behavior problems when there has been a severe drop in income, resulting in significant changes at home (Stevenson & Black, 1995). Dreman (2000) notes that when income is controlled, children in divorced families look more similar to children in two-parent families, although having a low income and having a change in income may result in different family issues and dynamics. Although knowledge of these risk variables does not indicate particular counseling strategies, it can be used to identify children and families who are more likely to need counseling.

The impact of the child's age on outcomes after a divorce is not clear. Examination of this factor is complicated for a number of reasons. First, studies on children of divorce often cover a wide age range, thus masking potential developmental differences. Second, even when children are categorized by age, as they often are in school-based studies, they are grouped by how old they are *at the time of the study,* not how old they were *at the time of the divorce.* Neither the age of the child at the time of the divorce nor the time since the divorce is controlled. Furthermore, the time at which the study occurs can affect one's responses. For example, in their longitudinal study of children of divorce, Burns and Dunlop (1999) found that people retrospectively recalled having more problems with the divorce when they were younger than they had reported at that earlier time. Whether this is a function of having an adult perspective on the past, denial as a child, or other factors has not been determined.

Kot and Shoemaker (1999) reviewed studies on the impact of divorce on children in four different age groups: infancy and toddlerhood, childhood, adolescence, and young adulthood. They found few studies that identified age-specific responses to divorce. In one example, Chase-Landsdale, Cherlin, and Kiernan (1995) noted that adolescents had more difficulty adjusting to divorce because of their need to feel secure within their families, which they needed to develop autonomy. Overall, however, studies do not find that age at the time of parental divorce has a significant impact on child outcomes over other factors, including family functioning, conflict, and social support (Pryor, 1999). According to Kot and Shoemaker (1999), the age of the child at the time of the divorce is a factor only in that it determines the type of coping strategies needed by the child to manage.

Research suggests that similar factors affect children's adjustment to divorce regardless of their age. Although many children experience negative short-term effects after a divorce, a small proportion have long-term problems that they carry into adulthood (Amato & Keith, 1991; Chase-Landsdale et al., 1995; Kelly, 2000).

FAMILY PROCESS VARIABLES

Several aspects of family functioning, including interparental conflict, parent-child relationships, changes in parental disciplinary practices, and social support, affect the child's adjustment to divorce even more than does parental separation (Kelly, 2000; Kot & Shoemaker, 1999; Shaw, 1991). These family process variables are discussed next.

Interparental Conflict

Many of the problems noted in children of divorce can be accounted for by problems that occur before the divorce itself (Kelly, 2000). Parental conflict, in particular, is associated with behavioral problems for children both from intact and divorced families (Dreman, 2000). Exposure to parental conflict increases the child's risk for emotional distress, lower academic performance, and dysfunctional peer relationships (Baris & Garrity, 1997; Camera & Resnick, 1989; Forehand, 1993b; Kelly, 2000; Tschann, Johnston, Kline, & Wallerstein, 1990). Thus, parents with high levels of conflict who stay together and parents who maintain a high level of conflict after a divorce provide ongoing risks to their children. Forehand (1993b) states that "if parents divorce and continue to engage in high levels of conflict, this is the worst scenario for a child" (p. 174). On the other hand, to the extent that separation reduces conflict, divorce may mitigate some of the destructive effects of marital conflict (Kelly, 2000).

How does marital conflict affect children? Several theories have been offered, including (a) children learn to model ineffective problem solving and fail to learn effective social interaction skills, (b) children become emotionally unstable as a function of living in a tension-filled home, (c) children feel responsible for the marital conflict and carry this stress into other aspects of their lives, and (d) the relationships between parents and children are disrupted as a result of these conflicts. None of these theories have been fully tested. However, children who model verbal or physical aggression or withdrawal when conflict arises with their peers are more likely to be socially isolated or rejected (Camera & Resnick, 1989; Kelly, 2000).

Parental conflict can take many forms, from physical violence to verbal aggression to undiscussed hostility. Studies indicate that all forms of interparental conflict are damaging to children, even if the conflict is manifested in nonviolent and nonverbal ways (e.g., the "silent treatment"), if the conflict remains unresolved (Cummings, Vogel, Cummings, & El-Sheikh, 1989).

Parent-Child Relationships

The quality of the parent-child relationship is another predictor of how well a child will adjust to a divorce (Emery, 1988; Forehand et al., 1990). Studies find that a good relationship with at least one parent during this time can buffer the child's negative experiences associated with divorce (Forehand, 1993a).

However, even if parent-child relationships are satisfying before a divorce, these relationships may change during a divorce. In some instances, parents become more distracted and unavailable (physically and emotionally) from their children as a result of economic difficulties or emotional stress (Shaw, 1991).

The emotional stress associated with the divorce for the parents may affect the warmth and affection parents show toward their children (Kelly, 2000; Wallerstein & Kelly, 1980).

Furthermore, high levels of interparental conflict are likely to affect parent-child relationships either because the children are drawn into the conflict or because they are ignored (Baris & Garrity, 1997; Emery & Forehand, 1993). Parents who involve their children in interparental conflict before they divorce tend to have poor relationships with their children after they divorce (Tschann et al., 1990).

Few studies have examined differences in children's response to divorce as a function of race or ethnicity. In a recent study, Gutierrez (1996) found similar, significant relationships for interparental conflict, parent-child relationship problems, and children's adjustment for Latino and Anglo families. Although the data across ethnic groups are limited, it appears that the combination of interparental conflict and poor parent-child relationships puts children at risk for behavior problems at home, at school, and with their peers.

Discipline

After a divorce, parental disciplinary practices may change, and these changes also affect child adjustment (Tschann et al., 1990). Wallerstein and Kelly (1980) report that both parents experience a "diminished capacity to parent" following a divorce. Furthermore, to the extent that single parents depend on their child for emotional support, they are at risk for becoming too permissive in their disciplinary style (Shaw, 1991). In other instances, parents react to the emotional and financial stress they experience by developing a more rigid parenting style, becoming more authoritarian and coercive and less responsive to their child's needs (Buehler & Legg, 1992).

The problems associated with ineffective parenting practices reverberate within a family. That is, overly authoritarian, or permissive, parenting increases defiance in children, whereas parents who perceive their children as out of control experience greater stress, further reducing their capacity to parent. On the other hand, studies show that single-parent mothers who perceived themselves as having more control had children who exhibited fewer behavioral problems, had fewer somatic complaints, and had higher self-esteem than children whose mothers perceived themselves as having less control (Machida & Holloway, 1991).

Few studies have addressed differences in parental styles across ethnic groups. Martinez (1993) reports that the child-rearing styles and disciplinary practices of Mexican Americans are diverse, ranging from permissive to authoritarian to authoritative. In a recent study on Latino and Anglo parents who were separated or divorced (Gutierrez, 1996), Latino parents reported more difficulty in disciplining their children. These problems may have been related to economic stresses, as the Latino families in this sample were larger and earned less income than Anglo families. Given the lack of systematic study of divorced families from diverse backgrounds and the confounds presented by differences in socioeconomic status across ethnic groups, caution is required in generalizing current findings across ethnicities. Current evidence suggests, however, that both the stability and quality of postdivorce events affect child adjustment (Sandler, Wolchik, Braver, & Fogas, 1991).

Social Support

Social support has also been associated with child adjustment to divorce. Some studies have reported that children of divorce, as a group, have a smaller social support network, spend less time in outside activities, and have fewer friends than children from intact families (Wyman, Cowen, Hightower, & Pedro-Carroll, 1985). However, there is great variation in perceived support both among children from intact families and among children of divorce. Nevertheless, children of divorce who perceived themselves as having a stronger support system rate themselves as better adjusted (Cowen, Pedro-Carroll, & Alpert-Gillis, 1990; Pruett, Calsyn, & Jensen, 1993).

Children from cultural backgrounds that value strong family ties and extended family relationships may rely on different types of social support after a divorce. Amato (1991) suggests that close extended family ties serve a protective function for Latinos because relatives are available to assume caretaking responsibilities. On the other hand, it has been argued that family conflict may have a greater negative impact on Latino adolescents because they have not developed strong social ties outside their extended family (Mechanic & Hansell, 1989). Few studies have considered the impact of different cultural values on the divorce process. Mirowsky and Ross (1980) state that extra-familial support buffers the negative effects of divorce among African Americans, Anglos, and Latinos. Furthermore, for some, religion and the church may provide support at times of family crisis (Breault & Kposowa, 1987).

In sum, a number of risk factors are associated with child behavior problems after a divorce. Use of this knowledge can help inform the development of effective prevention- and intervention-oriented counseling programs.

IMPLICATIONS FOR PREVENTION

One cannot know for certain which couples will obtain a divorce. However, factors that are linked to the development of emotional and behavioral problems in children can be addressed in all families before a parental separation.

Forehand (1993a) notes that a low degree of interparental conflict, a satisfying relationship with at least one parent, consistent parental discipline, and a good support system with other family members and friends can buffer a child from the negative effects of divorce. Thus, community counseling programs that focus on these aspects of healthy family functioning could prevent, or at least ameliorate, child behavior problems that may emerge during or after a divorce. This type of effort could include working with pediatricians or other health care providers to develop and make available informational booklets that describe the positive impact that resolving parental differences can have on children's behavior. Counselors might also use baby fairs or other community events as opportunities to provide families with this information.

Caplan and Caplan (1999) describe a prevention program that was implemented in Israel. The purpose of this program was to prevent mental disorder among children whose parents had filed for divorce. It must be noted that the authors cite national Israeli statistics that indicate that 40% of their children of divorce develop serious psychological disturbance. This is a much higher figure than that reported in studies in the United States (e.g., Burns & Dunlop, 1999). There are many potential reasons for this difference. For example, a lower prevalence of divorce exists in Israel because of religious controls over the divorce court. Thus, the populations that divorce, as well as the social implications of divorce, differ across these countries. Nevertheless, their program is one of few described in the literature and appears to have broad applicability.

As part of this prevention program, information on how to tell children about divorce and how to provide children with the emotional and cognitive guidance through the divorce is provided to all parents initiating divorce proceedings. Caplan and Caplan (1999) acknowledge that this prevention approach is most likely to be beneficial to parents "who are mentally healthy and generally reasonably effective but who lack the knowledge needed to deal adequately with the stresses faced by children of divorce" (p. 111). They also recognize that it is not possible to identify those parents a priori; thus, booklets are provided to all parents entering the divorce court. No data on the effectiveness of this intervention are provided. The authors also note the need to identify parents who have greater personal problems and who may require interventions that are more intensive. They have established study groups to develop a plan to provide additional prevention services to children with greater needs, but no program has yet been published.

In another prevention effort, Gately and Schwebel (1992) describe a series of tasks faced by children, adolescents, and young adults when their parents divorce. These include acknowledging marital disruption, regaining the ability to pursue everyday activities, dealing with feelings of loss and rejection, forgiving their parents for separating, accepting the permanence of the divorce, and feeling comfortable in their own relationships. They recommend talking with family members about these tasks before problems emerge. They also acknowledge that those who cannot address these issues on their own may need further treatment. Knowledge of child risk factors can also be used to identify children who are more likely to have adjustment problems. Thus, the knowledge that children, and boys in particular, are more susceptible to behavior problems when exposed to unresolved parental conflict, and that changes in the family's economic circumstances also increase the likelihood that children will evidence emotional and behavioral problems, suggests early identification of children in these "risk" categories for further assessment and possible counseling.

However, it is clear that many children of divorce are exposed to interparental conflict for long periods of time before they come to anyone's attention (Baris & Garrity, 1997). The predivorce home environment, if conflictual, contributes to children's behavior problems before a divorce takes place (Cherlin et al., 1991). In addition to the community-based programs described earlier, prevention of child adjustment problems, particularly in families with high conflict, could be addressed through public awareness campaigns, via the media, in which long-term exposure to parental conflict is identified as unhealthful for children. As parents consider divorce and the impact it may have on their children, counselors can effectively use psychoeducational strategies to help them see the deleterious impact of conflict over that of the divorce itself. In this sense, predivorce marital counseling and mediation may also circumvent problems in child adjustment, whether or not a divorce occurs.

Because child adjustment problems are heavily linked to processes occurring within the family, parental involvement would appear to be a critical element in such programs. Thus, many counseling programs designed to help with child adjustment require parental participation, whereas others work directly with children. Examples of each type of counseling program are discussed next.

FAMILY COUNSELING

Most of the factors associated with child adjustment problems are related to parental or family interactions, or both. Family functioning prior to the divorce and the ability of the adults to develop a cooperative postdivorce relationship particularly in relation to parenting are key factors in subsequent child adjustment. Thus, family counseling, depending on when it occurs, can help prevent, reduce, or address child behavior problems.

Counselors can help children of divorce by working with their divorcing parents on practical, child-oriented problems. Psychoeducational, structural, and behavioral approaches, including concrete directives, are recommended. For example, the focus of counseling may be to facilitate contact with the noncustodial parent or to help with transitions around visitations (Walsh, Jacob, & Simons, 1995). An important consideration is not to overburden either parent with new tasks, as this will only increase their stress and feelings of helplessness.

From the perspective of the counselor concerned with child adjustment, the focus of counseling should be to help the divorcing adults separate their parental and spouse roles (Brown et al., 1989). A major goal of the counselor is to help both parents remain responsible for their children and develop their roles as parents even though their roles as spouses have ended (Bird, 1992). This includes helping parents "encapsulate" their conflicts by not fighting in front of their children, separating their needs from those of their children, and helping each of them establish effective parenting practices on their own (Hetherington, Law, & O'Connor, 1993). Counseling strategies to accomplish this might include having separate discussions of parenting and spousal concerns at different times or using concrete materials (such as boards or lists) to categorize items that arise in session into one of these two domains. In a similar vein, Baris and Garrity (1997) suggest the use of a parenting coordinator during mediation, whose role is to make sure at some point during the divorce proceeding that child-rearing issues are addressed and that they are considered separately from other spousal concerns.

The postdivorce relationship between spouses also affects children's adjustment to divorce (Brown et al., 1989). If parents are motivated to work on their relationship after their divorce, counselors can help them develop a positive alliance by learning to convey respect for the other parent, maintain constructive communication about the children, and develop a way of sharing responsibly the child-rearing tasks (Ahrons & Rodgers, 1987). As noted by the investigators, a realistic goal of counseling would be to develop "cooperative colleagues" rather than "perfect pals."

Another counseling goal—helping parents reduce their stress—will also translate into better child adjustment. Counselors can achieve this objective in several ways. Herz (1989), for example, suggests counseling single-parent households about how to reduce financial pressures, improve parenting skills, and increase social relationships. In a different vein, Hetherington et al. (1993) note that by increasing parenting skills parents gain a sense of competence with their child, and this can enhance the child's self-esteem. Either approach establishes a family cycle in which parents are less stressed, are more confident, and have more energy to focus on the needs of their children.

Questions about different custodial arrangements are likely to arise in counseling. If there is little conflict and both parents remain involved with the children, a variety of custodial arrangements can be effective for children (Walsh et al., 1995). Nevertheless, some distress about custodial arrangements during the first year after a divorce is common. Parents can be counseled that the stability of visitation is more predictive of child adjustment than the frequency of visits (Isaacs, 1988).

Approximately 20 to 30% of divorced couples maintain high levels of conflict for years following their divorce (Emery, 1988; Johnston & Campbell,

1988; Maccoby & Mnookin, 1992). Factors that predict chronic problems include the length of negativity in their marriage, individual vulnerability in managing grief and loss, and the degree of injury (emotional and physical) sustained in the divorce process. Parental conflict (and conflict resolution) is a major factor in child adjustment after a divorce. Families with high conflict need help structuring their parenting arrangements while maintaining distance and disengagement in other areas of their lives (Baris & Garrity, 1997). The problems that sustain the conflict, however, tend to have long roots; for example, the ability to adjust to loss is related to the quality of early relationships and attachments. Using a combination of psychoeducational and structured counseling techniques may not be sufficient with some families. In these instances, providing support and coping skills for the children directly may also contribute to their adjustment.

Finally, little has been written about counseling families with alternative lifestyles after a separation. A growing issue is how to help lesbian and gay couples who have child custody and visitation issues after a separation (Chambers, 1998). Because gay and lesbian couples are not married, they do not share the legal rights for division of property afforded to opposite-sex married couples. Only a few states, such as California, enforce such agreements between unmarried same-sex couples going through a separation. The impact this has on a child of a lesbian couple is that unless the nonbiological mother has formally adopted the child, she has no legally enforceable rights or duties. However, if the nonbiological mother has adopted the child, she can be considered for custody, visitation, and child support. In some cases, the sperm donor, even if he has not been involved in the child's life, has been given legal status as a father (Benkov, 1994).

Thus, the lack of legal protection for both parents puts children of divorced lesbian and gay couples at greater risk for adjustment problems if their parents cannot resolve these issues on their own (Morton, 1998). Benkov (1994) adds that the lack of acknowledgment of lesbian and gay couples leads to a lack of legal and economic protection for children whose parents are getting a divorce. In these instances, counseling the family (and working with mediation) to clarify the future nature of the partners' relationship with the children is essential. Chambers (1998) encourages lesbian and gay couples to discuss custody arrangements and resolve disputes out of court, because judges may be biased against them. Chambers (1998) also advises mental health practitioners to become familiar with state rules and the practices of judges in their district so that they can understand the unique legal positions of their clients.

Most of the risk factors in the literature point to the importance of parental and family interventions. Although the aforementioned approaches to counseling address these needs, few have been empirically tested. A variety of child-oriented counseling groups have also been recommended and evaluated and are presented next.

CHILD COUNSELING

The literature describes group and individual child-oriented counseling for children of divorce. Most of the interventions, however, are small group, short term, and school based and are designed to help children understand more about the divorce process and their reactions to it. Although these programs do not affect the family stressors most associated with child adjustment problems, they serve an important auxiliary function by helping children build their personal resources for dealing with the changes in their lives. This is particularly important in light of Wallerstein and Blakeslee's (1989) finding that fewer than 10% of the children from divorced families reported having an adult speak to them sympathetically during the divorce. Thus, directly counseling children about divorce provides a forum to hear child concerns and to facilitate their understanding of and adjustment to factors they cannot control.

Child-focus counseling is designed to help the child understand and work through the emotional effects of the divorce when primary intervention efforts fail (e.g., Gately & Schwebel, 1992). Ciborowski (1989) frames the goals of the counselor as helping children work through the stages associated with this loss, which are denial, grief, guilt, anger, fear of abandonment, depression, and the desire to reunite their parents. Counseling strategies include (a) helping children become aware of their feelings and behavior in relation to the divorce, (b) encouraging children to talk about their anger and guilt in a rational manner, (c) allowing children to grieve, (d) discussing fear of abandonment or, in cases where one parent has left the family, dealing with the pain of actual abandonment, and (e) helping children maintain positive activities outside the family.

For example, a counselor can expect children who seek assistance after a divorce to be experiencing distress but not to be able to identify or understand their feelings. Furthermore, it is common for children to internalize the responsibility or blame for their negative feelings and possibly for the divorce. A combined psychoeducational and developmental approach might be used to help children understand the reasons for the divorce and to reattribute what has happened to their parents. This is congruent to the approach used in counseling parents in that children are asked to examine the divorce from another perspective—that of the adults in their lives. However, in this instance, children are asked to take less responsibility for what has occurred and instead to understand how the decision to divorce has affected their physical existence, their emotions, and their behavior. These changes in understanding are expected to change the child's expression of affect. At first, children are likely to express few feelings in session or to express feelings that are strong but diffuse. As children gain in their understanding of the divorce, they are likely to experience sadness and anger that is more focused on their actual losses. Sessions can then be used to allow the child to mourn and to understand and accept the changes in their family life.

Group counseling is commonly used both because it is cost-effective and because it offers children the opportunity for peer support (Sanders & Riester, 1996). The literature contains a variety of counseling groups (e.g., Crosbie-Burnett & Newcomer, 1990; Garvin, Leber, & Kalter, 1991; Pedro-Carroll & Albert-Gillis, 1997; Sanders & Riester, 1996; Slavkin, 2000; Yauman, 1991). These groups range in length from 6 to 12 sessions and serve children across the school-age spectrum. Common goals include (a) normalization of the experiences of divorce, (b) increasing the child's understanding of divorce and divorce-related concepts, (c) facilitating identification, acceptance, and appropriate expression of feelings, (d) teaching problem-solving skills; (e) addressing common problems such as feeling caught in the middle, visitation issues, and parents who don't maintain contact with them, (f) assisting in the development of coping strategies, and (g) enhancing perceptions of themselves and their families within a supportive group environment.

Evaluation of these groups has yielded equivocal findings. Several likely reasons for these poor outcomes include the small sample sizes (ranging from 10 to 20 in most studies) and the inclusion of all children of divorce who obtain parental consent to participate rather than those who demonstrate a need for counseling. Outcomes typically include measures of self-esteem and scales to assess understanding of divorce concepts. Most studies report little change in self-concept over time (e.g., Garvin et al., 1991; Sanders & Riester, 1996); however, some children show significant changes and many participants have relatively high levels of self-esteem before the programs start. In a post hoc analysis, Garvin et al. (1991) found that children who scored lowest on self-esteem at the beginning of the study were more likely to demonstrate gains at the end. In a recent study of children and adolescents participating in a Healthy Families program (Slavkin, 2000), the efficacy of specific group counseling modules on changing students' attitudes in those areas was examined. Participants had significant changes on responses to questions on anger management, responsibility for parents, and responsibility for being pulled between parents; responses to questions on alcohol and drug abuse, neglect, and sexual abuse were more equivocal. However, the impact of these written responses on subsequent behavior was not examined.

Pedro-Carroll et al. have published a number of studies on group counseling of children of divorce (e.g., Alpert-Gillis, Pedro-Carroll, & Cowen, 1989; Pedro-Carroll & Cowen, 1985; Pedro-Carroll, Cowen, Hightower, & Guare, 1986). Their Children of Divorce Intervention programs have been assessed across a wide age span of children and yield some of the more promising findings. For example, Pedro-Carroll and Alpert-Gillis (1997) compared 37 participants (5- and 6-year-olds) with 26 waiting list controls from divorced families and 39 controls from nondivorced families. The objectives of the 12-week counseling groups were to (a) foster a supportive group environment, (b) facilitate identification, acceptance, and appropriate expression of feelings, (c) promote understanding of divorce-related concepts, (d) teach communicative and problem-solving skills, and (e) enhance perceptions of themselves and their families. At the end of the study, teachers, parents, and children on a variety of measures noted significant changes for children in the treatment group relative to the control groups. The authors note that in these groups, as in others they have developed, providing children with a combination of support and coping skills appears to be the most effective counseling strategy. Although this strategy is promising, the authors also note that the generalization of their findings is limited by the self-selection of participants.

EXAMPLE OF A GROUP FOR CHILDREN OF DIVORCE

A group for children of divorce was offered after school for children whose parents had been separated for less than 2 years. This criterion was set because the 2 years following a parental separation can be the most difficult time for a child. The group was limited to eight children who were identified by parents or teachers (or both) as having difficulty adjusting to the divorce/ separation.

The group met once a week for a total of 12 weeks. The first two sessions focused on introductions and education on adjustment to divorce. An ice breaker technique ("If I had three wishes, I would wish . . ." or "I am a ____ but I would like to be a ____," using animals, vegetables, cars, flowers, etc.) was used to facilitate introductions. Group norms and confidentiality were discussed. The reasons why people marry and divorce were discussed, and the children were offered the opportunity to tell their story.

Sessions 3 through 6 addressed feelings of loss and abandonment. Children also described feelings of shame and anger. Group leaders normalized children's feelings by educating them on the stages of grief. To encourage the children to express their feelings, they participated in a grieving exercise in which they drew pictures of the different stages of grief (denial, sadness, anger, guilt, worry, confusion, hope, acceptance) and then shared the pictures with the group.

Sessions 7 and 8 focused on exposure to parental conflict and being caught in the middle. Children were given the opportunity to draw or role-play scenes of parental conflict. A discussion followed each role play, and problem-solving strategies were offered. Children were given "tools" to use to protect themselves from being placed in the middle.

Sessions 9 and 10 focused on stepfamily issues. Many times, children feel loyalty conflicts when their parents begin to date and remarry. Negotiating two homes, different rules, new family members, and realistic expectations were addressed.

Sessions 11 and 12 addressed termination issues. Progress was reviewed, and coping strategies were highlighted. Social supports were identified. Children were encouraged to maintain positive activities outside the home.

SUMMARY

Children vary in their reactions to divorce. Many of the factors that influence their adjustment are evident prior to the divorce, including the level of interparental conflict they experience, the quality of parent-child relationships, disciplinary problems, and social supports. The strong impact of these family behaviors on child adjustment indicates the need for prevention and early intervention efforts, including parental education programs on the impact of spousal conflict on children. The divorce itself can exacerbate children's problems as parents become more conflictual or too stressed or both to attend to their children's needs. Resolution of spousal conflicts, however, through mediation or divorce may reduce their children's behavior problems. Thus, parental involvement is a critical component to counseling when children are not adjusting well after a divorce. By helping parents separate spousal roles and conflicts from their parenting responsibilities and relationship to their children, counselors can help ameliorate children's adjustment problems. Specifically, children do better when their parents present a nonconflictual, caring presence to them, regardless of whether the parents live together or apart. In instances where efforts to reduce parental conflict are not effective, counselors may work with children directly, either individually or in small groups. Counselors working with children of divorce can help them understand the divorce process, reduce their sense of responsibility for their family's problems, assist them in identifying their feelings about divorce, allow them to express those feelings in session, and help them accept the changes in their families and adapt to them as well as possible.

VIGNETTES

Vignette 1: School-Based Prevention Program

You are working as a school counselor in an elementary school. The fourth-grade teacher has identified six children, and the fifth-grade teacher has identified eight children in their respective classes with mild "acting out" problems. Nine of the 14 children identified come from families who have experienced a divorce. The principal asks you to start a group for children of divorce with these nine students.

----

1. What are your goals for this group?

2. How will you know if this group has been successful?

3. How important is it to involve the parents of these children in treatment?

4. How effective do you think a group will be in decreasing problem behaviors?

Vignette 2: Family Versus Child-Centered Counseling

You are working in a community mental health agency. Mrs. Martinez has brought Jaime, her 10-year-old, to you because his behavior is a concern to her and to his teacher. At school, Jaime has been falling asleep during class and not turning in his homework. Eight times in the past month he has pushed and yelled at other students during recess. According to Mrs. Martinez, Jaime has recently been uncooperative at home.

A parent interview yields the following information: Mrs. Martinez (29) is employed as a nurse's aide, and Mr. Martinez (31) is a supermarket manager. Mr. and Mrs. Martinez met in high school. Mr. Martinez graduated and started working at the supermarket full time. Two years later, when Mrs. Martinez graduated, she enrolled in the community college. During her first year, Mrs. Martinez became pregnant with Jaime. Once Jaime was born, Mrs. Martinez withdrew from school. One year after Jaime's birth, his brother, Luis, was born, and his sister, Carmella, followed 2 years later. When Carmella entered preschool, Mrs. Martinez began attending evening classes at the community college and was able to get her certification as a nurse's aide.

Mrs. Martinez describes Jaime as her *amor de mi vida* ("love of my life"). He has always known what to say or do to cheer her up. Even when he was a toddler, she could count on him to make her laugh, especially after a fight with her husband. Mr. and Mrs. Martinez frequently argued about finances. After Carmella's birth, Mr. Martinez was laid off from work and the arguments increased. This was the first time that Mr. and Mrs. Martinez separated. The separation lasted 7 months. Things improved for a while after Mr. Martinez found a new job, but the fighting never ceased. In the past year, the arguments have escalated, and 3 months ago, Mr. Martinez moved out again. He is currently living with one of his brothers. Mr. Martinez visits the children on Sundays and weekday evenings. Mrs. Martinez dreads those pick-up and drop-off times because they often end up yelling at one another.

Mrs. Martinez is very concerned about Jaime's behavior at school. She acknowledges that she has been busy lately and has not been able to check his homework at night. At this point, Mrs. Martinez becomes tearful and tells you that she is worried about money and that she feels tired all the time. She has tried talking to Jaime, but most of the time she ends up crying and pleading with him to "be a good boy" for her sake.

The next day, you meet Jaime. Jaime is a small and quiet boy dressed in jeans and a sweatshirt. He seems shy and reluctant to engage in eye contact. He starts to doodle with the pen and paper on the table, and you ask him if he would like to draw. He draws a picture of a soccer field and tells you that he likes playing soccer. You ask him to draw a picture of his family. He draws himself in the center and to his right his mother and younger siblings. Off to the left, he draws his father. All the figures are the same height except for him, and he is quite large. He tells you that his dad sleeps over at his uncle's house. You notice that he has become intrigued by the superheroes on your shelf. He picks up Superman and has him fly through the air and then crash. He repeats this with the rest of the superheroes. Next, Jaime notices the Talking, Feeling, Doing Game® and asks if he can play. He consistently offers aggressive actions as solutions for social dilemmas.

---

1. Given what you know about the variables affecting children's adjustment to divorce, what effect do you think that Mr. and Mrs. Martinez's conflict has on Jaime?

2. How would you characterize Mrs. Martinez's relationship with Jaime? What impact do you think this relationship is having on Jaime's behavior?

3. Jaime's problem-solving skills appear to be modeled after his parents' way of resolving conflict. What intervention would you consider for improving Jaime's coping skills?

4. Would Jaime benefit more from joining a social skills group or from having his parents work with you on their communication skills?

ADDITIONAL RESOURCES

Recommended Readings for Children

Brett, D. (1986). *Annie stories: A special kind of storytelling.* New York: Workman.
Brown, L. K., & Brown, M. (1986). *Dinosaurs divorce: A guide for changing families.* Boston: Little, Brown.

Krementz, J. (1994). How it feels when parents divorce. New York: Knopf.

Lansky, V. (1998). *It's not your fault, Koko bear: A read-together book for parents and young children during divorce.* Minnetonka, MN: Book Peddlers.

Nightingale, L. V. (1997). *My parents still love me even though they're getting divorced: An interactive tale for children.* Yorba Linda, CA: Nightingale Rose.

Rogers, F. (1994). *Let's talk about it: Divorce.* New York: Putnam.

Recommended Readings for Parents

Blau, M. (1995). *Families apart: Ten keys to successful co-parenting.* New York: Perigee.

Lyster, M. (1996). *Child custody: Building agreements that work.* Berkeley, CA: Nolo.

Shulman, D. (1997). *Co-parenting after divorce: How to raise happy, healthy children in two-home families.* New York: Winspeed.

Counseling Tools

Heegaard, M. (1991). *When mom and dad separate: Children can learn to cope with grief from divorce.* Minneapolis, MN: Woodland.

Internet Resources

Focus on Kids: The Effects of Divorce on Children:
    http://www.muextension. missouri.edu/xplor/hesguide/humanrel/gh6600.htm

The Divorce Support Page: http://www.divorcesupport.com

Family Law Advice on Divorce, Child Support, Custody, Visitation:
    http://www.divorcenet.com

PART III

Adolescence

A dolescence is frequently defined by either physical maturity (e.g., begins with onset of puberty and ends with fully developed adult characteristics) or chronological age (12-21 years). Although there is a high correlation between these two variables, the fact that the onset of puberty for girls has moved steadily downward over the past 100 years raises questions about the stability and utility of this index of adolescence. Although some girls manifest signs of puberty by age 10 or even younger, most developmental specialists agree that social and emotional aspects of adolescence do not take place until around age 12. For this reason, we have elected to follow the convention of defining adolescence as the period of life between ages 12 and 21, inclusive.

Despite the early onset of puberty for some girls, adolescence is a period of life characterized by rapid physical, emotional, and cognitive maturation. Physical changes for boys include increased height and weight, development of the testes and penis, and growth of facial and body hair. For girls, physical changes include increased height and weight, development of breasts, onset of the menstrual cycle, and growth of body hair. These physical changes contribute to emotional and social development during adolescence. In particular, physical changes during this time often affect how adolescents perceive themselves, how they are perceived by others, and how they believe they are perceived by others (Newman & Newman, 1991).

It is generally recognized that adolescents experience more variability in their emotions than they did at a younger age, and many observers suggest that they are more subject to moodiness and emotional outbursts than at other stages of life. Whereas younger children are often shielded from the stresses of life, adolescents are often fully experiencing them for the first time. Stress, feelings of inadequacy, and hormonal changes have all been cited as possible causes of depression among adolescents (Newman & Newman, 1991).

Furthermore, adolescence is a period of heightened sensitivity to peer relationships. Belonging to an identifiable group outside the family becomes extremely important, and adolescents begin spending more time with peer groups than in childhood. Various characteristics, such as physical attractiveness, athletic ability, social skills, racial or ethnic background, religious affiliation, and socioeconomic background, often determine which peer group is open to any individual adolescent. Although peer groups are often problematic, as many parents will attest, they can also help adolescents develop their social skills and self-identity (Newman & Newman, 1991).

Adolescence is also a time when serious behavioral and psychological problems can develop. Weight gains associated with normal adolescent development, combined with media and peer stereotypes about the perfect body, often motivate girls (in particular) to start dieting; for some individuals, dieting can be the precursor to eating disorders. An increased interest in sexual activity puts adolescents at risk of an unwanted pregnancy and sexually transmitted disease. Through peer groups, adolescents are often exposed to alcohol and drug use, which in turn can lead to alcohol and drug abuse. Stress and depression experienced during adolescence may contribute to the high incidence of suicides among this age group (Newman & Newman, 1991).

Fortunately, counselors can play a role in preventing many of the problems associated with adolescence that often have a lifetime impact. Many adolescents establish unhealthy lifestyles that stay with them for the rest of their lives. For example, in 1997, more than one in three adolescents failed to engage in at least 20 minutes of vigorous physical activity a minimum of three or more times a week. Between 1988 and 1994, 11% of children ages 6 to 19 were overweight or obese. In 1997, 36% of adolescents reported having smoked a cigarette in the past month. In that same year, 21% of adolescents reported drinking alcohol in the past 30 days (U.S. Department of Health and Human Services, 2000).

In Chapter 6, José M. Abreu and Michael D. Newcomb review a number of school-based programs designed to promote healthy lifestyles among adolescents. The authors begin by briefly reviewing theories of adolescent development that have implications for the interventions to be presented. They break the presentation of intervention strategies into two types: those designed to promote healthy behavior and those designed to prevent risk behaviors. Within the category of interventions to promote healthy behaviors, Abreu and Newcomb focus on the promotion of physical and psychosocial behaviors. Under prevention of risk behaviors, they focus on three behaviors: drug abuse, sexual behavior, and violence. Their chapter provides a comprehensive overview of programs that counselors in schools and other settings will find helpful when attempting to promote healthy development and prevent risk behaviors.

An essential task of adolescent growth is establishing a foundation of positive self-esteem and identity development. In Chapter 7, Susana M. Lowe and Jackqueline Mascher begin by discussing the many factors that contribute, positively and negatively, to adolescent identity development. They identify eight key dimensions of any intervention designed to foster positive identity development. This is followed by descriptions of four structured programs aimed at promoting identity development. They conclude the chapter by suggesting ways for counselors to work with adolescent clients who have special needs related to identity development.

In Chapter 8, V. Scott Solberg, Wendy Close, and A. J. Metz use a ship sailing across an ocean as a metaphor for students' self-identity and success pathways as the means of moving students toward desired academic, vocational, and life goals. The authors select Developmental Systems Theory as the organizing framework for a number of interventions designed to build students' confidence and enhance their understanding of how academic activities can move them toward their goals. Specific interventions that counselors in schools can employ to enhance student confidence and understanding are described.

In Chapter 9, William J. Lyddon and Karen D. Slaton discuss the prevalence of body image disturbance among adolescent girls and steps that can be taken to prevent and treat this growing problem. After defining and documenting the prevalence of body image disturbance, the authors identify sociocultural factors, family and peer influences, and developmental and intrapersonal influences that contribute to body image disturbances. Lyddon and Slaton review factors that must be taken into consideration when developing prevention and treatment interventions for body image disturbances. They then offer specific preventive (challenging cultural ideals and media influences, teaching effective communication skills, providing education about development, teaching effective parenting) and treatment (cognitive-behavior, feminist cognitive-behavioral, experiential) programs to address this concern.

Finally, in Chapter 10, Joan I. Rosenberg provides suggestions for preventing and treating adolescent suicide ideation. She begins the chapters by documenting the prevalence of suicide among adolescents and describes the economic and emotional costs associated with suicide. Rosenberg examines why suicides are on the rise and looks at differences in adolescent suicide rates and causes that are related to sex, ethnicity, sexual orientation, and giftedness. Risk factors for suicide and methods of attempting suicide are discussed. Eight strategies for preventing youth suicide identified by the Centers for Disease Control are briefly described, along with additional early intervention considerations. The chapter concludes with a discussion of treatment strategies when working with an adolescent who is already suicidal.

These five chapters provide an outstanding resource to counselors who work with adolescents. Collectively, they describe a number of programs to help prevent and treat the many problems that confront this population.

CHAPTER 6

Promoting Healthy Lifestyles Among Adolescents

José M. Abreu
Michael D. Newcomb

The view of adolescence espoused by G. Stanley Hall in 1904 as a time of unavoidable "storm and stress" has been difficult to shake. Hall conceptualized adolescence as a trouble-ridden phase, with youths anxiously looking for and then rejecting leadership or guidance from both peers and adults. He believed that the maturational changes taking place during adolescence emanated from purely biological factors and that nothing could be done to intervene, other than simply letting this period of time pass as "a stage." This trend to focus on pathology—rather than on healthy development—is captured succinctly in Smith and Rutter's (1995) justification for their study of problem behaviors among U.S. adolescents: "[Disorders] can be defined . . . whereas well-being and happiness are extremely vague concepts" (p. 1).

Although many writers continue to associate adolescence with risk factors and other negatives (Humphreys & Rappaport, 1993), some have begun to emphasize opportunities and potentials for growth. Newcomb (1996a) affirms that adolescence can be considered a time of "birth, preparation, independence, and evolvement; it is exciting and stressful. . . . It can be filled with hope and aspiration, at the same time as fear, dread, and uncertainty; the extremes

Authors' Note: Grant DA 01070 from the National Institute on Drug Abuse to the first author supported this research.

of emotion and demands are vast and generate equally powerful responses that reverberate throughout our lives" (p. 484).

Given the multitude and significance of life changes occurring during adolescence (Coleman, 1978), defining healthy or optimal development is rather complicated, generating at least a little sympathy for Smith and Rutter's (1995) stance noted previously. In addition, it is difficult to imagine all the changes that take place in adolescence without some form of risk (Gullotta, Adams, & Markstrom, 2000; Newcomb & Bentler, 1989). For example, in rebelling against a parent's directives and increasing their intimacy with peers, youths may be lured to begin smoking cigarettes, a behavior resulting from a developmental transition that could lead to substantial health problems. At the same time, transitions in adolescence can also lead to salutary outcomes (Newcomb, 1996b). For instance, increasing cognitive ability and a better understanding of cause-effect contingencies that occur in adolescence can give rise to a greater sense of control over personal choice in behaviors that promote health rather than disease. Similarly, acquisition of adaptive life skills and integration of adult roles can be the results of a successful adolescent experience.

THEORETICAL MODELS OF DEVELOPMENT

It stands to reason that theoretical insight or scientific understanding of the contingencies that promote healthy and unhealthy lifestyles among young people should inform intervention programs designed to optimize adolescent development (Takanishi, 2000). It is unfortunate, however, that although many theories have been offered to help us understand health risk and promotion behavior among adolescents, very few have been explicitly incorporated in intervention designs and strategies (e.g., Applegate, 1998). By way of addressing this shortcoming, in this section we introduce and briefly discuss some of the relevant theories and, whenever possible, refer back to them as we present specific programs designed to optimize adolescent development.

The most common theoretical approaches involve social cognitive models. These include Social Cognitive Theory (Bandura, 1994), Information, Motivation, and Behavioral Skills Consolidation Model (Fisher & Fisher, 1992), Health Belief Model, Theory of Reasoned Action, and Protection Motivation Theory (Conner & Norman, 1996). Each of these involves similar forces that include knowledge, intentions, attitudes, normative perceptions, and self-efficacy.

Other more generic perspectives also provide frameworks within which to understand and develop specific prevention/protection and enhancement programs. For example, the Public Health Model (i.e., Schinke & Gilchrist, 1985), which is a variant of the Biopsychosocial Model (e.g., Zucker & Gomberg, 1986), emphasizes the interactions between numerous factors, including (a) the *agent* (cause of the response or problem: drugs, hormones, depression, anger), (b) the *host* (reflecting individual differences among people: genetics, temperament, personality, attitudes), and (c) the *environment* (both social and physical: peers, family, school, neighborhood).

Another example of a generic framework is Catalano, Kosterman, Hawkins, Newcomb, and Abbott's (1996) Social Development Model (SDM). In our opinion, SDM is perhaps the most comprehensive and promising approach to understanding the sources of healthy (prosocial) and risky (antisocial) behaviors among adolescents. This model identifies three essential forces and processes that shape human development: *bonding, opportunities,* and *rewards.* Bonding can occur to either prosocial (e.g., school, church, healthy family) or antisocial (deviant peers, gangs, dropouts) groups or institutions. Opportunities represent occasions in which to engage in either prosocial (e.g., homework, exercise, volunteer) or antisocial (e.g., drugs, violence, delinquency) activities. Rewards are the reinforcements (e.g., praise, friendship, money, pleasure) that result from engaging in specific behaviors and that maintain those behaviors that are either prosocial or antisocial.

INTERVENTION STRATEGIES

The promotion of healthy behavior among adolescents cannot be separated from the prevention of health risks. Although most programs are designed to either enhance health or protect against harm, the theory, practice, and integration of these approaches have rarely been well articulated. Therefore, the commonalities and potentially powerful synergy between increasing health and reducing harm are not readily apparent. Because enhancement and protection approaches complement each other, it is reasonable to speculate that they may be more effective when combined. This combined approach is justified from both conceptual and theoretical bases, such as the SDM, which can be used as a basis for both prevention of and protection from problems as well as enhancement of prosocial behaviors and optimal development.

The remainder of this chapter focuses on programs and research that address both—promotion of optimal development (by way of diet, exercise, and social/coping skills) and the prevention of risk behaviors (such as drug use, unprotected sex, and violence).

PROMOTING OPTIMAL ADOLESCENT DEVELOPMENT

For the purpose of this section, optimal development during adolescence is defined as that which takes place when there is a good person-environment fit between the needs of the developing adolescent and the opportunities and rewards afforded by the social environment (Eccles et al., 1993). We organized the areas of optimal development in this section under two general domains: physical and psychosocial. Issues tied to these domains that focus on pathology (e.g., sexually transmitted diseases) rather than health are presented later in the "prevention" section of the chapter.

Optimizing Physical Development

One of the most important "opportunities" during adolescence is the possibility of enhancing physical development (Crockett & Petersen, 1993). Proper diet and exercise are essential components of healthy development, yet inspection of U.S. indicators of adolescent lifestyles led Sallis (1993) to conclude that the "most prudent conclusion is that adolescents in all major U.S. ethnic groups eat too much fat and sodium" (p. 216). Kimm, Gergen, Malloy, Dresser, and Carroll (1990), for example, found that total fat consumption by American teens was 20% more than the level recommended by nutrition experts.

Because schools are compulsory institutions with significant and sustained contact with children and adolescents, they are a logical location for health promotion (Consortium on the School-Based Promotion of Social Competence, 1994; Price, Cioci, Penner, & Trautlein, 1993). Schools have the potential to become the source of life skills that promote health and prevent disease; thus, society has increasingly looked to school-based programs for promotion of healthy lifestyles (Neumark-Sztainer, Martin, & Story, 2000).

School programs are typically curriculum based, which propagate knowledge about healthy and unhealthy activities. For example, the Stanford Adolescent Heart Health Program (Killen, Robinson, Telch, & Saylor, 1989) involves two class sessions that cover the relationship between diet and exercise and cardiovascular health and illnesses. Implemented within each of two school districts, one high school received the program and another served as the control. At 2-month follow-up, knowledge gains were significantly greater for the treatment high school students on nutrition/diet, physical activity, and cigarette smoking. A higher proportion of treatment school participants than controls who were not exercising regularly at baseline reported regular exercise at follow-up. Treatment group students were also more likely to report they would choose healthy-for-heart snacks. Beneficial treatment effects were observed for resting heart rate, body mass index, and triceps and subscapular skinfold thickness.

A variety of classroom-based health programs such as the one just described have been evaluated, but this research suggests that such knowledge-only approaches have a rather limited impact on adolescent behaviors (Dryfoos, 1993;

Hansen, 1992; Wagenaar & Perry, 1994). This is because knowledge may be relatively simple to increase, but attitudes and behaviors are much more difficult to change (Botvin, 1986; Rundall & Bruvold, 1988). David and Williams (1987) suggest that in addition to the provision of health-related knowledge (a social cognitive model approach), school-based health promotion should also support opportunities for healthy lifestyles, development of coping skills, and encouragement of responsibility at the level of the individual, family, and community.

Child and Adolescent Trial for Cardiovascular Health (CATCH), the largest school-based program ever sponsored by the National Institutes of Health, is an example of a comprehensive approach to health education. The CATCH is a four-pronged approach to promote healthy lifestyles that targets (1) classroom curricula, (2) physical education, (3) school food service, and (4) home programs. Here's how the program has been implemented. CATCH curricula documented in project manuals, curriculum guides, and resource files are provided to CATCH classroom teachers. Physical education specialists are given equipment, guidebooks, and a file of activity cards with instructions for recommended physical activities. Food service staffs receive manuals, recipes, tip sheets, and promotional materials. And finally, family activity packets are sent home with the students. Although the success of the CATCH trial is yet to be determined, a 3-year feasibility account implemented in 56 schools across four states reported high levels of participation, program fidelity, and compatibility with existing programs (Perry et al., 1997). Evaluation of the CATCH trial will include data on intervention elements, training and support of school staff, implementations, school staff characteristics, student characteristics, external and competing programs, student participation, and student outcomes.

We encourage mental health professionals interested in promoting adolescent physical health to approach program development from a comprehensive perspective. For example, high school counselors can approach health education using the CATCH program as a guiding framework. They could first convene a general meeting with school principals, physical education staff, biology or health science teachers, cafeteria staff, and parents to discuss the importance of promoting healthy eating and exercise habits at home and school. The idea is to get individuals who represent each of CATCH's four prongs into a dialogue. Then objectives can be identified, with health science or biology teachers taking on the responsibility to develop or implement a classroom-based health curriculum such as Killen et al.'s (1989) noted previously. Cafeteria staff can be asked to work conjointly with parents in providing more opportunities for students to have access to healthier fare. Likewise, physical education staff can be approached to develop ways to impress upon their students the importance of maintaining a viable regimen of exercise.

Optimizing Psychosocial Development

Masten and Coatsworth (1995) define psychosocial competence as the skills and processes enabling people to adapt effectively to their environment. A person's coping skills refer to his or her capacity to actively minimize or reduce tension when facing stressful situations. This ability is associated with flexibility and effort at reframing a stressful situation cognitively or generating multiple problem-solving alternatives or both (Compas, Worsham, & Ey, 1992; Jorgensen & Dusek, 1990). Felner, Lease, and Phillips (1990) conceptualized coping skills as one of the hallmarks in adolescent psychosocial competence. Effectively coping with stressful but normative life transitions and tasks is associated with high levels of adjustment (Compas et al., 1992; Ebata & Moos, 1994; Stern & Zevon, 1990). An example of effective coping is the ability to reach out to social support systems as a resource in maintaining high self-esteem and sustaining optimism (Helsen, Vollebergh, & Meeus, 2000). In turn, high self-esteem and an optimistic outlook have been consistently associated with successful adolescent transitions (Jorgensen & Dusek, 1990; Stern, Norman, & Zevon, 1991). Coping strategies based on self-blame, wishful thinking, and denial—apparently typical among many adolescents (Stern & Zevon, 1990)—foster poor or dysfunctional transitions (McCrae & Costa, 1986; Stern & Alvarez, 1992).

Social Skills and Social Networks

Considerable empirical support exists for the notion that social networks support effective coping and promote resiliency during adolescent development. For example, in their study of 660 adolescents, Bijstra, Bosma, and Jackson (1994) reported a direct correlation between participant social skills and four indicators of psychosocial functioning: self-esteem, well-being, coping, and social support. Herzberg et al. (1998) found that self-reported interpersonal competence of 137 adolescent females at initial evaluation predicted a significant proportion of the variance in chronic interpersonal stress 1 year later, indicating that poor interpersonal skills may function as a mechanism for generating ongoing interpersonal stress in late adolescence. Parker and Asher (1993) documented the importance of children having at least one "best friend," and Buhrmester (1990) found that elementary and junior high school students with more friends were described as being better adjusted and more competent.

These findings are in line with Hartup's (1992) premise that development of social networks early in life may be a prerequisite for adequate adolescent psychosocial adjustment and coping. Hartup (1992) identified four significant functions of childhood friendships: (1) provide opportunities for acquiring, practicing, and elaborating basic social skills, (2) provide sources of information about self and others and about the world, (3) provide intimacy sources of emotional support, and (4) afford learning opportunities for the mutual regulation and management of close relationships.

Malouff and Schutte (1998) developed and compiled a series of creative activities designed to assist educators and mental health professionals interested in teaching valuable social skills. A total of 66 games are provided according to the type of social-emotional goals desired. Briefly, these games involve players in ways that encourage identification and expression of feelings, how to empathize with others, and how to persuasively ask for what they want. In developing the game ideas, the authors created a standard presentation format that includes suggestions on how to help players use their skills in daily life. Two examples follow.

Making Contact or Not can accommodate up to 40 players and is a game specifically intended to increase the amount and quality of social interaction. Participants are assigned to groups of no more than 8. Each player is to take a few moments to decide how to avoid making positive contact with every other member of the group. Players may use different contact-avoiding methods such as avoiding eye contact or walking away. All players then leave the classroom momentarily and come back to enact the game. They are to start avoiding contact with group members immediately upon returning to the classroom. After this goes on for a while, the facilitator asks each participant how he or she is avoiding contact and then announces "Now let's take a few moments to discuss how you can make positive contact with each fellow group member. . . . What do you usually do to make positive contact with someone you don't know?" After a brief discussion, players are asked to go outside the classroom again and to start making contact as soon they reenter the room. After the second round of play is finished, the facilitator asks the following questions: "What were the most effective ways to avoid contact? To make contact?" "How did you feel when the other group members were avoiding contact with you?" "How did you feel when you made contact with others?" "Which contact/avoidance methods do you more often use in day-to-day life?" "What contact methods might you use more often in day-to-day life after playing the game?"

Red Light, Green Light, designed for 8 to 10 players, was developed to improve self-awareness during social interactions. The facilitator begins by saying "Have you ever talked to someone and needed to leave but the person wouldn't stop talking?" or "In talking to someone, have you ever wanted very much to say something but been unable to get a word in?" After some discussion, the facilitator goes on to explain that people wanting to speak out during a conversation (or wanting to end a conversation) send off nonverbal signals. Some people catch these signals and make the needed change, perhaps pausing so the other person can speak or bringing the conversation to a close. After these general principles are introduced, the activity is described as a game to help us see how good we are at detecting the signals that tell us when to continue talking (a green light) or to pause (a red light). Participants then form groups of 2 or 3. One person leads a conversation about a topic—any topic. One person will show signs of interest, for example, leaning forward and nodding, and then at some point show a sign of having to leave or wanting to speak. The third person, if there is one, observes the other two interact. If the person who is leading the conversation misses one signal, he or she sends another one and another until the speaker notices. At the end of the conversation, the group discusses all the green and red signals sent, whether missed or noticed. Then group members change roles until all have the chance to be speaker, listener, and observer. The activity concludes with a brief discussion about the value of detecting nonverbal signals and emotions.

Critical Thinking and Problem-Solving Skills

A considerable body of research has documented the tenability and effectiveness of deliberate decision making as a coping technique to enhance psychosocial competence. According to Normative Decision Theory (Edwards & von Winterfeldt, 1986; Raiffa, 1968), decision makers must engage in a series of cognitive tasks in order to act in their best interest, an endeavor recently boiled down by Beyth-Marom and Fishhoff (1997) to five simple steps: (1) identify the possible options, (2) identify the possible consequences of each option, (3) evaluate the desirability of each consequence, (4) assess the likelihood of each consequence, should each action be taken, and (5) combine everything according to a logical defensible "decision rule."

Beyth-Maron and Fishhoff (1997) suggest that adolescents making ill-advised decisions represent a failing in any one (or all) of these five steps. Furthermore, the steps suggest the interventions needed to optimize adolescent critical thinking when facing important choices. For example, an adolescent attending a party may overlook options that reduce the penalties for refusing to smoke marijuana (e.g., teasing from peers) and decide to engage in this risk behavior. A possible intervention strategy is teaching adolescents "refusal skills" needed to devise socially adroit ways to avoid taking risks (Botvin, 1986). Another source of ill-advised decision making may be the time pressure of making a choice, as an adolescent may not have the wherewithal to make sense of complex decisions and keep track of their details, resorting to quicker, less thoughtful, and impulsive solutions. A suitable intervention may involve teaching decision making as a general cognitive skill or to preprogram choices so decisions do not have to be made under real-time pressures.

Other approaches to problem solving involve mental simulation techniques. For example, Rivkin and Taylor (1998) asked college students to designate a stressful event that was going on in their lives. One group of participants was directed to deliberately focus on the unfolding event, a second group was told to practice an outcome simulation (picture the problem beginning to resolve it-self), and a third group served as control. Participants who focused on the on-going stressful events reported one week later that they had used more active coping and had sought more instrumental social support relative to the out-come simulation and control groups. In their recent review of the mental simu-lation literature—which included the Rivkin and Taylor experiment—Taylor, Pham, Rivkin, and Armor (1998) concluded that although imagining the *pro-*✶ *cess* for reaching a goal (or dynamics of an unfolding event) is an effective cop-ing technique, envisioning successful *completion* of a goal or resolution to a stressor is not. In fact, imagining goal resolution—a form of wishful think-ing—not only fails to help in the achievement of goals but may actually inter-fere with it (Oetinger, 1996).

PREVENTING RISK BEHAVIORS

Many behaviors can have serious physical and emotional consequences for adolescents. Some of these behaviors can even lead to death. We have selected three general areas or constellations of behaviors that have the potential for numerous adverse consequences: drug abuse, sexual behavior, and violence.

Preventing Drug Abuse

The leading cause of death among teenagers in the United States is drunk driving, accounting for more than 20% of all mortalities (Julien, 1998). Ciga-rette smoking is the leading cause of death among all U.S. citizens and accounts for more than 400,000 lost lives each year and will likely kill more current chil-dren and adolescents later in life than any other cause (Julien, 1998). Nearly 3,000 youngsters begin smoking cigarettes each day (Julien, 1998). The use and abuse of all other drugs lag far behind these socially approved drugs. Mar-ijuana is the most commonly used illicit drug among adolescents, with a 40% lifetime prevalence rate among high school seniors in 1997; more than one third (38%) reported marijuana use within 12 months, and 24% reported use within 30 days. In contrast, only one tenth of high school seniors reported that they had tried inhalants, stimulants, cocaine (powder or crack), or hallucino-gens anytime in their lives (Johnston, O'Malley, & Bachman, 1998).

Primary Prevention

Many programs exist that are aimed at reducing drug and alcohol use and abuse among children and adolescents. These include programs designed to address family- and community-based risk factors, social influence approaches, and interventions with teenagers at highest risk for addiction.

The most widely known and distributed early intervention program is DARE (Drug Abuse Resistance Education). It is typically cosponsored by local school and law enforcement officials and taught by active police officers. The curriculum is designed for preadolescents (fifth- to seventh-grade students) in hopes of reducing early experimentation with drugs or alcohol. Weekly classes during a 4-month period focus on four issues and skills: (1) the nature and consequences of drug use, (2) resistance techniques, (3) making decisions about risk-taking behaviors and critical analysis of media messages about drugs and violence, and (4) positive role models and choosing drug- or violence-free activities. However, an extensive and consistent body of research does not support the efficacy of the DARE program (e.g., Dukes, Ullman, & Stein, 1996). Unfortunately, the political and social construction of drug problems often favors a simplistic and personal deficit model of drug use (e.g., Humphreys & Rappaport, 1993) that leads to ineffective approaches, such as DARE, rather than to more comprehensive and ecologically based interventions that may have a greater likelihood of success (Arthur & Blitz, 2000; Hawkins, Catalano, & Miller, 1992; Newcomb, 1992; Sloboda & David, 1997).

The success of *any* prevention program is partially dependent on the adolescent's initial beliefs about drugs, drug-using behavior, and most important, what type of message and messenger will best encourage resistance to drug use. This may be why peer-directed prevention programs appear to have the greatest impact on cognitive risk factors such as perceived consequences of drug use, normative beliefs, resistance self-efficacy, expectations of future use, knowledge about drugs, and drug use itself (Bangert-Drowns, 1988; Ellickson, Bell, & McGuigan, 1993; Tobler, 1986). In contrast, adult-directed programs sometimes produce early beneficial effects that quickly fade (Ellickson et al., 1993). A number of innovative programs that target early (family-based) risk factors have also been examined. These include community- and school-based parenting skills training and early childhood and family support programs (Perry et al., 1996) that address culture-specific needs/risks for teen drug use (Botvin, Schinke, Epstein, Diaz, & Botvin, 1995; Myers et al., 1992; Schinke et al., 1988; Tobler, 1986). Unfortunately, these may not attract participation by parents of adolescents at highest risk for use (Cohen & Litton, 1995).

In a recent summary of the prevention literature, Sloboda and David (1997) identified several common factors associated with greater drug abuse prevention efficacy. The basic notion is to enhance protective factors at the same time as reducing risk factors. Effective programs should (a) target all forms of drug abuse, including tobacco, (b) include skills training and interaction experiences, (c) be long term, (d) change perceived norms of drug use, (e) involve parents and family, (f) be age specific and adapted for cultural diversity, and (g) include media campaigns and policy changes. One specific model, called Preparing for the Drug-Free Years program, combines many effective interventions (Kosterman, Hawkins, Spoth, Haggerty, & Zhu, 1997). This is a comparatively successful approach (Spoth, Reyes, Redmond, & Shin, 1999) and is based on early identification and intervention with risk and protective factors. It is theoretically grounded in the Social Development Model (Catalano et al., 1996) and assumes that the most important influences on drug use occur early and primarily in the family. It is designed to both delay the onset of drug use initiation and inhibit the progression of adolescent drug abuse. It has demonstrated effectiveness for both of these goals.

Specifically, the Spoth et al. (1999) intervention is targeted at elementary school students and their parents. This intervention involves five 2-hour sessions spaced over a 5-week period. The focus of these group meetings is to enhance protective parent-child interactions while at the same time reducing family risk factors for drug use initiation. The child is required to attend only one session, whereas parents are expected to attend all meetings. The primary content of the sessions involves (a) educating parents about risk and protective factors for drug abuse, (b) helping them develop clear guidelines for drug-related behaviors, (c) monitoring compliance with the guidelines and providing appropriate consequences, (d) enhancing parent-child bonding, (e) teaching anger management and family conflict skills, (f) enhancing positive child involvement with family tasks, and (g) teaching the children peer resistance skills. Videotapes are used to standardize delivery of the content, and two-person teams run all the sessions.

Preventing Sexual Risk Behaviors

Experimenting with sex is a natural aspect of adolescence, but many risks are involved in unprotected intercourse. Becoming sexually active at a young age also has risks (Newcomb, 1996b). Although most consequences of sexual activity during adolescence are physical and health related (e.g., pregnancy and sexually transmitted diseases), some sequelae of sexual activity are developmentally inappropriate, and all the risks for these adverse outcomes are psychosocial (dropping out of school, drug involvement, delinquency, failure to learn life skills).

The teen birth rate in the United States is the highest of all industrial countries in the world (Bok & Morales, 1998). U.S. teenage sexual involvement has been steadily rising over the past few decades, and adolescent pregnancy and childbearing have been considered a serious public health crisis (Flinn, Shah, Davis, Zare, & Pasarell, 1998). More than 80% of teenage pregnancies are unintended, most are unwanted, and they create a major life change and stress (Flinn et al., 1998). Recently, however, some promising declines have been noted (Bok & Morales, 1998). In the past couple of years, more teens are delaying intercourse, and if they are sexually active, they are using contraception and condoms more frequently. Nevertheless, pregnancy, HIV, and AIDS remain serious problems among teenagers.

Although adolescents represent only 1% of the AIDS cases in the United States, one in four new HIV infections occurs in people less than 22 years of age (Rosenberg, Biggar, & Goedert, 1994), indicating that HIV infection is increasing most rapidly among young people. AIDS has now become the sixth leading cause of death for youths between the ages of 15 and 25 (Rios-Ellis & Figueroa, 1998), a statistic clearly revealing the need for HIV infection prevention efforts.

Not all youths are equally at risk for HIV infection. Certain adolescents or particular behaviors are more vulnerable to HIV transmission. For various cultural and background reasons, certain ethnic minority youths (African Americans and Latinos) are particularly at risk for HIV infection (e.g., Newcomb et al., 1998). Other high-risk categories for adolescents include (a) men who have sex with other men, (b) drug users and abusers, not limited to injection drug use, (c) runaway and homeless youths, (d) those with multiple sexual partners, and (e) those who do not use condoms during intercourse (Bok & Morales, 1998).

Nearly all schools have some form of AIDS education. Most of these programs are not based on sound theoretical approaches nor have any proven efficacy (Bok & Morales, 1997). However, there is a recent trend for more programs that do have theoretical grounding (Applegate, 1998). Most of the models used to design these prevention efforts are among those identified in the theories section of this chapter.

In evaluating AIDS prevention programs, several targets of change are considered (Kirby, 2000). These include knowledge, attitudes, behavioral intentions, and actual behavior (e.g., using condoms). In general, most programs have been able to increase knowledge about HIV infection and AIDS when comparing an experimental to a control group (Applegate, 1998). However, increased knowledge does not necessarily lead to changing behavior. Changes in attitudes were more difficult to achieve and often dissipated at follow-up testing (Applegate, 1998). Even more difficult to change were behavioral intentions (i.e., planning to use condoms, not use drugs during sex, not having multiple sex partners). Finally, the most important target of change was actual behavior, which also proved to be the most difficult to influence. Most programs failed to make significant changes in actual risk-reducing behaviors (Applegate, 1998). These findings provide a rather bleak perspective for reducing HIV transmission among adolescents and other youths.

Nevertheless, among those programs with a theoretical basis, some clearly effective approaches have begun to emerge (Basen-Engquist, 1994; Jemmott III, Jemmott, & Fong, 1992; Smith & Katner, 1995), indicating that effective HIV prevention programs should take a multipronged approach incorporating several different techniques. Three particular interventions used in concert seem particularly promising. First, information and knowledge need to be imparted to the teenagers from a credible, expert source. Smith and Katner (1995) incorporated physicians who were AIDS specialists and presented a 50-minute slide show, instructed about the basic facts of AIDS, and emphasized the personal stories of several AIDS patients they had treated. Second is the use of peer-directed discussion groups, where the peer facilitators were given extensive training. The third aspect is role playing. This can be guided by either trained teachers or trained peers. Role playing appears to be the critical component necessary for actual behavioral change (Smith & Katner, 1995). Role-play activities "provide the greatest opportunity for social interaction and learning called for in Social Cognitive Theory, . . . [and] students who practice skills in the relatively low-risk role-play situation are likely to experience increased self-efficacy" (Smith & Katner, 1995, p. 393). An example of a role-play activity involves groups of four students. They act out a scenario in which two of the four are a sexually active couple and the other two are each of their best friends. The crisis and focal point of the role play is the discovery that the male partner in the couple is HIV positive.

A final point about HIV prevention through education needs to be made. One concern that many have raised about HIV prevention programs is that "sex-related education" should not be provided in schools because it is likely to increase sexual activity and that only abstinence-oriented programs should be encouraged. In particular, fears have been voiced that providing condoms to students to prevent HIV transmission will encourage sexual activity. These concerns have been researched for many years, and the results are consistent and conclusive. Sex education, AIDS prevention, and distribution of condoms do *not* increase sexual activity among youths and adolescents (e.g., Sellers, McGrew, & McKinley, 1994).

Violence Prevention

The homicide rate among adolescents and young adults in the United States increased 55% from 1979 to 1991, becoming the leading cause of death among African American youths and the second leading cause of death among all adolescents (Sells & Blum, 1996). Among youths under age 18, murder, rape, robbery, and aggravated assault rose nearly 70% between 1986 and 1995 (U.S. Department of Justice, 1996); nonfatal violence victimization among adolescents is triple that of adults (Sickmund, Snyder, & Poe-Yamagata, 1997). A recent U.S. national survey revealed that about 10% of high school students claimed to have carried a handgun or a knife in the month previous to the survey and that 16% participated in a physical fight (Centers for Disease Control and Prevention, 1996). At the junior high school level,

25% of students surveyed had been victims of violence, and another 14% were either "very worried" or "somewhat worried" about being victimized while at school (Everett & Price, 1995). These sobering statistics clearly demonstrate the need to address the increasing violence among U.S. youths. The government publication *Healthy People 2000* (U.S. Department of Health and Human Services, 1991) recognized school violence as one of the most urgent problems in modern society.

Violence Prevention Programs

This section reviews a series of programs designed to prevent violence from occurring or to reduce its occurrence among aggressive youths. Because youths spend a great deal of their time in schools—about a quarter of their waking hours (Miller & Spicer, 1998)—violence prevention and mitigation programs are typically school based. Though not explicitly, these programs tend to share the same theoretical base (Social Learning Theory), focusing on changing individual attitudes and beliefs about violence via prosocial learning and self-regulation of emotional or cognitive processes.

Violence Prevention Curriculum for Adolescents, one of two middle school programs reviewed by DuRant et al. (1996), focuses on teaching students to recognize the risk factors for violence, how to deal with anger, and how to avoid fights. This program was implemented over a 5-week period, encompassing ten 50-minute class sessions taught by a trained instructor. The second program reviewed by DuRant et al., Conflict Resolution: A Curriculum for Youth Providers, focused strictly on personal skills to deal with conflict and was implemented by the same trained instructor over the same number of class sessions as the first program. DuRant et al. reported that participants in both programs used less violence in hypothetical and actual situations at posttest (see also Farrell & Meyer, 1997). In yet another study, Hausman, Pierce, and Briggs (1996) supplemented a violence prevention curriculum with other school-based activities and extensive contact with students' families. The suspension rate (based largely on overt acts of violence) among the high school sophomores participating in the intervention was reduced by 17%, compared to no change in rates of suspension for sophomores assigned to a control condition.

The Second Step: A Violence Prevention Curriculum, comprising fifteen 50-minute class sessions, is another approach to violence prevention, unique in its use of *peer leaders* in addition to adult instructors (Orpinas, Parcel, McAlister, & Frankowski, 1995). The curriculum covers information about the contingencies of violence, development of empathy toward others, anger management, and problem solving. Two Texas middle school classes were assigned to either an adult instructor-only condition or an instructor-plus peer leaders condition; a third class served as control (Orpinas et al., 1995). Results indicated that compared to the control condition, both instructor-only and instructor-plus-peer-leader interventions reduced violence among boys, although only the latter condition differed significantly from the control group.

Because the Orpinas et al. (1995) program is fairly representative of the curriculum-based violence prevention programs previously reviewed, we describe it in some detail. Unit 1 of the program curriculum describes violence as a societal problem, with basic information about the magnitude of interpersonal violence and factors associated with violence such as previous abuse, uncontrolled emotions, lack of conflict resolution skills, or being a witness to violence. Unit 2 trains students in empathy, which is implicated in a number of social behaviors such as altruism, generosity, and regulation of aggression. Empathy is defined using a three-component model that focuses on both cognitive and affective behaviors. The components are the ability to (1) determine the emotional state of another person, (2) assume the perspective and role of another person, and (3) respond emotionally to another person. Role plays are introduced to train students on the first two components. Responding emotionally is encouraged through learning to find a common ground with others, avoiding labeling and stereotyping, using "I" messages, and active listening. Unit 3 combines anger management and interpersonal problem solving for reducing impulsive and aggressive behavior. Anger management is taught following the model developed by Novaco (1975) based on the use of "self-talk" and the labeling of psychological arousal as anger. Training in problem solving is based on the model developed by Spivack and Shure (1989), which includes skills such as problem identification, brainstorming solutions, evaluating solutions, choosing a solution and using it, and evaluating whether the solution is working and changing to an alternative solution if necessary. Unit 4 applies the skills learned in the previous units to five specific situations: making a complaint, dealing with peer pressure, resisting gang pressure, dealing with bullying, and diffusing a fight. The most important strategy used in this unit is behavior modeling through videotapes and guided practice through role plays.

It is worth noting that an important component of this program is the use of peer leaders who are trained to reinforce classmates for nonviolent responses and expected to model verbal and behavioral commitment to nonviolence (see also Lerner & Barton, 2000). According to Orpinas et al. (1995), the rationale for using peer leaders stemmed from the notion that among adolescents, credibility, attractiveness, and power—all characteristics of persuasive communication—are greater when communicators are peers rather than adults. They go on to point out that Social Cognitive Theory predicts that knowledge and skills are necessary but not sufficient components to modify behavior. Thus, peer leaders apparently give the program the "additional component" needed for behavior change: the modification of perceived social norms and social support, as well as attitudes toward the behavior.

A Comprehensive Approach

Writers in the field of violence prevention are increasingly favoring programs that address violence *comprehensively,* pointing to the violence risk-factor literature to support their case (Boswell, 2000; Howard, Flora, & Griffin, 1999). For example, violence among adolescents has been associated with parental/guardian factors such as child neglect (Buka & Earls, 1993), poor communication (Resnick et al., 1997), harsh or inconsistent discipline, and criminal behavior (Buka & Earls, 1993; Loeber & Stouthamer-Loeber, 1986). The mass media, which often glorifies violence, is yet another factor apparently contributing to aggressive behavior (Huesmann, Eron, Lefkowitz, & Walder, 1984; Schooler & Flora, 1996; Williams, 1986).

To address the apparent multidimensionality of violence, Howard et al. (1999) present a framework for violence prevention implementation in three different environments (informational, social, and physical) at three different levels (school, home, and community). To illustrate the structure of this framework, school curriculum-based programs—as most reviewed in this section are—would be classified as *informational* in terms of "environment" and at *school* in terms of "level." *Informational* interventions at *home* would target parental disciplinary styles and ability to function as role models to their children. At the *community* level, interventions would target public education campaigns about violence and its portrayal in the mass media. *Social* interventions at the *school* level would be predicated on the manipulation of peer influences and student-teacher interactions. At *home,* communication of the importance of school and discussions about violence prevention can form the basis of possible interventions. At the level of *community,* neighborhood cohesion and increases of community ties could be the goals of violence prevention. *Physical* interventions at the school, home, and community levels could entail, respectively, metal detectors and security patrols, limiting access to guns and increasing parental presence, and promotion of social/health services and restriction of drug trafficking.

SUMMARY

This chapter began with a brief description of adolescent development and an overview of the theories and models that explain the incidence of health and risk factors during the life span. This was followed by sections detailing specific approaches and programs designed to promote optimal development and reduction of risk behaviors among adolescents. These sections focused on the rationale behind program development, how they were implemented, and the nature and level of their effectiveness. Generally, comprehensive programs appear to yield better results than programs with a more limited focus. This is not surprising, as risky and healthy behaviors do not occur in isolation but, rather, reflect a complex interplay that involves a multitude of factors (McGee & Newcomb, 1992).

Accordingly, more effort has been placed on approaching health promotion from a unified and multitargeted approach (Travis, 2000). For example, McCroskey and Einbinder (1998) and Perry (1999) both offer blueprints for models targeting various health-related outcomes that involve multiple components, including parents, classroom, school environment, and community. More specifically, McCroskey and Einbinder provide training plans, cost-benefit analyses, and implementation procedures for developing interprofessional liaisons to create school-based health promotion facilities accessible to entire communities. Similarly, Perry presents a detailed guide to create health behavior change programs for youths that require communitywide participation. Both of these are powerful approaches that have the potential for creating healthy and responsible citizens for the next century. Indeed, there is reason to believe we have come a long way since G. Stanley Hall's (1904) laissez-faire view of adolescence as a time of unavoidable storm and stress.

WORKSHOP FOR COUNSELING TRAINEES: OPTIMIZING ADOLESCENT DEVELOPMENT

Process

1. First meeting (20 minutes)

   ▶ Class is divided into groups of 5 to 7 students.

   ▶ Forming a circle, participants of each group pretend to be school counselors or administrators in charge of addressing Objective 1 stipulated below. Working together, group members use the content of the present chapter to develop a proposal that specifies an intervention program for this objective.

   ▶ Each group assigns a "secretary" who takes notes.

   ▶ Possible issues to consider:
   Definition/operationalization of objective
   Type/level of interventions needed (individual, family, community)
   Programmatic integration of interventions
   Implementation of interventions/program
   Evaluation

   ▶ Each group elects two "representatives" for the second meeting.

2. Second meeting (10 minutes)

   ▶ All participants reconvene as follows:

▶ Group representatives sit around a tight circle.

▶ Others form a circle around the representatives, creating a circle within a circle.

▶ Objective of this meeting is to synthesize or integrate the proposals worked out during the first meeting.

▶ A secretary takes notes.

▶ At the conclusion of this meeting, the original groups are reconstituted to address Objective 2. The cycle is repeated until all three objectives are addressed.

3. Plenary Session (20 minutes)

▶ All participants discuss the integrated program interventions that aim to optimize adolescent development.

Objectives

1. Improve nutrition and physical conditioning. Promote psychosocial development.
2. Prevent and decrease drug use and sexually transmitted diseases.
3. Prevent and decrease violence.

ADDITIONAL RESOURCES

Print Resources

Backer, T. E., Rogers, E. M., & Sopory, P. (1992). *Designing health communication campaigns: What works?* (p. 181). Newbury Park, CA: Sage.

Baron, J., & Brown, R. (1991). *Teaching decision making to adolescents.* Hillsdale, NJ: Lawrence Erlbaum.

DeMarsh, J., & Kumpfer, K. L. (1986). Family-oriented interventions for the prevention of chemical dependency in children and adolescents. In S. Griswold-Ezekoye, K. L. Kumpfer, & W. J. Bukoski (Eds.), *Childhood and chemical abuse: Prevention and intervention* (pp. 117-151). New York: Haworth.

Schinke, S. P., & Gilchrist, L. D. (1984). *Life skills counseling with adolescents.* Baltimore, MD: University Park Press.

Stoil, M. J., & Hill, G. (1996). *Preventing substance abuse: Interventions that work.* New York: Plenum.

Vernon, A. (1998). *The PASSPORT program: A journey through emotional, social cognitive, and self-development, grades 9-12* (p. 273). Champaign, IL: Research Press.

Videotapes

Goldstein, A. P., & McGinnis, E. (Producers). *The skillstreaming video.*
  Footage of actual training sessions showing specific prosocial skills. (Available from Research Press, Dept. 20, P.O. Box 9177, Champaign, IL 61826. Phone: 800-519-2707; e-mail: rp@researchpress.com)

Prothrow-Smith, D. (Producer). *Youth violence: A new public health issue.*
  Violence prevention through public-health strategies (order code #34x1660). (Available from Insight Media, 2162 Broadway, New York, NY 10024-0621. Phone: 800-233-9910; e-mail: www.insight-media.com/teachered.html)

Strumpf, F., & Crawford, D. K. (Producers). *The peer mediation video.*
  Video and print material provide a comprehensive peer mediation program. (Available from Research Press, Dept. 20, P.O. Box 9177, Champaign, IL 61826. Phone: 800-519-2707; e-mail: rp@researchpress.com)

CHAPTER 7

Fostering Positive Identity in Adolescents

Perspectives on Teens in the United States

Susana M. Lowe
Jackqueline Mascher

In her acceptance speech delivered during the nationally televised Teen Choice Awards, supermodel Tyra Banks told teens, "Don't ever give up" (Teen Choice Awards, 1999). She said, to paraphrase, "When I started modeling, people shut doors on me. They'd say you're too tall, too short, too Black, not Black enough, blah, blah, blah . . ." The crowd roared, and her heartfelt message was clear—despite external barriers, persist and you shall succeed.

What does a supermodel have to do with counseling adolescents? In contemplating this chapter, we were interested in taking a perspective that acknowledges traditional theories on adolescent identity development but at the same time incorporates contemporary contextual viewpoints. We believe Tyra Banks administered a form of therapy in that moment; she recognized her position as a role model, her demeanor was authentic, she demonstrated appropriate self-disclosure, and she instilled hope (especially in teens who don't fit society's narrowly defined beauty ideal).

Steele and Brown (1995) recognized the importance of the dialectical process between media, as cultural agents, and adolescents, who interact with media from their own developmental, social, and cultural perspectives. Piggybacking on Banks's inspirational speech, comedian Adam Sandler addressed the boys in the audience, to paraphrase, "Study hard. But if you don't do well, don't worry too much. I didn't do well, and I'm a multimillionaire."

It is perhaps impossible to know what specific role the media, arts, and entertainment industry, World Wide Web, schools, religion, books, sports, families, teachers, friends, peers, and counselors play in supporting or hindering adolescent identity development. There are a number of variations on the theme of building identity. Despite these variations, we've identified a strong need for the literature to be more focused on positive and preventive efforts. This chapter serves as an introduction to counselors in conceptualizing and facilitating positive identity among adolescent clients.

CONCEPTUALIZING ADOLESCENT IDENTITY

It is important to consider adolescent identity within a given sociocultural context, in our case the United States. Adolescence itself can be regarded as a largely Western concept, one that has transformed over the centuries (Arnett, 1999; Cummings, 1995). Non-Western and agrarian societies tend to delineate clear roles for their members and rarely involve self-exploration and choice in determining those roles (Hofstede, 1980). The beliefs about how older children and young adults can and should fill sociocultural roles varies according to the spirit and values of a given time and place. In the United States today, adolescence is clearly upheld as an identity, and some might even say adolescents have their own culture.

What portion of our society do teenagers represent? With the exception of the baby boom bulge circa 1970, the teenage population in the United States has been in gradual decline. Between the decades of the 1980s and 1990s, the total population of teens aged 10 to 19 decreased from 17% to 14% (Dacey & Kenny, 1997). According to the same source, in 1992, White teenagers represented 11% of the total population, African American teens 2%, Hispanic origin teens 1.8%, Asian and Pacific Islander teens 0.4%, and Native American teens 0.14%. The general population of the United States is expected to become a non-White majority by the year 2020, with expected growth in Latino and Asian American populations in particular. Approximately 20% of children live in poverty in the United States, a problem that is on the rise. Furthermore, children who live in poverty are disproportionately represented in non-White communities. McKinney, Schiamberg, and Shelton (1998) have documented several other relevant trends: (a) Geographic distribution of youths is predominantly metropolitan, (b) diversity of living arrangements is increasing, (c) employment of adults outside the home is increasing, and (d) availability of and exposure to technologies are increasing.

Considering the diverse environments and social conditions in which adolescents live, we see a host of variations on the theme of identity. In addition to theories on general identity achievement (Erickson, 1968; Marcia, 1980), many other forms of identity have emerged in the psychological literature, including gender, ethnic, sexuality, career, academic, regional, and class identities (Brannon, 1976; Heath & McLaughlin, 1993; Phinney, 1990; Super, 1990; Troiden, 1989). Whether or not these identities should be conceptualized as constellations of a central identity or are otherwise related to one another is outside the scope of this chapter. However, we do feel it is important to give consideration to multiple contextual factors that are salient for adolescents, including those mentioned previously. For example, Banks's speech at the Teen Choice Awards is indicative of an increasing acknowledgment of diversity in teen media discourse. Television geared toward teens has been tackling controversial "adult" issues such as race relations, sexuality, gender, and existential questions with a maturity and complexity not seen a generation ago. Counselors will increasingly see teen clients who are plugged in to a world of information technology and are grappling with identity on multiple fronts. Juggling variations on the theme of identity will be one of our most important tasks.

How do we as clinicians make sense of all this multiplicity? Despite some evidence to the contrary (Dacey & Kenny, 1997; Eckert, 1989), popular conceptions of adolescence maintain that teens live in the stormy and stressful margins of society on their way toward becoming respectable normal citizens (Arnett, 1999). Perhaps adults are uncomfortable with the multiple ways that adolescents challenge adult norms, so that teen identities are marginalized as stormy and stressful. This perspective is so pervasive that it may behoove us to look closely at the development of "marginalized" identities in order to conceptualize how lack of fit to the norm contributes to adolescent identity exploration more broadly defined.

Examining ethnic and racial identities can help us understand how other identity formations on varying points of the conformity-disconformity and majority-minority continuum affect teen self-concept. For example, the ethnic identity search is itself a developmental task that adolescents take on to differing degrees, depending on how explicit or supported such development is made and how receptive or hostile the environment is (Rotheram-Borus & Wyche, 1994). Cummings (1995) remarked that barriers to minority identity development include the existence of conflicting values between mainstream culture and underrepresented cultures, the lack of identity-achieved role models, and the lack of culture-focused guidance. To extrapolate, exploration of any aspect of identity is likely to be dependent on receptivity in the person's environment to give credence to and foster certain identities. We have only to look at the suppression of gay and bisexual identity development in teens (McConnell, 1994), the dismissal of so-called burnouts in high school (Eckert, 1989), and the invisibility of non-Christian identities among U.S. adolescents to see examples of the dominance of majority ideology. In contrast, many communities expressly promote jock and beauty queen identities in high school.

Let's take racial identity development as another stimulus for discussion. The phenotypical features of ethnic minority persons affect how others respond to them and may influence the degree to which persons may purposely engage in identity exploration (Helms & Cook, 1999). There is an interaction between physical attributes and the messages people receive from others that cue them to suppress or enhance exploration of their identity. Going back to Tyra Banks, who said modeling agencies deemed her either too Black or not Black enough and either too short or too tall, we wonder how those messages affected her self-concept, her willingness to explore her racial identity, her sense of being good enough. If a supermodel was rejected for her looks as a teen, imagine what most adolescent girls undergo. Adolescents experience discrimination from society in many forms: directly at the individual and institutional levels and symbolically through the media and so forth. We believe this societal oppression creates numerous barriers to healthy identity development in adolescents who don't fit the ideal profile in their given context. And because it's impossible to become the ideal under any circumstances (especially because the definition keeps shifting), we as counselors need to examine the barriers our adolescent clients face in achieving a healthy identity.

We all can claim a cultural heritage, but cultural and ethnic identity tend to be much more socially important for non-European American adolescents than European American adolescents. European American identity development in the United States has been treated as standard, unproblematic, and without need for intervention or research. Outbreaks of violence by White middle-class boys in several U.S. public schools shocked the nation and prompted many in society to question what went wrong. Steinem (1999) suggested that the shock the nation felt over violent crimes committed at Columbine High School is due in large part to our collective assumption that boys from normal, well-adjusted European American families don't commit violent crimes. She said our society expects such crimes to be committed by poor minority youths, and when they don't, we are at a loss for an explanation.

As counselors, we have a responsibility to see past the trappings of what mainstream society defines as normal and be inquisitive about aspects of identity that seem relegated to minority individuals. We urge counselors to explore the ethnic identity in White European American adolescents, the gender identity in boys, and the sexual orientation in heterosexuals. It is important for counselors to permit and even promote the act of exploring what exists in the margins (i.e., the unacceptable or the taboo) within every adolescent. This is a process that will foster a holistic sense of self in clients, one that does not succumb to the pressures of standard definition. Inviting clients to look into the meaning of that which is considered "normal" will also deepen the process of identity exploration.

For Phinney and Rosenthal (1992), a central task of adolescence is "to select and integrate childhood identifications, together with personal inclinations and the opportunities afforded by society, in order to construct a sense of who they are and what they will become" (p. 145). Broadly speaking, in U.S. society we encourage adolescents to seek and explore their identity, yet we strongly influence their identity choices and the timing of those choices by asserting dominant customs, traditions, morals, and values (Josselson, 1994b). Interventions to support identity development can therefore occur at both the individual and the societal level. We can help individuals understand their own capacities and predispositions, guide them in making realistic decisions, and help them cope with affective distress. At the societal level, we need to ask ourselves what options society makes available and to whom. Are there social gatekeepers to initiate adolescents into adulthood? Is entry into adult society difficult for some, and why (Josselson, 1994b)? Thus, the extent to which an individual can achieve a sense of identity within society is determined by how well society defines itself, how flexible or rigid society is in accommodating various expressions of identity, and how well the individual is able to explore and commit to a sense of identity (or identities).

KEY DIMENSIONS IN FOSTERING POSITIVE IDENTITY DEVELOPMENT

To form new intervention programs and to make ongoing assessments of existing programs, it may be helpful to identify key dimensions of prevention and intervention efforts. Programs vary widely along these dimensions, and they can help guide program implementation, assessment, and adjustment. Key dimensions include the foci of the effort, degree of multilevel collaborative networking, amount of tailoring to a situation's variability, intervention philosophy, self-reflexivity, outcome, commitment, and technology. Although this is not an exhaustive list, we can think about how to introduce new dimensions or alter existing dimensions to more effectively promote positive identity development.

Focus of Effort

McKinney et al. (1998) categorized prevention efforts into four arenas: (1) education, (2) community organization and systems intervention, (3) competency promotion, and (4) natural caregiving. Your focus may differ, depending on your role within a system, and we encourage thinking about ways that efforts can have overlapping effects. For example, a guidance counselor may provide educational seminars on career development to high school seniors and run counseling groups on interpersonal skills competencies for the same group; these education and competency promotion interventions are likely to build on one another, ideally contributing to career self-efficacy and positive identity.

Multilevel Collaborative Networks

Brown and Theobald (1998) called for strengthening connections of different learning environments in the following ways: (a) eliminate duplication of effort among learning contexts, (b) reconnect community, extracurricular, and academic activities, (c) broaden participation in community and extracurricular activities, (d) use extracurricular activities to promote school bonding between members of all peer groups, and (e) increase communication between all contexts. Collaborative networks are difficult to establish, but counselors can be essential in facilitating communication across community and academic contexts. For example, a counselor might establish biweekly meetings in order to process student volunteer experiences (e.g., visits with the elderly, organizing sporting events for kids with disabilities, taking care of animals at a local shelter, and tutoring children). The purpose would be to help adolescents make meaningful connections between activities they do and their individual and collective development. The same counselor might work with social studies teachers to create for-credit assignments that involve researching the group with whom they volunteer and making presentations to educate their peers. To take it a step further, some students might be advised to mentor younger students in volunteer activities, with the help and supervision of a counselor. Counselors are in a unique position to help adolescents make meaning of their community activities and link their experiences to family, community, social, and political purpose.

Variability

With so much variability in adolescents and their environments, interventions need to be differential, tailored, and individualized (Goldstein & Conoley, 1997). Successful efforts can be modeled in treatment manuals, but the effectiveness of an intervention is truly due to the unique combinations and relationships between participants in various contexts. Consider the varied and multilayered factors affecting adolescents of immigrants: educational background, resilience, knowing the culture of opportunity (e.g., the rules for success in the United States), immigrant status, gender issues, and other intergenerational conflicts, social challenges, economic hurdles, schooling mismatches, language barriers, and school sociopolitical structures (Calderon, 1998). We suggest that counselors assess these variables in their counseling work. For example, a counselor might construct profiles of immigrant clients that account for these diverse factors, ask students to create their own personal narratives, observe (in some cases, videotape) their classroom experiences, and perhaps arrange to meet with nuclear and extended kin.

Counseling is often considered an art because there is no cookie cutter way to do the job. You will constantly come across populations or individuals who challenge your basis of knowledge and your understanding of the norm. Counselors have wonderful opportunities to be creative in how they promote the welfare of their clients. We advise counselors to take advantage of supervision, if available, and to consult with colleagues on the development of programming. Collaboration, particularly when it occurs with people whose skills and backgrounds are diverse, makes it easier to respond to situations with huge variability.

Philosophy

Developing a clear philosophy is an essential ingredient to the success of an intervention program (Goldstein & Conoley, 1997). It is also critical to include and involve people who represent the intervention's target group in the development of a program (Goldstein & Conoley, 1997). We have already discussed one aspect of our philosophy, that of making marginal aspects of identity a bigger part of mainstream counseling. Operationalizing that philosophy requires inviting clients to explore what seem like undesirable aspects of their identity. Spend some time thinking about your philosophy or orientation toward working with clients. Try to articulate your philosophy in writing and discuss it with colleagues or supervisors.

Self-Reflexivity

It is important that prevention efforts emphasize aspects of self-reflexivity in caregivers or competency promoters. Sometimes, adults feel unable to relate to adolescents. People ask questions such as "Do you have to fit in and be like them to be effective?" "How do you get them to trust you?" (Eckert, 1989). Think back to your own adolescence. Try to remember how you felt, how you viewed others and yourself, politics, love. Although the scene may have looked very different, rest assured that you can draw on your own development to help you relate to adolescent clients. Counselors who are reflective about their own adolescence are more likely to be able to communicate with clients and encourage them to be self-reflective. Counselors from their adult vantage point can introduce a broader spectrum of alternatives and possibilities than the usual social categories to which adolescents are exposed (Eckert, 1989).

Outcome

Along with the flexibility and creativity required of the job comes the responsibility to demonstrate that our methods have helpful effects. Proper evaluation procedures can help us to assess the magnitude and longevity of changes that take place. Whenever possible, it is useful for counselors to do pre- and postintervention assessments. Determining the appropriate method of assessment is often as tricky as devising the intervention itself, but at the very least, invite client feedback about a workshop or counseling experience.

Commitment

One way to encourage commitment is to communicate the value of participation in programs. What kind of change can clients expect? Will they gain tangible skills? Are there intrinsic benefits, such as doing what is morally good? Another way to ensure commitment and reduce the likelihood of burnout in a program is to make it fun for the participants. Positive humor and focus builds safety and trust. In addition, a fun experience reduces tension and threat for all participants (Goldstein & Conoley, 1997). There are many ways to introduce fun in counseling, especially in a group setting. Some easy methods include (a) providing opportunities to meet in a new place such as outside, when the weather is good, (b) bringing food, especially if it can be related to a relevant theme, and (c) varying the kinds of engagement elicited from clients such as experiential, affective, cognitive, film, art, or athletic activities.

Technology

Technological advances are far from accessible to every adolescent. Using technology as an intervention tool for adolescence, however, has many advantages, including user control, personalization, branching, flexibility, open access, and anonymity (Bosworth, Espelage, & DuBay, 1998). Exercises located on the World Wide Web have been used to augment textbooks for professional training in prevention and intervention issues (Hanson & Venturelli, 1998). In addition, countless Web sites invite adolescent participation and seek to promote positive identity development.

INNOVATIVE PROGRAMS

The following section describes several programs and ideas for prevention and intervention that we find particularly inspiring and interesting. Our aim is to whet your appetite for researching interesting programs in your community or developing your own. In most cases, descriptions of how counselors can implement these programs or strategies are provided.

Teens Against Gang Violence

Teens Against Gang Violence (TAGV), found at http://www.tagv.org, is a good example of an intervention/prevention program accessible through the World Wide Web. TAGV is a volunteer community-based peer leadership program that provides violence prevention education to parents, teens, schools, and community groups. Participants can find online the founding principles of the group and an explicitly stated philosophy of the program, a contract of responsibilities, criteria for advancement, a book list, a code of conduct, awards, a model of change, and other pertinent information about the group.

TAGV's objectives are to dispel the myth that all inner-city youth are involved in violent street gangs and to promote healthy identity development and leadership in its members. TAGV consider themselves a positive gang, and their philosophy includes the following 10 C's Model of Awareness and Change.

The 5 C's of Awareness

Color. In a literal sense, color refers to individual/group identity based on race/the color of one's skin that is either self-determined or defined by those in power. However, we use this C symbolically to also mean aspects of the self/group that are part of one's core identity or essence—especially attributes that are not changeable, such as color, gender, and sexual orientation. For example, color "just is," but it is culture and context that define color as "race" and give it either positive or negative value.

Culture. The values, beliefs, symbols, behaviors, ways of living, and shared history of a group of people (that may or may not belong to the same ethnic, racial, or gender group) that are continually changing and are passed on from one generation to the next. Culture interprets meaning of color, class, character, and context.

Class. Refers to power relations and examines individual/group identity relative to power, authority, hierarchy, status, and the degree of access to, control over, or ownership of resources, including wealth, education, employment, housing, etc.

Character. The unique aspects of each individual person, including personal preferences, idiosyncrasies, and personality traits. People who share similar color, culture, class, and context still possess aspects of the self that are unique to the individual.

(Continued)

Context. The reality in which individuals/groups currently exist in time, location, environment, and the socio-political, economic, and historical conditions which influence individual and group experience. Color, culture, class, and character cannot be seen in isolation from context and cannot be fully understood when removed from the context that shapes their meaning.

The 5 C's of Change

Confidence. Faith in yourself and your abilities, and the belief that you, alone and with other people, can make a difference. Understanding and taking pride in your "5 C's of Awareness," including race, ethnicity, gender, class, and sexual orientation.

Courage. The capability to take action, in spite of fear. It means acting as a leader and being willing to take risks that leadership demands. It is the "inner resolution to go forward in spite of obstacles and frightening situations" (Dr. Martin Luther King, Jr.).

Commitment. Focus, strategy, determination, and consistency driven by love and grounded in knowledge.

Conflict. The reflection, struggle, and creative tension that promotes growth and justice. Conflict is a positive and necessary part of the process of change.

Community. Working collectively and collaboratively with others toward a shared vision that acknowledges, values, and affirms human diversity as essential to the whole.

Reprinted with permission of the author, Ulric Johnson, PhD.

TAGV is a comprehensive program that trains its teen members in antiviolence education, prevention, intervention, peer leadership, conflict resolution management, and gang/drug refusal skills. Members in turn conduct services in the community under the supervision of the group's leadership. Members have clear criteria for advancement within the organization to senior peers, which include participation in the group, service in conducting workshops and presentations, a record of nonviolence, and role-modeling proper respect for the program's goals and philosophy. The Web site offers a variety of contact points for those interested in learning more or getting involved.

Perhaps what is most impressive about this program is that teens are respected for all aspects of their personhood. The program engages youths in social action through violence prevention, self-reflection, community building, and basic human concern and respect. Perhaps you might want to consider set-

I, _____, on this day of _____, pledge to work together with the members of my family, school, community, city, and nation to educate about and eliminate violence in all its forms, including racism, sexism, heterosexism, guns, drugs, gangs, crime, and fighting. I promise to support others in efforts for peace and justice.

In support of non-violence, I will try to:

▷ Refuse to participate in any form of physical, verbal, or emotional violence.

▷ Model language and behavior that is non-biased and inclusive of all persons regardless of race, gender, ethnicity, disabilities, sexual orientation, class, age, or religion.

▷ Educate myself about the valuable cultural diversity which exists in each of us and in our society, and seek out opportunities to participate with culturally diverse groups.

▷ De-escalate situations which can lead to violence.

▷ Intervene to let others know that I will not tolerate jokes, comments, slurs, or actions that demean any person or group.

▷ Join with others in efforts to overcome prejudice and violence.

▷ Share this pledge with a friend and encourage them to share it with others.

> I pledge to reject hate and embrace love,
>
> Support, and care for myself and others,
>
> And to make a difference with my life.

SOURCE: Reprinted by permission of the author, Ulric Johnson, PhD.

NOTE: This pledge was adapted from the Youth Against Violence Pledge of Martin Luther King Jr. Center for Social Change in Atlanta, GA, and the Count on Me pledge of the Fair Housing Committee of Weymouth, MA, by Patti DeRosa of Cross-Cultural Consultation in Randolph, MA, the Cambridge Youth Peace and Justice Corps, and Teens Against Gang Violence, Boston, MA, 1994.

Figure 7.1   TAGV Pledge of Non-Violence

ting up a chapter of TAGV in the school or community where you practice. If you are interested, visit the Web site (http://www.tagv.org) and contact Dr. Ulric Johnson via e-mail or by the phone number listed on the site. Figure 7.1 presents an excerpt from their member pledge, which we see as an exemplar of how to affirm positive, multifaceted identity.

Narratives

Garrod, Smulyan, Powers, and Kilkenny (1999) provide an excellent illustration of how to use adolescent narratives to explore identity development in *Adolescent Portraits: Identity, Relationships, and Challenges.* Their work is a good training tool for counselors who have limited experience with adolescents. The cases are written by college students who reflect back on various periods in their adolescence. The authors provide a window into the worlds of an impressive array of people, and the narratives are quite compelling—a refreshing change from strictly theory-based discussions. Another function of the narratives is to integrate them in group counseling settings or to encourage adolescents to write their own stories to process in counseling.

The insight the authors bring to these narratives is striking. We would be hard-pressed to find a group of adults who could articulate their development this clearly. There is an undeniable power in allowing the participants to tell their story without interruption or imposition of an agenda other than to hear their reflections. It's unlikely most clients would be as articulate as those in the book, but having clients read others' narratives gives them a glimpse of how to process issues, even if they can't readily express what's going on personally. These stories make adolescent identity real and tangible, providing a way for adult counselors to truly relate.

These narratives can easily be used as a tool for developing theme-centered groups around a variety of identity issues such as sexuality, gender identity, family relationships, ethnicity, and careers. The stories provide intricate and complex examples of identity development in the context of psychosocial stressors such as child abuse, eating disorders, bicultural conflict, drugs/alcohol, and pregnancy/abortion. Counselors can select cases for their groups using the index, which is organized by theme. Prior to implementing interventions, counselors can also refer to a number of expert reflections on cases provided in the book.

One might arrange to bring copies of a narrative to an ongoing theme-centered group such as one on promoting healthy women's identities. In the group, members could take turns reading the case out loud and then the group would process their reactions to the case. The counselor might ask group members to share what most struck them about the person's story. The group could discuss any feelings expressed that they could relate to. The counselor could facilitate a discussion that moved around themes of individual self-reflection, making connections to relationships inside or outside the group, cognitive framing of identity, linking personal experiences to societal context, and more.

Another suggestion is to ask group members to write their own reflection paper to either process or share with the group. The assignment could be to focus on a clearly demarcated period of time such as freshman year in high school or junior high. The reflection paper could examine the messages clients received about what it means to be, for example, women or citizens from their family, school, and community. We recommend a similar process to that of the previously described intervention, in which people share stories out loud without interruption of questions or comments and then have the group process how people as individuals and as group members related to or responded to the narrative.

Adolescent Room Culture

Steele and Brown (1995) identified a relationship between teens and their bedroom space. Empirical data exist that support the existence of an "adolescent room culture," referring to the material things in a teen's space as well as the activities that the teens engage in when they are in such a space. Through everyday activities, adolescents incorporate, appropriate, motivate, attend to, evaluate, and interpret their surroundings. Although Steele and Brown (1995) are primarily interested in developing a theory on the effects of adolescent interactions with media, their work opens up some interesting counseling possibilities.

The notion of a private bedroom space is perhaps a European American ideal and is certainly determined by socioeconomic status, but all teens can be empowered to create environments that are extensions of themselves. Adolescents might value a locker, a place out of doors, or a space that is shared with many others. A lack of space can be an interesting segue into an assessment of the clients' perceptions of privacy and collectiveness, serving as a window to culture or lifestyle. Counselors can assess the spaces that are available to a client and the ways a particular space mirrors or changes along with the teen's identity. Various continuities and discontinuities—for example, the way items such as photos of significant others appear or disappear from a space—can be an indication of the flexible and transitory nature of adolescence. Beyond assessment, counselors can also help teens create shared or private spaces of their own. Spaces are palettes of experimentation as the adolescent retains aspects of youth or investigates adult possibilities.

We can use how teens consciously incorporate media and material items into their lives (a function Steele & Brown, 1995, identify as appropriation) to devise meaningful counseling interventions. Steele and Brown found that adolescents use their possessions and the media for the following purposes:

1. *To enhance a mood or cope with feelings:* "When I need to get pumped up, like before a party, I listen to wild, loud music" (White female, 16).
2. *To sort through cultural values and norms:* "Sometimes I try to figure out what I would have done" (White female, 13).
3. *To make a statement about identity:* "I like it just cuz it's weird and not many people have stuff like that. I like to be different. It's just me" (White female, 16).
4. *To emulate admired behavior:* Asked why she had dyed her hair, Asta replied, "Because that's what you got to do today, Mama" (Black female, 13).
5. *To fantasize about possible selves or situations:* "I would love to meet David Lee Roth one day. He would be a snob but I think it would be neat" (White female, 14). (p. 565)

Any one of these five themes could be highlighted in an individual or group counseling context. For example, to assess adolescents' coping behaviors, counselors can inquire about what kind of music clients listen to when they feel depressed, lonely, elated, or anxious. Similarly, counselors can discuss clients' favorite television shows, books, or movies in terms of characters with whom the clients identify and what they extract morally or culturally from the actions of their heroes or antiheroes. Such efforts tend to be relatively non-threatening to clients and afford the counselor opportunities to conceptualize their clients within their own chosen media microcosm. Such interventions obviously require that counselors keep themselves media savvy, a good excuse to watch lots of television for the good of one's profession.

What is very intriguing indeed is to engage clients in fantasizing about choices they would make if they projected themselves into a song or onto the silver screen as one of the characters. In the film *The Matrix,* the protagonist is given a choice between two pills to swallow: one is guaranteed to return him to his familiar life and the other is guaranteed to show him the truth. Although the film is controversial for its display of gun violence, it is also a film that was widely seen by teen audiences and one that grapples with the Orwellian theme of whether, in a complicated world, ignorance is bliss. Counselors might ask clients to describe which pill they would choose and why, or even whether they would choose at all. Counselors may also gain insight into clients' lives by exploring which behaviors and images they choose to emulate. What does it mean to a client to practice tae kwon do like the television character Buffy the Vampire Slayer or dress like the singer Jennifer Lopez?

Capitalizing on the dialectical process between teens and the culture of the rooms can take many forms. Assessment of coping strategies, decision processes, and values, as described above, is one form. Developing interventions using preselected media is another. Keeping in mind that individuals are very selective about the media they interact with (Steele & Brown, 1995), counselors can plan to use relevant media to stimulate discussion of a specific theme. For instance, one might incorporate the film *Double Happiness* (which is about a second-generation Asian Canadian adolescent who struggles with her bicultural identity) into a workshop on Asian American identity development. The film would serve as a stimulus for discussing how members of the group feel about their Asian heritage and their U.S. cultural heritage. Counselors might use the minority identity development model (Atkinson, Morten, & Sue, 1998) to help frame attitudes that members have about themselves and others in different cultural groups.

Another strategy is to employ media and art. Counselors could bring in magazines they know their clients read, scissors, and construction paper for a group on male identity development. Clients would be instructed to make collages of images of men working as a group, individually, or in pairs. The group could then discuss what it feels like to receive messages through these magazines and how they interact with these messages in their chosen behaviors, concerns, or fantasies. A group focused on male identity development might also involve client discussion of female media images, images of men and women together, images of men together, images of older men, and so forth. In this way, counselors would encourage exploration of messages that are less obvious or less popular but nonetheless powerful influences on male identity development. The possibilities in using media in counseling adolescents are numerous.

Tools for Tomorrow

Tools for Tomorrow (TFT) is a new classroom-based intervention geared toward promoting the psychosocial and career development of urban high school students (Blustein, Jackson, Jackson, Kenny, & Sparks, 1999). The following discussion highlights how the TFT program addresses key intervention dimensions outlined earlier in this chapter. We hope that by illustrating how a program can apply to the various dimensions in intervention development, we might motivate readers to pursue organizing and developing appropriate programming for clients in their communities.

Focus of Effort (McKinney et al., 1998)

TFT focuses on education and competency promotion. Blustein et al. (1999) based much of their work on the career development and school engagement literatures. They hypothesize that if students find their education relevant to their identity, broadly defined, they will become more engaged and perform better in school. TFT incorporates a variety of educational strategies to enhance student competencies in career exploration, decision making, and planning as well as coping with family pressures, interpersonal skills, cultural/racial identity, and internal motivation.

Multilevel Collaborative Networks (Brown & Theobald, 1998)

A variety of professionals were involved in all levels of the development of the program (i.e., assessment, intervention, and evaluation), including psychologists, education specialists, high school administrators, and teachers. Blustein (personal communication, 1999) remarked that putting together such a project takes a huge amount of effort, but because of the collaborative links, he anticipates the program will have sustaining power. The program also actively employs collaboration between teachers, counselors, and peers. For example, Theme Centered Interaction groups (Shafer & Galinsky, 1989) are facilitated by both teachers and counselors and revolve around relationships, spirituality, culture, and so forth.

Variability (Goldstein & Conoley, 1997)

TFT incorporates an impressive variety of activities to facilitate its goals. It employs multiple methods such as the use of narratives, fantasy, writing, listening to music, career inventories, and values checklists. References for these exercises can be found in the Additional Resources at the end of this chapter. A sampling of activities are (a) the vocational daydream—guided fantasy that begins with a relaxation exercise and leads to the participant's imagination of events during a typical workday 5, 10, or 15 years from the present (Spokane, 1991), (b) seeing yourself from different perspectives—clients indicate how their friends might describe them, how they would describe themselves, how teachers might describe them, and what symbols represent important aspects of their identity (Ducat, 1999), (c) structured autobiography—an age-appropriate writing exercise that guides clients in describing relevant experiences and roles. For example, in the life-roles component, clients are given examples of a variety of roles people play. Then they are instructed to list several roles, what they liked or valued most about a given role, sources of satisfaction/dissatisfaction from a role, and what skills were used in each role (Lock, 1992).

Philosophy (Goldstein & Conoley, 1997)

Blustein et al. (1999) clearly assert that TFT is an effort to face the moral challenge of helping students who experience a legacy of deprivation in urban schools. They believe that by helping students internalize the critical connections between school and work, they will be more engaged in their academic pursuits.

Self-Reflexivity

The team members reflect on their own development. One investigator noted that music was a major influence on how he made meaning of class, culture, and identity. One of the intervention components derived from this self-reflection involves discussing the lyrics to songs such as "Every Ghetto, Every Child" by Lauryn Hill and "Across the Border" by Bruce Springsteen. They use these music examples to stimulate discussion of a variety of important themes such as socioeconomic class and the meaning of change in one's life. TFT employs many intervention strategies that call for student reflection on their values, dreams, identity, and more.

Outcome

One of the multidisciplinary teams is designated to develop a psychosocial needs assessment and evaluation protocol. Outcome will be measured by both quantitative and qualitative methods. They expect to gather information on school engagement, academic performance, and other measures of development.

Commitment

By organizing the TFT program with multilevel school support, participants get a clear message that administrators, teachers, and counselors are on board. Classroom-based interventions have an advantage not only because of the captive audience, but because participants are more likely to invest themselves when they know a program has the support of the institution.

The Tools for Tomorrow program is one example of a comprehensive prevention/intervention program geared toward fostering healthy identity development in adolescents. Using the key dimensions as a guideline, think creatively about the kinds of programs needed in your community, school, or agency.

SUMMARY

We recommend that you develop your knowledge base in a variety of theories on adolescent identity development but think critically about the social and cultural bases for each of the theories. Archer's (1994) text is an excellent source for this endeavor. We found that with the exception of the career literature, there is a paucity of resources on specific counseling strategies for developmental concerns. Rather, most of the adolescent psychology literature focuses on clinical interventions for problems and disorders. We encourage you to work creatively with adolescents to develop a positive sense of self-in-context. Although clinical hours are often filled with cases requiring direct intervention, devoting time to healthy adolescents and helping them shape their identities is both worthy and rewarding.

We hope this chapter has been useful in helping you conceptualize positive identity development for adolescents and in thinking about practical counseling approaches. We conclude with a vignette so you can begin integrating the information presented in this chapter. In addition to referring to our suggestions, we encourage you to expand the list of criteria for developing interventions with your personal sociocultural knowledge base. Finally, lists of readings and audiovisual materials are provided to facilitate further development.

VIGNETTE

Imagine you're a practitioner at an urban community health center. You and your colleagues are working with numerous families who have recently immigrated to the United States and who share the same ethnic background (e.g., the culture of Cape Verde, Mexico, Russia, or Taiwan). You see an opportunity to promote positive identity development among the adolescents in these families by designing a preventive outreach.

––––––

1. *Focus of Effort.* What are some salient aspects of identity to explore with these adolescents?

2. *Multilevel Collaborative Networks.* Describe the kind of networking you believe would be appropriate to meet your counseling goals. Who might you collaborate with and how? Identify who would actually benefit from these collaborations (you? the teens? others?).

3. *Variability.* Identify some of the key factors you'll need to investigate in order to tailor your intervention to both your population and their specific identity development needs.

4. *Philosophy.* Articulate your philosophy of working with adolescents in terms of fostering their identity development. What adjustments, if any, might be warranted as you think about working with this population?

5. *Self-Reflexivity.* How can you personally relate to this population? What are the ways in which you don't relate or aren't familiar with this population? How might your reflections relate to your philosophy and to your intended approach to counseling this population?

6. *Outcome.* Describe how you would evaluate the impact of your outreach.

7. *Commitment.* Factoring in your answers to the above questions, how can you maximize the commitment of the participants (i.e., the adolescent clients as well as the network of professionals involved)?

8. *Technology.* What strategies would you use to access technological resources for your outreach? If they weren't readily available, what would you do?

9. How might you attend to marginalized aspects of identity in your counseling intervention?

10. What are some examples of activities you would consider doing with this population?

How might your approach to developing and implementing an outreach program for White middle-class adolescents (at least third- or fourth-generation to the United States) be similar or different to this vignette? Why and why not?

ADDITIONAL RESOURCES

Print Resources

Adams, G. R., Montemayor, R., & Gullotta, T. P. (1996). *Psychosocial development during adolescence.* Thousand Oaks, CA: Sage.

Archer, S. L. (Ed.). (1994). *Interventions for adolescent identity development.* Thousand Oaks, CA: Sage.

Barber, B. K., & Olsen, J. A. (1997). Socialization in context: Connection, regulation, and autonomy in the family, school, and neighborhood, and with peers. *Journal of Adolescent Research, 12*(2), 287-315.

Bosma, H., & Jackson, S. (Eds.). (1990). *Coping and self-concept in adolescence.* New York: Springer-Verlag.

Brookins, C. C. (1996). Promoting ethnic identity development in African American youth: The role of rites of passage. *Journal of Black Psychology, 22*(3), 388-417.

Carlson, J., & Lewis, J. (1995). *Counseling the adolescent: Individual, family, and school interventions* (3rd ed.). Denver: Love.

Carnegie Council on Adolescent Development. (1995, October). *Great transitions: Preparing adolescents for a new century.* New York: Carnegie Corporation of New York.

Coakley, J. (1992). Burnout among adolescent athletes: A personal failure or social problem? *Sociology of Sport Journal, 9,* 271-285.

Eccles, J. S., Early, D., Frasier, K., Belansky, E., & McCarth, K. (1997). The relation of connection, regulation, and support for autonomy to adolescents' functioning. *Journal of Adolescent Research, 12*(2), 263-286.

Grotevant, H. D. (1997). Family processes, identity development, and behavioral outcomes for adopted adolescents. *Journal of Adolescent Research, 12*(1), 139-161.

Gubitz, K. F., & Kutcher, J. (1999). Facilitating identity formation for adolescent girls using experientially-based outdoor activities. *Texas Classical Association Journal, 27,* 32-39.

Head, J. (1997). *Working with adolescents: Constructing identity.* Washington, DC: Falmer.

Heath, S. B., & McLaughlin, M. W. (1993). *Identity and inner-city youth: Beyond ethnicity and gender.* New York: Teachers College Press.

Hollander, G. (2000). Questioning youths: Challenges to working with youths forming identities. *School Psychology Review,* Special Issue: Mini-Series: Lesbian, gay, bisexual, transsexual, and questioning youths, *29*(2), 173-179.

Horne, A. M., & Kiselica, M. S. (1999). *Handbook of counseling boys and adolescent males: A practitioner's guide.* Thousand Oaks, CA: Sage.

Horton, C. B., & Bucy, J. E. (2000). Assessing adolescents: Ecological and person-environment fit perspectives. In W. E. Martin Jr. & J. L. Swartz-Kulstad (Eds.),

Person-environment psychology and mental health: Assessment and intervention (pp. 39-57). Mahwah, NJ: Lawrence Erlbaum.

Magen, Z. (1998). *Exploring adolescent happiness: Commitment, purpose, and fulfillment.* Thousand Oaks, CA: Sage.

Mattaini, M. A., & Thyer, B. A. (1996). *Finding solutions to social problems.* Washington, DC: American Psychological Association.

Muuss, R., & Porton, H. D. (1998). *Adolescent behavior and society: A book of readings* (5th ed.). Boston: McGraw-Hill.

Okun, B. F., Fried, J., & Okun, M. L. (1999). *Understanding diversity: A learning-as-practice primer.* Pacific Grove, CA: Brooks/Cole.

Rutter, M. (Ed.). (1997). *Psychosocial disturbances in young people: Challenges for prevention.* Cambridge, UK: Cambridge University Press.

Shorter-Gooden, K. (2000). Finding the lost part: Identity and the Black/White biracial client. In L. C. Jackson & B. Greene (Eds.), *Psychotherapy with African American women: Innovations and practice* (pp. 194-207). New York: Guilford.

Vernon, A. (1999). *Counseling children and adolescents.* Denver: Love.

Audiovisual Resources

Castle, S. (Producer). (1998). *In the mix: Reality television for teens* [Television series and videotape]. New York: Public Broadcasting Service.

Dupre, J. (Director, Producer). (1997). *Out of the past: The struggle for gay and lesbian rights in America* [Film].

Goodman, B., & Dretzin, R. (1999). *The lost children of Rockdale County* [Film].

Grodner, A. (Director, Producer). (1998). *Teenfiles: The truth about hate* [Film].

Jhally, S. (Director). (1999). *Tough guise: Violence, media, and the crisis in masculinity* [Film].

Lee, C. (Director, Producer), & Yang, D. (Producer). (1998). *Yellow* [Film].

Menendez, R. (Director). (1988). *Stand and deliver* [Film].

Rajski, P. (Director), & Stone, R. (Producer). (1994). *Trevor* [Film].

Redford, R. (Director), & Schwary, R. L. (Producer). (1980). *Ordinary people* [Film].

Shum, M. (Director), Hegyes, S., & Waddel, R.L. (Producers). (1994). *Double happiness* [Film].

Singleton, J. (Director). (1991). *Boyz 'n the hood.* [Film].

Audiovisual Media Distributors

California Newsreel, 149 Ninth St., San Francisco, CA 94103; phone: 415-621-6196; http://www.newsreel.org

National Asian American Telecommunications Association (NAATA), 346 Ninth St., 2nd Floor, San Francisco, CA 94103; phone: 415-863-0814; http://www.naatanet.org

National Latino Communications Center, 501 South Bixel, 2nd Floor, Los Angeles, CA 90017; phone: 323-663-8294; fax: 323-663-5606

New Day Films, 22-D Hollywood Ave., Hohokus, NJ 07423; phone: 201-652-6590; http://www.newday.com

Internet Resources

Adolescence Directory On-Line Counselor Resources:
    http://www.education.indiana.edu/cas/adol/counselor.html
Media Education Foundation: http://www.mediaed.org
National Film Board of Canada Collections:
    http://www.nfb.ca/FMT/E/cate/C/Childhood_and_Adolescence.html
National Resource Center for Youth Services: http://youthlifeskills.nrcys.ou.edu
Parenting Adolescents: http://www.parentingadolescents.com
Project YES: http://www.projectyes.org
Public Broadcasting Service: http://www.pbs.org
The Teen Files: http://www.teenfiles.com
Teen Focus: http://webhome.idirect.com/~mccann/index.html

CHAPTER 8

Promoting Success Pathways for Middle and High School Students

Introducing the Adaptive Success Identity Plan for School Counselors

V. Scott Solberg
Wendy Close
A. J. Metz

It's about making school successful for all students.

S uccessful navigation in the world of work demands educational success. Without completing high school and some college, individuals entering the workforce increasingly fail to acquire jobs providing livable wages. Roughly one third of all students in the United States drop out of high school without receiving a high school diploma (Hammack, 1986). Rather than focusing on identifying the "causes" of school failure, this chapter focuses on how school counselors can design educational interventions that promote success for all students. According to Walsh, Howard, and Buckley (1999), school counselor training in human relationships, prevention programming, and focus on the whole child provide the foundation for building interventions that create what we refer to as success pathways. Walsh et al. (1999) also emphasize that such interventions must be organized within a framework that is "developmentally ap-

Authors' Note: The authors wish to thank Don Krueger, Rosana Benishek, Rick Anderson, the Allied Health family, the Business Technology Family, the Engineering families, and the Travel and Tourism families, whose hard work and dedication to the ASIP project made this chapter possible. Correspondence concerning this chapter and requests for offprints should be addressed to V. Scott Solberg, PhD, Enderis Hall, P.O. Box 413, Milwaukee, WI 53202; e-mail: ssolberg@uwm.edu.

propriate, grounded in a comprehensive approach, research based, and have defined measurable outcomes" (p. 354). This chapter describes such a framework originally developed for college settings (Solberg et al., 1998) that integrates Developmental Systems Theory (Ford & Lerner, 1992), Social Cognitive Theory (Bandura, 1986), Diathesis-Stress Models, and Social Integration Theory (Tinto, 1987). This framework emphasizes the importance of designing interventions that build success pathways. Success pathways promote students' success identities that serve as a cognitive and emotional template for making effective school-to-work-to-life transitions. Within this proposed framework, students who possess a success identity make effective school-to-work-to-life transitions because they focus on learning how to learn the tasks associated with the transition, effectively manage stress and time, and effectively establish relationships with peers and authority figures. Examples for building success pathways are then described. On the basis of the adaptive success identity plan (ASIP), these classroom- and community-based interventions offer prescriptive solutions for school counselors to create the environmental context necessary to promote students' success identities.

DEVELOPMENTAL SYSTEMS THEORY AS THE ORGANIZING FRAMEWORK FOR BUILDING SUCCESS PATHWAYS

For many students, dropping out of school results from a series of failure experiences, as a result of which, students possess self-identity systems that define education as a negative self-defeating experience. One of the most comprehensive attempts to integrate theories of human development, Developmental Systems Theory (Ford & Lerner, 1992) prescribes strategies for school counselors designing academic environments that promote positive self-identity systems. Self-identity consists of a constellation of self-conceptions that emerge and evolve within social transactions (Mead, 1934; Shibutani, 1986). Within social transactions, the division of labor creates roles for the participants. Within a school setting, this division of labor consists of a teacher and student role. The type of activities associated with a given role determines the content of a self-concept, and the quality of the role performance determines the value of esteem associated with a self-concept. Students engaged in math activities, for example, possess an understanding of the content associated with performing a math self-concept, which consists of efficacy expectations, self-rated abilities, and schemas associated with performing math problems. Students also possess value information related to whether they "like" math, enjoy learning about math, and believe that learning math is important. The quality of feedback received from the environment, combined with predisposing valuations of "Can I do it?" and whether "I like it," interact to either maintain or modify one's current math self-concept. Taking into account the constellation of self-conceptions employed at school, dropping out becomes an adaptive solution when students do not believe they possess the ability to adequately perform these roles and/or do not value the performance. Education becomes self-defeating when students consistently feel inadequate and incapable.

According to Developmental Systems Theory (Ford & Lerner, 1992), students enter middle and high school with predispositions about their student self-conceptions. These predispositions operate through unconscious "feed-forward" processes that actively seek confirming information about their student role definition. Thus, students enter given situations with preconceptions of what is going to occur, including what are their roles, what are others' roles, and how others perceive them. Students attend to or cue in on specific stimuli that support their preconceptions and ignore other stimuli, thereby creating interactions that confirm their schemata. Thus, students with a history of school failure remain sensitive to information confirming their inability to learn. Self-conceptions actively seek confirming information in order to maintain a stable view of one's self-identity. In addition to remaining selective to information that confirms one's definition for a given self-conception, individuals actively select social transactions that express desired self-conceptions. Together, these two processes of selective attention and selection of social transactions allow individuals to maintain a stable sense of self (i.e., "autopoesis"). Unless school counselors offer interventions that provide discrepant feedback, maladaptive student role self-conceptions become elaborated with continued accumulation of failure experiences.

Unconscious constellations of self-conceptions generate probabilities of success or failure within recurring social transactions. Students failing to attend school, prepare for examinations, or pay attention during class increase the likelihood of maintaining a behavior trajectory resulting in the accumulation of academic failure experiences. These behavior episode schemata serve as templates forged within one's self-conceptions that guide behavior performances during a given social transaction (Ford & Ford, 1987). Behavior episode schemata provide blueprints from which behavior becomes constructed during a social transaction. Students who fail in school often possess behavior episode schemata that define the student role as resistant, antagonistic, or uninvolved with the learning process. These negative behavior episode schemata increase the likelihood of receiving successive failure experiences unless school counselors establish interventions that challenge these negative views or that activate more positive behavior episode schemata that increase the likelihood of experiencing successful outcomes. For example, interventions designed to improve math skills for a failing student attempt to challenge the student's view that "I can't do math." Alternatively, offering theatre training to this student may provide a successful school experience.

School counselors need to consider that the full environmental context consists of the school and school system, families, and community. School counselors must design interventions that respond specifically to students entering middle and high school with maladaptive behavior episode schemata in a number of ways. Interventions need to focus on improving the quality of student relationships with teachers, peers, and administration, offer behavior management programming, alternative education programming, and create other resources that allow students to activate desired self-conceptions (e.g., after-school programming, sports, arts). School counselors must work with their districts to acquire the resources needed to create support services that improve attendance and offer summer job opportunities and avenues for nontraditional learning contexts. School counselors must create opportunities for families to play an important role in educational success by establishing the structure to connect parents to the educational process.

The transition into middle or high school offers students the opportunity for reevaluation of their self-identity. Effective interventions early in the school year create opportunities for students' negative self-definitions to be met with new discrepant information and experiences that call into question their current negative self-conception. Students entering high school with behavior episode schemata consisting of expectations to be bored, not listened to, and sitting idle throughout the day likely fail unless discrepant information is perceived. Students experience a shift in definition when school counselors offer interventions that connect students to teachers, link academic performance to desired vocational goals, and connect parents to the educational process. Although some students with rigid maladaptive self-conceptions sabotage this environment, many will not. But more important is the fact that unless school counselors create different possibilities for defining one's student role, students with negative student role behavior episode schemata continue to accumulate failure experiences.

It is important to note that the proposition regarding the role of school counselors in facilitating changes in student outcomes should not imply that student outcomes are "caused" by poor teachers or ineffective learning environments. However, the locus of responsibility for creating change begins with the environmental context. All student outcomes result from a complex interaction between the student behavior episode schemata and the environmental context, but the impetus for changing students begins with school counselors establishing a framework and plan of action to attack negative self-identity systems and actively promote success identities.

CONSTRUCTS THAT FACILITATE BUILDING SUCCESS IDENTITIES

Three theoretical perspectives establish a framework for what school counselors need to focus on when attempting to design interventions that promote success identities. Students possess a success identity when their self-identity incorporates the constructs described by these theoretical perspectives. Students possessing a success identity approach life transitions with a focus on "learning how to learn" the tasks associated with the transition activities (e.g., learning job requirements), effectively managing stress and time, and building effective social relationships with peers and persons in authority. The theoretical perspectives include Social Cognitive Theory (Bandura, 1986, 1992), Diathesis-Stress Models (Hobfoll, 1989), and Social Integration Theory (Tinto, 1987).

Social Cognitive Theory

Consistent with Developmental Systems Theory, Social Cognitive Theory emphasizes academic outcomes as resulting from a complex interaction of person, environment, and behavior determinants (Bandura, 1977, 1986). Social Cognitive Theory focuses on the personal constructions students place on school events and emphasizes both the students' roles in promoting success or failure and the simultaneous influence of the environmental context as either supporting or changing the probability of success or failure.

Two constructs drawn from Social Cognitive Theory—self-efficacy and outcome expectations—influence how students define their student self-conceptions. Self-efficacy refers to students' beliefs in their ability to organize their behavior in a way that creates positive academic outcomes. School counselors may operationalize self-efficacy as the degree of confidence a student possesses in successfully performing a range of concrete academic tasks. Academic outcome expectations refer to one's belief that performing specific learning activities result in desired outcomes. Although self-efficacy may not always match ability and perceived outcome expectations may not always be accurate, one's self-efficacy beliefs and outcome expectations relate directly to whether the activity is performed, the amount of effort expended when performing the activity, and persistence to succeed in performing the activity. The direct role of self-efficacy beliefs and outcome expectations on academic interests, persistence intentions, career goals, academic performance, and student well-being are well documented. (Betz & Hackett, 1986; Fouad & Smith, 1996; Gainor & Lent, 1998; Lent, Brown, & Hackett, 1994; Multon, Brown, & Lent, 1991).

By creating interventions that focus on building academic self-efficacy, school counselors produce students who expect to succeed in school. Students receiving such interventions learn that they have the ability to learn new tasks and thus enter transitions with an understanding that occupational and life skills are not innate but must be learned. Students with high self-efficacy focus on learning how to learn the skills associated with making successful transitions. Alternatively, students entering middle and high school with low self-efficacy expect and often experience successive failure. By creating interventions that focus on building outcome expectations, school counselors increase students' motivation to perform well in school. Thus, counselors will want to create interventions designed to help students understand how successful performance with the subject matter translates into more extensive 2- and 4-year college major or training options and ultimately improved vocational options. Outcome expectations become directed through career planning that begins with evaluating students' current school persistence intentions and range of career aspirations.

School counselors build students' academic self-efficacy expectations when interventions include four sources of self-efficacy information: (1) mastery experiences, (2) watching others, (3) verbal inspiration, and (4) anxiety management (Bandura, 1986). Successfully performing a specific math task, for example, increases confidence in performing related math activities when students actively practice the task and receive concrete feedback regarding the performance. Watching someone solve aloud a difficult math equation improves confidence when a student identifies with the model and incorporates the solution strategies employed. Having adults who believe in the student's ability to succeed results in improved confidence when presented with insights into how previous performances in related activities relate to current tasks. One counselor used an American Indian woman's intricate beadwork skills as consisting of skills needed to succeed in school. Beadwork, like school, often demands learning from a number of successive failure experiences, which is similar to the type of persistence needed when learning how to master complex math problems. Often, ability judgments emerge from emotional reasoning—"If I could do this activity, I wouldn't feel so nervous." Learning to reduce math anxiety or test-taking anxiety through deep breathing and cognitive restructuring increases confidence by taking away the emotional feeling of doom often associated with anxiety.

In summary, for school counselors to create success identities, they must design interventions that build confidence for performing academic and social tasks (self-efficacy) and insight into how performing well academically translates into meaningful outcomes (outcome expectations).

Diathesis-Stress Models

Diathesis-Stress Models address factors that moderate or mediate the potentially debilitating role of high stress on one's well-being. Although stress caused by class assignments and examinations plays a motivating role for students, when too many pressures build up, one's immune system becomes compromised. Recent definitions of stress emphasize how pressure experienced within a given social transaction or activity results from one not having the skills or emotional resources necessary to manage the transaction or perform the activity (Hobfoll, 1989). Academic stress consists of difficulty in a number of areas, including meeting course requirements, getting along with peers, and writing papers (Solberg et al., 1998; Solberg, Hale, Villarreal, & Kavanagh, 1993). School counselors can help with students' well-being in a number of ways by conducting classroom interventions that discuss academic and life stress and avenues for maintaining well-being such as improving diet, exercise, relaxation, and positive social relationships. School counselors can also help students manage stress and maintain well-being by establishing pathways for family to connect to school and activities that facilitate peer support. The important role of perceived availability of family and peer support on maintaining well-being has been clearly documented (Cohen & Wills, 1985). It is believed that social support systems mobilize during high stress periods to buffer one from the potentially negative impact on well-being (Caplan, 1974; Cassel, 1974) by adding resources during high-pressure times. Recent research focusing on the role of the perceived availability of family indicates that family support provides resources that decrease the possibility that social transactions and activities will result in stress (Solberg et al., 1998; Solberg, Close, & Stark, 1999; Torres & Solberg, 1999). From working with diverse student populations, it has been found that perceived availability of family support results in lower reported academic stress (Solberg et al., 1999). In addition, family support directly improves the level of academic self-efficacy, which in turn relates to lower perceived academic stress (Torres & Solberg, 1999). With respect to family, school counselors need to find ways to connect the student's family to the education process. Community outreach activities, establishing home visits for low-attending students, and school Web pages offering advice and information to parents create multiple pathways for making such connections.

Thus, the emergence of success identities demands more than interventions designed to build self-efficacy and outcome expectations. School counselors must also design interventions that connect families to the educational process, create environmental support systems that buffer students from the potentially negative impact of stress, and provide learning experiences that help students learn effective ways to deal with academic and life pressures.

Social Integration Theory

Students stay in school when they feel connected to teachers, peers, and the learning environment (Tinto, 1987). Students who feel they belong within an educational setting will report stronger intentions to complete their academic goals (Pascarella & Terenzini, 1977, 1980), and students who possess stronger academic self-efficacy will report more social integration and subsequently stronger persistence intentions (Solberg et al., 1999).

Success identities also emerge when students feel connected to the environmental context. In addition to self-efficacy, outcome expectations, family support, and stress management, school counselors must design interventions that create strong relationships between teachers and students and between students. Students invest more of themselves in completing their education when they feel they *belong* within the school environment.

Theoretical Integration

A student's self-identity can be represented as a ship embedded in the ocean (Figure 8.1). Although effective navigation toward desired life and occupational outcomes demands possession of these constructs, the environmental context made up of many factors such as the educational system, students' economic status, and community resources operate as the ocean tide and wind. To possess a success identity, school counselors must create interventions that build the sails and cargo needed for students to navigate toward desired vocational and life aspirations.

Academic self-efficacy serves as a mainsail for two reasons: (1) It contributes to lower academic stress, stronger social and teacher integration, stronger persistence intentions, and better mental and physical well-being, and (2) it improves when school counselors design interventions that provide opportunities for successful mastery and vicarious experiences, inspirational support, and anxiety management skills. Outcome expectations also provide important motivation for the journey as well. Interventions providing students with insight into the link between educational attainment and vocational opportunities increases their motivation to attain those aspirations. Interventions must help students develop essential cargo such as knowing how to manage stress and time effectively, build connections with individuals in authority (teachers, staff, and community advocates), and build effective social skills to connect with peers. By designing interventions that build success identities, school counselors help students chart a life course toward positive future possibilities based on the combination of clear goals, high aspirations, stronger self-confidence, and high motivation.

The ship metaphor demonstrates Developmental Systems Theory's central tenets. Although many students from middle- and upper-middle-class backgrounds often find opportunity and clear direction, many students from lower income and diverse backgrounds find the seas choppy and the wind, if blowing at all, blowing against them. School provides a powerful developmental harbor for school counselors to create interventions that focus on building stronger mainsails and cargo for all students. Students exposed to such interventions build success identities that provide the navigational tools necessary for making successful school-to-work-to-life transitions. Students possessing success identities begin their school-to-work voyage by perceiving new events and

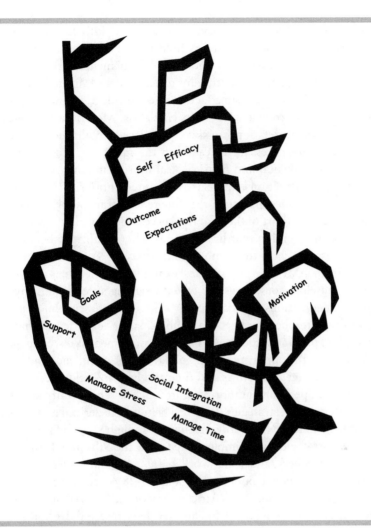

Figure 8.1 Ship Embedded in the Ocean as a Metaphor for Developmental Systems Theory's Central Tenets

learning experiences as challenges and seeking relationships and social transactions that support an evolving positive view of self.

INTERVENTION STRATEGIES FOR BUILDING SUCCESS PATHWAYS

School counselors serve a unique role within the school that makes them especially poised for creating interventions that build success pathways. Success pathways offer students opportunities to redefine their relationships with adults, peers, and themselves by offering supportive, encouraging relationships, mastery learning experiences, and social skills that transfer into the world of work. School counselors hold primary responsibility for building success pathways because they understand fundamentally the range of health, social, and emotional factors that influence student learning. School counselors understand that these same factors affect the degree to which students can learn the content knowledge of a specific class. Moreover, school counselors possess the human relationship skills necessary to build the community partnerships that are necessary to establish the range of success pathways that provide needed mental and physical health programming, vocational experiences, family connections, and classroom interventions (Walsh et al., 1999).

Interventions incorporating the theoretical framework described above were developed as part of the adaptive success identity plan (ASIP). ASIP is one method of intervention that links various school staff members together in a common vision of how to promote student success. A number of interventions derived from ASIP are provided as examples of the types of interventions school counselors could consider when designing success pathways. ASIP establishes interventions as success pathways to help students build stronger connections with teachers and peers, establish mastery experiences that build confidence, and provide students with stress management skills. Success pathways allow students the opportunities to build their self-confidence and learn how to effectively manage their stress and time and how to build effective social relationships with peers and authority figures such as school staff and other adults.

The intervention strategies described below were derived as part of an ongoing implementation with a low-income urban high school. Specifically, the intervention strategies were implemented with the 9th- and 10th-grade school counselors, teachers, and social workers ($N = 44$) and students ($N = 588$). Demographics of student population included 78% receiving free meals; 62% were Latino American, 21% African American, 7% Asian, 9% Euro/Slavic American and 1% American Indian. Teachers received 16 hours of training prior to the academic year and weekly support during the academic year. Training consisted of learning about the theory and empirical foundations of ASIP, an overview of curriculum, and brainstorming as to effective implementation strategies. Follow-up support consisted of modifying curriculum to meet the needs of the student population and teacher resources, cofacilitation of the curriculum implementation, and teacher inservice development activities.

Success Pathways That Build Student Success Identities and Teacher Investment

An essential prerequisite to constructing interventions that create success pathways involves gaining teacher buy-in. ASIP begins creating teacher buy-in by meeting with individual teachers to discuss the role that school counselors can play in making all students more successful. Teachers understand intuitively that learning outcomes improve when students build their confidence for learning, effectively manage stress, and build stronger relationships with peers and teachers. Establishing school counselor credibility occurs in two ways: (1) School counselors must offer an understanding of what limits student learning and solutions in the form of success pathways, and (2) school counselors must provide in-class interventions that (a) promote stronger connections between teachers and students, (b) build student confidence for learning, and (c) promote effective stress management strategies. Once teachers buy in to a plan of action, school counselors must offer inservice training prior to the beginning of the school year as well as ongoing meetings during the year. ASIP worked with the school principal to obtain funding for 2 days of training prior to the beginning of the school year. Teachers were also organized into common planning groups that allowed for weekly meetings during the school day, and therefore additional after-school funding was not necessary. It is important for teachers to "own" their role in working with the classroom interventions by cofacilitating with the school counselors. Establishing a common vision among teachers about the nature of promoting learning outcomes and creating collaborative classroom interventions discourage maladpative patterns of behavior and invite patterns of behavior that build success identities.

Assessment and Evaluation Using the ASIP Navigator

Following Developmental Systems Theory, students will not change negative patterns of behavior unless they perceive a discrepancy between how they currently define their student role and more effective behavior patterns. This is represented in Developmental Systems Theory as confronting the students' behavior episode schemata. To create the opportunity for this perceived discrepancy, students participating in ASIP receive a modified version of the College Experience Survey (Solberg et al., 1998) called the High School Experience Survey. In addition to modifying items to address middle and high school activities, the survey requires a fourth-grade reading level and is available in Spanish. Survey items address academic self-efficacy, academic stress, family and peer support, teacher connections, well-being, career decision needs, and high school persistence intentions. Scales associated with each measure are established using a sample of students from a given school. As part of the inservice training, teachers learn about the purpose of the items and goals of the survey process. School counselors, working in collaboration with teachers, explain the rationale of the survey to students in order to improve the administration validity. Completing the survey is voluntary. The rationale given to students is that the evaluation is the first step in a year-long program designed to improve academic and life success and that completing the survey results in their receiving an individualized report 2 weeks following administration.

The results from the survey generate an individualized report called the ASIP Navigator, which consists in part of bar graphs that compare the students' results to students who are deemed "successful" at the school. The average levels for each of the constructs represents one means of assessing students' "feedforward" processes associated with their student role. Although students often possess high educational and vocational aspirations, the survey attempts to assess the current behavior episode schemata trajectory pattern. Some students report "wanting" to succeed, for example, but do not expect to graduate from high school.

Individualized student reports in the form of bar graphs provide students with information about how their current attitudes and ratings relate to a norm group of successful students (e.g., students demonstrating high attendance and high grade point averages). Bar graphs represent each factor of a given construct. For academically at-risk students, the discrepancy between their confidence, stress, well-being, connections, career decision needs, and persistence ratings are self-evident. This represents feedback about the current behavior episode schemata and its relative likelihood of leading to successful academic outcomes. As a process note, school counselors and teachers prompt students to create their own definitions regarding whether the bar graph discrepancy represents a "problem."

Each bar graph contains a corresponding worksheet in which students elaborate on each construct. The worksheet prompts students to write about their personal issues in a language and at a level of self-disclosure with which they feel comfortable. For example, the stress section prompts students to identify specific stressors, how they physically and emotionally experience stress, and how others know they are stressed. The bar graph discrepancy and corresponding workbook enable students to develop a definition of the barriers and challenges they face in attempting to succeed in school.

Therapeutically, the ASIP Navigator confronts students' feedforward processes with environmental feedback, and any discrepancy creates the need for self-evaluation. School counselors and teachers support students' self-evaluation by providing a safe, affirming atmosphere for exploration and avenues for additional support programming when needed. For example, many students realize during this process that their sleeping, eating, or agitation levels are different from the norm sample. School counselors or teachers may report attention problems or problems managing anger and stress, and this feedback provides the student with an opportunity to define these areas as potential problems.

Each ASIP construct consists of a bar graph comparison and worksheet, enabling students and teachers to explore the range of possible issues affecting academic success. Whereas one student may dislike school because of feeling disconnected to peers or teachers, another may indicate low confidence, and someone else may report emotional/psychological issues. The ASIP Navigator facilitates exploration of the range of issues involved and creates an opportunity for students to define the challenges that affect their academic success. The ASIP Navigator also establishes a common language for school counselors, teachers, and students to use regarding issues that block academic success.

The ASIP Navigator possesses many characteristics that Developmental Systems Theory prescribes as necessary to facilitate change. Bar graph displays serve as feedback about whether current behavior episode schemata increase the likelihood of positive or negative outcomes. The feedback and corresponding worksheets offer students an opportunity to define whether a problem exists and creates a language that teachers and students can use to build change strategies.

Personal Narratives

A powerful method for establishing relationships between students, school counselors, and teachers involves personal narratives. Two personal narrative methods described below allow students to tell their own story, which breaks down any stereotypes school counselors and teachers may hold regarding why students fail to achieve. These methods effectively challenge school counselors and teachers regarding any inaccurate stereotypes and create the opportunity for establishing a stronger relationship with students.

The first personal narrative discussion involves a feedback session. During the interim between completing the survey and administering the individualized reports, school counselors and teachers facilitate a classroom discussion regarding the ASIP constructs. Using a transparency, each small group of students addresses one of the ASIP constructs by writing down examples associated with the construct and providing an oral report to the rest of the class. For example, students address self-efficacy by generating responses to the question "What does a student need to do well in order to succeed in school?" Stress is addressed by answering the question "What pressures do students experience?" Each construct is associated with questions such as these, and 10 responses are requested for each. The group discussion and oral reports create a context in which success identities become articulated, challenges to academic success become identified, and solutions are explored. School counselors and teachers participate by providing their own experiences associated with each of the constructs during the discussion. As a result, the classroom becomes a safe place to discuss and explore these issues. School counselors and teachers create a common language with students about the skills, resources, and strategies needed to be successful and learn about the range of issues confronting their students. With respect to Developmental Systems Theory, this first personal narrative session enables students to express themselves on meaningful issues. School counselor and teacher interest and self-disclosure create a new environmental context that responds to helping students learn about the issues involved in establishing a success identity.

The second type of personal narrative assessment directs students to write about challenges, barriers, and goals using open-ended statements. Sample statements include the following: "Tell me about school," "Tell me about your life in 5 years," and "Tell me about what gets in the way of learning." These sample questions are just a few possibilities. Students respond in writing that provides school counselors and teachers with insight into the range of issues confronting students, and classroom discussions offer opportunities for further understanding. The result is that students feel respected by the school counselors and teachers. This respect translates into increased motivation to learn and the likelihood that school counselors and teachers will be sought out when issues occur.

Charting Your Course Curriculum

After students define areas of needed improvement using the ASIP Navigator, the Charting Your Course curriculum creates a contract with the school counselor and teacher regarding behavior changes that increase the likelihood of academic success. Charting Your Course begins with students writing out the current course schedule and their grade expectations if they perform their hardest. This first activity affects the interactive style the teacher uses with the student. Research indicates that individuals who do not engage in success behaviors for which they possess high confidence (e.g., "If I tried my hardest, I could get an A in math") need to be confronted about the discrepancy between their self-rated ability and current behavior patterns (Oettinger, in press). However, students with low self-efficacy (e.g., "If I tried my hardest, I could get a C in math") respond to confrontation with avoidance. For a student with low confidence for performing math, calling attention to how their attitude or absence rate "causes" poor outcomes actually strengthens poor attitudes and increases absenteeism. Therefore, for students possessing low self-efficacy for a given course area, school counselors and teachers must provide a supportive interactive process that includes evaluation and involvement of other school support services.

The next section of the Charting Your Course curriculum asks students to select one course and identify school, home, and work challenges that prevent them from performing successfully. The perception of challenges represents in part their definition of the barriers that affect their ability to perform successfully. The ASIP Navigator and feedback session create a number of opportunities for students to generate this definition. After identifying the challenges, students choose which issues they want to change by writing them in a contract that is signed and monitored by the school counselor and teacher. To facilitate identification of observable behaviors, students select the wording from a list of behavior areas common to most students.

The Charting Your Course curriculum enables students to articulate their definition of the challenges that keep them from succeeding academically and individualize a contract to improve on those outcomes, but most of the behaviors identified generalize across the group. Rather than keeping track of as many as 35 different student contracts, most identify issues such as homework completion, attitude, and preparation as key elements to their success. Charting Your Course makes students a part of the success process and helps teachers connect with students directly to those concrete behaviors. This affords school counselors and teachers the opportunity to respond to student success behaviors as they occur. According to Developmental Systems Theory, the environmental context now contains a feedback mechanism that supports effective student self-conceptions. The Charting Your Course curriculum also provides school counselors with a means of working with students experiencing learning or other emotional/psychological problems. As a structured intervention, this curriculum enables school counselors to establish a set of measurable goals.

Skill-Building Workshops

Additional classroom workshops need to address specific issues such as exposure to violence, career exploration, gender/racial identity, and communication skills. Workshops should address how these topics facilitate effective school outcomes and school-to-work transitions. ASIP's career exploration module, for example, directs student exploration by researching careers on the Internet. Using a career exploration worksheet, students identify duties and responsibilities associated with the career, education requirements, salary range, and other information one would need when conducting a job search. The exploration creates outcome expectations associated with current academic performance needs while it simultaneously teaches job search skills.

Other Success Pathways That Build Success Identities

Life Skills Groups

Life skills groups offer students structured experiences that promote skills to deal with anger, stress, grief or loss, and exposure to violence. By offering structured group counseling experiences, school counselors provide an important resource for students experiencing a range of issues. ASIP provides a structured 8-week program for angry students who experience difficulty managing their frustrations. Incorporating social justice theater, personal narratives, and cognitive-behavioral techniques, students identify their role in problem behavior, the manner in which others' actions serve as antecedents to problem behavior, and resolution strategies (Evanow, 2000).

Mentoring and Tutoring

An important success pathway that school counselors need to consider includes mentoring and tutoring experiences for lower-achieving students. Such activities need to be coordinated with in-school resources as well as community resources. Beginning with teacher and staff volunteers, mentor relationships offer connections between students and adults outside teaching and counseling settings. Many successful adults who once experienced academic difficulty refer to an educator's encouragement as the change event in their life. After-school tutoring by teachers and other school educators provide these opportunities. Limited school personnel resources demand that school counselors work with community partners to create additional pathways for mentoring and tutoring support. Many community-based organizations (e.g., universities, Boys Club, Girls Club) or businesses seek partnerships in the form of precollege programming (e.g., Upward Bound, talent search programs), opportunities for volunteerism, and active vocational development opportunities. School counselors create success pathways by establishing the structure for linking students to adults and bringing adults from the community into direct contact with students.

Leadership and Service Learning Activities

Another success pathway that school counselors should consider is leadership training and service learning activities. Beginning with student leaders, school counselors create a new role for students by facilitating discussion and action directed at service learning projects. As part of the service learning activity, school counselors enlarge the number of students involved by directing student leaders to design projects that involve outreach to other students. ASIP works to facilitate students' self-directed activities. Adults serve to provide structure and encouragement, but students design the project, seek funding, and create the means to gather other student support. These activities provide an important success pathway by helping students understand the power they have to affect their community, build the skills necessary to work with other students and adults, and engage students in real-world issues.

Success Pathways for Connecting With Parents

Parent "involvement" provides a powerful success pathway. However, for many reasons, parent involvement wanes during middle and high school. More important than establishing involvement avenues, school counselors must create a means for parents to become connected to their child's educational experience. This means educating parents about how to use the school effectively to address their child's needs. For example, many parents from diverse racial or ethnic backgrounds need information about who to contact for what types of problems. Periodic letters home, in their native language, provide opportunities to educate parents about how to help their students prepare for examinations and how to set up a structured routine at home that contributes to school performance.

School counselors also create success pathways for parents when they establish ways for parents to successfully gain information. School Web pages provide parents with access through home, library, or other computer settings to information about colleges, how to help their child study, and when and how to talk with school staff about their child's performance. School counselors also facilitate parents having a positive experience at school when they create structured intake programs for parents the moment they walk into the school. Support components include a waiting area with information parents can read about the meeting they will be attending, consultation with a school counselor prior to meeting with teachers, and advocacy by the school counselor when parents meet with teachers.

Success Pathways for Special Education

Most of the interventions described previously work effectively for students with mild cognitive or behavioral deficits or both. In addition, school counselors need to use outcome information to create a school-to-work transition portfolio. Beginning with self-management skills, school counselors need to work with community resources to establish a graduate assessment and intervention process to help students build the skills and experiences necessary to enter the least restrictive vocational and life environment possible. Students with mild disabilities and severe behavior problems become more invested in their development when they help define the range of issues and work cooperatively in creating goals. The skills needed to adapt to a work environment center on the same success identity areas described above. Successful work adjustment relies on being able to learn how to learn the occupational tasks, managing stress and time, and connecting with both peers and one's boss. Middle and high school offer a contained environment in which school counselors can work cooperatively with special and regular education teachers to design effective school-to-work transition plans.

Integration of Proposed Interventions With Theoretical Framework

Following the recommendations of Walsh et al., (1999), we present in Table 8.1 an outline of how the various activities relate to the proposed theoretical

TABLE 8.1 Integration of Theory, Practice, and Outcomes

Activity	Developmental Systems Theory	Constructs Addressed	Measurable Outcomes
ASIP Navigator	• Assesses student's predispositions toward being a student • Confronts negative behavior episode schemata	• Self-efficacy • Outcome expectations • Stress • Family and peer support • Distress and well-being • Career needs • Teacher connection	• Each construct generated using validated measures
Charting Your Course	• Student defines challenges to success • Student creates a success plan	• Student learns to identify stresses and create short-term goals to improve educational outcomes • Successful performances lead to increased self-efficacy	• Student selects from list of observable tasks
Personal Narratives	• Periodic assessment using open-ended questions provides insight into student's Behavior Episode Schemata	• Builds connections to school counselors and teachers	• Qualitative narratives
Skill Building Workshops	• Environment creates opportunities for directing behavior episode schemata toward positive educational outcomes	• Self-efficacy • Stress management • Teacher connection • Career development • Distress and well-being	• Designed based on concrete objectives

Life Skills Groups	• Emotional support creates opportunity to maintain educational activities while addressing mental health needs • Anger management groups offer reexamination of roles associated with creating anger episodes	• Stress management • Self-efficacy • Connection with school • Distress and well-being	• Weekly personal narratives offer access to changes in behavior episode schemata • Gather weekly attendance, teacher ratings, and quarterly grades
Mentoring and Tutoring	• Environment creates opportunities for directing behavior episode schemata toward positive educational outcomes	• Connection with school • Self-efficacy • Stress management • Career development	• Weekly personal narratives offer access to changes in behavior episode schemata • Gather weekly attendance, teacher ratings, and quarterly grades
Leadership and Service-Learning Activities	• Environment creates opportunities for directing behavior episode schemata toward positive educational outcomes	• Connection with school • Self-efficacy • Stress management • Career development	• Weekly personal narratives offer access to changes in behavior episode schemata • Gather weekly attendance, teacher ratings, and quarterly grades
Connect With Parents	• Environment creates opportunities for changing how parents relate to school	• Family support	• Survey of parents assesses pre- and postattitudes about connection to school

framework and identify measurable outcomes. The *ASIP Navigator* addresses all the constructs (self-efficacy, stress, etc.) and helps students assess their own student predispositions while they confront maladaptive student self-conceptions (i.e., behavior episode schemata). The Navigator provides students with the opportunity for self-examination in a supportive atmosphere.

Charting Your Course creates the opportunity for students to define the range of challenges they face in performing academically and facilitates the development of a success plan in conjunction with school counselors and teachers. Charting Your Course teaches students that "challenges" represent stressors that can be overcome by establishing short-term plans of action and successfully performing these plans of action to increase confidence.

Personal Narratives enable students to tell their own story, which affords insight into how students define their role as a student and how they define their life experiences. Personal Narratives offer a glimpse of students' behavior episode schemata, and communication of these narratives, when met with support and understanding, forge strong connections with school counselors and teachers. Classroom-based *Skill-Building Workshops* conducted together by the school counselors and teachers continue building solution strategies. Positive educational outcomes become more likely when continued efforts challenge students' maladaptive behavior episode schemata while offering effective plans of action. Workshops that incorporate the sources of self-efficacy described above create a method for building confidence in specific skill areas. As students gain confidence in performing these skills, they approach future difficult tasks as challenges and therefore demonstrate stronger motivation for learning. Skill-Building Workshops should be designed to cover specific "success identity" topic areas.

Life Skills Groups move away from traditional one-to-one counseling and bring together students experiencing specific issues into a structured therapeutic setting. Many adolescents experience a wide range of emotional and anger management issues that create rigid maladaptive behavior episode schemata. Structured group activities offer students opportunities to reexamine and modify these negative behavior patterns. Using the sources of self-efficacy described above, structured activities that involve role plays, personal narrative discussions, and incorporate cognitive-behavioral techniques create a powerful group process.

Mentoring and Tutoring offer students adult relationships and connections that allow for a powerful opportunity for transforming maladaptive behavior episode schemata into positive behavior patterns. Many students lack positive relationships with encouraging adults. Mentoring and Tutoring programs create these opportunities for students to find out that they do matter and are capable of being cared about. In addition to creating stronger connections to school, mentoring and tutoring activities build confidence, stress management skills, and vocational development when school counselors design training opportunities to address these issues. Providing mentors and tutors with a frame-work for their role with the student increases the likelihood of pointing the student in the direction of positive educational and life outcomes.

Leadership and Service-Learning Activities also offer a powerful means of transforming maladaptive behavior episode schemata into positive patterns of behavior. Students who engage in leadership and community service activities gain an understanding of how their influence translates into affecting the community in which they live. Students' perceptions of the world shift as they gain confidence in performing service-learning activities. Connections to others and stress and time management skills emerge in response to working with peers and adults in worthwhile activities. By offering Leadership and Service-Learning Activities, school counselors transform the student role from a casual observer within the classroom to an active participant in directing meaningful activity.

Activities designed to more effectively *Connect With Parents* creates additional resources for helping low-achieving students to improve their academic outcomes. Parents possess a Behavior Episode Schemata regarding their role in education and their relationship to the school. By prescribing active roles for parents, creating ways for parents to successfully communicate with teachers, and creating technological links to the school, school counselors offer parents the opportunity to become active agents in supporting their child's academic outcomes.

Table 8.1 also describes a number of measurable outcomes associated with the various activities. The combination of quantitative and qualitative assessment strategies provides a strong evaluation strategy. As a portfolio assessment, students can track their own outcomes as well and assess changes in their own personal narratives. The goal of the evaluation is to provide information that the interventions promote change, but also important is that students and teachers perceive the changes taking place. Finding an overall grade point average or standardized test score improvement for a school is important but may not translate to school counselors and teachers feeling especially confident in their ability to bring about these changes.

SUMMARY

This chapter prescribes a role for school counselors as active intervention specialists who work in classroom settings with teachers and with community partners to create success pathways for all students. Using Developmental Systems Theory, students' self-identity was equated metaphorically with a ship sailing across an ocean toward desired or expected outcomes. Education serves as a harbor for building the cargo and sails necessary to make effective school-to-work-to-life transitions. Constructs associated with the cargo and sails were drawn from Social Cognitive Theory, Diathesis-Stress Models, and Social Integration Theory. Building confidence to learn and possessing an understanding of how academic activities create positive outcomes serves as the ship's sails. Essential cargo includes family connections to the learning process, stress management, strong connections between students and teachers and among peers, and articulated goals and aspirations. The chapter argues that school counselors must take responsibility for designing the learning experiences that challenge students possessing maladaptive behavior episode schemata. Working with teachers and community partners, counselors must create the interventions needed to help students build the cargo and mainsails needed for making success pathways toward desired vocational and life aspirations.

VIGNETTE

Juan and Elizabeth, two ninth graders, both attend an urban high school. As the fall term progressed, Juan began skipping school. His bitterness and anger were apparent when he did attend, and he was suspended twice after verbal altercations with his math teacher. Juan arrived in the United States 3 years ago, and his English proficiency was low enough to warrant continued bilingual instruction. However, the math class consisted of a monolingual English-speaking teacher and an English as a second language (ESL) paraprofessional aide. Juan's science teacher sees him as a potential leader and feels a special bond with him. Juan often shows up just for science class, but he does not turn in work or complete any tests.

Elizabeth tries hard in class but continues to struggle. She is included in regular education curriculum but receives special education services in her English class and 1 hour of tutoring. She struggles to keep up with the teacher's lectures and sleeps a lot during class. A quiet girl, Elizabeth has some friends but is perceived more as someone who follows the group.

---

1. Describe interventions that may help Juan's math teacher become more connected with him. Theoretically, why do you think your interventions will result in change?

2. Describe the types of interventions that may help Juan gain insight into his current maladaptive behavior episode schemata and help him design a success plan. Theoretically, why do you think your interventions will result in change?

3. What interventions may help Juan gain a stronger connection to the school? Theoretically, why do you think your interventions will result in change?

4. What interventions may help Elizabeth? Theoretically, what are the goals of your intervention?

5. What interventions will help in designing a school-to-work transition plan for Elizabeth?

ADDITIONAL RESOURCES

Print Resources

Howard, K., Barton, C., Walsh, M., & Lerner, R. (1999). Social and contextual issues in interventions with children and families. In S. Russ & T. Ollendick (Eds.), *Handbook of psychotherapies with children and families: Issues in clinical child psychology* (pp. 45-66). New York: Plenum.

Solberg, V. S., Gusavac, N., Hamann, T., & Felch, J. (1998). The adaptive success identity plan (ASIP): A career intervention for college students [Monograph]. *Career Development Quarterly, 47,* 48-95.

Some things DO make a difference for youth: A compendium of evaluation of youth programs and practices. Contact American Youth Policy Forum, 1001 Connecticut Avenue NW, Suite 719, Washington, DC 20036-5541.

Videotape

School-to-careers: Connecting youth to the future. Contact American Youth Policy Forum, 1001 Connecticut Avenue NW, Suite 719, Washington, DC 20036-5541.

ASIP Materials

Contact V. Scott Solberg, PhD, at Enderis Hall, P.O. Box 413, Milwaukee, WI 53202 (e-mail: ssolberg@uwm.edu) for information about the ASIP Navigator, ASIP High School Experience Survey, and ASIP Charting Your Course curriculum.

CHAPTER 9

Promoting a Healthy Body Image Among Adolescent Women

William J. Lyddon
Karen D. Slaton

Adolescence is most often conceptualized as a time of transition between childhood and adulthood and as a period of preparation and development for adult living (Graber & Brooks-Gunn, 1996; Schlegel & Barry, 1991). From a developmental perspective, the adolescent is challenged to adjust and adapt to significant physical, cognitive, social, and emotional changes (Hoffman, 1996; Scheer, Unger, & Brown, 1996) and successfully integrate these changes into an emerging sense of self, or personal identity, that is perceived to have continuity over time (Erikson, 1963). Thus, one of the key developmental tasks facing Western adolescents is the construction of a coherent identity that provides a sense of continuity between past, present, and future. In Erikson's (1968) words,

> The wholeness to be achieved [during adolescence] I have called a sense of inner identity. The young person, in order to experience wholeness, must feel a progressive continuity between that which he has come to be during the long years of childhood and that which he promises to become in the anticipated future;

Authors' Note: Correspondence regarding this chapter should be addressed to William J. Lyddon, Professor and Director of Training, Department of Psychology, Counseling Psychology Program, University of Southern Mississippi, Hattiesburg, MS 39406-5025.

between that which he conceives himself to be and that which he perceives others to see in him and to expect of him. (p. 87)

Although developmental formulations of Erikson and others (see Flum, 1994; Marcia, 1980, 1994; Valde, 1996) have helped highlight both the developmental significance of identity formation during adolescence and individual differences in adolescent identity achievement, they have been criticized for the way in which they portray identity as an autonomous, bounded, independent entity created by the individual (Oyserman, Gant, & Ager, 1995, p. 1217). By way of contrast, contemporary writers and researchers in the field emphasize both the *multidimensional* nature of adolescent identity (Josselson, 1994a; Marsh, 1989) and the *social and cultural contexts* in which identities are constructed (Bosma, Graafsma, Grotevant, & Levita, 1994; Gossens & Phinney, 1996). For example, rather than viewing identity in singular terms, researchers suggest that the adolescent self-concept is multidimensional— often organized into academic and nonacademic self-concepts. Academic self-concepts are divided into subject-specific dimensions (e.g., English and mathematics), and nonacademic self-concepts are divided into social, emotional, and physical dimensions (Marsh, 1989). With regard to social and cultural influences, many contemporary writers have emphasized the way in which *social* constructions of gender differentially influence the *personal* identity constructions of males and females. For example, Archer (1989), Gilligan (1988), and Josselson (1994a) maintain that Erikson's model of personal identity— with its emphasis on separation and individuation—may be helpful in understanding male identity development, but they question its relevance to female identity development and the way in which "women's sense of self is organized around the ability to make and maintain relationships" (Josselson, 1994a, p. 83).

Together the focus on the multidimensional features of identity and the increased attention to social and gendered constructions of identity have contributed to significant research designed to examine the different ways adolescent males and females may evaluate various dimensions of their identities and self-images (Brown & Gilligan, 1992; Holland & Andre, 1994; Josephs, Markus, & Tafarodie, 1992; Marsh, 1989; Peters, 1994). One of the most consistent findings associated with this literature is that adolescent girls tend to report significantly lower physical appearance self-concepts than adolescent boys (Marsh, 1989). Girls appear to value their physical attractiveness more than boys, report feeling unattractive more frequently, and are more self-conscious about their appearance (Abell & Richards, 1996). In particular, of all age and gender groups, preadolescent and early adolescent girls report the most dissatisfaction with their body shape and weight (Rauste-von Wright, 1989; Wood, Becker, & Thompson, 1996). Although bodily development during puberty is an important catalyst for adolescent body image reappraisal, adolescent boys typically take pride in their changing bodies and abilities, whereas adolescent girls often have a difficult time finding anything they appreciate about their changing bodies (Rosenbaum, 1993). Given the relationship between body image and attitudes about eating, adolescent girls with poor body images tend to diet excessively and run the risk of developing serious eating disorders (Keel, Fulkerson, & Leon, 1997).

The purpose of this chapter is to examine the problem of body image disturbance among adolescent girls and young women, with a focus on the prevention and treatment of this growing problem. Toward this end, the nature and scope of body image disturbance are first described, followed by an overview of the salient factors believed to play a role in the development of body image disturbance. We conclude the chapter by enumerating a number of considerations and specific strategies for both the prevention and treatment of body image disturbance and provide illustrative examples of contemporary prevention programs.

BODY IMAGE AND BODY IMAGE DISTURBANCE

In a recent national survey, Garner (1997) found that 62% of 13- to 19-year-old females and 67% of women age 30 and above were unhappy with their weight and had negative feelings about their body. Eighty-nine percent of all women surveyed indicated a desire to lose weight, with 24% reporting that they would give up 3 to 5 years of their life to be at their ideal weight. Srebnik and Saltzbert (1994) describe these high rates of dissatisfaction with appearance to be "nearly normative for women" (p. 119) and suggest that rates of dissatisfaction are increasing for women of color and lesbians as well. Although, as previously noted, negative attitudes toward physical appearance usually become more negative during early adolescence (Rosen, Orosan-Weine, & Tang, 1997), Hill, Oliver, and Rogers (1992) found girls as young as 9 to be both dissatisfied with their bodies and to report idealized body shapes significantly slimmer than their actual bodies.

Definition of Body Image Concerns

The term *body image* sounds simple, but it is difficult to conceptualize. Hutchinson (1994) suggests that body image is central to personal identity and offers a particularly comprehensive definition of body image:

> Body image is the image of the body that a person sees with the mind's eye; it is the image of the body that allows a person to know about emotions, sensations, bodily needs, and appetites, and to negotiate the physical environment; it is the

image of the body that a person hears about as she listens to her inner speech. . . . Body image describe[s] the psychological space where body, mind and culture come together—the space that encompasses our thoughts, feelings, perceptions, attitudes, values, and judgements about the bodies we have. (p. 153)

Over the years, various terms have been used to describe body image problems, including body image disturbance, body dissatisfaction, body cathexis, body image preoccupation, and body dysmorphic disorder. Recently, the term *body image disturbance* has gained general acceptance and refers to the distress associated with one's subjective evaluation of one's appearance, with body dissatisfaction being the most important global measure of this distress (Thompson, Heinberg, Altabe, & Tantleff-Dunn, 1999). Body image disturbance can be further divided into perceptual and subjective components (Stormer & Thompson, 1996). The perceptual component typically involves the tendency to overestimate one's body size, whereas the subjective component generally refers to affective, cognitive, or behavioral (or all three) aspects of body dissatisfaction. For example, if individuals experience distress, anxiety, or frustration about their appearance, the disturbance is thought to exist in the affective arena. A cognitive disturbance might consist of adherence to an unrealistic cultural ideal—for example, the belief that one must look like a fashion model to be considered attractive. A behavioral disturbance might include avoiding looking at oneself in the mirror or avoiding situations where one is likely to be evaluated based on appearance. An individual with body image disturbance may have disturbance in one or more of these domains.

Body image disturbance is most easily conceptualized as existing on a continuum, with levels of disturbance ranging from none (body image satisfaction) to extreme (body dysmorphic disorder/preoccupation). Body image disturbance can either exist as part of an eating disorder or can be a significant issue for individuals who exhibit no symptoms of disordered eating. Recently, researchers have begun to investigate factors that may contribute to the development of body image disturbance as well as ways to prevent the problem (Rieves & Cash, 1996; Rosen et al., 1997; Stormer & Thompson, 1996; Thompson et al., 1999).

FACTORS INFLUENCING THE DEVELOPMENT OF BODY IMAGE DISTURBANCE

Several factors are thought to contribute to body image disturbance. These may generally be grouped into three categories: (1) sociocultural factors, (2) family and peer influences, and (3) developmental and intrapersonal influences.

Sociocultural Factors

Sociocultural factors are believed to play a prominent role in the development and maintenance of body image disturbance (Heinberg, 1996; Rosen et al., 1997; Stormer & Thompson, 1996). Sociocultural theories of body image disturbance highlight the influence of cultural ideals of beauty and the role of the media in perpetuating and shaping these ideals, as well as the influence of a person's gender, racial/ethnic background, and sexual orientation.

Cultural Ideals

Current societal beauty standards for thinness are pervasive and are becoming increasingly unattainable for most women (Srebnik & Saltzberg, 1994; Thompson et al., 1999). Just a century ago, women who were tall, full busted and full figured with "dimpled" flesh were considered attractive. Fat was equated with strength and energy and was a sign of emotional well-being (Seid, 1994; Thompson et al., 1999). By way of contrast, the current "culture of thinness" has its origins in the post-World War II fears that people in the United States were becoming physically (and morally) soft. Health insurance companies began to encourage weight loss as a means of health promotion, resulting in a shift in self-perceptions to that of a diseased, unhealthy group. During the 1950s, a slimmer yet curvaceous form, represented by Marilyn Monroe, was considered ideal. This trend continued until the 1960s, when preferences for feminine beauty shifted to embrace the gawky, bare-boned, adolescent frame represented by Twiggy. At 5 feet 7 inches, Twiggy weighed only 98 pounds (Seid, 1994). It is interesting to note that Miss America contestants and *Playboy* centerfolds have progressively become thinner over the years (Raudenbush & Zellner, 1997; Turner, Hamilton, Jacobs, Angood, & Dwyer, 1997). For example, Heinberg (1996) reports that Miss America contestants from 1979 to 1988 weighed 13 to 19% below expected weights for women their height. More recently, the ideal has been altered to include larger breasts and a more toned, muscular shape. Because this ideal is sometimes contradictory to having a thin body, some women have resorted to plastic surgery (for example, breast implants). Interestingly, the taunt, lean, muscular body that women are currently encouraged to achieve is actually more like that of a male than of a female and suggests that the secondary sexual characteristics that accompany women into adulthood are considered undesirable. Dimpled flesh, plump thighs, buttocks, and hips are all to be suppressed. As a consequence, contemporary women in the United States seem to be "pitted in a war against their own biologies" (Seid, 1994, p. 9).

The Media

The media have been harshly criticized for their role in communicating the thin standard to women. Women receive daily messages telling them that their skin is too dry, their hair color is wrong, they are fat, they have vaginal odor, and they need to shape up. Women are presented with images of young, thin women as role models and are told that they do not measure up. Media photographs are airbrushed, edited, and even computer manipulated so that the image presented is sometimes not even of a real woman. Thompson et al. (1999) state that women experience a significant rate of exposure to the print media, which strongly endorse the thin ideal as well as present the means for achieving it (diet and exercise). Turner et al. (1997) studied the influence of fashion magazines on the body image satisfaction of college women. These researchers found that women who viewed fashion magazines for only 13 minutes wanted to weigh less, were less satisfied with their bodies, were more frustrated about their weight, were more preoccupied with the desire to be thin, and were more afraid of becoming fat than were their peers who viewed news magazines for the same amount of time. These findings suggest that the media may play an important role in shaping, rather than merely reflecting, societal expectations. Women in the two groups in this study did not differ in terms of mean height and weight. It was the women's *perception* of being overweight that appeared to be influenced by exposing them to either fashion or news magazines. These findings were corroborated by Pinhas, Toner, Ali, Garfinkel, and Stuckless (1999), who found that viewing images of female fashion models had an immediate effect on women's mood. Women were reported to feel angrier and to have a more depressed mood after viewing only 20 images of thin models.

Gender, Race, and Sexual Orientation

A recent meta-analysis by Feingold and Mazzella (1998) found that when compared to men, women's dissatisfaction with their bodies has dramatically increased over the past 50 years. This trend has also been borne out by two large national surveys (Cash & Henry, 1995; Garner, 1997). Further evidence for gender differences in body image is provided by Muth and Cash (1997), who report that compared to men, women have more negative body image evaluations, a stronger investment in their appearance, more frequent dysphoria related to body image, and more self-ideal discrepancies. These findings suggest that women may spend more time in appearance-related activities such as grooming, dieting, and exercising for appearance management and that they may also experience more bad feelings related to their appearance. Feingold and Mazzella (1996) report that these gender differences are more pronounced during adolescence, but other evidence suggests that women continue to be dissatisfied with their weight and appearance well into their middle-age years and beyond (Allaz, Bernstein, Rouget, Archinard, & Morabia, 1998; Garner, 1997).

In most studies comparing the body image concerns, Caucasians appear to be more concerned about weight than any other racial or ethnic group. Altabe (1998), for example, found that African American women exhibit more positive body-related beliefs that did Caucasian, Asian American, or Hispanic women. Among these groups, Caucasian and Hispanic women showed the greatest body image disturbance, African American women had the most positive self-view, and Asian American women placed the least importance on physical appearance. A recent national survey (Cash & Henry, 1995) also found African American women to report significantly more favorable appearance evaluations, more body satisfaction, and less overweight concerns.

Siever (1994) investigated sexual orientation and gender as vulnerability factors for body dissatisfaction and eating disorders. He found that gay men and heterosexual women are more dissatisfied with their bodies and more vulnerable to eating disorders. The high incidence of dissatisfaction among gay males is suggested to be the result of (a) a shared emphasis on physical attractiveness and thinness and (b) the desire to attract and please men. Although heterosexual men place high value on attractiveness in evaluating female partners, they are less concerned with their own physical attractiveness and therefore less dissatisfied with their bodies. Lesbian women were found to be the least concerned about physical attractiveness. Despite being larger and dissatisfied with their weight, lesbians in this sample were less likely to express weight concerns with dysfunctional attitudes and behaviors typically associated with eating disorders. More recently, Ludwig and Brownell (1999) found that lesbian and bisexual women who rated themselves as "feminine" reported lower body satisfaction than those who identified themselves as "masculine" or "androgynous." Furthermore, these researchers found that the women in their sample who had mostly lesbian or bisexual women friends had higher body satisfaction than those with mostly heterosexual friends.

Family and Peer Influences

The great majority of family influence studies have focused on the role of the family in the development of eating disorders, rather than exclusively on body image concerns. For example, families of individuals with eating disorders have been described as being rigid (Waller, Slade, & Calam, 1990), less supportive and cohesive, less open to expression of feelings (Hodges, Cochrane, & Brewerton, 1998), and less able to achieve mutual understanding (Steiger, Liquornik, Chapman, & Hussain, 1991). In fact, researchers suggest that when compared to individuals without eating disorders, individuals with eating disorders perceive their family environments as more conflictual, disengaged, and less cohesive and nurturing, and they perceive their family interactions as more enmeshed, intrusive, hostile, and insensitive to their emotional needs (Strober & Humphrey, 1987).

Attachment Theory (Ainsworth, Blehar, Walters, & Wall, 1978; Bowlby, 1969, 1973, 1977, 1980) may provide a useful perspective for identifying family influences that contribute to the development of body dissatisfaction and eating disorders. Attachment Theory is based on the notion that there are individual differences in the way infants become emotionally attached to their primary caregivers and that these differences influence a child's perceptions of self, others, and resources for emotional self-regulation in times of crisis (Bowlby, 1977). Attachment patterns are believed to vary as a function of caregivers' responses to infants' behavior. If the caregiver is warm and responsive on a consistent basis, the relationship is characterized as secure attachment. Caregiver inconsistency or rejection (or both) of the infant's bids for attention and care, on the other hand, are believed to form insecure attachments. Attachment theorists contend that through continued interaction with a caregiver, children develop internal working models (beliefs and expectations) about the caretaker's trustworthiness and responsiveness along with their own personal sense of being worthy of care and attention.

Although most research on attachment style and eating disorders has been conducted with an adult population (e.g., Armstrong & Roth, 1989; Calam, Waller, Slade, & Newton, 1990; Palmer, Oppenheimer, & Marshall, 1988), Sharpe et al. (1998) studied the relationship between attachment style and weight concerns among 305 preadolescent and adolescent girls and found that insecurely attached girls exhibited lower self-esteem and had significantly greater weight concerns than securely attached girls. The authors suggest that a decreased sense of self-worth and a heightened expectation of rejection by others may make insecurely attached girls more reliant on gaining acceptance from others. As a result, they may also be more likely to internalize and idealize societal standards for appearance in order to gain acceptance from others. In the only known study on the relationship between attachment and body image disturbance, Slaton, Lyddon, and Dale (1999) found that body image satisfaction varied as a function of paternal rather than maternal parental bonding. Specifically, women who reported an optimal and secure bonding relationship with their fathers were significantly more satisfied with their bodies than women who characterized their paternal relationship as either absent or affectionless and controlling.

Teasing and negative verbal criticism also seem to play an important role in the development of body image dissatisfaction. Heinberg (1996) and Rosen et al. (1997) describe several studies that demonstrate a relationship between recurrent childhood teasing and adult body dissatisfaction. For example, Rieves and Cash (1996) found that greater appearance-related teasing and criticism during childhood and adolescence was associated with a more dysfunctional body image in adulthood. The majority of women in their study reported such experiences, with 38% reporting that these experiences had been detrimental to their body image development. Similarly, Schwartz, Phares, Tantleff-Dunn, and Thompson (1999) found that parental teasing about weight predicted body image disturbance in young women. Rosen et al. (1997) reported that teasing ranked number 16 out of 19 "critical experiences" in the development of body image dissatisfaction. Stormer and Thompson (1996) studied several variables thought to contribute to body image disturbance and found that teasing explained only a small portion of the variance when compared to the relative influence of maturational status, internalization of sociocultural pressures, and degree of social comparison. They suggest, however, that teasing in the formative years may lead to excessive social comparison or internalization (or both) of societal standards of beauty.

Developmental and Intrapersonal Factors

Attitudes about physical appearance usually become more negative during early adolescence—about the time that physical development is peaking (Rosen et al., 1997). The timing of this development (maturational timing) has been implicated in the development of body image disturbance. Girls who mature later than their peers (after age 14) tend to have a more positive body image than those who reach puberty early (before age 11) or on time (age 11 to 14) (Heinberg, 1996). This may be due to the fact that later maturation appears to result in less body fat and weight or, more important, that early maturation and subsequent physical changes may place an adolescent at higher risk for being teased (Heinberg, 1996). Puberty was reported to rank 7th out of 19 "critical experiences" contributing to the development of body image (Rosen et al., 1997) and was listed more frequently than teasing by individuals interviewed about influences that were related to physical appearance.

An important intrapersonal variable that seems particularly significant to body image dissatisfaction is level of social comparison. This involves the degree to which persons compare themselves to others in order to examine their standing on various attributes. For example, women high in social comparison may compare their appearance, weight, or body shape with that of other women and may experience a great deal of distress if they perceive themselves as somehow being less attractive. In fact, women who demonstrate high levels of social comparison have been found to report greater body dissatisfaction (Thompson et al., 1999). For example, Rieves and Cash (1996) found that having a more attractive sibling may foster unfavorable self-evaluations in women, and Stormer and Thompson (1996) reported that degrees of social comparison significantly predicted college women's drive for thinness and bulimic behavior over and above the influence of maturational status, negative verbal commentary, and internalization of social pressures. High levels of social comparison may result in a discrepancy between one's perceived "real" and "ideal" body image and thus contribute to greater body dissatisfaction (Thompson et al., 1999).

CONSIDERATIONS FOR PREVENTION AND TREATMENT OF BODY IMAGE CONCERNS

Prevention

Prevention of body image disturbance is an important consideration for mental health professionals for two reasons. First, a growing body of research has linked body image concerns to increased rates of dieting, weight preoccupation, and eating disorders (Attie & Brooks-Gunn, 1989; Bruch, 1962; Cash & Hicks, 1990; Grubb, Sellers, & Waligroski, 1993; Killen et al., 1996; Killen et al., 1994; Paa & Larson, 1998; Thompson, 1996). Thus, increasing a young woman's body image satisfaction may help mitigate the strong desire for thinness found in women with eating disorders. Second, body image concerns are often associated with lower levels of psychological well-being (Butters & Cash, 1987; Dworkin & Kerr, 1987). Women who perceive themselves as unattractive may also have low self-esteem, increased social anxieties and inhibitions, sexual difficulties, and vulnerability to depression.

A number of authors have discussed possible approaches to the prevention of disordered eating (Carter, Stewart, Dunn, & Fairburn, 1997; Crisp, 1988; Franko, 1998; Friedman, 1996; Mann et al., 1997). However, although prevention efforts have been successful in increasing knowledge and awareness about eating disorders, they have not been shown to be effective in reducing disordered eating behaviors. In fact, in two recent studies (Carter et al., 1997; Mann et al., 1997), participants actually showed an increase in eating disorder symptoms after participating in the prevention programs. Mann et al. (1997) explained these results by pointing out that their study combined primary and secondary prevention by including women with no symptoms of eating disorders and women at high risk for developing an eating disorder. The goals of primary and secondary prevention are very different and require very different intervention strategies. Primary prevention seeks to prevent the onset of a disorder, and it works by stressing that eating-disordered behavior is abnormal and can have dire consequences. In contrast, secondary prevention is directed toward early detection and intervention for individuals in the early stages of an eating disorder and encourages them to seek help by suggesting that disordered eating is treatable and common. Combining both primary and secondary prevention may inadvertently normalize disordered eating for those who do not have a problem as well as introduce them to new weight control methods (such as vomiting and the use of laxatives and diuretics) that precede the development of eating problems.

Recently, Franko (1998) evaluated a secondary prevention program for college women thought to be at risk for developing eating disorders and found that positive changes are possible, especially in the areas of body image concerns and appearance orientation. These results are encouraging and suggest that matching appropriate prevention programs to appropriate samples is important.

Specific Preventive Approaches

Strategies for the prevention of body image concerns are inherently related to the primary factors that are believed to influence the development of such concerns. Specifically, prevention can take the form of (a) challenging cultural ideals and media influences, (b) teaching effective communication skills, (c) providing education about female physical development and body image issues, and (d) teaching effective parenting.

Challenging Cultural Ideals and Media Influences

A number of writers highlight the importance of learning to challenge cultural ideals of beauty and provide useful strategies for counselors to consider. For example, women can be taught to challenge and change culturally prescribed roles that are oppressive and to develop strengths that are generally devalued by the culture (Berel & Irving, 1998). Srebnik and Saltzberg (1994) suggest that it is important for women to explore whom they are trying to please with their appearance, to move from external to internal evaluations of effectiveness, and to redefine self-worth in terms broader than appearance alone.

Katzman, Weiss, and Wolchik (1986) provide exercises for challenging the cultural expectations of thinness for women. In one exercise, women are encouraged to describe characteristics that are usually attributed to the "perfect woman." Typically, women name physical characteristics (she must be tall and thin, have flawless skin, be immaculately dressed and groomed) as well as personal characteristics (she must be intelligent and successful, a wonderful wife and mother, and a gourmet cook). This exercise often brings laughter from women as they begin to realize the absurdity of trying to live up to such impossible standards.

Encouraging young women to critically evaluate the way women are portrayed in movies, television, books, and magazines constitutes another important preventive strategy for counselors involved in outreach projects in schools and colleges. Berel and Irving (1998), for example, have called for the development of a media literacy program to teach women and girls to think critically about appearance-related media. Such a program would target appearance-related media by reducing the perceived realism of media messages, decreasing acceptance of the thin ideal, and reducing the positive expectancies associated with being thin. This could be accomplished by having women ask questions such as "Do real women look like the models on television?" "Does this person look like this because they use this product?" and "Does thinness really guarantee happiness and success?" By encouraging young women to critically evaluate various media, they may be in a better position to reject as unrealistic certain media messages that may contribute to personal body image dissatisfaction.

Teaching Effective Communication Skills

Some young women may have difficulty expressing their emotions directly or assertively. This may affect their ability to assertively respond to teasing, criticism, or negative comments about their appearance and may lead them to turn to food as a way of dealing with hurt feelings (Katzman et al., 1986). Young women can be encouraged to learn to communicate assertively by saying no without feeling guilty and by expressing anger directly and appropriately. Role play is often helpful for modeling and practicing communication skills. One example of using role play involves learning to say no. In this exercise, one person tries to get the other to do something and the response can only be "No" or variations of "No." Another exercise involves teaching assertive anger expression. This may involve asking women to explore their beliefs about the emotion of anger, their reactions to others' anger, and their possible fears about the consequences of expressing anger to others. Young women may learn to distinguish between passive, aggressive, and assertive expressions of anger. Other important skills involve learning to match words, voice, and facial expressions in order to maximize the effectiveness of the message and to learn to assertively express anger using "I am" statements rather than "You are" statements.

Providing Education About Development

From a preventive perspective, it is important to provide young women with a forum to discuss their reactions to their own development and bodily changes. Friedman (1996) describes a prevention program called Girls in the 90s. This program is based on the notion that as girls approach womanhood, they begin to negate their own culture (which is relational and contextual) in an attempt to fit into the dominant, male culture. According to Friedman, girls learn to deal with the changes in their life by focusing on their bodies. Their bodies become the context for their experiences, and the "language of fat" (p. 240) becomes their way of expressing themselves. Friedman suggests that when girls speak of feeling fat, they are usually not referring to how much they weigh; rather they are feeling angry, lonely, jealous, or disappointed. Girls in the 90s provides a forum for girls to recognize and "decode" the language of fat before it can become internalized and develop into a way for them to respond to stressful life situations. Utilizing role play, movement, and art, girls are encouraged to express their feelings, practice new behavior, and support each other as they experiment with new behavior outside the group.

Crisp (1988) suggests that prevention should focus on providing information to young women about risk factors associated with the development of body image problems and eating disorders. Additional information might include the following topics: (a) sociocultural pressures on women to diet and to be thin, (b) body weight regulation and the effects of dieting, (c) characteristics of eating disorders, (d) healthy eating, and (e) resisting pressures to diet (Carter et al., 1997). It is important to remember the lessons learned from Mann et al. (1997) and pay attention to the population for which the intervention is designed. As previously noted, there seems to be a risk associated with including too much information about eating-disordered behaviors in a primary prevention program. According to the findings of one study, "School-based prevention programs may do more harm than good" (Carter et al., 1997, p. 167).

Teaching Effective Parenting

Quite often, parents are not aware that their parenting style may be influencing the development of body image concerns in their young girls. Parents can learn to foster development of healthy body image in several ways. For example, parents can learn to respond to the needs of their children in a consistent, warm manner while allowing them the opportunity to experience the world around them. Parents can also teach young girls that appearance does not need to be central to one's identity. Children can learn that "inner beauty" is as important as "outer beauty." This may assist young women in challenging media and cultural messages that tell them they should look a certain way. It may be helpful for parents to watch television or read magazines with their daughters and to discuss the messages being presented. This may assist young women in learning to critically evaluate the messages they are hearing and seeing. Parents can also be taught to refrain from comments about their daughters' appearance and to be cognizant of the impact of such remarks. Finally, parents can become aware of their own beliefs and concerns about physical appearance and learn to challenge cultural ideals for themselves.

Treatment of Body Image Concerns

Treatment goals for body image dissatisfaction include helping women appreciate their bodies and view their bodies more realistically as well as realize that weight and physical appearance are not the sole criteria for attractiveness, success, and relationships (Katzman et al., 1986). Three prominent approaches to the treatment of body image concerns are used: cognitive-behavioral, feminist cognitive-behavioral, and experiential.

Cognitive-Behavioral Approach

Cognitive-behavioral therapy (CBT) has achieved the most empirical support (Brouwers, 1990; Butters & Cash, 1987; Dworkin & Kerr, 1987; Fisher & Thompson, 1994; Grant & Cash, 1995; Rosen, Orosan, & Reiter, 1995; Rosen, Reiter, & Orosan, 1995). CBT focuses on correcting distorted perceptions of body size, changing dysfunctional attitudes and beliefs, confronting avoidance behaviors, and encouraging pleasurable body experiences and is applicable to either a group or an individual counseling setting as well as in a format with minimal counselor contact. An important emphasis of CBT is helping young women identify judgmental, evaluative, and self-degrading self-descriptions they make regarding their body or their appearance (negative body talk) and assisting them in brainstorming and rehearsing more neutral, objective descriptions. For example, this may involve encouraging the use of alternative descriptions of body parts such as substituting "a round stomach" for "a disgusting jelly belly." Once specific examples of negative body talk are identified, women are encouraged to self-monitor their negative statements using a diary and to generate less critical statements for themselves. Grant and Cash (1995) suggest that effective CBT can be provided in as little as 20 minutes per week with appropriate homework assignments between meetings. Cash's (1995) book *What Do You See When You Look in the Mirror?* is a valuable CBT self-help guide for women who are highly motivated to work on body image concerns outside a counseling setting.

Feminist Cognitive-Behavioral Approach

An important adaptation of CBT for negative body image is feminist cognitive-behavioral therapy (Srebnik & Saltzberg, 1994). This approach integrates traditional CBT with an emphasis on sociocultural issues. Thus, in addition to techniques such as cognitive restructuring, feminist CBT also draws attention to the historical, patriarchal, and societal influences on body image. For example, an important strategy associated with this approach is to help young women examine whom they may be trying to please with their appearance and to move from external to internal evaluations of effectiveness and attractiveness. From a feminist perspective, it is important to show young women that they can learn to redefine self-worth in terms broader than body shape and size alone.

Experiential Approaches

Experiential approaches to the treatment of body image problems involve the use of creative arts such as guided imagery, body work, psychodrama, art, and journaling and are based on the notion that the creative arts may assist persons in using their bodies as positive vehicles for self-expression and the exploration of personal feelings, thoughts, and conflicts (Kaslow & Eicher, 1988). Experiential approaches are most often employed in a group counseling format. Two common types of experiential strategies are body image distortion exercises and body image dissatisfaction exercises. One example of a body image distortion exercise involves asking each group member to view a range of body silhouettes and to rate the one that she believes best represents herself currently and the one that represents her ideal body image. Each member shares her selections, receives feedback from the other members, and is encouraged to consider the accuracy of her perception. An example of a body image dissatisfaction exercise involves asking group members to draw themselves and color in their body parts, using red for what is good, yellow for what is neutral, and black for what is bad. Members discuss perceived positive parts of themselves, followed by neutral and then negative. Throughout the exercise, the group leader emphasizes the functions of the various body parts rather than their appearance.

Kinesthetic exercises have been suggested to be useful in facilitating greater body awareness and ownership and to help bridge the mind-body split that many women with body image problems experience. Srebnik and Saltzberg (1994), for example, suggest regular exercise, progressive muscle relaxation, stretching, and dancing as ways of achieving better mind-body integration. Other helpful experiential and expressive techniques designed to improve body awareness and facilitate the expression of personal feelings related to one's body image include body movement to music, projective artwork, and various psychodrama and imaginal exercises (Kaslow & Eicher, 1988).

Illustrative Prevention Programs

Eating Disorders Awareness and Prevention (EDAP)
and the Just for Girls Program

Prevention of body image disturbance and eating disorders has become the primary focus of many researchers and organizations. For example, Eating Disorders Awareness and Prevention, Inc. (EDAP; 603 Steward Street, Suite 803, Seattle, WA 98101) was created to increase the awareness and prevention of these concerns through education and community activism. EDAP provides free and low-cost educational information for educators, parents, health professionals, and the public at large.

EDAP provides four basic principles for prevention of body image disturbance and eating disorders:

1. Body image problems and eating disorders are serious and complex problems. Their expression, cause, and treatment have many dimensions. Therefore, one should avoid thinking of these problems in simple terms such as "Anorexia is just a plea for attention" or "Bulimia is just an addiction to food."

2. Prevention programs are not just for women and girls. Males can also develop eating disorders and dangerous shape control practices such as steroid use. Moreover, objectification and other forms of mistreatment of women by men contribute directly to two underlying features of an eating disorder: obsession with appearance and shame with one's body.

3. Prevention efforts will fail, or worse, inadvertently encourage body image disturbances and disordered eating if they concentrate solely on warning parents and children about the signs, symptoms, and dangers of these problems. Any attempt to prevent body image disturbance and eating disorders should also address cultural obsessions with slenderness, the distorted meaning of masculinity and femininity in today's society, and the development of self-esteem and self-respect.

4. Prevention programs should ideally be coordinated with opportunities for audience members to speak confidentially with a trained professional and, if appropriate, to receive a referral for counseling.

One of the primary prevention programs recommended by EDAP for adolescent girls is Just for Girls. Just for Girls is based on the belief that body image disturbance and disordered eating are coping mechanisms that girls develop in order to deal with the changes in their lives and bodies as they grow up female. The program consists of a series of open discussion groups designed to help girls (a) learn how to recognize what Friedman (1999) refers to as "grungies"—the negative voice that tells them they are fat, stupid, or ugly—and (b) understand some of the reasons why they may feel the way they do. The Just for Girls program is described in Friedman's book of the same name. In addition to information on differences in male and female culture, eating disorders, depression, and numerous issues that girls face during adolescence, this book contains a special section devoted to prevention groups for boys and specific group activities with reproducible handouts. The core of the Just for Girls program is contained in 14 units:

1. *Self.* This unit is designed to help girls learn about the different roles they may play and the various situations they may find themselves in.

Specific activities are focused on the development of a healthy sense of self.

2. *Self-Esteem.* This unit helps girls build positive self-esteem by encouraging them to become aware of and to value their qualities, characteristics, skills, and talents.

3. *Feelings.* This unit helps girls build a feeling vocabulary, become aware of different feelings, and express feelings either in role plays or through various symbolic activities.

4. *Stress.* This unit teaches girls to identify stressors, become aware of bodily signs that signal stress, and to practice different relaxation strategies.

5. *Our Bodies.* This unit contains information on how girls' bodies develop. Girls learn about puberty, body image and body awareness, weight concerns, and physical activity.

6. *Our Relationship to Food.* This unit provides girls with information about food, explores eating habits and attitudes, and examines myths about good and bad food.

7. *Dieting.* This unit provides information about dieting, including myths about dieting, what happens when girls diet, and a description of Set Point Theory (i.e., the theory that the body resets its metabolic rate at a lower level when caloric intake is restricted).

8. *Building Communication Skills.* This unit teaches good communication skills, including assertiveness training, giving and receiving feedback, dealing with defensiveness and conflict, and fighting fairly.

9. *Families.* This unit prompts girls to discuss issues they may face with their families. The idea is emphasized that families come in different forms and each girl can compare the ways her family is similar to other families along with ways it is different.

10. *Friendships.* In this unit, girls learn about friendships and discuss issues and concerns about friendships. Girls learn about appropriate boundaries and the importance of separating their feelings and experiences from those of their friends.

11. *Choosing a Partner.* This unit is designed to help girls think more proactively about the choice of a partner. Activities in this unit are designed for heterosexual girls and provide information about relationships with boys, choosing a partner, and dealing with abusive relationships.

12. *School.* This unit affords discussion of how schools often teach a "hidden curriculum" that reinforces gender roles and attitudes. Girls discuss how learning materials do not always show girls and women in realistic ways, how classroom language can be sexist, how boys often domi-

nate classroom interaction, and how sexual harassment can occur in schools.

13. *Media.* This unit provides information about the media and encourages girls to be informed consumers of media messages. Girls learn to counteract media messages and to become media literate.

14. *Bullying.* This unit describes different types of bullying, including physical, verbal, and relational bullying. Girls learn that bullying is an issue of power and are taught ways of fighting back that enable them to feel empowered.

Empirically Supported School-Based Prevention Programs

A number of authors have suggested that the school environment is an opportune context for the development and implementation of educational programs designed to promote healthy body image and prevent eating disorders (Button, Loan, Davies, & Sonuga-Barke, 1997; O'Dea, 1999; Scarano & Kalodner-Martin, 1994). Students are accessible and tend to be motivated to become involved in educational activities, and the discussion of health and personal development issues are already a part of many school curricula (O'Dea, 1999).

EDAP Puppet Program

The EDAP puppet program was designed by Pabst (1996) to promote in children in Grades K-5 an acceptance of diverse body shapes (including one's own body shape), a positive self-concept, and healthy attitudes about food and eating. The program features four life-sized, multicultural puppets: Josh, a Caucasian boy who is teased by his peers for being fat; Heidi, a Caucasian girl who is preoccupied with her weight and what she eats; Tamika, an African American girl who is a supportive friend to both Josh and Heidi; and Ms. Helen, an African American teacher who helps the children cope with being teased or pressured. The puppet program consists of three different "shows"—one for Grades K-3 and two for Grades 4-5, an accompanying presenter's manual (Smolak, 1999), and educational and follow-up class activities designed to reinforce messages contained in the programs (Pabst, 1996). Each puppet program, in developmentally appropriate language, teaches children that human body shapes are naturally diverse, that families and peers should not exert unusual pressures about weight and shape, and that teasing and dislike of overweight people are forms of discrimination and prejudice that can have adverse effects on people (Irving, 2000). Each program performance lasts 15 to 20 minutes and is followed by a 10 to 20-minute opportunity for student questions that are fielded and answered by the puppets themselves rather than by the humans operating the puppets.

Irving (2000) provides preliminary empirical support for the EDAP puppet program. Following the presentation of the puppet program to approximately 2,400 children at 12 different elementary schools, 152 children (18% first grade, 19% second grade, 35% third grade, and 27% fourth grade) at one of the schools completed an evaluation of the program. At a different school location, 45 fifth-grade girls completed the Figure Rating Scale (Brylinsky & Moore, 1994) either before ($N = 20$) or after ($N = 25$) watching the puppet program. The student evaluations suggested that the puppet program achieved its intended goal of promoting greater acceptance of diverse body shapes by discouraging teasing in general and on the basis of body shape. The fifth-grade girls' responses to the Figure Rating Scale suggested that the program was able to reduce negative attitudes about large body shapes. However, as Irving (2000) correctly points out, because (a) there was no control group and (b) the rating scale was administered as a pretest to one group and a posttest to a second group, differences between the two groups may or may not have been exclusively a function of the puppet program. As a result, Irving recommends replication of the study using larger samples, intervention, control groups, and longer-term outcomes.

The Everybody's Different Program

Everybody's Different (O'Dea, 1995) is an educational program designed to improve body image by focusing on self-esteem development in the context of a cooperative and interactive student learning environment. The program consists of nine consecutive weekly lessons of 50 to 80 minutes' duration. They are Lesson 1: Dealing With Stress; Lesson 2: Building a Positive Sense of Self; Lessons 3, 4, and 5: Stereotypes in Our Society; Lesson 6: Positive Self-Evaluation; Lesson 7: Involving Significant Others; Lesson 8: Relationship Skills; Lesson 9: Communication Skills. Also included are some home-based activities such as family discussions of lessons and positive parental input. The program was developed in conjunction with principals, teachers, school counselors, parents' groups, pediatricians, and youth workers.

O'Dea (1999) provides empirical support for the Everybody's Different program in improving body image and eating attitudes in her study of 470 seventh- and eighth-grade students (63% female). In this study, students were randomly assigned to either the intervention (Everybody's Different program) or a control group. The Everybody's Different program was integrated into the regular school personal development and health curriculum, and the teachers (including those delivering the intervention) and students were unaware of the aim to examine the program's effect on body image and eating attitudes. Results indicated that when compared to the control students, students in the intervention group exhibited significantly improved body satisfaction and higher self-esteem related to particular dimensions of the self. For example, social acceptance, physical appearance, and athletic ability became less important for the intervention students and more important for control students. Female students in the intervention group rated their physical appearance as perceived by others significantly higher than control students and were also able to avoid the dieting behaviors and consequential weight loss observed in the female control group. One year after the intervention, body image and attitude changes were still present. A particularly important outcome of this study was the fact that these findings also held for the 116 students (63% female) in the intervention group who were considered at risk for the development of eating disorders because of their initial lower self-esteem and higher anxiety scores. Control at-risk students, on the other hand, significantly decreased their body weight over the 12-month duration of the study.

A Resiliency Promotion Prevention Program

Phelps, Sapia, Nathanson, and Nelson (2000) have developed a school-based prevention program designed to promote resiliency factors and mitigate risk factors associated with the development of body dissatisfaction and disordered eating. The design of the program is based on the results of a path analysis from a large sample of adolescent females (Phelps, Johnston, & Augustyniak, 1999). In the path analysis, higher physical self-esteem and personal competence were shown to significantly reduce the internalization of cultural mores related to the current ideal of extreme thinness, which in turn was related to diminished body dissatisfaction. On the basis of this etiological model, Phelps et al. (2000) developed a six-session prevention program designed to strengthen specific personal attributes (physical self-esteem and feeling personal competence) in order to attenuate the sociocultural pressures that promote body dissatisfaction. Integrated into existing school curricula, the overall goals of the program are to facilitate a critical evaluation of contemporary sociocultural mores of beauty and thinness, encourage individual values clarification, and enhance personal resilience in the context of a cooperative and interactive learning environment. Phelps et al. (2000) provided empirical support for the program in their study involving three female student samples: 530 middle school (aged 11 to 15 years), 312 high school (aged 13 to 16 years), and 45 college (aged 18 to 25 years). Each sample was divided into an experimental group that received the program and a control group. The program was successful in (a) facilitating an acknowledgment of the societal pressures to attain the model skeletal look, (b) changing attitudes about beauty standards, (c) increasing physical self-esteem and personal competence, (d) reducing body dissatisfaction, and (e) altering participants' current and future intended use of either pharmaceutical aids or disordered eating behaviors as methods of weight control. However, only experimental-control group posttest comparisons in the college sample reached statistical significance. The authors suggest that this was due to the fact that the middle school and high school female participants were not participating in eating-disordered activities to the extent to allow for a statistically significant drop. Likewise, middle school and high school sample scores on the Body Dissatisfaction and Drive for Thinness subscales of the Eating Disorders Inventory-2 (Garner, 1991) were well within the normative range.

Healthy Body Image: Teaching Kids to Eat and Love Their Bodies, Too!

Kater (1998) developed a school-based program designed to prevent negative body image and disordered eating among elementary school children. The program—Healthy Body Image: Teaching Kids to Eat and Love Their Bodies, Too!—teaches fourth and sixth graders how to critically evaluate the current societal standards for beauty and desirability, to understand the intrinsic and behavioral determinants of size and weight, to develop an incentive for healthy, balanced eating and activity patterns, and to construct an identity based on interests, competence, and self-acceptance rather than image and appearance. Using poems, stories, humor, experiential games, activities, and discussions, the curriculum consists of 10 separate lessons. Four of the lessons emphasize the biological determinants of body size, shape, and hunger that cannot be controlled. Topics include information about the expected changes in appearance during puberty, genetic predisposition for body size, shape, and composition, components of the internal weight regulatory system (such as metabolism), and consequences of dieting behaviors. The next four lessons emphasize controllable factors that influence weight and body image and offer choices such as eating well to satisfy hunger, energy, and nutritional needs, limiting sedentary activities, embracing a balanced sense of identity (rather than focusing exclusively on appearance), and selecting realistic role models. The final two lessons focus on sociocultural issues, including a historical perspective on current societal body image attitudes. Students are taught to interpret and critically evaluate media messages that encourage body image prejudice.

Preliminary empirical support for the Healthy Body Image program comes from a recent pilot study (Kater, Rohwer, & Levine, 2000). In this study, 222 fourth- and sixth-grade boys and girls completed a 30-question pretest designed to assess student attitudes and behaviors regarding body image, eating, and dieting. Following the administration of the pretest, volunteer classroom teachers implemented the 10-lesson curriculum over a period of 6 weeks. Posttest survey results suggested that the curriculum positively influenced knowledge, attitudes, and intentions related to (a) body image, (b) the limits and hazards of dieting to control weight, and (c) unrealistic media messages.

The researchers concluded that the positive impact of the Healthy Body Image curriculum was related to four primary factors: (1) the fact that the targeted age range was just prior to or at the beginning of puberty—that is, before attitudes about weight and shape become more engrained, (2) the hands-on and student-friendly (rather than didactic) learning activities in the curriculum, (3) the curriculum's emphasis on constructing identity based on competencies and preferences rather than appearance, and (4) the strong focus on identifying cultural values and pressures that are in conflict with human biology and health needs. The researchers also recommend that following the implementation of the curriculum booster lessons be provided to students throughout middle school in order to sustain positive changes in body image attitudes and reduce the risk of unhealthy and disordered eating.

SUMMARY

In this chapter, we have drawn attention to the multidimensional and gendered nature of adolescent identity development and suggested that one of the most salient developmental challenges for young adolescent women involves the construction of a healthy physical self-concept, or body image. Young women in the United States seem particularly prone to the development of body image disturbances. Strategies for the prevention of body image disturbances are directly related to the sociocultural and interpersonal factors believed to influence the development and maintenance of body image disturbances and include encouraging young women to (a) critically evaluate cultural ideals and portrayals of women in the media, (b) learn how to assertively respond to teasing, criticism, or negative comments from others about their appearance, and (c) become more knowledgeable about development and body image issues. Because of the foundational role parents play in the identity and emotional development of their children, the effective parenting skills may also foster healthy body image. In addition to parenting strategies, cognitive-behavioral, feminist cognitive-behavioral, and experiential approaches represent three prominent perspectives for the treatment of body image disturbance. School-based prevention programs appear to hold considerable promise, particularly those designed for elementary and middle school children. Because body image disturbance appears to place young women at risk for the development of serious eating disorders (Keel et al., 1997), it is imperative that counselors and mental health professionals be aware of this growing problem and the various ways they can work to promote healthy body image among their clients.

VIGNETTE

As a local mental health professional, you have been invited to talk to a high school sociology class on the topic "Do Media Portrayals of Women Promote Positive Self-Image Among Teenagers?"

---

1. What are some important issues to consider in your preparation for your talk?

2. What are two or three lessons about this topic that you would like your young audience to remember after your presentation?

3. What kind of media examples might you bring to the class to share and discuss?

4. How might you go about helping the young women (and men) in the class critically examine some of the explicit and implicit messages associated with the portrayal of women in popular magazines, newspapers, television shows, and movies?

ADDITIONAL RESOURCES

Books for Professionals

Friedman, S. S. (1999). *Just for girls.* Vancouver: Salal Books. (Available from EDAP, 603 Stewart Street, Suite 803, Seattle, WA 98101.)

Thompson, J. K. (Ed.). (1996). *Body image, eating disorders, and obesity: An integrative guide to assessment and treatment.* Washington, DC: American Psychological Association.

Thompson, J. K., Heinberg, L. J., Altabe, M., & Tantleff-Dunn, S. (1998). *Exacting beauty: Theory, assessment, and treatment of body image disturbance.* Washington, DC: American Psychological Association.

Videotapes

Beyond the looking glass: Body image and self-esteem [Video]. Hourglass Productions, Inc., phone: 914-723-2065.

Frontline: Fat [Video]. Public Broadcasting System.
    Available: http://shop.pbs.org/ OYEfeyEoOC/products/NOO52/

Books for the General Public

Cash, T. F. (1997). *Body image workbook: An 8-step program for learning to like your looks.* Berkeley, CA: New Harbinger.

Rodin, J. (1993). *Body traps: Breaking the binds that keep you from feeling good about your body.* New York: William Morrow.

Internet Resources

Eating Disorders Resources: http://www.gurze.com
   Contains information and resources on eating disorders and body image disturbances.

Eating Disorders Awareness and Prevention, Inc. (EDAP):
   http://members.aol.com/ edapinc/home/html
   Contains body image resources, including a prevention curriculum.
   Mailing address: EDAP, 603 Stewart Street, Suite 803, Seattle, WA 98101

CHAPTER 10

The Challenges of Preventing Adolescent Suicide

A Guide for Practitioners

Joan I. Rosenberg

Although we may think about who we are, our place in the world, what life means to us, and, even at some point, contemplate our death or committing suicide, it is less common for us to act out any thoughts of suicide. As much as adults struggle with these issues, it was unthinkable, even as recently as a couple of decades ago, that children or adolescents became depressed or suicidal. We now know this to be false. Children and adolescents do get depressed, think of suicide, and are, in increasing numbers, taking their own lives. In fact, suicide rates among youths (15 to 24 years) have increased more than 300% since the 1950s (Berman & Jobes, 1995); the suicide rates for those between the ages of 10 and 14 have increased 196% in the past 15 years (American Association of Suicidology, 1996). On the basis of the increasing importance of adolescent suicide as a national public health problem, the focus of this chapter is to discuss adolescent suicide and similarly to highlight suicide prevention and intervention strategies for this age group.

CONTEXT OF THE PROBLEM

Demographics and Related Statistics

Although adolescence is generally considered to be between 12 or 13 years of age to about 20 years of age, the National Center for Health Statistics

(NCHS) reports epidemiologic data in 5-year (e.g., age 15 to 19) and 10-year (e.g., age 15 to 24) age increments. Consequently, most suicide research encompassing this age group defines this period (youth) as occurring between the ages of 15 and 24 years. The NCHS identifies childhood between 5 and 14 years of age. To remain consistent with the NCHS and existing suicide research literature, the period of adolescence will be defined more broadly in this chapter and will also include the earliest years of adulthood.

Consider the following statistics gleaned from the 1996 and 1997 NCHS final reports (Hoyert, Kochanek, & Murphy, 1999; Peters, Kochanek, & Murphy, 1998). Suicide is either the second (15- to 19-year-olds), third (15- to 24-year-olds), or fourth (10- to 14-year-olds) leading cause of death for adolescents, following accidents and homicides (Berman & Jobes, 1995). Among 15- to 19-year-olds, for every female suicide there are 4.4 male suicides. Among 10- to 14-year-olds, this ratio is 2.7:1 (American Association of Suicidology, 1996). Furthermore, it has been estimated that there are 100 youth suicide attempts for every youth suicide, and in the 15- to 19-year-old age group, girls make two of every three of these attempts (U.S. Public Health Service, 1999). Approximately every 1 hour and 3.1 minutes, an average of one young person kills him- or herself.

Studies of high school students have found that up to 60% have experienced some degree of suicidal ideation or action (e.g., Friedman, Asnis, Boeck, & DiFiore, 1987). Despite a geographic variation in rates of suicide, it is likely that within a typical high school classroom, three students (one boy, two girls) have made some form of suicide attempt in the past year (American Association of Suicidology, 1996). A study by Lewinsohn, Rohde, and Seeley (1996) found that the lifetime occurrence of suicidal ideation was much more prevalent in girls as opposed to boys. In the same study, they found that lifetime suicidal ideation rates tended to increase through age 16 but then stabilized for the 17- to 18-year-olds.

Lifetime prevalence rates regarding suicide attempts are estimated at between 6 to 10% of high school-aged adolescents (Friedman et al., 1987), with approximately 1 in 10 adolescent girls and 1 in 25 adolescent boys making some form of suicide attempt. Suicide attempts appear much less common before puberty.

What is particularly disturbing about these numbers is that statistics on suicide are generally considered to be low estimates of true incidence. Researchers believe that the tendency to underreport suicide may be due to religious implications, concern for the family, and concerns regarding restrictions on insurance payments. In addition, underreporting may be a result of the difficulty in differentiating "accidents" from suicidal behaviors—for example, sudden deaths resulting from drug overdose or alcohol use and recklessness, where it is often hard to tell whether the death was planned or truly accidental.

These statistics highlight only one aspect of the suicide problem. Consider the financial and emotional costs involved when a suicide occurs. One economic study completed in 1980 in the United States indicated that each youth suicide resulted in an average loss of 53 years of life and $432,000 of economic productivity, which nationally totaled up to 262,000 actual lost years of life and $3.19 billion each year. Costs in lost economic productivity using the value of a dollar in the year 2000 would clearly be much higher than the figures computed in 1980. In Canada, it is estimated that 12% of hospital critical care and 2% of insurance co-payouts are suicide related.

However, these economic and health costs pale in comparison to the emotional costs of suicide. A lost loved one cannot be replaced. It is estimated that every suicide intimately affects at least six other people. In sheer numbers, this means that there are approximately 3.68 million American survivors of suicide, and this number grows by approximately 180,000 each year.

Although these statistics are sobering and may seem overwhelming at first glance, there is still much reason for hope. In 1986, Schneidman noted that at least 80% of those thinking about suicide signal their intent before attempting suicide. As a result, counselors have many opportunities to intervene. This means that clinicians may be able to help prevent both attempts and actual suicides from occurring.

RISK FACTORS ASSOCIATED WITH ADOLESCENT SUICIDE ATTEMPTS AND COMPLETIONS

Researchers studying adolescent suicides have extensively used a method called psychological autopsy (using extensive interviews with family members and peers to construct psychological profiles of adolescents who have committed suicide) to identify risk factors associated with adolescent suicide. Results from these psychological autopsies have identified several primary risk factors for adolescents considered at risk of attempting suicide. These results indicate that, on average, greater than 90% of suicide victims have at least one diagnosable psychiatric illness at the time of their death (Brent et al., 1988; Conwell et al., 1996; Shaffer et al., 1996), and the disorders most closely associated with suicide are affective disorders and substance abuse (Brent & Perper, 1995).

Lewinsohn et al. (1996) noted that the strongest predictors for future attempts are a history of past suicide attempts and a current episode of major depression. In their research, they found that variables predictive of future suicide attempts included (a) indicators of interpersonal problems (low social support from friends, low self-rated self-competence), (b) a history of drug/

alcohol problems, (c) hopelessness, (d) recent suicide attempt by a friend, and (e) functional impairment due to a physical illness or injury. Their research also reflected that (a) stressful life events, (b) low self-esteem, (c) depressotypic cognitions (negative attributional style, dysfunctional attitudes) and (d) excessive emotional reliance on others may act as predispositions to a suicide attempt.

Their findings are consistent with other researchers who note, in order of importance, factors associated with increased risk of youth suicide, which include (a) prior suicide attempts, (b) affective illness, especially a major depression (for adolescents, depression may also appear as anger or irritability) and dysthymic and bipolar disorders, (c) drug and alcohol abuse, (d) conduct disorder, (e) antisocial or aggressive behavior, (f) psychiatric comorbidity (e.g., depression and substance abuse together), (g) a family history of suicidal behavior, (h) parental psychopathology (e.g., depression, substance abuse, and antisocial behavior), (i) hopelessness, and (j) the availability of firearms in and outside the home (e.g., Brent et al., 1988; Brent & Perper, 1995; Dixon & Scheckel, 1996; Ebert, 1987; Shaffer, 1988; Shaffer, Garland, Gould, Fisher, & Trautman, 1988; U.S. Public Health Service, 1999). For instance, firearms are used in approximately 62.5% of youth suicides. It appears that the best single predictor of death by suicide is a prior suicide attempt.

Researchers suggest that similar risk factors exist for boys and girls (Groholt, Ekeberg, Wichstrom, & Haldorsen, 1997); however, there are differences in the relative importance of these risk factors (Shaffer et al., 1996). For girls, the most important risk factors appear to be the presence of major depression or a previous attempt or both, whereas for boys, important risk factors include previous attempts, depression, disruptive behavior, and substance abuse.

Researchers have also found that suicidal ideation becomes increasingly predictive of future suicide attempts as it increases in frequency of occurrence. Risk of a suicide attempt in the near future increases in almost a linear fashion, with the risk of an attempt increasing as a function of frequency of suicidal ideation. Also, as suicidal intent increases, so does lethality. And suicide attempts made by older adolescents, especially by males, often have more serious intent. The risk of a repeated suicide attempt appears to be highest in the first 3 months immediately following the first attempt, although realistically the risk can remain greater than the base rate for the general population for at least 2 years (see Lewinsohn et al., 1996).

Although there have been many claims that various aspects of family dysfunction are risk factors for completed suicide or suicidal symptoms in children or adolescents, Wagner (1997) disputed most of these claims in an extensive review of the literature in 1997. He notes, however, that consistent evidence shows that a history of physical or sexual abuse is a risk factor. Furthermore, some evidence reveals that poor family or parent-child communication (negative parenting or negative parent-child relationships), loss of the caregiver to separation or death, and psychopathology in first-degree relatives are other risk factors. Similarly, Davis and Brock (in press) and Davis and Sandoval (1991) suggest that economic stress, significant family strife, and family loss are associated with increased risk and that suicidal children appear to have experienced more parental separations, divorces, and remarriages.

Rising Adolescent Suicide Rates: Do Risk and Social Factors Matter?

Adequate empirical support is lacking to provide a clear answer to this question, although certain hypotheses can be made regarding the noted increase. Berman and Jobes (1995) have highlighted a number of possibilities. First, suicide risk is clearly related to psychopathology; affective (Brent et al., 1993) and conduct disorders (Berman & Jobes, 1991) are seen as key risk factors for completed suicides in youth. Suicide attempts almost always occur in the presence of significant psychopathology (Andrews & Lewinsohn, 1992) and, with few exceptions, as noted by Marttunen, Aro, Henriksson, and Lonqvist (1994), adolescents with no lifetime history of psychiatric disorder do not attempt suicide. Similar to adults, the likelihood of suicide attempt increases greatly in the presence of more than one diagnosable psychiatric disorder (Lewinsohn, Rohde, & Seeley, 1995). Furthermore, it is generally acknowledged that individuals are experiencing depression in greater numbers and at earlier ages since the 1920s, with the first onset of depression occurring at younger and younger ages (Nolen-Hoeksema, 1998).

Active substance use or abuse is common in adolescence, and this has long been established as a key risk factor in adolescent suicide (see, e.g., Brent, Perper, & Allman, 1987). In fact, researchers have suggested that changing patterns of drug and alcohol abuse may be related to the rise of adolescent suicides, both in the United States as well as in Europe. For example, in the United States, between the years 1978 and 1983, the percentage of adolescents committing suicide under the influence of alcohol increased by 46% (Brent et al., 1987). Furthermore, Diekstra (1989) examined trends in suicide rates in Europe and found that the rate of change in alcohol consumption had the highest single correlation with changes in suicide rates. More recently, Moscicki (1995) noted that intoxication is present in half of all youth suicides.

Stressful life events such as changes in the nuclear family that include separation from or rejection by parents or both, changes in caretaker or living situation, and poor family communication and problem solving are issues that have been implicated in the increase of youth suicidal behaviors (e.g., deWilde, Kienhorst, Diekstra, & Wolters, 1992; Spirito, Brown, Overholser, & Fritz, 1989).

The availability and presence of a firearm in the home is often cited as being related to the overall increased incidence of suicide, as well as the increased use of firearms by adolescents who suicide (Boyd & Moscicki, 1986; Brent et al., 1991). Boyd and Moscicki noted that between 1968 and 1979, the number of firearms per 100 Americans increased by 47%, and they suggest that this may offer a partial explanation for why the rate of suicide by firearm has increased three times faster than the rates of all other methods for 15- to 19-year-olds. By 1994, roughly 50% of U.S. households possessed a firearm (U.S. Department of Justice, Bureau of Justice Statistics, 1994). Recently, O'Donnell (1995) high-lighted the number of teens who have easy access to acquiring and carrying guns. He further noted that by the teen years, most suicides occur with fire-arms. Statistics from the Federal Bureau of Investigation (1993) indicate that about 60% of all youths (aged 15 to 19) who commit suicide use a gun.

Social imitation offers another possible explanation for teen suicide. In this case, the media has been implicated in what are described as "cluster" or "copycat" suicides. Adolescents seem to be vulnerable to the impact of tele-vision or newspaper coverage of a suicide, and often suicide rates increase fol-lowing such coverage. When teenagers commit suicide using the identical method portrayed in a book or movie they just watched or read, this is consid-ered a copycat suicide (also known as the Werther effect; Phillips, 1974).

Suicide and Specific Populations

Sex and Ethnic Differences

The suicide rate is higher among males than among females. Although males *complete* suicide approximately four times as often as females, females *attempt* suicide at least three times as often as males (Berman & Jobes, 1991). Overall, the suicide rate is higher for Caucasians than for other ethnic groups. However, elevated suicide rates are present for all ethnic youths, especially Native Ameri-cans in certain tribes.

Although there is great variability among tribes, Native Americans (and particularly Native American adolescent males) are still the highest risk group and have the highest suicide rates for persons of color in the United States (e.g., Howard-Pitney, LaFromboise, Basil, September, & Johnson, 1992). The rate in the Indian Health Service areas was the highest in the nation at 62 per 100,000 population (Wallace, Calhoun, Powell, O'Neil, & James, 1996). High sui-cide rates in the Native American population have been associated with high rates of alcoholism, substance abuse, availability of firearms, unemploy-ment, and child abuse and neglect (Berman & Jobes, 1991; Garland & Zigler, 1993).

These elevated suicide rates are also present for young, urban, African American and Hispanic men. For instance, Black adolescent males between the ages of 15 and 24 have shown the greatest increase in suicide completion rates in the 1990s relative to other races and ethnicities (American Association of Suicidology, 1996). Their rate has risen 67% over the past 15 years (American Foundation for Suicide Prevention, 1996). Furthermore, Hovey and King (1996) have suggested that heightened levels of acculturative stress may result in critical levels of suicidal ideation in Mexican American adolescents. High rates of unemployment and poverty, especially in the absence of a strong, positive self-identity, are seen as factors that contribute to a higher rate of suicide in these ethnic groups.

Although there are statistics about rates of death, as yet there is almost no epidemiologic data on the *spectrum* of suicidal behaviors among diverse ethnic adolescent populations. This includes an absence of data on prevalence, incidence, duration, and recurrence for ethnic teens as it relates to (a) nonfatal suicidal behaviors (e.g., suicidal ideation and suicide attempts), (b) comorbid psychiatric disorders in children and adolescents (e.g., Bird, Gould, & Staghezza, 1993; Brady & Kendall, 1992), and (c) the role of developmental factors in suicidal behaviors (e.g., Costello & Angold, 1993) or the relation between developmental stages and suicidal behaviors. Furthermore, the requisite data for explaining the etiology of mental disorders and suicidal behaviors (prospective longitudinal studies assessing the roles of multiple risk factors drawn from both biologic and psychosocial domains) are not available for ethnic youths (Roberts, 1999).

In addition, Roberts (1999) has highlighted the need for more research on the role of ethnicity in suicidal behaviors, yet he believes that future research should focus on an expanded conceptualization of the ethnic experience as it relates to all aspects of suicidality. This means using measures that assess in at least three domains: (1) natal (place of birth), (2) behavioral (e.g., affiliation, language spoken in home, style of dress, and foods eaten), and (3) subjective (e.g., attitudes and beliefs about their ethnicity, acculturative stress). As Roberts noted, virtually no epidemiological studies have incorporated such a strategy when examining what it is about ethnicity that affects either an increase or a decrease in psychiatric outcomes such as suicide.

Roberts has, however, hypothesized a relationship between a number of relevant personal and environmental attributes to suggest why ethnicity might be a protective factor. These include (a) family history (biological and relational information), (b) status attributes or placement factors (age and gender), (c) stressors (chronic, catastrophic, acute, victimization), and (d) resource or protective factors (social, financial, socioeconomic status, personal) and personal factors (self-esteem, coping style, fatalism, and attributional style). Using family history (biological or relational) and placement (age and gender) attributes, Roberts hypothesizes that if ethnicity increases stressors and decreases resources, then there may be increased suicidal risk. Using these same attributes (family history, age, and gender), if ethnicity decreases stressors and increases resources, then there may be decreased suicidal risk.

Gay, Lesbian, and Bisexual Youths

As a result of cumulative stresses (e.g., stigmatized sexual orientation, fear of reprisal or rejection from family or friends on disclosure, being at risk for victimization), gay, lesbian, and bisexual youths may be at particularly high risk for suicide. Gibson (1989) suggested that lesbian and gay male youths are 200 to 300% more likely to commit suicide than their heterosexual counterparts, with gay youths comprising as many as 30% of completed youth suicides. Though figures vary for the percentage of gay and lesbian youths who have attempted suicide, published research has reported disproportionately high suicide rates for gay persons (Harry, 1989). In 1991, Harry concluded that "homosexuals of both sexes are two to six times more likely to attempt suicide than heterosexuals . . . especially during late adolescence and early adulthood" (p. 120). Reported rates for attempted suicide range from 21 to 42% for gay adolescents (D'Augelli & Hershberger, 1993; Hershberger & D'Augelli, 1995; Martin & Hetrick, 1988; National Lesbian and Gay Health Foundation, 1987) as opposed to high school suicide attempt rates, which reportedly range between 6 and 13% (e.g., Friedman et al., 1987; Garland & Zigler, 1993; Shaffer, Garland, Vieland, Underwood, & Busner, 1991).

For instance, in a recent study conducted in the north-central United States using a sample population of approximately 35,000 junior and senior high school students, the highest rates of suicidal intent and attempts were found among homosexual boys and girls, respectively, followed by heterosexual girls and boys (Remafedi, French, Story, Resnick, & Blum, 1998). Results of youth risk behavior surveys (see Grunbaum et al., 1999; Kann et al., 1998) suggest that adolescents who identified themselves as gay, lesbian, or bisexual reported significantly higher rates than their heterosexual peers regarding (a) considering suicide (54% vs. 22%), (b) making a suicide plan (41% vs. 18%), (c) attempting suicide (37% vs. 8%), and (d) requiring medical attention for a suicide attempt (19% vs. 3%). Though still debated somewhat in the literature, it is more commonly believed that a homosexual sexual orientation, especially for young males, continues to be considered a risk factor for suicide. Moscicki (1995) suggests that, in general, research on this issue is complicated by the lack of accurate information on the true rate of homosexuality in the population.

Suicide Among Gifted Adolescents

The empirical research literature related to the suicide of gifted and talented adolescents is quite limited. Most of the work done in this area is conceptual, and some of the empirical studies completed did not adequately specify the definitional criteria for either suicidal behavior or for giftedness. Consequently, until a more adequate research literature develops in this area, clinicians will need to continue to apply the information and base rates pertaining to adolescents in general (Dixon & Scheckel, 1996).

REASONS, MEANINGS, AND METHODS
ASSOCIATED WITH ADOLESCENT SUICIDE

Suicide and Psychic Pain

In 1993, Schneidman implored researchers and clinicians to "address the problem of psychological pain—the psychache that is present in the mind and, if sufficiently severe, drives a person to suicide" (p. 297). Baumeister (1990) noted that the wish to commit suicide "emerges as an escalation of the person's wish to escape from meaningful awareness of current life problems and their implications about the self" (p. 91). Furthermore, Hendin (1991) noted that little research attention has been focused on an individual's capacity to "bear hopelessness, rage, anxiety, and other unpleasant affects without collapse or regression" (p. 1156). Hendin considers suicide an escape from an intolerable affective state, and he identifies these states as rage, hopelessness, despair, guilt, or desperation. He believes that the feeling of despair develops from aloneness and murderous hate, self-contempt, or from any state that "leads to the individual's inability to maintain or envision any human connections of significance" (p. 1151).

Adolescents may use many different expressions to alert others that they may be suicidal. These may include statements such as "I'm feeling suicidal," "I've been thinking about suicide lately," "I have suicidal thoughts," "I'm thinking about taking my life," "I just want everything to be over," "I just want to end it all," or "People would be better off if I were dead." So what does it mean when someone describes these thoughts or feelings? Most individuals who describe feeling suicidal (or use expressions as above) are very ambivalent about taking their lives. In fact, most really want to live rather than die. And if someone has reached the level of thinking about or feeling suicidal, the clinician should understand that this means that individuals who are expressing suicidal thoughts or feelings are experiencing emotional pain that they find either unbearable or intolerable.

Furthermore, when individuals describe themselves as "feeling suicidal," generally, counselors will immediately think, "Suicide = act of hurting oneself." Instead, clinicians are encouraged to reframe their thinking about suicide and understand that suicide equals a communication about experiencing deep (unbearable, intolerable) emotional pain or feeling—usually described as feelings of hopelessness, despair, or desperation (Rosenberg, 1999).

Overall, Leenaars (1999) suggested that more similarities than differences exist across the lifespan of those who are at risk for, attempt, and complete suicide, so that many of the risk factors that have been identified for adults are applicable as well to adolescents. Essentially, adolescents kill themselves largely for the same reasons as adults. In particular, he notes these factors to be (a) *intrapsychic* (unbearable psychic pain, cognitive constriction, indirect expression of feelings, inability to adjust), (b) *interpersonal* (poor interpersonal relations, rejection, abandonment from loss, anger), and (c) *identification-egression* (work toward a goal that a person is attached to is somehow thwarted; then person egresses). Teens tend to have tunnel vision and become singularly preoccupied with one trauma, tending also to show more confusion, contradiction, and ambivalence (love and hate toward same person) when loss occurs.

Meanings Attributed to Youth Suicide

Adolescents may attribute many meanings to suicide. Hendin (1991) and Katz (1995) discussed at length the meanings that adolescent suicide may have; these are noted below. Some of these meanings include (a) death as rebirth or reunion with a lost object (person)—this is reflective of the wish to reunite with someone from whom separation has occurred, (b) revenge, where suicide expresses a repressed wish to kill an ambivalently regarded lost love object (e.g., hatred toward a parent), (c) revengeful fantasies, where the individual has a fantasy of how sorry everyone will be following the suicide, (d) retaliatory abandonment, where there is an illusion of mastery over a situation through the adolescents' control of their living or dying, (e) reward fantasies, where one is compensated for a miserable life on earth with a much happier afterlife, (f) identification with a suicide—adolescents identify with someone who has committed suicide and feel that they must do the same, (g) reactions to losses, which may include such losses as romantic or other important attachments or loss of health, (h) guilt—adolescents blame themselves for some specific incident(s) and seek to expiate their guilt by suicide, (i) escape from a harsh superego—individuals feel guilty for everything they do and try to escape through death, and (j) self-punishment or atonement, where suicide is the final act of self-hatred.

In general, Hendin (1987) believes that all the psychodynamic meanings given to death can be conceptualized as responses to loss, separation, or abandonment. He noted that becoming the one who leaves is one way to avoid the feeling of having been left. Loss, however, needs to be conceptualized more broadly than loss of relationship; examples may include such losses as loss of a dream, health, or reputation (Rosenberg, 1999). Interestingly, Hendin also notes that elderly suicides are often preoccupied with conflicts centering on the end of their lives, whereas young suicides seem determined not to allow their lives to begin—as if individuals are trying to freeze time by deadening themselves long before they try to kill themselves. Regarding retaliatory abandonment, Hendin believes that some adolescents may keep the means for completing suicide readily available, whether or not they ever attempt it, in order to always keep possible the illusion of mastery or control over their situation.

Methods

The vast majority of suicide attempts are premeditated. Ingestion (overdose) and cutting are the most common suicide *attempt* methods used by adolescent girls; adolescent boys attempt by ingestion, cutting, firearm use, and hanging (Lewinsohn et al., 1996). Firearms are the most frequent method of *completed* suicide for both genders, followed by hanging and gassing, respectively. For *completed* suicides, males continue to use firearms and hanging more often than do females. The ratio between attempts and completions for males and females is probably reflected in the choice of method. Females attempt more frequently (three times as often as males) yet have tended to use less lethal means; males, however, have tended to use more violent and immediately lethal methods and complete suicide approximately four times as often as females.

SUICIDE PREVENTION: PROGRAM IMPLEMENTATION AND TREATMENT STRATEGIES

Prevention and Intervention: Clarifying the Terms and the Tasks

Silverman and Felner (1995) provided a comprehensive overview of suicide prevention. The following discussion is a condensation of that work. Silverman and Felner noted that the general assumption underlying a public health model (as it is applied to the full range of traditional medical, mental health, and human service interventions) involves a linear view of illness or disease. This means that disorders are seen to move sequentially from onset through clinical syndrome. In this type of situation, the "onset" of dysfunction can be readily identified.

However, this sequential movement is not applicable to someone who is suicidal, even though the onset of certain aspects of functioning may seem obvious (e.g., when one begins to use or abuse alcohol or other drugs, the occurrence of a recent loss). Thus, Silverman & Felner (1995) believe that following a public health model in its strictest sense (linear approach) is not well suited to suicide prevention, especially because suicidal ideation, attempts, and completions are more often the results of "complex, multicausal factors in which the interaction of a number of predisposing conditions are key to incidence, prevalence and course" (p. 73).

Using the descriptions set forth by Silverman and Felner, primary prevention activities seek to reduce new cases of individuals who are suicidal; the concept is that a prevention activity involves a "before the fact" action—before the event occurs, in this case, a suicide attempt. Furthermore, *prevention activities are targeted to entire populations* rather than to specific individuals. Secondary prevention activities (considered *early intervention* by Silverman and Felner) target those persons showing early signs of suicidality, with the goal of reducing the intensity, severity, and duration of symptoms. They consider tertiary prevention *treatment*; these strategies focus on individuals who are already displaying several aspects of suicidality. Thus, strategies in this last domain would likely include specific treatment and rehabilitation efforts. It is also important to remember that integral to prevention programming are efforts to promote strength, well-being, and positive developmental outcomes (e.g., health promotion activities).

Youth Suicide Prevention Strategies

Eight strategies designed to prevent youth suicide, described earlier in a guidebook for youth suicide prevention and compiled by the Centers for Disease Control and Prevention (1992), have been summarized by Berman and Jobes (1995) and Potter, Powell, and Kachur (1995). Suicide prevention programs should be linked as closely as possible with professional mental health resources in the local community. And communities should work toward developing a comprehensive prevention effort that incorporates several levels of strategies as opposed to relying on only one type of prevention strategy. The following strategies are included in the guide.

School Gatekeeper Training

This program is directed at school staff (teachers, counselors, coaches, etc.) to help them more readily identify, respond to, and refer students at risk of suicide. The program is also designed to teach staff how to respond in the event a tragic death or other crisis occurs. Trained school personnel are encouraged to (a) actively identify high-risk students, (b) facilitate social support and life-skills training programs for all youths and more tailored intervention programs or groups for high-risk students, (c) participate as a member of a crisis response team within the school, and (d) facilitate a supportive return of students to school following suicidal threats, suicidal behaviors, or hospitalization.

Community Gatekeeper Training

This program provides training to community members (e.g., clergy, police, businesspersons, and recreational staff) and all levels of medical and psychological practitioners who are likely to have frequent contact with youths. Programs at this level will also teach individuals how to correctly identify and refer youths at risk of suicide. The goals of community gatekeeper training are similar to goals for school personnel; these programs are designed to increase a potential gatekeeper's sense of confidence and competency in recognizing, referring, or accessing appropriate help (e.g., by increasing knowledge of referral resources within the community) for youths at risk of suicide. Community gatekeepers may also be involved by facilitating training for new gatekeepers and by participating in public education or media campaigns aimed at suicide prevention.

General Suicide Education

These school-based programs are classroom-centered, knowledge-based models intended for the adolescents themselves. They are designed to provide the adolescents with facts about suicide, alert them to warning signs, and provide information about how to seek help for themselves (encouraging self-referral) or for others. Common topics include discussion of relevant facts, statistics, myths, warning signs, available community resources, and how to use these resources. Often, these programs incorporate information intended to help increase self-esteem and social competence, teach stress management and communication skills, and develop help-seeking and problem-solving abilities. However, many school-based suicide prevention programs have been criticized for (a) their "stress model" orientation, (b) their universal approach rather than targeting only those considered most at risk of suicide, (c) negative effects of some of the programs, and (d) failing to adequately evaluate the prevention effort itself.

Programs with a stress model orientation are programs that have represented suicide as a response to a significant or extreme amount of stress; these programs have been highly criticized for ignoring the extensive research that has shown that adolescent suicide and suicidal behavior are strongly associated with psychopathology (Brent et al., 1988; Garland & Zigler, 1993; Mazza, 1997). The stress model "normalizes" suicide and suicidal behavior, suggesting that, given enough stress, everyone may be vulnerable to suicide (Ciffone, 1993). Consequently, portraying suicide as an outcome of stress may actually increase the likelihood of suicidal behavior, because suicide may be viewed as a viable alternative under stressful conditions (Shaffer et al., 1988).

Screening Programs

Screening entails the administration of an instrument to identify high-risk youths for the purpose of providing more detailed assessment and treatment. Typically, this is accomplished in a school setting, and it may include repeated administrations of the screening instrument(s) to measure change in attitude or behavior or to evaluate the effectiveness of prevention strategies.

Peer Support Programs

These school-based (e.g., Eggert, Thompson, Herting, & Nicholas, 1995) or community-based programs are designed to enhance peer relationships and foster social skill development and social competence for youths considered at high risk of suicide or suicide-related behaviors.

Crisis Centers and Hotlines

These programs provide either telephone counseling and referral or drop-in crisis center services (which may also include referral) for individuals who are suicidal. Trained volunteers typically staff the centers and hotlines. However, the preventive effect from these suicide prevention centers appears to be small and sometimes inconsistent (Lester, 1997).

Means Restriction

This level of intervention consists of activities designed to restrict access to drugs, alcohol, handguns, or other means of committing suicide. At this time, nearly two thirds of all youth suicides are by firearms. Although efforts may also need to be expended at a policy level, it is recommended that drug and alcohol prevention and restricting access to firearms become key foci for future prevention efforts.

Postvention and Cluster Prevention

Postvention efforts often include crisis debriefings and are intended to diffuse the crisis in order to prevent or contain suicide clusters (or copycat suicides) following a completed suicide. Often, this involves the use of crisis response teams. In this situation, the mental health professional targets interventions to help youths cope with feelings of anger or loss that often accompany the sudden death or suicide of a peer.

General Intervention Strategies for Schools

To combat the high rate of suicide among adolescent youths, comprehensive suicide prevention programs and intervention strategies must clearly be targeted at and developed for our schools. School personnel, especially the school psychologist or school counselor, will likely assume an essential role in these prevention efforts. Accordingly, Poland and Lieberman (2000) identified six critical tasks for the school psychologist or school counselor:

1. Promote primary prevention programs that address at-risk youths (substance/alcohol abuse, violence, dropout, and pregnancy programs).
2. Assist schools in linking with parents, community law enforcement, and mental health agencies.
3. Advocate for school crisis teams to implement and collaborate on appropriate intervention and postvention strategies.
4. Provide staff development on youth suicide risk factors, warning signs, and referral processes.
5. Advocate for mental health needs of students who return to school following expulsion, mental health hospitalization, or other traumatic events.
6. Support programs to reduce accessibility to firearms. (p. 11)

In addition, Poland and Lieberman (2000), in their discussion of best practices in suicide intervention, offered a summary of additional intervention strategies and responsibilities that school personnel (e.g., the school psychologist or school counselor) should consider. These include (a) collaboration with other colleagues (e.g., administrator or nurse) at the school, (b) assigning a "designated reporter"—a person or persons who are responsible for receiving and acting on all reports of students who may be suicidal, (c) actively supervising or monitoring the child at the school until a parent can assume responsibility for the child's supervision, (d) helping the suicidal child mobilize his or her social support network, (e) asking the child to sign a "no-suicide" contract, (f) "suicide-proofing" the environment by clearing the adolescent's environment of all potentially dangerous objects and medications, (g) calling the police when appropriate, and (h) documenting the efforts and actions taken to respond to the suicidal student.

Early Intervention Considerations

Given the high level of diagnosable mental health difficulties seen in adolescent suicides, the therapist must be well trained—especially in completing thorough diagnostic interviews and psychopathology. This means being aware of existing mental health concerns (e.g., depression, substance use or abuse, conduct disorders, and comorbidity) and related parental and family mental health history. The therapist must intervene aggressively, especially with the presence of clinical depression and substance abuse (Brent & Perper, 1995).

It is important to remember that violence—whether self- or other-directed—is a process, and there will almost always be some signs or signals that an adolescent is suffering and perhaps headed for a downfall. Counselors, friends, or family may notice a teenager exhibiting such indicators as (a) downward changes in school performance, (b) increased isolation from friends and family, (c) increased irritability, anger, or apathy, (d) increased use of alcohol or drugs, or (e) unremitting feelings of sadness or depression.

Treatment Strategies

In terms of overall assessment, the therapist must take an active role and take all talk of suicide seriously. Complete a thorough diagnostic interview when possible. Because depression has long been considered a risk factor for suicidality, the clinician must assess for existing depressive symptomology. Talk openly and directly about (a) suicidal ideation (thoughts or feelings), (b) intent, (c) plans, or (d) means for completing the suicide. An area often overlooked and underassessed is homicidal ideation. Consequently, a clinician is well advised to assess for homicidal thoughts and feelings while evaluating suicidal thoughts and feelings. In addition to the information described above, the therapist must also consider the variety of risk factors associated with adolescent suicide. Reviewing these areas should provide the clinician with the ability to make an overall assessment of the adolescent's level of suicide risk.

With regard to specific interventions, the clinician can engage adolescents in a discussion about what suicide means to them and explore why they feel so inescapably trapped. Provide support and reinforcement for talking about these difficult issues and feelings. Convey to them that the fact that an open discussion is occurring around these issues reflects both a desire for help and a desire to live. In addition, a therapist can address (a) feelings of anger, rage, or revenge, or (b) ambivalent feelings about suicide and death. It is also possible to discuss the finality of death and the impact suicide may have on family and friends the adolescent may leave behind. Furthermore, individuals often lose a realistic perspective regarding time when experiencing intense emotional pain; people frequently describe deep fears that the pain is interminable and will last forever. In this case, teenagers can be reminded that just as good feelings may pass, so too will bad feelings.

The therapist can help adolescents understand that what they really desire is to eradicate feelings of intolerable pain rather than to eradicate the self. The therapist can also help adolescents understand that thoughts or feelings of suicide can be considered a communication about the depth of feelings they are experiencing (despairing, desperate, or hopeless) versus an actual intent to take action. Acknowledging and discussing feelings of despair or hopelessness may help teenagers shift their concept of suicide from a physical or concrete act to understanding that "feeling suicidal" is about having intolerable emotional pain. As one considers possible treatment strategies, it is important to keep in mind both possibilities regarding suicide:

▶ Suicide = a communication about deep, unbearable, or intolerable emotional pain, and

▶ Suicide = an act or action(s) to hurt oneself.

It is quite conceivable that the therapist will need to respond to each aspect in an effort to help mitigate psychic pain while simultaneously addressing issues of physical safety.

Individuals who are suicidal often find it difficult to identify a range of options for dealing with their psychic pain. Thus, another intervention may be to help suicidal teens generate other avenues for handling such pain. This may include having teenagers write in a journal or use other safe modes of emotional expression. The therapist can also explore whether teenagers believe that they have any positive coping resources (means for solving problems that they have used effectively in the past) and other available resources (e.g., friends or family members) to whom they can turn and rely on for help.

Clinicians are often easily lulled into believing that every suicidal adolescent can be helped. However, this is not only a false assumption, but it can be an emotional trap for the therapist. Although at least 8 of every 10 persons can be helped, clinicians must accept that they may not be able to help everyone—especially those who refuse therapeutic help. Occasionally, therapists may experience some individuals who use threats of suicide as manipulation. In these situations, it is sometimes difficult to maintain objectivity in order to remain unaffected by the emotional coercion that threats of suicide can evoke. Counselors may be less vulnerable to this type of coercion if they are able to accept failure and accept that some suicidal individuals will, in fact, commit suicide. One has to remember that help can be provided only to those adolescents who truly desire help and that not all suicides can be prevented.

Suicide Attempts and Completions: Considering a Child's Needs

Many clinicians and researchers have offered suggestions for helping children who have been bereaved by suicide (see, e.g., Hoff, 1989; Shamoo &

Patros, 1990; Webb, 1993), and a compilation of their suggestions are offered here. If there has been a suicide attempt or a completed suicide in a family, often the first impulse of parents or caregivers is to shield the truth—especially from young children. This impulse is based on the belief that children need to be protected from the truth because they are too young to understand what is happening. For a number of reasons, it is better for parents or caregivers to tell children the truth. Children are expected to tell the truth; similarly, they should be able to rely on the adults in their life being truthful with them. Children are often able to accurately perceive much that is happening around them, and they will know something is wrong when other siblings and adults are grieving or a family member is no longer present.

Furthermore, beginning and maintaining a lie often becomes a preoccupation that can interfere with normal grief. It is possible that a child may find out the truth under less favorable circumstances (e.g., a schoolmate might tell the child). Not only do lies create an atmosphere of distrust, but the effect of not telling children the truth may lead them to believe, through magical thinking, that they are responsible for the suicide. Without the facts, children may attempt to fill in the details alone and may consequently imagine circumstances far worse than the truth.

Suggestions Therapists Can Make to Caregivers

Be honest and use explanations appropriate to the children's age and cognitive development. Talk with the children; convey that the death was a suicide and that the death was not their fault. Create and foster an emotional climate in which children feel comfortable asking questions and expressing emotions; this may mean answering the same questions repeatedly. Allow children to see your grief. This helps them learn how to master painful experiences. Help children generate many solutions to problems and explain that there are other ways than suicide to solve problems. Resume normal routines as soon as possible and seek professional help as needed.

SUMMARY

Because very little attention has been given to primary prevention models focused on individuals considered at high risk for suicide, prevention education and activities should be distinctly targeted to these high-risk groups (Mazza, 1997). On the basis of the existing research, these prevention programs clearly should (a) change to a mental illness rather than a stress model to explain suicidal behavior, (b) include assessment instruments that examine actual suicidal behaviors (ideation, attempts), along with changes in attitude and knowledge, and (c) focus on targeting the most-at-risk populations on *multiple* dimensions of suicidal behavior (ideation, attempts, self-destructive behavior) rather than targeting everyone. Furthermore, programs also need to gather empirical evidence over both the short term (several months) and long term (1 to 3 years) to show whether these programs were effective in reducing suicidal behavior.

Ciffone (1993) believes at least two messages should be delivered to all adolescents: They must understand (1) that suicidal attempts and completions are usually symptoms of treatable psychiatric illness, and (2) that they should prepare themselves for emergency emotional situations—given that adolescence is often such a period of disequilibrium, uncertainty, impulsivity, and recklessness. This means that all adolescents should be prepared with the knowledge of basic intervention and referral skills—especially because many potential suicidal adolescents tend to seek out one another, as opposed to adults, to discuss their feelings and intentions when in a psychosocial crisis. The goal, then, is to present referral information to them as "safety education"—that is, if the adolescent is told by a friend about depressive feelings, suicidal thoughts, or an intent to commit suicide, even if in confidence, it is important for the adolescent to inform a responsible adult. The friend should be discouraged from holding onto confidences and, if possible, refer the suicidal youth to the appropriate resource or mental health professional. As Cross, Cook, and Dixon (1996) note, "It is better to have a live enemy than a dead friend" (p. 408).

It is almost a certainty that counselors will encounter adolescents who will be depressed and also be suicidal. Thus, it is imperative that mental health professionals receive thorough training and develop skills in both assessment and intervention. Working with individuals who are suicidal often raises anxiety for clinicians. Consequently, clinicians are encouraged to seek appropriate supervision or consultation for themselves while they work toward reducing the individual's suicidality. Working with suicidal adolescents is a particularly sensitive and challenging area of practice, yet the rewards are priceless when lives have been saved.

VIGNETTE

You are a counselor working in the college counseling center, and you have just begun to interview Julie about why she is here. She states that she is in your office because she is "extremely concerned" about her roommate Sandy, and she is hopeful that you will be able to do something to help Sandy feel better. This is the information that Julie relates to you:

Seven months ago, 19-year-old Sandy left her home in Wisconsin and traveled to Texas to begin her undergraduate studies at a regional university. She chose an out-of-state college because she wanted to "test her wings" away from her family. Her father worked 12 hours a day and rarely even acknowledged Sandy's presence when at home with her. Instead, he could be found drinking his martinis, generally until he passed out in front of the television. Sandy's mother had committed suicide when Sandy was 12. Not only was Sandy instructed never to speak of her again, but she was left with the responsibility of caring for two younger siblings. She was not really ready for this level of responsibility, and the demands of completing household errands and chores often limited her ability to develop a good social network. She did manage to excel academically, thus allowing her to go away to college on scholarship.

Although shy and initially having difficulty making friends, Sandy persisted and began making friends and continued making high grades during her first semester. By second semester, she started feeling more comfortable around the men in her classes and began studying with one man in particular, Trevor. Within a few weeks, they began dating, though one evening after dinner, a movie, and a walk, talking stopped and was replaced by kissing. Their sexual activity intensified, Sandy insisted Trevor stop—and despite her verbal and physical efforts to stop him, Trevor raped her.

Sandy returned to her college room without talking to any of her friends and feeling very confused about what had just happened. She sought no medical or professional help, continued to go to classes, and tried to pretend nothing had happened. She had to continue to face Trevor in the classes they had together, though it appeared he moved right on by hanging out with other women. As the weeks passed, Sandy became overwhelmed by feelings of guilt, shame, sadness, humiliation, and fear and found it difficult to concentrate on her coursework. As a result, she began skipping classes and isolating herself in her room by sleeping most of the day. She was keeping more and more distance from her friends, and she ceased her involvement in a variety of school activities. She brushed off questions about changes in her mood and behavior despite being consumed with the pain and memory of what had happened. She also began drinking to cope. All these changes left her at risk of losing her scholarship—and possibly facing a return home to an unsupportive and undesirable family situation.

As a mental health professional,

---

1. What suicide risk factors or warning signs are you aware of?

2. What thoughts do you have about how to address this situation?

3. How will you proceed to help her? What resources will you suggest?

4. How will you evaluate her mental and emotional status?

5. What are your legal, ethical, and clinical concerns?

ADDITIONAL RESOURCES

Print Resources

Berman, A. L., & Jobes, D. A. (1991). *Adolescent suicide: Assessment and intervention.* Washington, DC: American Psychological Association.

Capuzzi, D., & Golden, L. (1988). *Preventing adolescent suicide.* Muncie, IN: Accelerated Development.

Leenaars, A., & Wenckstern, S. (1990). *Suicide prevention in schools.* Washington, DC: Hemisphere.

Parkin, R., & Dunne-Maxim, K. (1995). *Child survivors of suicide: A guidebook for those who care for them.* Newark: University of Medicine and Dentistry of New Jersey Mental Health Services.

Poland, S. (1989). *Suicide intervention in the schools.* New York: Guilford.

Poland, S., & McCormick, J. S. (1999). *Coping with the crisis: Lessons learned.* Longmont, CO: Sopris West.

Shamoo, T. K., & Patros, P. G. (1990). *Helping your child cope with depression and suicidal thoughts.* New York: Lexington Books.

Films and Videotapes

Adolescence: Current Issues II
Covers the subjects of depression, suicide, delinquency, violence, runaways and dropouts. (Available from Magna Systems, Inc., 95 West County Line Road, Barrington, IL 60010; phone: 800-203-7060; fax: 815-459-4280)

Before You Say Good-bye
Conversations with those whose lives have been intimately touched by suicide. (Available from Aquarius Health Care Videos, 5 Powderhouse Lane, P.O. Box 1159, Sherborn, MA 01770; phone: 508-651-2963; fax: 508-650-4216)

No Easy Way
Talking with family members who have lost a loved one to suicide; geared toward survivors of suicide and for training those who work with suicide survivors. (Available from Aquarius Health Care Videos, 5 Powderhouse Lane, P.O. Box 1159, Sherborn, MA 01770; phone: 508-651-2963; fax: 508-650-4216)

Teen Suicide
Examines the reasons why teens consider, attempt, or commit suicide. Information provided on warning signs in friends and relatives, how to help, and where to go for assistance. (Available from Films for the Humanities, P.O. Box 2053, Princeton, NJ 08543-2053; phone: 800-257-5126; fax: 609-275-3767)

Dying to Be Heard . . . Is Anybody Listening?
Offers specific advice on how to recognize teens in danger of committing suicide and successfully intervene. Talks to teens who have attempted suicide about their reasons for trying and about their lives after treatment. (Available from Films for the Humanities, P.O. Box 2053, Princeton, NJ 08543-2053; phone: 800-257-5126; fax: 609-275-3767)

Everything to Live For

Features stories of two teens who attempted and two teens who committed suicide. Addresses possible causes, cries that went unheard, and warning signs to which peers, parents, teachers, and counselors must be alert. (Available from Films for the Humanities, P.O. Box 2053, Princeton, NJ 08543-2053; phone: 800-257-5126; fax: 609-275-3767)

Agencies and Related Internet Sites

American Association of Suicidology (AAS), 4201 Connecticut Avenue, Suite 310, Washington, DC 20008; phone: 202-237-2280; fax: 202-237-2282; http://www. suicidology.org

American Foundation for Suicide Prevention (AFSP), International Headquarters, 120 Wall Street, 22nd Floor, New York, NY 10005; phone: 212-363-3500; fax: 212-363-6237; toll-free: 888-333-AFSP; http://www.afsp.org

Canadian Association for Suicide Prevention (CASP/ACPS), c/o The Support Network, #301, 11456 Jasper Avenue NW, Edmonton, AB T5K 0M1; phone: 780-482-0198; fax: 780-488-1495; e-mail: casp@suicideprevention.ca; http://www. suicideprevention.ca

Center to Prevent Handgun Violence, 1225 Eye Street, Room 1100, Washington, DC 20005; phone: 202-898-0792; fax: 202-371-9615; http://www.handguncontrol. org

Connecticut Committee for Youth Suicide Prevention, United Way of Connecticut/Infoline, 1344 Silas Deane Highway, Rocky Hill, CT 06067; phone: 860-571-7528

European Network for Suicidology (ENS), c/o Josephine Scott, St. Mary's Hospital, Castlebar, County Mayo, Ireland. Phone: +353 94 21333; fax: +353 94 27904; e-mail:joscott@tinet.ie; http://www.uke.uni-hamburg.de/ens

International Association for Suicide Prevention (IASP), c/o Professor David Clark, Rush Center for Suicide Research and Prevention, 1725 West Harrison Street, Suite 955, Chicago, IL 60612; phone: 312-942-7208; fax: 312-942-2177; e-mail: iasp@aol.com; http://www.who.int/ina-ngo/ngo/ngo027.htm

LivingWorks Education Inc., #208, 1615 10th Avenue SW, Calgary, AB; phone: 403-209-0242; fax: 403-209-0259; e-mail: living@nucleus.com

Suicide Information & Education Centre (SIEC), #201, 1615 10th Avenue SW, Calgary, AB T3C 0J7; phone: 403-245-3900; fax: 403-245-0299; e-mail: info@siec. ca; http://www.siec.ca

Suicide Prevention Advocacy Network (SPAN), 5034 Odin's Way, Marietta, GA 30068; phone: 888-649-1366; fax: 770-642-1419; http://www.spanusa.org

Washington State Youth Suicide Prevention Program, C/o Leona Eggert, PhD, RN, Box 357263, University of Washington, Seattle, WA 98195-7263; phone: 206-543-9455; fax: 206-685-9551; http://www.depts.washington.edu/ysp

Internet Resources

Befrienders International: http://www.befrienders.org
Kids Help Phone: http://www.kidshelp.sympatico.ca
SAVE: http://www.save.org
Suicide @ Rochford.org: http://www.suicide@rochford.org
Yellow Ribbon Suicide Prevention Program: http://www.yellowribbon.org

PART IV

Young Adulthood

The starting point of adulthood is ambiguous. Legally, the recognition of assuming adult responsibilities might occur at age 18 or 21 for various activities. Yet, adult responsibilities, including parenting, establishing long-term relationships, and caring for others, often begin much earlier. Furthermore, the point at which young adulthood transitions into middle adulthood can also vary. In this section, young adulthood is assumed to begin at the age corresponding to the completion of high school and extend through the formation of career and family roles.

According to Erikson (1963), the primary crisis of young adulthood is intimacy versus isolation. The resolution of this crisis is to connect to another person in an expression of intimacy. Relationships formed during this stage are likely to be more critically evaluated in terms of longevity and stability. Forming a relationship that is both intimate and lasting may become a high priority. According to the U.S. Bureau of the Census (1998), an estimated 58 million adults between the ages of 18 and 35 are married. An additional 3 million are divorced. In contrast, approximately 20 million adults between the ages of 18 and 24 have never married, and this number drops significantly, to less than 14 million, between the ages of 25 and 34. It is also important to note that data collected by the Census Bureau do not include people in long-term gay or lesbian relationships, who are also forming intimate relationships during young adulthood.

In addition to intimate relationships, young adults are entering a variety of new relationships with peers, professional colleagues, family members, and mentors. In addition, they may be taking on the role of responsibility for others in some of these relationships, particularly as they begin families and assume parenting responsibilities.

With these responsibilities comes the need to become self-sufficient, and new skills must be developed to meet financial and employment goals. As Levinson (1978) describes this process in the Entering the Adult World stage, young adults are forming and testing out preliminary life structures and creating a link between themselves and adult society. As new employees and new parents, young adults might be struggling with adjusting to significant adult roles.

The challenge of dealing with new, and sometimes unanticipated, situations on top of new life roles may be exhausting and stressful for many young adults. Such stress can contribute to domestic violence between partners and between parents and children. There are some indications that young adults are more likely to be the victims of assault within intimate relationships than other age groups. Bachman and Saltzman (1995) reported that women between the ages of 19 and 29, as well as women in low-income families, were more likely to be assaulted by an intimate partner than any other group of women. As discussed previously in this text, children continue to be at risk for abuse and violence as well.

Education and prevention programs can help young adults make the best possible choices, given the myriad decisions that face them in this developmental stage. By developing good relationship choices and life management skills, young adults may become more effective partners, parents, and workers, prepared to balance the multiple roles they will assume.

Chapters 11 through 15 address several of the issues commonly encountered by young adults. In Chapter 11, Gregory S. Lambeth and Marybeth Hallett identify several intervention programs focused on the variety of new relationships that young adults encounter. Using programs that have been developed in campus settings, which can and have been used in other community settings, these authors suggest ways to help young adults navigate relationships in both personal and professional environments. Changing family-of-origin relationships, peer and friendship issues, romantic, and professional or educational relationships are addressed, and implications for counseling practice and program evaluation are provided.

In Chapter 12, Stephanie San Miguel Bauman addresses the various emotional and social costs that can be avoided when parenting skills are developed. After a brief look at the history of parenting, she describes different parenting styles. She then considers ways in which the roles of the counselor might be broadened to promote positive parenting and provides examples of programs that can be used for parent education. The chapter concludes with a discussion of cross-cultural differences in parenting and the need to reach out to parents in minority groups.

Elizabeth Nutt Williams, in Chapter 13, addresses the important issues of role conflict, role overload, and role contagion that are increasingly experienced by both men and women who are maintaining active family and work lives. After considering the literature in these areas, which frequently acknowledges the benefits of multiple roles, the author discusses strategies for helping young adults avoid or prevent role strain and stress and presents an example program from a university counseling center. She then provides information about the treatment of role strain, once it is already present, and concludes with a case example.

The remaining two chapters in this section address the fact that violence and assault situations have become so common in our society that any individual is vulnerable to them. As highlighted in Chapter 14, young adults, especially women, are particularly vulnerable to sexual assault. In this chapter, Helen A. Neville and Mary J. Heppner provide an overview of the issues related to the prevention of sexual assault on college campuses, based on their extensive and ongoing research program in the area. They discuss important issues about the cultural issues, and misconceptions, related to sexual assault and describe various intervention programs that have been implemented in college settings. On the basis of their research, they present an important set of findings about the components of effective intervention programs. The authors then provide information on treatment approaches following rape and conclude with a call for counselors to intervene in violence against women on a systematic level.

Finally, in Chapter 15, Carolyn Zerbe Enns discusses the issue of violence in families and its prevalence across age groups. She describes the multiple factors that contribute to family violence, including specific risk factors and the complex ways they interact. Enns then discusses the need for counselors to try to stop violence before it begins, providing strategies for building communication skills, gender equity, and creating a social environment that does not promote violence. This is followed by a section on treatment issues for families where violence is already present, including the challenges of working with both victims and perpetrators.

In these five chapters, a number of issues relevant to work with young adults are thoroughly discussed. The counseling strategies provided can help support young adults as they navigate a series of challenging new life roles, ensuring that young adulthood is a time of challenge and exhilaration rather than stress and role strain.

CHAPTER 11

Promoting Healthy Decision Making in Relationships

Developmental Interventions With Young Adults on College and University Campuses

Gregory S. Lambeth
Marybeth Hallett

The transition from adolescence to young adulthood is an important developmental period that exposes individuals to a variety of challenging relationship tasks and issues (Arnett, 1999). The majority of young adults do not encounter serious psychological difficulties with these transitions, however, and therefore may not seek traditional mental health services. Nevertheless, many young adults could benefit from preventive interventions that target relationship concerns. These interventions are not only potentially effective in addressing individual psychological concerns, but they may also result in improved communities by assisting young adults with the development of necessary relationship skills such as conflict resolution, violence prevention, and cross-cultural understanding.

The early adult years are typically characterized by some degree of individuation from the family of origin and a concurrent emphasis on peer group and romantic relationships. These changes are frequently accompanied by more autonomy as well as a new emphasis on emotional and physical intimacy. As young adults complete high school and continue their education or enter the workplace, they will also develop additional relationships with employers, mentors, faculty, and/or advisers that provide skills relevant for future professional relationships. In addition, some young adults will have children, which requires the acquisition of unique parenting skills. The successful negotiation of these myriad relationships has a direct bearing on one's participation in the family, workplace, and community (Bellah, Madsen, Sullivan, Swidler, & Tipton, 1985).

Many young adults receive fairly extensive training in a variety of life skills, often in the secondary school system, which ranges from first aid to HIV/AIDS prevention, but they are unlikely to have been exposed to any prevention programs designed to improve relationship skills. Yet there is a tremendous need to recognize and understand that young men and women do need some guidance as they negotiate so many new types of relationships (Pipher, 1994; Pollack, 1998). Pollack (1998), for example, starts his book *Real Boys* with the assertion that "boys today are in serious trouble" (p. xxi) because of confusions they experience regarding the development of healthy relationships. Pipher (1994) makes a similar argument regarding young women, who, she contends, are bewildered by conflicting expectations regarding how they should participate in relationships. The fact that these books have been bestsellers may in part reflect the culture's readiness to engage in a larger conversation about what constitutes healthy relationships, what skills are necessary for their promotion, and what types of programs are most likely to produce meaningful outcomes.

These are ambitious goals that cannot be addressed solely through the implementation of a relatively limited prevention program. Nevertheless, research has indicated that some basic skills are necessary for the development of healthy relationships, and prevention programs that emphasize skill acquisition can ameliorate some of the psychological, economic, and social costs associated with relationship problems (Drum & Lawler, 1988). These skills include, but are not limited to, the ability to negotiate the increased autonomy that generally accompanies the transition to young adulthood and provides the basis for more mature relationships with parents. In addition, many young adults will be required to interact with a more diverse group of peers and colleagues, including persons of different racial, ethnic, religious, and sexual orientation backgrounds. The development of interpersonal skills to understand and manage the conflicts that sometimes emerge between groups is another necessary relationship skill often formed at this stage of development. Many young adults also become involved in more intimate dating relationships, which require the ability to sustain a commitment to another person. A variety of skills are necessary for healthy dating relationships, including self-awareness, empathy, the ability to communicate feelings, sexual decision making, and conflict resolution. Finally, many young adults are developing more complex professional relationships with supervisors, faculty, and advisers, which require, among other things, the recognition of power differentials and the ability to work within these boundaries.

Numerous psychological, social, and economic costs are directly and indirectly associated with unhealthy relationships. Some of these costs are borne primarily by individuals in the form of social isolation, loneliness, anxiety, depression, low self-esteem, low self-confidence, shame, alcoholism, and substance abuse. These intrapersonal issues also have social dimensions that may include academic difficulties, employment problems, legal concerns, and increased health care utilization. The interpersonal costs associated with unhealthy relationships range from conflicts with roommates to dating abuse and sexual assault. In fact, some of the most problematic issues currently facing society are related to the violence frequently associated with various types of young adult relationships. The statistics on domestic violence, battering, sexual assault, and hate crimes testify to the extensive personal and social repercussions of unhealthy relationships.

This chapter examines four relationship categories: family or origin, peer/friendship, romantic, and professional/collegial relationships. The primary emphasis is to evaluate the skills necessary to navigate successfully through these various types of relationships and review the types of developmental interventions currently being used in college and university settings. By narrowing the focus in this way, it is possible to examine a variety of programs that have been designed specifically to enhance the relationship skills of young adults and reduce the risk of interpersonal violence and other deleterious outcomes. The chapter concludes with recommendations for conducting assessment and evaluation of programs designed to promote healthy decision making in relationships.

All the programs reviewed in this chapter originated on college and university campuses, but nothing is intrinsic to the programs that binds them to this context. The relationship issues that these programs have been designed to address are broader than any particular institutional setting, and it is our contention that the majority of programs described in this chapter are relevant to young adults not attending colleges or universities. In fact, comparable programs have frequently been developed elsewhere and have similar goals and purposes. The structured theme groups described in this chapter, for example, are similar to those being run in some community mental health centers. In addition, civic groups and local, faith-based organizations have begun to develop programs that examine sexual orientation differences and seek improved understanding, tolerance, and acceptance. In addition, many communities have developed programs that promote dialogue between groups of different ethnic, religious, and socioeconomic backgrounds. These examples illustrate that the programs described in this chapter are representative of the kinds of approaches being developed to assist young adults in developing healthy relationship skills irrespective of their academic and vocational choices.

FAMILY-OF-ORIGIN RELATIONSHIPS

The perception that adolescence is a period of "storm and stress" has an extensive history in the psychological literature, beginning with Hall's (1904) early work on the subject. Although contemporary psychologists have increasingly emphasized individual and cultural differences in how adolescents manage the developmental tasks of this period (Offer & Shonert-Reichl, 1992), they agree that adolescence is a particularly difficult developmental period for many individuals. Arnett (1999), for example, defined conflict with parents, mood disruptions, and risk behavior as the three key elements of adolescence. Moreover, it is also apparent that these developmental issues are frequently still present in early adulthood (Kett, 1977). This section examines how two of the issues identified by Arnett—mood disruptions and conflict with parents—affect the relationships between young adults and their families of origin. The issue of risk behaviors is addressed in a later section.

The presence of mood disruptions have been identified as a facet of adolescent and young adult existence (Arnett, 1999), and the factors that appear responsible for the mood disruptions evident in adolescence are often still present in the lives of young adults. Among college students who were seeking mental health services at university counseling centers, for example, anxiety and depression were two of the most frequently reported symptoms (Drum & Baron, 1998). The early adult years are a time of significant transition, which may be accompanied by predictable mood disruptions that can adversely affect relationships with family and peers. Many young adults experience low self-confidence, social isolation, romantic rejections, poor academic performance, uncertainty about the professional identity, and family discord. In addition, college students often face the challenge of developing a new peer group with a far more diverse cohort than they had encountered in their home communities.

Hallett and Carter (1995) developed a structured theme group titled Experiencing and Expressing Emotions, which focuses on how early childhood experiences influence the way affect becomes incorporated into the emotional life of adults. The group used a variety of formats, including didactic training, structured exercises, psychoeducational materials, interpersonal process, and homework assignments to assist group members with the task of incorporating emotion into their everyday lives. The authors presumed that the family of origin constitutes the learning environment in which children begin to understand their emotional life and assumed that many group members experienced difficulties identifying, interpreting, and communicating their feelings.

The interplay between emotional functioning and relationships has been a consistent theme in the group. The structured exercises, for example, are designed to encourage group members to identify their emotional reactions to relationship events. Some group members may have difficulty acknowledging feelings of anger in relationships, whereas others may rely exclusively on anger because they feel uncomfortable with feelings of sadness or rejection. These structured exercises may also reveal the existence of family messages regarding emotions such as "Feelings are private," "Your feelings aren't important," or "You aren't entitled to your feelings." Once these family messages are identified, group members can determine how they have affected present relationships and consider alternative ways of experiencing and expressing their emotions.

In addition to mood disruptions, the tasks of separation, individuation, and identity formation are frequently a source of conflict between young adults and their parents. A national survey of college students who were seeking mental health services at university counseling centers, for example, revealed that 43% of students had experienced "frequent family arguments" (Drum & Baron, 1998). These conflicts often emerge as adolescents achieve more autonomy and make an increasing number of independent decisions regarding dating relationships, sexuality, curfews, alcohol and substance use, academic responsibilities, and financial obligations. These conflicts also may serve a useful function, because they provide young adults with the opportunity to clarify values and develop more autonomy while they are still reliant on their parents for guidance and direction (Steinberg, 1990). Nevertheless, the presence of excessive conflict can be detrimental to the relationships between young adults and their parents. Therefore, a successful transition between adolescence and young adulthood requires a variety of communication, negotiation, and conflict resolution skills.

Powell and Carter (1996) designed a structured theme group titled My Family/My Self for young adults who want to engage in a process of "exploration, identification, observation, and appreciation" of their family histories and personal identity (p. 2). The group examines family dynamics from a variety of perspectives, which include family roles, communication styles, physical and emotional boundaries, and the experiences of emotional safety and vulnerability. A principal goal of the group is the development of skills and resources that will allow individual group members to more effectively manage issues such as family conflict. The group encourages individuals to identify what factors have been responsible for family discord and to formulate alternative coping strategies. In addition, the group recognizes that culture, religion, and social class mediate how group members will experience their family of origin. Consideration is given to these individual differences.

These structured theme groups recognize that young adults frequently bring the interpersonal and emotional conflicts initially experienced in their family of origin with them to college. Sometimes, young adults hope that the transition from family life to college will enable them to separate from their families and leave their childhood problems behind. Unfortunately, young adults frequently encounter similar problems in the relationships they develop with friends, colleagues, and partners. These structured theme groups strive to prevent the repetition of these familial patterns of interpersonal conflict, neglect, abuse, and addiction by providing young adults with the skills necessary to identify how specific problems have affected their family lives and to apply these insights to issues they are facing as young adults.

PEER/FRIENDSHIP RELATIONSHIPS

The most significant change in higher education during the past several decades may have been the dramatic change in the composition of students who are attending college (Levine & Cureton, 1998). A recent survey by the U.S. Department of Education (1996) indicated that fewer than 16% of undergraduates conform to the conventional image of a full-time student, 19 to 22 years old, and living on campus. In addition, these progressive changes in student demographics have been mirrored by changes that are occurring in the broader culture. Sue and Sue (1999) report that more than one third of the current American population consists of ethnic minorities, and projections indicate that the United States will have a majority minority culture sometime between 2003 and 2005 (see also U.S. Bureau of the Census, 1992b).

As college campuses have become increasingly diverse institutions, the need to develop a more tolerant and affirming social climate has been an important topic for the past several decades (Perry, 1968). The importance of cross-cultural understanding has been further emphasized in recent years by the continued occurrence of hate crimes or bias-related incidents on college campuses (Beckham, 1981), which include verbal harassment, physical assault, racial slurs, and the use of racial stereotypes. Far from subsiding, there is convincing evidence that the prevalence of these bias-related incidents continues to increase (see Hively, 1990; Levine & Cureton, 1998). Dalton (1991) has proposed that "bias-related incidents are predictable outcomes of increasingly self-interested values and limited personal experience with racial and ethnic diversity [among students]" (p. 3).

A variety of factors are probably responsible for the increase in bias-related incidents on campuses, but limited contact between racial and ethnic groups may be especially relevant. There have been widespread concerns that college students do not understand or appreciate other cultures (Ikenberry, 1988) and that they have increasingly fragmented into homogeneous groups that seldom communicate with one another (Levine & Cureton, 1998). The experience of diversity itself has become more threatening to college students, who often perceive themselves to be increasingly isolated on their campuses and are uncomfortable socializing with peers of other races (Levine & Cureton, 1998). Some authors have suggested that the adjustment to a diverse peer culture in college may be somewhat less difficult for African American, Latino, and Asian American students because many will have already lived in a multicultural world (Dalton, 1991). Nevertheless, the segregated social climate that exists on many college campuses impedes intercultural dialogue and prevents the sort of mutual understanding that can challenge racial and ethnic stereotypes, reduce prejudice and oppression, and facilitate peer relationships among diverse groups.

The Program on Intergroup Relations, Conflict, and Community (Program on Intergroup Relations, 1999) developed at the University of Michigan was initiated in the late 1980s in response to heightened racial and ethnic tensions on that campus. The program sought to "advance student understanding of and respect for diversity and to augment [skills] in responding to intergroup conflicts" (p. 1) by engaging students who represent at least two different social identity groups in semester-long dialogue courses. The intergroup dialogue groups have focused on issues of race, ethnicity, gender, sexual orientation, social class, physical ability or disability, and religion. The groups are facilitated by trained peer educators who emphasize listening and dialogue rather than debate, challenge the existence of stereotypes, prejudice, and privilege, encourage the productive resolution of intergroup conflicts, and collaborate in the development of constructive solutions.

The University of Illinois at Urbana-Champaign developed a similar program in 1994, which provides students with the knowledge and skills necessary to participate in culturally diverse group interactions (Landrum-Brown & Khuri, 1998). The program recognizes that topics related to multiculturalism and social justice are threatening to many undergraduate students, and without adequate preparation, participants in the intergroup dialogues frequently become defensive, contentious, or silent. To ameliorate these difficulties, the program has an educational component that provides participants with a background in social justice issues such as racism, oppression, and privilege so that they become more prepared to engage in intergroup dialogues. A three-semester course sequence is offered, for example, that provides instruction in social justice issues, group facilitation, and supervised experiences as a peer group facilitator of intergroup dialogues. The program has found that intergroup conflicts frequently persist, but students who have participated in the dialogue courses have achieved greater understanding of how intercultural differences affect the perceptions and experiences of their peers (Landrum-Brown & Khuri, 1998).

These intergroup dialogue programs provide a context in which students can examine a variety of group identities and develop greater understanding, appreciation, and acceptance of peers who represent different social identity groups. In addition, the programs encourage students to "reformulate their own communicative strategies as questions of social justice and awareness are brought to the fore" (Program on Intergroup Relations, 1999, p. 1). The opportunity to engage in sustained discussion with peers who represent different social identity groups can result in the identification of shared values, comparable interests, and similar concerns that may have been obscured by persistent conflict and the emphasis on intergroup differences. The initial recognition of these communalities may pave the way toward stronger peer relationships, irrespective of social identity differences, and provide the basis for a more tolerant and affirming community.

Another concern on many college campuses has been the social climate for gay, lesbian, and bisexual students, and especially the continued presence of homophobia, prejudice, and interpersonal violence. The coming-out process, which frequently begins during late adolescence and extends through the early adult years, is complicated by the harmful myths and stereotypes that pervade the social discourse regarding sexual orientation. The development of a positive sexual identity is further hindered by the lack of an affirming social environment for gay, lesbian, and bisexual persons. These factors contribute to the social isolation, internalized homophobia, and self-acceptance difficulties that may impede the development of peer group relationships between gay, lesbian, and bisexual students and their heterosexual counterparts.

The University of California at Los Angeles has developed a program for mentoring gay, lesbian, and bisexual persons with a primary goal of providing resources to students who are experiencing difficulties with self-acceptance, identity confusion, and coming-out issues (Alford-Keating, 1999). The mentors are themselves gay, lesbian, or bisexual students, faculty, and staff who understand and appreciate the difficulties associated with self-acceptance, coming out, and making connections with positive role models. The program encourages mentors to challenge negative and inaccurate stereotypes of gay, lesbian, and bisexual persons and provide alternative ways of understanding sexual identity. The mentoring program recognizes that transformation of the social climate for gay, lesbian, and bisexual persons will often be a long-term endeavor, and in the short term, exposure to positive role models and connections with a supportive community are meaningful outcomes.

The programs described in this section are examples of how colleges and universities can become involved in fostering positive peer group relationships among young adults. As college and university campuses have become increasingly diverse institutions, however, it has also become more apparent that how young adults interact with and relate to one another is a political issue. The involvement of universities in these programs has been controversial on some campuses, as indicated by a recent court decision that prevented the use of mandatory student fees at the University of Wisconsin to support initiatives that appear to advance specific political agendas (Guernsey, 1996). These political issues cannot be entirely disentangled from questions about the types of peer group relationships young adults are developing, because whom we consider to be a part of our communities has always been a moral, ethical, and political issue. These programs and others like them do not evade difficult issues such as social justice and civic virtue but, rather, include them as part of their analysis of peer group relationships.

ROMANTIC RELATIONSHIPS

Young adults encounter numerous challenges as they attempt to form meaningful romantic relationships. Many of these challenges have been exacerbated by a "retreat from intimacy," according to Levine and Cureton (1998), which has altered the traditional structure of dating relationships. These authors report that the dating relationship has largely been replaced on college campuses by "group dating," which allows peer groups to socialize with one another without forming committed relationships. The social activities available for group dating are diverse, but the activity most frequently cited by college students in a recent survey involved alcohol consumption (Wechsler, 1996). This fact is alarming, considering the concomitant increase in binge drinking in recent years, which may increase the risk of interpersonal violence. The Commission on Substance Abuse at Colleges and Universities (1994), for example, found that 90% of all rapes that occur on college campuses involve alcohol consumption.

Although group dating appears to have become more common in recent years, many young adults continue to form intimate relationships with a single partner. These couples will face many challenges, which run the gamut from sustaining a long-distance relationship to coping with family reactions to an intercultural or interracial dating relationship. Moreover, a lesbian, gay, or bisexual couple may encounter homophobia, prejudice, harassment, or violence, which complicates the coming-out process and may contribute to stress within the relationship. In addition, sexual decisions often need to be made in romantic relationships, which may include the choice to remain abstinent, selection of birth control, and STD/HIV prevention. This section reviews a sample of prevention programs designed to assist young adults in managing some of these relationship issues.

The University of Illinois at Urbana-Champaign has developed a program called Tuesdays at 7, which offers a series of workshops designed in part to address the concerns of college students, including relationship concerns. These workshops are frequently well attended, and evaluations from participants indicate that programs focusing on relationship issues are among the most beneficial. The workshop titles during the past several years have included Intercultural/ Interracial Dating Relationships, Loving in a Long-Distance Relationship, Is It Love or Infatuation?, and When Your Relationship Ends. These workshops use a semistructured format, which allows workshop leaders to present didactic information and facilitate group discussion. The workshops are peer facilitated by trained paraprofessionals, which allows students to interact with other students on relationship topics. The workshop goals include the provision of basic information on specific relationship issues, self-assessment of relationship concerns, and normalization of various relationship difficulties.

A more comprehensive prevention program has been developed by Hallett and Shan-Dechaine (1992), who designed a structured theme group called Women, Identity, and Intimacy With Men. The authors contend that Western cultural values encourage heterosexual women to focus their attention on finding and keeping a man, which Gilbert (1988) termed the "over-valuation of love." An intimate relationship with a man was traditionally considered to be desirable because it offered the promise of lifelong security. As women attended to the emotional needs of men, many neglected their own emotional lives due to concerns that it might disrupt the relationship. As a result, some women may have attained a committed relationship, but it was at the expense of themselves.

The group assists participants in recognizing cultural influences on women's identity development and encourage them to seek a balance between connection and autonomy in their relationships. The group examines gender-role expectations, for example, which often encourage women to be responsible for the emotional well-being of the relationship. The group explores potential adverse consequences of these gender-role expectations and proposed alternative ways of constructing relationships. The group participants frequently describe their interactions with men as more intimate after they engaged in more equitable relationships.

The problem of date or acquaintance rape has also become an increasing concern, especially since the advent of the drug Rohypnol (Smith, Wesson, & Calhoun, 1997), and many colleges and universities have attempted to develop successful prevention programs to address the problem. The University of Illinois at Urbana-Champaign, for example, initiated a mandatory First Year Care program in 1995, which focused on sexual assault violence prevention. The workshops are conducted by trained peer educators, who facilitate gender-specific group discussions that focus on sexual assault avoidance strategies for women and issues of consent for men. In addition, a short film addressing the dynamics of sexual assault in acquaintance and dating relationships is presented to all participants. These workshops are designed to promote increased awareness of violence potential in relationships and to encourage risk reduction behaviors between men and women.

As more attention has been paid to violence prevention on college and university campuses, it has become apparent that these institutions can play a role in promoting healthy romantic and dating relationships. Many of the programs being developed are utilizing technology and other innovative program designs to convey their messages to young adults. These programs have increasingly recognized the complexity of issues facing young adults who are participating in romantic relationships, and the programs have incorporated education on such topics as alcohol and substance abuse because of its correlation with interpersonal violence. The Alcohol 101 CD-ROM (Reis & Riley, 1997), for example, enables participants to engage in self-assessment of their alcohol and substance abuse patterns and determine whether they may potentially be at risk for interpersonal violence. These programs, which combine an emphasis on acquisition of relationship skills while recognizing violence potential, are particularly encouraging developments.

PROFESSIONAL/COLLEGIAL RELATIONSHIPS

Many young adults develop their first important professional relationships during college, and the skills acquired during these years will form the basis for future relationships with colleagues, mentors, and supervisors. Although young adults will have had previous experiences with high school teachers, sports coaches, or employers, the professional relationships formed during the early adult years often provide the opportunity to refine interpersonal skills necessary for the workplace. In addition to the technical skills required for professional work, young adults are also developing the communication, negotiation, conflict resolution, and diplomatic skills that will facilitate interactions with colleagues and enhance their productivity.

Young adults are developing professional relationship skills in a variety of contexts. Many college students, for example, are working part-time or full-time while completing their degrees. Levine and Cureton (1998) report that at least 60% of students work part-time while attending college, and 24% of undergraduate students attending 4-year universities and 39% of students at 2-year colleges were working full-time while attending school. These statistics represent substantial increases from previous generations of college students (Levine & Cureton, 1998). The remarkable number of students working while pursuing their education suggests that they are developing and utilizing relationship skills in the workplace at an earlier age than did their counterparts from previous generations, particularly those students already employed in a professional capacity.

In addition to these workplace relationships, many college students have the opportunity to develop research projects that enable them to collaborate with faculty on topics that range from research design and methodology to data analysis and interpretation. These interactions between students and faculty often extend beyond scientific topics and may include interpersonal issues such as distribution of responsibilities, supervision and evaluation of work, group decision making, disagreement, and compromise. Lovitts (1996) reported, for example, that recent graduates of doctoral programs cite positive working relationships with their advisers as a key element to a successful graduate education. Moreover, poor adviser-student relationships were a primary factor in the attrition of doctoral students, particularly those who left relatively late in their graduate careers (Nerad & Miller, 1996). This section discusses intervention programs designed to improve relationships between graduate students and their advisers, although it should be emphasized that many of the conflict resolution skills examined are applicable to other professional relationships.

The adviser-student relationship is not only professionally important to graduate students, but it is also an emotionally significant relationship. The relationship frequently becomes a crucible through which graduate students attempt to resolve questions of competency, self-confidence, and creativity. Ideally, graduate students participate in a variety of mentoring relationships with faculty, which provide the students with opportunities to develop the intellectual and technical skills necessary to succeed in the workplace. The adviser-student relationship sometimes becomes fettered by conflict, however, particularly in failed expectations. Many graduate students desire approval from their advisers, for example, and feelings of disappointment and resentment are common whenever students perceive their advisers to be indifferent to their work. The power differential between the faculty adviser and graduate student sometimes exacerbates these negative feelings and can be a source of conflict that impedes productive work. The perception that graduate school is a culture of "passive neglect" and the appearance of graduate student unions on many campuses may be signals of a broad-based discontent.

The Graduate School at Michigan State University has initiated a program called Setting Expectations and Resolving Conflict (Klomparens & Beck, 1998) designed to improve the communication, negotiation, and conflict resolution skills of faculty and graduate students. The program use a series of video vignettes to illustrate the types of conflicts that can emerge between faculty and graduate students while providing a basis for discussion. The program also introduces "interest-based negotiation strategies" to faculty and graduate students, which offer specific skills in setting expectations and resolving conflicts. Klomparens and Beck (1998) report that "interest-based negotiation strategies focus on the underlying interests and concerns of the involved parties, with an emphasis on crafting options that satisfy multiple parties and their interests" (p. 2).

The program assumes that all conflict cannot be avoided, because contrasting viewpoints on ideas is a necessary aspect of academic discourse and graduate education. The program focuses instead on how traditional negotiation frequently impedes conflict resolution, because both parties become increasingly committed to their positions and focus on differences between them. An interest-based negotiation strategy, by contrast, addresses the problem and not the people involved in the conflict. A primary goal of interest-based negotiation is the development of options that advance the shared interests of both parties and emphasize values of fairness and equity. The criteria developed must take into account the inherent power differentials in graduate education, but flexibility is expected from both parties. A successful negotiation should generate a variety of options for consideration and provide the opportunity for compromise.

The conflict resolution program developed at Michigan State University provides graduate students with the skills and resources necessary to engage in constructive negotiations with colleagues, faculty, and advisers and seeks to preempt the negative outcomes sometimes associated with protracted conflicts, which sometimes result in formal grievances, interpersonal violence, and suicide. In addition, the program recognizes that the next generation of faculty will be comprised of today's graduate students. It is hoped that graduate students who have received training in interest-based negotiation skills will be more effective faculty, advisers, and mentors for future generations of students.

SUMMARY

The focus of this chapter has been on promoting healthy relationship decisions in young adults, with special attention being devoted to the types of developmental interventions currently being used in college and university settings. The chapter has also highlighted those programs that emphasize primary prevention of relationship concerns. The interest in primary prevention has often necessitated the development of innovative programs that depart from standard practices and procedures. A recent survey of university counseling centers, for example, indicated that almost one quarter of staff time is currently devoted to outreach and consultation activities (Stone & Archer, 1990), which represents a substantial departure from previous decades, in which the emphasis was primarily on clinical services (see Chickering, 1969). Although not all the programs described in this chapter are university counseling center initiatives, nor are they all outreach and consultation programs, these statistics do suggest the extent of change that higher education institutions have made to assist young adults make healthy decisions in their relationships and prevent more serious problems from occurring in the first place.

Along with these changes in the types of programmatic work frequently being conducted within student affairs divisions at many colleges and universities, a new emphasis has been made on assessment and evaluation as a means of demonstrating the effectiveness of these services. The goals of assessment are generally considered distinct from those of research (see Erwin, 1991), be-cause the former emphasizes the effectiveness of a single program in a particu-lar institutional context whereas the latter focuses on the analysis of empirical data and the formulation of theory. In order to conduct a comprehensive as-sessment of student affairs programs, Upcraft and Schuh (1996) suggest that the focus should be on basic questions regarding program effectiveness. These questions should include information on who uses the program, demographic data on whether attendees are representative of the campus population, assess-ment of client needs (e.g., do those individuals attending alcohol awareness programs identify as binge drinkers?), evaluation of client satisfaction, and as-sessment of changes to the campus environment and culture.

The challenge facing student affairs divisions will be to demonstrate that programs that are intended to promote healthy decision making in relation-ships are in fact effective in reaching these goals. Administrators will generally want to know, at a minimum, what the goals of the program are, what types of outcomes are desired, and if the program was successful in achieving these out-comes. Moreover, it may also be important to demonstrate that improvements in the quality of relationships have a bearing on the academic mission of the university or the campus climate. Therefore, outcomes that demonstrate a pos-itive correlation with student retention, learning, campus culture, or academic success are especially helpful. A campus that begins to use the Alcohol 101 CD-ROM as part of freshman orientation, for example, may use interpersonal violence statistics to determine whether there is a decrease in these incidents following the adoption of the program.

Another example of these types of assessments is being conducted by Khuri (2001), who is examining how anxiety mediates involvement in intergroup di-alogue. This assessment focuses on how anxiety may limit some individuals from participating in intergroup dialogue exercises, which reduces opportuni-ties to learn about, interact with, and develop understanding of persons with different cultural backgrounds. A primary objective of the intergroup dialogue program is to decrease harmful stereotypes that have been shown to provoke intergroup conflict on college and university campuses. Khuri observes that "the nature of the intergroup dialogue process entails that students have some capacity to tolerate affect, ambiguity, and multiple perspectives" (p. 16) and that fears about negative experiences such as intergroup conflict cause suffi-cient anxiety for some persons that they withdraw from the process. Informa-tion from this assessment will be used to evaluate ways of increasing the emo-tional safety of individuals enrolled in the course so that they can participate more fully in the intergroup dialogue exercises.

The development of an increasing number of programs targeting relation-ship concerns on college and university campuses has partly been a response to the recognition that many young adults are experiencing serious relationship problems. Stone and Archer (1990), for example, note that "larger numbers of students are coming to our campuses with psychological problems that have difficult and complicated antecedents, [including] sexual, physical and emotional abuse, alcoholic and dysfunctional families, sexual violence, and substance abuse" (p. 559). All these issues are either the result of relationship dysfunction or will inevitably lead to relationship concerns. Likewise, Levine and Cureton (1998) report that "one of the things undergraduates have been most eager to escape is intimate relationships" (p. 109), which appears at least partly to be a response to the psychological issues students bring to campus. In their study, Levine and Cureton (1998) found that "again and again, deans of students reported on the growing rate of dysfunctional families among their students. They talked of violence; instability; blended families; and emotional, sexual, and financial problems" (p. 95). Many of the programs described in this chapter were developed to assist young adults in coping with relationship concerns that have their origins in the family.

The chapter has also examined some of the interpersonal skills young adults will require to negotiate successfully the peer group, romantic, and professional relationships they are forming at this stage of their lives. The increasing diversity of college and university campuses as well as demographic changes throughout the United States suggest that young adults will be socializing with peers and colleagues who represent different racial, ethnic, social class, and sexual orientation backgrounds. The heterogeneity of U.S. society presents new challenges to peer group relationships that are being addressed through initiatives such as the Program on Intergroup Relations, which brings students from diverse backgrounds together for the purposes of dialogue and understanding. Finally, the chapter has discussed some of the relationship skills, tasks, and issues that are imperative for the successful transition from adolescence to young adulthood. The desire to develop long-term committed relationships with a partner, the need to develop intimate relationships unfettered by violence, and the opportunity to work with professional colleagues, advisers, and mentors are significant developmental milestones for many young adults. It is hoped that programs such as those described in this chapter will play a role in promoting healthy decision making in these relationships.

VIGNETTE

As a mental health professional at a university counseling center, you have become aware that many college students routinely use e-mail and Internet chat rooms to meet people and develop relationships. Some of your clients have reported meeting romantic partners though the Internet, and others are talking regularly in various chat rooms. A large number of students routinely communicate with parents and family via the Internet. You have also found that students are increasingly utilizing the Internet to communicate with faculty, advisers, prospective employers, and other professional colleagues. Many of your clients describe the Internet and chat rooms as "a tool" they use, but others have expressed concerns about the relationships they have developed through this medium. Some of these concerns include compulsive use of the Internet, e-mail harassment, and compromised safety (e.g., agreeing to meet in person someone met over the Internet).

You have been assigned the task of developing either a brochure or workshop to help students consider how they are utilizing technology to initiate, develop, and maintain relationships. You should consider the following questions as you design the brochure or workshop:

1. What are the goals and objectives of the brochure or workshop?

2. What are the critical issues that should be addressed in this brochure or workshop?

3. What relationship skills are being expressed through the Internet and chat rooms, and how does the use of technology facilitate or impede intimacy?

4. What types of risks should the brochure or workshop mention, and what kinds of prevention strategies can be recommended?

ADDITIONAL RESOURCES

Print Resources

Bass, E. (1996). *Free your mind: The book for gay, lesbian and bisexual youth—and their allies.* New York: HarperPerennial.

Betz, N. E., & Fitzgerald, L. F. (Eds.). (1987). *The career psychology of women.* Orlando, FL: Academic Press.

Burns, D. D. (1985). *Intimate connections.* New York: Penguin.

Chen, G., & Starosta, W. J. (1998). *Foundations of intercultural communication.* Needham Heights, MA: Allyn & Bacon.

Eichenbaum, L., & Orbach, S. (1987). *Between women: Love, envy, and competition in women's friendships.* New York: Penguin.

Fisher, R., Ury, W., & Patton, B. (1991). *Getting to yes: Negotiating agreement without giving in.* New York: Penguin.

Hallett, M. B., & Shan-Dechaine, T. (1992). *Women, identity, and intimacy with men.* Unpublished manuscript, University of Texas at Austin. Inquiries should be made to Marybeth Hallett, University of Illinois at Urbana-Champaign, Counseling Center, 610 East John Street, 110 Turner Student Services Building, Champaign, IL 61820.

Lerner, H. G. (1989). *The dance of intimacy: A woman's guide to courageous acts of change in key relationships.* New York: Harper & Row.

Levine, A., & Cureton, J. S. (1998). *When hope and fear collide: A portrait of today's college student.* San Francisco: Jossey-Bass.

Napier, A. Y. (1988). *The fragile bond: In search of an equal, intimate and enduring marriage.* New York: Harper & Row.

Napier, A. Y., & Whitaker, C. A. (1978). *The family crucible.* New York: Harper & Row.

Wolin, S. J., & Wolin, S. (1993). *The resilient self.* New York: Warner.

Audiovisual Resources

Mosbacher, D., Reid, F., & Rhue, S. (Producers/Directors). (1996). *All God's children* [Film]. (Available from Woman Vision Films, San Francisco, CA)

Reid, F. (Producer/Director). (1995). *Skin deep: College students confront racism* [Film]. (Available from Iris Films, San Francisco, CA)

Reis, J., & Riley, W. (1997). *Alcohol 101* [CD-ROM]. Urbana-Champaign: University of Illinois Board of Trustees and The Century Council. (Inquiries should be made to Ilene Harned, University of Illinois at Urbana-Champaign, Alcohol and Other Drug Office, McKinley Health Center, Urbana, IL 61801.)

Wah, L. M. (Producer/Director). (1994). *The color of fear* [Film]. (Available from Stir-Fry Productions, Oakland, CA)

Presentations

Alford-Keating, P. (1999, March). *Mentoring for gay, lesbian, bi and transgender students: We get by with a little help from our friends.* Paper presented at the annual conference of the American College Personnel Association, Atlanta, GA. Inquiries should be made to Pat Alford-Keating, University of California at Los Angeles, Student Psychological Services, Box 951556, Los Angeles, CA 90095-1556.

Hallett, M. B., & Carter, A. L. (1995, February). *Experiencing and expressing emotion: A structured theme group approach to working with affect.* Paper presented at the Big Ten Counseling Center Conference, Ann Arbor, MI. Inquiries should be made to Marybeth Hallett, University of Illinois at Urbana-Champaign, Counseling Center, 610 E. John Street, 110 Turner Student Services Building, Champaign, IL 61820.

Powell, J. D., & Carter, A. L. (1996, February). *My family/My self: Examining the past for a better present.* Paper presented at the Big Ten Counseling Center Conference, State College, PA. Inquiries should be made to John D. Powell, University of Illinois at Urbana-Champaign, Counseling Center, 610 East John Street, 110 Turner Student Services Building, Champaign, IL 61820.

Programs

First Year Care. Inquiries should be made to Patricia Morey, University of Illinois at Urbana-Champaign, Office of Women's Programs, 610 East John Street, Turner Student Services Building, Champaign, IL 61820.

Tuesdays at 7. Inquiries should be made to John D. Powell, University of Illinois at Urbana-Champaign, Counseling Center, 610 East John Street, 110 Turner Student Services Building, Champaign, IL 61820.

Internet Resources

Klomparens, K., & Beck, J. (1998). *Setting expectations and resolving conflict: Michigan State University.* http://www.msu.edu/user/gradschl/conflict/proposal.htm
Inquiries should be made to Karen Klomparens, Associate Dean, The Graduate School, 118 Linton Hall, Michigan State University, East Lansing, MI 48824.

Landrum-Brown, J., & Khuri, L. (1998). *Program on intergroup relations: University of Illinois at Urbana-Champaign.* http://www.intergrouprelations.uiuc.edu
Inquiries should be made to Joycelyn Landrum-Brown, University of Illinois at Urbana-Champaign, Counseling Center, 610 East John Street, 110 Turner Student Services Building, Champaign, IL 61820.

Program on Intergroup Relations. (1999). *The program on intergroup relations, conflict, and community: University of Michigan at Ann Arbor.*
http://www.umich. edu/~igrc/index.html
Inquiries should be made to the Coordinator of the Program on Intergroup Relations, Conflict and Community, Michigan Union, Room 3000, 530 South State Street, Ann Arbor, MI 48109-1349.

CHAPTER 12

Promoting Parenting and Child-Rearing Skills

Stephanie San Miguel Bauman

Whether through pregnancy, adoption, or the assumption of stepparent status, many young adults become parents and, in the process, experience the excitement and the challenge of a new role. "Parents protect the child's health, transmit social and cultural tradition, are the principal guides for the young child's development as a thinking, acting, and feeling person, and are the unique persons who enable the child to experience intimacy, security and love" (Beckwith, 1990, p. 400). Faced with the charge of raising children who will become productive adults, parents grapple with issues of providing discipline, nurturing self-esteem, developing independence, instilling responsibility, and improving communication skills (Conroy & Mayer, 1994). Meanwhile, parents must also attend to other relationships within and outside the family (Seitz & Provence, 1990). A child with a difficult temperament, a parent's own limited psychological resources, or stress in the ecosystem in which the family lives might present additional challenges (Belsky, 1984; Strand & Wahler, 1996). Clearly, parenthood is demanding and generates both emotional and practical stress (Silverstein & Auerbach, 1999).

Despite its complexity as a multilevel, multiskill task that changes over time, parenting often is assumed to be a skill that comes naturally (Einzig, 1996). Research on parenting behaviors during the newborn period and 1 year later (e.g., Lamb, 1987) challenges this assumption. Neither mothers nor fathers necessarily are "natural" parents at the newborn stage. Most young adults who become parents learn how to parent from the parenting practices of their own parents (Santrock, 1986) or on a trial-and-error basis (Gladding, 1999). They often rely on the informal support of extended family, friends, and neighbors for emotional support and concrete or material assistance with parenting (Keller & McDade, 2000). Meanwhile, they may sort through plentiful yet frequently contradictory advice on topics such as basic child care and discipline (Scarr, 1984). Fortunately, although parenting does not necessarily come naturally, people can build on relevant skills and develop into sensitive and competent caregivers with experience over time (Kaitz, Chriki, Bear-Scharf, Nir, & Eidelman, 2000).

From their professional vantage point, mental health practitioners appreciate the challenge, the complexity, and the importance of parenting. Seitz and Provence (1990) observe, "A continuum of parental risk conditions exists that ranges from lack of knowledge to alterations in affect and deficits in judgment. The conditions may be either transitory or persistent, and mild or severe" (p. 63). Counselors regularly encounter clients who have experienced or still encounter such risk conditions. Indeed, clients' concerns often may be conceptualized as linked to their current or past experiences with inadequate or harmful parenting. For instance, clients may seek counseling services to come to grips with early experiences with punitive parents or to learn ways to deal with the unruly behavior of their own child.

The costs of not addressing parental risk factors and not promoting child-rearing skills are sobering, as evident in families that are filled with continual conflict, children who develop serious emotional disorders that carry into adulthood, and parents who resort to ineffective, abusive, and potentially lethal methods of discipline. The benefits of promoting parenting skills are equally compelling. Under conducive circumstances, a child can give a parent the gifts of unqualified love, absolute trust, the thrill of discovery, and the heights of emotion. In return, a parent can give a child the gifts of unconditional love, self-esteem, value and traditions, joy in life, good health, secure surroundings, and skills and abilities (Shelov, 1993). Even children raised under dire circumstances such as poverty, parental alcoholism, or war are more likely to circumvent risk factors and demonstrate competence if they bonded with someone who provided them with stable care and adequate and appropriate attention during the first year of their life (Werner, 1990).

Despite the likelihood of encountering client issues related to parenting, training in working with parents as part of counselor preparation is often lacking. For example, in one survey of elementary, middle or junior high, and high school counselors in the state of Ohio, only 21.6% of the participants had received specific training in working with parents (Ritchie & Partin, 1994). Growing numbers of counselors, however, are assuming a more preventive and proactive stance and turning their attention to parent support and education in addition to the more traditional functions of a counselor (Einzig, 1996).

This chapter examines key aspects of parenting and ways counselors can promote child-rearing skills. First, while acknowledging changing views of children and child rearing, dimensions of effective parenting and specific parenting behaviors are reviewed. Second, a broadened role for counselors is introduced. This view of the counselor supplements traditional counselor activities with preventive, proactive activities.

The chapter ends with a discussion of how mental health practitioners can respond to different levels of parent involvement in counseling services and to multicultural issues in the promotion of child-rearing skills. Helping professionals tend to view parents who are involved in prevention or intervention programs as "good parents" and parents who refrain from participation as "bad parents" (Fine & Gardner, 1991). A more productive alternative is considered.

Multicultural considerations include the recognition that much theory, practice, and research on parents and families revolves around a model of the European American, middle-class, nuclear family in which a married couple raise their own biologically related children, the father acts as financial provider, and the mother serves as nurturer (Nugent, 2000). This definition overlooks the fact that caregiving functions can be performed by parenting figures of either sex, regardless of their biological relation to the child. It also ignores the fact that positive child outcomes can be attained in diverse family structures, including households with single fathers, two-parent families in which the father is the primary caretaker, and families headed by gay fathers (Silverstein & Auerbach, 1999). Other diverse family structures are those headed by cohabitating couples, lesbian parents, and a grandparent as primary caretaker. The dramatic rise in different kinds of family structures during the 1980s and the steady increase of non-White immigrants to the United States underscore the importance of counselors' considering and being responsive to the wider contexts of race, gender, ethnicity, and culture when working with parents (Sciarra, 1999).

PARENTING

Throughout history, Western views of children and the practice of child rearing have changed as times changed. Initially, in light of alarming infant and child mortality rates, the question was not how to parent children but, rather, whether people would have children to rear. By the 18th and 19th centuries, the influence of the Industrial Revolution and the "Protestant work ethic" led to an emphasis on strict moral behavior, integrity, honesty, industriousness, orderliness, and courtesy. In the early 20th century, hygiene and prevention of illness were emphasized in an attempt to reduce further the high mortality rates (Grusec & Lytton, 1988). Beginning in the 1920s, debate arose among influential child experts about the nature of children. For instance, Arnold Gesell felt that children possessed an inborn tendency to the best development possible. They could benefit from good parenting but would be largely unaffected by parental mistakes unless abuse and neglect were involved. In contrast, John Watson viewed children as blank pages to be inscribed or malleable material to be shaped through intensive training on the part of their parents (Scarr, 1984). By the 1940s and 1950s, permissive parenting notions derived from Sigmund Freud's theories gained popularity (e.g., Spock, 1946). The conclusion of these post-Freudians (who selectively used and misinterpreted some of Freud's notions) was that a child would grow into a well-adjusted individual if early experiences were pleasurable. Warmth and understanding, rather than frustration, should surround children (Grusec & Lytton, 1988).

Contemporary Western views of children and parenting tend to strike a balance between Gesell and Watson. Scarr (1984) reflects, "Today's child requires less intense parenting to achieve optimum development than the pure Watsonian child. But today's child needs more attention to detail than the pure Gesellian child" (p. 79). Faced with ever-changing views of children and child-rearing practices, parents typically use a combination of several methods to raise their children and will vary them depending on the situation. Whether or not a particular style of parenting is optimal under all circumstances is a matter of debate. In fact, different styles of parenting may be adaptive, depending on circumstances (Grusec & Lytton, 1988).

Undoubtedly, parenting is multidimensional and involves a number of distinct behaviors. Two particular dimensions of parents' child-rearing practices, however, recurrently have emerged in factor analytic studies of parents' child-rearing practices: warmth-hostility and restrictiveness-permissiveness (Grusec & Lytton, 1988). Other labels for these major parenting dimensions are nurturance and control (Jacob, Moser, Windle, Loeber, & Stouthamer-Loeber, 2000). Two specific classes of parenting behavior also have been identified as important in parent-child interactions: attunement and conflict resolution (Strand, White, & Touster, 1998). Our discussion now turns to these parenting dimensions and behaviors.

Dimensions of Parenting

Few people would debate the importance of warmth, an attitudinal dimension of parenting. A warm or nurturing relationship expresses caring, support, and feelings of love and acceptance. Although a warm parent may at times disapprove of a child's negative, unacceptable behavior, the parent remains committed to the child's welfare.

In the research literature, parental warmth has been related to the development of a child's internalized moral orientation, compliance, cognitive competence, achievement, and good social adjustment. Extreme lack of parental warmth has been associated with poor social adjustment on the part of the child. An attitude of warmth is also highly correlated with one of the two parenting behaviors that will be discussed later in the chapter, namely a parent's responsiveness to a child's social signals, demands, or distress (Grusec & Lytton, 1988).

Although most people agree that children benefit from parenting that is loving, caring, and supportive, the issue of whether parenting should reflect authoritarian or democratic relationships between adults and children inspires more controversy (Harry, 1997). Research on the issue of control versus permissiveness is exemplified by the work of Diana Baumrind (1971, 1973), who distinguished three parenting styles: authoritarian, authoritative, and permissive. The authoritarian parent values obedience, order, and firm enforcement of rules. This parent discourages independence and restricts the child's autonomy. In turn, the authoritative parent sets standards for behavior and desires compliance with reasonable rules. The authoritative parent, however, also respects and encourages the child's autonomy, individuality, and independence. There is a balance of high control and high responsiveness. When compared with the authoritarian and authoritative parent, the permissive parent refrains from restraining the child's impulses and actions and acts in an affirmative, acceptant manner.

Research on child outcomes related to the various parenting styles suggests that both democracy and control are necessary ingredients of child rearing. For instance, authoritative parenting that balances high control and high responsiveness has been demonstrated to have beneficial and adaptive consequences such as social responsibility, independence, self-esteem, and cognitive competence in children. In contrast, negative effects such as aggression are associated with extreme restrictiveness that is combined with hostile punitiveness or overlax discipline that reflects parental indifference (Grusec & Lytton, 1988).

Parenting Behaviors

Consideration of warmth-hostility and restrictiveness-permissiveness leads to questions about specific parenting behaviors. How is warmth demonstrated? How is parental control reflected in the ability to resolve conflict? As previously mentioned, parental warmth is correlated with responsiveness. The parental behavior of attunement examines the extent to which a parent's behavior is responsive to the child's behavior. Attunement is a necessity from birth and requires a fairly constant process of tracking and responding to the child. Two examples of attunement are the ability to respond to infant signals regarding feeding (Seitz & Provence, 1990) and the capacity to soothe a crying newborn (Kaitz et al., 2000). Conflict resolution, the second type of parenting behavior, includes issues of discipline and behavior control and becomes important once the child grows old enough to display oppositional behavior. Conflict resolution strategies are often situation specific.

The research of Strand and colleagues (Strand & Wahler, 1996; Strand et al., 1998) provides interesting information about factors that impede effective attunement and conflict resolution. Strand and Wahler (1996) found that poor parental attunement behavior was related to parent self-reports of inter-personal difficulties rather than to expressions of personal inadequacy or poor ability to focus on a specific task. In a later study, Strand et al. (1998) found that poor parental conflict resolution behavior (i.e., failure to remain firm in the face of child disobedience) was related to expressions of personal inade-quacy and difficulty remaining focused on a particular task but not to parent self-reports of interpersonal functioning. In short, different factors may get in the way of the effectiveness of different parenting behaviors. By implication, a particular maladaptive parenting behavior may require a specific counseling approach. Indeed, a counselor may find it more productive to explore a client's sense of personal adequacy and competence and less productive to discuss the client's interpersonal relationship issues in the case of clients who struggle with the discipline of their child. Generally, mental health practitioners are advised to consider an approach that combines education about responsiveness and be-havior management with exploration of issues of personal inadequacy, ability to attend to specific tasks, and interpersonal functioning.

PROMOTING PARENTING AND CHILD-REARING SKILLS BY BROADENING THE ROLE OF THE COUNSELOR

How can counselors promote child-rearing skills once they are equipped with knowledge of different dimensions of parenting and specific parenting behav-iors? It stands to reason that some parents may expect mental health practi-tioners to facilitate the development of their skills and resources, whereas oth-ers may expect counselors to provide emotional guidance. Thus, an effective counselor must be prepared to assume a variety of professional functions and roles. Simeonsson and Bailey (1990) have developed a framework that repre-sents the full spectrum of professional involvement in the area of early inter-vention, or the services provided for young children with special needs. This framework can easily be applied to services provided to promote parenting and child-rearing skills. Using a numbering system that reflects a successive in-crease in the active involvement of the practitioner, Simeonsson and Bailey propose the following professional functions: (a) informing families about available services and offering such services, (b) tracking and advising fami-lies, (c) providing or brokering child-related services, (d) consulting or teach-ing families as part of information sharing, (e) working on practical concerns in the role of family advocate and focusing on personal concerns through relationship building, (f) setting goals to develop practical strategies and coordinating resources to help the family manage their ongoing needs and demands, and (g) providing help with psychological or existential issues through counseling or therapy.

Although a growing number of promising parenting support initiatives with core services such as information and knowledge, problem-solving support, and community resource information are being implemented (e.g., Mertensmeyer & Fine, 2000), the discussion of the specific role of mental health practitioners is often truncated. Thus, Simeonsson and Bailey's framework (1990) provides a vehicle for acknowledging ways in which counselors promote parenting and child rearing. The framework supports traditional counselor functions and roles such as individual, couple, and family. It also encourages functions and roles of a preventive, proactive nature. These roles include (a) advocate, mediator, or liaison, (b) consultant, and (c) parent educator. The following section discusses the components of the broadened role for a counselor in greater detail.

Advocate, Mediator, or Liaison

For some families, the first step toward promoting parenting skills may be to address basic survival needs such as acquiring medical care or providing a physically safe environment with opportunities for exploration. Indeed, parents who are without substantial or steady income often find themselves and their children in need of numerous services from an increasingly complex bureaucracy of social, medical, and mental health agencies. Even when services are available, the ability of agencies to make coordinated, effective services accessible is extremely limited (San Miguel, Morrison, & Weissglass, 1995).

Imagine a counselor who literally reaches out to clients in schools and in the community. Picture a counselor who knows about a broad range of educational and support services, who maintains good professional relationships with referral sources, who works to smooth relations between parents and agencies, or who works to change administrative policies and procedures that impede access to services (Fine & Gardner, 1991; Nugent, 2000). In all of these examples, the counselor acts as an advocate or mediator. A related role would be that of a school-home-community liaison who serves as an interface between school and home, school and community, and home and community. This may entail identifying, developing, coordinating, and utilizing the resources of the family, the child's school, and services in the community such as social services, job training, and child care (Atkinson & Juntunen, 1994; Seitz & Provence, 1990). Generally, the responsibilities and functions of an effective liaison will vary with the needs of the parents and child.

Consultant

Consultation with families is a function that increasingly has been assumed by school counselors and mental health practitioners in child guidance clinics and mental health centers (Brown, 1997; Campbell, 1993). Benefits of consultation include an efficient use of time, exploration of multiple factors that contribute to a problem, parent ownership in the creation and implementation of a solution, and increased parent involvement with schools (White & Mullis, 1998). Parents seek consultation as problems associated with their children arise. These problems may be behavioral, attitudinal, or social in nature (Campbell, 1993). For instance, a parent may consult with a school counselor due to concerns about a child's academic performance, lack of friends, low motivation in school, or unruly behavior at home (Nugent, 2000).

Consultation is distinct from counseling in terms of the number of parties involved, the directness of the activity, and the focus of the communication (Gladding, 2000). In consultation, three parties are involved: the consultant (the counselor), the consultee (the parent or parents), and a third party (the child). The parent forms a working relationship with the consultant and receives direct assistance, but the child receives only indirect service from the consultant through the actions of the parent (Dougherty, 1990). The consultant serves as the expert on child development. In turn, the parent is the expert on the child and a key source of information about the child's medical history and social, emotional, and intellectual development (Campbell, 1993). As in other counseling activities, the consultant listens, attends, questions, clarifies, confronts, and summarizes. The initial focus, however, is on content rather than feeling (Gladding, 2000), because consultation is essentially a problem-solving process. The actual solution often involves the acquisition of parenting skills that promote a child's educational and personal functioning. Indeed, changes in the way adults interact with a child or with each other often lead to the desired changes in the child's behavior (White & Mullis, 1998).

Parent Educator

Parent education is a productive and relatively nonthreatening way for a counselor to work with parents (Fine & Gardner, 1991). Given the critical phases of development that take place during pregnancy, parent education also is appropriate and important for expectant parents. In fact, pregnancy often creates much excitement about parenthood, the motivation to be good parents, and a receptivity to advice about parenting (Fox, Bruce, & Combs-Orme, 2000).

A typical format for parent education is a psychoeducational group (Gladding, 1999) that consists of a series of scheduled meetings with a specific agenda and prepared materials. Commonly addressed topics include providing basic child care, understanding child development, building a positive parent-child relationship, establishing effective communication with children, and using positive discipline. Audiovisual aids may be incorporated such as Active Parenting's (Popkin, 1993) videotaped segments that provide examples of typical child behaviors and inappropriate and appropriate parent responses. Generally, parent education strives to enhance the parent-child relationship and increase parent effectiveness. Although the following discussion highlights formalized parent education programs, alternatives include parent drop-in programs or home-visitor programs (Fine & Gardner, 1991).

Parent education includes a variety of approaches united by efforts to be nonjudgmental and open to different parental values. Mental health practitioners may select from parent education programs that are eclectic in orientation or that are based on Rogerian, Adlerian, Rational-Emotive Behavior Therapy, and Transactional Analysis approaches (Gladding, 1999). The existing research on the effectiveness of different approaches to parent education is generally positive. Research with increased methodological rigor is still needed, however. The most popular approaches at present include Adlerian parent education, Rogerian programs, hybrids of Adlerian and Rogerian programs, and behavioral parent education (Fine & Gardner, 1991; Gladding, 1999; Ritchie & Partin, 1994).

In Adlerian parent education, the goal is to foster a democratic atmosphere and cooperation among family members. Consequently, regular family council meetings in which all members voice concerns and needs are encouraged. Logical and natural consequences are also emphasized in an effort to avoid power struggles (Gladding, 1999). Systematic Training for Effective Parenting or STEP (Dinkmeyer & McKay, 1976) follows the Adlerian tradition. STEP strives to encourage children to behave in socially appropriate ways to achieve a positive social identity. To that end, parents are encouraged to adopt a style in which children have choices within limits set by the parents. Parents are trained to identify how their children's misbehavior results from discouragement and becomes a negative means of establishing an identity. Parent-child communication is also emphasized (Fine & Gardner, 1991). There are downward extensions of STEP (Dinkmeyer, McKay, & Dinkmeyer, 1989) for parents of infants, toddlers, and prekindergartners and upward extensions of STEP (Dinkmeyer, McKay, & Dinkmeyer, 1998) for families with adolescents.

Rogerian parent education hypothesizes that individual growth is promoted and family conflicts decrease by active listening and acceptance. In active listening, a parent hears both what is actually said and what is implied. Through acceptance, a parent acknowledges what is happening in the child's life rather than evaluating it (Gladding, 1999). Parent Effectiveness Training or PET (Gordon, 1970) is a parent education program that reflects this orientation. In PET, parents learn to listen actively, to determine who owns the problem, to present a concern in a nonjudgmental manner, and to work out a solution in which both parent and child experience a feeling of success. PET is applicable to toddlers and, perhaps to a greater extent, to preschoolers who have more well-developed verbal skills (Fine & Gardner, 1991).

When compared to Adlerian or Rogerian approaches, behavioral parent education programs target more specific behaviors. Parents are often provided with training manuals so they can observe and record child behaviors as well as their efforts to use positive reinforcement to promote change (Fine & Gardner, 1991; Gladding, 1999). A number of programs with a behavioral thrust exist (Dangel & Polster, 1984). Effective Black Parenting (Alvy & Marigna, 1985) is one example of a cognitive behavioral parenting skill-building program. It teaches parenting strategies and child management skills within an African American perspective. Sessions focus on topics such as life goals, socialization, successful living, traditional African American discipline, family rules, and appropriate consequences to behavior.

Counselor

In a counseling role, mental health practitioners can effectively promote parenting and child-rearing skills in individual clients, in couples, and in families. Research in the area of attachment and object relations is building support for the notion that a person's past relational experiences with caregivers is internalized. Once internalized, these experiences affect current patterns of thinking, perceiving, and behaving. These experiences also affect a person's pattern of relating with others, especially a person's own children (Strand & Wahler, 1996). Although the specific focus and process of counseling will vary with the client's concerns and the practitioner's theoretical orientation, individual counseling provides time and space for clients to explore how they were parented or how they parent or both. Individual counseling is a particularly appropriate forum for parents who are likely to show special difficulties with parenting such as parents who are depressed or who were abused as children (Beckwith, 1990).

Although concerned parents will want to work on their capacity to develop a strong parent-child relationship, they will also continue to seek or maintain healthy, intimate adult relationships and friendships (Santrock, 1986). Just as individuals move through developmental stages, so do couples and families. Starting a family is a major transition point in the family life cycle that creates intense stress. When children come along, a couple must learn to make space for their children and to negotiate joint responsibility for child-rearing and household responsibilities (Carter & McGoldrick, 1988). Counseling services that focus on the relationships between the adults may be warranted (Seitz & Provence, 1990), because the relationship between parents and their spouse or partner affects their parent-child relationship. In fact, research suggests that a good marital relationship or coparental interaction not only increases parenting quality (Fox, Bruce, & Combs-Orme, 2000) but also is linked to competence in the child (Grusec & Lytton, 1988).

In some instances, a counselor may work with an entire family to improve members' relationships with one another and, in the process, promote individual and familial growth and development (Nugent, 2000). The aim is change on a systemic level, that is, in the system in which parents and children reside (Dykeman & Appleton, 1999). Lebow and Gurman (1995) reviewed family therapy efficacy research and found support for family therapy as an intervention with parenting issues as well as with a variety of mental health concerns.

Couple or family counseling and individual counseling have both similarities and differences (Gladding, 2000). Success rates in marital therapy and family therapy are comparable to those of individual therapy (Nugent, 2000). Another similarity is that some of the individual counseling theories also are employed with couples or families. These include the person-centered approach and Adlerian counseling. On the other hand, other theoretical approaches are more commonly used or were specifically developed for use with couples or families. For instance, many theories designed for counseling with couples reflect the social learning school in their emphasis on learning skills and educational information (Nugent, 2000). A focus on couples or families means that additional entities are considered in the process of counseling—not only the individuals involved but also the couple or the family are considered. A final distinction is that when compared with individual counseling, there is a stronger emphasis on dynamics and a decreased emphasis on linear causality in marriage and family counseling (Gladding, 2000).

LEANING FORWARD: CONSIDERING PARENTAL INVOLVEMENT AND MULTICULTURAL ISSUES

Harry (1997) uses the concepts of leaning forward and bending over backward to suggest guidelines for working with families, especially when parents and professionals have differences in viewpoint. She comments, "If I feel like I'm bending over backwards in working with families, then I'm probably doing something wrong! Not only am I doing something unnatural, but, by bending backwards, I'm actually looking away from the person I'm trying to help" (p. 62). Harry goes on to suggest that practitioners assume a "posture of reciprocity" in which the practitioners are clear about their beliefs or values on points of contention yet lean toward the parent in order to understand the parent's stance. Harry elaborates, "Your goal is to arrive at a point which, though it may stretch you, feels natural, and enables collaboration rather than alienation" (p. 72).

Bearing the notion of a posture of reciprocity in mind, counselors who effectively promote parenting and child-rearing skills in young adults remember that issues surrounding parenting are often sensitive. More specifically, regardless of their role as a counselor, they recognize, respect, and respond to variations in the level of parent interest and involvement in counseling services that promote child-rearing skills. Finally, they address multicultural issues.

Variations in Parental Involvement

Earlier in the chapter, variations in a professional's function, role, and level of involvement were presented using Simeonsson and Bailey's (1990) framework. Notably, parents' roles vary with the professional's role due in part to parents' comfort with parent-professional interaction and involvement in counseling services. When the practitioner's function is to provide information or to track and advise families, family involvement is modest. At the middle of the spectrum, when professionals take on the role of consultant or provide other guidance for families, families actively seek both information and skills. For example, parent education requires a commitment of time and a willingness to learn on the part of the parent. At the highest levels of Simeonsson and Bailey's framework, parents pursue counseling and thus invest much of themselves in personal, behavioral, and psychological terms.

Unfortunately, rather than recognize and respect variations in involvement, practitioners tend to criticize parents who refrain from participation. Realistically, nonuse of services and limited involvement may signal extreme sensitivity, apathy, or resistance on the part of parents. In these cases, counselors can employ strategies such as setting a positive tone, using active listening skills, or using written or verbal contracts to clarify expectations (Campbell, 1993). Low parent involvement may reflect other issues, however. For instance, parents may feel distracted or overwhelmed by financial, health, or job-related issues. Perhaps they value their privacy (Campbell, 1993) and will not disclose family concerns until their counselor earns their trust. In most cases, there is no one best way for parents to be involved at any point in time. Ideally, a full range of services should be available to meet parents' current and evolving needs and desires for involvement (Fine & Gardner, 1991; Weissberg, Caplan, & Harwood, 1991).

Multicultural Considerations

Although parenting is a basic human behavior, how it is applied is culturally determined (Keller & McDade, 2000). Counselors must remember that their own life experiences and cultural values affect their perceptions of how

parenting should be done. Cultural background even determines one's definition of a family. In Eurocentric culture, the term *family* is typically associated
with a nuclear family that consists of a mother, a father, and children. In contrast, in traditional Hispanic American, American Indian, and Asian American
culture, *family* includes parents, children, grandparents, aunts, uncles, cousins,
and family friends. Moreover, ethnicity affects the way parents think about
children, their parenting goals, and their behavior toward their children. Of
note are the differences between ethnic groups in the United States that emphasize independence and autonomy (e.g., European Americans) and those that
stress interdependence and group identity (e.g., Latinos and Asian American
Pacific Islanders) (Okagaki & Johnson-Divecha, 1993). Thus, Eurocentric
parenting approaches might be effectively applied to culturally diverse families
in some instances but not in others (Brown, 1997). For example, preferences
for the content, facilitators or leaders, delivery strategies, location, and scheduling of parent education all may reflect cultural differences (Martin,
Chenoweth, & Engelbrecht, 2000). Caution is warranted.

In order to build bridges between the counselor's and parents' points of
view through a posture of reciprocity, a counselor can undertake the following
specific actions: (a) identify issues that divide the counselor and the family the
counselor is working with, (b) identify beliefs or values that underlie the counselor's position, (c) inquire into the beliefs and values that underlie the family's
position, (d) explicitly discuss two different but equally valuable points of
view, and (e) identify a point of similarity between the counselor's and the
family's views as the first step in the process of collaboration (Harry, 1997).
Cultural empathy also can be fostered by increased direct involvement with
families from diverse cultural groups and by acquisition of multicultural information germane to specific counselor roles (e.g., Alvy & Marigna, 1985;
Atkinson & Juntunen, 1994; Brown, 1997; McGoldrick, Pearce, & Giordano,
1982).

SUMMARY

Parenthood brings both excitement and complex challenges into the lives of
young adults. Counselors who know about the importance of parental
warmth, attunement behavior, the balance of democracy and control, and
conflict resolution can use existing expertise and counseling skills in the promotion of parenting and child-rearing skills in their clients. Practitioners may
also build new skills in order to assume the preventive, proactive roles of consultant, parent educator, and liaison. For instance, mental health practitioners
may pursue continuing education opportunities to build their working knowledge of child development or to become versed in a family systems approach

(Fine & Gardner, 1991). They may attend a training workshop and receive a certificate in a parent education approach geared toward culturally diverse families. Increased familiarity with public and private and formal and informal organizations that can provide educational and community support services may also be a professional goal (Atkinson & Juntunen, 1994). As counselors develop a range of counseling services to meet parents' current and evolving needs and desires for involvement, they may find ideas in promising parenting support initiatives that are comprehensive, integrated, flexible, and responsive to community needs (e.g., Mertensmeyer & Fine, 2000).

At its core, parenting is a challenging journey in which adults grow and develop alongside the children they are raising. At its best, parenting is a process that not only fosters the well-being of the next generation but also provides a sense of fulfillment and moments of wonder. Clearly, if counselors are prepared to promote parenting and child-rearing skills through a variety of roles and in a posture of reciprocity, then important benefits are likely to accrue to parents, children, and their social environment.

VIGNETTE

You receive a phone call from a parent whom you met during a parent information night at a local elementary school. The parent had stopped by to look at the various brochures on child rearing that you provided and later had asked you to recommend a book on parenting. During the phone call, the parent says, "Thanks for mentioning that book the other evening. We got some helpful ideas from it, and things with our daughter have started to improve. She is less likely to throw a tantrum when we drop her off at school, and we are less short-tempered too. But I'm calling because we feel like we still need some guidance. We think we have a close relationship with our daughter and want that to continue. We also want her to know that we have our limits and have certain expectations about how she'll behave both at school and at home. I know you do counseling, but that seems unnecessary and a little too personal at this point. Other than recommending books or being our counselor, can you provide us with some help? We would really like to see what options we have."

1. What different roles could a counselor assume to promote this parent's child-rearing skills?

2. What counselor roles might best complement the parent's level of interest and likely level of involvement in services?

3. What else would you like to know about the family as you apply these counselor roles to this particular situation?

ADDITIONAL RESOURCES

The following guidebooks, using a four-star rating system, contain full-page reviews of hundreds of resources focused on parenting and child rearing. Reviewed resources include books, CD-ROMS, Web sites, and videotapes.

Ganz, J. (Ed.). (1998). *Raising teenagers: The best resources to help yours succeed.* Issaquah, WA: Resource Pathways.

Montgomery, A. (Ed.). (1999). *Having children: The best resources to help you prepare.* Issaquah, WA: Resource Pathways.

Soto, J. (Ed.). (1998). *Infants, toddlers & preschoolers: The best resources to help you parent.* Issaquah, WA: Resource Pathways.

CHAPTER 13

Preventing and Managing Personal and Professional Role Strain

Elizabeth Nutt Williams

Men and women in the United States are working more hours than ever in the paid workforce (Bond, Galinsky, & Swanberg, 1998). In addition, more women continue to enter the paid workforce, comprising nearly half of all individuals working in the United States (U.S. Bureau of Labor Statistics, 1993). Although there is a greater emphasis on paid work, especially in women's lives, there seems to be no less emphasis on home and family (Morgan, 1992). Family roles continue to be perceived as the main source of life satisfaction for a majority of working women and about half of working men (Parker & Aldwin, 1994). Interestingly, although past research has often focused on the workplace as a source of stress, Baruch, Biener, and Barnett (1987) noted that domestic activities and parenting can also be highly stressful.

Thus, both men and women have to juggle multiple roles and may experience conflicts between their work demands and home responsibilities (Bird & Ford, 1985). The demands of personal and professional role conflicts can lead to what has been called *role strain* (Goode, 1960), or the difficulty fulfilling one's demands and others' expectations. Three specific elements of role strain have been identified (Greenhaus & Beutell, 1985; Home, 1998).

First, *role conflict* (or behavior-based conflict) is defined as the psychological experience of being faced with simultaneous or incompatible demands. In this instance, the behaviors appropriate for one role conflict with the behaviors necessary for a different role. For example, a lawyer who is a single father may feel guilty when he has to work late and leave his child in extended day care; his need to stay at the office late is incompatible with his need to pick up his child. Second, *role overload* (or time-based conflict) refers to the inability to meet all demands or expectations. Role overload is often felt as the predicament that "there are not enough hours in the day to accomplish everything." For example, the father cannot fulfill both his job demands (stay at the office) and home demands (pick up his child) at the same time; he may begin to feel stress as he tries to accomplish all his tasks concurrently (i.e., he picks up his child but continues to work by dictating notes by audiotape in his car and typing documents while holding the baby at night). Third, *role contagion* (or strain-based conflict) refers to preoccupation with one role while engaged in a different role. In other words, there is intrusion from the strain of one role into a different role. Thus, the father cannot concentrate at work because he is so worried about his child in day care.

The purpose of this chapter is to investigate the existence and effects of role strain and to examine models for its prevention and treatment. Therefore, the conceptual framework of role strain is reviewed, highlighting both theoretical and empirical findings. Second, a model for role strain prevention is presented. Third, the key issues in role strain management are discussed. Finally, resources and suggested exercises are provided that may be useful in designing interventions related to role strain.

OVERVIEW OF ROLE STRAIN AND THE IMPACT OF MULTIPLE ROLES

Vulnerability to conflict between personal and professional roles is an issue with which most working adults must contend. This vulnerability to role strain cuts across issues of income (e.g., Home, 1998), sexual orientation (e.g., Elliott, 1993), and ethnic background (e.g., Watts-Jones, 1990), although it appears that combining parenting and employment may be less stressful for Black women than for White women (Waldron & Jacobs, 1989). Despite the potential universality of role strain, there continue to be persistent gender differences in how men and women think about and react to their work and family roles (Covin & Brush, 1991; Gilbert & Brownson, 1998). In fact, most of the research on multiple roles and role strain has focused on women (Stanfield, 1998). For example, women juggling work and family roles tend to experience more role "spillover," greater work-family interference, and more distress than men (Hughes & Galinsky, 1994; Williams & Alliger, 1994). Several factors have been identified that often have a particularly negative effect on women in the workforce. For example, factors such as caring for children and elderly parents, having high personal expectations and standards, adhering to traditional sex role attitudes, and feeling a lack of social support can all contribute to role conflict and strain (Reifman, Biernat, & Lang, 1991). Cook (1993) suggested that we need to challenge our assumptions about work life (and what it takes to succeed) and the outdated idea that the home is solely the woman's responsibility. Although the workforce has been slow to adapt to changing family needs (Gilbert, Hallett, & Eldridge, 1994), it does appear that the focus is moving toward conceptualizing personal and professional role strain as a family and employment issue rather than a purely intrapsychic or purely female issue (Stanfield, 1998; Thompson & Walker, 1989).

A number of theories have also been proposed to address the meaning of different roles in women's work lives. Two theories, however, have gained the most attention. The first, the *scarcity hypothesis* (Goode, 1960), suggests that individuals have only a limited amount of energy available to them; thus, engaging in multiple roles increases the likelihood of role strain. By contrast, the *enhancement hypothesis* (Marks, 1977) assumes that energy is limitless and is actually enhanced by multiple roles. This hypothesis suggests that multiple roles increase one's self-esteem and available resources, thus enriching rather than detracting from one's quality of life. The question emphasized by these competing hypotheses is really about whether engaging in multiple roles is necessarily equated with experiencing role strain.

Although there are clearly stressors associated with engaging in multiple roles, it appears that the benefits outweigh the costs (Kirchmeyer, 1993). Thus, most evidence supports the enhancement hypothesis. Specifically, combining multiple roles appears to have few negative physical impacts (Hibbard & Pope, 1991) and few negative psychological impacts (Moen, Dempster-McCain, & Williams, 1992). In fact, engaging in multiple roles has been associated with higher self-esteem (Kopp & Ruzicka, 1993), greater life satisfaction (Burke & McKeen, 1993), and better physical health (Waldron & Jacobs, 1989). As Reid and Hardy (1999) found for midlife women, satisfaction with a role appears to be more important than the number of roles in which a person engages. Thus, merely engaging in multiple roles does not in and of itself lead to role strain.

However, when conflict between roles does occur, it has been associated with several negative mental health impacts such as problems with alcohol abuse (Frone, Russell, & Cooper, 1993) and reduced marital quality (Hughes, Galinsky, & Morris, 1992). In addition, the higher the amount of role strain experienced, the lower the person's job satisfaction (Greenglass, Pantony, & Burke, 1988). Fortunately, the more importance one places on one's career, regardless of other life roles, the less strain is experienced (Parker & Aldwin, 1994). Overall, the effects of multiple roles seem positive, although there are certainly some negative effects associated with role strain. It is important to keep in mind that it is not the existence of, or even quantity of, one's multiple roles that creates problems; rather, it is individuals' interpretation of their roles, the meaning of those roles, that is more important to assess (Wiley, 1991).

Because of the potential negative effects of role strain, prevention and planning efforts are increasingly needed for both men and women. Much of what we know about role strain (and its prevention and treatment), however, rests on empirical studies of young women (e.g., McCracken & Weitzman, 1997). We know much more about how young women respond to multiple roles than we do about how young men do. For example, it appears that combining parenting and employment may be particularly stressful for some women (Marshall & Barnett, 1991). Although women's career aspirations have increased (Regan & Roland, 1985) and more women expect to combine work and family (Tangri & Jenkins, 1986), many young women remain unaware of the consequences associated with different career choices and make decisions that are inconsistent with their future family goals (Machung, 1991). Thus, both the prevention and treatment of role strain are critical. The following sections of this chapter detail the key elements of an effective intervention program aimed at preventing role strain, treatment strategies to help men and women better manage multiple roles, and the resources available to help the practitioner address issues of personal and professional role strain with their clients.

ISSUES IN THE PREVENTION OF ROLE STRAIN

Career planning is something that most people now recognize as important. We live in a high-tech, fast-paced global economy in which job stability cannot always be counted on. Those who want to pursue a particular career, whether it is in banking, education, public service, entertainment, or athletics, generally recognize the need for training and advance planning. We are all less likely, however, to believe that the same amount of effort should go into planning our family lives. And yet we see that planning for work and family interactions *does* help reduce role strain and stress (Steffy & Ashbaugh, 1986).

To address this issue, Weitzman (1994) proposed a comprehensive model for helping individuals plan ahead for combining work and family. Her Multiple Role Realism Model highlights the importance of attitudes, knowledge, and planning, focusing on the prevention of role strain rather than just learning to cope with current demands. Specifically, Weitzman suggested that practitioners help young people (young women in particular) identify actual strategies they can use to integrate the roles of family and work. She also suggested that most young women are unprepared for managing the realities of their multiple roles (Spade & Reese, 1991). Weitzman noted that "the *how* of multiple-role planning is much less thought out relative to the simple desire to have both a career and family" (p. 18). They may be somewhat naïve about the realities of combining work and family, including the necessity of deciding on when (or if) to have a child (Sullivan, 1992), what employer leave policies are in place (Baber & Monaghan, 1988), and where to find adequate child care (Tetrick, Miles, Marcil, & Van Dosen, 1994). McCracken and Weitzman (1997) also emphasized the importance of engaging in multiple role planning as a developmental process. Although young women and men may perceive decisions about multiple roles to be "far in the future," waiting until role strain occurs is not helpful. Thus, helping men and women plan for multiple roles when they are young is an important part of preventing potential role strain.

Weitzman (1994) proposed three main areas that are important for making specific decisions and choices in the planning for multiple roles (and thus possibly preventing future role strain). First, she highlighted the need to make decisions regarding career interruption after the birth of a child. She suggested that young women "consistently *underestimate* their future work involvement" (p. 21); it may no longer be possible to "take time off" after having children. Reentry into the fast-paced workforce may become more difficult over time. Thus, young parents need to assess if planning for a career interruption is a viable option. Second, Weitzman emphasized the importance of reviewing the financial consequences of *not* planning for multiple roles and the possibility of job interruption. Gaps in employment are associated with a drop in income (Schneer & Reitman, 1990), a fact not always considered when planning for work-family commitments. Finally, Weitzman acknowledged the importance of seeking support. Although not all researchers have found social support to be beneficial (Reifman et al., 1991), others have noted the buffering effect that social support can have on the psychological effects of stress (Greenglass, 1993). On the basis of the general outline of Weitzman's model, I detail several specific elements crucial to an effective prevention effort: (a) assessment of attitudes and values, (b) education and knowledge, and (c) planning and decision making.

Assessment of Attitudes and Values

Before even dealing with the issue of potential role strain, it is important to understand individuals' attitudes toward work and the values they hold important. In proposing a developmental model of career counseling, Donald Super (1957) emphasized the importance of individuals' self-concepts in their vocational decisions. He also emphasized the interdependence of a person's multiple roles and thus highlighted role salience (i.e., degree of personal relevance of each role) as an important issue for both men and women. Super's model included several distinct roles such as child, student, leisurite, citizen, worker, spouse, homemaker, parent, and retiree through which we cycle during our lifespan. The importance or salience of each role can be assessed by examining a person's commitment or attachment to the role, participation or time spent in the role, and knowledge of or experience with the role (Nevill & Super, 1986). Super believed it was important to assess the salience attached to each role in a person's life when helping a person determine the most satisfying and successful pathways in that person's career development (Super, 1980).

In assessing a person's attitudes and values regarding multiple roles, a wide variety of measurement instruments are available (see Additional Resources at the end of this chapter). Whether you use an established measure of role conflict or values salience, or whether you use an open-ended interview format to identify a person's values and attitudes toward engaging in multiple roles, the most important issue to identify is the extent to which individuals have thought through their career plans, planned for multiple roles, and identified strategies to help them maximize their plans. For example, people who see themselves as high-powered professionals may assert different needs than people who wish they could be the primary caregiver in the home. Both will likely have to juggle multiple roles, but they may need different strategies to help them attain their goals.

Although it is clearly important to assess a person's current values and goals, it may also be interesting to examine with individuals how their attitudes developed. What kind of messages did they receive as children? Were they expected to act in traditional or nontraditional ways with regard to their gender and cultural backgrounds? What kind of dreams did they have for themselves when they were much younger? Finally, the attitudes of others (such as a partner, friends, or other family members) toward multiple role management may also be important to understand. For example, neighbors or co-workers might comment on or criticize a person's lifestyle choices (e.g., using day care, eating out or at fast food restaurants, relying on a partner who stays home to care for children). Wiersma (1994) noted that Rapoport and Rapoport (1969), who first coined the term *dual career family,* referred to this as the "normative dilemma." It is also important to understand the cultural context in which these "normative" attitudes were formed. Knowing all the parameters involved in a person's planning process will make strategizing ways to manage multiple roles that much more successful.

Education and Knowledge

Education regarding factual knowledge about options and the world of work are an important next step in helping to prevent role conflict. Once we understand individuals' attitudes, we need to be sure they have all the information necessary to make decisions. Both Weitzman (1994) and Sullivan (1992) have emphasized the need for women to be aware of their options in balancing work and family. For example, young women in particular should consider if and when to have children and plan their career paths accordingly. That is not to say that career planning will always be accurate or never change. Plans change all the time. And there are some things that happen which we never plan on. However, it appears that there is a real advantage to thinking through options in terms of reducing role conflict. In other words, one might emphasize the need to be prepared for a variety of contingencies and the importance of making family *and* career planning a conscious and informed process.

Once individuals begin to settle on a career- or work-related choice and make plans to pursue a certain vocation, it may also be important to assess the flexibility of the job itself. For example, Marshall and Barnett (1994) found that workers who had more flexible jobs (i.e., professionals in colleges, doctors' offices, law firms, and other professional services who were able to set their own hours) reported greater job satisfaction. In addition, the flexibility of the employer, in terms of flextime, job sharing, personal days, availability of child care, and family leave policies, among other issues, will be important issues to explore. Following Weitzman's view, decisions about managing multiple roles should be realistic and thus based on accurate information about the world of work.

Planning and Decision Making

Finally, we turn to the issue of finalizing plans and implementing action strategies. In establishing a plan for managing multiple roles and preventing role conflict, Gilbert et al. (1994) suggested that individuals identify several resources for support: personal resources, family resources, and societal resources. For personal resources, they included such ideas as personality attributes (e.g., competitiveness, drive for success, need for affiliation), ability to cope with stress, beliefs about work and love, and overall outlook (i.e., idea of how things "should" be). Gilbert et al. noted that the "most essential" family resource is the support of one's partner, followed by the support of friends and other relatives. In other words, one should assess how much one gains empowerment and strength from one's relationships. In particular, support between partners (both emotional and instrumental support) can moderate stressful events and help couples find suitable solutions. Gilbert et al. suggested that couples should ask themselves a variety of questions such as how many hours each partner plans to work in a week. Finally, societal resources refer to general support from society at large, including family-friendly employers, flexible work conditions, and adequate child care. One specific organizational resource to consider is how much an employer will assist with relocation for a spouse or partner (Wilcox-Matthew & Minor, 1989).

These types of personal, family, and societal issues can arise in working with individuals and couples, but they can also be addressed in groups. Gerken, Reardon, and Bash (1988) redesigned a career course to include planning for family and partner issues. Although none of the 196 participants expected to gain information about marriage or family during the course, Gerken et al. found that the career planning course did help raise awareness of the complex issues involved with combining work and family. Specifically, they incorporated many exercises designed to get people thinking about their preconceived career notions (Catalyst, 1984, 1987). The results of their intervention suggest that although individuals may be unaware that they lack knowledge about how to successfully plan for multiple life roles, group and classroom formats can be an effective method for disseminating this information. As Gerken et al. (1988) stated, college students in particular want to (and believe they can) "have it all—career, spouse, and children, although they are unaware of the paradoxes and conflicts inherent in their life expectations" (p. 269). Clearly, efforts to prevent role strain can be quite useful and should be included in career counseling interventions with youth (particularly high school and college students). The following section outlines an example of one possible type of prevention program.

Example of a Prevention Program

A university counseling center decided that it would like to provide services to both undergraduate and graduate students making career decisions (but who had not yet begun to deal with home-career conflict). Specifically, the center began to offer a career-focused support group for both men and women, centered on issues of preventing role conflict. Four stages of the group were implemented: Stage 1 (group formation and identification of attitudes, interests, and values), Stage 2 (gathering information about the world of work), Stage 3 (clarifying personal plans and recognizing resources and potential pitfalls), and Stage 4 (implementation of action plans and group termination). Ideally, the group would run for a semester (around 16 weeks).

In Stage 1, group facilitators would help group members become acquainted and acclimated to the expectations of a career counseling group (highlighting issues of confidentiality, group norms, etc.). In addition, the initial weeks of the group would be dedicated to assessing the clients' attitudes toward career and home life, vocational interests, and work-family values. Several Catalyst (1984) campus resource exercises could be used here, such as the ones on fathering, spouse/partner expectations, and sex-role stereotypes. Other traditional career assessment instruments could also be useful, including the Strong Interest Inventory, the Values Inventory, and the Salience Inventory. Several role conflict measures outlined above could also be useful. At the beginning of the group, it might also be helpful to conduct a pretest assessment of the clients' attitudes regarding home-career conflict in order to assess the degree of success of the counseling program at the end of treatment.

In Stage 2, clients would spend time between counseling sessions gathering information about the world of work by interviewing employers and searching for specific career information on the Web and in the library. Several resource books can be quite helpful, including *Dictionary of Occupational Titles* and *Occupational Outlook Handbook*. In the counseling sessions, clients would discuss what they had found and whether the new information was consistent with their expectations. For example, preconceived salary expectations may be inflated before reviewing the actual employment trends (Catalyst, 1987).

In Stage 3, the clients would work on synthesizing the information they have obtained about themselves and the world of work. The focus would be on helping them draw up accurate personal goals that reflect the realities of combining work and personal demands. It would also be important to identify future resources (e.g., support system, certain employer benefits to seek out, time management skills) and potential pitfalls (e.g., taking time off to care for young children, experiencing overload if one tried to do it all).

Finally, Step 4 would be dedicated to helping clients begin to implement their plans. For example, they may make some particular decisions regarding their choice of major or future careers. They may sign up for certain classes or seek employment that would further their career plans. If they already have a steady partner, they may begin a dialogue about the issues of home-career conflict and how domestic responsibilities will be handled. Although this stage marks the termination of the counseling group, it is also just the beginning in terms of putting a realistic career plan into action. To complete the entire intervention, the facilitators should also plan for a posttest to investigate how the intervention has been successful in altering attitudes and behaviors.

As has been stated before, planning ahead for work and family interactions can help reduce role strain and conflict (Steffy & Ashbaugh, 1986). Therefore, the issue of prevention should be the primary line of defense against role strain. Helping men and women identify the potential problems and plan for ways to be successful when juggling multiples roles will help reduce the occurrence of role strain and thus the need to treat role strain in a remedial sense. However, not all people have planned ahead nor do all plans cover every possible scenario. Thus, we also need to consider how we can successfully treat role strain in those for whom it already exists. The following section outlines several useful treatment strategies.

TREATMENT STRATEGIES FOR MANAGING ROLE STRAIN

Although it would be ideal to prevent role strain in all cases before it becomes a problem, role conflict and strain is already a daily issue for many seeking counseling. Thus, in addition to prevention strategies, it is helpful to have on hand a set of useful tools to help clients manage the role strain already present in their lives. The literature on strategies and techniques to treat role strain can be divided into three sections by the focus of the intervention: task-focused strategies, relationship-focused strategies, and self-focused strategies.

Task-Focused Strategies

Task-focused strategies refer to those techniques designed to address time management, delegation of tasks, and work restructuring. In other words, the person experiencing the role strain can gain relief by changing the work and family demands. Specifically, several strategies have been found to be quite useful. First, McLaughlin, Cormier, and Cormier (1983) found that handling two or more tasks at one time is a particularly helpful time management strategy. The concept of "multitasking" may be a way to get more done at one time; however, harried overworking may also increase role contagion and overload over time.

McLaughlin et al. (1983) also found that a large number of the women in their sample noted the importance of saying no to additional time demands. This idea of limiting one's obligations has also been suggested by other researchers (e.g., Epstein, 1970). The ability to say no may be invaluable. Many men and women may feel, for both personal and professional reasons, that they should continue to take on additional responsibilities. However, there are still only 24 hours in a day, and we should be able to prioritize the tasks and demands before us and work to schedule and organize tasks in a way that is more manageable (Voydanoff, 1988).

Wiersma (1994) also highlighted the issue of domestic chores as a focus for time management strategies. Specifically, Wiersma suggested hiring outside help and dividing chores among family members, suggestions also made by Rapoport and Rapoport (1972) and McLaughlin et al. (1983). However, it is also important to note that some women of color may feel ambivalent about hiring domestic help because of the expectations that the domestic worker may likely also be a woman of color (Comas-Diaz & Greene, 1994). Many people do, however, have partners and children they can rely on to participate fully in domestic activities. An important point to be emphasized is that many people experiencing role strain might think about delegating chores as asking for help. However, it is important to avoid labeling the work of other family members as merely "helping" the person experiencing role strain. It may be more useful to frame family members' domestic chores as "sharing" in the household work. This issue may be about semantics, but language has a powerful effect on our perceptions and motivations.

Finally, Karambayya and Reilly (1992) suggested the need for work restructuring (or fitting work to family needs). They found that the most common methods of work restructuring involved altering work hours (both arrival and departure times and total number of hours spent at work) to match family schedules and limiting work hours on weekends. Other methods of restructuring included limiting evening work hours and the amount of time spent traveling for a job. On average, about 40% of men and 70% of women in dual-career couples reported restructuring their regular work activities. Counselors may be able to help individuals and couples make changes in their daily routines to accommodate family needs. It is also important to note, however, that although some jobs may allow greater flexibility in one's schedule or in one's financial status, not all work environments can be restructured by the individual. Thus, it may also be crucial to work toward larger organizational change, including work-at-home options and flexible time schedules.

Overall, there are several effective time management and task-focused strategies for helping individuals manage role strain. In addition, King, Winett, and Lovett (1986) found that training in time management was effective for increasing the amount of time spent in high-priority activities, increasing self-efficacy feelings, and decreasing felt-stress. Once individuals can identify their priorities, time management tools can help keep those priorities in order.

Relationship-Focused Strategies

Several researchers have also acknowledged the interpersonal nature of role strain and therefore the interpersonal nature of its treatment. Although some have gone so far as to suggest that men and women reduce the size expectations of their families (e.g., have one child instead of three) as a way to manage role strain (Epstein, 1970; Van Dusen & Sheldon, 1976), decisions about children are highly personal and individual. Thus, other strategies focused on relationships have been proposed.

For example, Wiersma (1994) emphasized the importance of maintaining social relations. In addition to sharing domestic chores with other family members, Wiersma suggested that couples share work-related friends and activities. In order to share in both work and family, one partner may become involved in the other's work activities. Wiersma also noted the need to plan time for couples to be alone together. Engaging in activities such as a weekly date night might help strengthen the couple and their ability to meet their many multiple demands as partners, parents, workers, and members of the greater community. McLaughlin et al. (1983) also suggested allowing a special time for each child and engaging in family activities as a way to manage role strain.

The issue of social support in general (beyond the couple and family) has also been addressed extensively in the literature. Although many have suggested that social support can be quite helpful, others have found that social support is not always a buffer against the effects of stress (Reifman et al., 1991). Belle (1987) even thought that the demands of maintaining one's social network (e.g., telephone calls, e-mail messages, going out with friends, and writing letters) might be a stressor in and of itself. Specifically, for individuals in certain ethnic or racial groups (e.g., African Americans, Latinos), there may be pressure or an expectation that individuals will also serve their community (Gilkes, 1982). Again, it seems that the emphasis needs to be on the choices of the individual. Some people feel energized by seeing friends, working within the community, and keeping up correspondences, whereas for others, these activities feel like an overload to what they are already doing at work and in the home. Thus, all these strategies need to be tailored to the needs of each specific individual.

Self-Focused Strategies

Finally, a focus on self-care seems critical to the management of multiple roles and role strain. McLaughlin et al. (1983) referred to a grouping of self-focused strategies as self-care. They included such strategies as eating nutritionally balanced meals, exercising, and engaging in a hobby. Stress management skills can be particularly helpful in reducing emotional strain and exhaustion (Higgins, 1986). Rapoport and Rapoport (1972) also emphasized the importance of setting aside leisure time in the reduction of stress and role strain. Essentially, the idea is to not forget oneself in the mix of work demands and family responsibilities. Furthermore, it is important not to forget to have fun in the midst of juggling one's many obligations.

Beyond enjoying life through leisure and maintaining a healthy physical state, one should also attend to one's cognitive self. Wiersma (1994) suggested the need for "cognitive reappraisal," and Epstein (1970) emphasized the redefinition of roles. For example, one may give money, rather than time, to charities. One might also reappraise the need to have a spotless house; perhaps cleaning once a week rather than every other day could be relabeled as sufficient. McLaughlin et al. (1983) also suggested that lowering one's standards for housework and giving oneself permission to be less than perfect can be particularly effective in managing role strain.

Finally, the most important aspect of self-focused strategies seems to be an emphasis on personal power. The more individuals feel in control of their life (e.g., by employing many of the strategies discussed), the less role strain they will likely experience. In fact, Trocki and Orioli (1994) found personal power to be the strongest predictor of low stress. They even suggested that several of the more common stress management skills usually emphasized (e.g., the importance of gaining social support) "turn out *not* to be the most important factors that help individuals deal with stressful environments" (p. 19). Similarly, Piechowski (1992) emphasized the importance of personal power in control also highlighted in Karasek's (1979) job strain model, which equates stress with the combination of high demands and low control.

Thus, a focus on the self may be quite beneficial. However, one must be careful not to bandage over stress with an emphasis merely on fun and physical health. The most important quality to emphasize and help a client achieve is a sense of personal control and empowerment. The case example provided below illustrates how several of the intervention strategies may be used in a counseling context.

CASE EXAMPLE

Joan, a 32-year-old African American woman, has just sought individual counseling from Dr. Practicality for the first time for depression and anxiety. Immediately after college, she entered a 2-year MBA program and received a degree in business. She has been in her current job as a high-ranking manager in a national corporation for 8 years, steadily advancing in rank and salary since she started. She reports that her career has always been important to her and that her parents always encouraged her to "make it" in business. She has also always felt that it is important, as an African American woman, to succeed in the business environment.

In terms of relationships, she met and married her husband, Bill, in graduate school. Bill just recently became a partner in a start-up computer business. They decided to have children after she had been working for 3 years but before Bill ventured out into his own business. Now, 5 years later, they have two young children (ages 4 and 1½).

After the birth of her second child, Joan began to feel even more stressed than she had before. At first, she attributed her anxiety and feelings of being out of control to the "maternity blues." She assumed that when she returned to work after her maternity leave, she would feel better. However, she has been back at work for a year and things continue to get worse. She feels guilty that her children are in day care from 6:00 a.m. to 6:00 p.m. Monday through Friday. At work, she feels less productive. At home, she feels exhausted and can't keep up with her expectations that her home be spotless for Bill's business entertaining. Bill does not help much with the domestic work because he is busy with his own start-up company. She does not have time to see friends, and they do not live near family. She is, however, active in her church and community service projects. They have also been struggling financially due to paying off graduate school bills, investing in Bill's business, and buying the necessities for two quickly growing children. Joan thinks there is "something wrong" with her and thinks she may need medication for depression.

After assessing Joan's situation, Dr. Practicality identifies several sources of external stress in Joan's life. Joan, like many in her generation, did not plan ahead for home-career conflict. Because she is an able and capable woman, she assumed she could do it all with grace and ease. Joan and Dr. Practicality began by discussing Joan's need to be Superwoman both at work and at home (and her subsequent guilt at not meeting her own standards). They discussed Joan's upbringing, cultural background, and the values she holds dear regarding work, community involvement, marriage, and motherhood. For example, Joan believed that her house was a reflection on her; the messier the house, the worse she felt about herself as a mother and wife. She was no longer sure how she could juggle her demanding career and her family responsibilities.

Together, Joan and Dr. Practicality outlined several strategies to help her ease the role strain she was experiencing. First, Dr. Practicality helped Joan change her self-imposed expectations about doing it all to perfection. This cognitive reappraisal helped Joan let herself off the hook for not having a perfectly clean home at every moment of the week. Next, Dr. Practicality helped Joan find ways to discuss with Bill his own role in the domestic chores. Together, they worked out a plan to slowly increase Bill's home chores. Most important, however, Bill and Joan spontaneously decided that Bill would begin to entertain business colleagues at restaurants rather than at home.

Next, Dr. Practicality helped Joan make some financial decisions that enabled her to hire a cleaning service twice a month to take care of the larger cleaning jobs. Before making the decision to hire domestic help, Joan and Dr. Practicality discussed Joan's feelings about seeking outside help and her concerns about potentially hiring another woman of color. Also, in terms of task-focused strategies, Joan began to look into ways to restructure her workday, investigating her employer's policies on flextime. With some of the task-focused and relationship-focused strategies underway, Dr. Practicality began to address with Joan how she could better nurture herself. It turns out that Joan used to love photography and hiking. Although she was not even sure where her camera and hiking boots were at first, she sought them out and began taking a few hours on Saturday with her children to hike nature trails in the park and take pictures. Dr. Practicality also encouraged Joan to renew old friendships and build new ones, particularly with others who could help share in child-care activities. She began to focus more on making stronger connections with other mothers in her church. As Joan began to feel better and more energized, she also found ways to create "personal time" for each member of the family (each person could choose their activity such as reading, napping, playing quietly inside, or playing a sport). By working together, she and Bill were also able to designate time each week that was purely "couple's time."

Once Joan felt empowered again, able to make changes in her own life that could help her manage her various roles, she began to feel less anxious and was no longer depressed. Her multiple roles were not gone, but she felt in control of implementing ways to help her family manage the conflicting demands. Before leaving therapy, Dr. Practicality and Joan planned ahead for setbacks and identified all the coping resources that Joan had at her disposal.

In summary, there seems to be agreement that active coping styles are associated with stress reduction (Wells, Hobfoll, & Lavin, 1997) and that the more strategies used, the less stress a person experiences (McLaughlin et al., 1983). This is certainly the case with Joan's example. She worked with her counselor to identify different task-focused, relationship-focused, and self-focused strategies to help manage her multiple role strain. Because she felt empowered to help herself and because she had several resources to aid her (e.g., her husband, some money, a flexible job), she felt less anxious and depressed. One important point to note is that Joan was not forced to give up any one of her roles. In fact, she ended up adding roles (photographer, active friend) that she found pleasurable and that gave meaning to her life. Along with specific strategies, it is the meaning one places on one's multiple roles that eventually determines the level and type of stress one might experience.

SUMMARY

It appears that the existence of multiple roles is here to stay. Men and women both must learn how to juggle a variety of often disparate roles. They must also learn to prevent role strain (role conflict, role overload, and role contagion). Those professionals in a counseling role are in an excellent position to help. With prevention, assessment, and education, we can help reduce strain and add to the quality of life. With remedial treatment efforts, we can also help correct a home-career path that has gone off course. Thus, with the prevention and treatment strategies outlined in this chapter, we can help men and women become better parents, partners, and workers.

VIGNETTE

To gain practice in implementing some of the strategies detailed in this chapter, use the following scenario to highlight the major prevention and treatment issues in this case. After reading through the scenario, take a few minutes to jot down some notes about what you see as the potential problems or causes of the problems and how you might begin to intervene. Also think about what concerns you would have in working with the client(s) and what you think the outcome might be. Then take a look at the questions at the end of the scenario. Although you can certainly do this exercise on your own, it may be helpful to work in a group to discuss the questions and the scenario.

You work as an in-house counselor for a utility company. A male worker comes to you because he and his wife are having marital problems. He doesn't want to seek outside therapy but wants to bring his wife in for a few sessions so you can "straighten her out." They have three children (ages 5, 8, and 12). She has recently gone back to work now that their youngest has started kindergarten. She is enjoying working, but he feels all the housework has been "dumped" on him to do. They both feel stressed and unhappy. They feel confused about their work and home roles and responsibilities, given the recent change in her work status. You check with the company and find that they allow (and even expect) their in-house counselors to work with couples. Therefore, you agree to start seeing both the husband and wife as long as the wife is a willing and voluntary participant.

———————

1. What do you imagine are the major issues with which you would be faced?

2. What are some of the potential problems you might experience doing counseling in this setting?

3. How would demographic factors such as racial or ethnic group or socioeconomic status affect your work with this couple?

4. What do you think may be "causing" some of the discord the couple is experiencing?

5. In what ways would you intervene to address issues of role strain?

ADDITIONAL RESOURCES

Print Resources

Comas-Diaz, L., & Greene, B. (1994). *Women of color: Integrating ethnic and gender identities in psychotherapy.* New York: Guilford.

Keita, G. P., & Hurrell, J. J. (1994). *Job stress in a changing workforce: Investigating gender, diversity, and family issues.* Washington, DC: American Psychological Association.

Walsh, W. B., & Osipow, S. H. (1994). *Career counseling for women.* Hillsdale, NJ: Lawrence Erlbaum.

Videotapes

Work and family. (Available from Insight Media, 2162 Broadway, New York, NY 10024-0621; phone: 800-233-9910; http://www.insight-media.com)

Managing your career and your personal life. (Available from Managing Work & Family Inc., 912 Crain St., Evanston, IL 60202; phone: 847-864-0916; http://www.mwfam.com)

Organizations

Catalyst, 120 Wall Street, New York, NY 10005; phone: 212-514-7600; http://www.catalystwomen.org

The Dependent Care Connection (DCC), P.O. Box 2783, Westport, CT 06880; phone: 203-226-2680; http://www.dcclifecare.com

Families and Work Institute, 330 Seventh Avenue, 14th Floor, New York, NY 10001; phone: 212-465-2044; http://www.familiesandworkinst.org

9 to 5, National Association of Working Women, 231 W. Wisconsin Avenue, Suite 900, Milwaukee, WI 53203; phone: 414-274-0925; 800-522-0925 Job Survival Hotline; http://www.9to5.org

Work & Family Connection, 5197 Beachside Drive, Minnetonka, MN 55343; phone: 800-487-7898; http://www.workfamily.com

Inventories

Amatea, E. S., Cross, E. G., Clark, J. E., & Bobby, C. L. (1986). Assessing the work and family role expectations of career-oriented men and women: The Life Role Salience Scales. *Journal of Marriage and the Family, 48,* 831-838.

Berry, J. O., & Rao, J. M. (1997). Balancing employment and fatherhood: A systems perspective. *Journal of Family Issues, 18,* 386-402.

Holahan, C. K., & Gilbert, L. A. (1979). Conflict between major life roles: Women and men in dual career couples. *Human Relations, 32,* 451-467.

McCracken, R. S., & Weitzman, L. M. (1997). Relationship of personal agency, problem-solving appraisal, and traditionality of career choice to women's attitudes toward multiple role planning. *Journal of Counseling Psychology, 44,* 149-159.

Nevill, D. D., & Super, D. E. (1986). *The Salience Inventory: Theory, application, and research.* Palo Alto, CA: Consulting Psychologists Press.

Tipping, L. M., & Farmer, H. S. (1991). A home-career conflict measure: Career counseling implications. *Measurement & Evaluation in Counseling & Development, 24,* 111-118.

CHAPTER 14

Prevention and Treatment of Violence Against Women

An Examination of Sexual Assault

Helen A. Neville
Mary J. Heppner

A shley and Tanisha are undergraduate students at the same university. They have very little in common because they move in different social circles: Ashley is an English major and is active in her predominantly White sorority; Tanisha, an African American nontraditional student, majors in computer science and spends most of her free time at home with her daughter. However, they share one life-transforming experience: They were raped by a trusted friend they were dating. In high school, Ashley was thrilled to be dating someone she admired from afar. Then one day her dream come true became a living nightmare. Near the close of one date, her new boyfriend parked the car in a remote location to "neck." When Ashley rebuffed his advances, he raped her. Tanisha was in college when she was raped by her boyfriend. It happened shortly after she had given birth to his child. He came over to her house to visit and check in on her and the baby. As the evening progressed, he insisted they become romantic. She refused, and he proceeded to have sex with her against her will.

Ashley's and Tanisha's accounts are based on 2 of the nearly 100 narratives we have heard during interviews conducted as part of our research examining general and culture-specific aspects of the postrape recovery process. Although their stories are heartbreaking, they unfortunately are all too common. Data consistently suggest that approximately 14 to 25% of women across racial and ethnic lines in the United States will be sexually assaulted by a man sometime in their lifetime (see Neville & Heppner, 1999). Although girls and women of all ages are sexually assaulted (i.e., experience attempted or completed rape), the incidence rate is higher for young adults between the ages of 16 and 19 (Koss, Gidycz, & Wisniewski, 1987). And about 50% of the women in one large-scale college sample experienced some form of sexual abuse (Koss et al., 1987). Although some women are raped by a stranger, the majority of sexual assault survivors, similar to Ashley and Tanisha, know their assailants (Bachman & Salzman, 1995).

Ashley's and Tanisha's stories are more than another number or statistic. Rape has had a very real and lasting impact on their lives. For example, Tanisha reported experiencing a "nervous breakdown" as a result of the stress related to both the rape and the sexual abuse she experienced as a child by her stepfather. Immediately following the rape, she tried to report the crime; the officer dismissed her claim because she previously had had sex with the perpetrator and had just given birth to his child. At the time of the research interview, Tanisha reported significant levels of depression, anxiety, and social isolation. Ashley, on the other hand, reported no history of previous sexual abuse during the research interview. For a long time following the rape, Ashley blamed herself for what happened. When she finally disclosed the incident to a close friend in high school, her friend did not believe her; in fact, her friend said that she was initially happy for her. Apparently, the perpetrator communicated to the friend that they "made love." Her friend dismissed the seriousness of the rape and even encouraged Ashley to continue seeing him and shared this information with others. When she entered college, Ashley shared her experiences with others and received positive social support. At the time of the interview, she reported moderate levels of anxiety and minimal levels of depression.

Rape has deleterious acute and longer-term consequences for many survivors similar to Ashley and Tanisha. Three interrelated psychological postrape responses receiving the most empirical attention include depression, fear and anxiety, and posttraumatic disorder symptomology (Neville & Heppner, 1999). Depression is one of the most common postrape responses. Upwards of 43% of rape survivors experience clinical levels of depression 1 month following the assault (Frank & Stewart, 1984), with a significant decline in depressive symptomology generally 3 months after the incident. However, researchers have found that compared to women who have not been raped, rape survivors expressed greater levels of depression 1 year (Kilpatrick & Veronen, 1984) to more than 10 years following the incident (Kilpatrick et al., 1987). A number of women experience rape-related fear and anxiety as well, primarily expressed in situations that may remind them of the rape such as blind dates, going out with new people, or being awakened at night. Research suggests that compared to women who have not been raped, rape survivors experience greater levels of anxiety and fear 6 months (Kilpatrick, Veronen, & Resick, 1979), 1 year (Kilpatrick, Resick, & Veronen, 1981), and even 2 to 3 years after the incident (Resick, 1993).

More recently, researchers have conceptualized rape responses within the framework of posttraumatic stress disorder (PTSD), which consists of three interrelated symptoms: reexperiencing the rape, avoiding feelings around the rape and/or numbing oneself, and elevated arousal. The most methodologically sophisticated work has been done in this area. Prospective studies indicate that upwards of 50% of survivors meet the diagnostic criteria for PTSD 3 months following the trauma (Rothbaum, Foa, Riggs, Murdock, & Walsh, 1992). It has also been estimated that a little more than 12% of rape survivors develop chronic PTSD or meet the criteria for PTSD for 6 months or more than 6 months following the assault (Resnick, Kilpatrick, Dansky, Saunders, & Best, 1993). Sexual assault survivors with PTSD may also have related problems that may be under- or misdiagnosed such as sleep-breathing and sleep-moving disorders (Karkow et al., 2000).

Although some initial findings suggest a difference in racial and ethnic group recovery process from rape (e.g., Williams & Holmes, 1982), other results indicate little or no differences between women (e.g., Morelli, 1981; Wyatt, 1992). What is clear is that the empirical data indicate that no racial or ethnic group is immune to negative psychological or behavioral postrape sequelae; rape is a traumatic experience for most people irrespective of social classifications. It is also important to note that after controlling for class, there is no significant difference between the incidences of rape for Black and White women (see Neville & Heppner, 1999). And the overwhelming majority of rapes (more than 95%) are intraracial, not interracial. This is important because, historically, people have erroneously argued that Black men are more prone to rape women. This simply is not the case. Men across racial groups rape, and women across racial groups, unfortunately, are raped.

We began this chapter with case studies to illustrate the deleterious effects of sexual assault on women's lives and to underscore the social need to ameliorate sexual violence. Psychologists, student personnel, educators, and rape activists have long fought to institute programs designed to prevent traumatic experiences such as what happened to Ashley and Tanisha from befalling other girls and women. In this chapter, we outline current college campus intervention efforts intended to decrease the incidence of rape within a given context. We also recognize the inherent limitations in these types of efforts in changing the attitudes and behaviors of all potential rapists within the specified environment and moreover in society in general. So, while many institutions have implemented rape prevention programs, the incidences of new rapes have not abated. It is thus critical to provide effective interventions designed to treat and in some cases prevent chronic psychological distress among rape survivors. To this end, we also review current effective treatments with rape survivors. We conclude by discussing systemic interventions that counselors can implement to address the overarching concern of sexual violence against women.

RAPE PREVENTION INTERVENTIONS
ON COLLEGE CAMPUSES

Given the pervasiveness of sexual violence in American society, many intervention programs have been designed in an attempt to prevent this violence from occurring. Although sexual violence can happen at any age, junior high, high school, and college students have been prime recipients of these interventions because they are in the primary age group where victimization occurs. All college campuses that receive federal dollars, for example, are now mandated to provide some type of intervention program (National Association of Student Personnel Administrators, 1994).

Findings from investigations evaluating the effectiveness of college rape interventions are equivocal. They indicate that sometimes the interventions have been successful, other times not; sometimes, the interventions have been effective only with women, not men, and vice versa; sometimes, participants' change on one outcome measure but not on others (Breitenbecher, 2000; Ullman, in press). It is thus difficult to draw definitive conclusions about the effective elements of rape prevention interventions. Part of the problem is that few researchers in this area have conducted programmatic research, allowing for greater precision in identifying the most effective strategies in creating change. Another problem is the methodology employed. Most studies only provide pre/posttest assessments and do not include follow-up data collection (e.g., Foubert & McEwen, 1998). Without follow-up assessments, our knowledge about the extent of change is misleading. On the surface, it may seem that the programs are effective; however, immediate changes may erode over time.

In this section, we review programmatic research conducted at the University of Missouri that provides initial data regarding the critical elements of sexual violence interventions. We first briefly describe the evolution of these investigations, and then we highlight findings that may be helpful for future programming. The programmatic research was conducted in four major studies over the course of 6 years. Each investigation was built on the knowledge gained from the previous effort, and each ensuing investigation was enhanced in terms of methodological sophistication.

Our programmatic work builds on the innovative research of Gilbert, Heesacker, and Gannon (1991), which used the Elaboration Likelihood Model (ELM) of attitude change (Petty & Cacioppo, 1981, 1986) as its theoretical base. Because an understanding of the ELM is important to conceptualizing the results of our investigations, we briefly describe it first. The ELM conceptualizes attitude change on a continuum, the anchors being peripheral route processing and central route processing of the persuasive message. In peripheral route processing, the individual attends to superficial issues such as the attractiveness of the speaker. In central route processing, the individual attends to the central core of the message itself. The model suggests that an important goal of interventions is to provide the conditions for central route processing to occur. When this happens, the participant finds personal relevance in the message, thoughtfully evaluates the message, judges the quality to be good and the level to be appropriate, feels motivated to listen to the message, engages in issue relevant thinking, and subsequently demonstrates more stable attitude change.

In the first investigation, Heppner, Good, et al. (1995) evaluated a prototypic rape prevention intervention on a coed sample. Results indicated that women in the sample were much more likely to find the message personally relevant and to use central route processing; men in the sample were more likely to attend to peripheral cues. We also found that both men and women evidenced significant increases in awareness about rape and sexual violence immediately after the intervention. However, this change rebounded to preintervention levels at a 2-month follow-up.

In addition to examining quantitative changes on attitude measures, Hillenbrand-Gunn (1995) also conducted an extensive examination of the qualitative data collected in this investigation. She found that one third of the men expressed negativity or hostility about aspects of the intervention and included such statements as "This is male bashing," "Why are you talking to me about this, I am not a rapist," and "Why don't you talk about male rape victims?" These data emphasize the need to directly address the ways in which male defensiveness is fostered so as not to turn men off to listening to the message. Data also suggest the need to identify and present aspects of rape that are more personally relevant for men in order to help them engage in the kind of issue-relevant thinking that, according to ELM, could produce more lasting change.

To address these concerns, in the third study, we evaluated the efficacy of two types of interventions and a no-treatment control (Heppner, Humphrey, Hillenbrand-Gunn, & DeBord, 1995). We specifically examined whether an innovative interactive drama intervention that was designed to be more personally relevant and motivating (Gibson & Humphrey, 1993) would produce more central route processing and thus more stable change than a standard intervention (e.g., didactic portion, video, discussion). The interactive drama intervention consisted of actors portraying a typical dating scenario that ended in date rape. After the scenario, the audience actively engaged in rewriting the script to avoid the occurrence of rape. The actors then reenacted the scene using the audience suggestions. Results indicated that compared to the standard intervention and the no-treatment control group, the interactive drama intervention was more effective in promoting central route processing, helping participants identify what constitutes consent and coercion in sexual situations, and promoting change on five behavioral indicators immediately following the intervention. However, similar to the first investigation, a pattern of rebounding scores occurred over time for both the interactive drama and the standard intervention. This second finding of a rebound of scores is important; to evaluate the potency of change, it is not adequate to assess attitudes only immediately following the intervention.

One of the most consistent arguments raised by researchers is that attitudes toward rape have formed over a considerable length of time, and thus a one-shot intervention, no matter how well designed, will not produce lasting change. Researchers have also consistently called for more in-depth, multi-session interventions that may have a greater possibility of producing lasting effects. To this end, a fourth large-scale intervention study was conducted with White and Black fraternity members. Participants were randomly assigned to one of two treatment conditions (a generic/"colorblind" or a culturally relevant group) or a no-treatment control group. The two treatment interventions consisted of three 90-minute sessions focused on cognitive, affective, and behavioral dimensions of attitudes and were aimed at providing a more in-depth intervention as well as strengthening the personal relevancy of rape prevention with racially diverse men (Heppner, Neville, Smith, Kivlighan, & Gershuny, 1999). Specifically, we wanted to test if, compared to a generic (colorblind) rape intervention, a culturally relevant intervention (e.g., include specific information about race-related rape myths, using Black and White speakers to discuss their sexual violence experiences in a cultural context) would increase the personal relevance of the message and thus encourage Black, and potentially White, participants to process the message centrally.

Briefly, the cognitive component of the intervention examined myths and facts about rape through the use of an interactive myths and facts quiz, which enabled participants to get actively involved in the intervention. The culture-specific intervention used incidence and prevalence figures for both Black and White populations and discussed the historical context of Black and White women's and men's sexuality. The affective component consisted of a panel of rape survivors and male allies talking about the lasting impact of rape on their lives. This component was designed to increase participant empathy for rape survivors. The panelists in the culture-specific condition were racially diverse and specifically discussed how race and culture may have played a role in their recovery process. The behavioral component taught skills through role-played scenarios on recognizing consent and coercion in a sexual situation and in understanding what is helpful to do to support a friend who has been raped. In the culture-specific intervention, one of the teams of actors was Black and the other White. The dating scenarios were placed in a cultural context, and special attention was given to avoid stereotypical behavior.

In contrast to our first two studies, which indicated a rebound of scores to preintervention levels for all participants, the current investigation found three different treatment responses. About one third of the participants demonstrated the typical rebound pattern, another third deteriorated, and another third improved, and their improvement remained stable at 5 months. Those who improved were more likely to have attended more sessions than participants in the other two conditions. In addition, Black students in the culturally relevant condition were more motivated and cognitively engaged in the intervention than their Black peers in the generic intervention.

Taken together, these four studies offer some initial data and support previous findings about what makes for more effective prevention programs. What we see as the five most important findings from these investigations are highlighted as follows:

1. *We know that more substantial and sustained interventions have greater long-term benefit.* Thus, when designing programs, it may be more beneficial to provide longer, more in-depth interventions to fewer students than trying to provide one-shot sessions to greater numbers. The three-session intervention highlighted in our most recent study provides initial data that suggests that men who participated in more sessions demonstrated more lasting change (Heppner et al., 1999). Similarly, Lonsway et al. (1998) evaluated a semester-long course on rape prevention designed for students who wanted to become rape facilitators and also found stable change at a 2-year follow-up. Thus, it seems useful to examine what length of intervention is sufficient to produce longer-term change in individuals.

2. *We know that increasing personal relevance increases the likelihood of change.* Several studies have now demonstrated that when men find the message about sexual assault to be more personally relevant, they are more likely to make immediate changes in their attitudes about rape. Some ways of making the message more relevant are by (a) use of local statistics, (b) use of realistic scenarios or role plays, (c) talking about local sexual violence issues that students may be aware of in their own community, or (d) use of actual rape survivors or allies who can share their stories either in person or on video. On this last point, however, disturbing evidence from a new study by Berg, Lonsway, and Fitzgerald (1999) indicates that men who listened to an audiotape of women describing their experience of rape actually reported more likelihood to engage in rape-supportive behavior following an intervention aimed at increasing empathy. Thus, it may be important, as was done in the Heppner et al. (1999) study, to highlight the psychological and physical impact of the rape rather than describe the rape itself when attempting to alter men's empathetic response to rape survivors.

3. *We know that getting students more actively involved in the presentations in personally relevant ways produces more immediate change.* In our intervention that actively involved participants, we found that those participants were more likely to (a) describe themselves as more motivated to hear the presentation and find it more personally relevant to them, (b) recognize consent and coercion in sexual situations, and (c) demonstrate behavioral change (Heppner, Humphrey, et al., 1995). The interactive drama is one strategy that promotes active learning. Other ways of creating active learning include the use of role plays or the "think-pair-share" technique in which a question is posed, students are asked to think about it, pair with a peer to briefly discuss their thoughts, and then share with the larger group.

4. *We know that attending to the specific racial and ethnic makeup of the audience will increase their motivation and willingness to engage in the message.* In our most recent study (Heppner et al., 1999), we specifically altered both the content and the process of one of the interventions to make it more relevant to African Americans. We did this by having African Americans as presenters, rape survivors, and role players and by infusing content such as statistics related to African Americans into the intervention. We found that African Americans in the culturally specific intervention were more likely to report that they found the intervention personally relevant and felt more motivated to engage in the message. Thus, because it is our intention to engage individuals in the intervention, attending to the unique characteristics of the audience may be helpful in producing more long-term, positive change.

5. *We know that prototypic rape prevention programming can create defensiveness in males, which can then shut down their willingness to engage in the message.* Although it is important to acknowledge that rape is a male issue and that men need to provide the solution for stopping it, it is also increasingly apparent that some rape prevention programming fosters a level of defensiveness in men that may cause them to shut down cognitively and emotionally and thus not benefit from the intervention. In Hillenbrand-Gunn's (1995) qualitative study, she found that 30% of men in a prototypic rape prevention intervention reported some sort of bored or hostile response to the presentation. This finding emphasizes the need to directly address how male defensiveness is fostered so as not to turn men off to listening to the message. This can be done by (a) using male presenters, including teachers, coaches, or other respected males, (b) communicating that men can be part of the solution if they educate themselves about sexual violence and stop others when they see the potential for sexual assault occurring, or (c) discussing the prevalence of male rape and acknowledging the pain and trauma that men experience from rape as well.

The descriptions of rape prevention interventions with males, especially high school and college students, have increased considerably over the past decade. Many of the interventions implemented in such institutions are single-session programs aimed at increasing participants' awareness of the detrimental effects of sexual violence on girls and women and in society as a whole. Although it seems as though this type of programming may initially increase sensitivity to the topic, the dosage of the typical rape awareness intervention is much too weak to create sustained change.

Within the context of school environments, professionals must begin to implement more systematic interventions (i.e., more than one session), paying close attention to the racial and ethnic composition of the target audience. Although the Heppner et al. (1999) study was one of the first actual prevention studies to examine a culturally specific intervention, there is growing evidence of the importance of providing culturally specific models of rape perpetration (Hall, Sue, Narang, & Lilly, 2000), providing culturally inclusive models of rape recovery (Neville & Heppner, 1999), and examining culturally specific survivor patterns of responding following an assault (Neville & Pugh, 1996). Developing ways to decrease defensiveness of the participants is also necessary in reducing the incidence of sexual violence against high school and college students.

TREATMENT INTERVENTIONS

Rape prevention programming is certainly one of many steps needed to challenge and change our cultural belief system that serves to condone rape in our society. However, because rape persists, it is not only important to design interventions to significantly curb the incidence of rape but also to provide effective treatment to survivors when it has occurred. In this section, we briefly review the current treatment interventions that have been proven to significantly reduce psychological distress in rape survivors. We then spotlight one specific intervention: cognitive processing therapy.

Historically, health practitioners have implemented a variety of methods to assist women in dealing with the trauma of sexual assault, including crisis, pharmacological, and psychodynamic interventions. However popular these methods may be in the real world, systematic data supporting the effectiveness of these treatment modalities are scant. The bulk of the empirical research on treatment with rape survivors has evaluated the effectiveness of cognitive behavioral interventions on survivors' posttraumatic stress, depressive, and anxiety symptomology. The three general cognitive behavioral interventions receiving the most theoretical and empirical attention with rape survivors include prolonged exposure, anxiety management training, and cognitive processing therapy. The systematic work of Edna Foa et al. (e.g., Foa & Rothbaum, 1998; Foa et al., 1999) and Patricia Resick and Monica Schnicke (e.g., 1993) have contributed greatly to our understanding and explication of the intervention approaches and specific techniques useful in helping survivors process the trauma successfully and, consequently, improve psychological functioning. The three forms of therapy are briefly described below, followed by a summary of key research findings. We conclude the section by providing case examples using cognitive processing therapy and prolonged exposure therapy.

Prolonged exposure treatments have received the most empirical support. Most prolonged exposure interventions include a combination of imagination exposure (or a cognitive reliving of the event) and an in vivo exposure (or real-life exposure to a rape-related stimuli, e.g., going to a similar place where the person was raped). A typical prolonged exposure treatment program consists of the following four techniques: (1) education about common trauma reactions, (2) controlled breathing techniques, (3) repeated reliving of the trauma, and (4) in vivo confrontation in safe environments that remind the survivor of the trauma. A more recent development in prolonged exposure is eye movement desensitization and reprocessing (EMDR), in which the survivor imagines a scene from the trauma while "tracking" the therapist's moving fingers. Findings from at least one study support the effectiveness of a brief EMDR intervention (one session per week for 4 weeks) in substantially reducing PTSD symptoms for up to 3 months postintervention (Rothbaum, 1997).

Stress inoculation therapy (SIT) is the primary form of anxiety management training evaluated in research. Essentially, SIT is designed to assist clients in developing more effective skills primarily to handle anxiety and fear. Common SIT activities include skills building and education components around cognition (e.g., cognitive restructuring and thought stopping) and behavior (e.g., deep muscle relaxation, role playing). Cognitive processing therapy, on the other hand, is grounded in information processing and is designed to assist clients to challenge faulty assumptions about the rape and to better integrate the rape experience. Incorporating both cognitive- and exposure-based techniques, cognitive processing therapy consists of imaginal exposure (writing or reading, or both, an account of the rape), breathing exercises, and cognitive restructuring.

Although findings differ from study to study, research generally provides two suggestions: (1) Systematic and properly administered cognitive behavioral interventions are effective in significantly reducing the negative psychological effects of rape, and (2) no one therapy is superior to the other, and a combination of therapies does not produce greater therapeutic effects. First, research suggests that each of the three treatments described above is highly effective. For example, findings from controlled empirical studies suggest that prolonged exposure significantly decreases PTSD symptomology (see Foa & Rothbaum, 1998). In one of the studies showing the greatest gains, Richards, Lovell, and Marks (1994) found a 65 to 80% reduction in PTSD symptomology following the intervention, and at a 1-year follow-up, none of the participants met the diagnostic criteria for PTSD. Similarly, results from Resick and Schnicke's (1993) work indicate that participants in cognitive processing therapy experience a significant reduction in PTSD, depression, anxiety, and general psychological distress for up to 6 months postintervention. For example, nearly all of the participants in their study (96%) met diagnostic criteria for PTSD prior to the intervention, but only 8% met the criteria at the 6-month follow-up. Second, the various cognitive behavioral treatments appear to be, in general, equally effective. Foa et al. (1999) have conducted several studies evaluating the comparative effectiveness of prolonged exposure therapy and situational inoculation therapy and a combination of the two on PTSD and related symptomology. Consistent with existing literature, results from one of their recent investigations indicated that, compared to a wait-list control group, participants in each of the three treatment groups experienced a substantial reduction of PTSD and depression for up to 1-year postintervention.

To help better understand the nature of cognitive behavioral interventions with rape survivors, we next briefly describe prolonged exposure (PE) therapy and then cognitive behavior therapy using Ashley's narrative to highlight central processes. PE therapy generally consists of nine weekly 90-minute sessions; however, if there is not a significant reduction (70%) in PTSD symptoms, then three additional sessions are added. Foa and Rothbaum (1998) outlined several therapy conditions that should be created regardless of the type of treatment modality, including the following: creating a nonjudgmental and caring atmosphere, demonstrating expertise about rape-related symptoms, communicating confidence that the treatment will be effective, and normalizing postrape responses.

In the first PE session, the overall treatment program is described, personal and trauma history is collected, and breathing exercises are introduced. Clients are able to describe the assault and its impact on them in more detail in the second session. During this time, therapists normalize the women's experiences by discussing common postassault responses. In this session, in vivo exposure is also introduced, and a list is created of situations, places, and people the clients avoid because they remind them of the rape. The logic here is that it is essential to directly confront feared situations that are realistically safe as a way to process the rape and to reduce anxiety resulting from the trauma. If Ashley were in treatment, her list might consist of items such as being alone in a car with a male, going hiking, driving by deserted areas, and talking to someone about the assault. Clients assign each situation on the list a subjective unit of discomfort between 0 (no anxiety) and 100 (extreme discomfort). In homework assignments and, in some cases, in actual therapy sessions, clients imagine themselves in a specific situation on their list with a moderate subjective unit of discomfort rating (between 40 and 60) for an extended period of time (at least

30 minutes). The goal is for clients to remain in the imaginary situation until their discomfort is reduced by at least 50%. By the end of therapy, clients' level of discomfort should be relatively low for each of the items on the list.

In sessions three through eight, clients are guided through imaginal exposure, or a vivid recalling of the trauma in the present tense. In initial sessions, clients are asked to describe the trauma gradually, and in subsequent sessions they are asked to describe the trauma progressively in more detail, paying attention to psychological and physiological sensations. Time permitting, clients retell the trauma several times in each session, and therapists record the clients' subjective units of discomfort approximately every 10 minutes. If Ashley were seeking this type of treatment, the latter sessions would consist of her retelling her story in the here and now, describing her feelings of intense fear as her date pinned her down in the car; she would detail physical sensations such as her heart racing and cognitive reactions such as thinking she was going to be killed during each stage of the attack. By retelling the event in a safe environment and practicing relaxation breathing techniques along with the other ingredients of therapy, by the ninth session, Ashley's level of PTSD, anxiety, and depression should be significantly decreased, and thus therapy would be terminated.

Cognitive processing therapy (CPT) consists of 12 structured 60-minute individual (or 90-minute group) sessions, incorporating weekly homework assignments. Therapists using this form of therapy also try to create a safe therapeutic environment, as described earlier. In the first session, general education about rape reactions and the treatment are covered. The next couple of sessions are devoted to understanding the meaning of and emotional reactions to the rape. In these sessions, clients identify an activating agent that is associated with the rape and resulting beliefs and consequences of these thoughts. For example, if Ashley were in CPT treatment, she may have identified riding in a car with a male as the activating agent, with corresponding internal messages such as "I am vulnerable" and "I should protect myself." The consequences of these thoughts may lead her to respond to the event by feeling anxious and terrified during the ride. Treatment in this phase focuses on challenging the internal messages.

The next four sessions center on remembering the rape and processing thoughts and feelings. This process includes writing and rewriting one's story and analyzing past and present feelings about the trauma as well as challenging conflicting cognitions and faulty assumptions about the event. If Ashley had sought therapy prior to coming to college, she might have described feeling sadness and shame about the trauma because she minimized the event by not identifying it as a "real rape" and because she assumed she was able to somehow prevent the event from transpiring. These faulty thinking patterns would be challenged by identifying more accurate and adaptive thoughts (e.g., she was at least 20 pounds lighter and 4 inches shorter than the person she was dating; she was not physically strong enough to stop the rape). In the remaining sessions, the client continues to process the rape in terms of the following rape-related recovery issues (one session is devoted to each area): safety, trust, power and control, esteem, and intimacy (for additional information on cognitive therapies with trauma survivors, see Muran & DiGiuseppe, 2000; Rothbaum, Meadows, Resick, & Foy, 2000).

It is important to note that the manualized treatments in the research described above are not designed for all survivors. Because of complicating factors, specific populations have been excluded from participation in most studies, including women with a history of incest such as Tanisha, women with borderline personality disorder, and women with active substance abuse. In addition, it is also important to emphasize that therapists who perform these interventions must have advanced training and skill. Otherwise, these interventions may very well do more harm than good.

Although many of the studies reviewed reflect sophisticated methodology and the treatments across the board are proving to be effective, challenges remain for future work. First, although high-school age girls fall within the age range of most assault victims, there is scant literature evaluating the effectiveness of interventions targeting this population. It is unclear at this point whether the level of adolescent cognitive development plays a role in current treatment processes, especially in CPT, which incorporates information processing theory. Another major concern rests with the consideration of potential ethnocultural variables. For example, in Tanisha's case, she rated culture-specific attributions (e.g., "Black women are portrayed negatively in the media") as significant reasons for understanding why she was assaulted. She also identified racism as a significant factor in explaining why she was mistreated by the police officer she disclosed the assault to. The research did not examine how these factors may be incorporated into the therapy process. Future researchers may want to consult the literature on multicultural counseling and therapy to assist in efforts to systematically include ethnocultural factors into their treatment protocols. Research evaluating the effectiveness of culturally relevant interventions compared to traditional colorblind interventions is clearly needed, especially with racial and ethnic minority samples.

Over the past decade, our knowledge base about the effectiveness of individual and group therapy with rape survivors has significantly increased. We know that three general types of cognitive behavioral therapy (i.e., prolonged therapy, anxiety management training, and cognitive processing therapy) are quite effective in reducing the negative psychological effects of rape, especially PTSD and clinical levels of depression. However, additional information about the effectiveness of these treatments with diverse populations (e.g., high school students) and other postassault symptoms (e.g., risky sexual behavioral practices, eating disorders) is needed. And consistent with our discussion of the limitations of rape prevention programming on college campuses, we need more information about what counseling professionals can do to prevent rape or its negative sequelae beyond the individual (e.g., cognitive behavioral therapy) and her immediate environmental context.

SYSTEMIC INTERVENTIONS

To help describe risk and protective factors influencing psychological adjustment, we developed a culturally inclusive ecological model of sexual assault recovery (Neville & Heppner, 1999), which we later adapted to contextualize prevention and intervention work (Neville, Heppner, & Spanierman, in press). A main premise of the model is that human behavior is multiply determined by complex interactions between individuals and their environments. We argue that in order to contextualize rape survivors' experiences it is critical to examine the general and culture-specific factors present at the individual level as well as at the microsystem (immediate environments such as family and school the individual has contact with), exosystem (social institutions or practices that have an indirect impact on individuals), and macrosystem (societal practices, values) levels. We also note the importance of practitioners to intervene on multiple levels to prevent rape from occurring and in treating rape survivors.

Consistent with our observations, Lee and Brydges (1998) provide concrete strategies that practitioners can implement to intervene on systemic levels to address the general concern of violence against women. Relevant intervention strategies include (a) promoting public awareness about rape via a variety of activities, including facilitating community forums on the topic, circulating critical statistics and information to key sectors in the public, developing public service announcements or public statements for media outlets, (b) building coalitions with professionals within other fields and environments to help challenge violence against women (e.g., coalitions with health professionals or K-12 educators, or both, and administrators), and (c) supporting public policy and legislation. Specifically related to the college environment, practitioners can assist with campus rape prevention efforts by providing theoretical and practical guidance to prevention interventions with men. Practitioners can also work with the campus administration to devise strategies to increase women's safety on campus, including installing lighting in parking areas and emergency phones strategically located throughout campus as well as security escorts to walk women to their cars or across campus at night.

SUMMARY

Rape has reached epidemic proportions in the United States. This form of violence has had profound personal and social implications. Over the years, mental health professionals have played a key role in helping women process the rape and, moreover, in designing programs to significantly reduce the incidence of rape in specific contexts. Working collaboratively with other professionals, psychologists can also begin to find creative, yet effective, interventions designed to promote exo- and macrosystem changes.

VIGNETTE

Michael, a popular, well-liked senior and star tennis player at Kennedy High School, knew Kendra casually, a junior attending the same school. After a neighborhood party in which both had been drinking alcohol, Michael offered to drive Kendra home. Instead of taking Kendra home immediately after the party, he took her to a deserted dirt road and had sex with her both inside and outside the car. Kendra screamed, yelled, kicked, and punched Michael to get him to stop assaulting her. However, she was physically too small to thwart his aggressions. Michael dropped her off at home in the morning. After some reluctance, Kendra told her mother about the previous night's incident. Against Kendra's wishes, her mother forced Kendra to file formal charges against Michael, and her mother met with school officials to inquire about disciplinary actions. Michael swears he didn't do anything wrong and that Kendra wanted to have sex with him. Rumors of the rape quickly spread throughout the school; the school newspaper even included commentaries of the incident in a recent issue, in which some students supported Michael's claims in blaming Kendra for what happened and others supported Kendra, making affirming statements. Kendra lost several close friends for "going public" with the "misunderstanding." As a result of the publicity around the assault, several girls have come to the school counselor to discuss similar experiences they have had while attending high school.

---

1. What interventions would you implement if you were hired as a psychological consultant to (a) intervene in the current situation and (b) assist in devising a concrete plan to prevent future incidents? In your response, consider the following: the various points of interventions possible (e.g., school officials, newspaper, family, students, survivors) and possible legal and ethical issues involved. Be very specific and outline the suggested interventions.

2. How would your intervention and programmatic plan differ depending on the following:

- It was a predominantly (a) White suburban high school, (b) White rural high school, or (c) racial and ethnic minority urban high school.
- It was a college campus instead of a high school (predominantly White campus vs. historically Black college or university).
- It was a community church.

ADDITIONAL RESOURCES

Books on Prevention Intervention

Books can be purchased at http://www.amazon.com

Berkowitz, A. D. (Ed.). (1994). *Men and rape: Theory, research and preventive programs in higher education.* San Francisco: Jossey-Bass.

Marshall, W. L., Fernandez, Y. M., Hudson, S. M., & Ward, T. (1998). *Sourcebook of treatment programs for sexual offenders.* New York: Plenum.

Parrot, A. (1994). *Rape 101: Sexual assault prevention for college athletes.* Holmes Beach, FL: Learning Publications.

Books on Psychological Treatment Intervention

Foa, E. B., & Rothbaum, B. O. (1998). *Treating the trauma of rape: Cognitive-behavioral therapy for PTSD.* New York: Guilford.

Resick, P. A., & Schnicke, M. K. (1993). *Cognitive processing therapy for sexual assault victims: A treatment manual.* Newbury, Park, CA: Sage.

Bibliotherapy Books

Books can be purchased at http://www.amazon.com

Francisco, P. W. (1999). *Telling: A memoir of rape and recovery.* New York: Cliff Street Books.

Pierce-Baker, C. (1998). *Surviving the silence: Black women's stories of rape.* New York: Norton.

Raine, N. V. (1998). *After silence: Rape and my journey back.* New York: Crown.

Warshaw, R. (1994). *I never called it rape* (Rev. ed.). New York: Harper & Row.

Videotapes

Videotapes can be purchased at http://www.intermedia-inc.com

When a kiss is not a kiss (1995)
  A 38-minute interactive presentation about date rape.

Scars (1999)
  A 22-minute video profiling rape, molestation, and date rape.

Responding to rape (1992)
  A 30-minute overview of rape and its implications on society.

Internet Resources

Campus & Community Victim Assistance Resources: Security on Campus, Inc.:
  http://www.campussafety.org/assistance/index
Men Can Stop Rape: http://www.mencanstoprape.org
RAINN (Rape, Abuse, & Incest National Network): http://www.rainn.org

CHAPTER 15

Prevention and Treatment of Family Violence

Carolyn Zerbe Enns

The American Psychological Association (APA) Presidential Task Force on Violence and the Family (1996) defined family violence and abuse as "the physical, sexual, and emotional maltreatment of one family member by another" (p. 3). Family violence encompasses a diverse array of behaviors, including battering, child physical and sexual abuse, dating violence and marital rape, and elder abuse. The dynamics of family violence are highly complex, and acts of family violence are "disturbingly common" (Emery & Laumann-Billings, 1998, p. 122), even when conceptualized by the most conservative of definitions.

Given the complexity, diversity, and frequency with which counselors are likely to encounter counseling issues related to family violence, it is necessary for counselors to be knowledgeable about the dynamics of violence. To provide counselors with this essential background, this chapter (a) provides a brief commentary about the prevalence, risk factors, and forms of family violence, (b) summarizes prevention and early intervention priorities, and (c) identifies general principles for intervening effectively with victims and perpetrators of family violence.

COMPLEXITY OF FAMILY VIOLENCE, PREVALENCE, AND RISK FACTORS

Across all forms of violence, children are more likely than adults to be victimized. Children also experience victimization by being observers of violence, with approximately 3.3 million children being exposed to violence against adult women partners or caretakers in a given year (APA, 1996). Gender is another important factor associated with family violence in that the most significant risk factor associated with becoming a victim of violence in the home is being female (APA, 1996; Chalk & King, 1998a). Within adult partner relationships, approximately one in three women experiences partner assault (Browne, 1993). Women are 13 times more likely to be victims of violence than are men, and girls are twice as likely to experience sexual abuse than are boys (APA, 1996; Finkelhor & Dzuiba-Leatherman, 1994).

Elder abuse, which has only received attention during the past decade, has also been recognized as a serious form of family violence. Neglect is the most common form of elder abuse, and adult children are the most common abusers of elders (APA, 1996). Elders at greatest risk are women who reside with their adult offspring and who have limited economic resources (Barnett, Miller-Perrin, & Perrin, 1997).

Various forms of family violence such as partner battering and child abuse often coexist, and individuals may be victims of multiple forms of family violence over a lifetime (Barnett et al., 1997). For example, approximately 50% of women who have experienced adult abuse also report a history of child abuse (McCauley et al., 1997), and when children live with an abused mother, they are 12 to 14 times more likely to experience sexual abuse (McCloskey, Figuerdo, & Koss, 1995). Between 40% and 75% of children who are observers of adult violence in the family are also likely to be victims of physical abuse (Emery & Laumann-Billings, 1998). Family violence is not only related to other forms of family violence but is associated with other types of aggression, gender-related violence, and violence in the community (APA, 1996; Barnett et al., 1997).

High rates of family violence, especially domestic violence, are present in both heterosexual and homosexual relationships and within a wide range of cultures around the world (APA, 1996; Walker, 1999; Wiehe, 1998). Although issues of power are associated with intimate violence across cultures and many types of relationships, the dynamics and forms of violence are often influenced by racism, sexism, heterosexism, and cultural attitudes and values (APA, 1996; Barnett et al., 1997; Chalk & King, 1998a).

Barnett et al. (1997) indicated that similarities across the various forms of family violence include being a young parent or spouse, economic hardship, victimization during childhood, and violence or criminal behavior outside as well as inside the family. One of the strongest predictors of family violence is the act of perpetrating violence in the past (APA, 1996). The following personal characteristics have also been associated with the use of abusive or violent acts: personal isolation, emotional neediness or immaturity, power and control needs, a sense of worthlessness or low self-esteem, and inappropriate expectations of significant others. Other factors associated with family violence include high levels of stress, alcohol and drug abuse, exposure to parental violence and conflict in one's family of origin, and the use of coping methods marked by aggression, anxiety, impulsiveness, and defensiveness (APA, 1996; Chalk & King, 1998a; Emery & Laumann-Billings, 1998). Although it is "firmly established" (Finkelhor & Dzuiba-Leatherman, 1994, p. 181) that experiencing abuse as a child is associated with an increased likelihood of becoming a perpetrator of violence, an important qualification is that only a minority, or roughly one third, of those who are exposed to violence in the home are violent as adults (Belsky, 1993). Social isolation, poverty, and lack of community cohesion are also risk factors associated with family violence. For people living in poverty, financial stress and unequal access to opportunities appear to contribute to high levels of frustration in the family. However, social cohesion, mutual caring, and community identity play important protective roles within impoverished communities (Coulton, Korbin, Su, & Chow, 1995).

In addition to being aware of the relationship between risk factors and violence, counselors should also be attentive to the support systems (e.g., community, kinship bonds, nurturing relationships with adults outside the family), coping and social skills, personal attitudes (e.g., respect for others, empathy, self-esteem), and other protective factors (e.g., psychological hardiness) that may decrease a person's or a family's vulnerability to violence. When working with potential victims of violence, counselors should ask open-ended questions that facilitate discussion of both risk and protective factors as well as explore the full range of life experiences that may account for the presence of risk factors in clients' lives.

Many researchers and commentators contend that family violence cannot be understood apart from larger sociocultural influences such as the acceptance of violence in the media, rigid gender-role socialization, violence in the larger culture, and strong beliefs about the privacy of the family. Emery and Laumann-Billings (1998) observed that "societal policies may not cause family violence, but many of our practices appear to condone it" (p. 127). In general, simplistic or unidimensional models of family violence are inadequate. It is more likely that multiple pathways and multiple risk factors, including a confluence of individual and environmental issues, contribute to family violence.

PREVENTION OF AND EARLY INTERVENTION WITH FAMILY VIOLENCE

Chalk and King (1998b) noted that "after-the-fact" treatment interventions for family violence are more common than proactive and prevention strategies. To effectively address the developmental needs of families, however, it is necessary for human service professionals to work toward stopping violence before it begins as well as intervene efficiently and effectively at the earliest signs of violence. The following brief discussion emphasizes three areas of prevention and early intervention: building skills, changing attitudes about gender roles, and altering cultural norms that condone violence.

Building Skills in Communication and Coping

A substantial number of psychoeducational programs have been developed, and in general, these programs target the major risk factors of family violence, including high levels of stress, coping and social skills deficits, and family isolation and lack of social support (Andrews, 1994). Training in negotiation, compromise, conflict management, and collaborative problem solving can be offered to both adults and children in a wide array of settings, including schools, churches, early intervention programs, and other community settings. In general, successful prevention and education programs for both children and adults emphasize the development of social-cognitive skills, including perspective taking, negotiation skills, and methods for avoiding violence. These programs are likely to be active and involving, focus on specific goals and skills, and include both educational and practice components (Guerra, Tolan, & Hammond, 1994; Wurtele & Miller-Perrin, 1992). The use of role playing and modeling may be especially helpful to family members as they write new scripts for coping with specific situations that are associated with the escalation of conflict. Interventions designed to help individuals restructure flawed parent-child relationship schemas (e.g., unrealistic or developmentally inappropriate expectations) also facilitate more productive problem solving in families (Azar, 1997).

Although many psychoeducational programs show short-term changes in attitudes and behavior, new behaviors are not necessarily maintained over time. Furthermore, short-term educational programs that focus solely on skills may be inadequate for addressing the multiple and complex contributors to family violence (Blau & Long, 1999; Chalk & King, 1998b). Skill-building programs designed to counteract risk factors for violence also need to be sensitive to the developmental stages and life tasks of participants, and they need to emphasize the development of competence and empowerment rather than remediation. Also important are community-based neighborhood programs that use peer leadership and self-help, counteract isolation and foster neighborhood networks and pride, and mobilize the entire community to counteract both family and nonfamily violence (Benjamin, 1998).

Research suggests that family support and home visitation programs associated with early infancy projects and family support are some of the "most promising" (Chalk & King, 1998a, p. 301) programs for preventing family violence. These programs are designed to facilitate the skills of at-risk parents such as young, single, poor mothers of very young children. Chalk and King

(1998a), whose book summarized the findings of the National Research Council on family violence, indicated that parenting practices are often resistant to change. Early intervention with young persons coping with the early challenges of parenting helps ensure that ineffective parenting practices do not become the foundation for dealing with the ongoing challenges of family development. In general, home visitation (sometimes referred to as parental competence programs) establish relationships between expectant and new parents and a mentor, sometimes a volunteer or paraprofessional, who provides parenting information and social support (Barnett et al., 1997; Wiehe, 1998). Comprehensive programs (e.g., the Good Start Program) not only provide in-home assistance but also include prenatal and infant health services, developmental assessments, parent-child programs, referral to various community services, transportation to service locations, assistance with seeking child care, and social advocacy (Chalk & King, 1998a; Harrington & Dubowitz, 1999; Wiehe, 1998). Evaluation research reveals that these parent intervention programs appear to be more successful when they (a) provide support for parents as close in time as is possible to the birth date of the first child, (b) focus on building clients' self-efficacy and competence, (c) are based on a positive, sustained working alliance between the client and educator-consultant, and (d) help mobilize the client's community and family support network (MacMillan, MacMillan, Offord, Griffith, & MacMillan, 1993; Olds, 1997). Home visitation programs may be effective, in part, because intervention occurs at multiple levels: the individual level, family level, and community level (Harrington & Dubowitz, 1999). In addition, these programs facilitate more accurate, complete assessments of clients' unique situations, allow for the modeling of new behaviors within the environments in which they will be enacted, and support family empowerment and self-esteem by building on personal resources (Blau & Long, 1999).

Modified forms of preventive home visitation programs can also be useful for early intervention after abuse has occurred. The Family Crisis Care (FCC) project provides three phases of service: (1) 6 weeks of crisis intervention, (2) 2 to 6 weeks of in-home visits with therapists and concrete services such as food, clothing, and shelter, and (3) a 4- to 12-month follow-up phase that includes counseling and making connections with a variety of community agencies. Throughout the program, therapists are on call 24 hours per day (Harrington & Dubowitz, 1999). Another project, the Homebuilders Program, provides crisis intervention and multidimensional services for high-risk families and less intensive in-home counseling for lower-risk families (Wiehe, 1998).

Group interventions that incorporate skill-building components with other goals (e.g., decreasing isolation, providing support, and helping clients keep a perspective) also play significant prevention and early intervention roles. For example, one group treatment model includes information and general discussion about the cycle of family violence, which is characterized by (a) increased tension, (b) is followed by violent actions, and (c) typically culminates in a calm phase marked by apologies and promises for change (Blau & Long, 1999). When integrated with communication skills training, an awareness of the dynamics of violence may help families cope with stresses more effectively. Self-help groups such as Parents Anonymous provide peer support and make use of mentors or sponsors for assisting abusive parents seeking to make changes. Members who learn to consistently implement nonviolent negotiation skills may graduate to positions of mentoring, which can further empower group members. These types of groups are not time limited and thus can also offer longer-term support (Wiehe, 1998).

When working with individuals at later phases of the life development span, skill building and coping training may need to take different forms. The needs of elderly family members are often unique because they may be experiencing a decreased ability to engage in the physical and cognitive functions that they took for granted earlier in their lives. Skill-building and education programs are useful for helping family members gain practical caregiving skills, develop new tools for communicating effectively with elderly parents or spouses, and feel confident and competent about their abilities to provide necessary care. In addition, psychoeducational programs can be augmented with supportive services such as foster or day care, transportation services, financial planning assistance, and respite care. These supportive services decrease caregiver stress and increase the elderly family member's sense of independence (APA, 1996).

Many of the programs described above call on counselors to think flexibly about their roles as well as the context in which they implement their roles. They may need to step out of their offices and into the homes and institutions of their clients in order to enact comprehensive and effective programs.

Working Toward Gender Equality

A significant factor associated with family violence is male dominance in society and the associated beliefs that men are entitled to hold special executive power in the family (Barnett et al., 1997; Straus & Smith, 1990). Several recent books have focused on the "emotional miseducation" of boys, the potential connection between this socialization and violence, and the importance of changing the ways society trains boys to become men (e.g., Garbarino, 1999; Pollack, 1998).

During the past two decades, significant attention has been paid to the concept of male gender role conflict, which consists of (a) restrictive emotionality, (b) overvaluing of control, power, and competition, (c) homophobia, (d) restricted ability to show affection and the sexualization of intimacy, (e) obsession with achievement and success, and (f) a variety of health care problems (O'Neil, 1990). In addition to being related to a variety of psychological problems in men (Mahalik, 1999), gender role conflict is associated with the use of immature psychological defenses such as turning against others (Mahalik, Cournoyer, DeFranc, Cherry, & Napolitano, 1998). The significant predictive link found between the restrictive emotionality aspect of men's gender role conflict and men's psychological distress suggests that intervention and prevention efforts designed to facilitate men's expression of vulnerable emotions are important (Fischer & Good, 1997). If men develop a repertoire of nonviolent coping methods and are able to express a wide range of emotions other than anger, they are likely to be prepared to deal with conflict in the family more effectively.

The Youth Relationships Project curriculum (Wolfe et al., 1997) emphasizes gender-related issues and the importance of establishing nonviolent intimate adolescent relationships. This curriculum clarifies the relationship between relationship violence and abuse of power and redefines positive powerful relationships as those in which equality, empathy, and emotional expressiveness are present. It also explores linkages between violence, sexism, and gender socialization and encourages adolescents to become involved in a social action event designed to counteract violence against women. Another similar program, the Skills for Violence-Free Relationships (SVFR), targets 13- to 18-year-old young people and incorporates activities that challenge traditional gender roles and promotes nonviolent conflict management (Barnett et al., 1997).

It is important to note that the use of aggression is not restricted to men. Research findings reveal that men and women often report using similar amounts of physical and verbal aggression. However, women are more likely to report their aggressive behaviors, rely on aggression for self-defense purposes, and are more likely to limit their aggression to domestic domains. Men are more likely than women to perpetrate multiple and severe forms of aggression (Koss et al., 1994). Helping both men and women share power and express a full range of emotions is central to creating nonviolent family environments. In addition to family and cultural socialization factors, it is important to remain cognizant of the reality that men continue to hold greater power than women within society in general. Efforts designed to promote equality in the family, the work domain, and within institutional power structures are also likely to have preventive effects (Straus & Smith, 1990).

Changing Social Values to Promote the Acceptance of Violence

Straus and Smith (1990) proposed that one major contributor to family violence is the reality that conflict is inherent within the family, as it is in many groups in which members may have competing needs and goals. This conflict is exacerbated by cultural norms and socialization factors that condone family violence and view physical punishment and hitting as normal and appropriate ways of disciplining others. Straus and Smith (1990) noted that "the family operates on the basis of different rules than those that apply outside the family.

The rule outside the family is that, with the exception of self-defense, you cannot hit anyone, even if he or she behaves terribly" (p. 516). Within American society, approximately 90% of parents use some form of physical punishment, and this use of force against children is associated with the increased violence of children toward their siblings (Straus, 1990). Finkelhor and Dzuiba-Leatherman (1994) argued that if spanking were labeled a form of family violence, roughly two thirds of children would be labeled victims. Physical punishment may lay the groundwork or "script" for other forms of violence. These realities underscore the importance of helping parents learn alternative approaches to discipline as well as working to implement broad cultural change.

High levels of both legitimate violence and criminal violence are pervasive in American society, and "violence in one sphere of life tends to spill over into other spheres of life" (Straus & Smith, 1990, p. 521). Given these realities, prevention and public education efforts should focus on a wide range of issues such as violence in the media, the legislation of gun control, and even the use of "legitimate" military intervention. Counselors and prevention workers should not limit their efforts to local or small group interventions but should consider becoming involved in social change and advocacy programs designed to change public opinion and public policy. For example, by supporting legislation that increases access to family leave and child care or that implements legal sanctions that deter violence, the counselor supports systemic changes that are likely to decrease the stresses associated with family conflict (Andrews, 1994). Harrington and Dubowitz (1999) argued that recent federal welfare and child protection reforms have contributed to the dismantling of services available to disadvantaged families and may increase the vulnerability of some families to various forms of disruption. Being cognizant of such changes and speaking out about their effects are additional issues that prevention-oriented counselors may wish to address.

WHEN FAMILY VIOLENCE OCCURS: THE PSYCHOLOGICAL COSTS

Research about the psychological consequences of family violence reveals that all forms of family violence are related to a wide range of psychological problems such as depression, anxiety, self-destructive behaviors, aggression, and other posttraumatic reactions (APA, 1996; Emery & Laumann-Billings, 1998). Many of the psychological problems associated with family violence can be conceptualized as forms of posttraumatic stress. Posttraumatic symptoms, especially those associated with cumulative traumas or stressors, are often accompanied by depression, anxiety and panic disorders, and substance use (APA, 1996; Breslau, Davis, Peterson, & Schultz, 1997). Depression is so common among traumatized individuals that Davidson and Fairbank (1993) suggested using the phrase "posttraumatic depression" to conceptualize many mood-related reactions to violence. The use of a posttraumatic stress framework for unifying the wide-ranging effects of family violence may facilitate assessment, the organization of the diverse effects of abuse, and the designing of appropriate interventions.

One important cautionary note is that children and adults may experience the effects of trauma in different ways. Furthermore, some childhood victims exhibit few behavioral changes, whereas others display severe psychological problems marked by diverse symptoms such as depression, aggression, anxiety, or sexualized behavior (Saywitz, Mannarino, Berliner, & Cohen, 2000). Many of the cognitive, affective, behavioral, and physiological symptoms experienced by traumatized children and adolescents are consistent with posttraumatic stress disorder (PTSD), but the classic conceptualization of this diagnosis may be inadequate for understanding the manner in which trauma may affect the whole person (Armsworth & Holaday, 1993). A sense of stigma, betrayal, and powerlessness as well as distorted perceptions of the self are frequent consequences of abuse experienced by abused children (Friedrich, 1996).

Herman's (1992) description of complex PTSD may be especially useful for linking the diverse array of symptoms associated with long-term and cumulative family violence. According to her conceptualization, posttraumatic reactions associated with long-term exposure to abuse may be manifested by alterations of (a) affect (e.g., depression or anger), (b) consciousness (e.g., amnesia, reliving experiences, dissociation, or depersonalization), (c) self-perception (e.g., feelings of shame, helplessness, and stigma), (d) relationships (e.g., isolation or relationship disruption), and (e) systems of meaning (e.g., sense of hopelessness or loss of faith). Victims may also experience changes in their perceptions of a perpetrator, which may involve idealizing the perpetrator or believing she or he holds unrealistic levels of power. To summarize, the psychological consequences of abuse are often diverse and may affect a wide range of human functioning. Counselors need to be aware of the unique and varied ways in which clients manifest trauma-related symptoms and to be attentive to how these symptoms facilitate clients' efforts to cope with significant psychological or physical threats to their well-being.

Counseling and Psychotherapy for Victims of Family Violence

Challenges Associated With Intervention

Effective family violence intervention programs (a) are based on sound conceptual models and assessment procedures, (b) consider the specific needs, life circumstances, gender-related issues, and developmental phases of victims, (c) are designed to stop violence and limit future exposure to violence, (d) use techniques that help clients cope with intrusive symptoms and avoid repeated discussions of abuse that may retraumatize clients, and (e) are culturally appropriate and sensitive to family and social belief systems and traditions (APA, 1996).

Feelings of helplessness and loss of personal control are often consequences of victimization, and thus it is important for the counseling relationship to reflect a cooperative, collaborative partnership that helps counteract the effects of disempowering relationships (Enns, Campbell, & Courtois, 1997). Because of the multidimensional nature of family violence, it is also essential that counselors use assessment procedures that attend to a wide range of influences, including intrapsychic factors, the developmental phase of victims, family dynamics and influences, power dynamics within the family, and the social context in which violence occurs.

Disclosure of abuse is often difficult for clients, especially when it has occurred in intimate relationships. Victims may fear retaliation, may believe that disclosure violates a code of loyalty, or may have experienced a kind of traumatic bonding with the perpetrators that allow them to define the relationship as normal. Alternatively, clients may experience limited memory of abuse or may use denial in order to cope with abuse (Freyd, 1996). Because victims frequently experience multiple forms of family violence and because the effects of interpersonal violence may be cumulative, it is important that assessments be based on open-ended, nonsuggestive questions about the wide range of traumas individuals and members in their household may have encountered, including domestic and elder violence, physical or psychological abuse and neglect, accidents, and medical trauma. Although the posing of such questions does not guarantee disclosure, this practice may provide permission or a gentle prompt to clients who may feel reluctant to raise issues of abuse without an invitation to do so. When the counselor's questions about abuse are embedded within a comprehensive assessment and when clients are treated as knowledgeable about their own experiences, clients are most likely to feel empowered and explore their concerns openly and nondefensively (Enns et al., 1998).

When clients disclose abuse, counselors must be aware of occasions when they are mandated to report abuse and must be prepared to implement crisis intervention procedures. When children or elderly individuals are victims, state mandates about reporting violence and abuse are clear. In contrast, the counselor's ethical and legal obligations when working with adult victims of domestic violence are more ambiguous. Counselors face the challenge of emphasizing the unacceptability of violence while also respecting the autonomy and choices of the client. Instead of imposing a specific course of action on the client, the counselor faces the tasks of providing information and sound advice and helping the client sort through the costs and benefits of remaining in a relationship while also recognizing the realities that influence the victim's choices (e.g., the fact that staying in a relationship may be a financial necessity or the reality that violence often escalates after a woman leaves a batterer) (APA, 1996; Enns et al., 1997).

Dimensions of Counseling Victims of Trauma

Despite the fact that the adult or child status of clients will dictate very different courses of action and treatment, there is increasing consensus that psychotherapy with abuse survivors attends to three major themes or stages: (1) a safety, psychoeducation, and stabilization stage, (2) a trauma resolution phase, and (3) a reintegration phase (Enns et al., 1998; Herman, 1992). However, clients do not necessarily proceed through these experiences in an orderly or straightforward fashion. Furthermore, some clients may resolve some of these tasks outside the counseling context.

During the initial phase, safety, the counselor's relationship-building, crisis-intervention, psychoeducation, and referral skills are essential. To ensure the physical safety of clients, counselors must be knowledgeable about mandatory reporting and the social service agencies that provide protection to children and adults, shelters for battered women and their children, and sources of legal aid and protection. When working with battered women and children, counselors must not only be knowledgeable about shelter resources but must also be prepared to help clients who remain in their homes develop escape and safety plans (Enns et al., 1997; Walker, 1994). Other important tasks of this phase include helping clients (a) feel a sense of psychological safety, stability, and control, (b) develop skills for daily living and self-care, and (c) cope with intrusive and immediate trauma symptoms. Counselors may also educate the client about the nature of abuse, the process of recovery and counseling, and the challenges of coping with the aftermath of abuse.

The special needs of individuals at different life stages must be considered during the safety phase. When working with children, structure and predictability in the counseling relationship are particularly important for increasing children's feelings of safety and trust (Friedrich, 1996). Issues of safety may also be especially complex for elderly victims, who may be experiencing functional or cognitive impairments and who may be physically or psychologically dependent on their caregivers and perpetrators. These elderly clients may be fearful of losing connections with their abusive partners or children, of being abandoned by their families, or of bringing shame to their families.

As a part of the second dimension of counseling, clients learn how to come to terms with trauma, grieve losses associated with abuse and violence, and re-create a sense of meaning. The activity of recognizing and working through painful memories in a safe, therapeutic environment is often central, although not necessarily essential, to decreasing the distorted processing of material, reconstructing a positive self-concept, and developing new perspectives and goals for the future. Through the use of emotionally corrective experiences, memories are no longer associated with shame but with the dignity and new beliefs about the capacity to thrive (Herman, 1992).

Careful pacing and timing is essential to ensure that clients are not overwhelmed by the emotional content they are attempting to resolve (Herman, 1992). When clients are exposed to painful content in manageable increments, they are more likely to maintain a sense of safety while experiencing emotions associated with traumatic events. Friedrich (1996) suggested that when working with children it may be helpful to schedule times for discussing abuse or to develop words or phrases that make it easier to discuss abuse. These structural supports may add predictability for children and decrease the likelihood of regression or decompensation.

It is important to note that the resolution of traumatic memories often cycles through approach and avoidance phases. Avoidance is sometimes a useful temporary solution because it reduces immediate anxiety and allows individuals to pursue important tasks. Paradoxically, relying too heavily or exclusively on avoidance may be associated with an increase in intrusive symptoms, emotional numbing, and difficulty completing daily tasks.

The third phase, reintegration, involves dealing with unresolved issues such as relational, sexual, family, and social concerns as well as the consideration of new directions that are consistent with a person's new self-knowledge. Important outcomes of the counseling process include (a) control and authority over memories about abuse, mastery over abuse and trauma-related symptoms, and a tolerance for strong emotions that may reemerge at times, (b) a sense of integration, including the ability to integrate emotion and memory as well as feelings of self-cohesion, self-acceptance, and purpose, and (c) the ability to develop trusting relationships.

Although these three dimensions are relevant to the counseling of both children and adult victims, the different developmental needs as well as cognitive, affective, and verbal skills of clients will influence the manner in which these phases are negotiated. When working with children, the expression and working through of feeling and mastery of traumatic material is likely to be facilitated by a variety of play therapy techniques that make use of art, music, sand trays, and dolls. Cognitive-behavioral skills (e.g., stress inoculation, relaxation, thought stopping, desensitization, the use of positive mental imagery) are useful for helping both adults and children cope with and control posttraumatic intrusive memories (APA, 1996).

Interventions With Perpetrators of Family Violence

The motivations and characteristics of those who perpetrate violence are varied, and the treatment of perpetrators must take this diversity into account. For example, recent research has revealed several different typologies of men who physically abuse their adult partners. Jacobson and Gottman (1998) found physiological differences among abusers, with one group of men demonstrating heart rate increases and emotional arousal during conflict and the other group showing a slowing heart rate. Men who demonstrated this second pattern, which was evident in about 20% of batterers, also showed more antisocial behaviors and more calculating, humiliation-focused, and pain-focused intentions. Similarly, a review of the literature noted three major types of batterers: (1) those who are antisocial and violent across situations and who are most likely to abuse alcohol, (2) those who batter within the family context alone, are less likely to engage in less severe acts, more likely to suppress anger, and feel remorse after violence, and (3) those individuals who are emotionally volatile and are more likely to have personality disorders (Holzworth-Munroe & Stuart, 1994). It is likely that those who show remorse and physiological arousal in response to their own violence and engage in less aggressive acts will be more responsive to psychotherapy than those who show severe levels of pathology.

There have also been efforts to classify sexual offenders of children. Current systems categorize perpetrators according to their motivations, their use of children as primary erotic attachments or as surrogates for adult sexual contact, the type of strategy used to lure children into sexual activity, and their level of social competence or incompetence (Wurtele & Miller-Perrin, 1992). However, limited information is available about the relationship between typologies and potential interventions. Salter (1995) concluded that, in general, sexual offending is characterized by repetitive and compulsive behavior patterns, suggesting that successful intervention is likely to be complex and elusive. Programs that have shown some success involve the offender's acceptance of responsibility and cognitive behavioral methods that help minimize the risks of reoffending (e.g., by avoiding situations that may trigger motivations and behaviors associated with offending) (APA, 1996).

Although limited evaluation data are available, a variety of programs for perpetrators of domestic violence exist and include interventions by the criminal justice system, social skills training, anger management, and psychoeducation (APA, 1996; Jacobson & Gottman, 1998). The results of some studies have suggested that mandatory arrest for domestic violence is the most successful deterrent to future violence (e.g., Sherman & Berk, 1984), but these finding have not been replicated consistently in other studies (Buzawa & Buzawa, 1993). Sherman (1992) reported that mandatory arrest was an effective deterrent for married employed men. However, men who were not married to victims, were unemployed, had limited community support, or did not respond to social pressure were often more violent after an arrest than before the arrest. Arrest can also be associated with increased physical violence, especially when abusers have limited community support or do not respond to social pressure (Dunford, Huizinga, & Elliot, 1990). Studies of short-term intervention programs have generally found that although these programs are sometimes associated with immediate decreases in violence they are often ineffective for helping individuals maintain violence-free relationships (APA, 1996). On the basis of their review of existing programs and their effectiveness, Jacobson and Gottman (1998) recommended that psychotherapy or psychoeducation should be available to batterers on a voluntary basis but should not be required or provided as an alternative to legal consequences. Psychotherapy, if chosen voluntarily, may be successful in combination with legal sanctions.

Jacobson and Gottman (1998) proposed that men are most likely to discontinue physical violence when they (a) are held accountable and do not deny or minimize their responsibility for violence, (b) subscribe to a code of ethics that does not condone violence, (c) discover that battering is not an effective means of controlling others or solving problems, and (d) engage in low levels of domineering behavior, emotional abuse, and alcohol abuse. They cautioned that "cobras," or the 20% of batterers who demonstrate a calculating, antisocial pattern, may not benefit from any current education or rehabilitation programs.

In contrast to the limited optimism researchers convey about programs for batterers and perpetrators of child sexual abuse, intervention programs for abusive parents are promising and "quite effective" (Feindler & Becker, 1994, p. 409). Comprehensive programs are designed to increase parents' competence and include instructions about positive parenting, the modeling of appropriate parenting behaviors, and rehearsal of desired behaviors. These programs often challenge faulty expectations and cognitions that abusive parents hold about their children's behaviors and focus on helping parents develop new social skills for communicating, providing positive reinforcement to children, and using time-out options as alternatives to punishment (APA, 1996; Feindler & Becker, 1994; Wolfe & Wekerle, 1993).

Given the fact that family violence occurs within a family context, family and couples therapy would seem to be especially appropriate methods of intervening within the family system. However, researchers caution that the use of family approaches is sometimes associated with an increase in violence toward the most vulnerable individuals in the family. Dutton (1992) warned that a flawed assumption underlying many forms of couples and family therapy is that equality of power exists within the family and that batterers and perpetrators are generally amenable to change. Couples and family therapy are only appropriate if violence has stopped and abusers have taken responsibility for violent behavior (APA, 1996; Dutton, 1992). When relationships are free of violence, couples therapy may be useful for helping adult partners (a) explore and understand personal vulnerabilities (e.g., the need to control) and patterns of communication that are related to violence, (b) reconnect and rebuild the positive dynamics that initially attracted partners to each other, and (c) explore ways to modify behavior and engage in the mutual sharing of power (Gauthier & Levendosky, 1996).

Limited information is available about working with perpetrators of elder abuse, in part because elder abuse has only recently been identified as a major social problem, and efforts to identify risk factors and facilitate the reporting of elder abuse have consumed the energy of many practitioners and researchers. The APA's Task Force (1996) noted that life partners commit many forms of elder abuse and that general principles for working with batterers represent appropriate methods of treatment. Abusers with other types of relationships to elderly victims are likely to benefit from interventions that focus on anger management, coping skills, and working through the dependency needs of both perpetrators and victims. Other resources such as support groups, respite care, and stress management education for caregiver stress can be used in conjunction with individual interventions.

In summary, perpetrators of family violence rarely seek counseling voluntarily, and working with clients to stop abuse is challenging. In general, interventions for perpetrators should focus on three major goals: (1) changing personal behaviors that are abusive, (2) addressing personal issues, attitudes, and characteristics that support abusive behavior, and (3) protecting victims by altering aspects of the situation and context that contribute to abuse (APA, 1996).

SUMMARY

This brief discussion of the family reveals the complexity of family violence issues and the necessity of thorough preparation for working with issues of family violence. During the past several decades, researchers have documented the high prevalence of family violence, and mental health workers have identified effective methods for working with victims. As we enter the 21st century, it will also become increasingly important that counselors and psychologists become involved in prevention programs for at-risk groups as well as to develop effective education and prevention programs that address the larger social forces that support the acceptability of violence within the home. In addition to applying individual and group interventions in traditional office settings, counselors must expand the focus of their work to encompass creative collaborative efforts with multidisciplinary teams and to offer services in a broad array of community settings.

VIGNETTE

Maria is an 8-year-old second grader who was placed in foster care after being hospitalized for a major arm fracture inflicted by her mother's 26-year-old live-in boyfriend, Larry. Maria's 25-year-old mother, Julia, has been in several battering relationships and recently sought short-term emergency housing in a domestic violence shelter. As a result of her most recent battering experience, Julia has "broken up" with Larry.

Maria misses her mother a great deal, and her foster parents report that her moods and behaviors have been volatile, ranging from "clingy" behavior to angry temper tantrums to sadness and crying. Maria repeatedly asks to be reunited with her mother and states that it is her fault that she is separated from her mother.

---

1. What types of interventions do you believe would be most useful for Larry, for Maria, for Julia? How would you go about exploring the significance of Maria's changeable behavior?

2. What types of assessment questions might you pose in an interview with each of these three individuals? What types of risk factors and strengths would you hope to explore?

3. What types of ethical considerations would you need to consider before recommending reunification of Maria with her mother? Assuming that reunification with Maria's mother is a goal, what types of interventions might be useful for enhancing Julia's self-care skills? Her parenting skills?

4. It is likely that Maria witnessed the battering of her own mother. It is also possible that she experienced abuse other than physical battering (e.g., emotional or sexual abuse or both). What impact might the witnessing of violence have on Maria? How might you explore the possibility that Maria has experienced multiple forms of abuse without inappropriately suggesting abuse?

5. What other support systems might be mobilized to provide the most comprehensive treatment plan possible for each of these three individuals?

ADDITIONAL RESOURCES

Print Resources

Barnett, O. W., Miller-Perrin, C. L., & Perrin, R. D. (1997). *Family violence across the lifespan: An introduction*. Thousand Oaks, CA: Sage.

Briere, J., Berliner, L., Bulkley, J. A., Jenny, C., & Reid, T. (Eds.). (1996). *The APSAC handbook on child maltreatment*. Thousand Oaks, CA: Sage.

Jacobson, N., & Gottman, J. (1998). *When men batter women: New insights into ending abusive relationships.* New York: Simon & Schuster.

Wiehe, V. R. (1998). *Understanding family violence: Treating and preventing partner, child, sibling, and elder abuse.* Thousand Oaks, CA: Sage.

Films and Videotapes

The abused woman: A survivor therapy approach
   Training video featuring Lenore Walker. (Available from Newbridge Educational Publishing)

The amazing normal story
   Documentary about the childhood sexual abuse of filmmaker Flavyn Feller. (Available from Filmakers Library: http://www.filmakers.com)

Elder abuse: Five case studies
   Explores the ambivalent feelings of elderly abuse victims as well as interventions for stopping abuse. (Available from Fanlight Productions: http://www.fanlight.com)

The golden years?
   A comprehensive overview of elder abuse. (Available from Fanlight Productions: http://www.fanlight.com)

A room full of men: Therapy for abusive men
   A documentary about three men who participate in group therapy for abusive men. (Available from Filmakers Library: http://www.filmakers.com)

Internet Resources

Center for the Prevention of Sexual and Domestic Violence: http://www.cpsdv.org
Family Caregiver Alliance: http://www.caregiver.org
National Center on Elder Abuse: http://www.elderabusecenter.org
National Domestic Violence Hotline: http://www.ndvh.org
National Organization for Women: http://www.now.org/issues/violence

PART V

Midlife

Middle adulthood might generally be viewed as those years between the mid-30s and the early 60s, given some flexibility on either end of that range. Midlife has tended to receive less attention than many other life stages (Erikson, 1963; Savickas, 1995). Perhaps because midlife covers such a large portion of the lifespan, midlife adults are not frequently categorized as a group with specific issues. However, partly because of the extended time period, midlife individuals do encounter a substantial range of life events, moving through significant physical, emotional, sociocultural, and family changes.

An important activity of midlife is recognizing the contribution one has made, and is still making, to the world. Erikson (1963) suggests that the developmental crisis that emerges in midlife is that of generativity versus stagnation. The resolution of this crisis is to recognize that one has made a contribution to society. As people enter midlife, they may become aware of themselves as one generation of an ongoing family. They may be considering the impact of their working life, their family life, and their personal life on the world around them.

For many midlife adults, development includes new roles in the family and in the work world. During this stage of life, for example, many individuals are filling more family-related roles than they might at any other point in life—child, sibling, partner, parent, grandparent, and possibly great-grandparent. In addition, some combination of blended family experience might cause this number of roles to grow larger, and divorce and death of a spouse are increasingly likely to occur during midlife. U.S. Bureau of the Census (1998) figures indicate that approximately 70% (72 million) of adults between the ages of 35 and 64 are married. An additional 14 million are divorced, and slightly more than 3 million midlife adults are widowed. Women are much more likely to be widowed in midlife, accounting for 2.5 million of the adults in the widowed category.

In the work world, midlife individuals may be employees, supervisors, mentors, and leaders. In addition, they may find that work situations are being influenced by cultural and economic change as well as by the advancement of younger colleagues. In the year 2000, the oldest baby boomers were 54 years old and the youngest were 36. Numbering 78 million individuals, the work-related decisions of this group will have a significant impact on the U.S. labor market (Purcell, 2000). Interestingly, the employment rate for people between the ages of 54 and 63 rose between 1994 and 2000 (Purcell, 2000) for both men and women. This greater participation in the workforce indicates that counselors need to attend more closely to the career transition issues of midlife adults, which have often been overlooked relative to other career development stages (Savickas, 1995).

Rather than an extended time of stability, midlife can often be full of changes, both expected and unexpected. In order to provide effective service to midlife adults, counselors need to be aware of the developmental issues that are likely to emerge in both the family and work arenas during this time period and consider ways to facilitate positive response to role changes.

In Chapter 16, Lori R. Kogan and Tammi Vacha-Haase provide an extensive look at the myriad family roles that midlife adults might experience. They begin the chapter with a discussion of the dynamic nature of the midlife stage of development, noting that people experience the generation versus stagnation crisis in a number of ways. The authors then move into a discussion of issues commonly emerging in couplehood relationships, including changes in the status of intimate relationships. This section is followed by the changing roles of parenthood and grandparenting. The chapter concludes with consideration of the role of the adult child, particularly as midlife adults might be encountering the caretaking needs or death of a parent. For each issue presented, the authors include options for counseling strategies that can help clients adapt to the changes they are encountering.

The focus of Chapter 17 is on the various factors affecting midlife career transitions. After describing the interaction of factors, including family, financial, and sociocultural forces, Cindy L. Juntunen, Krislea E. Wegner, and Linda G. Matthews identify several types of career transitions that might occur during midlife. This discussion is accompanied by two case examples in which different factors are relevant for two very different career transitions. Counseling strategies and issues that need to be addressed are presented, and the chapter concludes with an illustrative case example.

These two chapters provide a broad range of strategies that can be used to foster positive adjustment to both anticipated and unanticipated changes in midlife. Such adjustment increases the likelihood that a positive resolution to the generativity versus stagnation crisis will be achieved.

CHAPTER 16

Supporting Adaptation to New Family Roles in Middle Age

Lori R. Kogan
Tammi Vacha-Haase

*Each age of life is new to us, and we find ourselves hampered
by inexperience regardless of our years.*

—Francois Duc de La Rochefoucauld
(translated from the French by John Heard)

How do relationships change within the family system as individuals reach middle age? How do people adapt to these changes? And how can counselors help with these transitions? These questions reflect the unique journey of those going through the uncharted territory of middle age—the focus of this chapter. Answers to the questions provide counselors the foundation to effectively prevent difficulties or intervene in times of crisis for clients in midlife.

Unfortunately, middle age has received less attention than any other lifespan period although the number of individuals within this age period continues to grow. From 1990 to 2015, the number of people in middle age will increase from 47 million to 80 million, a 72% increase (Willis & Reid, 1999). Given this dramatic demographic trend, the need for more information concerning this population, its assets and its limitations, its successes and its problems, is essential (Bahr & Peterson, 1989).

In the past, middle age has been viewed as a transitionary period to old age. However, today it is increasingly recognized that middle age involves numerous role changes within the family structure, complete with new stressors and challenges. Social class, gender, and individual differences create difficulty in placing an actual time period on middle age; instead, the boundaries are often viewed as being more fluid (Farrell & Rosenberg, 1981). Some have suggested that middle age begins around age 35 and includes the middle stages of parenting (i.e., when children reach early adulthood and move out from their parents' house) (Brooks-Gunn & Kirsh, 1984). Others have defined middle age as "later-life families," or families who are beyond the child-rearing years and have begun to launch their children. These families consist of the remaining members of the family after children have begun creating their own families (Troll, 1983).

Erikson (1963) described middle age within his psychosocial model as the stage of generativity, a time when developmentally mature adults attempt to improve life conditions for future generations. Generativity includes "procreativity, productivity, and creativity, and thus the generation of new beings, as well as new products and new ideas, including a kind of self-generation concerned with further identity development" (p. 67). For Erikson, the opposing pole is stagnation, in which adults become self-centered and withdraw into their own small worlds.

Erikson provides the opposing poles, but there is, most likely, a middle ground. As middle age occurs, some people do not have the ability to make generative contributions to society, nor do they have an interest in doing so, but at the same time, they do not stagnate or withdraw. They do not necessarily contribute directly to the growth of others or produce creative products that enhance society, but they continue to grow personally. Some simply increase their involvement in activities, hobbies, or recreational activities; some take up new activities. Many build or maintain friendships with others. These individuals may be closer to the norm than either Erikson's generative contributors or his stagnant withdrawers.

> The years like great black oxen tread the world,
> And God, the herdsman goads them on behind,
> And I am broken by their passing feet.
> —William Butler Yeats
> *The Countess Cathleen*

If middle age is a time of multiple changes, is it also a time of despair and crisis, given the loss of youth? Although the concept of the midlife crisis is slowly dissipating, for many people, aging within Western culture remains a negative phenomenon. Many individuals cling to their youth (Angel, 1987), evidenced by the billions of dollars spent on "age defying" cosmetics every year. However, the idea that everyone experiences a midlife crisis has not been supported; in fact, numerous studies have found little empirical evidence for this proposed phenomenon (Chiriboga, 1989a, 1989b). It has been found that younger adults actually tend to report more distress than those in middle age. Consequently, Rosenberg, Rosenberg, and Farrell (1999) state that the support for the midlife crisis is "absolutely ethereal" (p. 47).

Rather than filled with despair, these years are described by Rosow (1976) as relatively satisfying years, those shaped by individual choice and personal initiative. Individuals in middle age have had time to learn about themselves and their family members. They are often more comfortable with themselves in comparison to when they were younger, including both the positive and negative characteristics. Middle age is often a time of increased freedom, in which people have greater opportunity to explore new interest areas and open doors to different experiences and relationships (Fry, 1996).

But there are important changes during these years, and, similar to earlier developmental stages, how one progresses through the challenges of middle age depends on multiple factors, including environmental aspects, individual coping skills, and adaptability to change. Middle age demands numerous changes in family roles: attending to aging parents, relating to grown children, adapting to changes within marriages, and facing mortality. Individuals who struggle with these changes often face strained family relationships, reduced morale, and a decline in physical and mental health (Scott, 1997). Although it may, therefore, not be accurate to describe this period as a "crisis," it is a time that offers new challenges and opportunities, and a failure to meet these can lead to feelings of frustration, loneliness, and depression. For some, these challenges will evolve into crises, whereas others will learn to change and adapt to new roles.

This chapter is devoted to describing the relationship dynamics, including the positive factors and the challenges, that occur as people make the transition into middle age. The focus is on a specific group: people who have formed bonds, become couples, and established families of their own. Couplehood, defined in this chapter as two people involved in an intimate relationship, is explored in detail and includes the following issues pertaining to marriage and long-term relationships: role changes within a couple, love and compassion, ruts and stagnation within a relationship, and sexuality and physical affection. Other topics discussed relevant to couplehood are divorce and the ending of intimate relationships, remarriage or repartnering, and the death of a partner. In addition to relationships with partners, this chapter explores issues pertaining to adult children, aging parents, and grandparenting.

Unfortunately, this discussion excludes many people, including single men and women, gay and lesbian couples, heterosexual couples without children, and individuals who choose to have children when they are older. Although the adjustments of middle age clearly bring important challenges and issues for people in any of these groups, a specific discussion of those challenges is outside the scope of this chapter. Selected books that focus on these specific lifestyles are included in the Additional Resources at the end of the chapter.

Each of the following sections of this chapter discusses a particular issue related to middle age, followed by comments on counseling centered on that specific issue. Although there are some general principles that are crucial for counseling middle-aged clients, good counseling is good counseling, regardless of the client's age. The ability to listen, empathize, reflect, and provide therapeutic feedback paramount to therapeutic interactions. However, in addition, knowledge of the transitions and unique challenges faced by middle-aged clients is crucial when working with this population. These clients often require support and education to understand they are not "abnormal" or alone in their experiences. Thus, a primary role of the counselor may be to assist clients in realizing the normalcy of role changes as families and individuals age.

In addition, counseling middle-aged clients requires that counselors explore their own feelings, beliefs, and stereotypes pertaining to people in middle age. What does the term *middle age* bring to mind? Is it a picture of one's own parents? Of oneself? Is it an abstract view based on media depictions? The first task of an effective counselor often begins with a deeper understanding of oneself. After one has explored one's own "picture" of middle age, it may be helpful to examine the different topic areas in much the same way. What are the connotations of middle-age relationships? Divorce? Remarriage or recoupling? Recognizing that counselors have some beliefs and stereotypes about these topic areas is an important step toward consciously recognizing attitudes and biases that may be conducive to, or interfere with, effective counseling of people in middle age.

COUPLEHOOD

Couplehood in middle age can involve numerous changes, providing both opportunities and challenges. Roles change individually as well as within the twosome. Relationships continue to evolve, with unique issues arising.

Role Changes

As individual family members reach midlife, individual roles often change. The role changes for a man are often closely linked to work, career, and the role as family provider. Role changes for a woman, however, tend to be more influenced by the behaviors of other family members such as a child's decision to leave home, a husband's change in career or retirement status, or a parent's physical decline (Weiss, 1990).

These individual role changes may also influence roles within the relationship. For example, wage earners are often at a stage of increasing work responsibility or may be dealing with the knowledge that they will never meet their dream goals. Women who have been occupied by child raising may now find themselves with increased time. Some may return to school, start businesses, or seek other activities. Obviously, as individual roles change, decisions are made, or perceptions change, the relationship is influenced.

In addition, midlife changes the primary role of parenting for most couples. Although beyond the scope of this chapter, it is important to recognize that parents with special-needs children often do not experience the same launching stages and indeed may need support for their lack of role change. Most children, however, leave home either to attend school, begin a career, or marry, thereby creating major changes within the relationship. Unbeknown to many adult children, most couples view the launching of their children as a positive factor in their marriage through the creation of additional freedom (Lauer & Lauer, 1986). For some families, however, the launching of their children can be a difficult time, particularly if the relationship between the parents and children has been challenging.

When children move out of their parents' home, middle-age couples often must relearn how to live together and relate to each other without the presence of children. They must love and support each other in new ways as the level of dependence changes for one or both partners. Although the role of wife remains a central feature for most women throughout midlife (Scott, 1997), many women become more equal to their husbands and assertive over the duration of the marriage. It has been suggested that women display more masculine traits and become less dependent on their husbands as they explore the new freedoms that come from being released of the role as primary caretaker. Men are often likely to display an increase in feminine traits and become more emotionally dependent on their wives, perhaps due to changes in their work roles (McGee & Wells, 1982). Ideally, the couple grows from a position of "you" and "me" to one of "we-ness" (Keith & Schaefer, 1991) and can view themselves as a partnership and not solely as interacting individuals (Walster, Walster, & Berscheid, 1978).

Counselor Focus Areas

Role changes can be challenging to a couple that has different expectations or preconceived notions of what is appropriate or desired within a relationship. It is important to openly explore each person's feelings and thoughts pertaining to the changes they perceive happening within the relationship. Clients can be encouraged to discuss their perceptions of their present roles and how they would like their roles to be different. Sometimes, clients are unaware of old messages they received from their parents about how they "should" act and have not made a conscious decision about whether those expectations fit their own image. Every couple is different. To best facilitate this type of awareness, it is essential that counselors be aware of their own perceptions and stereotypes of appropriate roles for middle-age men and women and how this may bias the counseling process.

Therapeutic Activities and Tools

Exploration With Pictures. It is important that couples understand the naturally occurring role changes for themselves and their partners. One way to help clients explore role changes is for each partner to bring pictures of themselves throughout various life phases to the counseling session. During the session, the partners can discuss how they viewed themselves during the depicted time periods. After the partners discuss their own different roles, it can be helpful for the partners to discuss how they remember each other's role for each picture. The partners can than continue the developmental discussion to current times.

Role Play. Sometimes, partners can more easily express themselves through role-playing than through direct verbalization. Role-playing can be used to help partners demonstrate how they perceive their own roles or their partners' roles. It can also be successfully used to help clients demonstrate the type of behavior they would prefer to see in their partners. Have each partner role-play the other within his or her role. Be sure to have clients process what it was like to play the other's role in addition to how they experienced their partner playing their role.

Relationship Dynamics

As couples mature into middle age, inevitable changes occur. For most couples, the focus on children tends to decrease, and the focus on the couple's relationship increases. Experiences within the relationship can strongly influence the personal identity of each partner. Through the process of sharing personal information about one another, partners stimulate their identity assimilation (Whitbourne & Ebmeyer, 1990). This type of feedback is especially powerful due to the long connection and history shared between partners and can instigate growth or lead to a negative self-evaluation, depending on the nature of the relationship. Aging often brings more interdependence to the relationship, especially if the number of outside social contacts decreases. When other sources of support are reduced, the need for communication and support between a couple increases (Stinnett, Collins, & Montgomery, 1970). Middle age does not dictate a reduction of social contact; many people actually increase their social activities as their child-raising responsibilities abate.

When assessing the changes that occur during midlife, it is important for counselors to remember that although many midlife couples experience the same events (e.g., aging parents), it is not realistic, or wise, to assume that all middle-age couples are affected similarly. It is important to keep the individuality of couples in mind and not rely on stereotypic assumptions of midlife behavior or problems. For example, one could consider the transition that occurs when a child leaves home. Depending on the relationship and dynamics between the parents and child, the event could be distressing, relieving, natural, difficult, or relatively easy. Every family is different, and every child is different, even in the same family. Some children hang on and need to be pushed out, and some leave so early that discomfort is caused for the parents.

Numerous exploratory studies have been conducted on midlife marriages. These studies, however, must be interpreted cautiously, due to the inevitably biased sample from the attrition rates of divorce, separation, and death. Because these events do not happen randomly, it is assumed that couples that stay together through midlife are healthier and represent happier marriages than the original sample of newly married couples (Troll, 1971). Despite the bleak predictions of marital success, Lauer and Lauer (1986) do not predict gloom for future marriages. They note that most people prefer stable, monogamous relationships. The keys to success appear to be teaching skills that help people stay together: tools for coping with changes in roles, love, compassion, sexuality, division of labor at home, career, and equality issues.

What are the benefits of a lasting intimate relationship, and why are they worth the hard work they require? The largest benefit appears to be intimacy. Long-term relationships offer a unique kind of intimacy, one that can be an "emotional salvation in an impersonal, competitive world" (Lauer & Lauer, 1986, p. 22). Happiness appears to be another benefit. One study discovered that marital happiness contributed more to general happiness than any other factor (Norval & Weaver, 1981). Physical and mental health may also benefit from marriage or couplehood, perhaps by protecting partners through support and intimacy (Korbin & Hendershot, 1977). In addition, coupled people tend to be healthier psychologically; they report less loneliness and more happiness than uncoupled people (Carin & Shaver, 1982).

Counselor Focus Areas

A crucial element in working effectively with couples is the ability of a counselor to gain a clear understanding of the relationship dynamics and the goals of each partner. Counselors need to provide an atmosphere that allows both members of a relationship the freedom and comfort level to express themselves. Each partner should be allowed the opportunity to speak without inter-

ruption. The physical environment should be conducive for interaction between the couple as well as with the counselor. Because numerous aspects
influence how a couple perceives the dynamics within the relationship and how
they cope with change, it is important to remain cognizant of the influence of
family history, ethnic background, and individual styles within a relationship.

Therapeutic Activities or Tools

Communication Skill Building. Communication is essential within any relationship. One technique used to improve communication skills is to ask couples to sit facing one another. Ask one person to begin speaking while the
other person listens. When the first person has finished talking, ask the listener to paraphrase what he or she has just heard. The speaker is then given
the opportunity to provide feedback about the accuracy of the paraphrasing.
This should then be repeated with the speaker in the role of listener and the
listener in the role of speaker.

Schedule Time to Talk. Some partners may find it helpful to schedule a specific time devoted to verbal communication. This would be a commitment by
both partners to devote a specific time to share experiences, feelings, or concerns that have arisen. Assist clients in setting times to meet, agendas, and so on.

Love and Compassion

Although some studies have indicated that passionate and even compassion-
ate love do not last (Peterson & Payne, 1975; Traupmann, Hatfield, & Wexler,
1981), other studies have produced more positive findings. Traupmann and
Hatfield (1981) suggest, "The prospects of love's lasting (for most couples)
seem to be reasonably good" (p. 263). Therefore, what are the important components of a successful, lasting relationship? When Lauer and Lauer (1986)
asked couples that had remained together for more than 10 years to list the
most important ingredients (out of 39 potential factors) in the success of their
marriages, the following top seven reasons were given in the same order by
both men and women: "My spouse is my best friend," "I like my spouse as a
person," "Marriage is a long-term commitment," "Marriage is sacred," "We
agree on aims and goals," "My spouse has grown more interesting," and "I
want the relationship to succeed." This illustrates the point that men and
women share many of the same thoughts and feelings about the important
components of a successful marriage. Often, the key is helping couples express
themselves in ways that convey this commonality.

Counselor Focus Areas

Education is a key component in helping middle-age couples prevent problems and deal effectively with difficulties that have arisen related to love and compassion. The ability for partners to listen to one another and be able to define the problems or risk areas in the partnership may be the first step toward maintaining or mending a relationship. Many people have false notions of love through the media and their interactions with other people. Realizing that a loving relationship is a process and one that takes continual work may be crucial.

Therapeutic Activities and Tools

One Nice Thing. A number of couples fall into routines that do not include tangible expressions of affection. One way to help couples express their feelings through behaviors is to ask each partner to identify one nice gesture each would like to do for the other during the week. Then, during the following week, partners follow through on their plans but do not inform their partners of the nature of the task. Examples are making dinner, taking over a chore, and purchasing theater tickets. This can help encourage couples to focus on displaying behaviors that indicate their commitment and affection.

Comfort Jar. Partners often have a wish list but may expect their partners to read their minds. To increase the likelihood of having these wishes come true, clients can designate a jar that is to be filled with wishes. Each partner is instructed to write several wishes on individual pieces of paper and place them in the jar. The wishes should consist of small, inexpensive requests that can be easily fulfilled. Examples are back rubs, dances in the kitchen, and hugs. Each partner then draws from the jar one slip of paper weekly, and the wish is "granted" by the other partner.

Avoiding the Ruts in Long-Term Relationships

Long-term relationships enjoy many benefits that come from building a history with another individual. Ideally, it is a sanctuary where one can relax and feel free to express oneself without fear of criticism or disapproval. Long-term relationships also, however, involve the risk of falling into repetitive patterns and ruts. The antidote to stagnation is change. In order to keep a healthy relationship, two people must change in ways that enhance compatibility and keep the relationship new (Lauer & Lauer, 1986). Change is inevitable, yet it can be a positive or negative factor in the relationship, depending on how it is perceived. Partners may be viewed as more interesting as they mature and are able to bring more substance into the relationship. Successful couples also learn how to be more accepting, patient, and tolerant of each other. One long-time coupled woman expressed this growth, "We have become much more tolerant of each other's quirks of personality. We know who we are. Often we can predict the other's reactions to events or attitudes. The relationship has sweetened over the years. I wouldn't change places with anyone I know" (Lauer & Lauer, 1986, p. 140).

Mutual education and the interjection of small spontaneous activities are two of the best ways to help ensure the types of change that will bring people together (Lauer & Lauer, 1986). Contrary to the notion that people should never marry with the intent of changing another person, Krantzler (1981) recognizes that people need to be both teachers and students with each other. In fact, it is suggested that couples that do not mutually educate their partners may actually jeopardize their relationship (Lauer & Lauer, 1986). The myth that partners who "really love each other" will know intuitively what the other needs is a dangerous one. It is only through communication and education that two people continue to meet each other's changing needs.

Counselor Focus Areas

The counselor can help clients identify potential at-risk areas for boredom and ruts within the relationship. Specifically defining problem areas allows the couple to begin creating solutions. It is also important to share with clients the normalcy of experiencing boredom in a long-term relationship. Exploring the positive aspects that accompany long-term relationships (e.g., trust, security, and understanding) may help clients deal more effectively with the negative potential aspects of tedium and monotony.

Therapeutic Activities and Tools

Risk Area Identification. Defining risk or problem areas is often the first step in preventing boredom and making positive changes. Counselors can suggest that clients come to a session with several potential risk areas. During the counseling session, the couple can then explore how to define a risk area and how to measure when something becomes a problem. Once an area has been defined as problematic, the couple can generate ideas to transform the area into something more exciting. For example, if a couple identifies a nighttime behavior of television watching as a problem, they can generate options of behavior for that time period. Communication and mutual goal setting are skills to help clients focus on during this exercise.

New Activities. Some clients may not be able to visualize new activities and may need suggestions. If clients require assistance developing new ideas, the counselor may suggest that each partner explore new activities and come back to counseling with a list of five new activities the couple could do together. These ideas could then be implemented on a weekly basis.

Sexuality and Physical Affection

In a society that glamorizes youth and sex, it is often believed that aging is synonymous with reduced sexual activity and desire. Research, however, suggests this is not always true. One study found that only 5% of men and 10% of women married for 20 years were indifferent or averse to sex (Ben & Ard, 1977). Many middle-age partners find that sexual intimacy is a strong and fulfilling part of their relationship, although others may be satisfied in relationships where physical intimacy plays only a minor role (Lauer & Lauer, 1986). So, although frequent sexual activity is not mandatory for a successful partnership, agreement between two people about the kind and frequency of sexual relations is a necessary element. Because sexual needs change along with other needs, a positive sexual relationship is something requiring continual attention and communication between partners.

In addition to sexual activity, there are numerous ways to show affection. One study found that 98% of happily married couples kiss each other every day or almost every day (Lauer & Lauer, 1986). Physical displays of affection should not only be exchanged during times of sexual intimacy but also on a regular basis. The tendency for couples to take one another for granted is a dangerous one and should be guarded against carefully.

Counselor Focus Areas

The meaning of sexuality is different for everyone, and sensitive counselors are aware of the need to understand their clients' views of sexuality and physical affection. Counselors should also be aware of their own feelings and attitudes toward sex. When counselors are uncomfortable discussing sexual topics, they often subtly redirect their clients when sexual topics arise. Furthermore, clients can often sense when counselors are uncomfortable discussing sexual topics, and they may therefore refrain from disclosing information. In addition to sexual topics in general, counselors should be aware of their feelings and stereotypes pertaining to middle-age people engaging in sexual activities. A counselor's views within these areas can negatively affect therapeutic intervention and preventive education practices. When counselors feel comfortable with sexual topics, they can then encourage their clients to openly communicate about sexual and intimate needs. Suggestions to clients on ways to increase the comfort level of sexual communication (e.g., atmosphere, timing) may prove beneficial.

Therapeutic Activities and Tools

Beginning (or Ending) Some Activities. Sexual intimacy is often one of the most difficult topics for couples to discuss. They often rely on their partner's reading their mind. Clients should, therefore, be encouraged to discuss specific examples of behaviors that they would like to see changed. For example, one partner may begin by stating that she or he would like the relationship to be more physically intimate. The counselor could then help the client learn how to be more specific in asking for what is desired. By helping clients feel more comfortable with specific sexual words, a counselor can help clients eliminate vague references that can be misunderstood.

Hugs and Physical Strokes. Some couples fall into routines that do not include regular hugs, kisses, and other physical displays of affection. It is important to help clients explore each other's need level for these activities. If both partners need a minimum level of physical contact, there is little relationship risk in this area. However, if there is a discrepancy in need level between partners, compromises should be explored. Perhaps a "hug jar" or some type of reminder cue to help couples incorporate physical contact into their schedules would be helpful.

Balance. One crucial element to a healthy relationship is a balance between giving to a partner and taking care of oneself. When this balance is disturbed for one or both partners, education on boundary and limit setting may be helpful. This may include setting aside time for oneself or learning to say no to a partner's requests. Regardless, open communication is necessary between partners.

INTIMATE RELATIONSHIP STATUS

Many couples evolve during their middle years and create new roles and expectations within the relationship. Other middle-age couples, however, face the process of their relationships coming to an end. Ending the relationship may be the choice of one or both partners or as a result of death. However, the ending of a long-term relationship for middle-age clients, whether for the best or not, can be a difficult transition.

Divorce or Ending a Long-Term Relationship

Although long-term relationships offer many positive elements, these relationships are not always possible or desirable. The termination of a long-term relationship is a reality for many middle-age individuals. In fact, research suggests the number of people in midlife who are in their first marriage is decreasing. Furthermore, the rates of divorce are higher for ethnic minorities, especially African American females (Hooyman & Kiyak, 1993).

Men and women demonstrate different areas of vulnerability associated with divorce or the ending of a relationship. Although many men have difficulty with loneliness and unhappiness (Chiriboga, 1982), women have been found to often feel anger and a sense of being overwhelmed, often related to financial hardships. Because many middle-age women have chosen to stay at home with their children or have not worked full-time, divorce often places women at an economic disadvantage.

The ending of a relationship does not always have to be negative, however. For some couples, this can be a step in the right direction. Much of what makes the ending of a relationship either a devastating or positive event depends on the coping abilities of those undergoing the experience. Coping can be defined as any activity aimed at reducing distress (Lazarus & Folkman, 1984) and often includes the following components (Chiriboga, 1989c): Coping individuals (a) perceive themselves as having personal control over the situation (i.e., planning what to do, making decisions); this does not imply that they have to be the ones that initiated the ending—instead they can redefine the situation; (b) involve themselves in meaningful and pleasurable activities and develop a sense of commitment; and (c) develop and maintain good social support systems.

Counselor Focus Areas

To assist clients going through a divorce, counselors must be aware of their own views on divorce or other types of relationship termination, including issues pertaining to judgment, blame, and responsibility. Some clients may experience the loss of a well-established identity. When someone has defined him- or herself primarily as a husband, wife, or partner, the loss of this role can affect self-appraisal and identity. It is also pertinent to explore clients' views on divorce or the ending of relationships. Background information concerning religion and family views on divorce can be helpful in identifying potential stressors, as these issues help shape clients' coping strategies during this transition.

Clients may also need to explore feelings related to starting over. Newly single individuals are often apprehensive about the prospect of dating. Many have not dated since early adulthood and feel out of touch with current dating practices. Concerns about AIDS and other sexually transmitted diseases can inhibit middle-age people from beginning to date. Discussions pertaining to worries and concerns as well as education of current issues for single individuals can help normalize clients' feelings and help them take new risks.

Therapeutic Activities and Tools

Visualization. For clients who have a hard time imagining life as a single adult, role-playing can be useful. Clients who are apprehensive about being alone can visualize what actually might happen when they are home alone. In this way, fears can be exposed and plans of intervention generated. Visualization can also be used for clients who have fears about dating. For example, clients can visualize going out on a dinner date and holding hands. How would they react? How do they judge their reaction?

Self-Describe. Clients having difficulty with role loss can often benefit from exercises in which they describe themselves. In this way, they can begin to identify who they are beyond *husband, wife,* or *partner.* Although some people like to use lists of words, other more artistic clients can draw pictures that represent themselves. After they have generated some type of depiction, they can explore what aspects of themselves they would like to keep and which ones they would like to modify. Another representation 3 to 6 months later can be useful to help clients identify where they are and how they have changed.

Death of a Partner

The death of a partner is typically thought of as a problem for the elderly (Demi, 1989), and therefore little information is available in the area of spousal death during middle age. Demographics, however, indicate that many women are widowed in middle age. Although 5% of women ages 45 to 54 are widowed, the number increases to 17% for women ages 55 to 64 (U.S. Bureau of the Census, 1992a). Women are widowed six times more often than men (U.S. Bureau of the Census, 1992a), with the number even higher for minorities and in particular African Americans (Matras, 1990).

The death of a partner is seen as one of the most stressful events during one's lifespan. The level of difficulty is based on numerous aspects, including type and timing of death, the relationship between the couple, and an individual's coping skills. Studies have found that men and women share many of the same hardships when a partner dies. Loneliness and practical problems are major factors for both genders (Demi, 1989), although men and women may deal with these problems differently. Women tend to have larger social networks and consequently often choose to date less often and wait longer after the death of a spouse to date when compared to men.

Kubler-Ross identified five sequential stages that people experience in the grief process. These include denial, anger, bargaining, depression, and acceptance (Kubler-Ross, 1969). Parkes (1972) described four stages of grief in somewhat different terms. The first stage is numbness and is often accompanied by physical signs, including loss of appetite and weeping. The second stage is intense yearning, during which time the bereaved longs for the deceased. The third stage is marked by depression. Often, the second and third stages alternate and do not follow a sequential order. The fourth stage is the period of recovery as the grief abates.

Counselor Focus Areas

Working through grief is important for maintaining and regaining mental health. Clients need a safe environment in which to explore their grief and come to terms with their loss. It can be helpful to emphasize the normalcy of their grief reaction and encourage them to be gentle and patient with themselves. Counselors' knowledge of the grief process can be helpful in identifying the current stage of a grieving client.

Therapeutic Activities and Tools

Focus on Self. Counselors can help encourage clients to think of ways to focus on their own needs during this time. Learning to be their own best friend, clients can begin distinguishing healthy and nonhealthy thought and behavior choices. Helping clients make lists of potential activities to be accomplished or enjoyed during the week can help them stay focused on positive aspects of daily living.

Rituals. Some clients may find it helpful to create a ritual to mark the passing of their partner. This could be lighting a special candle, reading a poem, or visiting somewhere meaningful. The ritual can help acknowledge the importance of the deceased individual, yet it allows the bereaved to continue living productively.

Remarriage/Repartnering

In addition to dating less often, women tend to remarry less often than men. Hayes and Anderson (1993) found that 41% of women ages 45 to 49 and 46% of women ages 50 to 59 preferred to remain single. Due to the tendency for women to remain single and the fact that women tend to marry older men, it is more likely for men to remarry in midlife (Scott, 1997). When two middle-age people begin a new intimate relationship, making changes and adaptations is inevitable. People have expectations, schedules, and habits that can be deeply embedded and difficult to change. One potential problem for remarried or repartnered couples is intolerance to different lifestyles (Visher & Visher,

1979). Learning tolerance and flexibility, however, is mandatory for a successful second marriage or committed relationship. So how does one help ensure a successful remarriage or repartnership? McKain (1972) suggests that partners should know each other well, adjust to age-related changes, receive approval from family and friends, and set up a new home.

Relationships within a blended family can be a major stressor within a new marriage or partnership. Although the children may no longer be physically present in the home, they are always present within the partner relationship. This can cause challenges for the new relationship in many ways. For example, dynamics with an ex-partner can be a difficult additional component. Boundary setting and clear communication can help ease the feelings associated with ex-partner contact. In addition to ex-partners, stepchildren can create stressors for a new relationship. Although some stepchildren form immediate positive bonds with a new parent or their children, most children need time to adapt to the major changes. Couples need to stay united when dealing with the children to keep the children from "dividing and conquering." Children in intact families will often try to play one parent against the other, but if an actual threat to the relationship arises, children will usually try to keep their parents together. The same does not hold true for stepfamilies (Visher & Visher, 1979).

Most first marriages or relationships have a time period in which people begin to learn about one another without the presence of children, but this is not often the case for second marriages or relationships. Some partners feel insecure about their place or hierarchy when children are involved; other partners feel guilty about forming bonds with another adult and feel they are betraying their children. Modeling a positive, healthy adult relationship, however, can benefit everyone. Choices that can lead to a successful remarriage or repartnership include emotional sharing, a lack of criticism and withdrawal, and an awareness of the importance of the relationship. To help the new relationship develop, it may be beneficial for stepparents and children to spend time in subgroups (e.g., parents alone, children with their own parents, and children with stepparents). Patience is mandatory when developing new family relationships; parents should be encouraged to allow interpersonal connections to develop slowly. Parents can promote positive change through communication in the form of family negotiation sessions and creating a general atmosphere that permits the discussion of feelings and thoughts.

Counselor Focus Areas

The counselor can play an active role in educating people as to realistic expectations pertaining to blended families and remarriage or repartnership in middle age. New relationships take time, patience, and good communication skills. Counselors can help family members define clear role expectations and create open channels for communication. Some new families find it helpful to schedule regular times to discuss progress and problems in a nonthreatening atmosphere.

Therapeutic Activities and Tools

Role Play. The use of role-playing for new family roles can help members visualize what other family members expect. Family members can play the role of another person, indicating how they would like that person to act.

Family Sculpture. The sculpture is made by one family member arranging the other members into one "sculpture." This involves physical movement and touching, as one family member decides how to have each of the other family members come together in a living statue. Decisions that must be made include whether family members should be standing or sitting, what direction they should face, who they should be touching, and how the rest of their bodies are "molded." All family members should be given an opportunity to sculpt and explain their artwork when completed.

PARENTHOOD

Parenthood for individuals in middle age involves several roles. Often faced with aging parents, many middle-age parents are also forging new relationships with their grown children and perhaps beginning new relationships with their grandchildren. With a new generation comes the role of grandparenting and new ways to relate to one's own children.

Adult Children

The role of parents obviously does not end when children reach adulthood. The relationship in midlife, however, often is a time of transitioning from a state of dependence to one of equality. There are, however, important cultural influences that can affect the relationships between grown children and their parents. Many cultures do not encourage independence to the same degree as Western families. Extended family households are more common for African American and Latino families than for White families (Mindel, Haberstein, & Wright, 1988). African American women tend to continue performing instrumental familial roles much longer than White women, whereas Latino families often have a highly integrated family structure, and mutual support is often the norm (Mindel, Haberstein, & Wright, 1988). Culture, therefore, can play a large role in the level of independence desired by adult children and their parents. For traditional Western families, it is a time when young adults continue to develop their autonomy (Huyck, 1989), and most parents experience a reduction in their children's dependency level. Other cultures may show very small changes in dependency or authority levels.

For families that experience their children leaving home, several components are involved in this transition period for both children and their parents. One step toward a successful launching is for parents and children to acknowledge and mourn the loss of the previous parent-child relationship. In addition, parents must forgive themselves for any past inadequacies, release negative memories, and transition themselves into the important role as family stabilizers (Huyck, 1989; Troll, 1983). It is a time to accept new people into the family circle as children form their own intimate relationships and begin their own families.

Much has been written about the "empty nest" stage, defined as the time when all one's children have left home. Although some parents feel the loss of their clear social roles as parents or feel that an important structuring element in their lives has changed, these losses seem most problematic for women who have focused entirely on motherhood and therefore did not develop other roles (Huyck, 1989). The number of parents faced with an overwhelming feeling of loss is expected to continue to decrease as women place more emphasis on their careers (Huyck, 1989). In contrast to a minority of women who struggle with multiple loss issues during this time, most parents find that they welcome their new freedom. In fact, studies have shown that marital and life satisfaction increase when there are no adult children living at home (Mattessich & Hill, 1987). It has been discovered that as children leave home, marital happiness tends to increase (White & Edwards, 1990). In fact, many couples describe this time period as a postlaunch honeymoon (White & Edwards, 1990).

A relatively new phenomenon seems to be occurring for many during their middle years, and that is that adult children are returning home. Some parents find their adult children suddenly living with them again. The young adult may be in transition between jobs or involved in a separation or divorce and may need a place to live. Some young adults even have their own children live with them and their parents.

As families develop, the importance of one's children in middle age does not decrease; it merely changes form. Children provide a unique source of information regarding parents' identity or a way for parents to evaluate themselves for both positive and negative qualities (Whitbourne & Connolly, 1999). Many parents' sense of well-being is linked to their children's level of personal adjustment (Keys & Ryff, 1999), regardless of whether or not they are in the home.

Counselor Focus Areas

Helping clients cope effectively with the changing relationship they have with their grown children first involves understanding the meaning placed by clients on their children leaving the home or returning home, if this is the case. Through this exploration, clients can explore the troubling aspects of this transition. Counselors can help clients by teaching them how to focus on themselves, beyond their roles as parents. It may be helpful to encourage clients to remember their dreams and aspirations before they had children and recognize which ones hold appeal. Counseling can also be used to encourage clients to explore new areas within themselves.

Therapeutic Activities and Tools

Self-Reflection. Counselors can help clients relate to their children by encouraging parents to remember how they felt when they were 18 to 20 years old. What did they want and need from their parents during this time period? How can they offer these things to their own children?

Role Play. If adult children come to counseling with their parents, role-playing can be used as an alternative form of communication. Ask family members to role-play each other and demonstrate what they need from specific family members. Following role-playing sessions, counselors can facilitate open discussion pertaining to new roles and expectations.

Dream List. If clients are experiencing difficulty with their new role, they can be encouraged to write a "dream list" of activities they put off doing because of child-rearing responsibilities. The counselor can help the couple brainstorm, creating a list with a wide variety of topics, from extravagant vacations to a quiet candlelight dinner at home. By focusing on new and resurfaced dreams, counselors can help clients reframe their new relationships with their grown children.

Grandparenting

The role of grandparenting has increased in importance and duration as people continue to live longer and healthier lives. It is estimated that 94% of older adults with children are grandparents, and most grandparents see at least one grandchild regularly (Hooyman & Kiyak, 1988). Cherlin and Furstenberg (1992) found that 70% of grandparents surveyed indicated they had seen at least one grandchild within the last week. Benefits from grandparenting include love, affection, and the ability to share in grandchildren's achievements (Cherlin & Furstenberg, 1992). Different cultural backgrounds can play an important role in grandparenting, demonstrated by the number of minorities who place the role of grandparenting higher than typically found within the White culture.

As blended families continue to become more prominent, the role of grandparents continues to evolve. Because most divorced spouses remarry, a large proportion of grandparents have stepgrandchildren. Although it is possible they will no longer have contact with their own biological grandchildren in the case of divorce, one study found that more than 50% of grandparents whose adult children divorced did not change the contact they had with their grandchildren (Ahrons & Bowman, 1982). Divorce and new relationships can create problems for grandparent-grandchild relationships if not handled appropriately. The role of grandparenting can also sometimes dramatically increase in the event of a divorce, whereby many grandparents take on a more active role in the child rearing.

Numerous programs have been developed to help grandparents identify the stressors faced by children in this time period (Strom & Strom, 1988). An example of one of these programs, Becoming a Better Grandparent, helps people improve their attitudes and behaviors within the grandparenting role. People who have taken the program reported gaining a broader perspective, more confidence, higher self-esteem, and strengthened intergenerational communication and relationships (Strom, Strom, & Collinsworth, 1990).

The past two decades have witnessed the increasing phenomenon of custodial grandparenting, with grandparents from all socioeconomic levels, race, age, and gender becoming the primary caretakers for their grandchildren (Fuller-Thomson, Minkler, & Driver, 1997). Grandparents are increasingly serving as full-time surrogate parents to their grandchildren due to factors such as incapacitating illness, substance abuse, incarceration, child abuse and neglect, and domestic violence affecting parents' ability to care for their children (Aaron, 1992). Custodial grandparents often find their personal resources stretched to the limit in their role as surrogate parents for their grandchildren (Strom & Strom, 1993). The challenges and obstacles faced by custodial grandparents are numerous, often with psychological challenges and emotional stressors. Custodial grandparents may experience changes in their lifestyle (Jendrek, 1993) that include loss of freedom and control, disruption of friendships with age-mates, conflict with their offspring who are unwilling or unable to raise their own children, as well as emotional stress such as shame, anger, self-doubt, disappointment, and fear (Aaron, 1992; Creighton, 1991).

Counselor Focus Areas

Grandparenting has different meanings to people based on their own life situation, experiences with their own grandparents, their ethnic background, and their perception of the role. It can be helpful to explore what "being a grandparent" means to clients. For some grandparents, it is a positive time in which they can enjoy children without the parental responsibility, but for others it can be a time when they are asked to step into roles they had not expected. By exploring the perceptions clients hold, counselors can help clients decide how they would like to integrate the grandparenting role into their lifestyles.

Therapeutic Activities and Tools

Past Experiences. Counselors can help clients reminisce about their own grandparents to help them evaluate the importance of the grandparenting role. What were those relationships like? What were the positive or negative aspects? Counselors can then encourage clients to relate their past experiences to the type of relationship they would like with their grandchildren. Do they want to be closely involved? Do they want to visit occasionally but not be involved in the day-to-day aspects of their grandchildren? Clear communication between parents and adult children can help everyone understand the roles within the family unit.

Family Communication. Counseling can help the family explore different expectations for each member's role. Family counseling may help clients gain an understanding of how each generation fits together, how to express needs and boundaries, and how to solve problems when difficulties arise.

Boundary Setting. Some grandparents may have a difficult time setting boundaries with their children and might benefit from practicing boundary setting and saying no in counseling sessions. Counselors can role-play with clients to encourage new behaviors and techniques to take care of themselves.

Custodial grandparents often face serious challenges and require specialized interventions. Support groups for custodial grandparents may be located through the American Association for Retired Persons Grandparent Caregiver Information Center (de Toledo & Brown, 1995).

ADULT CHILD RESPONSIBILITIES

Middle-age clients often assume responsibilities when interacting with their own parents. Relationships between adult children and their parents are often one of the most enduring and important relationships within the lifespan. Unfortunately, these bonds have not yet been studied to the extent of other relationships (Brubaker, 1983). Many studies have been done that pertain to young children and parental attachment, but how the child-parent relationship changes and endures over time is not well known. It does seem clear that the roles and levels of dependency change as parents age, with adult children assuming more caretaking roles. Many middle-age individuals experience a role reversal with their parents as their parents become more dependent and less autonomous. This intergenerational dependency is seen as a widespread phenomenon (Stanford, Peddecord, & Lockery, 1990). With these changes come the opportunity to create new satisfying relationships as well as challenges to accept the loss of old relationships and roles. In contrast to the perception that many older parents are often left feeling alienated and abandoned, Shanas (1979) found in his interviews that 53% of older parents had seen their children within the past 2 days. Furthermore, 94% of older parents had grandchildren and 46% had great-grandchildren who offered assistance.

Aging Parents

The "sandwich generation" is defined as people (usually women) caught in the middle of caring for children and parents. As young adults continue to wait until they are older to move out of the house and people live longer lives, the number of people who care for children and aging parents will continue to increase (Bengtson, Rosenthal, & Burton, 1996). Although several studies have described the multiple caretaking roles as stressful and overwhelming (Brody, 1985; Pearlin, Mullan, Semple, & Skaff, 1990), others have argued that the numerous roles lead to increased social support and feelings of competence (Lopata, 1993; Stoller & Pugliesi, 1989). For many, the fear pertaining to the sandwich generation is the assumption that older parents need extensive support from their grown children. Research has indicated, however, that most parent-older child relationships are based on reciprocity (Spitze & Logan, 1992). Therefore, multiple roles are not seen as negative in themselves and can actually be an asset (Logan & Spitze, 1996). At the ultimate level of difficulty, however, is the question of whether or not to place a parent in a nursing home when that time arises.

The role of the extended family is often stronger in ethnic minorities such as African Americans, Native Americans, Asian Americans, Mexican Americans, and Latinos than in Whites (Mindel, Haberstein, & Wright, 1988). The research on African American families has shown that they tend to be more involved in exchanges of help across generations (Mutran, 1985). Black women are more likely than White women to give and receive help from grandchildren (Kivett, 1993).

Counselor Focus Areas

Watching one's parents grow older can be a difficult process for many people. As older parents become more dependent, roles often reverse between parent and child, leaving the child in the role as caretaker. Honoring the loss of the previous parent-child relationship is one aspect of coping with the new role as provider. The counselor can normalize the processes involved with watching one's parents age. Most people view their parents as immortal, and the shock of seeing them age can be a stark reality. The realization that one's parents are aging may remind clients that their parents may not always be there, leading to thoughts of death and mortality.

Therapeutic Activities and Tools

Loss Issues. Counselors can help clients identify and process the aspects of the parent-child relationship they feel they have lost with the aging of their parent.

Making Amends. Counselors can help clients recognize, acknowledge, and articulate any amends to aging parents that need expression.

Education. Many older people go through changes that can be distressing to their loved ones. Diseases like Alzheimer's and Parkinson's can be devastating to the entire family. It is important that family members are educated regarding changes that come from physical diseases. It can be difficult for people to not react personally when a family member displays personality changes such as inappropriate anger or sadness or does not recognize loved ones. Although it cannot take away the loss and grief that comes with a debilitating disease, education can help family members cope better with the changes.

Death of a Parent

As medicine has increased longevity, many aspects of parental death have changed. Although people in the past normally died at home with their family gathered around, today three quarters of the deaths in the United States occur in institutions (Huyck, 1989). It is suggested that when people regularly died in their 40s and 50s, death was more intimately related. It reminded people of life's frailty and therefore helped families stay together (Kalish & Huyck, 1989). The increase of institutionalization has led to many changes, including an increase in feelings of guilt on the death of a parent. Adult children often wonder if they did enough or did the right thing. Most people actually did do all they could and therefore need to work through their unrealistic expectations of themselves and come to terms with the death process. Some adult children may have a legitimate reason to feel they could have done things differently and need help working through their regret. The death of a parent can also change adult children's views of their own mortality. Anderson (1980) suggests that parental death removes the buffer of death, making one's own death more tangible.

The feelings associated with the death of a parent and the styles people use to cope with death depends on a multitude of things, including the past relationship and individual coping mechanisms. Kalish (1989) suggests that mourning too little or too much is an indication that the relationship was potentially problematic. Mourning is also affected by the final good-bye. When people have the opportunity to reaffirm their love, ask and give forgiveness, and come to a reconciliation if the relationship was troublesome, people react better to the death (Kalish, 1989). If the final meeting went poorly, the mourning process will often be more difficult. The adult child might require additional support or counseling. In the event of a sudden death, people generally do not have the opportunity to say good-bye. In these instances, it is often the relationship characteristics up to that point that determine the mourning status of the adult child. If the relationship was primarily positive, it is likely the adult child will be able to focus on those aspects and learn to deal with the lost opportunity of saying good-bye. If the relationship was a negative one, however, it may be more difficult for the adult child to come to terms with not being able to obtain some closure.

Counselor Focus Areas

Many of the same focus areas mentioned previously under the subject of death of a partner apply to the death of a parent. Counselors can offer insight into the grieving process and let clients know what they might expect as they grieve. Be cautious about generalizing, however, as everyone has different relationship histories with their parents and will respond differently to their death. Likewise, people have different concepts of death and what death means to them. How a parent died (e.g., suddenly or after a long illness) will also affect the grieving process. Whether the adult child had the opportunity to say good-bye often is a fundamental aspect involved in the healing process. As the counselor explores these issues, it is important to be sensitive to cultural and gender differences.

Therapeutic Activities and Tools

Saying Good-Bye. If clients were not able to say good-bye to their parents in a way that provided the closure they needed, counseling can offer options for filling this void. Clients can be encouraged to write a good-bye letter and possibly keep it, share it during counseling, or burn it as a sign of closure. Using the *empty chair technique,* clients can be encouraged to say what they needed to say to their parent.

Symbolic Gesture. Some clients may benefit from performing an activity that allows their relationship with their parent to continue through a tangible yet symbolic form. Clients may want to plant a tree in honor of a deceased parent or create a special ceremony to symbolize the death.

Amends After Death. When clients experience the death of a parent, they may need to explore ways to make amends in order to purge themselves of guilt and remorse. Possibilities include visiting the grave or volunteering at a hospital or hospice.

SUMMARY

Middle age offers both challenges and rewards to midlife clients and their families. Clients in middle age seek and require preventive education and counseling for multiple reasons. As their roles change, clients may need assistance with their intimate relationships or relationships pertaining to parenthood and grandparenthood. Clients come with the influence of their own histories, ethnic backgrounds, and gender influences. By understanding typical transitions and challenges within this time period, counselors can help their clients understand the changes they are experiencing and accept the fact that they are not unusual in their concerns or difficulties.

People in middle age come to counseling with many strengths. It can be a time when people know what is important to them and have some idea of who they are. It can be a time when people are ready to make decisions. It can be a time of power and freedom. It can be a time when, having learned from past mistakes, people in middle age can be wiser than when they were younger. They have lived through numerous experiences but still have uncharted territory in which to travel. The counselor can provide them with maps for this journey and help them on their way.

"Middle age can be the masterpiece of your life" (Kalish & Huyck, 1989, p. 315).

VIGNETTES

Vignette 1

Mary has been referred to counseling following a difficult separation from her partner. Mary, who is 46 years old, was with her partner for 24 years and is now concerned about starting over. She has not dated since her early 20s and is uncertain how to begin. She is not sure she wants to enter the dating scene.

Mary discusses her fears about being alone and explains that she does not want to live the rest of her life by herself.

———————

1. What are the main issues for this client?

2. What other information would you want to know about Mary?

3. As Mary's counselor, what would be your main areas of focus?

4. What tools and techniques might be beneficial when working with Mary?

How would your approach and answers change if

1. Mary were a male client?

2. Mary were a lesbian client?

3. Mary had two grown children who believed Mary is too old to begin dating?

4. Mary had two children at home and was taking care of her elderly mother?

Vignette 2

Jane and Steve have come to counseling with concerns about their grown child, Kevin. Although Kevin has lived outside the home for several years, he recently lost his job and has asked his parents if he can return home. Although Jane feels their lives would change very little if Kevin moved back into the house, Steve is concerned that there would be many negative changes as a result of Kevin's moving back. Steve reminds Jane that their child has been employed sporadically over the past several years and has had problems with alcohol. Jane acknowledges these concerns but believes it is their parental duty to allow Kevin to move back home.

———————

1. What are the main issues concerning this family?

2. What other information would you want to know about this family?

3. As their counselor, what would be your main areas of focus?

4. What tools and techniques would be beneficial for working with this family?

How might your approach and answers change if

1. Jane and Steve were Asian American? African American? Native American? Hispanic/Latino? Caucasian?

2. In addition to problems with alcohol, Kevin had a newborn daughter whom he is raising?

3. Together, Jane's and Steve's salaries placed them below the poverty line?

Vignette 3

Roger and Kim met 3 years ago and have enjoyed an intimate relationship for 2 years. They have come to counseling because they would like to marry yet are concerned about how family members will react. Roger has three children, one of whom lives at home. Kim has two young children who come to visit every other weekend and during the summer months. During the time that Roger and Kim have been together, the children have had several fights. These fights have usually led to arguments between Roger and Kim, because they tend to take the side of their own children. Kim's ex-spouse lives within 2 miles and calls Kim regularly, always with questions concerning the children. The ex-spouse clearly does not like Roger and has made derogatory comments concerning the children living with "someone like that."

———

1. What are the main issues concerning Roger and Kim?

2. What other information would you want to know about this family?

3. As their counselor, what would be your main areas of focus?

4. What tools and techniques would be beneficial for working with this family?

How might your approach and answers change if

1. Kim's religion discouraged relationships outside marriage?

2. Roger and Kim both had teenage children, and Kim's son had made sexual advances toward Roger's daughter?

3. Roger's elderly parents were currently living with him?

4. Roger and Kim were both males?

ADDITIONAL RESOURCES

Print Resources: General

Brody, S., & Brody, C. (1999). *Renew your marriage at midlife*. New York: Putnam.

Brooks, J. (1999). Midlife orphan: Facing life's changes now that your parents are gone. New York: Berkley.

Gerzon, M. (1995). *Listening to midlife: Turning your crisis into a quest*. Boston: Shambhala.

Hollis, J. S. (1993). *The middle passage: From misery to meaning in midlife*. Toronto, Canada: Inner City.

Polston, B. L. (1999). *Loving midlife marriage: A guide to keeping romance alive from the empty nest through retirement*. New York: John Wiley.

Sadler, W. A. (2000). *The third age: Six principles of growth and renewal after forty*. Cambridge, MA: Perseus.

Print Resources: Cross-Cultural

Adleman, J., & Enguidanos, G. M. (Eds.). (1995). *Racism in the lives of women: Testimony, theory, and guides to antiracist practice*. New York: Haworth.

Adler, L. L. (Ed.). (1989). *Cross-cultural research in human development: Life span perspectives*. New York: Praeger.

McGoldrick, M., Giordano, J., & Pearce, J. K. (Eds.). (1996). *Ethnicity & family therapy* (2nd ed.). New York: Guilford.

Sotomayor, M., & Garcia, A. (1993). *Elderly Latinos: Issues and solutions for the 21st century*. Washington, DC: National Hispanic Council on Aging.

Stanford, E. P., & Torres-Gil, F. M. (1992). *Diversity: New approaches to ethnic minority aging*. Amityville, NY: Baywood.

Print Resources: Middle-Aged Childless Couples

Bell, J. E., & Eisenberg, N. (1985). Life satisfaction in midlife childless and empty-nest men and women. *Lifestyles, 7*(3), 146-155.

Bram, S. (1985). Childlessness revisited: A longitudinal study of voluntarily childless couples, delayed parents, and parents. *Lifestyles, 8*(1), 46-65.

Print Resources: Gay and Lesbian

Cabaj, R. P., & Stein, T. S. (Eds.). (1996). *Textbook of homosexuality and mental health.* Washington, DC: American Psychiatric Press.

D'Augelli, A. R., & Patterson, C. J. (Eds.). (1995). *Lesbian, gay, and bisexual identities over the lifespan: Psychological perspectives.* New York: Oxford University Press.

Greene, B. (Ed.). (1997). *Ethnic and cultural diversity among lesbians and gay men: Psychological perspectives on lesbian and gay issues.* Thousand Oaks, CA: Sage.

Print Resources: Grandparents as Parents

Cohen, J. (1994). *Helping your grandchildren through their parents' divorce.* New York: Walker.

Cox, C. B. (2000). *To grandmother's house we go and stay: Perspectives on custodial grandparents.* New York: Springer.

de Toledo, S., & Brown, D. E. (1995) *Grandparents as parents: A survival guide for raising a second family.* New York: Guilford.

Endicott, I. M. (1992). *Grandparenting redefined: Guidance for today's changing family.* Lynwood, WA: Aglow.

Kornhaber, A. (1996). *Contemporary grandparenting.* Thousand Oaks, CA: Sage.

Internet Resources

MIDMAC Midlife Research: The John D. and Catherine T. MacArthur Foundation Research Network on Successful Midlife Development: http://midmac.med.harvard.edu

HRS AHEAD Health and Retirement Study and Asset and Health Dynamics Among the Oldest Old: http://www.umich.edu/~hrswww

Craig Nathanson, Making a Difference: http://www.craignathanson.com/index.htm

Midlife Mommies: http://www.midlifemommies.com

50 Something.net: http://www.50something.net

50+ Friends Club: http://www.50plusfriends.com

CHAPTER 17

Promoting Positive Career Change in Midlife

Cindy L. Juntunen
Krislea E. Wegner
Linda G. Matthews

A fundamental task of midlife, or middle adulthood, may be characterized by the process of coming to terms with the past and preparing for the future (Erikson, 1963). In many instances, this task includes a significant career transition as individuals evaluate their work life and determine a need for change. External forces also create the challenge and opportunity of midlife career transition. Job loss due to downsizing, illness or disability, or compulsory retirement constitutes a significant portion of midlife career changes. Job entry, whether planned or in response to a financial or personal crisis, is also a significant midlife experience.

An important lifespan model of career transition, developed by Donald Super (1957, 1969, 1990), posits that careers will develop across a set of predictable stages, offering a parallel to Human Developmental Theory. A full exploration of Super's Career Theory is beyond the scope of this chapter, and readers are referred to Super's original works for further information. Briefly, however, individuals are expected to progress across five stages of career development: growth/birth, exploration, establishment, maintenance, and disengagement or decline. Each of these stages includes significant career tasks that lead to the next developmental level. Although Super suggests age ranges corresponding to each stage, these ages are not predictive. In fact, an important component of the theory is the recognition that people might recycle, or move back one or more stages, as career changes arise.

Within Super's theory of career development (1990), the midlife career role might be consistent with advancing (a substage of establishment), during which a person is moving into positions of increasing responsibility, and the stage of maintenance, which occurs after an individual is solidly established in a career. In addition, we will consider another important group of clients in this chapter—chronologically midlife (mid-30s to mid-50s)—who have never had a career experience or significant work history or who are returning to the workforce after a prolonged absence. People who are seeking entry-level or re-entry work career positions during midlife face a different set of challenges. They might be actively involved in the exploration stage, according to Super, yet be simultaneously experiencing the demands of midlife tasks in other aspects of their lives. Career intervention would necessarily differ for these two groups of clients, yet each is addressing issues related to a midlife change in career role.

Despite the potential for major midlife career change and the complexity of issues accompanying such change, career counseling programs are seldom designed with adults in mind (Zunker, 1998). Most of the work-transition literature has focused on the transitions from education into work (exploration- and establishment-stage activities) and work into retirement (disengagement activities). Yet, midlife workers represent the fastest growing sector of the population in career transition (Newman, 1995). Furthermore, the complexity of career transition for adults is substantial. Career transition in midlife is affected by numerous personal, family, workplace, and cultural factors, each of which can be significant and the combined force of which can be tremendous. The potential for struggle and the opportunity for growth both accompany such a transition. Savickas (1995) has pointed out that "the realities of contemporary life no longer allow clients and counselors to slight the maintenance stage in career development" (p. 3).

In this chapter, we address three major aspects of promoting positive career change in midlife. First, we identify the myriad factors that contribute to or affect midlife career transitions. Second, we describe four different types of career transition that can occur during midlife. Finally, we suggest strategies and techniques to help midlife clients negotiate the maintenance of midlife career development and move toward a healthy and satisfying career transition.

FACTORS AFFECTING MIDLIFE CAREER TRANSITIONS

Career transitions are always affected by numerous factors, regardless of the age or life-stage of the individual. However, the implications of these factors may vary considerably for adults at various stages of life. For midlife adults, sociocultural, personal, economic, and family factors are likely to play an important contextual role in the decision-making process leading up to a career transition and in the career transition itself.

The workforce of the United States has changed dramatically in the last 15 years (Zunker, 1998). Unemployment is notably low, at less than 4.2% throughout late 1999 and early 2000 (Bureau of Labor Statistics, 2000). However, the situations of many individuals do not reflect this apparently positive situation. In the past 2 decades, many millions of jobs have been eliminated. Even more have been created, but they generally have lower pay and fewer benefits (Zunker, 1998). Furthermore, in recent analyses, the apparent success of welfare-to-work programs has been seriously tempered by the recognition that many people are moving off welfare simply to become members of the working poor in low-paying jobs with few, if any, benefits (Loprest, 1999).

The growth of technology is having a significant effect on employment opportunities and security. Technology is growing so rapidly that many workers can barely keep up, and the failure to stay current may create a distinct disadvantage in the job market. Technological equipment, including computers and communications systems, appears to become obsolete within months. New workers immediately out of educational or training programs often have technological skills far superior to established workers and pose a new threat to employment stability. In addition, the growth of e-commerce may have an even greater change on the work environment, although the potential nature of such change is not yet clear.

The nature of change in the workforce highlights a potential "generation gap" that many midlife adults making career transition might encounter. The current social climate of North America is heavily influenced by the value placed on youth and vitality, easily demonstrated in the emphasis of media and advertising. In a youth-obsessed culture, it is not uncommon for individuals in their middle years to feel disregarded and neglected. The social construction of midlife as "over the hill," among other stereotypes, can create barriers to a positive career transition. In the employment arena, this generation gap may be even more keenly experienced, because older workers have long been encouraged to retire to make room for new workers.

In addition to barriers introduced by age, women and people of color are also likely to encounter sex or racial discrimination, as they might at any level of career development. Discrimination might make the transition more difficult by limiting options for new employment, particularly distressing if it is work being sought out of necessity. Similarly, discrimination might affect an individual's access to training or other means for career advancement. In some situations, cultural or gender factors might have contributed to a delayed entry into the workforce. One example of this is the transition that displaced homemakers, usually women, might make into the workforce at midlife. Midlife entrants frequently are women, and assumptions made about women who stayed home with their families, for example, might serve as barriers to later employment.

In addition, midlife adults might be working in an environment that requires greater multicultural and gender awareness than ever before, as the civil rights of women, ethnic minorities, gay males and lesbian women, people with disabilities, and other disenfranchised groups are increasingly recognized. The proportion of working racial and ethnic minorities is increasing, as is the number of women (Zunker, 1998). Issues such as diversity training and sexual harassment are more frequently addressed in the work setting, and unwillingness to attend to these issues is more likely to be challenged in today's work environment.

A variety of personal factors are likely to contribute to the career transition process. Values, emotions, and attitudes will all come together to affect individual career transitions. Personal values may play a particularly important role in the career decisions of midlife adults (Brown, 1995). Given the developmental task of coming to terms with the past and preparing for the future (Erikson, 1963), it is possible that a midlife reevaluation of values may serve as the precipitating event for a career change.

Emotional responses to a career transition are also an important variable. Possible emotional factors include insecurity, anxiety, excitement, anger, fear, depression, relief, and joy. Different emotional factors will be more relevant, depending on the circumstances, such as whether a career change is voluntary or involuntary, expected or unexpected.

Self-efficacy is also an important emotional, or attitudinal, factor to consider with the midlife career changer. For example, in a recent study of individuals making the transition from welfare to work, a primary theme developed around the participants' concerns about their ability to make it on their own, or working without the support of social services (Juntunen, Cavett, Clow, & Suzen, 2000). Career beliefs and attitudes about the barriers that need to be overcome to make an effective career change also contribute to the process.

Economic or financial factors may also affect the adjustment to a change in work status or career role change. Financial factors can frequently trigger the decision to seek a career transition. Financial freedom or restriction may also have a significant impact on whether a desirable transition can be considered. Retirement incentives such as a secure Social Security basis and employer pension benefits are increasingly eroding, contributing to decisions by many midlife adults to extend employment into later years (Brewington & Nassar-McMillan, 2000).

Finally, midlife adults are more likely than any other age group to have responsibilities to other family members. As such, the family will potentially play a major role in any decisions made regarding career transition. In a recent study of unemployed women in Israel, job content and work conditions were the most frequently cited reasons for rejecting a work opportunity, regardless of age group. However, young and midlife adults were more likely than women of other age groups to turn down job offers due to family concerns (Kulik, 2000). The presence of a family may serve as either (or both) a barrier or a support when a career transition is encountered.

Multiple Factors in Context

The impact of these factors (and likely others not considered here) will vary for clients, depending on their unique situations. As the following two cases demonstrate, similar factors may be relevant for a career transition process and still present very differently for two different clients.

Consider Liz, who at 40 years old is chief financial officer (CFO) for a large acquisitions firm. She spent 15 years planning and following a career course that would bring her to that point, and 3 years ago she was appointed the first woman CFO in the history of the company. Now she has an option to move to a vice president's position, again as the first woman to hold such a position. However, she is surprised at her ambivalence about this opportunity. As she approached her 40th birthday, Liz began to feel like she had not accomplished some of her personal goals, despite her success at work and a happy family life. Her self-assessment brought her to the conclusion that she needed to revisit an old dream of pursuing an early talent for writing. Over the past year, Liz has written several short stories during her leisure time, and just 1 month ago the first one was accepted for publication. That success has reinforced Liz's desire to devote more time to writing. Increasing her corporate job duties now would seriously curtail that option.

In addition to her own personal satisfaction, Liz has family members to consider. Her partner, Sue, works full-time in a well-paying position, and the two of them have the financial freedom to travel as they like. The promotion to VP would increase this financial freedom but probably limit available time. In addition, Liz's mother is in a residential care facility that is quite expensive, and Liz expects to assume financial responsibility for her mother within the coming year. The VP salary would certainly cover any of those costs.

Liz enters counseling seeking help for making a career decision. She is having difficulty prioritizing her options and is somewhat discouraged with her inability to act. She will need to indicate her interest in the VP's position very soon if she wants to pursue it, but she is very reluctant to do that.

In contrast to Liz, Mark, a 40-year-old single father of three children, needs to reenter the workforce in order to support his family. Mark worked as a music director briefly after obtaining his bachelor's degree in music education, until he was seriously injured in a car accident. The injury limited Mark's ability to stand or walk for extended periods of time, thereby making it impossible to continue in his chosen field of work. Mark's wife, Jan, had a successful career at the time, and the couple decided that Mark would stay at home with their first child, who was then 10 months old. This allowed them to meet two important goals: increased parental contact with their child and decreased child care expenses. Also, Mark was able to pursue his interest in music composition from an office at home, and he spent several hours a week composing and critiquing musical scores. The financial rewards were small and relatively infrequent, but the emotional rewards were great.

Mark and Jan had two more children in the next 7 years, and both found satisfaction in their family and work lives. Although Mark had some physical discomfort at times, he was able to manage most household and child-rearing tasks. He missed working with music students, and the family never had a large amount of discretionary money, but he was pleased with his life overall. Then Jan was killed in a bicycle accident. She died after 24 days in the hospital. The hospital bills, even after health insurance, wiped out all of the family's savings and also a good portion of the life insurance policy Jan had held.

Mark has been referred for career counseling by a social service worker. Ten months after Jan's death, Mark is unemployed and relying on various welfare agencies to house, clothe, and feed himself and his family. He receives a small amount of money in disability and Social Security payments each month, but it is insufficient for his family of four. Mark wants to change his situation, but he is depressed, anxious, and grieving the loss of his wife.

Mark and Liz certainly need to consider some of the same factors in their career transition; family members, finances, and emotional factors are going to be important for both of them. They each have others depending on them, they are each facing a change, or the need for a change, in their financial situation, and they will each experience a number of feelings about the career transition. Both are also likely to encounter some sex discrimination: Liz, as the first woman in a senior executive position, and Mark as a late-entry stay-at-home father. However, they also have very different issues to consider. Mark is more likely to need some education or training to adjust to new work demands, and this may also bring about greater self-efficacy concerns. In addition, he might experience some discrimination based on age. Mark's financial situation is also more immediately critical than that of Liz. However, the potential for her to incur some important financial concerns is clear. Self-efficacy may be an issue for Liz, as she considers the appointment to VP and also as she considers increased writing activity. However, this might be tempered by her previous successes. Prioritizing and evaluating her personal values might be a very important task for Liz, because her choice seems to be related to her feelings of personal dissatisfaction.

Although Mark and Liz both face career transition and decision-making tasks, they are beginning the task from two very different perspectives. Mark is approaching the career transition from a position of vulnerability, with a basic need to support the survival of himself and his family. He is seeking to reenter the workforce from which he has had an extended absence. Liz is well entrenched in the workforce and is faced with the apparent luxury of deciding between two rewarding options, yet making a decision between those options may prove emotionally difficult. In these two scenarios are represented a number of factors that can influence several types of career transitions at midlife.

TYPES OF MIDLIFE CAREER TRANSITIONS

Career transitions can develop in countless ways at midlife. Isaacson and Brown (2000) suggest that there are two groups of midlife career changers: voluntary and involuntary. Voluntary career changers are those who make a planned and deliberate decision to change their career path or goals. This decision for a change could come from many possible sources. Dissatisfaction with a current career or a desire to pursue new kind of work or leisure activity might lead to a career change or the decision to leave the workforce. Another possible change in career goals can occur when a person decides to enter the workforce after a period of voluntary work inactivity (e.g., time off to spend with family, travel).

Involuntary changers are those whose career goals are changed for them, for reasons of health, economics, age, or other unexpected or imposed event. An involuntary change in career interests or goals may result from termination from a job or job loss due to inability to satisfactorily meet job requirements. One possible scenario is physical injury resulting in decreased productivity or a complete inability to meet the demands of a job. One factor that may lead someone to enter or reenter the workforce involuntarily is economic hardship. That might occur due to the death of a spouse or partner, divorce, or other circumstances resulting in increased financial burdens or responsibilities.

The voluntary (or involuntary) nature of the career transition has significant implications for counseling interventions. However, it is also important to consider the types of change that are occurring, in addition to the nature by which they have occurred. To better organize the myriad options for midlife career change, we have identified four types, or categories, of career transitions for this chapter: maintenance transitions, advancement transitions, entry (or reentry) transitions, and leave-or-seek transitions.

Maintenance Transitions

Maintenance transitions are those career changes that result in some change in the role of the individual, without an actual change in career or even job title. The maintenance stage of career development has been characterized by the stance of "holding your own." In Super's conceptualization, maintenance-stage career activities consist of maintaining the current position, doing what is necessary (e.g., continuing education or advanced skills training) to retain a position in the face of competition, and making new contributions as required by the position (Super, 1990).

In many ways, maintenance signals the end of the "rising" career and the beginning of the "arrived" career. For some people, this is disappointing and an indication that they have nothing new to contribute. For others, this will be a welcome relief or reward and an opportunity to mentor and show the ropes to new, rising colleagues. The voluntary or involuntary nature of this transition is likely to affect the role any individual will adopt. If an employer suggests that an employee needs to sit back and let junior colleagues take the lead, the employee may be more likely to feel like he or she hasn't held out against the competition. However, an employee who chooses the role of mentor may achieve satisfaction from the contribution he or she is making to the career of another.

A maintenance transition may not appear, outwardly, to be a transition at all. But internal individual awareness of one's role as leader or follower, student or teacher, agent or mentor is an identity transition that deserves acknowledgment. Whether the role was chosen or imposed, it is likely to change the experience of work.

One unique type of maintenance change that clearly affects the person externally as well as internally is that of relocation. Limited research is available on the issue of relocation. However, it is estimated that companies were relocating approximately half a million employees annually in 1990 (Fusco, 1990). Frequently, employees resist relocation, and this seems to have a significant relationship to a spousal unwillingness to relocate (Eby & Russell, 2000). Relocation may well be a maintenance transition that is encouraged by an employer, but the decision to relocate is complicated by family as well as career needs.

Advancement Transitions

Super (1990) identifies advancing as part of the establishment stage of career development, in which the person is beginning a meaningful working life. After a stable career or working life is established, advancement involves making plans for getting ahead and improving opportunities for promotion.

Earlier in this chapter, Liz, who is considering a promotion to vice president, is encountering an advancement transition. She has already made substantial career achievements and is now being offered even greater rewards. With advancement come several changes: in role, in relationship with colleagues, in responsibility, and in time commitment, as well as rewards. For some individuals, this transition would be welcomed with enthusiasm, as validation of hard work and dedication. For others, enthusiasm might be tempered with concern for the impact of the corresponding changes. And for still others, it might be more trial than opportunity, where the costs far outweigh any rewards.

Deciding not to accept an advancement opportunity also carries with it a transition. The employee who does not pursue advancement may be viewed as less committed or even as deadweight. Future opportunities might be curtailed, and suggestions or innovations made by the employee might be seen as less important.

Advancement transitions are unique in the importance played by choice. Certainly, choosing between a job and an even better job is an enviable problem. It might seem that decision making in this instance would be easy, for the change appears voluntary. Yet factors such as economics, family responsibilities, and even employer expectations can all contribute to making advancement transition decisions as difficult as any other.

Entry (or Reentry) Transitions

Entry transition refers to midlife adults who are entering the workforce for the first time or entering after a prolonged absence. Mark, in the earlier example, was experiencing an entry transition. Issues related to education, training, age, and life experience might be particularly relevant for midlife entry transitions.

Midlife adults might consider entering the workforce for a variety of reasons. In many cases, the motivation is involuntary, as may accompany the death, illness, or disability of a wage-earning partner. In other instances, however, delayed entry may have been a planned part of the career path. Remaining at home while children are growing up, for example, is an option that women and, increasingly, men have chosen with the assumption that career activities would follow. In addition, some adults may be entering the workforce for the first time because they have previously been unable to do so, due to incarceration, illness, or other factors. Adults with limited access to education and work opportunities may have been trying to enter the workforce and been unsuccessful until their midlife years.

Moving into the work environment will influence relationships both with new colleagues and with friendships that were established while working in the home. In addition, the new role of worker is likely to have an impact on the adult's self-perception, as new skills and behaviors are adopted for the work environment. Also, the midlife adult entry worker is likely to be working with, and supervised by, younger adults, which can create discomfort for some individuals.

For many adults, a period of earlier work experience was interrupted for some reason, with the opportunity or necessity for employment returning during midlife. Reentry career seekers are likely to experience some of the same transitions as new-entry career seekers, such as changing relationships. However, their work transition will also be affected by their earlier experience. In some aspects, this earlier experience is likely to be helpful, providing some preparation for the work environment and its demands. However, changes in the workforce, such as those brought about by technology, may be very confusing for a reentry employee.

Entry transitions are often complicated by serious financial concerns, because in many cases the adult is returning to work out of financial necessity. However, even when the decision to work is completely voluntary, late-entry workers encounter unique adjustments. The world of work has changed dramatically in even the past decade, and some adjustment time can be expected.

Leave-or-Seek Transitions

Adults who decide to leave their current career or find or move to a new career are experiencing a leave-or-seek career transition. Different from maintenance or advancement transitions, these changes reflect a major change in career focus and content. Both Liz and Mark might eventually make such transitions, in addition to the transitions they currently face. Should Liz decide to leave her job and pursue writing full-time, she would be making a voluntary leave transition. If Mark looks for work in a field completely unrelated to music, a seek-career transition would be encountered.

Some types of occupations are almost automatically going to result in a leave transition. Leaver occupations (Isaacson & Brown, 2000) such as professional athletics, military positions, and modeling typically have a lifespan much shorter than the potential career span of the occupant. Workers in such positions are very likely to experience an involuntary leave transition, which may then transform into a seek transition if they shift their attention to other opportunities.

Employees encounter involuntary leave transitions under many circumstances: (a) when they are fired, laid off, or downsized, (b) when illness or disability affects their work ability, (c) when technology renders a position obsolete, and (d) various other situations. Voluntary leave transitions might occur due to job dissatisfaction, changes in personal values or priorities, or in response to family considerations, among other things.

COUNSELING ISSUES AND STRATEGIES

Unlike most of the other chapters in this book, prevention per se will not be a major emphasis of the counselor's activities. Preventing career transitions is often impossible, because they can arise from so many sources. In addition, preventing such transitions is also often not a goal of counseling, because career transition can result in greater satisfaction and happiness for the client. However, effectively promoting a positive career transition can lead to the prevention of potential negative consequences, including decreased life satisfaction, distressing emotional responses, and reduced employability or employment rewards.

Gysbers, Heppner, and Johnston (1998) propose that counselors have a checklist of roles that are important for effective career counseling within a good working alliance. These roles, listed below, provide a useful framework for considering the issues likely to be encountered by midlife adults in career transition.

1. Help clients view themselves and their situations holistically, so that they can see connections and relationships in their lives, families, and work.
2. Help clients understand and deal with the intertwined issues of psychological adjustment and career adjustment.
3. Help clients appreciate diversity in the workplace.
4. Help clients appreciate changing gender roles in the workplace.
5. Empower clients with disabilities.
6. Help clients understand and work through the stages of life transitions.
7. Help clients separate their successes and failures at work and at home from who they are as people.
8. Help clients develop support systems to buffer workplace and family stresses and strains.
9. Help clients recognize that grief and loss are natural reactions to change.
10. Help clients deal with resistance to change.
11. Help clients turn workplace and family frustration and anger energy toward positive solutions. (Gysbers et al., 1998, pp. 27-28)

Inherent in these roles is an orientation toward positive and healthy career development, with emphasis placed on client understanding, as well as skills development. In the following section, our emphasis is on the various issues that clients might need to consider during a career transition and the actions that counselors can take to promote a positive career transition and increased client understanding. Counselors need to assess and explore a substantial range of issues with clients in this situation. It is important to note that the combination of issues will vary, depending on the nature of the transition (voluntary or involuntary) and the type of transition (maintenance, advancement, entry, seek, or leave), as discussed above.

It is also important to note that emotional reactions to the career transition are likely to vary, depending on the nature and type of transition. Clients may be having problems with self-esteem, depression, distress over loss, displacement, loss of identity, fear of the unknown, anxiety about change, and other painful feelings. In contrast, other clients may be excited, happy, relieved, enthusiastic, or looking forward to the change in any number of optimistic ways. It is reasonable for the counselor to expect a wide variety of reactions, emotions, feelings, and behaviors.

The discussion of the issues below is meant to introduce various ways counselors might foster a positive career transition experience. While reading this discussion, consider that a given strategy might need to vary for different types of career transitions. In addition, consider the way in which different counselor roles are coming into play, or might come into play, with the suggested strategies.

Issues Related to Aging and Age Discrimination

For those adults seeking a career change, stereotypes about middle age may exacerbate self-esteem and self-concept issues and may also be a barrier to employment opportunities (Newman, 1995). If they are perceived as lacking the vitality of youth, midlife adults might be overlooked by employers or disregarded as viable applicants for new positions. Ironically, however, many midlife career seekers have developed skills that employers are likely to appreciate: work experience, dependability and reliability, transferable job skills, and other work behaviors garnered through personal experience (Newman, 1995).

Not all clients will be concerned about age or age discrimination—in fact, with an increasing awareness of midlife and aging issues regarding health and fitness, many clients may be perfectly happy about their age and not even consider discrimination an issue. We hope that will become a trend. However, for those who are concerned about this issue, counselors can help midlife career seekers consider issues related to aging and the potential for discrimination in a number of ways. First, it will be important for counselors to assess their own biases about aging and "middle age," in order to determine how such stereotypes can affect the counseling process. This self-assessment may well result in some insight into the type of barriers clients might encounter.

Clients may also hold stereotypes about midlife that can serve as barriers to a successful career transition. One way this can be explored is by asking clients to discuss their perceptions of themselves as a worker, family member, individual, and member of society. Within that discussion, look for indications of how aging is viewed. Do the clients use words that reinforce their role as contributing, experienced, wise, mentoring, exciting, capable, involved, or other positive descriptors? If so, build on these positive aspects of development and apply them to the career transition process.

Alternatively, do the clients focus on the negative aspects of aging, reflecting on time passed by, opportunities missed, competition from youth, or other concerns? If so, work with clients to reframe some of those aspects to look toward ways the clients might achieve more satisfaction in the future. It is possible that many clients will have internalized social stereotypes about midlife and minimized aspects of value to themselves. Often, values clarification (Brown, 1995) will be a useful exercise in this situation. A number of values exercises, including card sorts, values inventories, or assigning priority points to a selection of values, might be helpful here in helping clients change their perspective toward what they want to achieve, not what they feel they have missed. Of course, most clients are likely to have both positive and negative perceptions of midlife. The important task will be clarifying those perceptions and helping clients view themselves from a more holistic perspective (Gysbers et al., 1998).

In addition to understanding the personal and internalized stereotypes around aging, it is important for clients to explore the impact of age discrimination on the career transition they are facing. Here, counselors can play an important role in helping clients explore the realities of the work world. Several questions can be asked of the client: How receptive does a chosen career option seem to you? Are there employees in this company about your own age? If this is a very "young" field or firm, what will your challenges possibly be? How can you highlight your strengths and attributes so that potential employers might better see you for your qualities rather than your age? If this does seem to be a career area where age is a major factor, is it a desirable enough goal to take on the challenges that might be posed for you? If not, are alternative options available that are also acceptable?

In some situations, clients may believe they have been forced to leave work because of age discrimination. A different set of issues then becomes more salient. First, it may be necessary to help the client express and process the emotional reactions to such an event. Anger, sadness, and a sense of injustice may be likely responses. Also, grieving the loss of work, particularly if it was both emotionally and financially important, is an important step. Finally, a client seeking a new work position after such an event is likely to have increased concerns about potential age bias from employers.

Social Support Issues

Families are a primary source of social support for many people. The ways in which families might be affected by a career change are numerous. The working adult might be caring for children and for parents simultaneously. A change in income might have consequences, either positive or negative, for multiple generations of a family. Dual-career couples might be very limited in their options for career transition when one or the other is satisfied with a current position and unwilling to relocate. The relative importance of the family will vary for each client. For some, family needs will come first, without hesitation. For others, individual needs will be of primary importance, with family preferences serving as just one of many considerations. Regardless, the presence of a family may serve as either (or both) a barrier or a support when a career transition is encountered.

In a recent study, Eby and Buch (1995) found that family flexibility was an important factor in promoting career growth after job loss among displaced white-collar women workers, although family support was a relatively unimportant factor. In a counseling situation, therefore, it might be important to consider the potential for the family to respond to a career transition with some flexibility or ability to accept change. Family factors tended to rank relatively low on the list of career growth-promoting factors for men in this study, yet it stands to reason that considering family factors is likely to be an issue for clients of both sex, at least to some degree.

Relocation is an issue that affects an entire family. Eby, Dematteo, and Russell (1997) suggest that counselors can assist relocation partners with a variety of employment assistance services, including counseling, networking with other relocated spouses, job search strategies, and self-efficacy development. In a study of 503 relocating spouses, only 17% had ever received employment assistance services, but 68% expressed an interest in such services (Eby et al., 1997).

Counselors can help clients assess how a career change is affecting, or is likely to affect, their family system. A career change can lead to increased stress for the family, which might exacerbate any anxiety the client is feeling about the career change itself. This is particularly likely if the change is involuntary, but may be relevant in any major change situation. A career change that results in greater reward might also require more responsibility, thereby limiting the time a client has available for family attention. This is also potentially a source of family stress and conflict. The financial, social, and emotional impact of career changes on family members may need to be explored as well. If communication about the career concerns is strained within the family setting, it may be useful to include relevant family members in counseling. This can reinforce support for the primary client and also reassure family members that positive change can occur.

Friends and co-workers are another source of social support that might be helpful during a career transition. Eby and Buch (1995) found that support from friends and co-workers was a significant factor in positive career growth for displaced men, although not for women. Any change in career position, whether leaving a position, advancing, or being demoted, is likely to affect work-based friendships in some way. Counselors can help clients understand that this is an expected response and to seek strategies for maintaining relationships, even if barriers seem to exist. Although this might be especially important for men, positive social support from peers is likely to be helpful for women as well.

Financial Issues

Financial considerations are likely to be an issue in most career decisions and are even more likely to influence the decisions of midlife adults who are responsible for people other than themselves. Loss of income, decreased income, and incurring new costs are possible sources of financial strain. In addition, job loss or change is likely to have a negative effect on insurance, retirement savings, and other benefits.

On the other hand, financial factors may be the motivating issue for considering a career change. The presence of extra discretionary income might allow consideration of a desired career change. Loss of an employed partner may require that a client begin, increase, or advance in their work situation.

In some instances, counselors will choose to refer clients to a financial counselor for consultation with these issues. Complex financial concerns are often best resolved with the assistance of certified credit counselors or financial planning experts. In other cases, however, counselors can help the client negotiate this issue directly. The counselor working with financial issues will need to help the client identify resources related to financial needs. Such resources could include phone numbers and applications from financial support institutions and agencies, regional and national salary studies, cost of living analyses, and labor force projections. It is important to be familiar with resources regarding these topics, including Internet sites, journals, magazines, and government publications.

Counselors can also help clients make decisions and begin problem-solving strategies related to financial concerns. For clients with an immediate financial need, counselors might serve as advocates to connect clients with the appropriate public and private social service system. Local food cupboards, jobs programs, social welfare offerings, and similar programs may be an important resource to help a client get through an immediate financial crisis. When not in crisis, it might be helpful to have clients look to the future and describe the lifestyle they hope to have at a given point (1, 5, or 10 years, for example). Then, determine the financial resources to achieve that goal and help clients identify how their current financial situation might be leading toward or away from that goal. Counselors can help clients isolate particular facilitators and barriers in their current saving and spending habits, level of resources, and potential for financial growth. Counselors can then work with clients to develop problem-solving strategies for each issue that might be serving as a barrier to achieving the desired goal and to practice those strategies with increasingly complex barriers.

Education or Reeducation Needs

Frequently, a career transition will be accompanied by the need, or strong encouragement, to develop new or advanced skills. The counselor can help clients explore a number of questions related to this area. First, will the client need to learn new skills to successfully negotiate the career change? If so, the client will need to gather information about the skills, including descriptions and relevance, training options, characteristics of training programs, and basic competency information for each skill.

Second, does the client possess the potential for learning these skills? This question needs to be considered regarding both ability and resources. It might be necessary to complete ability assessments with the client to see if training is realistic. If the client is capable, then it is important to explore whether the client has access to adequate resources, including finances, social support, and past experience, that will foster attainment of the skills. It is also important to ask whether there are any obvious factors that would keep the individual from the set goal. If that is the case, the counselor can work with clients to identify other options that fit their ability level, which are also desirable occupations or contain components of the original goal.

In many instances, some new level of formal education may be required to obtain a desired position. In such instances, it will be important to explore the implications of embarking on an advanced training path. Clients will need to fully explore the level of commitment necessary (length of program, cost, etc.). The decision to pursue extended training will have implications for income expectations, family members, delay for entrance into the field, and other lifestyle factors.

CASE EXAMPLE

Sue, a 40-year-old housewife of 20 years, is ready to enter the workforce. Sue has been thinking about her career goals since her youngest child entered junior high, and recently she decided to move forward on her own education and career. Sue has a strong interest in medicine and wants to become a pediatrician. She has spent substantial time researching the medical field, the daily activities of physicians, and her own values and interests related to this field. She has completed 12 credits of undergraduate education, including 6 credits of premed coursework, with a 4.0 GPA. Her academic success is reinforcing her desire to pursue medical school. However, she worries about the time and expense that such training would involve.

Sue comes to counseling for help with her dilemma and reports that her husband is supportive of her goals. However, her kids are frustrated that she is studying for exams and visiting the library in the evenings, leaving little time to attend their high school activities or even sit down and talk with them. In addition, with her oldest child soon entering college, the financial strain of two tuition bills (and a third in the next few years) may be more than they can handle. In addition, Sue recently learned that the average age for first-year medical students at the state university was 25.6 years old. Only one person over 35 has been accepted in the past 10 years. Sue had never thought about age being an issue in admission before and is now worried that she might not have a chance at medical school.

Despite all of these concerns, Sue is committed to moving ahead with her goal. To that end, the counselor explores a wide range of issues with Sue. What social support does she have for this change besides her husband? What do her friends think about her moving her attention to these activities outside the home? What financial resources might she be eligible for as she continues her education? What is it about being a pediatrician that is most important to Sue? Would any other job option meet those same needs? How will she feel about being the oldest person in a class if she is admitted to medical school? What concerns does she have about her relationships with her children? What personal rewards are most important? How does she feel when she's writing papers and studying in the library? How can she begin to prioritize all these things?

Sue's dilemma is clearly multifaceted. Issues related to age discrimination, social support, finances, and education are all relevant. However, by exploring all the components of the decision she is encountering, Sue can come to a decision that will work for her.

SUMMARY

Midlife career transition provides many opportunities, as well as challenges. In this chapter, we have introduced a few of the factors and issues that are most likely to be important in the career transition process. Many career transitions are positive changes, accompanied by excitement and new opportunity. However, many other transitions pose a threat to security, self-confidence, and career satisfaction. Counselors who are able to help clients explore the various issues most relevant for their individual career transitions can foster a positive transition experience, even in the face of involuntary and negative career change situations.

VIGNETTE

Johnna is a 40-year-old male. He was a medical technician in his home country. In the last year, Johnna has been transferred from one refugee camp to another because of the unrest and warring in his own country. He has been in the United States for 3 months and is having difficulty finding work. He speaks English but not fluently. He attempted to send for his transcripts and certification papers from his country, only to learn that these buildings and paperwork no longer existed because of the bombings. He is having nightmares and an increased level of anxiety. He is married and has one child, but he and his daughter were separated from her mother. They are still awaiting contact from someone who knows her whereabouts. Johnna and his daughter are living in the area with a family that is sponsoring them. He is eager to get a job and be able to support his family, as he once did. He really enjoyed his career and would like to remain in the medical field. His country allowed him more duties and medical responsibility with less education. He is open to other career path options but is resistant to obtaining education within the United States because he already spent 6 years obtaining his education.

This is a complicated example for any career counselor, but there is an increasing chance that one will encounter such a case. Use this information for the following questions:

----

1. What factors are at play in Johnna's career transition?

2. What is the type and nature of his career transition?

3. What are the possible social changes he and his family will have to address?

4. What will Johnna's career path be, and how will he obtain it?

5. What counselor roles will you be using as you work with these various questions?

How would your approach and assessment differ based on the following:

1. Imagine Johnna without any formal education, separated from his family, and otherwise in the same situation. How would you proceed?

2. How would this case differ if Johnna had the same circumstances but was born and educated in the United States and lived in a foreign country with his family for 2 years?

3. Consider the same circumstances with the genders reversed. The woman had a career, supported the family, and was displaced from her husband.

ADDITIONAL RESOURCES

Print Resources

Birkel, J. D., & Miller, S. J. (1998). *Career bounce-back: The Professionals in Transition guide to recovery and reemployment.* New York: American Management Association.

Career Development Quarterly. (1995). Special issue on career transition. Volume 44, Number 1.

Goodenough, D. (Ed.). (1999). *Career transitions: The best resources to help you advance.* Issaquah, WA: Resource Pathways.

Internet Resources

iVillage.com: http://www.ivillage.com/workingdiva
Monster.com: http://www.monster.com

PART VI

Older Adults

There is universal agreement that the final stage of life ends with death, but there is less agreement about when it begins. For example, in his eight stages of psychosocial development, Erikson (1963) identified age 60 as the beginning of late adulthood. In deliberations aimed at identifying an age at which Americans would qualify for Social Security payments, the Committee on Economic Security considered ages 60, 62, 68, 70, 72, and 75 before arriving at age 65 (now, of course, the age at which full benefits will be paid is being increased). The U.S. Bureau of the Census tracks statistics on older Americans and uses 65 or older to determine membership in this population (Federal Interagency Forum on Aging-Related Statistics, 2000). The Census Bureau has also adopted the convention used by social scientists of separating this final life stage into two substages: the young-old (referring to persons in the 65 to 84 age group) and the old-old (persons 85 of age and older). For our purposes, we have used age 65, coinciding with the typical age of retirement, as the beginning age for our older adult life stage. However, we want to acknowledge that various factors, including each individual's unique biological aging process and age of retirement, can determine when a person qualifies as an older adult.

There is also disagreement about how to refer to members of the final stage of life. In addition to more pejorative terms, older adults are often referred to as seniors, senior citizens, and elders. As already noted, the Census Bureau and others further distinguish between the young-old and the old-old among older adults. We have adopted the term *older adults* to use in reference to individuals 65 years of age and older, but we readily acknowledge that some members of this population will prefer that other terms be used in reference to them.

The population growth rate for people 65 years of age and over far exceeds the growth rate for people under 65. Between 1900 and 1994, the 65-and-older age group increased eleven-fold, whereas those under 65 increased only three-fold (U.S. Bureau of the Census, 1996). This faster rate of growth is expected to continue at least until 2050. In 2000, there were an estimated 35 million people age 65 and over, making up more than one eighth of the U.S. population. The older population is expected to double to 70 million by 2030 (Federal Interagency Forum on Aging-Related Statistics, 2000), and by 2050, there is expected to be 79 million people 65 and over, making up one fifth of the U.S. population (U.S. Bureau of the Census, 1993).

Furthermore, life expectancy is on the increase. In 1900, individuals who reached age 65 could expect to live, on average, an additional 12 years; in 2000, they could expect to live an additional 18 years. As most people know, women live longer than men, and this accounts for the fact that in 2000, women made up 58% of the population 65 and older and 70% of the population 85 and older (Federal Interagency Forum on Aging-Related Statistics, 2000). The longer lifespan for women may be the result of a healthier and safer lifestyle; older men are more likely than older women to smoke, smoke heavily, drink, drink heavily, commit suicide, and die in a motor vehicle accident (U.S. Bureau of the Census, 1996).

The stereotype that most older adults are senile and living in nursing homes is simply not true. Although memory loss does increase with age, in 1998 only 4% of persons aged 65 to 69 were reported to have moderate or severe memory loss. Even among persons 85 or older, only about 36% had moderate to severe memory loss. In 1997, only about 4% of persons aged 65 or older resided in nursing homes. In fact, the proportion of older adults residing in nursing homes actually decreased from 1985 to 1997 (Federal Interagency Forum, 2000). Among those not living in nursing homes, three in four aged 65 to 74 and two in three aged 75 or older rate their health as good, very good, or excellent (U.S. Bureau of the Census, 1996). Most older adults report being socially active and satisfied with their level of social activities (Federal Interagency Forum on Aging-Related Statistics, 2000).

These data notwithstanding, there is room for improvement in the lifestyles, health, and mental health of older Americans. In 1995, about one in three older adults reported that they had a sedentary lifestyle, and in 1996, 80% of older adults reported diets that were poor or needed improvement. Approximately 23% of persons aged 85 or older reported severe symptoms of depression in 1998 (Federal Interagency Forum, 2000). At the same time, however, current trends suggest that future older adults will live longer, healthier, more active lifestyles. They are also likely to be more educated and economically advantaged than past generations of older adults (U.S. Bureau of the Census, 1996).

As with other age groups discussed in this book, older adults can benefit from counseling prevention and treatment interventions. Counselors can certainly play an important role in promoting active, healthy lifestyles among older adults. They can also help older adults adjust to the inevitable losses (e.g., spouse, career, mobility) associated with the final stage of life. These are the themes discussed by Sue C. Jacobs and Karissa K. Adams in Chapter 18. The authors first provide an overview of social trends and issues in an aging society by documenting the increasing numbers of older adults, highlighting differences in aging due to gender, race, class, and residence, discussing diversity in health, disease, and disability, and examining the social impact of an aging population. They then discuss in some detail the activities that promote healthy aging, including exercise, nutrition, social activity, and adjusting to loss. They conclude by describing what counselors can do to promote healthy aging, including the provision of both prevention and treatment interventions.

One of the major adjustments that most older adults have to make at some point is the transition to retirement. In Chapter 19, Diane J. Tinsley and Monica Bigler describe some of the stressors associated with this transition. The authors describe how changing lifestyles and increased diversity in the United States have contributed to changing needs associated with retirement. They go on to present a structured group approach that can facilitate the retirement transition, identifying six essential issues that need to be addressed in group discussions. In addition, they offer guidelines for counselors who plan to offer retirement transition groups, and they discuss sources of referral for such groups.

Erikson (1963) described the major task of the final stage of life as the resolution of the conflict between ego integrity and despair. In Chapter 20, William J. Lyddon and Darlys J. Alford examine how personal narratives can be used to help older adults achieve ego integrity by reviewing and evaluating their life. After documenting the need for life review, the authors provide a theoretical base for the Self-Confrontation Method, a method they espouse for conducting a life review and evaluation. The phases of the Self-Confrontation Method, which provide a framework for identifying important client issues and life themes, are presented. A case example of the Self-Confrontation Method is described and discussed.

These three chapters provide a solid foundation of information and interventions that counselors can apply to the prevention and treatment of concerns addressed by older adult clients. We hope you find them helpful when working with older adult clients.

CHAPTER 18

Promoting Aging Well in Older Adults

Sue C. Jacobs

Karissa K. Adams

*Aging well and successfully is the extent to which a
person is able to interact effectively with the environment
and adapt, accommodate and adjust to age-related changes.*

—Teri, McCurry, and Logsdon (1997, p. 269)

How successful any individual is at aging well depends to some extent on
genes, socioeconomic status, disease states, cultural factors, environmental factors, and lifelong health and mental health attitudes, habits, and behaviors. In this chapter, however, we limit the focus to older adults, those aged 65 or
older, living in the United States. The population of older adults is increasing,
and counselors, counseling psychologists, and other mental health and health
care providers (hereafter referred to as counselors) face increasing opportunities and challenges to promote healthy aging. Counselors can both engage in
primary preventive activities, which foster the maintenance of physical health,
functioning, a healthy sense of self and well-being, and provide secondary prevention and remediative interventions to increase quality of life and reduce
health and mental health problems associated with disease, disability, and functional loss.

In this chapter, we provide an overview of older adults today and their incredible diversity, followed by information on normal aging and the contexts of many older adult lives. This background is fundamental to any work with older adults, especially that which is intended to promote healthy aging.

OVERVIEW OF SOCIAL TRENDS AND ISSUES IN AN AGING SOCIETY

Increasing Older Adult Population

Trends are important when considering working with older adults. The most important is that the older adult population has grown dramatically. According to the Administration on Aging (2000), one in eight Americans was an older adult in 1999. Life expectancy in the United States was 76.7 years in 1998 compared to 47.5 years in 1900. Since 1900, the percentage of Americans over age 65 has tripled (from 4.1% to 12.7%), and the absolute number has increased 11 times (from 3.1 million to 34.5 million). The oldest old (persons 85 years old and over) is now the fastest growing group within the total older adult population. In 1994, the oldest old comprised 3.5 million persons, 28 times larger than in 1900 (Administration on Aging, 2000). From 1960 to 1994, this group increased 274% (U.S. Bureau of the Census, 1994). An estimated 25,000 U.S. citizens now living are 100 years or older. In summary, turning age 65 no longer means death and demise. Turning 65 in the first decade or so of the 21st century is almost a given, with many individuals having one fourth or more of their lives yet to live. As many as one in five Americans will be over 65 by the year 2050.

Differences in Gender, Race, Class, and Residence

The older one gets, the more likely she will be a woman, because the sex ratio (number of males per 100 females) decreases as age increases. The sex ratio is 82 for persons 65 to 69 years old, 44 for persons 85 to 89 years old, and 26 for persons 95 to 99 years old (U.S. Bureau of the Census, 1994). In 1999, approximately 16.1% of older adults were minorities, including 8.1% Black, 2.3% Asian or Pacific Islander, 5.3% of Hispanic origin, and less than 1% American Indian. Life expectancy is affected dramatically by racial background (Administration on Aging, 2000). White females have the highest life expectancy (79 years), followed by Black females (74 years), White males (74 years), and Black males (67 years) (National Center for Health Statistics, 1999). In 1999, the poverty rate was 9.7%, with about 3.2 million older persons below the poverty level. Older women have a higher poverty rate (11.8%) than older men (6.9%). The rate is substantially higher for older Blacks (22.7%) and Hispanics (20.4%) than for Whites (8.3%) (Administration on

Aging, 2000). In 1999, the median income was $19,079 for older men and $10,943 for older women (Administration on Aging, 2000). Significant disparities are evident in income among older adult subgroups, with the income of older White men double that of the Black and Hispanic women ($6,220 and $5,968).

The education level among older adults has substantially increased. Older adults who had completed high school rose from 28% to 68% between 1970 and 1999. Furthermore, by 1999, 15% had a bachelor's degree. This is another key trend, as better-educated older adults tend to be healthier longer and better off economically.

Geographically, California has the most numbers of older adults (3 million), but Florida has the highest percentage (19%), followed by Pennsylvania (16%) (U.S. Bureau of the Census, 1994). Fourteen percent or more of older adults reside in farming states such as North Dakota, Nebraska, Iowa, and Arkansas. Most older adults live in urban environments, with 31% in large cities, 42% in suburbs, and 27% in rural areas (Cockerham, 1991).

The majority of older adults live in age-integrated communities in their own homes or with family members. Some live in age-segregated, independent living communities ranging from high-priced retirement communities to Housing and Urban Development-subsidized housing to mobile home parks. A much smaller number live in a variety of increasingly supportive and restrictive residential settings. These include supported independent living, assisted living, residential care, locked residential care, intermediate care, skilled nursing care, and locked skilled nursing care (Zarit & Knight, 1996, p. 4).

Diversity in Health, Disease, and Disability

Variability in health is increasing between individuals as they age. This is due to differences in genetic factors, environment, past injuries, infections, experiences, behavioral patterns, and resources. An 80-year-old legally blind high school graduate (who is still working part-time, has a great group of friends, eats well, and walks with his dog daily) may be aging well and actually be "younger" than his 66-year-old cousin, a retired English professor (who lives alone, has few friends, and has limited activity due to a rapid degeneration of her vision from diabetes). Understanding increasing individual differences with age is as important as understanding the usual aging process and disorders outside that process.

Older adults experience the same range of psychological problems found in other age groups. Serious mental disorders are found in 15 to 25% of older adults and in 70 to 90% of nursing home residents. Approximately 2.5% of older adults are clinically depressed, with up to 27% reporting depressive symptoms. Anxiety disorders are reported in 3.6% of older men and 6.8% of older women. Older White men are at the greatest risk for suicide of all age groups. Dementia increases with age, with at least 15% of those over age 85 affected (Knight, Teri, Wohlford, & Santos, 1995).

The psychological problems associated with physical ailments are major mental health issues for many older adults. Approximately 80% must cope with multiple acute and chronic physical conditions such as hearing and vision loss, metabolic changes, orthopedic impairments, sinusitis, diabetes, cardiovascular problems, arthritis, hypertension, and the effects of medications taken to control or treat these conditions (Knight et al., 1995). With advancing age, chronic health conditions interfere with and limit activities of daily living.

Social Impact

How successfully and healthfully older adults age affects and is influenced by their families, caregivers, and the health and social service systems. Some understanding of the social context of older adults is important for the counselor who works with them, their families, or caregivers. The economic costs to care for an unhealthy older population are often talked about, as evidenced by debates surrounding health care, Medicare, and Medicaid. Equally important and emotionally and socially costly are the stresses that the rules, regulations, and social norms of medical care settings often cause in the lives of older adults and their loved ones. This is doubly so for the many older adults who are caring for other older adults or grandchildren or both.

A variety of social services are available to older adults, although access to these can be confusing and limited. These include senior recreation centers, multipurpose centers, congregate and home-delivered meals, adult day care centers, legal aid, in-home supportive services, volunteer support, and long-term care ombudsman programs (Zarit & Knight, 1996, p. 5). Other programs, such as community fitness programs, adopt-a-grandparent programs, elder hostels, and retired senior volunteer programs, are geared toward healthy older adults.

With the steady increase in life expectancy, we are faced with two fundamental choices. As counselors, we can help our clients, our communities, and ourselves age well and maximize the number of healthy, productive, quality years. Conversely, clients, communities, and we can age poorly and be continuously at substantial risk for disease and/or disability.

THE AGING PROCESS

The keys to enjoying later life involve understanding the normal aging process and planning for what lies ahead. An understanding of the aging process and the socioeconomic context in which older adults live is imperative in counselors' preventive and intervention work with older adults. Rowe and Kahn (1998) propose the term "usual aging" to describe the normal physical, mental, and physiological functions that gradually change or decline, or both, with advancing age. It is important to differentiate normal physiological, physical, and cognitive changes that are intrinsic to the aging process from disease or disability.

Psychosocial developmental similarities also exist among 65-year-olds that may differ from those of 90-year-olds or 50-year-olds. Erik Erickson's perspective on vital involvement in old age and stages of human life (Erikson, Erikson, & Kivnick, 1986) is important reading for counselors working with older adults, as also is some basic background in the psychosocial factors important in older adulthood (e.g., Cavanaugh, 1996). Although controversy exists about how stable personality is with age, most researchers agree that normal aging does not include a deterioration of personality (for a brief summary of research into normal processes of aging, see Zarit & Zarit, 1998, pp. 9-30). It is also important to emphasize the fact that older adults are heterogeneous, with differences in gender, ethnicity, cultural and cohort expectations, life expectancy, economic resources, and support systems.

The aging process, therefore, can be thought of as a dynamic change process that is influenced by a multitude of factors, situations, and individual characteristics. Teasing apart and considering the various factors that shape the aging process is critical for the development and implementation of prevention and counseling interventions for older adults. We will highlight some of the factors that influence the aging process.

The Usual Aging Process

Physical and cognitive changes that are the result of the normal aging process include changes in mobility, cardiovascular functioning, the respiratory system, excretory system, digestion, and the central nervous system. Mobility changes include a decrease in muscle and bone strength and a decline of joint functioning, which can restrict movement, increase bodily pain, and consequently infringe on daily functioning and recreation (Whitbourne, 1996).

Aging also directly affects a number of central nervous system functions, including perception, short-term memory, fine motor coordination, and large muscle control. Age-related changes have been found in reaction time, memory, and fluid intelligence (Whitbourne, 1996). Changes in sensory abilities also occur gradually with age and affect energy levels, hearing, sight, taste, memory, response time, and concentration.

The rate at which individuals experience these changes is highly variable, as is how they adapt or cope with such changes. These body and brain changes do not necessarily signal degeneration and inevitable, dysfunctional declines.

Many of these age-related changes or their effects can be minimized and even reversed through lifestyle changes.

Life Events and Sociocultural Factors

Older adults often face multiple life transitions in the later years of life, including changes in health, roles, occupation, housing, social support, transportation, financial and economic position, function, and loss of a spouse, friends, or other supports. The unique social, economic, political, and cultural factors and events that face older adults could potentially affect the aging process and serve as a strong determinant in how well a person ages. These are also important factors to which counselors need to attend.

Demographic changes have affected family life, resulting in more heterogeneous family structures. Older adults play a variety of roles in their families and have different levels of support and demands placed on them. More than one third of older adults are married. Older marriages face unique challenges of changes in income, occupational status, residence, and health. These changes hold the potential for either dysfunction or loss or relationship growth and change (Pruchno, 1995). Between 10 and 13% of older adults are divorced. They often have more physical and mental health problems and are economically disadvantaged compared to older adults who are not divorced (Pruchno, 1995). The percentage of older adults who are lifelong singles is expected to increase as baby boomers age. Lifelong singles appear to have a better quality of life than widowed or divorced older adults but age less well than married older adults (Pruchno, 1995). These individuals also are part of various family constellations with parents, siblings, nieces, and nephews and may have strong relationships with other older adults but never chose to marry.

One half of older women have lost at least one spouse. In 1997, there were four times as many widows (8.5 million) as widowers (2.1 million) (Administration on Aging, 1998). Marital status and mortality are strongly linked. The highest mortality rate is among the never-married, followed by those who were widowed or divorced and then by those who were married at the time of death (National Center for Health Statistics, 1999). Carr et al. (2000) found that widowhood was associated with elevated anxiety among older adults who were highly dependent on their spouses and lower levels of anxiety among those who were not dependent on their spouses. The loss of friends and relatives tends to be more difficult for women, whereas the loss of a spouse is more difficult for men. Widowers are particularly vulnerable and have increased mortality rates following the death of their wives.

The most common stresses for older adults are health related. Chronic stresses include chronic illness and medical problems, difficulties related to diminished functioning (e.g., having to give up a driver's license or use a hearing aid), or role strains (taking care of a parent with Alzheimer's disease, an alcoholic child, or grandchildren). As with younger adults, older adults differ in terms of what they perceive as stressful and how they cope. They have a lifetime of coping skills and strengths that they can use to deal with stresses and losses as they age.

Social support is believed to buffer the impact of losses or otherwise help with healthy aging. However, social support appears to act differently in men and women. For example, marriage has more positive physical and mental health consequences for men than for women. This may be because women often are the support givers as well as support receivers; they care for older relatives, grandchildren, children, sick spouses, and friends and often are in support-giving occupations such as teaching, counseling, or nursing. On the other hand, women recover from the loss of a spouse more quickly than men do, most likely because they have many confidants, whereas men in traditional marriages tend to only have their wives. Social isolation appears to result in health problems for both genders. For example, older adults with no social ties are at increased risk of developing cognitive decline or a poor prognosis following a heart attack.

Perceived control among older adults also plays a key role in psychological and mental health. In a recent study, for example, it was found to mediate the relationship between social support, psychological well-being, and perceived health in two independent samples of adults aged 65 and older (Bisconti & Bergeman, 1999). It is particularly important for counselors to understand this relationship between psychological well-being/health and the capacity to achieve and retain power over one's own life and make decisions about one's own situation. Not understanding this, a counselor could, with the best of intentions, inadvertently encroach on an older adult's perceived control in the name of providing service and thereby decrease the well-being and self-care abilities of the elderly person involved (Beckingham & Watt, 1995; Waters & Goodman, 1990).

Poverty is a serious concern among older adults. Millions of older adults in the United States live below the poverty level, with a marked difference in poverty level among different ethnic groups. The lower the socioeconomic status and education level, the higher at risk the individual is for aging poorly. Scheidt, Humpherys, and Yorgason (1999) assert that it is presumptuous to assume that there is only one route to aging well. Instead, they stress that it is important to recognize that not every older adult can age "successfully," because some have lack of access to environmental resources. There is a strong relationship between economic status and health, with higher socioeconomic status resulting in better health (Adler, Boyce, & Castelli, 1993). In a review of socioeconomic status, race, and heart disease, Escobedo, Giles, and Anda (1997) suggested that socioeconomic status might be a marker for insufficient medical care. There appear to be interactions between race and income in the health status and access to medical care of older adults. According to 1993

Medicare administrative data, older Black patients (men and women) and low-income patients (both Whites and Blacks) had fewer physician visits, fewer mammograms, and fewer immunizations than median-income older adults had. In all groups except Black women, the lowest income group of older adults had the highest mortality rate, and the highest income group had the lowest mortality rate (Gornick et al., 1996). Current research further supports the association between race, ethnicity, socioeconomic status, and psychological distress. In a recent study, older Blacks were found to be significantly less psychologically distressed than Whites when socioeconomic status was controlled (Kubzansky, Berkman, & Seeman, 2000). These relationships between socioeconomic status and mental and physical health differences in older adults raise important prevention and intervention counseling concerns that must be acknowledged and considered in our work with older adults. A client's economic status affects stressors, access to and acquisition of resources, needs, concerns, and the ability to engage in certain activities or follow through on recommendations.

Stereotypes of older adults prevail. Older adults are often described as sick, helpless, senile, childlike, sexless, a drain on their families' finances, a burden on hospitals and the social security system, and so forth (Friedan, 1993). Such ageism can have detrimental effects on both counselors' work with older adults and on the way older adults perceive themselves. Ageism differs from racism, sexism, or homophobia in that it is directed against us. We too will be older adults. Ageism attempts to deny our own age and separate us from the older folks. Lack of attention to prevention, misdiagnosis, inadequate or inappropriate treatment or interventions, lowered expectations for prognosis, and premature termination of care can all result from equating usual aging with dependency, disease, and disability. Such ageism can be deadly, as indicated by the mini-AIDS epidemics affecting some retirement communities. Approximately 12% of male and 7% of female cases of AIDS and 7% of male and 2% of females cases of HIV have been diagnosed in individuals over age 50 (Gott, 1999). In Maryland, as an example, AIDS in persons 55 to 79 appears to be increasingly contracted heterosexually, particularly in women (Allison-Ottey et al., 1999). The erroneous beliefs that older adults don't have sex, that they only have monogamous, heterosexual sex, and that they don't need to use prophylactics since they won't catch HIV can be lethal.

In all these areas, it is important that counselors both understand their ageism and other stereotypes and learn about normal aging. In terms of sexuality, for example, although there is a general decline with factors related to sexual function with aging, there is relative stability in sexual satisfaction (Hillman, 2000; Zeiss & Zeiss, 1999). Counselors need to be able to discuss sexuality with older adults, refer them for help for sexual dysfunction (most likely to an interdisciplinary team able to evaluate medical, pharmacological, and psychological factors; Zeiss & Zeiss, 1999), and talk about prevention of sexually transmitted diseases. There is some evidence, for instance, that increased sexual activity because of Viagra could increase the spread of HIV infection and other sexually transmitted diseases among older adults who may lack factual knowledge about the transmission of these diseases and perceive themselves as nonsusceptible to such diseases. Counselors can again play an important prevention role in this regard, especially since information on sex and aging is not as readily available as sexuality resources for other age groups (as regards Internet resources for older adults with sexual concerns, see Harris, Dersch, Kimball, Marshall, & Negretti, 1999).

If ageism is combined with other biases such as gender, race, sexual orientation, disability, or socioeconomic status, some older adults face even greater challenges to aging well and successfully. The challenge is to provide preventive programs, services, and interventions that help break down or overcome these barriers and promote healthy aging. Counselors must therefore acknowledge their own fears of getting old and examine their own ageism or stereotypes about the aging process.

Cultural contexts and cohort histories are varied among older adults. To provide effective counseling interventions or to promote aging well, counselors must understand and learn about their clients' cultures and beliefs. There are distinct cohorts of older adults. The economic, political, and political histories of cohorts will affect how they understand and adapt to aging. Crose, Leventhal, Haug, and Burns (1997) illustrate this with examples of three cohorts of older women whom health care providers and counselors will encounter in the first decade of the millennium. Differences in education, experience with the medical system, and political events such as war, the Great Depression, boom economies, Rosie the Riveter, women's rights, and the move of women into the professions all affect how these cohorts interact with and what they expect from the health care system. These histories also affect the importance they attach to aging successfully. For example, women born in 1918 or earlier tend to be passive and compliant with the health care system. These women may not comply, however, with instructions, for example, to get out of the hospital bed and walk following surgery or a heart attack because of a belief that exercising is unladylike. Women born in the 1920s, on the other hand, had more access to health care and the concepts of preventive health behaviors and thus tend to accept professional advice and assistance more readily. Those born between 1929 and 1938 are more assertive with health care providers and have increased information. However, these women have responsibilities for their mothers, grandchildren, and jobs. Although they value prevention, health promotion, and stress management, caregiving stresses put them at risk of aging poorly.

In summary, a variety of factors distinguish usual aging from disability or disease. And some generalizations can be made about usual life events and circumstances for various cohorts of older adults. It is important, however, to stress again the heterogeneity of older adults. The interactions of psychological, physiological, socioeconomic, cultural, social support, belief systems, cognitive, and behavioral factors become increasingly important and complex with age.

ACTIVITIES THAT PROMOTE HEALTHY AGING

Primary health promotion and disease prevention goals for older adults are to increase the years of healthy life and decrease the years of dependence on others (U.S. Department of Health and Human Services, 1998). Counselors can help meet these goals by using their skills to facilitate older adults' behaviors that foster healthy aging. This includes promoting regular exercise, good nutrition, health and mental health screens, and the social support essential to the health, independence, and well-being of older adults. Counselors can help identify older adults who are at risk for problems and provide interventions to reduce risk. This might be recognizing the high risk for suicide of a new widower and assessing and intervening for support systems, confidants, and depression. Or it might be running a wellness group for older women to reduce their risks for osteoporosis, cancer, and heart disease. Simple interventions such as providing telephone reminders can increase prevention behaviors by increasing the rate of medical appointments kept.

Exercise and Physical Activity

Regular exercise can help increase the number and quality of healthy years of life and help sustain older adults' health, abilities, and independent living. Often when older adults have difficulty doing things on their own, it is not because of usual aging but because of inactivity, which leads to a decrease in endurance, strength, balance, and flexibility. Exercise (e.g., walking, stretching, weight-bearing exercises) can improve these four areas that are fundamental for staying healthy and independent (National Institute on Aging, 1998). It doesn't matter how fit or how old a person is prior to initiating an exercise program. The key requirements to gaining the health benefits of exercise include frequency, intensity, and duration of activity.

Counselors can educate older adults about the considerable benefits that exercise can have on their physical, mental, and emotional functioning. The Surgeon General's Report on Physical Activity and Health (1996) noted that regular sustained physical activity can substantially reduce the risk of developing or dying from heart disease, diabetes, colon cancer, and high blood pressure. Exercise also increases metabolism, helping to keep weight and blood sugar at healthy levels and prevent obesity and diabetes, two major health problems.

Exercise can increase an older adult's sense of independence. Endurance exercises, for example, increase the stamina required to live and do things independently. Balance exercises can help prevent injuries that are common among older adults. Falling is a major cause of broken hips and fractures that often lead to disability and loss of independence. Balance exercises can improve overall balance by 50% and build leg muscles to help prevent falling. Stretching exercises can accelerate the injury recovery process and help prevent future injuries.

Exercise has also been shown to improve older adults' psychological functioning. Specifically, exercise can alleviate symptoms of depression, anxiety, tension, and stress, and improve self-esteem, feeling states, energy, mood, sexual activity, memory, and concentration.

However, despite the physical and psychological benefits of exercise, the prevalence of vigorous and frequent activity in the United States is estimated at only 8 to 20%, whereas the estimated rate of sedentary living is approximately 25% (U.S. Department of Health, 1996). The percentage of the population reporting no leisure-time physical activity is higher among women than men, higher among African Americans and Hispanics than Whites, higher among older than younger adults, and higher among those with lower education and lower income (U.S. Department of Health, 1998). Studies show that in the long term, older adults in all age groups hurt their health far more by not exercising than by exercising. After tobacco smoking, the lack of exercise and poor dietary habits were found to be the second leading underlying causes of all the deaths that took place in the United States in 1990 (not counting genetic causes).

Unfortunately, there is a relative lack of research studies that investigate specific behavioral or program-based strategies promoting physical activity in the older adults to guide counseling interventions (for a review of existing studies, see King, Rejeski, & Buchner, 1998). Still, counselors can help promote and facilitate the adoption and maintenance of exercise as a permanent lifestyle habit in several ways. They can (a) educate clients about the benefits of exercise and the potential risks of not exercising, (b) address some of the possible fears and apprehensions about adopting an exercise routine, (c) assist clients who have adopted an exercise program in generating ways to expand and add variety to their program, (d) direct older adults to resources that address ways to begin a safe exercise program and stay motivated, and (e) develop a repertoire of exercise interventions that are applicable and accessible to older adults who may be of different socioeconomic status, ethnic background, gender, age, or level of education.

Nutrition

Healthy eating habits are also vital for aging well. A number of changes typically occur as a function of age in older adults' nutritional requirements. These changes can lead to insufficient protein and calcium intake, dehydration, vitamin D deficiency, and a lack of vitamins such as B6, iron, or zinc (Rolfes,

DeBruyne, & Whitney, 1998; Rowe & Kahn, 1998). Counselors working with older adults need to educate themselves about these common changes in nutritional requirements in order to help their clients age well.

Counselors can foster healthy aging by asking about eating habits, fluid intake, vitamin intake, prescriptions, and alternative medications. Because of multiple health problems, older adults may take multiple medications. Medication side effects are seven times more likely to occur in older adults than in young adults. Interactions between multiple medications increase the possibility of side effects and symptoms. Since common medications can contribute to delirium, depression, anxiety, mania, and other problems, it is important that the counselor help prevent further problems by referring older adults with such symptoms to someone trained to work with older adults for a nutritional, medical, and pharmacological consultation.

There is some evidence that conducting community-based health promotion programs are effective. For example, Wallace et al. (1998) conducted a 6-month, multicomponent randomized trial with older adults recruited at a senior center. The experimental group all received nutrition counseling, exercise interventions, and a home safety assessment. Adherence was excellent, and both health and psychosocial functioning improved. The authors suggest that conducting such prevention programs in senior community centers provides a promising model for preventing functional decline.

Maintaining Mental Health

The factors that go into maintaining mental health are similar to the ones necessary for aging well overall. Ruth Jacobs (1997), in her popular book *Be an Outrageous Older Woman*, reprints a useful acronym from a 1992 issue of *Hot Flash* (vol. II, no. 3) on mentally aging well:

> *Aging Mental Health:* Activities that satisfy; Growth continues; Income adequate; No undue stress; Good nutrition; Meaningful interactions; Emergency supports; New friendships; Transportation available; A good physical checkup; Lots of mental stimulation; Helping others; Exercise faithfully; Ask for help when needed; Let go of clutter; Take time for self; Have a religious community. (pp. 27-28)

Wisdom (i.e., a combination of cognitive, reflective, and affective personality qualities) in later life has also been found to be an important predictor of aging well (Ardelt, 2000). Specifically, wisdom is linked positively to women's life satisfaction, physical health, and familial relationships. Sustaining mental ability requires effort and an active attempt to preserve mental sharpness. Older adults who engage in low-demand leisure activities, for instance, have been found to also have high mental health scores (Everard, Lach, Fisher, & Baum, 2000).

Inevitable mental changes accompany the aging process. The cognitive domains that are typically affected include verbal meaning (recognition vocabulary), spatial orientation, inductive reasoning (ability to generate novel concepts or relationships), number skills (simple addition), and word fluency (verbal recent memory). Performances on all the above cognitive domains begin to decline by age 74 (Teri et al., 1997).

Optimizing Successful Cognitive Aging

Several factors optimize and protect cognitive functioning despite advancing age. One of the strongest predictors of cognitive functioning in later years of life is educational achievement. Another is physical health status and includes such factors as number of illness episodes, chronic disease, exercise participation, and subjective reports of health and health-related activities such as alcohol and tobacco use (Teri et al., 1997).

Mental health and emotional state are also highly related to cognitive function in later life. Studies have found a relationship between cognitive functioning and self-efficacy (i.e., what a person believes he or she is capable of doing), depression, and anxiety. Older adults functioning at a high cognitive level score higher on scales of self-efficacy and report fewer symptoms of anxiety and depression than those functioning at a lower cognitive level (Teri et al., 1997).

The MacArthur study (Rowe & Kahn, 1998) illustrates the characteristics of "successful agers," older adults who are functioning very well on a mental and physical level. Successful agers credit their pursuit of activities and use of techniques such as reading, discussing current events, daily crossword puzzles, and playing bridge to keep their minds busy and challenged. Social support or verbal encouragement while completing tasks, memory training (which involves the learning of mnemonic techniques) (Teri et al., 1997), and cognitive training sessions targeted to improve spatial orientation and inductive reasoning (Rowe & Kahn, 1997) have each been found to be effective in improving cognitive function in older adults.

Maintaining Social Connections

Essential to our well-being and a vital component of aging well is connectedness. Social connection includes such behavior as talking, touching, and relating to others. Rowe and Kahn (1998) suggest six primary forms of support: confiding, reassuring, providing sick care, expressing respect or affection, talking about health problems, and talking about problems. Social isolation, defined as a lack of social ties, is a serious risk factor for poor health. People who are strongly connected with others will generally live longer (Rowe & Kahn, 1998). One study found that a strong predictor of high functioning among older women was the presence of strong social networks such as close friends, relatives, and the presence of a confidant (Michael, Colditz, Coakley, & Kawachi, 1999). Social support has both direct positive and buffering effects on health and some of the health-related effects of aging. It appears to protect people from premature death and disease. For example, members of church and secular organizations live longer than people do without such group affiliations, and men who report a high level of social support have been found to have significantly lower levels of three "stress hormones"—epinephrine, norepinephrine, and cortisol (Rowe & Kahn, 1998).

Dealing With Loss

Older adults experience many forms of loss and bereavement, a normal reaction to the loss of someone to whom there has been a strong, loving attachment (Scrutton, 1995). The emotions that are generated by bereavement are typically described as grief, which produces feelings such as despair, guilt, fear, anguish, hopelessness, anger, regret, sadness, depression, bitterness, and self-pity. Grief can affect physical health and produce symptoms (e.g., loss of weight, exhaustion, tension, restlessness, and loss of appetite) that make daily functioning difficult. Grief often impedes social functioning and affects involvement in social activities.

Recovery from bereavement is a very personal process. Each individual will grieve loss(es) in a unique way. Often, older adults are ready to accept their dying sooner than their loved ones. Family counseling can be helpful during such times. Bereavement groups or other ways to enrich social ties are important, especially for widowers who have lost their confidants (Hanson & Hayslip, 2000). Formal intervention programs have also been designed to help older adults adjust to widowhood (Raveis, 2000). For older adults, grief work involves both accepting losses and finding a new life without their loved ones.

THE COUNSELOR'S ROLE IN PROMOTING AGING WELL

The counselor's role in promoting healthy aging is multifold. It involves intervention and prevention. It includes teaching ourselves and others about the issues facing older adults and society, the distinctions between usual aging and illness or disability, what we know about successful agers and effective activities, and the diversity and heterogeneity of older adults. To promote aging well, counselors also need to develop an understanding of how to change behaviors that damage health and maintain behaviors that promote health, utilize interventions that optimize older adults' psychological functioning, and help older adult clients maximize and maintain productivity into late adulthood. This will require tapping the wealth of older people's experience, wisdom, and expertise as well as the expertise of other professionals.

Throughout this chapter, we have provided information on aging. Palmore (1988) developed the Facts on Aging Quiz (Table 18.1) to test individuals' knowledge about aging. We have reproduced this quiz at the end of this chapter. Taking this quiz is a good way for counselors interested in working with older adults to assess their own current knowledge and stereotypes about aging.

There are many organizations of interest to counselors, counseling psychologists, and other mental health providers with interests in promoting aging well or otherwise working with older adults. These include sections of larger organizations such as the Association for Adult Development and Aging, a division of the American Counseling Association; the American Psychological Association (especially Division 20, Adult Development and Aging; Section II of Division 12, Clinical Geropsychology; and Special Interests Groups in Divisions 17, Counseling Psychology, and 38, Health Psychology); and the Behavior Therapy and Aging Special Interest Group of the Association for the Advancement of Behavior Therapy. All these organizations are useful for continuing education on healthy aging and older adults, for information on education and training to work with older adults, and for networking. The Internet sites (see Additional Resources at the end of this chapter) of the Gerontological Association of America, the National Institute on Aging, and the American Association of Retired Persons are particularly useful for keeping current on issues and pointing to information on normal aging and geriatrics.

Prevention

Prevention is the promotion and preservation of health and mental health. It has three levels: primary, secondary, and tertiary. Primary prevention aims at preventing the onset of disease or disability by preventing or removing precipitating causes. Secondary prevention involves the timely detection and treatment of disease. Tertiary prevention aims at the reduction or elimination of further disability among those who already have a disease or disability. Counselors intervene at all three levels of prevention in order to promote healthy aging.

Traditionally, prevention follows either a high-risk medical approach or a population approach (Derby, Winkleby, Lapane, & Stone, 1997, p. 44). The high-risk approach targets those most at risk due to behaviors, exposures, genetic predisposition, or other situations that place them at high risk for a certain disease or disability. Examples include (a) education or group intervention programs aimed at older caregivers of Alzheimer's disease patients, (b) support groups for recent widowers, (c) an education program for primary care physicians about the high risk of depression and suicide among recently widowed men, and (d) a program to increase screening behaviors for breast cancer or cardiovascular disease in older women. Besides the interventions cited earlier at senior centers, other interventions for high-risk groups have been shown to be effective. For example, Gallagher-Thompson et al. (2000) found that psychoeducational interventions geared to increasing life satisfaction were more effective in reducing the depression of family caregivers of physically or cognitively impaired older adults. They found that problem-solving psychoeducational classes were more effective in reducing the caregivers' subjective burden and increasing their use of cognitive or behavioral coping strategies. Their results suggest that intervention programs targeted to specific psychological symptoms or to improve specific coping skills can significantly affect caregivers' distress.

The population approach targets all people in a community or other population to reduce overall incidence of disease or disability. Community prevention approaches assume that lifestyle choices that contribute to the risk of aging poorly are a function of social and physical milieus. The community prevention approach is based on Social Learning Theory (Bandura, 1977) and assumes that personal, environmental, and cultural factors, knowledge and skills, and individuals' level of confidence in their ability to succeed all interact to determine behavior. An example of the community prevention approach might be a program geared to increasing exercise in a retirement community, which provides low-cost or free and safe access to exercise facilities, walking, jogging, or bicycling trails, education about how to exercise, and supports and rewards for exercise. The two approaches can be complementary and both used to promote aging well in the older population.

Group programs in universities, through Elderhostel (Masunaga, 1998), in retirement communities, churches, nursing homes, and senior centers have all been effective in addressing older adults' psychological, social, and physical health concerns. They can serve to assist older adults in normalizing the aging process and optimizing their potential through increased social support from peer support, improving social skills, learning coping skills, addressing issues of grief and loss, and enhancing well-being through exercise, music, mental activities, humor, discussions, learning to "surf the Net," and other self-expression. These include wellness programs that stress preventive activities such as stress management, exercise, nutrition, and cognitive therapy; group counseling; educational adventures and programs at universities and elsewhere; and programs that pair retired older adults with jobs, volunteer activities, elementary school children, or grandchildren.

Counselors also play a role in tertiary prevention programs. Examples are providing stress management and cognitive therapy to cardiac rehabilitation patients and social support and cognitive therapy for depression to older adults who are isolated and depressed.

Counseling Interventions

Although this chapter's focus has been on problem prevention and the promotion of aging well, counselors often are called on to help with the alleviation of preexisting problems in which the goal is to change some situation or behaviors or assist in coping with, adjusting to, or accepting the problem. Those interventions are sometimes with the individual older adult but are more often with family members or other caregivers such as nursing home staff or health care providers. Such effective interventions require individual counseling skills, family and couple therapy skills, behavioral assessment and teaching skills, consultation skills, and skills necessary to work with inter- or multidisciplinary teams. When working with older adults, it is important that counselors ask about recent or past medical problems, trauma or injuries throughout the lifespan, exposure to toxins, substance or alcohol abuse, current activity level and exercise patterns, current eating habits, current social supports, stresses, and caregiving responsibilities. It is important that counselors ask older adults and their caregivers about the medications they are taking. In studies of older hospitalized adults, for example, medications have been found to be responsible for delirium in at least 11 to 30% of cases (Moore & O'Keefe, 1999). Because iatrogenic reactions such as delirium and falls are both more common and more preventable in adults over age 65 (Rothschild, Bates, & Leape, 2000), such a simple intervention as getting older adults to take all their medications (prescribed and over-the-counter) to each of their doctor visits could be lifesaving.

Counselors also need to adapt some of their treatment approaches for some older adults, keeping in mind individual differences and possible slowing or losses in sensory and cognitive functions. On all individual counseling and group or community prevention programs, it is important to provide demonstrations and present materials both verbally and visually. Counselors need to say it, write it, and show or demonstrate it, and then ask clients to say and demonstrate in return.

In both prevention and problem intervention, the counselor's attitude is crucial. We therefore end this chapter with a poem in which an older woman speaks well to that attitude:

Older Woman's Advice to a Therapist

What I need from you
Is support for my strengths
Rather than reminders of my flaws
And the reinforcement of them.
What I crave from you
Is unconditional caring
Which is available nowhere else
And never has been for me.
What I expect from you
Is that my pain and terror
Will not make you turn away
Or offer unwanted palliatives.
What I want is that you recognize
I have surmounted huge obstacles
And have reservoirs of strength
Even when hidden below despair.
What I desire is your wisdom
A place to cry for lost dreams
Gathering strength to go on
Imperfectly in an imperfect world.

Excerpt from *Be an Outrageous Older Woman* by Ruth Harriett Jacobs (pp. 28-29). Copyright © 1997 by Ruth Harriett Jacobs. Reprinted by permission of HarperCollins Publishers, Inc.

VIGNETTES

Vignette 1

Dean Phillips is a 75-year-old European American man referred to you for counseling by his physician because he has gone to the doctor's office multiple times over the last few weeks with somatic complaints. Dean's wife of 51 years died 3 months ago after a battle with Alzheimer's disease. He says he is fatigued, lonely, and "forgets a lot." He is "mad" at the doctor for sending him to you because "being dizzy" is "not in my head."

1. What aspects of Dean's concerns would you explore in greater detail?

2. What additional information would you gather from him?

3. What types of problem interventions or preventive activities would you implement with or suggest for Dean?

4. How could you discover and integrate Dean's unique strengths as a person into the counseling session, treatment goals, and further activities to foster his aging well?

Vignette 2

You have been hired by a local health center and a coalition of religious, spiritual, and political leaders to develop a program to cut down on the high incidence of heart disease, cancer, and early deaths. You and a team of professionals from other disciplines have been asked to create and implement a viable, effective program for helping the older adults in the community age well. Although the community is incredibly impoverished with many socioeconomic stresses, the leaders are behind you 100%.

1. What factors do you need to find out about the community and the older adults living there?

2. Given those, what are your goals?

3. Who are the ideal other members of the planning and intervention team? Why? What is your role on the team and with the other members?

4. List and describe the key elements needed to achieve your "aging well" goals.

5. How would this change if a different ethnic group was involved? If it was a rural community? An inner-city community? If it was an age-segregated community? An age-integrated community?

ADDITIONAL RESOURCES

Print Resources for Professionals

American Psychological Association. (1993). *Vitality for life: Psychological research for productive aging.* Reston, VA: Author.

Hillman, J. L. (2000). *Clinical perspectives on elderly sexuality.* New York: Plenum.

Jacobs, S. C., & Formati, M. J. (1998). Older adults and geriatrics. In S. Roth-Roemer, S. E. Robinson Kurpius, & C. Carmin (Eds.), *The emerging role of counseling psychology in health care*, (pp. 309-329). New York: Norton.

Knight, B. G., Teri, L., Wohlford, P., & Santos, J. (Eds.). (1995). *Mental health services for older adults: Implications for training and practice in geropsychology.* Washington, DC: American Psychological Association.

Palmore, E. B. (1988). *The facts on aging quiz.* New York: Springer.

U.S. Department of Health and Human Services. (1998). *Healthy People 2010 objectives: Draft for public comment.* Washington, DC: Government Printing Office.

Zarit, S. H., & Knight, B. G. (Eds.). (1996). *A guide to psychotherapy and aging: Effective clinical interventions in a life-stage context.* Washington, DC: American Psychological Association.

Zarit, S. H., & Zarit, J. M. (1998). *Mental disorders in older adults: Fundamentals of assessment and treatment.* New York: Guilford.

Films

Anderson, L. (Director). (1997). *The whales of August.*

Brown, D. (Producer), & Duke, B. (Director). (1993). *The cemetery club.*

Cohen, S. H., & Whiteford, W. A. (Producers), & Whiteford, W. A. (Director). (1993). *Living with grace: A guide to understanding and caring for persons with Alzheimer's disease or related dementing disorders.*

This is a particularly useful film for understanding Alzheimer's disease and its impact on caregivers. Available from Video Press, University of Maryland at Baltimore, 100 Penn Street, Baltimore, MD 21201.

Gilbert, B. (Producer), & Rydell, M. (Director). (1981). *On Golden Pond.*

Hartley, E. (Director). (1994). *Green winter.*

Thoughtful meditation on various cultures' attitudes about the aging process, raising questions about death, the nature of retirement, and caring for aging family members and spouses.

Pelletier, K. (1991). *Healthy aging.*

A documentary that is part of a senior wellness series. Dr. Pelletier discusses factors that determine our longevity and successful aging: good nutrition, regular exercise, managing stress, and nurturing vitality through supportive relationships and positive attitudes.

Van Wagenen, S., & Foote, H. (Producers), & Masterson, P. (Director). (1985). *The trip to Bountiful.*

Zanuck, R. (Producer), & Beresford, B. (Director). (1989). *Driving Miss Daisy.*

Internet Resources

The Age Pages: http://www.agepage.com

American Association of Retired Persons (AARP): http://www.aarp.org

American Psychological Association, Division 20: Adult Development and Aging: http://www.apa.org/about/division/div20.html

Food and Nutrition Information Center: http://www.nal.usda.gov:80/fnic; or write: Agricultural Research Service, USDA, National Agricultural Library, Room 304, 10301 Baltimore Avenue, Beltsville, MD 20705-2351; 301-504-5719

Gerontological Society of America (GSA): http://www.geron.org; or write: 1030 15th Street NW, Suite 250, Washington, DC 20005

National Institute on Aging. http://www.nih.gov/nia; toll-free information line: 800-222-2225

TABLE 18.1   Facts on Aging Quiz

Mark the statements "T" for true, "F" for false, or "?" for don't know.

1. A person's height tends to decline in old age.
2. More older persons (65 or over) have chronic illnesses that limit their activity than do younger persons.
3. Older persons have more acute (short-term) illnesses than do younger persons.
4. Older persons have more injuries in the home than younger persons.
5. Older workers have less absenteeism than do younger workers.
6. Blacks' life expectancy at age 65 is about the same as Whites'.
7. Men's life expectancy at age 65 is about the same as women's.
8. Medicare pays over half of the medical expenses for the aged.
9. Social Security benefits automatically increase with inflation.
10. Supplemental Security Income guarantees a minimum income for needy aged.
11. The aged do not get their proportionate share of the nation's income.
12. The aged have higher rates of criminal victimization than younger persons.
13. The aged are more fearful of crime than are younger persons.
14. The aged are the most law abiding of all adult age groups.
15. There are about equal numbers of widows and widowers among the aged.
16. More of the aged vote than any other age group.
17. There are proportionately more older persons in public office than in the total population.
18. The proportion of Blacks among the aged is growing.
19. Participation in voluntary organizations (churches and clubs) tends to decline among the healthy aged.
20. The majority of old people live alone.
21. The aged have a lower rate of poverty than the rest of the population.
22. The rate of poverty among aged Blacks is about three times as high as among aged Whites.
23. Older persons who reduce their activity tend to be happier than those who do not.
24. When the last child leaves home, the majority of parents have serious problems adjusting to their "empty nest."
25. The proportion widowed among the aged is decreasing.

The key to the correct answers is as follows: Alternating pairs of items are true or false; that is, 1 and 2 are true, 3 and 4 are false, 5 and 6 are true, and so forth, and 25 is true.

SOURCE: Reprinted from *The Facts on Aging Quiz* by E. B. Palmore, 1988, p. 11. Copyright © 1988 Springer Publishing Company, Inc., New York. Used by permission.

CHAPTER 19

Facilitating Transitions in Retirement

Diane J. Tinsley
Monica Bigler

The U.S. Supreme Court held in a 5 to 4 decision that Congress exceeded its authority when allowing lawsuits against the states under 1974 amendments to the Age Discrimination in Employment Act of 1967. "The Supreme Court said Congress does not enjoy the same power to enforce the 14th Amendment's equal protection guarantee when seeking to protect people against age discrimination as it does when the bias is based on race, national origin, religion or sex." O'Connor wrote that "older persons . . . have not been subjected to a history of purposeful unequal treatment" (p. 3A). She also wrote that "old age also does not define a discrete . . . minority because all persons, if they live out their normal life, will experience it." An AARP attorney "accused the justices of making protection against age bias a 'second-class civil right.' "

—A January 11, 2000 news flash
reported in *Gainesville Sun*

The United Nations declaration of 1999 as the International Year of Older Persons stimulated multiple activities across the world focusing on the situations of older adults, the aging of populations, and lifelong individual development. Yet in the United States, with its emphasis on youthfulness, negative stereotyping of older Americans persists. They are thought of as senile, boring, cranky, dependent, and opinionated persons who are characterized by declining health, decreasing productivity, and increasing withdrawal from a life of purpose and fulfillment. The description of retirement as "being put out to pasture" and going to "po' farms" illustrates Americans' negative view of this transition (Carter, 1998). These stereotypes can lower older Americans' sense of self-worth and become self-fulfilling prophecies, as revealed by the research on stereotype vulnerability (Myers, 1999). The fears of aging, the negative stereotypes of old age, and the failure to plan effectively for their senior years negatively affect older Americans' quality of life.

In addition, economic, biological, social, and psychological issues such as financial adversity, unmet health care needs, social isolation, and a decreased sense of personal fulfillment also trouble older Americans. For example, more than 17% of people 65 years or older were classified as poor or near poor in 1999; that percentage was 8% for elderly Whites, 23% for elderly Blacks, and 20% for elderly Hispanic Americans. Almost 95% of all Americans aged 51 to 61 will have no appreciable personal savings at retirement and will have to rely on their Social Security benefits and a small pension. Moreover, one in seven of these people has no health insurance, and 20% are disabled (Administration on Aging, 2001).

Retirement is relatively stressful, ranking ninth (i.e., 79th percentile) among 43 stressful events studied by Holmes and Rahe (1967). Among the factors that contribute to people's anxiety and apprehension about an impending retirement are a low sense of self-efficacy, a low degree of planfulness, and concerns about finances and health (Fretz, Kluge, Ossana, Jones, & Merikangas, 1989). The increasingly fluid and mobile nature of American society also creates substantial stress for older Americans by separating them geographically from their families and support networks and requiring more personal adjustment to living in a different location.

Although the literature suggests that individuals who plan for retirement cope more successfully with the transition than those who do not plan (Robbins, Lee, & Wan, 1994; Tinsley & Schwendener-Holt, 1992), fewer than 10% of older people actually participated in retirement planning programs (Kragie, Gerstein, & Lichtman, 1989). Most people develop no systematic plan for retirement. There is a need for counselors to take initiative in developing innovative, psychologically oriented educational strategies to help these persons plan more effectively for their later years. Yet the diversity of this generation, which spans a 20-year age range (American Association of Retired Persons, 1998), poses a special challenge to counselors to match people with appropriate, innovative interventions. The need for social services to individuals approaching retirement will increase dramatically in the next decade as the "age wave" baby boomers enter later phases in their lives. This is especially important, argues Atchley (1989), because satisfactory adjustment to retirement depends on the degree to which individuals' expectations are met.

In this chapter, we describe changes in the needs for retirement planning that are necessitated by changing American lifestyles and the increasingly diverse nature of the U.S. population. We provide guidelines for designing structured group interventions for assisting clients to deal with the transition to retirement and discuss six essential issues to cover in retirement planning programs. Sample activities and additional counselor resources are provided at the end of the chapter. In addition, Table 19.1 lists objectives for a group counseling intervention, and Table 19.2 presents the Basic Data Form (Tinsley & Bigler, 1999) assessment instrument. We conclude with information about the source of referral and a summary. Throughout this chapter, we emphasize psychologically oriented educational interventions to prevent personal problems and concerns from escalating into a crisis.

CHANGING NEEDS OF RETIREMENT PLANNING IN OUR SOCIETY

Conceptions of retirement changed dramatically in the 20th century. In 1900, most men worked outside the home until close to death. Only 4.1% (or 3.1 million) of U.S. citizens were 65 years or older in 1900, whereas in 1997, 12.7% (or 34.1 million) were 65 years or older (American Association of Retired Persons, 1998). This situation began to change with the widespread unemployment and poverty brought about by the onset of the Great Depression. Jobs were scarce and the opportunity to work until close to the end of life no longer existed for many in the United States. This crisis stimulated the 1935 passage of Social Security legislation to provide a government-sponsored old-age insurance program. The idea was that people who paid into the program while they were working would receive subsistence benefits during their retirement years or when they became incapable of working. This legislation also forced workers covered by the program to exit from their jobs at 65 years of age. Historically, retirement signaled the individual's exit from full-time paid employment as a result of declining health and old age; retirement was synonymous with termination, withdrawal, and departure.

Despite its noble intent, the benefits of Social Security were not applicable to most Caucasian women and ethnic minorities. Most women were not employed outside the home in jobs covered by the Social Security legislation, so they qualified for benefits only through their husbands' participation in the system. Elderly African Americans were more likely to have worked part-time throughout their lives, so they did not receive benefits comparable to those of Caucasian men. Furthermore, they were more likely to continue to work at least part-time after age 65 to support their families (Mutchler, Burr, & Massagli, 1997).

The view of retirement held by scholars during the 1970s primarily reflected the experiences of White middle-class men, despite the different retirement patterns of women and racial or ethnic minority group members. For example, Atchley (1976) defined retirement as a "condition in which an individual is forced or allowed to be employed less than full time and in which his income is derived at least in part from a retirement pension earned through prior years as a job holder" (p. 1). This definition focuses on individual choice by men who have been employed full-time and contributed to the government pension plan for years. It ignores the tremendous variability that exists in the work patterns and needs of older Americans.

Cultural and other legislative changes have begun to influence psychologists' changing views of retirement in the United States. For example, women began to experience increased job opportunities outside the home in the expanding post-World War II economy. Although women experienced psychological barriers, restrictions due to family commitments, and discriminatory policies in employment, the proportion of women engaged in paid employment outside the home increased from 25% in 1940 to about 58% in the late 1990s (U.S. Department of Labor, 1999). Beginning in the 1960s, the strong influence of the women's movement, technological advances that modified women's work in the home, the growing availability of day care for children, and changes in legislation have contributed to women's changing life roles across the lifespan. Recent studies show that a woman's career is a central component of her self-concept that she seeks to integrate with other important components of her life such as family and children (Cook, 1993). Gallos (1989) argued that scholars need to develop models of adult development that recognize the importance to women (and an increasing number of men) of expressing and coordinating both their productive and their nurturing roles across the lifespan. However, information about women's retirement planning is still sketchy (Phillips & Imhoff, 1997).

Other cultural changes such as advances in the biological sciences have contributed to improving health and increasing longevity for men and women. Through most of the 18th and 19th centuries, life expectancy for Americans was in the low 40s. At the turn of the 20th century, the average life expectancy of Americans was about 47 years of age, and people spent an average of only 2% of their lives in retirement. In the year 2000, the average life expectancy is now 78 years for men and 84 years for women. About 13% of our population is age 65 and older. That proportion will increase to 21% by 2030, and most people will spend more than 20% of their lives in retirement.

Changes in Social Security legislation eliminated compulsory retirement at age 65 for federal employees in 1978, and subsequent legislation in 1986 extended that benefit to those outside the federal system working for companies with 20 or more employees. Also, early retirement became a more widely adopted voluntary choice for individuals whose private pensions and savings allowed them to retire early in life. Others in selected occupations (e.g., the military, education, and professional sports) traditionally retire at an early age and spend their time in further paid work, volunteer work, education, leisure, increased travel, and multiple other options.

Given these governmental and societal changes, retirement no longer represents a marked shift from work to nonwork at a prescribed time. The event of retirement is no longer uniquely defined as the point at which an individual begins to collect a Social Security pension or an annuity from a company or organization, for those events do not necessarily signal a withdrawal from the workforce and physical decline. In fact, more than one third of all American Association of Retired Persons (AARP; 1999) members are currently working. Retirement has now taken on more of an individual psychological significance as that time in life when people make subjective decisions that they have achieved the status of retirement.

In this chapter, we view retirement not as an organizationally determined state but as a developmental process during which individuals redefine and renegotiate their roles and activities. For that reason, we will henceforth refer to the retirement transition. For most adults, retirement now represents a continuation of adult development that is characterized by more freedom than they have experienced since adolescence. This increased freedom provides the opportunity to lead active, personally rewarding lives, but it also carries with it the challenge to make intentional choices that will have the desired effects. The retirement process is influenced by the individual's culture, gender, health, work history, personal history, social support, ethnic background, and economic circumstances (Tinsley & Schwendener-Holt, 1992). The cultural and ethnic diversity of the U.S. population and the variety of ways in which individuals can retire challenge those who assist persons with retirement-related issues to recognize the changing and complex nature of retirement and each individual's unique approach to it.

THE RETIREMENT TRANSITION

A Structured Group Approach

The retirement transition involves a process of self-assessment, goal identification and prioritization, learning to apply existing skills to new roles and situations, and developing new skills as needed. In many instances, however, the individual's work ethic, fears of the unknown, and the ageism and negative connotations about nonworkers that are pervasive in U.S. culture undermine self-esteem and disrupt the retirement transition. When that occurs, counselors need to help individuals examine their attitudes and the external barriers that lessen their quality of life in retirement.

TABLE 19.1   Objectives for Developmental, Structured Group Intervention for Retirement Transitions Counseling

During this group you should

1. Increase your awareness of myths and stereotypes regarding ageism, sexism, and other isms in American culture.
2. Identify attitudinal blocks and other potential barriers to effective retirement planning.
3. Learn about a model for dealing effectively with change.
4. Clarify your understanding of retirement planning tasks.
5. Learn more about your interests, skills, values, and personal strengths and the relation of these to potential future roles.
6. Develop optimism about your ability to handle your changing life roles and responsibilities.
7. Learn how to create optimally challenging opportunities in your life.
8. Evaluate your preferences for geographic location and living arrangement.
9. Assess your social support networks and develop new networking techniques.
10. Explore issues of loss and learn effective strategies for dealing with loss.
11. Develop your financial management plans.
12. Develop plans to improve and maintain your physical health and spiritual well-being.
13. Explore safety issues related to the changes associated with growing older.
14. Develop your plans and ability to [specify]

15. Other [specify]_____

A structured small group intervention can be an effective means of helping relatively normal individuals make satisfying decisions and changes during the retirement transition. The supportive, positive atmosphere of a small group can help the participants think critically about their goals and facilitate their adjustment to retirement. We recommend having two counselors work together to provide diversity and balance to the process and content of the group work. The general objectives of retirement transition counseling are to provide clients with information and help them make decisions about future plans, to increase their awareness of how their attitudes affect their approach to retirement, and to help them change their attitudes, and, if necessary, their behaviors. The outcomes can be increased self-esteem, personal growth, and improved life satisfaction. Table 19.1 presents a specific set of objectives.

Potential group participants should complete the Basic Data Form (Tinsley & Bigler, 1999; see Table 19.2) and participate in an individual interview prior to their inclusion in a group. The criteria to use in deciding whether each individual should be included in a structured group (or the structured group you presently are forming) depend in part on your theoretical orientation. Some therapists believe that groups that are homogeneous in factors such as gender, ethnicity, socioeconomic level, and life experience more quickly achieve mutual

(Text continued p. 384)

TABLE 19.2   Basic Data Form: Group Participation Assessment

Today's date _____/_____/_____

Name [First/Middle/Last] _____/_____/_____

Address [Street/City/State/ZIP] _____

_____

Phone [Area code first] (____)_____

Background:
Gender [Female/Male] _____ Date of Birth [Month/Day/Year] _____/_____/_____

Racial Background: [please check]
_____African Descent/Black _____American Indian _____Asian _____Hispanic/Latino/a
_____Caucasian/White _____Multiracial: specify nationality: _____
Languages: 1._____2._____3._____

What other identities are especially meaningful to you (e.g., ethnic cultural background, marital status, physical abilities, religion, senior citizen, sexual orientation)?

Summarize briefly your work history and current occupational status:

What are your main retirement planning concerns?

List individuals who have been very important in your life. Explain.

What factors in your family relationships provide joy and a sense of fulfillment for you?

What factors in your family relationships are displeasing or unsatisfying to you?

Do you want your family relationships to be different? If so, what would you change?

List leisure activities you pursue now:

List new leisure activities you want to consider:

(Continued)

TABLE 19.2   Continued

How much assistance would you like to increase
your self-awareness in the following areas?

	None	*Some*	*Much*
Abilities and skills	( )	( )	( )
Interests	( )	( )	( )
Personal attitudes	( )	( )	( )
Personal strengths	( )	( )	( )
Personal values	( )	( )	( )
Work motivations	( )	( )	( )

How much help do you need in the following areas?

	None	*Some*	*Much*
Assessing emotional readiness for retirement	( )	( )	( )
Assessing retirement benefits	( )	( )	( )
Developing and implementing retirement plans	( )	( )	( )
Evaluating compatibility of your values, interests, and skills with your choices	( )	( )	( )
Overcoming barriers	( )	( )	( )

How much assistance do you need with the following
specific aspects of the retirement transition?

	None	*Some*	*Much*
Financial management	( )	( )	( )
Housing and geographical	( )	( )	( )
Legal planning	( )	( )	( )
Leisure planning	( )	( )	( )
Promoting healthy living	( )	( )	( )
Setting long-term goals	( )	( )	( )
Setting short-term goals	( )	( )	( )
Other_____	( )	( )	( )

How much help do you want in the following areas?

Time and stress management:

	None	*Some*	*Much*
Dealing with stress	( )	( )	( )
Scheduling my time wisely	( )	( )	( )
Setting priorities	( )	( )	( )
Other_____	( )	( )	( )

	None	Some	Much
Developing:			
Assertiveness skills	( )	( )	( )
Communication skills	( )	( )	( )
Other_____	( )	( )	( )

Anxiety and depression management:

	None	Some	Much
Anxiety management	( )	( )	( )
Fear of aging	( )	( )	( )
Fear of failing	( )	( )	( )
Irrational thoughts	( )	( )	( )
Depression	( )	( )	( )
Other_____	( )	( )	( )

Rate the topics you would most like to cover in the retirement planning group.

	None	Some	Much
Caregiving	( )	( )	( )
Continuing education	( )	( )	( )
Exercise	( )	( )	( )
Family roles	( )	( )	( )
Finding a new career	( )	( )	( )
Full-time work	( )	( )	( )
Leadership roles	( )	( )	( )
Leisure roles	( )	( )	( )
Meditation	( )	( )	( )
Mentoring	( )	( )	( )
Part-time work	( )	( )	( )
Political activism	( )	( )	( )
Safety issues	( )	( )	( )
Spirituality issues	( )	( )	( )
Sports/club member	( )	( )	( )
Starting my own business	( )	( )	( )
Volunteering	( )	( )	( )
Other:			
Specify_____	( )	( )	( )
Other Comments			

Source: D. J. Tinsley and M. Bigley, personal communication (1999).

understanding and acceptance, whereas others believe that heterogeneous groups lead to better outcomes. However, some pragmatic issues and some attributes of the individual need to be considered when deciding whether to include an individual in a structured group. For example, clients who live too far away from the meeting place, those who must travel frequently for business or other reasons, those who have unpredictable but unavoidable obligations (e.g., employment, legal problems, or child care), and those who have serious physical health problems may find it difficult to meet with the group regularly. It is better to see those individuals in individual counseling. In addition, individuals who suffer from organic brain damage, who have psychoses that are not well controlled (e.g., paranoid, hypochondriacal, or sociopathic), those who are addicted to alcohol or drugs, and those whose agitation, anxiety, or depression seem likely to impede group progress should be seen in individual counseling (Yalom, 1995).

Six interrelated issues are critical to designing effective, developmentally oriented group retirement interventions: (1) understanding the changing life roles that accompany the retirement transition, (2) increasing clients' self-understanding, (3) reevaluating social networks and relationships, (4) considering relocation and safety issues, (5) revising financial and legal issues, and (6) maintaining physical health and spiritual well-being. We describe each of these briefly and refer readers to our Additional Resources at the end of this chapter and other chapters in this book.

Changing Life Roles

Theories of normal adult development (Fassinger & Schlossberg, 1992) and counselors' theoretical approaches to change are useful in understanding the changing life roles associated with the retirement transition. It is critical to understand, however, that the age norms implied by these theories are no longer accurate. For example, improved health care and the maintenance of an active lifestyle will allow some baby boomers to redefine middle age as 65 and old age as 85 years of age. Counselors must help clients consider the consequences of decisions made at age 50 to 65 in this changing context to create positive opportunities in later life.

Developmental models emphasize the typical changes associated with aging. Erikson, Bordin, and Super have useful insights for counselors working with the retirement transition. Erikson (1963) argued that the changes associated with old age create an identity crisis that must be resolved by developing integrity (e.g., looking back on life with acceptance and self-respect) or falling into a life of despair (e.g., viewing previous life events with regret and remorse). Identity issues are central to the retirement transition, and an important function of the counselor is to help clients maintain a positive sense of self-acceptance as they progress through the transition. Super (1994) emphasized that persons fulfill multiple, evolving life roles across the lifespan (e.g., worker, citizen, homemaker, leisurite, and annuiant). This model nicely depicts the multiple roles of contemporary seniors as they progress through the retirement transition. Super also highlighted the importance of congruence between individuals' self-concepts and their perceptions of their life roles across the lifespan. Counselors can best help clients understand the retirement transition as an evolving series of roles. Bordin's (1979) view that balancing work, leisure, and other aspects of life are essential goals across the lifespan is another useful perspective to keep in mind when helping clients during the retirement transition. The essential message of these models, therefore, is that a central component of the retirement transition is the planful evolution of the multiple life tasks and roles the clients choose to pursue.

The individual transitions model (Schlossberg, 1984) extends developmental models by focusing on significant life events (e.g., early retirement, death of a spouse or companion, or an accident causing long-term disability) that influence the roles and future goals of the individual. Schlossberg's analysis focuses on factors that caused the transition, the perceived locus of control over the precipitating events, the client's ability to cope with change, and the identification of ways to improve the client's skills (Schlossberg, 1984).

For many adults, work provides a social niche in the form of a recognized status in an organization and in society, and work interactions promote a sense of purpose and meaning in living. The retirement transition is a significant life event that causes a shift in individuals' interpersonal relationships and disrupts some social networks. Some work values (e.g., influencing others, having structured time, and socializing with work acquaintances) may cause difficulties in retirement for those who fail to find new ways to satisfy these values. Nonwork roles (e.g., caregiver and leisurite) may also require redefinition. Structured group activities can help clients consider a variety of means for replacing work-related roles in retirement (e.g., continuing education opportunities, expanded leisure activities, entering part-time or full-time employment, self-employment, and volunteer work).

The losses that clients experience as job related can be compounded by the loss of contacts with friends and family due to death or relocation to a different part of the country. The uncertainties of growing older, thoughts about the potential decline of health, and the need for clients to discuss long-term plans and desires with their aging parents all create feelings of grief and loss that heighten clients' sense of vulnerability too. Dealing with the emotional aspects of death and dying is often a critical part of helping clients continue to grow and create positive retirement experiences (Hundley, 1993). As individuals accept losses and experience internal peace, they are more likely to create more positive experiences that are reciprocally rewarding for themselves and others and to experience meaning in their lives (Pargament, 1997).

As noted previously, it is also important to recognize that some individuals may require referral to individual counseling, crisis counseling, or some other type of intervention because of the nature or severity of their psychological stress. Underlying psychopathology, the existence of long-standing emotional stresses, or personal characteristics may interfere with the facilitative conditions of the group. The need for crisis counseling may arise as a result of an unexpected termination of employment where feelings of shock, guilt, fear, and anger may be interfering with normal life patterns. Potential signs of such distress may include denial, projection, extreme distractibility, and hopelessness. If the counselor is not prepared to provide crisis work, immediate referral is necessary. The need for specialized assessment for emotional, physiological, and medical problems that are identified in the screening interview may necessitate referral because of the time involved in assessment and in the prior scheduling of the retirement groups.

Increasing Self-Understanding

Assessing older clients is a challenging undertaking because of the lack of instruments specifically designed for use with older clients, lack of norm groups, clients' longer life histories, and clients' multiple concerns about later life changes. Furthermore, much of the research and writing on assessment has neglected the instruments specifically designed for use with older clients (Kaszniak, 1996). Nevertheless, psychological assessment is an important component of a developmentally oriented retirement planning program (Zunker & Norris, 1998). Counselors need to use their assessment skills to develop an understanding of the individual's level of functioning in multiple situations. Accurate assessment is an essential prerequisite to choosing relevant topics to address in the group, to determining alternative referrals, and establishing goals.

Skillful assessment can be critical in providing clients with information that is essential in making decisions and in making behavioral changes that promote an effective adjustment to the retirement transition. Some of the issues that confront younger individuals considering a career choice (e.g., lack of self-knowledge, inadequate decision-making skills, and unfamiliarity with options) also confront clients during the retirement transition (Bolles, 1995). Many older clients need to gain a more explicit understanding of their values, personal interests and preferences, and transferable skills. Like younger clients, retirement transition clients may need help in understanding the implication for their choices of future roles of the changes that are occurring in their physical abilities, knowledge, skills, and financial situation (Smith & Smith, 1999).

Support Networks and Changing Relationships

Individuals' social support networks vary considerably as a function of gender, personality characteristics, and values, but a stable, well-functioning social support network contributes to an individual's sense of safety, coherence, stability, and meaning in life. Friends and family can provide emotional buffers in times of distress (Reeves & Darville, 1994). The absence of preretirement activities and the associated loss of social contacts can overwhelm clients who do not have an effective substitute for the lost social interactions. Divorce or the death of a companion also can create a devastating loss of personal support during the retirement transition (Blieszner & Bradford, 1995).

Group interventions designed to teach clients about social networks and relationships should assess the present situation and its potential, elaborate on the qualities of a good social network and relationships, and discuss ways that individuals can improve their social networks. Mini-lectures and experiential activities can be used to help clients develop their support networks. It is important that counselors help clients examine their support networks, whether working with individual clients or couples, and match the interventions to the composition of the group members. One possibility is to have clients list people who are sources of support. Encourage them to consider multiple factors (e.g., geographic distance, frequency of contact, marital status, and the quality of contacts) that influence their overall satisfaction with their current situation. Use strategies to help clients identify appropriate contacts and resources by exchanging information with each other. Then counselors can help their clients plan ways to maintain and redefine their social networks and relationships during the retirement transition with their companion or on their own.

Couples entering retirement together are faced with a number of unique internal and external challenges (Blieszner & Bradford, 1995; Silverstone & Hyman, 1998). Aging couples may fear for the physical health and psychological well-being of their companions. Once stable roles may actually be disrupted by declining health or disability (Smith, 1997). Often, couples making the transition to retirement face the possibilities of sharing considerably more time together. This may cause them to feel constrained by the perceived loss of independent activity. Alternatively, they may want to examine more broadly their changing needs for activities (e.g., sexual activity and other means of expressing affection) to take advantage of their increased flexibility. Sexuality is a highly valued aspect of many healthy relationships for older couples.

Clients' communication skills, openness for change, and their use of negotiation skills are essential for maintaining a mutually satisfying relationship through the retirement transition. Clients can learn to express mutual respect more clearly and better understand important people in their lives during this retirement transition. Counselors can help clients reevaluate their attitudes and beliefs about important people in their lives, improve these communication skills, and identify other ways to create and maintain healthy relationships.

Relocation and Safety Issues

Group facilitators should help individuals who are planning the retirement transition consider the implications for their safety and quality of life of their preferences and needs for geographic location, type of residence, and physical features of their residence (Smith & Smith, 1999). Counselors can help clients make these decisions by helping them assess their values, obtain relevant information, and consider several issues jointly before making changes (Cleveland, 1996). For example, interrelated choices include moving to a different geographic location, moving to a different kind of residence to reduce safety hazards and increase accessibility, and modifying a current residence in response to declining physical abilities and other special needs.

About 20% of baby boomers expect to move to a new geographic area when they retire, and many more individuals consider options for retirement-style living in Florida, Texas, California, Arizona, and other Sun Belt locations (AARP & Roper, 1998). Some of the factors that influence clients' choices of these locations include the distance from family and relatives, weather conditions, and the cost of living (e.g., most affordable housing, lowest property taxes, and least expensive utility bills). The availability of services (e.g., convenient shopping, medical facilities, and public transportation) and other community characteristics (continuing education opportunities, entertainment, and public safety) are also important considerations. These decisions are complex, and counselors need to help their clients determine the factors that are most important for them, prioritize their options, and make realistic decisions.

Clients also have multiple options regarding the kind of dwelling they consider (Fox, 2000). Single-family homes can be in the general community or in planned retirement communities. Active adult communities and assisted living dwellings can be in age-integrated communities or in age-restricted resort communities. Some individuals may choose to travel full-time, live in a recreational vehicle, or spend extended periods of time with children, other family members, or friends. Some may prefer communal living based on other interests and personal preferences (e.g., educational and religious services or sexual orientation).

Other options for clients having special health concerns are lifetime care facilities that provide room, board, recreation, and medical care in close proximity for residents. Generally, at least three levels of care are available. Independent living could include owning or renting a private home, an apartment, or a condominium. The amenities provided can include food, cleaning, and maintenance services. Assisted living includes the provision of nursing care in one's residence and works well for couples in which one person needs additional help and the second requires assistance with the caregiving process. Finally, acute care typically occurs in a nursing home-like facility in which more substantial medical care services are provided.

Most individuals want to remain independent and comfortable as they grow older, but to do so frequently requires making adjustments to their living environments (AARP, 1995). Clients may need to remodel to improve accessibility and remove hazards to their safely living independently. Home modifications can include the installation of additional lighting, handrails or grab bars, lever faucets, disability planks, fire safety features, emergency response systems, and ways to protect the residence from forced entry and other criminal activity.

Other safety concerns can deal with high-pressure sales tactics, telemarketing, cons, and frauds that try to take advantage of unsuspecting individuals (Smith & Smith, 1999). Counselors could help clients consider helping their residential area develop a community watch program. Counselors could also invite local police representatives as a resource to help retirees think critically about their physical security. Alternatively, a community health advocate could develop a mini-lecture and provide a discussion around clients' specific health and safety needs.

Financial and Legal Concerns

For the past 60 years, most descriptions of retirement planning programs have dealt exclusively with financial planning; most still do (Hayes & Deren, 1990). An Internet search for references to retirement yielded 807,520 hits, with the highest proportion of those related to financial planning. Some books and articles on financial planning provide excellent didactic information; others present biased views favoring products and services the authors represent. However, very few resources help the retirement planner deal with the anxiety and stress associated with financial decision making. Although mental health practitioners are not qualified to provide certified financial planning, counselors can help clients become aware of and deal with the attitudes and beliefs that interfere with effective financial decision making.

A general guideline is that most retirees will need only 60 to 80% of their earlier income, depending on their needs and desired lifestyles (Fullner, 1996; Keating, 1996). Clients can consult the numerous resources available to learn about increasing retirement income and cutting expenses (e.g., Yolles & Yolles, 2001). For example, Keating (1996) suggested reducing expenditures and preserving savings by completely paying off the house mortgage, eliminating debt, driving cars longer before buying new ones, taking advantage of senior discounts, and donating time instead of money to charities. The role of counselors in this aspect of the retirement transition is not that of a financial consultant but that of helping clients manage the stress and the anxiety associated with the planning process, gain greater clarity about their values, and evaluate the consistency between their values and the alternatives that confront them.

Counselors can help clients deal with the cognitive and emotional barriers that interfere with their efforts to develop a system to organize, review, and modify financial and legal documents (e.g., wills, life insurance policies, annuities, and medical insurance). It is important that retirees review these periodically to ensure that they reflect their current and anticipated future situation. Wills should be reviewed every few years or when a significant change occurs (e.g., a second marriage, relocation to a different state, or a shift in financial status). For some clients, it may be important to include legal affairs and estate planning issues in the retirement planning group work. This depends on the individual's financial status, prior planning, personal priorities, and other special circumstances. Fullner (1996) advocated inviting financial planning specialists to attend one group session to provide relevant information (e.g., the tax implications of alternative income sources and procedures for obtaining all their Social Security and other pension benefits). An alternative is to invite a company representative to inform prospective retirees about the retirement benefits available through the organization. Counselors can provide referrals to specialized professionals (e.g., estate planning issues) to help individuals decide issues after the psychological aspects of financial and legal planning are resolved and basic information has been made available in the developmental intervention.

Physical and Spiritual Well-Being

Individuals search for meaning in their lives through their physical activities, relations with others, and their personal views regarding a higher spiritual purpose. By one estimate, two thirds of our physical ailments and premature deaths are caused by our lifestyle choices (Carter, 1998). Health problems can be delayed or prevented by eliminating harmful practices (e.g., smoking, drinking alcohol excessively, and driving after drinking alcohol) and by increasing health-promoting behaviors (e.g., improving strength, endurance, flexibility, and balance; maintaining recommended body weight; exercising regularly; and having regular medical checkups). Thus, one group objective may be to help clients develop health-enhancing lifestyles (Doress & Siegal, 1987). Counselors can include psychoeducational interventions in the structured group that help clients increase their understanding of the health risk behaviors and factors that are likely to affect their long-term health.

The challenges of the retirement transition and the aging process can have a considerable influence on a person's religious faith (Worthington, 1989). Many individuals value personal spirituality but do not necessarily take part in traditional communities of faith (Roof, 1999), but their reactions to the myriad changes occurring in the retirement transition may stimulate them to explore and reorganize their spiritual lives. The striving of many older Americans for personal development and meaning transcends their physical and psychological well-being and includes an increased or renewed concern with religion and spirituality (Fiske & Chiriboga, 1990). Spirituality beliefs may provide comfort, emotional support, and a sense of connection with others. The belief that they are connected with a greater goodness and part of something larger than their own lives provides a sense of meaning and stability to many clients grappling with issues of continuity and change. Whether these issues are best addressed through quiet, individual reflection (Larrivee, 1996) or become an important group focus depends on the goals of the group members and the comfort and skill of the counselor in working with individuals who are experiencing a deepening awareness of their spiritual beliefs. Eanes (1997), Fowler (1984), and Stoltz-Loike (1997) have described models to help individuals create personal and spiritual balance across their multiple life roles that build on Super's (1994) career development stages and Erikson's (1963) life cycle stages.

Planning and Providing a Retirement Transitions Group

At the end of the chapter, we provide three vignettes that you can use to practice the application of the basic principles underlying retirement transitions counseling. Table 19.1 lists more specific objectives for a 12-session intervention that can be used with a relatively homogeneous group of 8 to 12 clients, and Table 19.2 provides the Basic Data Form (D. J. Tinsley & M. Bigler, personal communication, 1999) that can be used in screening individuals for inclusion in the group. Following are some guidelines for counselors to consider when planning a retirement transitions group.

First, it is important to recognize that effective groups are the outcome of the skillful blending of planning, sensitivity, flexibility, and skill. The planning comes first; skillful counselors should carefully plan the group intervention in detail with their particular clientele in mind before the first session. Begin by reviewing the information obtained from evaluations of previous structured group interventions. Think about what worked, what did not seem to be as effective, and why. Review your expectations for the structured group and think carefully about how it differs from group therapy (which you may also practice). Carefully plan the structure for the group sessions, and once the group begins, communicate that by providing an overview of each session at its beginning.

Some counselors have argued against planning too much, protesting that they want to retain the flexibility to respond to their clients' needs. That is quite important, of course, and counselors must take care to remain sensitive to their clients' needs and be flexible about following the planned schedule of group topics and experiential activities. It is important to monitor the group and individual progress throughout the sessions and to be willing to modify the focus and timing of interventions to better accomplish unmet goals. Also consider the possibility that topics covered in earlier sessions may require further group attention as a result of outside activities or unmet goals.

Two critical functions of developmental group interventions are to provide support and encourage self-exploration. Incorporate specific activities into the group sessions to promote and maintain a supportive group environment. Also take care to include activities that will help participants become aware of any apprehensions or perceptual blocks that may prevent them from engaging in effective problem solving about the retirement transition. Emotional blocks can occur as a result of fear of taking risks or fear of being wrong, impulsivity, and lack of perseverance. Blocks to effective planning can take the form of internal stressors and mental pressures that clients place on themselves and external pressures in the form of major life changes and the expectations of others.

A variety of techniques can be helpful in retirement transition counseling groups. The use of specific techniques will depend, of course, on the counselors' theoretical views, the clients' needs, and the setting in which the group occurs (e.g., employer-sponsored program, community college or other academic setting, regional-sponsored Professional Business Women's conference, private practice, or church/synagogue-sponsored program). Nevertheless, we advocate an eclectic approach. Behavioral techniques such as modeling, systematic desensitization, assertiveness training, and self-management strategies are useful in helping clients make changes in their behavior. Modeling effective coping strategies and encouraging mutual support within the limits of a structured group intervention are effective in creating a facilitative environment and enabling behavioral change. Use of values clarification, guided fantasy, and journal writing enable individuals to explore deeply personal issues while retaining control over what they choose to share verbally in the group. Assign homework to encourage active participation in planning and to maximize the outcomes that can be accomplished during the 12 sessions. Be sure to discuss completed homework and help participants use the results to monitor their progress.

Once the group sessions begin, use the first three sessions to introduce the topic of transitions, preview topics and group expectations, establish group cohesion, and initiate self-exploration activities. Building trust and mutual understanding in order to safely explore new facets of the self is an important aspect of the helping relationship. Help clients adopt a problem-solving approach to retirement planning and identify the types of activities and resources they can use during the group intervention. Lead clients through an exploration of their interests, values, expectations, and cognitive styles and engage them in a consideration of how they can use their abilities and prior experiences in new or modified life roles. During the early sessions, you may decide to use standardized assessment instruments to aid your clients in self-exploration and in understanding that they can create alternatives for retirement. The use of informal assessment activities should be an ongoing process throughout the group sessions. By the end of the third session, you should be in a position to prioritize the group's needs using the information obtained from the Basic Data Form, the individual interviews, and the initial sessions.

During the fourth session, have clients contract for individual goals that match the major issues you plan to cover over the next four to six sessions (e.g., life roles, financial and legal concerns, and support networks). Help clients develop plans for implementing their contracts and begin to consider one of the major issues more in depth. Devote parts of three to five sessions to each of the issues. Clients need the time between sessions to come to an understanding of the issues, acquire information, explore their attitudes, determine their strengths, problem-solve, practice skill building, and complete the tasks that are necessary to reach their goals. Also provide opportunities to help clients recognize and grieve their losses (e.g., declining physical health, changing financial resources, and changes in social networks) and develop plans for enriching their lives. Some clients may need to examine their stereotypic beliefs (e.g., uncritical acceptance of ideas about ageism) and learn to replace their negative thoughts with a more positive outlook. An important key to helping clients accommodate is to help them recognize that some events associated with the retirement transition may be outside their control, but their reactions to those events are within their personal control. In this regard, distinguishing between primary control (i.e., behaviors individuals use to engage the external world) and secondary control (i.e., cognitive processes localized within the individual) may be efficacious.

Use the final three sessions to review accomplishments, consolidate clients' gains, strategize ways each person can continue independent action after the group ends, and express appreciation for the contributions all group members have made to each person's development. Discuss with participants the desirability of having a single booster session in the future (e.g., 1 to 3 months) during which individuals can report on progress and strategize future plans. Be sure to obtain written feedback from clients about their reactions to the group process and the content of the activities. This will be invaluable in continuing your own development as a counselor and in planning future retirement transition groups.

Source of Referral

Counselors can recruit clients for retirement transition groups from an already established clientele base, from a specific community, or from organizations that desire designated services for their employees. Although counselors working with a familiar clientele already have essential knowledge about the potential clients' background, special needs, and relevant risks, it is still essential to screen individuals prior to accepting them into a retirement transition group. Regardless of the source of clients, group cohesion and the openness of the participants to one another are essential to achieve the level of self-disclosure that is a prerequisite to personal development (Sue & Sue, 1999). We stipulated a limitation on group size of 8 to 14 clients to allow time for the meaningful exploration of sensitive issues by each client within a 12-week period.

Alternatively, counselors may want to provide retirement transition services to a specific target population. Clients such as these may be associated with a specific environment (e.g., a housing complex, country club, or religious institution) or clients having certain characteristics in common (e.g., couples, family members, gay/lesbian or bisexual individuals, or persons of a common ethnic heritage). Individuals who are of the same gender, socioeconomic status (Brown, Fukunaga, Umemoto, & Wicker, 1996), religion, racial background, culture, and occupation can be expected to have more in common. Nevertheless, counselors need to focus their intervention strategies to deal with the unique situation of the participants. For example, Riddick and Stewart (1994) found that the life satisfaction and active participation in leisure activities of older Black and White female retirees were influenced by their perceived health, leisure repertoire planning, and income.

When counselors work with a target population that is different from their typical clientele, the initial screening interviews are of greater importance. Furthermore, counselors must follow these with a more detailed needs assessment during the first three group sessions to better tailor their intervention to meet the unique needs of these clients. For example, counselors may find that attachment and separation issues require greater attention when working with couples or extended families than when working with individuals. Issues of control, autonomy, and interdependency also will be more salient when working with couples and families, and these issues could interfere with progress in developmental groups. Counselors may find it necessary to refer such parties to private therapy sessions so that their individual needs can be met without disrupting the group process.

Sensitivity to individual differences in personality and life experiences is essential in designing effective retirement transition interventions. For example, women who have been very social throughout their lives might welcome the additional time that retirement brings because it allows them to spend more time with friends and relatives. Alternatively, those who have been strongly task oriented may feel a sense of void and disengagement. The retirement transition, with its inherent readjustments in social support networks, will be more stressful for the second type of person. Clients who take on increased caregiving responsibilities during retirement could find themselves working overtime to provide care to grandchildren and those in their own and their parents' generations.

When counselors are asked to provide assistance to a special group, it is important to assess the needs, expectations, and goals of the contact person making the request. For example, employers may have complex reasons for requesting that the counselor provide a retirement planning program (e.g., encouraging deadwood to consider leaving their employment or encouraging early retirement to prepare for company downsizing). Employers also may want to limit the focus of the retirement planning sessions (e.g., to providing information about employee benefits). Confidentiality issues also may be of concern. Counselors need to establish their obligation to report sensitive information to the employer and to limit client self-disclosure unless confidentiality can be assured. It is critical that these issues be resolved before the screening of potential group members begins.

In these or other instances, counselors may focus on a limited range of retirement planning issues (e.g., leisure counseling, relocation workshops, and coping with the stresses of retirement planning). Whenever this occurs, counselors must be clear that the goals of the intervention are psychological development and that the interpersonal focus that is the essence of counseling is maintained (Tinsley & Tinsley, 1982).

SUMMARY

Before counselors can provide effective retirement transition counseling, they need to become aware of their own stereotypes and prejudices toward aging and retirement and their own work-related values. It is essential for the counselor to understand the client's worldview and cultural values and avoid imposing their own personal view of a desirable outcome on the client. Clients differ greatly in the values they place on factors such as family, friendships, and attitudes toward volunteering, full- or part-time work, and leisure. Counselors can help clients reevaluate and work through the consequences of earlier events and remain sensitive to the individual's willingness and ability to change. For example, it may be critical for the counselor to address with clients whether they retired voluntarily or were forced into retirement. The literature shows that individuals who choose to retire are more ready to explore alternative roles than persons who are forced to retire.

Retirement planning is a complex, multitask process that involves client self-reflection, reevaluation, and decision making. The changes and new possibilities that are associated with the retirement transition can be both exciting and anxiety provoking. Retirement transition clients are faced with the challenge of negotiating the meaning of retirement in their own lives in the face of social inequities (e.g., ageism, sexism, racism, and other discrimination) and negative stereotypes about aging and older citizens. Clients need the opportunity to acknowledge, understand, and accept the complex emotional reactions they are experiencing and to engage in meaningful planning for their future.

VIGNETTES

To complete these three exercises, imagine that you are an experienced counselor beginning a new position in which a part of your responsibilities will be to co-lead developmentally oriented structured groups to facilitate the retirement transition. A notice has been printed in the local community newspaper advertising a series of structured groups for participants who anticipate a retirement transition with the next 2 years. Each group will consist of 8 to 15 individuals who have been evaluated by an intake counselor as being ready to benefit from the structured group intervention. Inclusion in this first set of groups will be limited to participants who are interested in learning more about themselves and the implications of their values and skills for the upcoming transition. Specific issues you will address are improving physical and mental health, leisure planning, and thinking through the possible ramifications of a pending geographical relocation.

Vignette 1

Study the Basic Data Form in Table 19.2 and determine what other information you would want to obtain about potential participants prior to the individual interview to assess the individual's appropriate placement. Then use the results of several imagined sample forms to help you determine what specific information you want to obtain from the potential client in the individual interview. Finally, what are your primary goals for giving and receiving information in that individual assessment interview?

Vignette 2

Outline a structured group intervention of approximately 8 to 10 sessions to address the needs of these participants. What factors would you consider in determining the number of groups to offer, the size of each group, the number and length of the sessions provided, and the spacing of the sessions across the coming weeks or months? In doing this, consider each of the objectives in Table 19.1 and decide whether and how you and your co-leader would address each in the structured group.

Vignette 3

Suppose that the potential participants first learned through a newsletter about the availability of the retirement counseling services you are offering.

How would you and your co-leader individualize the group interventions to better meet the anticipated needs of participants if the newsletters were published by the following organizations?

———————

1. A large financial institution

2. A religious organization

3. A community organization such as the YMCA, a fitness center, or a golf and country club

4. The volunteer workers organization in a medical facility

5. The continuing educational division of a community college

ADDITIONAL RESOURCES

Print Resources

Birnbach, L. (1997). *1003 great things about getting older.* Kansas City, MO: Andres McMeel.

Hodgson, H. (1999). *Smart aging: Taking charge of your physical and emotional health.* New York: John Wiley.

Howells, J. (1998). *Where to retire: America's best and most affordable places* (3rd ed.). Old Saybrook, CT: Globe Pequot.

Morris, K., Siegel, A. M., & Morris, V. B. (1998). *The* Wall Street Journal *guide to planning your financial future.* New York: Simon & Schuster.

Orman, S. (1997). *The 9 steps to financial freedom: Practical and spiritual steps so you can stop worrying.* New York: Crown.

Sheard, R. (2000). *Money for life: The 20 factor plan for accumulating wealth while you are young.* New York: Harper Business.

Wasik, J. F. (2000). *Retire early—and live the life you want now.* New York: Henry Holt.

Internet Resources

American Association for Retired Persons: http://www.aarp.org
Medicare and Medicaid information: http://www.hcfa.gov
National Wellness Institute: http://www.nationalwellness.org
Social Security information: http://www.ssa.gov

CHAPTER 20

Life Review and the Self-Confrontation Method With Older Adults

William J. Lyddon
Darlys J. Alford

If you want to know me, then you must know my story, for my story defines who I am. And if I want to know myself to gain insight into the meaning of my own life, then I, too, must come to know my own story. I must come to see in all its particulars the narrative of the self—the personal myth—that I have tacitly, even unconsciously, composed over the course of my years. It is a story I continue to revise, and tell to myself (and sometimes to others) as I go on living.

—McAdams (1993, p. 11)

One of the most fundamental constructs in psychology is the concept of the self. In personality and counseling theory, for example, the self is often the centerpiece of the theory—a central focus of assessment and change. Traditionally, however, the self has often been described in terms of a substance or thing—a kind of container of traits, motives, or properties, or all three (Cox & Lyddon, 1997; Polkinghorne, 1991). Within this view, knowing and understanding the self involves measuring, describing, or mapping out the component properties "contained" in the self.

In recent years, the emergence of the narrative perspective in psychology and counseling offers an alternative way to conceptualize the self and its development (Gonclaves, 1995; Howard, 1991; McAdams, 1985; Polkinghorne, 1988; Sarbin, 1986; White & Epston, 1990). Viewing the self as a narrative, or continuously unfolding story, refashions the construct of self from a traditional focus on properties and structure to that of process. Narratives and stories highlight the temporal and developmental dimensions of human existence and provide a framework for organizing the self and one's life into a meaningful and coherent whole (Polkinghorne, 1991). Just as a written story possesses a beginning, a middle, and an end, so too do persons organize their lives temporally, in sequential and meaningful storied patterns or plots. As Polkinghorne (1991) notes, these stories "are stories about the self. They are the basis of personal identity and self-understanding and they provide answers to the question 'Who am I?'" (p. 136).

It is important to note that achieving narrative coherence in one's life story is never a once-and-for-all accomplishment. Human identities are not static, but they continually evolve and are influenced by the events and social interactions throughout one's life history. It is also important to note that developing stories of self-identity are embedded in and constructed out of a person's particular cultural environment and language forms (Scheibe, 1986), and thus every individual's personal story is constructed out of the fabric of the larger, overarching "cultural tale" of his or her place and time (Howard, 1991). As Mair (1988) points out,

> Stories are habitations. We live in and through stories. They conjure worlds. We do not know the world other than as story world. Stories inform life. They hold us together and keep us apart. We inhabit the great stories of our culture. We live through stories. We are *lived* by the stories of our race and place. (p. 127)

Although it is widely held that individuals begin to construct storied identities in late adolescence (McAdams, 1993), a particularly salient developmental task beginning in midlife and extending into late life involves a review and evaluation of one's life. In other words, during adolescence and young adulthood, the personal narrative helps define an emerging sense of self and address the question "Who am I?" By way of contrast, in midlife and late life, an important function of the personal narrative is to effectively integrate the temporal dimensions of past, present, and future. At this juncture, the narrative is decidedly more evaluative in tone and seeks to answer the questions "What kind of person have I been, am I now, and can I still become?" In developmental terms, the person in later life has begun the process of *life review* (Butler, 1963).

In his seminal work, the distinguished geriatrician Robert Butler (1963) argued that—rather than being a symptom of degeneration—life review among the elderly is a "naturally occurring, universal mental process characterized by the progressive return to consciousness of past experiences, and particularly, the resurgence of unresolved conflicts" (p. 66). The function of the life review is to aid in the assessment of one's life as a whole and contribute to the process of psychological integration. Thus, life review is a normative developmental process, catalyzed by the pressure of the eventual ending of life, in which individuals strive to view and evaluate their whole life as if it were a coherent narrative. It is important to note that because life review may likely involve the resurgence of unresolved conflicts, it also holds the potential for significant personal change, and even reconciliation.

The purpose of this chapter is to highlight a narrative approach to life review. In particular, we want to introduce counselors to a narrative-based life assessment strategy known as the Self-Confrontation Method (Hermans & Hermans-Jansen, 1995) and suggest its utility for working with older clients in the process of life review. Toward this end, we first provide a brief overview of Valuation Theory—the conceptual basis of the Self-Confrontation Method. A description of the method and guidelines for its use with clients is then presented. Finally, a case example is offered to illustrate the use of the Self-Confrontation Method as a vehicle for life review.

VALUATION THEORY

Inspired by the philosophical thinking of James (1890) and Merleau-Ponty (1945/1962) as well as the contemporary narrative psychology perspectives of Bruner (1986) and Sarbin (1986), Hermans developed Valuation Theory as a framework for the study of personal experience, its ordering into a narrative structure, and its development over time (Hermans, 1987, 1988, 1989). Within Valuation Theory, the self is conceptualized as "an organized process of valuation" (Hermans & Hermans-Jansen, 1995, p. 14). The *process* feature of his view of self emphasizes the historical and temporal nature of personal experience—that is, people live in the present but at the same time may orient toward the past and the future from the unique position they occupy in the present (which, of course, is always changing). The *organizational* feature draws attention to the unique way each person, through self-reflection, orders life experiences into a coherent and meaningful whole, or self-narrative.

Valuation is the theory's central concept and refers to anything that people find significant when telling their life story. As Hermans (1995) notes, a valuation is "any unit of meaning that has a positive (pleasant), negative (unpleasant), or ambivalent (both pleasant and unpleasant) value in the eyes of the individual" (p. 248). Thus, a valuation may include a broad array of experiences— an early grade-school memory, an unanticipated loss, a future goal, a proud accomplishment, a beloved person, and so forth. According to Hermans, through the process of self-reflection, either in dialogue with oneself or with another person, valuations become organized into a narratively structured system. As new valuations become significant, old ones may be deleted or reworked. Thus, the self may be viewed as a dynamically maintained narrative system of valuations that is always subject to potential reorganization and change.

It is also important to point out that, according to Valuation Theory, the construction of a valuation is both a cognitive and an emotional process. In fact, Hermans (1995) emphasizes that each valuation implies a specific pattern of affect. In short, when people value something, they always *feel* something about it. The emphasis on the affective quality of a valuation as a unit of meaning is consistent with the general notion that affect plays an integral role in the organization and meaning of one's self-narrative (Bamberg, 1991; McAdams, 1985).

In sum, Valuation Theory and its model of self serve as a conceptual base for the study of personal meaning. As a result, Valuation Theory has become an important perspective for exploring the personal meanings associated with the difficulties and concerns that clients present in counseling. A particularly significant application of Valuation Theory has been the development and use of the Self-Confrontation Method (Hermans & Hermans-Jansen, 1995). Consistent with the growing body of literature on constructivist assessment in counseling (Neimeyer, 1993; Sexton & Griffin, 1997), the Self-Confrontation Method is an idiographic (rather than standardized or normative) approach to assessment and self-exploration that focuses on how clients uniquely organize their sense of self and world. The method is conducted in three phases that are next explained in order: (1) formulation of valuations, (2) affective exploration, and (3) evaluation and integration.

Formulation of Valuations

The first step in the Self-Confrontation Method involves the client generation of salient past, present, and future valuations. Valuations have personal meaning and "can be seen as part of an interpreting self that is extended to the event in question. . . . It is the workings of the interpreting self that make a given event highly significant for one person but meaningless to another" (Hermans & Hermans-Jansen, 1995, p. 18). Three sets of valuations are created to begin the procedure. Hermans and Hermans-Jansen (1995) suggest posing open-ended questions about the past, present, and future as shown in Table 20.1.

TABLE 20.1   Stimulus Questions for Writing Valuation Statements

Past These questions are intended to guide you in reviewing one or more aspects of your past life that may have been of great importance to you.	1. Has there been anything of major significance in your past life that still continues to exert a strong influence on you? 2. Was there in the past any person, experience, or circumstance that greatly influenced your life and that appreciably affects your present existence?
Present This set consists of two questions referring to your present life that will lead you, after a certain amount of reflection, to formulate a response.	1. Is there anything in your present existence that is of major importance to you or exerts a significant influence on you? 2. Is there in your present existence any person or circumstance that exerts a significant influence on you?
Future The following questions referring to your future should again guide you to a response. You are free to look as far ahead as you wish.	1. Do you foresee anything that will be of great importance for or exert an major influence on your future life? 2. Do you feel that a certain person or circumstance will exert a significant influence on your future life? 3. Is there any future goal or object that you expect will play an important role in your life?

After the participant in the method has seen or heard the questions, it is helpful to provide a few suggestions for creating valuation statements. It is important to emphasize that valuations should overtly concern the *self*. Group leaders or therapists who are assisting persons in constructing valuations may need to paraphrase, reflect, and clarify initial attempts that respondents offer in order to reach the goal of generating a sentence or two that contain a single unit of meaning for each of the valuations. It is essential to compose a minimum of five valuations for each of the time orientations so that recurrent themes and dominant affective experiences can be identified. Some samples of valuations that might be created by persons in later adulthood are as follow:

Past

▶ My mother died when I was 12, and I raised my little brother, who continues to seek out my advice on decisions and problems.

▶ My job as a university staff supervisor helped me discover how competent I could be in difficult and demanding situations.

▶ My sister's death served as a wake-up call to live my life fully each day.

Present

▶ My father is in the hospital again (heart disease), and I feel I should drop everything and fly across country, even though I was there just 2 months ago.

▶ I'm embarrassed that my adult son cannot manage his money well or pay his bills on time.

▶ The demands of keeping up a yard and big house overwhelm me right now.

Future

▶ Traveling in Europe has been my dream since I was a young girl, and I now have the time and money to actually start making plans to go.

▶ I don't want to spend the rest of my life obsessing about my health and not taking any risks to avoid accidents.

▶ I want to write a novel.

Affective Exploration

The second phase of the Self-Confrontation Method involves rating each of the valuations on four affective dimensions: (1) self-enhancement—self *(S)*, (2) social connectedness—other *(O)*, (3) positive affect—positive *(P)*, and (4) negative affect—negative *(N)*. The self-enhancement *(S)* dimension indicates the extent to which individuals see themselves as autonomous, competent, and strong enough to cope with a given situation. The other *(O)* dimension refers to the "experience of participating with someone or feeling close to someone or something (e.g., a group of people, a particular place, an animal, a gift that functions as a symbol)" (Hermans & Hermans-Jansen, 1995, p. 39). The positive *(P)* and negative *(N)* dimensions provide an overall measure of affective pleasure, ambivalence, or discomfort for the valuations. Having both positive

TABLE 20.2   Affective Terms Used in the Self-Confrontation Method

1. Joy (P)	9. Unhappiness (N)
2. Self-esteem (S)	10. Tenderness (O)
3. Happiness (P)	11. Self-confidence (S)
4. Worry (N)	12. Intimacy (O)
5. Strength (S)	13. Despondency (N)
6. Enjoyment (P)	14. Pride (S)
7. Caring (O)	15. Disappointment (N)
8. Love (O)	16. Inner calm (P)

NOTE: S affect, self-enhancement; O affect, desire for contact with others; P affect, positive affect, and N affect, negative affect.

and negative affect dimensions makes it possible for clients to acknowledge that they have both positive and negative feelings about a particular person or event at one time. Understanding the human capacity for such ambivalence can be crucial in helping people move beyond confusion and contradictions that can sometimes paralyze decision-making processes.

All four affective dimensions are derived by having clients rate 16 affective terms (4 for each dimension) on a scale of 0 = *Not at all* to 5 = *Very much*. The terms are listed in Table 20.2 with the associated dimension identified.

Evaluation and Integration

Hermans and Hermans-Jansen (1995) provide instructions for generating a variety of matrices and indices as part of the evaluation process. The most basic matrix involves listing each valuation with corresponding numerical totals for S (sum of ratings for self-esteem, strength, self-confidence, and pride), O (sum of ratings on caring, love, tenderness, intimacy), P (sum of ratings for joy, happiness, enjoyment, inner calm), and N (sum of ratings for worry, unhappiness, despondency, disappointment).

A number of comparisons between S, O, P, and N totals may also be made. For example, differences between S and O can be calculated to determine the balance of self and other focus in the past, present, and future. Comparisons between P and N show the general well-being reflected by the valuations in the three time orientations. More advanced analyses can be conducted on the raw score ratings by correlating valuations. When affective patterns are similar or dissimilar for two valuations, emotional themes can be identified within a particular time frame or between past, present, and future. Additional ratings can be obtained by asking respondents to rate each valuation a second time according to how they would ideally like to feel in the past, present, or future. This information can then be analyzed to guide counseling goals or to determine new directions for future growth and exploration.

Hermans and Hermans-Jansen (1995) propose that assessment take place at least twice in the course of counseling to evaluate progress in reframing self-information about the past, present, and future in a way that promotes acceptance of the self and enhances a feeling of well-being. For example, as (a) self-narratives about the past change from "I regret . . ." to "I understand why I . . . ," (b) sentences describing the present change from "I worry about . . ." to "I've decided to . . . ," and (c) descriptions of the future change from "I'm afraid that . . ." to "I intend to . . . ," these become indications that personal narratives are changing in the direction of greater self-understanding, autonomy, and integration.

For adults in later life, narratives about the past can seem to be cast in stone. Carrying heavy emotional baggage that is laden with negative emotional experiences can taint thinking about the present and future. By confronting the past through the Self-Confrontation Method, clients can become more creative and active rather than trapped by their repeated recitations about what has happened in the past. This narrative creativity can then be extended into the present and future with potentially powerful results.

The Self-Confrontation Method provides counselors and clients with a useful framework for identifying important client issues and life themes about self and relationships. Because the method provides persons with the opportunity to highlight both positive and negative life experiences, emotional reactions, and prospects for the future, the method often provides more of a balanced life narrative picture in contrast to many assessment approaches that place a nearly exclusive focus on client deficits and so-called psychopathology. A second important advantage of the Self-Confrontation Method is that it is relatively culture neutral. The need for adapting counseling services to accommodate ethnic minority clients has been well documented (Atkinson, Morten, & Sue, 1993). Because of the constructivist foundation of the Self-Confrontation Method, clients write valuations *in their own words* and select the valuations that are most important to them. This leaves each client free to select the extent to which one's own valuations contain ethnic content, collectivistic or individualistic values, and personal problems. The cross-cultural counseling literature also suggests that comfort with affect differs for American ethnic minorities. As a result, it would be expected that older members of minority groups who value stoic suppression of personal emotions might have more difficulty using the affective terms to rate their valuations. However, a recent study conducted by Atkinson, Kim, Ruelas, and Lin (1999) comparing the attitudes of elderly

Chinese Americans, Mexican Americans, and European Americans toward "facilitated reminiscence" suggests that these groups may actually differ very little in the reasons they give for engaging in reminiscence. For example, in their study, all groups rated "share past experiences," "enhance self-understanding," "elevate mood," and "resolve problems" as legitimate reasons to engage in reminiscence. Atkinson et al. (1999) state that "elders from all three ethnic groups in the current study gave their lowest mean scores to sharing past experiences and their highest mean ratings to enhancing self-understanding as reasons for reminiscing with a facilitator" (p. 78). According to these data, the Self-Confrontation Method is likely to lead to satisfying outcomes for ethnic minority elderly persons because of its emphasis on facilitating self-understanding of the past, *present*, and *future*.

THE SELF-CONFRONTATION METHOD AS A RESEARCH TOOL

In recent years, researchers have begun to employ the Self-Confrontation Method as a research strategy for the study of a range of topics and issues, including research on counseling process (Hermans, Fiddelaes, de Groot, & Nanta, 1990), attachment style and working models of emotion (Lyddon, Schreiber, & Alford, 2000), affective organization of self in value crisis (Hermans & Oles, 1996), the relationship between self-esteem and psychological well-being (Hermans, 1992), valuations and coping styles (Rim, 1989), and *fugit amour* (the loving orientation to another unreachable person) (Hermans, Hermans-Jansen, & Van Gilst, 1987).

Because of its focus on the affective features of personal meanings, the Self-Confrontation Method has shown particular promise as a research strategy for understanding emotional patterns and themes associated with human change and adaptation. For example, Hermans and Oles (1999) investigated valuation differences among men with high, medium, and low scores on the Midlife-Crisis Scale (Oles, 1994, 1995). In their study, midlife crisis was defined as a process of intensive self-transition characterized by (a) the replacement of a "time since birth" perspective with a "time left to live" orientation, (b) a reevaluation of life values and goals, (c) a focus on one's mortality, and (d) the development of a plan for the second half of life (Hermans & Oles, 1999). Using the Self-Confrontation Method, Hermans and Oles found affective differences among low, medium, and high midlife crisis groups. As expected, when compared to low and medium midlife crisis groups, the high crisis group reported significantly lower P, lower S, and higher N indices. Contrary to the researchers' expectations, the high midlife crisis group was not different from the other groups on the O index. In addition, when past, present, and future valuations were compared, Hermans and Oles found that high midlife crisis men had a more negative emotional orientation to the future than they did to their past and present, whereas low and medium crisis groups were consistently positive on all three time orientations. The authors concluded that these data suggest that men experiencing a midlife crisis may not be able to envision the potential for positive gain that can come from personal transformation. Assessment that includes a temporal component is particularly relevant with individuals who are in the later part of life. In fact, it may be the degree of positive and negative affect associated with the future self and social connections that might best predict the mental health and adjustment of older individuals. Hermans and Oles's (1999) study of men in midlife crisis suggests that the Self-Confrontation Method can be a viable research tool for investigating the cognition and affect associated with the developmental transitions of older adults.

The idiographic focus of the Self-Confrontation Method has also been shown to be particularly well suited to case study research (Hermans, 1987, 1996, 1997; Hermans & Oles, 1996). To illustrate the self-confrontation process and how it can be used with a person in later life, we now turn to the composite case example of "Daniel," who is (a) evaluating past experience and pondering the meaning of career changes precipitated by dissatisfaction and (b) yearning for new challenge in his life.

THE SELF-CONFRONTATION PROCESS OF DANIEL

Daniel earned an advanced degree in divinity during his 30s. Most of his 40s he spent leading a church that served a university population. He married while completing his studies and became a parent of two sons. In his middle 40s, he divorced, left the ministry, remarried, and began teaching high school English. Now in his late 50s, Daniel is contemplating another career change in which he plans to venture into retail sales as a co-owner of a specialty garden shop. Daniel has sought the assistance of a counselor to help him understand the confusion he is experiencing about his current change of direction and especially to reconcile his apparent progression from a life guided by deep devotion to altruistic social activities to what appears to be a "capitalistic vocation" based on "mere product exchange."

As previously noted, the first step in the Self-Confrontation Method involved the client's generation of salient past, present, and future valuations. Daniel's valuations were as follows:

Past Valuations

1. "I was forced out of the ministry because of my divorce and the general suspicion people in the church had about my relationships with women."
2. "Going through the divorce was one of the most painful experiences I have had to endure; visitation with my boys was not at all what my idea of parenting should be."
3. "The time I had spent preparing for and serving as a pastor felt like the right thing for me intellectually and socially. I felt so useful and good."
4. "When I started teaching, it was humiliating to work for administrators who were less educated than I, and depressing being so limited by the structure of the school schedule, when I had been able to plan my schedule with great flexibility before."
5. "Marrying Jean and having her become a parent to my boys was the delight of my life, although the adjustment period was challenging."

Present Valuations

1. "Teaching allows me to express myself in creative ways and challenges me to 'entice' young people to learn."
2. "After a week of teaching, I feel depleted and used up, because my efforts are not often recognized or appreciated. I'm tired of hearing other people's problems, and at the same time I feel guilty when I admit it."
3. "When a woman friend at work misinterpreted my interest in her as a sexual advance, I felt sad and experienced that same old feeling of being morally inadequate, like when I was forced out of the church."
4. "I've decided to leave teaching to own and operate a plant shop with specialty items for the garden like statues and fountains."
5. "I wish my wife were more sexual, though in every other way our marriage is wonderful and reassures me of my worth."

Future Valuations

1. "It really excites me to imagine days filled with plant care and educating customers about how to create gardens like mine at home—the most beautiful, comforting, renewing place I know."
2. "I want to help others, although I'm not sure how I can do that in a retail business in the same way as I have in the ministry or through teaching."

3. "The future seems so free of public scrutiny. The fact that I will have my own shop means that I don't have to meet school administrators' expectations or be examined through someone else's moral code anymore."

4. "Gaining a sense of spiritual peace and continuing to learn and grow are important goals in my life. Education has always played a central role in my life: student, pastor, teacher."

5. "The fact that Jean and I will be in business together opens the possibility for us to grow even closer in our marriage and make decisions as a team."

After clarifying and writing out the 15 valuations, Daniel then rated each valuation using the 16 affective words, each anchored on a scale from 0 = *Not at all* to 5 = *Very much* (see Table 20.3, a blank Affective Rating Sheet).

Once the ratings were completed, the counselor was able to determine the S, O, P, and N numerical totals for each valuation. Each valuation was then inspected in terms of its affective dimensions. This detailed review provided Daniel with a more complex understanding of the emotional content of important aspects of his life. In addition, by totaling all the scores for each affective dimension for the past, present, and future, a more global picture of the emotional themes associated with these different periods of his life was achieved. These valuation scores and grand totals are summarized in Table 20.4 for the past, present, and future.

The impact of the Self-Confrontation Method as a life review strategy was quite productive for Daniel. In responding to the visual impact of the summation of his valuations and emotional themes associated with the past, present, and future, Daniel gained many valuable insights. In particular, he began to organize the changes he was experiencing at this point in his life in a manageable and meaningful way. Some of the significant themes that emerged from his self-confrontation life review process are summarized below.

Affect Directed Toward Self

As can be seen from Table 20.4, total scores for the S dimension suggest improvement in Daniel's self-enhancement (past = 44, present = 65, future = 78) and also reveal an increase in positive affect (past = 39, present = 48, and future = 78). This feedback was very reassuring for Daniel. One of the most critical values conflicts for Daniel had to do with the meaning of his basic commitment to serve others. In the past, he felt "called" to the ministry by God and spent every working day serving the members of his congregation. His "flock" sought out his expertise and reassurance on life-and-death matters that involved significant conflicts and decisions in their lives. On the other hand, when he was a teacher, students reluctantly read the English assignments he required of them and complained regularly about the irrelevance of the material. As Daniel approached the future in retail sales, he felt embarrassed

TABLE 20.3   Affective Rating Sheet

Valuation:_____

_____

_____

To what extent do you experience each of the following feelings in relation to this valuation?

	Not at all	A little bit	To some extent	Rather much	Much	Very much
Joy	0	1	2	3	4	5
Self-esteem	0	1	2	3	4	5
Happiness	0	1	2	3	4	5
Worry	0	1	2	3	4	5
Strength	0	1	2	3	4	5
Enjoyment	0	1	2	3	4	5
Caring	0	1	2	3	4	5
Love	0	1	2	3	4	5
Unhappiness	0	1	2	3	4	5
Tenderness	0	1	2	3	4	5
Self-confidence	0	1	2	3	4	5
Intimacy	0	1	2	3	4	5
Despondency	0	1	2	3	4	5
Pride	0	1	2	3	4	5
Disappointment	0	1	2	3	4	5
Inner calm	0	1	2	3	4	5

about how difficult it was to integrate the early self-confidence he had about his calling with the risky competition of an untried business venture. His search for self-value and the importance of his day-to-day social contributions were difficult to reconcile, yet his self-esteem appeared to be improving. The questions he was having difficulty answering began to formulate much more clearly now: "What can I contribute to others through this business?" "How important is service to others to my self-identity?" "How is it that I am feeling better about myself when I am moving further away from a social service career?" As he turned his attention to the O dimension of his self-confrontation, some potential answers to these questions began to emerge.

TABLE 20.4   Daniel's Valuation Scores

	PAST			
	Self (S)	Other (O)	Positive (P)	Negative (N)
1. Forced out of ministry	2	3	2	20
2. Divorce	5	9	6	11
3. Being a pastor	19	17	15	3
4. Becoming a teacher	7	8	2	14
5. Remarriage	11	19	14	5
Grand totals	44	56	39	53

	PRESENT			
	Self (S)	Other (O)	Positive (P)	Negative (N)
1. Creativity of teaching	18	11	11	6
2. Depleted by others	13	4	3	18
3. Rejection by friend	8	0	1	16
4. Quit teaching	9	12	16	5
5. Marriage	17	17	17	6
Grand totals	65	44	48	51

	FUTURE			
	Self (S)	Other (O)	Positive (P)	Negative (N)
1. Gardening environment	16	11	13	3
2. Helping others	13	8	10	1
3. Freedom from scrutiny	15	6	20	1
4. Seek peace and growth	18	12	18	5
5. Wife/business partner	16	19	17	6
Grand totals	78	56	78	16

Contact and Union With Others

The totals for Daniel's O ratings showed a surprising pattern. The totals for the past, present, and future were 56, 44, and 56, respectively. What Daniel found remarkable was that his O score for the future was identical with the past, during the time he had been a church pastor. He had expected that the past O score would be quite high, his present O score would be at a medium level, and his future O score would be the lowest. As he explored this surprising finding, Daniel discovered that what seemed to account for the moderate O score in the past had to do with the negative consequences that resulted when he gave so much of himself to both his parishioners and his family. Daniel concluded that one of the major causes of his divorce was that he counseled and nurtured his parishioners all day and came home exhausted and worn out when his former wife needed his support and energy. He found himself becoming more and more impatient with her and unwilling to accept her complaints about how much time he spent listening and showing compassion to the women of the church while at the same time expecting her to take care of everything at home and ask for little from him when he came home. Daniel also began to realize that at times he felt used by some of his church members, and rather than showing his irritation to those persons, he would instead show his irritation at home, where he could let down his guard. As his former wife became increasingly unhappy, he spent more of his time and energy with church members who idealized him and built up his self-esteem. The long work hours and his unwillingness to deal directly with his wife's anger eventually resulted in her suspicion that he was having an affair, and in fact, he was becoming close to a female work colleague who regularly sought his companionship.

A second theme that tainted his past relationships with others in the church had to do with the cold reality that hit when the church members began to see him in a less than perfect light. When Daniel's marriage problems surfaced, church members quickly began to question Daniel's motives, especially in his relationships with women. When his marriage ended in divorce, he was forced out of the position of pastor in the church. The betrayal that Daniel felt from the church members began to balance the fond memories he maintained about the "time when he was doing God's work."

As Daniel began to think about his present relationships with school colleagues and students, he was able to admit that his expectations about being a "servant" to others had not given him as much pleasure as he had hoped throughout his life. In fact, he had a persistent feeling that he had given much more to others than he had been offered or accepted in return. His decision to leave teaching was mainly motivated by this disappointment and emotional exhaustion. One important valuation for the future summed up the issue: Being in a retail garden business meant that he would be free from what he referred to as "someone else's moral code." He began to elaborate on this theme by saying that he was looking forward to having people come to him and *ask* for information, advice, help, or friendly conversation when they were *ready*, rather than being in the role of pointing out how others should strive for spiritual growth or trying to teach unmotivated students the *necessity* of learning. Of course, in the garden business, it wouldn't be necessary to check on his customers to see if they had followed through on his suggestions. He wouldn't have to evaluate his customers' progress in gardening or prepare another sermon or lesson for a reluctant audience. His relationships would now become simple exchanges in which customers would come with more specific needs and he would answer their questions (if he could) without feeling a sense of failure at not being able to provide the correct and right answers to the life dilemmas of others.

Best of all, Daniel expected that he might be able to *share* experiences with people who could tell him what they liked about listening to fountains or smelling the fragrances of fine plants. Focusing on the common meeting of minds (without the expectation that he should provide enlightenment for the soul) seemed to afford Daniel the possibility of finding happiness in life's simple pleasures without the baggage of needing to convince anyone of the moral correctness of a particular matter. The thought of having long hours working in a garden shop environment without even having to talk to anyone else was also wonderful for him to contemplate. In his words, he would no longer need to be constantly "talking and attempting to shove ideas down people's throats."

Positive and Negative Affect Dimensions

The total scores on P and N affective dimensions showed complementary changes over time. For P, past = 39, present = 48, and future = 78, whereas for N, past = 53, present = 51, and future = 16. Although positive feelings had been consistently increasing, negative feelings had persisted for Daniel's valuations of the past and present. The dramatic decrease in negative feelings associated with his future valuations, together with expectations about more positive feelings in the future, gave Daniel the sense that doing something for himself would lead to a satisfying and meaningful future life. He was reassured that his direction was right. His acceptance of the changed boundaries that he was setting for himself—the relief of not having to reach out to others so much and the prospect that others could reach out to him— gave him a new sense of purpose and life meaning and an emerging feeling of peace.

SUMMARY

In this chapter, we have emphasized (a) how the self may be viewed as a narrative, or unfolding story, and (b) how the Self-Confrontation Method may be used as a life review strategy for helping the older adult understand personal life themes, emotional patterns, and any unfinished business of persisting conflicts. This guided construction and reconstruction of emotions surrounding meaningful life events and central social relationships in the person's own words helps older adults organize their life story into a more coherent, integrative, and meaningful whole. Through the process of life review, one may not only become more aware of early originating events (those that helped form a particular life path), turning points (those experiences that redirected a life course), and past unresolved conflicts, but one also may gain greater insight into any current unresolved conflicts or unfinished business related to the past, present, or future. It is interesting to note that although life review appears to be a significant developmental process of later adulthood, researchers have recently suggested that significant life challenges or events during earlier life stages (e.g., adolescence, early adulthood) may also catalyze a life review (Staudinger, 1999).

Ultimately, at any age, the successful outcome of a life review involves new insight into the themes, values, emotions, and conflicts associated with one's personal life story and recognition of the possible need to revise parts of even fundamental aspects of one's life narrative. Regarding the potential need for story revision, Polkinghorne (1991) suggests that

> when the self is viewed in terms of narrative, the experience of *angst* and despair is understood to be symptomatic of the fact that one's personal plot can no longer hold together one's life events nor produce a unified and integrated experience of self. Overcoming these feelings of personal incoherence and disconnectedness requires a new or revised personal plot that makes sense of the events that have become disconnected. A plot that links together previously disparate events into a new whole provides for the reintegration and renewal of self. (p. 151)

Toward this end, we have suggested that the Self-Confrontation Method, as a guided and structured strategy for life review, is ideally suited to help persons refashion and reconstruct life stories in the direction of greater integration, coherence, and personal meaning.

VIGNETTE

In order to gain skills in facilitating the life review process for others, it is recommended that counselors apply the Self-Confrontation Method of life review to themselves. Begin the process by writing personal valuations for the past, present, and future using the questions presented in Table 20.1. Once class participants have completed writing their valuations, the instructor should divide the participants' class into dyads and have the partners tell each other about their valuations. Members of the dyads may assist each other in condensing the valuations into one or two sentences if necessary—always attempting to protect carefully the writer's own words. Once participants have clarified at least five valuations for the past, present, and future, they should use the Affective Rating Sheet to rate each of their valuations with regard to the 16 affective terms.

Then each participant should sum the scores for each of the S, O, P, and N terms. From these sums, matrices similar to those constructed for Daniel can be made. Grand totals for the four affective dimensions can be calculated and placed in the following chart:

Affective Dimensions

	S	O	P	N
Past	_____	_____	_____	_____
Present	_____	_____	_____	_____
Future	_____	_____	_____	_____

1. What patterns do you observe in your life narrative?

2. What are the relationships between the S and O affective dimensions for your past, present, and future valuations? How would you describe your well-being (P and N dimensions) for the past, present, and future?

3. Were there any originating events, turning points, or unfinished business that became clearer to you through your life review?

ADDITIONAL RESOURCES

Print Resources

Birren, J. E., & Deutchman, D. (1991). *Guiding autobiography groups for older adults: Exploring the fabric of life.* Baltimore: Johns Hopkins University Press.

Butler, R., & Lewis, M. (1991). *Aging and mental health: Positive psychosocial approaches.* St. Louis, MO: C. V. Mosby

Carlson, M. B. (1991). *Creative aging: A meaning-making perspective.* New York: Norton.

Hermans, H. J. M., & Hermans-Jansen, E. (1995). *Self-narratives: The construction of meaning in psychotherapy.* New York: Guilford.

Peake, T. H. (Ed.). (1998). *Healthy aging, healthy treatment: The impact of telling stories.* Westport, CT: Greenwood.

Waters, E. B. (1990). The life review: Strategies for working with individuals in groups. *Journal of Mental Health Counseling, 12,* 270-278.

REFERENCES

Aaron, L. M. (1992). The effects of raising grandchildren on the marital satisfaction, life satisfaction, and parenting stress of grandparents. *Dissertation Abstracts International, 53*(8-A), 2685. (University Microfilms No. 9300576)

Abell, S. C., & Richards, M. H. (1996). The relationship between body shape satisfaction and self-esteem: An investigation of gender and class differences. *Journal of Youth and Adolescence, 25,* 691-703.

Adler, N. E., Boyce, T., & Castelli, W. P. (1993). Socioeconomic inequalities in health: No easy solution. *Journal of the American Medical Association, 269,* 3140-3145.

Administration on Aging. (1998). *Profile of older Americans: 1998.* Washington, DC: U.S. Department of Health and Human Services. Retrieved July 1999 from the World Wide Web: http://www.aoa.gov/aoa/stats/profile/profile98.html

Administration on Aging. (2000). *Profile of older Americans: 2000.* Washington, DC: U.S. Department of Health and Human Services. Retrieved December 2000 from the World Wide Web: http://www.aoa.dhhs.gov/aoa/stats/profile/default.htm

Administration on Aging. (2001). *Profiles of older Americans: 2000–Poverty.* Washington, DC: U.S. Department of Health and Human Services. Retrieved April 17, 2001 from the World Wide Web: http://aoa.dhhs.gov/aoa/stats/profile/default.htm#poverty2

Ahrons, C. R., & Rodgers, R. H. (1987). *Divorced families.* New York: Norton.

Ahrons, C. R., & Bowman, M. (1982). Changes in family relationships following divorce of an adult child: Grandmother's perceptions. *Journal of Divorce, 5,* 49-68.

Aiken, L. R. (1998). *Human development in adulthood.* New York: Plenum.

Ainsworth, M. D. S., Blehar, M. C., Waters, E., & Wall, S. (1978). *Patterns of attachment: A psychological study of the strange situation.* Hillsdale, NJ: Lawrence Erlbaum.

Albee, G. W., & Ryan-Finn, K. D. (1993). An overview of primary prevention. *Journal of Counseling & Development, 72,* 115-123.

Alford-Keating, P. (1999, March). *Mentoring for gay, lesbian, bi and transgender students: We get by with a little help from our friends.* Paper presented at the annual meeting of the American College Personnel Association, Atlanta, GA.

Allaz, A., Bernstein, M., Rouget, P., Archinard, M., & Morabia, A. (1998). Body weight preoccupation in middle-aged and aging women: A general population survey. *International Journal of Eating Disorders, 23,* 287-294.

Allison-Ottey, S., Weston, C., Hennawi, G., Nichols, M., Eldred, L., & Ferguson, R. (1999). Sexual practices of older adults in a high HIV prevalence environment. *Maryland Medical Journal, 48*(6), 287-291.

Alpert-Gillis, L. J., Pedro-Carroll, J. L., & Cowen, E. L. (1989). The children of divorce intervention program: Development, implementation and evaluation of a program for young urban children. *Journal of Consulting & Clinical Psychology, 57,* 583-589.

Altabe, M. (1998). Ethnicity and body image: Quantitative and qualitative analysis. *International Journal of Eating Disorders, 23,* 153-159.

Alvy, K. T., & Marigna, M. K. (1985). *Effective Black parenting program.* Studio City, CA: Center for the Improvement of Child Caring.

Amato, P. R. (1991). Parental absence during childhood and depression in later life. *Sociological Quarterly, 32,* 543-556.

Amato, P. R., & Keith, B. (1991). Parental divorce and the well-being of children: A meta-analysis. *Psychological Bulletin, 110,* 26-46.

American Association of Retired Persons. (1995). *Planning your retirement.* Washington, DC: Author.

American Association of Retired Persons. (1998). *Baby boomers envision their retirement: An AARP segmentation analysis.* Retrieved October 2, 1999 from the World Wide Web: http://research.aarp.org/econ/boomer_seg_1.html

American Association of Retired Persons. (1999). Name change is official: We are now AARP. *AARP Bulletin, 40*(8), 3, 8.

American Association of Suicidology. (1996) Youth suicide by firearms task force. Retrieved January 2, 2001 from the World Wide Web: http://www.suicidology.org/youthsuicidetaskforce.htm

American Association of University Women. (1993). *Hostile hallways: The AAUW survey on sexual harassment in America's schools.* Washington, DC: Author.

American Counseling Association. (1995). *ACA code of ethics preamble.* Alexandria, VA: Author. Retrieved October 1999 from the World Wide Web: http://www.counseling.org/resources/codeofethics.htm.

American Foundation for Suicide Prevention. (1996). Retrieved January 2, 2001 from the World Wide Web: http://afsp.org

American Psychological Association. (1996). *Violence and the family: Report of the American Psychological Association Presidential Task Force on Violence and the Family.* Washington, DC: Author.

American Psychological Association. (1999). *Archival description of counseling psychology.* Washington, DC: Author. Retrieved October 1999 from the World Wide Web: http://www.apa.org/crsppp/counseling.html

Anderson, H. (1980). The death of a parent: Its impact on middle-aged sons and daughters. *Pastoral Psychology, 28*(3), 151-167.

Andrews, A. B. (1994). Developing community systems for the primary prevention of family violence. *Family and Community Health, 16*(4), 1-9.

Andrews, J. A., & Lewinsohn, P. M. (1992). Suicidal attempts among older adolescents: Prevalence and co-occurrence with psychiatric disorders. *Journal of the Academy of Child and Adolescent Psychiatry, 31,* 655-662.

Angel, M. D. (1987). *The orphaned adult: Confronting the death of a parent.* New York: Human Sciences.

Applegate, M. (1998). AIDS education for adolescents: A review of the literature. *Journal of HIV/AIDS Prevention & Education for Adolescents & Children, 2,* 5-29.

Archer, S. L. (1989). Gender differences in identity development: Issues of process, domain and timing. *Journal of Adolescence, 12,* 117-138.

Archer, S. L. (Ed.). (1994). *Interventions for adolescent identity development.* Thousand Oaks, CA: Sage.

Ardelt, M. (2000). Antecedents and effects of wisdom in old age: A longitudinal perspective on aging well. *Research on Aging, 22,* 360-394.

Armstrong, J. G., & Roth, D. M. (1989). Attachment and separation difficulties in eating disorders: A preliminary investigation. *International Journal of Eating Disorders, 8,* 141-155.

Armsworth, M. W., & Holaday, M. (1993). The effects of psychological trauma on children and adolescents. *Journal of Counseling and Development, 72,* 49-56.

Arnett, J. J. (1999). Adolescent storm and stress, reconsidered. *American Psychologist, 54,* 317-326.

Arthur, M. W., & Blitz, C. (2000). Bridging the gap between science and practice in drug abuse prevention through needs assessment and strategic community planning. *Journal of Community Psychology, 28,* 241-255.

Asher, S. R., Hymel, S., & Renshaw, S. (1984). Loneliness in children. *Child Development, 55,* 1456-1464.

Atchley, R. C. (1976). Selected social and psychological differences between men and women in later life. *Journal of Gerontology, 31,* 204-211.

Atchley, R. C. (1989). A continuity theory of normal aging. *The Gerontologist, 29,* 183-190.

Atkinson, D. R., & Juntunen, C. L. (1994). School counselors and school psychologists as school-home-community liaisons in ethnically diverse schools. In P. Pedersen & J. C. Carey (Eds.), *Multicultural counseling in schools* (pp. 103-119). Boston: Allyn & Bacon.

Atkinson, D. R., Kim, A. U., Ruelas, S. R., & Lin, A. T. (1999). Ethnicity and attitudes toward facilitated reminiscence. *Journal of Mental Health Counseling, 21,* 66-81.

Atkinson, D. R., Morten, G., & Sue, D. W. (1993). *Counseling American minorities: A cross-cultural perspective* (4th ed.). Madison, WI: Brown & Benchmark.

Atkinson, D. R., Morten, G., & Sue, D. W. (1998). *Counseling American minorities.* Madison, WI: Brown & Benchmark.

Attie, I., & Brooks-Gunn, J. (1989). Development of eating problems in adolescent girls: A longitudinal study. *Developmental Psychology, 25,* 70-79.

Aubrey, R. F. (1986). The professionalization of counseling. In M. D. Lewis, R. L. Hayes, & J. A. Lewis (Eds.), *An introduction to the counseling profession* (pp. 1-35). Itasca, IL: F. E. Peacock.

Azar, S. T. (1997). A cognitive behavioral approach to understanding and treating parents who physically abuse their children. In D. A. Wolfe, R. J. McMahon, & R. D. Peters (Eds.), *Child abuse: New directions in prevention and treatment across the lifespan* (pp. 79-101). Thousand Oaks, CA: Sage.

Baber, K. M., & Monaghan, P. (1988). College women's career and motherhood expectations: New options, old dilemmas. *Sex Roles, 19,* 189-203.

Bachman, R., & Saltzman, L. E. (1995). Violence against women: Estimates from the re-designed survey. In U.S. Department of Justice, Bureau of Justice, *Special report: National crime victimization survey.* (Report No. NCJ-154348). Washington, DC: Author.

Bahr, S., & Peterson, E. (1989). *Aging and the family.* Lexington, MA: Lexington Books.

Baker, S. B. (2000). *School counseling for the twenty-first century* (3rd ed.). Upper Saddle River, NJ: Prentice Hall.

Baltes, P. B. (1983). Life-span developmental psychology: Observations on history and theory revisited. In R. M. Lerner (Ed.), *Developmental psychology: Historical and philosophical perspectives.* Hillsdale, NJ: Lawrence Erlbaum.

Bamberg, M. (1991). Narrative activity as perspective taking: The role of emotionals, negations, and voice in the construction of the story realm. *Journal of Cognitive Psychotherapy, 5,* 275-290.

Bandura, A. (1977). Self-efficacy: Toward a unifying theory of behavioral change. *Psychological Review, 84,* 191-215.

Bandura, A. (1977). *Social learning theory.* Englewood Cliffs, NJ: Prentice Hall.

Bandura, A. (1986). *Social foundations of thought and action: A Social Cognitive Theory.* Englewood Cliffs, NJ: Prentice Hall.

Bandura, A. (1992). Exercise of personal agency through the self-efficacy mechanism. In R. Schwarzer (Ed.), *Self-efficacy: Thought control of action* (pp. 3-38). Washington, DC: Hemisphere.

Bandura, A. (1994). Social cognitive theories and the exercise of control over HIV infection. In R. DiClemente & J. L. Peterson (Eds.), *Preventing AIDS: Theories and methods of behavioral intervention* (pp. 25-59). New York: Plenum.

Bangert-Drowns, R. L. (1988). The effects of school-based substance abuse education: A meta-analysis. *Journal of Drug Education, 18,* 243-264.

Baris, M. A., & Garrity, C. B. (1997). Co-parenting post divorce: Helping parents negotiate and maintain low-conflict separations. In K. Halford & H. Markman (Eds.), *Clinical handbook of marriage and couples interventions* (pp. 619-649). New York: John Wiley.

Barnett, O. W., Miller-Perrin, C. L., & Perrin, R. D. (1997). *Family violence across the lifespan: An introduction.* Thousand Oaks, CA: Sage.

Barovick, H., Booth, C., Cole, W., Monroe, S., Nordan, D., Padgett, T., Roche, T., & Stodgill, R. (1999, May 31). Troubled kids. *Time,* pp. 33-38, 43.

Baruch, G. K., Biener, L., & Barnett, R. C. (1987). Women and gender in research on work and family stress. *American Psychologist, 42,* 130-136.

Basen-Engquist, K. (1994). Evaluation of a theory-based HIV prevention intervention for college students. *AIDS Education and Prevention, 6,* 412-424.

Baumeister, R. F. (1990). Suicide as escape from self. *Psychological Review, 97,* 90-113.

Baumrind, D. (1967). Child care practices anteceding three patterns of preschool behavior. *Genetic Psychology Monographs, 75,* 43-88.

Baumrind, D. (1971). Current patterns of parental authority. *Developmental Psychology Monographs, 4*(1, Pt. 2).

Baumrind, D. (1973). The development of instrumental competence through socialization. In A. Pick (Ed.), *Minnesota symposia on child psychology* (Vol. 1, pp. 3-46). Minneapolis: University of Minnesota Press.

Beckham, B. (1981). *The Black student's guide to college.* New York: Dutton.

Beckingham, A. C., & Watt, S. (1995). Daring to grow old: Lessons in healthy aging and empowerment. *Educational Gerontology, 21*(5), 479-495.

Beckwith, L. (1990). Adaptive and maladaptive parenting—Implications for parenting. In S. J. Meisels & J. P. Shonkoff (Eds.), *Handbook of early childhood intervention* (pp. 53-77). New York: Cambridge University Press.

Beers, C. (1908). *A mind that found itself.* New York: Longman.

Bellah, R. N., Madsen, R., Sullivan, W. M., Swidler, A., & Tipton, S. M. (1985). *Habits of the heart: Individualism and commitment in American life.* Berkeley: University of California Press.

Belle, D. (1987). Gender differences in the social moderators of stress. In R. C. Barnett, L. Biener, & G. K. Baruch (Eds.), *Gender and stress* (pp. 257-275). New York: Free Press.

Belsky, J. (1984). The determinants of parenting: A process model. *Child Development, 55*, 83-96.

Belsky, J. (1993). Etiology of child maltreatment: A developmental-ecological analysis. *Psychological Bulletin, 114*, 413-434.

Ben, N., & Ard, J. (1977). Sex in lasting marriages: A longitudinal study. *Journal of Sex Research, 13*, 274-285.

Benard, B. (1991). *Fostering resiliency in kids: Protective factors in the family, school and community.* Portland, OR: Northwest Regional Laboratory.

Benard, B. (1993a, September). Resiliency paradigm validates craft knowledge. *Western Center News,* pp. 4-5.

Benard, B. (1993b, March). Resiliency requires changing hearts and minds. *Western Center News,* pp. 4-5.

Bengtson, V., Rosenthal, C., & Burton, L. (1996). Paradoxes of families and aging. In R. H. Binstock & L. K. George (Eds.), *Handbook of aging and the social sciences* (4th ed., pp. 253-282). San Diego, CA: Academic Press.

Benjamin, M. P. (1998). The psychological impact of violence on children and families: Assessment and service system strategies. In H. Hernandez & M. R. Isaacs (Eds.), *Promoting cultural competence in children's mental health services* (pp. 169-183). Baltimore: Brookes.

Benkov, L. (1994). *Reinventing the family.* New York: Crown.

Benson, P. (1993). *The troubled journey: A portrait of 6th-12th grade youth.* Minneapolis, MN: Search Institute.

Benson, P. (1996). *Developmental assets among Minneapolis youth: The urgency of promoting healthy community.* Minneapolis, MN: Search Institute.

Berel, S., & Irving, L. M. (1998). Media and disturbed eating: An analysis of media influence and implications for prevention. *Journal of Primary Prevention, 18,* 415-430.

Berg, D. R., Lonsway, K. A., & Fitzgerald, L. F. (1999). Rape prevention education for men: The effectiveness of empathy-induction techniques. *Journal of College Student Development, 40,* 219-234.

Berk, L. E. (2000). *Development through the lifespan.* Needham Heights, MA: Allyn & Bacon.

Berman, A. L., & Jobes, D. A. (1991). *Adolescent suicide: Assessment and intervention.* Washington, DC: American Psychological Association.

Berman, A. L., & Jobes, D. A. (1995). A population perspective: Suicide prevention in adolescents (age 12-18). *Suicide and Life-Threatening Behavior, 25*(1), 143-154.

Betz, N. E., & Hackett, G. (1986). Applications of self-efficacy theory to understanding career choice behavior. *Journal of Social and Clinical Psychology, 4,* 279-289.

Beyth-Marom, R., & Fishhoff, B. (1997). Adolescents' decisions about risks: A cognitive perspective. In J. Schulenberg, J. L. Maggs, & K. Hurrelmann (Eds.), *Health risks and developmental transitions during adolescence* (pp. 110-125). New York: Cambridge University Press.

Bijstra, J. O., Bosma, H. A., & Jackson, S. (1994). The relationship between social skills and psycho-social functioning in early adolescence. *Personality & Individual Differences, 16,* 767-776.

Bird, G. W., & Ford, R. (1985). A source of role strain among dual-career couples. *Home Economics Research Journal, 14,* 187-194.

Bird, H. R. (1992). Psychotherapy with children of divorce. In J. D. O'Brien, D. J. Pilowsky, & O. W. Lewis (Eds.), *Psychotherapies with children and adolescents:*

Adapting the psychodynamic process (pp. 255-268). Washington, DC: American Psychiatric Press.

Bird, H. R., Gould, M. S., & Staghezza, B. M. (1993). Patterns of diagnostic comorbidity in a community sample of children aged 9 through 16 years. *Journal of the American Academy of Child and Adolescent Psychiatry, 32*(2), 361-368.

Bisconti, T. L., & Bergeman, C. S. (1999). Perceived control as a mediator of the relationships among social support, psychological well-being, and perceived health. *The Gerontologist, 39*(1), 94-103.

Blau, G. M., & Long, D. (1999). The prediction, assessment, and treatment of family violence. In R. L. Hampton (Ed.), *Family violence: Prevention and treatment* (2nd ed., pp. 309-337). Thousand Oaks, CA: Sage.

Blieszner, R., & Bradford, V. H. (1995). *Handbook of aging and the family.* Westport, CN: Greenwood.

Blustein, D. L., Jackson, J., Jackson, L., Kenny, M., & Sparks, E. (1999). *Tools for tomorrow: A classroom-based intervention for psychosocial and work readiness.* Manuscript in preparation.

Bok, M., & Morales, J. (1997). Effective HIV prevention interventions for adolescents and young adults: A theoretical approach. *Journal of HIV/AIDS Prevention & Education for Adolescents & Children, 1,* 9-35.

Bok, M., & Morales, J. (1998). HIV risk behaviors in youth, adolescents, and young adults. *Journal of HIV/AIDS Prevention & Education for Adolescents & Children, 2,* 81-95.

Bolles, R. N. (1995). *What color is your parachute? A practical manual for job-hunters and career-changers.* (25th ed.). Berkeley, CA: Ten Speed.

Bond, J. T., Galinsky, E., & Swanberg, J. E. (1998). *The 1997 national study of the changing workforce.* New York: Families and Work Institute.

Bordin, E. S. (1979). Fusing work and play: A challenge to theory and research. *Academic Psychology Bulletin, 1,* 5-9.

Bosma, H. A., Graafsma, T. L. G., Grotevant, H. D., & de Levita, D. J. (1994). *Identity and development: An interdisciplinary approach.* Thousand Oaks, CA: Sage.

Boswell, G. (2000). *Violent children and adolescents: Asking the question why.* London: Whurr.

Bosworth, K., Espelage, D., & DuBay, T. (1998). A computer-based violence prevention intervention for young adolescents: Pilot study. *Adolescence, 33*(132), 785-795.

Botvin, G. J. (1986). Substance abuse prevention research: Recent developments and future directions. *Journal of School Health, 56,* 369-374.

Botvin, G. J., Schinke, S. P., Epstein, J. A., Diaz, T., & Botvin, E. M. (1995). Effectiveness of culturally focused and generic skills training approaches to alcohol and drug abuse prevention among minority adolescents: Two-year follow-up results. *Psychology of Addictive Behaviors, 9,* 183-194.

Bowlby, J. (1969). *Attachment and loss: Vol. 1. Attachment.* New York: Basic Books.

Bowlby, J. (1973). *Attachment and loss: Vol. 2. Separation, anxiety, and anger.* New York: Basic Books.

Bowlby, J. (1977). The making and breaking of affectional bonds. *British Journal of Psychiatry, 130,* 201-210.

Bowlby, J. (1980). *Attachment and loss: Vol. 3. Loss, sadness and depression.* New York: Basic Books.

Bowlby, J. (1982). *Attachment and loss: Vol. 1. Attachment* (2nd ed.). New York: Basic Books.

Boyd, J. H., & Moscicki, E. K. (1986). Firearms and youth. *American Journal of Public Health, 76,* 1240-1242.

Bradley, R. H., Whiteside, L., Mundfrom, D. J., Casey, P. H., Kelleher, K. J., & Pope, S. K. (1994). Early indications of resilience and their relation to experiences in the home environments of low birthweight, premature children living in poverty. *Child Development, 64,* 346-360.

Brady, E. U., & Kendall, P. C. (1992). Comorbidity of anxiety and depression in children and adolescents. *Psychological Bulletin, 111*(2), 244-255.

Brannon, R. C. (1976). No "sissy stuff": The stigma of anything vaguely feminine. In D. David & R. Brannon (Eds.), *The forty-nine percent majority* (pp. 49-50). Reading, MA: Addison-Wesley.

Breault, K. D., & Kposowa, A. J. (1987). Explaining divorce in the United States. A study of 3,111 counties, 1980. *Journal of Marriage and the Family, 49,* 549-558.

Breitenbecher, K. H. (2000). Sexual assault on college campuses: Is an ounce of prevention enough? *Applied and Preventive Psychology, 9,* 23-52.

Brent, D. A., & Perper, J. A. (1995). Research in adolescent suicide: Implications for training, service delivery, and public policy. *Suicide and Life-Threatening Behavior, 25*(2), 222-230.

Brent, D. A., Perper, J. A., & Allman, C. J. (1987). Alcohol, firearms, and suicide among youth: Temporal trends in Allegheny County, Pennsylvania, 1960-1983. *Journal of the American Medical Association, 257,* 3369-3372.

Brent, D. A., Perper, J. A., Allman, C. J., Moritz, G. M., Wartella, M. E., & Zelenak, J. P. (1991). The presence and accessibility of firearms in the homes of adolescent suicides: A case control study. *Journal of the American Medical Association, 266,* 2989-2995.

Brent, D. A., Perper, J. A., Goldstein, C. E., Kolko, D. J., Allan, M. J., Allman, C. J., & Zelenak, J. P. (1988). Risk factors for adolescent suicide: A comparison of adolescent suicide victims with suicidal inpatients. *Archives of General Psychiatry, 45,* 581-588.

Brent, D. A., Perper, J. A., Moritz, G., Allman, C., Friend, A., Roth, C., Schweers, J., Balach, L., & Baugher, M. (1993). Psychiatric risk factors for adolescent suicide: A case control study. *Journal of the American Academy of Child and Adolescent Psychiatry, 32*(3), 521-529.

Breslau, N., Davis, G. C., Peterson, E. L., & Schultz, L. (1997). Psychiatric sequelae of posttraumatic stress disorder in women. *Archives of General Psychiatry, 54,* 81-87.

Brewington, J. O., & Nassar-McMillan, S. (2000). Older adults: Work-related issues and implications for counseling. *Career Development Quarterly, 49,* 2-15.

Brody, E. M. (1985). Parent care as a normative family stress. *The Gerontologist, 25,* 19-29.

Bronfenbrenner, U. (1979). *The ecology of human development: Experiments by nature and design.* Cambridge, MA: Harvard University Press.

Bronfenbrenner, U. (1985). Summary. In M. B. Spencer, G. K. Brookins, & W. R. Allen (Eds.), *Beginnings: The social and affective development of Black children* (pp. 67-73). Hillsdale, NJ: Lawrence Erlbaum.

Bronfenbrenner, U. (1986). Ecology of the family as a context for human development: Research perspectives. *Developmental Psychology, 22,* 723-742.

Brooks-Gunn, & Kirsh. (1984). Life events and the boundaries of midlife for women. In G. K. Baruch & J. Brooks-Gunn (Eds.), *Women in midlife* (pp. 11-30). New York: Plenum.

Brouwers, M. (1990). Treatment of body image dissatisfaction among women with bulimia nervosa. *Journal of Counseling and Development, 69,* 144-147.

Brown, B. B., & Theobald, W. (1998). Learning contexts beyond the classroom: Extracurricular activities, community organizations, and peer groups. In K. Borman & B. Schneider (Eds.), *The adolescent years: Social influences and educational challenges.* Chicago: University of Chicago Press.

Brown, D. (1995). A values-based approach to facilitating career transitions. *Career Development Quarterly, 44,* 4-11.

Brown, D. (1997). Implications of cultural values for cross-cultural consultation with families. *Journal of Counseling and Development, 76,* 29-35.

Brown, J. H., Portes, P. R., & Christensen, D. N. (1989). Understanding divorce stress on children: Implications for research and practice. *American Journal of Family Therapy, 17,* 315-325.

Brown, L. M., & Gilligan, C. (1992). *Meeting at the crossroads: Women's psychology and girls' development.* Cambridge, MA: Harvard University Press.

Brown, M. T., Fukunaga, C., Umemoto, D., & Wicker, L. (1996) Annual review, 1990-1996: Social class, work, and retirement behavior. *Journal of Vocational Behavior, 49,* 159-189.

Browne, A. (1993). Violence against women by male partners: Prevalence, outcomes, and policy implications. *American Psychologist, 48,* 1077-1087.

Brubaker, E. (1983). Providing services to older persons and their families. In T. H. Brubaker (Ed.), *Family relationships in later life.* Beverly Hills, CA: Sage.

Bruch, J. (1962). Perceptual and conceptual disturbances in anorexia nervosa. *Canadian Journal of Psychiatry, 26,* 187-194.

Bruner, J. (1986). *Actual minds, possible worlds.* Cambridge, MA: Harvard University Press.

Brylinsky, J. A., & Moore, J. C. (1994). The identification of body build stereotypes in young children. *Journal of Research in Personality, 28,* 170-181.

Buehler, C., & Legg, B. H. (1992). Selected aspects of parenting and children's social competence post-separation: The moderating effects of child's sex, age and family economic hardship. *Journal of Divorce and Remarriage, 18,* 177-195.

Buhrmester, D. (1990). Intimacy of friendship, interpersonal competence, and adjustment during preadolescence and adolescence. *Child Development, 61,* 1101-1113.

Buka, S., & Earls, F. (1993). Early determinants of delinquency and violence. *Health Affairs, 12,* 46-64.

Bureau of Labor Statistics. (2000). *2000 employment situations summary.* Washington, DC: Author. Retrieved December 10, 2000 from the World Wide Web: http://stats.bls.gov:80/news.release/empsit.nr0.htm

Burke, R. J., & McKeen, C. A. (1993). Career priority patterns among managerial and professional women. *Applied Psychology: An International Review, 42,* 341-352.

Burns, A., & Dunlop, R. (1999). "How did you feel about it?" Children's feelings about their parents' divorce at the time and three and ten years later. *Journal of Divorce and Remarriage, 31,* 19-35.

Burroughs, M. S., Wagner, W. W., & Johnson, J. T. (1997). Treatment with children of divorce: A comparison of two types of therapy. *Journal of Divorce & Remarriage, 27,* 83-99.

Butler, R. N. (1963). Life review: An interpretation of reminiscence in the aged. *Psychiatry, 26,* 65-76.

Butters, J. W., & Cash, T. F. (1987). Cognitive-behavioral treatment of women's body image dissatisfaction. *Journal of Consulting and Clinical Psychology, 55,* 889-897.

Button, E., Loan, P., Davies, J., & Sonuga-Barke, E. (1997). Self-esteem, eating problems and psychological well-being in a cohort of schoolgirls aged 15-16: A questionnaire and interview study. *International Journal of Eating Disorders, 21,* 39-47.

Buzawa, E. S., & Buzawa, C. G. (1993). The scientific evidence is not conclusive and arrest is no panacea. In R. J. Gelles & D. R. Loseke (Eds.), *Current controversies in family violence* (pp. 337-356). Thousand Oaks, CA: Sage.

Calam, R., Waller, G., Slade, P., & Newton, T. (1990). Eating disorders and perceived relationships with parents. *International Journal of Eating Disorders, 9,* 479-485.

Calderon, M. (1998). Adolescent sons and daughters of immigrants: How schools can respond. In K. Borman & B. Schneider (Eds.), *The adolescent years: Social influences and educational challenges* (pp. 65-87). Chicago: University of Chicago Press.

Camera, K. A., & Resnick, G. (1989). Styles of conflict resolution and cooperation between divorced parents: Effects on child behavior and adjustment. *American Journal of Orthopsychiatry, 59,* 560-575.

Campbell, C. (1993). Strategies for reducing parent resistance to consultation in the schools. *Elementary School Guidance and Counseling, 28,* 83-91.

Caplan, G. (Ed.). (1974). *Support systems and community mental health.* New York: Basic Books.

Caplan, G., & Caplan, R. B. (1999). Methods of preventive intervention in a program of primary prevention of psychosocial disorders in children of divorce. *Journal of Primary Prevention, 20,* 107-118.

Caplan, M. Z., Weissberg, R. P., Grober, J. S., Sivo, P. J., Grady, K., & Jacoby, C. (1992). Social competence promotion with inner-city and suburban young adolescents: The effects on social adjustment and alcohol use. *Journal of Consulting and Clinical Psychology, 60,* 56-63.

Carin, R., & Shaver, P. (1982). *In search of intimacy.* New York: Delacorte.

Carr, D., House, J. S., Kessler, R. C., Nesse, R. M., Sonnega, J., & Wortman, C. (2000) Marital quality and psychological adjustment to widowhood among older adults: A longitudinal analysis. *Journals of Gerontology: Series B: Psychological Sciences and Social Sciences, 55B,* S197-S207.

Carter, B., & McGoldrick, M. (1988). *The changing family life cycle* (2nd ed.). New York: Gardner.

Carter, J. (1998). *The virtues of aging.* New York: Ballantine.

Carter, J. C., Stewart, D. A., Dunn, V. J., & Fairburn, C. G. (1997). Primary prevention of eating disorders: Might it do more harm than good? *International Journal of Eating Disorders, 22,* 167-172.

Cash, T. F. (1995). *What do you see when you look in the mirror? Helping yourself to a positive body image.* New York: Bantam.

Cash, T. F., & Henry, P. E. (1995). Women's body images: The results of a national survey in the U.S.A. *Sex Roles, 33,* 19-28.

Cash, T. F., & Hicks, K. L. (1990). Being fat versus thinking fat: Relationships with body image, eating behaviors and well-being. *Cognitive Therapy and Research, 14,* 327-341.

Cassel, J. (1974). Psychosocial processes and "stress": Theoretical formulations. *International Journal of Health Services, 4,* 471-482.

Catalano, R. F., Berglund, M. L., Ryan, J. A. M., Lonczak, H. C., & Hawkins, J. D. (1998). *Positive youth development in the United States: Research findings on evaluations of positive youth development programs.* Seattle, WA: Social Development Research Group.

Catalano, R. F., Kosterman, R., Hawkins, J. D., Newcomb, M. D., & Abbott, R. D. (1996). Modeling the etiology of adolescent substance use: A test of the social development model. *Journal of Drug Issues, 26,* 429-455.

Catalyst. (1984). *Catalyst campus resource.* New York: Author.

Catalyst. (1987). *New roles for men and women: A report on an educational intervention with college students.* New York: Author.

Cavanaugh, J. C. (1996). *Adult development and aging* (3rd ed.). Pacific Grove, CA: Brooks/Cole.

Centers for Disease Control and Prevention. (1992). *Youth suicide prevention programs: A resource guide.* Atlanta, GA: Author.

Centers for Disease Control and Prevention. (1996, September 27). *Morbidity and Mortality Weekly Report, 45* (CDC Surveillance Summary No. SS-4). Atlanta, GA: Author.

Chalk, R., & King, P. A. (1998a). *Violence in families: Assessing prevention and treatment programs.* Washington, DC: National Academic Press.

Chalk, R., & King, P. A. (1998b). Assessing family violence interventions. *American Journal of Preventive Medicine, 14,* 289-292.

Chambers, D. L. (1998). Lesbian divorce: A commentary on the legal issues. *American Journal of Orthopsychiatry, 68,* 420-423.

Chase-Lansdale, P. L., Cherlin, A. J., & Kiernan, K. E. (1995). The long-term effects of parental divorce on the mental health of young adults: A developmental perspective. *Child Development, 66,* 1614-1634.

Cherlin, A. J., & Furstenberg, F. F. (1992). *The new American grandparent: A place in the family, a life apart.* Cambridge, MA: Harvard University Press.

Cherlin, A. J., Furstenberg, F. F., Chase-Lansdale, L., Kiernan, K. E., Robins, P. K., Morrison, D. R., & Teitler, J. O. (1991). Longitudinal studies of effects of divorce on children in Great Britain and the United States. *Science, 251,* 1386-1389.

Chickering, A. W. (1969). *Education and identity.* San Francisco: Jossey-Bass.

Children's Defense Fund. (2000). *Families struggling to make it in the workforce: A post welfare report.* Retrieved from the World Wide Web: http://www. childrensdefense.org/release001214.htm

Child Welfare League of America. (1997). *Children with reports of abuse and neglect and with reports substantiated/indicated, 1997.* Retrieved from the World Wide Web: http://ndas.cwla.org/Report.asp?PageMode=1&ReportID=134&GUID= {51CCDCEA-D546-11D4-895E-00A0C9CE08E4}#Table

Chiriboga, D. A. (1982). Adaptation to marital separation in later and earlier life. *Journal of Gerontology, 37,* 595-601.

Chiriboga, D. A. (1989a). Divorce at midlife. In R. A. Kalish (Ed.), *Midlife loss: Coping strategies* (pp. 179-217). Newbury Park, CA: Sage.

Chiriboga, D. A. (1989b). Mental health at the midpoint: Crisis, challenge or relief? In K. Hunter & M. Sundel (Eds.), *Midlife myths: Issues, findings, and practical implications* (pp. 116-141). Newbury Park, CA: Sage.

Chiriboga, D. A. (1989c). Stress and loss in middle age. In R. A. Kalish (Ed.), *Midlife loss: Coping strategies* (pp. 42-86). Newbury Park, CA: Sage.

Chung, H., & Elias, M. (1996). Patterns of adolescent involvement in problem behaviors: Relationship to self-efficacy, social competence, and life events. *American Journal of Community Psychology, 24,* 771-784.

Ciborowski, P. J. (1989). Counseling children of divorce. In *The Hatherleigh guides series (Vol. 6). The Hatherleigh guide to marriage and family therapy* (pp. 35-55). New York: Hatherleigh.

Ciffone, J. (1993). Suicide prevention: A classroom presentation to adolescents. *Social Work, 38*(2), 196-203.

Cleveland, J. (1996). *Everything you need to know about retirement housing: Finding the place at the right time.* New York: Penguin.

Cockerham, W. C. (1991). *The aging society.* Englewood Cliffs, NJ: Prentice Hall.

Cohen, D. A., & Litton, K. L. P. (1995). Parent participation in an adolescent drug abuse prevention program. *Journal of Drug Education, 25,* 159-169.

Cohen, M. A. (1998). The monetary value of saving a high-risk youth. *Journal of Quantitative Criminology, 14,* 5-33.

Cohen, S., & Wills, T. A. (1985). Social support and the buffering hypothesis. *Psychological Bulletin, 98,* 310-357.

Cole, M., & Cole, S. R. (1993). *The development of children* (2nd ed.). New York: Scientific American Books.

Coleman, J. (1978). Current contradictions in adolescent theory. *Journal of Youth and Adolescence, 7,* 1-11.

Coll, C. G., Lamberty, G., Jenkins, R., McAdoo, H. P., Crnic, K., Wasik, B. H., & Garcia, H. V. (1996). An integrative model for the study of developmental competencies in minority children. *Child Development, 67,* 1891-1914.

Comas-Diaz, L., & Greene, B. (1994). Women of color with professional status. In L. Comas-Diaz & B. Greene (Eds.), *Women of color: Integrating ethnic and gender identities in psychotherapy* (pp. 347-388). New York: Guilford.

Commission on Substance Abuse at Colleges and Universities. (1994). *Rethinking rites of passage: Substance abuse on America's campuses.* New York: Columbia University, Center on Addiction and Substance Abuse.

Compas, B. E., Worsham, N. L., & Ey, S. (1992). Conceptual and developmental issues in children's coping with stress. In A. La Greca, L. Siegel, J. Wallender, & E. Walker (Eds.), *Stress and coping in child health* (pp. 7-24). New York: Guilford.

Conner, M., & Norman, P. (Eds.). (1996). *Predicting health behavior: Research and practice with social cognitive models.* Buckingham, UK: Open University Press.

Conroy, E., & Mayer, S. (1994). Strategies for consulting with parents. *Elementary School Guidance and Counseling, 29,* 60-66.

Consortium on the School-Based Promotion of Social Competence. (1994). The school-based promotion of social competence: Theory, research, practice, and policy. In R. J. Haggerty, L. R. Sherrod, N. Garmezy, & M. Rutter (Eds.), *Stress, risk, and resilience in children and adolescents: Processes, mechanisms, and interventions* (pp. 268-316). New York: Cambridge University Press.

Conwell, Y., Duberstein, P. R., Cox, C., Hermann, J. H., Forbes, N. T., & Caine, E. D. (1996). Relationships of age and Axis I diagnoses in victims of completed suicide: A psychological autopsy study. *American Journal of Psychiatry, 153,* 1001-1008.

Conyne, R. K. (1994). Preventive counseling. *Counseling and Human Development, 27*(1), 1-10.

Conyne, R. K. (1997). Educating students in preventive counseling. *Counselor Education and Supervision, 36,* 259-269.

Conyne, R. K. (2000). Prevention in counseling psychology: At long last, has the time now come? *The Counseling Psychologist, 28,* 838-844.

Cook, E. P. (1993). The gendered context of life: Implications for women's and men's career-life plans. *Career Development Quarterly, 41,* 227-237.

Costello, E. J., & Angold, A. (1993). Toward a developmental epidemiology of the disruptive behavior disorders. *Development and Psychopathology, 5*(1-2), 91-101.

Coulton, C. J., Korbin, J. E., Su, M., & Chow, J. (1995). Community level factors and child maltreatment rates. *Child Development, 66,* 1262-1276.

Covin, T. J., & Brush, C. C. (1991). An examination of male and female attitudes toward career and family issues. *Sex Roles, 25,* 393-415.

Cowen, E. L., Pedro-Carroll, J. L., & Alpert-Gillis, L. J. (1990). Relationships between support and adjustment among children of divorce. *Journal of Child Psychology and Psychiatry, 31,* 727-735.

Cox, L., & Lyddon, W. J. (1997). Constructivist conceptions of self: A discussion of emerging identity constructs. *Journal of Constructivist Psychology, 10,* 201-219.

Creighton, L. A. (1991, December 16). Silent saviors. *U.S. News and World Report,* 80-89.

Crick, N. R., & Ladd, G. W. (1993). Children's perceptions of their peer experiences: Attributions, loneliness, social anxiety, and social avoidance. *Developmental Psychology, 29,* 244-254.

Crisp, A. H. (1988). Some possible approaches to prevention of eating and body weight/shape disorders, with particular preference to anorexia nervosa. *International Journal of Eating Disorders, 1,* 1-17.

Crockett, L. J., & Petersen, A. C. (1993). Adolescent development: Health risks and opportunities for health promotion. In S. G. Millstein, A. C. Petersen, & E. O. Nightingale (Eds.), *Promoting the health of adolescents: New directions for the twenty-first century,* (pp. 13-37). New York: Oxford University Press.

Crosbie-Burnett, M., & Newcomer, L. L. (1990). Group counseling children of divorce: The effects of a multimodal intervention. *Journal of Divorce, 13,* 69-78.

Crose, R., Leventhal, E. A., Haug, M. A., & Burns, E. A. (1997). The challenges of aging. In S. E. Gallant & G. P. Keita (Eds.), *Health care for women: Psychological, social, and behavioral influences* (pp. 221-234). Washington, DC: American Psychological Association.

Cross, T. L., Cook, R. S., & Dixon, D. N. (1996). Psychological autopsies of three academically talented adolescents who committed suicide. *Journal of Secondary Gifted Education, 7*(3), 403-409.

Cummings, E. M., Vogel, D., Cummings, J. S., & El-Sheikh, M. (1989). Children's responses to different forms of expression of anger between adults. *Child Development, 60,* 1392-1404.

Cummings, N. A. (1977). The anatomy of psychotherapy under national health insurance. *American Psychologist, 32,* 711-718.

Cummings, N. A. (1995). Impact of managed care on employment and training: A primer for survival. *Professional Psychology: Research and Practice, 26,* 10-15.

Cummings, N. A. (1997). Behavioral health in primary care: Dollars and sense. In N. A. Cummings, J. L. Cummings, & J. N. Johnson (Eds.), *Behavioral health in primary care: A guide for clinical integration* (pp. 3-21). Madison, CN: Psychosocial Press.

Cummings, N. A., Budman, S. H., & Thomas, J. L. (1998). Efficient psychotherapy as a viable response to scarce resources and rationing of treatment. *Professional Psychology: Research and Practice, 29,* 460-469.

Cummings, R. (1995). *Adolescence: A developmental perspective.* New York: Harcourt Brace.

Dacey, J., & Kenny, M. (1997). *Adolescent development* (2nd ed.). Madison, WI: Brown & Benchmark.

Dalton, J. (1991). Racial and ethnic backlash in college peer culture. *New Directions for Student Services, 56,* 3-12.

Dangel, R. G., & Polster, R. A. (Eds.). (1984). *Parent training: Foundations of research & practice.* New York: Guilford.

D'Augelli, A. R., & Hershberger, S. L. (1993). Lesbian, gay, and bisexual youth in community settings: Personal challenges and mental health problems. *American Journal of Community Psychology, 21,* 421-448.

David, K., & Williams, T. (1987). *Health education in schools.* London: Harper & Row.

Davidson, J. R. T., & Fairbank, J. A. (1993). The epidemiology of posttraumatic stress disorder. In J. R. T. Davidson & E. B. Foa (Eds.), *Posttraumatic stress disorder: DSM-IV and beyond* (pp. 147-169). Washington, DC: American Psychiatric Press.

Davis, J. M., & Brock, S. E. (in press). Suicide and the schools: Incidence, theory, research and response. In J. Sandoval (Ed.), *Handbook of crisis counseling, intervention, and prevention in the schools* (2nd ed.). Mahwah, NJ: Lawrence Erlbaum.

Davis, J. M., & Sandoval, J. (1991). *Suicidal youth: School-based intervention and prevention.* San Francisco: Jossey-Bass.

Deater-Deckard, K., & Dodge, K. A. (1997). Externalizing behavior problems and discipline revisited: Nonlinear effects and variation by culture, context, and gender. *Psychological Inquiry, 8,* 161-175.

Demi, A. S. (1989). Death of a spouse. In R. A. Kalish (Ed.), *Midlife loss: Coping strategies* (pp. 218-248). Newbury Park, CA: Sage.

Derby, C. A., Winkleby, M. A., Lapane, K. L., & Stone, E. J. (1997). Community-based prevention studies: Intervention lessons for women. In S. E. Gallant & G. P. Keita (Eds.), *Health care for women: Psychological, social, and behavioral influences* (pp. 405-424). Washington, DC: American Psychological Association.

DeRossa, P., & Johnson, U. (1992). *10 C's Model of Awareness and Change.* Boston: Teens Against Gang Violence. Retrieved March 11, 2001 from the World Wide Web: http://www.tagv.org/tencs.htm

DeShazer, S. (1985). *Keys to solutions in brief therapy.* New York: Norton.

de Toledo, S., & Brown, D. E. (1995). *Grandparents as parents: A survival guide for raising a second family.* New York: Guilford.

deWilde, E. J., Kienhorst, I. C. W. M., Diekstra, R. F. W., & Wolters, W. H. G. (1992). The relationship between adolescent suicidal behavior and life events in childhood and adolescence. *American Journal of Psychiatry, 149,* 45-51.

Diekstra, R. F. (1989). Suicidal behavior and depressive disorders in adolescents and young adults. *Neuropsychobiology, 22*(4), 194-207.

Dinkmeyer, D., & McKay, G. D. (1976). *Systematic training for effective parenting.* Circle Pines, MN: American Guidance Services.

Dinkmeyer, D., McKay, G. D., & Dinkmeyer, J. S. (1989). *Parenting young children: Helpful strategies based on STEP for parents of children under six.* Circle Pines, MN: American Guidance Services.

Dinkmeyer, D., McKay, G. D., & Dinkmeyer, J. S. (1998). *Parenting teenagers: Systematic training for effective parenting of teens.* Circle Pines, MN: American Guidance Services.

Dixon, D. N., & Scheckel, J. R. (1996). Gifted adolescent suicide: The empirical base. *Journal of Secondary Gifted Education, 7*(3), 386-392.

Doress, P. B., & Siegal, D. L. (1987). *Ourselves, growing older.* New York: Simon & Schuster.

Dougherty, A. M. (1990). *Consultation: Practice and perspectives.* Pacific Grove, CA: Brooks/Cole.

Dreman, S. (2000). The influence of divorce on children. *Journal of Divorce & Remarriage, 32*, 41-71.

Drum, D. J., & Baron, A. (1998, November). *Highlights of the research consortium outcomes project.* Paper presented at the annual meeting of the Research Consortium of Counseling and Psychological Services in Higher Education held in conjunction with the annual meeting of the Association of University and College Counseling Center Directors, Santa Fe, NM.

Drum, D. J., & Lawler, A. C. (1988). *Developmental interventions: Theories, principles, and practice.* Columbus, OH: Merrill.

Dryfoos, J. G. (1993). Preventing substance abuse: Rethinking strategies. *American Journal of Public Health, 83*, 793-795.

Ducat, D. (1999). *Turning points: The career guide for the new century.* Upper Saddle River, NJ: Prentice Hall.

Dukes, R. L., Ullman, J. B., & Stein, J. S. (1996). Three-year follow-up of Drug Abuse Resistance Education (DARE). *Evaluation Review, 20*, 49-66.

Dumas, J. E., Rollock, D., Prinz, R. J., Hops, H., & Blechman, E. A. (1999). Cultural sensitivity: Problems and solutions in applied and preventive intervention. *Applied and Preventive Psychology, 8*, 175-196.

Dunford, F., Huizinga, D., & Elliot, D. (1990). The role of arrest in domestic assault: The Omaha police experiment. *Criminology, 28*, 183-206.

DuRant, R. H., Treiber, F., Getts, A., McCloud, K., Linder, C. W., & Woods, E. R. (1996). Comparisons of two violence prevention curricula for middle school adolescents. *Journal of Adolescent Health, 19*, 111-117.

Durlak, J. (1980). Comparative effectiveness of behavioral and relationship group treatment in the secondary prevention of school maladjustment. *American Journal of Community Psychology, 8*, 327-339.

Durlak, J. A. (1995). *School-based prevention programs for children and adolescents.* Thousand Oaks, CA: Sage.

Durlak, J. A., & Wells, A. M. (1997). Primary prevention mental health programs for children and adolescents: A meta-analytic review. *American Journal of Community Psychology, 25*(2), 115-152.

Dutton, M. A. (1992). *Healing the trauma of woman battering: Assessment and intervention.* New York: Springer-Verlag.

Dworkin, S. H., & Kerr, B. A. (1987). Comparison of interventions for women experiencing body image problems. *Journal of Counseling Psychology, 34*, 136-140.

Dykeman, C., & Appleton, V. (1999). Family theory. In D. Capuzzi & D. R. Gross (Eds.), *Counseling and psychotherapy* (2nd ed., pp. 319-343). Upper Saddle River, NJ: Prentice Hall.

D'Zurilla, T. J., & Goldfried, M. R. (1971). Problem solving and behavior modification. *Journal of Abnormal Psychology, 78*, 107-126.

Eanes, B. E. (1997). Creating one's personal meaning throughout the cycles of life: Its development in career, professional, and faith realms. In D. P. & L. J. Richmond, *Connections between spirit and work in career development* (pp. 27-46). Palo Alto, CA: Consulting Psychologists Press.

Ebata, A. T., & Moos, R. H. (1994). Coping and adjustment in distressed and healthy adolescents. *Journal of Applied Developmental Psychology, 17*, 33-54.

Ebert, B. W. (1987). Guide to conducting a psychological autopsy. *Professional Psychology: Research and Practice, 18*, 52-56.

Eby, L. T., & Buch, K. (1995). Job loss as career growth: Responses to involuntary career transitions. *Career Development Quarterly, 44*, 26-42.

Eby, L. T., & Russell, J. E. A. (2000). Predictors of employee willingness to relocate for the firm. *Journal of Vocational Behavior, 57,* 42-61.

Eby, L. T., DeMatteo, J. S., & Russell, J. E. A. (1997). Employment assistance needs of accompanying spouses following relocation. *Journal of Vocational Behavior, 50,* 291-307.

Eccles, J. S., Midgley, C., Wigfield, A., Buchanan, C. M., Reuman, D., Flanagan, C., & MacIver, D. (1993). Development during adolescence: The impact of stage-environment fit on young adolescents' experiences in schools and families. *American Psychologist, 48,* 90-101.

Eckert, P. (1989). *Jocks & burnouts: Social categories and identity in the high school.* New York: Teachers College Press.

Edwards, W., & von Winterfeldt, D. (1986). On cognitive illusions and their implications. In H. R. Arke & K. R. Hammond (Eds.), *Judgment and decision making: An interdisciplinary reader* (pp. 642-679). Cambridge, UK: Cambridge University Press.

Eggert, L. L., Thompson, E. A., Herting, J. R., & Nicholas, L. J. (1995). Reducing suicide potential among high risk youth: Tests of a school-based prevention program. *Suicide and Life-Threatening Behavior, 25*(2), 276-296.

Einzig, H. (1996). Parenting education and support. In R. Bayne, I. Horton, & J. Bimrose (Eds.), *New directions in counselling* (pp. 220-234). New York: Routledge.

Elias, M. J., Gara, M. A., Schuyler, T. F., Branden-Muller, L. R., & Sayette, M. A. (1994). The promotion of social competence: Longitudinal study of a preventive school-based program. *American Journal of Orthopsychiatry, 61,* 409-417.

Ellickson, P. L., Bell, R. M., & McGuigan, K. (1993). Preventing adolescent drug use: Long-term results of a junior high program. *American Journal of Public Health, 86,* 856-861.

Elliott, J. E. (1993). Career development with lesbian and gay clients. *Career Development Quarterly, 41,* 210-226.

Emery, R. E. (1988). *Marriage, divorce and children's adjustment.* Newbury Park, CA: Sage.

Emery, R. E., & Forehand, R. (1993). Parental divorce and children's well being: A focus on resilience. In R. J. Haggerty, M. Rutter, & L. Sherrod (Eds.), *Risk and resilience in children* (pp. 56-85). London: Cambridge University Press.

Emery, R. E., & Laumann-Billings, L. (1998). An overview of the nature, causes, and consequences of abusive family relationships: Toward differentiating maltreatment and violence. *American Psychologist, 53,* 121-135.

Enns, C. Z., Campbell, J., & Courtois, C. A. (1997). Recommendations for working with domestic violence survivors, with special attention to memory issues and posttraumatic processes. *Psychotherapy, 34,* 459-477.

Enns, C. Z., Campbell, J., Courtois, C. A., Gottlief, M. C., Lese, K. P., Gilbert, M. S., & Forrest, L. (1998). Working with adult clients who may have experienced childhood abuse: Recommendations for assessment and practice. *Professional Psychology: Research and Practice, 29,* 245-256.

Epstein, C. F. (1970). *Woman's place.* Berkeley: University of California Press.

Erikson, E. H. (1963). *Childhood and society* (2nd ed.). New York: Norton.

Erikson, E. H. (1968). *Identity, youth, and crisis.* New York: Norton.

Erikson, E. H., Erikson, J. M., & Kivnick, H. Q. (1986). *Vital involvement in old age: The experience of old age in our time.* New York: Norton.

Erwin, T. D. (1991). *Assessing student learning and development: A guide to the principles, goals, and methods of determining college outcomes.* San Francisco: Jossey-Bass.

Escobedo, L. G., Giles, W. H., & Anda, R. F. (1997). Socioeconomic status, race, and death from coronary heart disease. *American Journal of Preventive Medicine, 13,* 123-30.

Evanow, M. (2000). *Innovations in adolescent anger management: Action theater as a vehicle for learning.* Paper presented at the 12th Annual School of Education Conference, University of Wisconsin at Milwaukee.

Everard, K. M., Lach, H. W., Fisher, E. B., & Baum, C. M. (2000). Relationship of activity and social support to the functional health of older adults. *Journals of Gerontology: Series B: Psychological Sciences and Social Sciences, 55B,* S208-S212.

Everett, S. A., & Price, J. H. (1995). Student's perceptions of violence in the public schools: The Metlife survey. *Journal of Adolescent Health, 17,* 345-352.

Farrell, A. D., & Meyer, A. L. (1997). The effectiveness of a school-based curriculum for reducing violence among urban sixth-grade students. *American Journal of Public Health, 87,* 979-984.

Farrell, M. P., & Rosenberg, S. D. (1981). *Men in midlife.* Boston: Auburn House.

Farrington, D. P. (1992). The need for longitudinal-experimental research on offending and antisocial behavior. In J. McCord & R. E. Tremblay (Eds.), *Preventing antisocial behavior* (pp. 353-376). New York: Guilford.

Fassinger, R. E., & Schlossberg, N. K. (1992). In S. D. Brown & R. W. Lent (Eds.), *Handbook of counseling psychology* (2nd ed., pp. 217-249). New York: John Wiley.

Federal Bureau of Investigation. (1993). *Uniform crime reports for the United States: Crime in the United States, 1992.* Washington, DC: Government Printing Office.

Federal Interagency Forum on Aging-Related Statistics. (2000). *Older Americans 2000; Key indicators of well-being.* Hyattsville, MD: Author. Retrieved November 5, 2000 from the World Wide Web: http://www.agingstats.gov/chartbook2000

Feindler, E. L., & Becker, J. V. (1994). Interventions in family violence involving children and adolescents. In L. D. Eron, J. H. Gentry, & P. Schlegel (Eds.), *Reason to hope: A psychosocial perspective on violence and youth* (pp. 405-430). Washington, DC: American Psychological Association.

Feingold, A., & Mazzella, R. (1998). Gender differences in body image are increasing. *Psychological Science, 9,* 190-195.

Felner, R., Lease, A. M., & Phillips, R. S. C. (1990). Social competence and the language of adequacy as a subject matter for psychology: A quadripartite trilevel framework. In T. P. Gullotta, G. R. Adams, & R. Montemayor (Eds.), *Developing social competency in adolescence* (pp. 245-264). Newbury Park, CA: Sage.

Fine, M. J., & Gardner, P. A. (1991). Counseling and education services for families: An empowerment perspective. *Elementary School Guidance & Counseling, 26,* 33-44.

Finkelhor, D., & Dzuiba-Leatherman, J. (1994). Victimization of children. *American Psychologist, 49,* 173-183.

Fischer, A. R., & Good, G. E., (1997). Men in psychotherapy: An investigation of alexithymia, intimacy, and masculine gender roles. *Psychotherapy, 34,* 160-170.

Fisher, E., & Thompson, J. K. (1994). A comparative evaluation of cognitive-behavioral therapy (CBT) versus exercise therapy (ET) for the treatment of body image disturbance. *Behavior Modification, 18,* 171-185.

Fisher, J. D., & Fisher, W. A., (1992). Changing AIDS-risk behavior. *Psychological Bulletin, 111*, 455-474.

Fiske, M., & Chiriboga, D. A. (1990). *Change and continuity in adult life.* San Francisco: Jossey-Bass.

Fitzgerald, L. F., & Osipow, S. H. (1986). An occupational analysis of counseling psychology: How special is the specialty? *American Psychologist, 41*, 534-544.

Flinn, S. K., Shah, J., Davis, L., Zare, R., & Pasarell, S. (1998). Adolescent pregnancy and too-early childbearing. In A. Henderson & S. Champlin (Eds.), *Promoting teen health: Linking schools, health organizations, and the community* (pp. 132-150). Thousand Oaks, CA: Sage.

Flum, H. (1994). The evolution style of identity formation. *Journal of Youth and Adolescence, 23*, 489-498.

Foa, E. B., & Rothbaum, B. O. (1998). *Treating the trauma of rape: Cognitive-behavioral therapy for PTSD.* New York: Guilford.

Foa, E. B., Dancu, C. V., Hembree, E. A., Jaycox, L. H., Meadows, E. A., & Street, G. P. (1999). A comparison of exposure therapy, stress inoculation training, and their combination for reducing posttraumatic stress disorder in female assault victims. *Journal of Consulting & Clinical Psychology, 67*, 194-200.

Foos, J. A., Ottens, A. J., & Hill, L. K. (1991). Managed mental health: A primer for counselors. *Journal of Counseling and Development, 69*, 332-336.

Ford, D. H., & Lerner, R. M. (1992). *Developmental Systems Theory: An integrative approach.* Newbury Park, CA: Sage.

Ford, M. E., & Ford, D. H. (1987). Humans as self-constructing living systems: An overview. In M. E. Ford & D. H. Ford (Eds.), *Humans as self-constructing living systems: Putting the framework to work* (pp. 1-46). Hillsdale, NJ: Lawrence Erlbaum.

Forehand, R. (1993a). Family psychopathology and child functioning. *Journal of Child and Family Studies, 2*, 79-85.

Forehand, R. (1993b). Twenty years of research on parenting: Does it have practical implications for clinicians working with parents and children? *The Clinical Psychologist, 46*, 169-176.

Forehand, R., Wierson, M., Thomas, A. M., Armistead, L., Kempton, T., & Neighbors, B. (1990). The role of family stressors and parent relationships in adolescent functioning. *Journal of the American Academy of Child Adolescent Psychiatry, 30*, 316-322.

Fouad, N. A., & Smith, P. L. (1996). A test of a social cognitive model of middle school students: Math and science. *Journal of Counseling Psychology, 43*, 338-346.

Foubert, J. D., & McEwen, M. K. (1998). An all-male rape prevention peer education program: Decreasing fraternity men's behavioral intent to rape. *Journal of College Student Development, 39*, 548-556.

Fowler, J. W. (1984). *Stages of faith: The psychology of human development and Christian faith.* San Francisco: Harper.

Fox, G. L., Bruce, C., & Combs-Orme, T. (2000). Parenting expectations and concerns of fathers and mothers of newborn infants. *Family Relations, 49*, 123-131.

Fox, R. L. (2000). *America's 100 best places to retire* (2nd ed.). Houston: Vacation.

Frank, E., & Stewart, B. D. (1984). Depressive symptoms in rape victims: A revisit. *Journal of Affective Disorders, 7*, 77-85.

Frankenburg, W. K., Dodd, J. B., & Fandal, A. W. (1973). *Denver developmental screening test.* Denver, CO: Ladora Project.

Franko, D. L. (1998). Secondary prevention of eating disorders in college women at risk. *Eating Disorders, 6,* 29-40.

Fretz, B. R., Kluge, N. A., Ossana, S. M., Jones, S. M., & Merikangas, M. W. (1989). Intervention targets for reducing preretirement anxiety and depression. *Journal of Counseling Psychology, 36,* 301-307.

Freud, S. (1905). Three essays on the theory of sexuality. In J. Strachey (Ed. and Trans.), *The standard edition of the complete psychological works of Sigmund Freud.* London: Hogarth.

Freyd, J. J. (1996). *Betrayal trauma: The logic of forgetting child abuse.* Cambridge, MA: Harvard University Press.

Friedan, B. (1993). *The fountain of age.* New York: Simon & Schuster.

Friedman, J. M., Asnis, G. M., Boeck, M., & DiFiore, J. (1987). Prevalence of specific suicidal behaviors in a high school sample. *American Journal of Psychiatry, 144,* 1203-1206.

Friedman, S. S. (1996). Girls in the 90s. *Eating Disorders, 4,* 238-244.

Friedman, S. S. (1999). *Just for girls.* Vancouver, Canada: Salal.

Friedrich, W. N. (1996). An integrated model of psychotherapy for abused children. In J. Briere, L. Berliner, J. A. Bulkley, C. Jenny, & T. Reid (Eds.), *The APSAC handbook on child maltreatment* (pp. 104-118). Thousand Oaks, CA: Sage.

Frone, M. R., Russell, M., & Cooper, M. L. (1993). Relationship of work-family conflict, gender, and alcohol expectancies to alcohol use/abuse. *Journal of Organizational Behavior, 14,* 545-558.

Fry, C. L. (1996). Age, aging and culture. In R. H. Binstock & L. K. George (Eds.), *Handbook of aging and the social sciences* (4th ed., pp. 117-136). San Diego, CA: Academic Press.

Fuller-Thomson, E., Minkler, M., & Driver, D. (1997). A profile of grandparents raising grandchildren in the United States. *The Gerontologist, 37,* 406-411.

Fullner, W. (1996). *Primer on personal money management. Women: Take charge of your money!* Washington, DC: American Association of Retired Persons.

Fusco, M. A. C. (1990). Employment relations programs. *Employment Relations Today, 17,* 79-82.

Gainor, K. A., & Lent, R. W. (1998). Social cognitive expectations and racial identity attitudes in predicting the math choice intentions of Black college students. *Journal of Counseling Psychology, 45,* 403-413.

Gallagher-Thompson, D., Lovett, S., Rose, J., McKibbin, C., Coon, D., Futterman, A., & Thompson, L. W. (2000). Impact of psychoeducational interventions on distressed family caregivers. *Journal of Clinical Gerontology, 6*(2), 91-110.

Gallos, J. V. (1989). Exploring women's development: Implications for career theory, practice, and research. In M. B Arthur & D. T. Hall (Eds.), *Handbook of career theory* (pp. 110-132). Cambridge, UK: Cambridge University Press.

Garbarino, J. (1990). The human ecology of early risk. In S. J. Meisels & J. P. Shonkoff (Eds.), *Handbook of early childhood intervention* (pp. 78-96). New York: Cambridge University Press.

Garbarino, J. (1995). *Raising children in a socially toxic environment.* San Francisco: Jossey-Bass.

Garbarino, J. (1999). *Lost boys: Why our sons turn violent and how we can save them.* New York: Free Press.

Garland, A. F., & Zigler, E. (1993). Adolescent suicide prevention: Current research and social policy implications. *American Psychologist, 48,* 169-182.

Garmezy, N., Masten, A. S., & Tellegan, A. (1984). The study of stress and competence in children: Building blocks for developmental psychology. *Child Development, 55,* 97-111.

Garner, D. M. (1991). *Eating Disorder Inventory-2.* Odessa, FL: Psychological Assessment Resources.

Garner, D. M. (1997). The *Psychology Today* 1997 body image survey results. *Psychology Today, 30,* 32-84.

Garrod, A., Smulyan, L., Powers, S. I., & Kilkenny, R. (1999). *Adolescent portraits: Identity, relationships, and challenges* (3rd ed.). Boston: Allyn & Bacon.

Garvin, V., Leber, D., & Kalter, N. (1991). Children of divorce: Predictors of change following preventive intervention. *American Journal of Orthopsychiatry, 61,* 438-447.

Gately, D., & Schwebel, A. I. (1992). Favorable outcomes in children after parental divorce. *Journal of Divorce & Remarriage, 17,* 57-78.

Gauthier, L. M., & Levendosky, A. A. (1996). Assessment and treatment of couples with abusive male partners: Guidelines for therapists. *Psychotherapy, 33,* 403-417.

Gavin, L. A., & Furman, W. (1989). Age differences in adolescent perceptions of their peer groups. *Developmental Psychology, 25,* 827-834.

Gelso, C. J., & Fretz, B. R. (1992). *Counseling psychology.* Fort Worth, TX: Harcourt Brace Jovanovich.

Gerken, D., Reardon, R., & Bash, R. (1988). Revitalizing a career course: The gender roles infusion. *Journal of Career Development, 14,* 269-278.

Gibson, D. B., & Humphrey, C. F. (1993). *Educating in regards to sexual violence: An interactional dramatic acquaintance rape intervention.* Unpublished manuscript, University of Minnesota, Sexual Violence Program, Minneapolis.

Gibson, P. (1989). Gay male and lesbian youth suicide. In ADAMHA, *Report of the Secretary's Task Force on Youth Suicide* (DHHS Publication No. ADM 89-1623, Vol. 3, pp. 110-142). Washington, DC: Government Printing Office.

Gilbert, G. J., Heesacker, M., & Gannon, L. J. (1991). Changing the sexual aggression-supportive attitudes of men: A psychoeducational intervention. *Journal of Counseling Psychology, 38,* 197-203.

Gilbert, L. A. (1988). *Sharing it all: The rewards and struggles of two-career families.* New York: Plenum.

Gilbert, L. A., & Brownson, C. (1998). Current perspectives on women's multiple roles. *Journal of Career Assessment, 6,* 433-448.

Gilbert, L. A., Hallett, M., & Eldridge, N. S. (1994). Gender and dual-career families: Implications and applications for the career counseling of women. In W. B. Walsh & S. H. Osipow (Eds.), *Career counseling for women* (pp. 135-164). Hillsdale, NJ: Lawrence Erlbaum.

Gilkes, C. T. (1982). Successful rebellious professionals: The Black woman's professional identity and community commitment. *Psychology of Women Quarterly, 6,* 289-311.

Gilligan, C. (1982). *In a different voice: Psychological theory and women's development.* Cambridge, MA: Harvard University Press.

Gilligan, C. (1988). Remapping the moral domain: New images of self in relationship. In C. Gilligan, J. V. Ward, & J. M. Taylor (Eds.), *Mapping the moral domain* (pp. 480-495). Cambridge, MA: Harvard University Press.

Gladding, S. T. (1996). *Counseling: A comprehensive profession* (3rd ed.). Englewood Cliffs, NJ: Prentice Hall.

Gladding, S. T. (1999). Groups for adults. In S. T. Gladding, *Group work: A counseling specialty* (3rd ed., pp. 290-319). Upper Saddle River, NJ: Prentice Hall.

Gladding, S. T. (2000). Consultation. In S. T. Gladding, *Counseling: A comprehensive profession* (4th ed., pp. 459-478). Upper Saddle River, NJ: Prentice Hall.

Goldschmitt, M., Tipton, R. M., & Wiggins, R. C. (1981). Professional identity of counseling psychologists. *Journal of Counseling Psychology, 28,* 158-167.

Goldstein, A. P., & Conoley, J. C. (Eds.). (1997). *School violence intervention.* New York: Guilford.

Goncalves, O. F. (1995). Cognitive narrative psychotherapy: The hermeneutic construction of alternative meanings. In M. J. Mahoney (Ed.), *Cognitive and constructive psychotherapies: Theory, research, and practice* (pp. 139-162). New York: Springer-Verlag.

Goode, W. (1960). A theory of role strain. *American Sociological Review, 25,* 483-496.

Gordon, K. A. (1995). Self-concept and motivational patterns of resilient African American high school students. *Journal of Black Psychology, 21,* 239-255.

Gordon, K. A. (1996). Resilient Hispanic youths' self-concept and motivational patterns. *Hispanic Journal of Behavioral Sciences, 18,* 63-73.

Gordon, R. S., Jr. (1983). An operational classification of disease prevention. *Public Health Reports, 98*(2), 107-109.

Gordon, T. (1970). *Parent effectiveness training: The "no-lose" program for raising responsible children.* New York: Peter H. Wyden.

Gornick, M. E., Eggers, P. W., Reilly, T. W., Mentnech, R. M., Fitterman, L. K., Kucken, L. E., & Vladeck, B. C. (1996). Effects of race and income on mortality and use of services among Medicare beneficiaries. *New England Journal of Medicine, 335,* 791-799.

Gossens, L., & Phinney. J. S. (1996). Commentary: Identity, context, and development. *Journal of Adolescence, 19,* 491-496.

Gott, C. M. (1999). Sexual risk-taking in later life. *Reviews in Clinical Gerontology, 9*(2), 139-150.

Gottfredson, L. S. (1981). Circumscription and compromise: A developmental theory of occupational aspirations. *Journal of Counseling Psychology, 28,* 545-579.

Graber, J. A., & Brooks-Gunn, J. (1996). Transitions and turning points: Navigating the passage from childhood through adolescence. *Developmental Psychology, 32,* 768-776.

Grant, J. R., & Cash, T. F. (1995). Cognitive-behavioral body image therapy: Comparative efficacy of group and modest-contact treatments. *Behavior Therapy, 26,* 69-84.

Green, R., Boots, S. W., & Tumoin, K. C. (1997). *The cost of protecting vulnerable children: Understanidng federal, state, and local child welfare spending.* Washington, DC: Urban Institute. Retrieved March 19, 2001 from the World Wide Web: http://newfederalism.urban.org/html/occa20.html#total

Greenglass, E. R. (1993). The contribution of social support to coping strategies. *Applied Psychology: An International Review, 42,* 323-340.

Greenglass, E. R., Pantony, K., & Burke, R. J. (1988). A gender-role perspective on role conflict, work stress and social support. *Journal of Social Behavior and Personality, 3,* 317-328.

Greenhaus, J. H., & Beutell, N. J. (1985). Sources of conflict between work and family roles. *Academy of Management Review, 10,* 76-88.

Groholt, B., Ekeberg, O., Wichstrom, L., & Haldorsen, T. (1997). Youth suicide in Norway, 1990-1992: A comparison between children and adolescents completing suicide and age- and gender-matched controls. *Suicide and Life-Threatening Behavior, 27,* 250-263.

Grubb, H. J., Sellers, M. I., & Waligroski, K. (1993). Factors related to depression and eating disorders: Self-esteem, body image, and attractiveness. *Psychological Reports, 72,* 1003-1010.

Grunbaum, J., Kann, L., Kinchen, S., Ross, J., Gowda, V., Collins, J., & Kolbe, L. (1999). Youth risk behavior surveillance: National alternative high school youth risk behavior survey, United States, 1998. *Morbidity and Mortality Weekly Report, Surveillance Summary 48,* 1-44.

Grusec, J. E., & Lytton, H. (1988). Social development: History, theory and research. New York: Springer-Verlag-Verlag.

Grynch, J. H., & Fincham, F. D. (1992). Interventions for children of divorce: Toward greater integration of research and action. *Psychological Bulletin, 111,* 434-454.

Guernsey, L. (1996, December 13). U.S. judge says mandatory fees at U. of Wisconsin violated first amendment. *Chronicle of Higher Education,* p. A-32.

Guerra, N. G., Tolan, P. H., & Hammond, W. R. (1994). Prevention and treatment of adolescent violence. In L. D. Eron, J. H. Gentry, & P. Schlegel (Eds.), *Reason to hope: A psychosocial perspective on violence and youth* (pp. 383-403). Washington, DC: American Psychological Association.

Guiliano, J. D. (1994). A peer education program to promote the use of conflict resolution skills among at-risk school age males. *Public Health Reports, 109,* 158-161.

Gullotta, T. P., Adams, G. R., & Markstrom, C. A. (2000). *The adolescent experience.* San Diego, CA: Academic Press.

Gutierrez, M. (1996). *Comparisons of interparental conflict, parent-child relationship, discipline, social support and children's adjustment to divorce between Latino and Anglo children.* Unpublished doctoral dissertation, University of California at Santa Barbara.

Gysbers, N. C., Heppner, M. J., & Johnston, J. A. (1998). *Career counseling: Process, issues and techniques.* Boston: Allyn & Bacon.

Hall, G. C. N., Sue, S., Narang, D. S., & Lilly, R. S. (2000). Culture-specific models of men's sexual aggression: Intra- and interpersonal determinants. *Cultural Diversity and Ethnic Minority Psychology, 6,* 252-267.

Hall, G. S. (1904). *Adolescence: Its psychology and its relations to physiology, anthropology, sociology, sex, crime, religion and education* (Vols. 1-2). Englewood Cliffs, NJ: Prentice Hall.

Hallett, M. B., & Carter, A. L. (1995, February). *Experiencing and expressing emotion: A structured theme group approach to working with affect.* Paper presented at the Big Ten Counseling Center Conference, Ann Arbor, MI.

Hallett, M. B., & Shan-Dechaine, T. (1992). *Women, identity, and intimacy with men.* Unpublished manuscript, University of Texas at Austin.

Hammack, F. M. (1986). Large school systems' dropout reports: An analysis of definitions, procedures, and findings. *Teachers College Record, 87,* 324-341.

Hammond, W. R., & Yung, B. (1991). Preventing violence in at-risk African American youth. *Journal of Health Care for the Poor and Underserved, 2,* 359-373.

Hammond, W. R., & Yung, B. (1993). *Evaluation and activity report: Positive adolescent choices training* (Unpublished grant report). Washington, DC: U.S. Maternal and Child Health Bureau.

Hansen, W. B. (1992). School-based substance abuse prevention: A review of the state of the art in curriculum, 1980-1990. *Health Education Research, 7,* 403-430.

Hanson, G., & Venturelli, P. (1998). *Drugs and society.* Boston: Jones & Bartlett.

Hanson, R. O., & Hayslip, B., Jr. (2000). Widowhood in later life. In J. H. Harvey, & E. D. Miller (Eds.), *Loss and trauma: General and close relationship perspectives* (pp. 345-357). Philadelphia: Brunner-Routledge.

Harrington, D., & Dubowitz, H. (1999). Preventing child maltreatment. In R. L. Hampton (Ed.), *Family violence: Prevention and treatment* (2nd ed., pp. 122-147). Thousand Oaks, CA: Sage.

Harris, S. M., Dersch, C. A., Kimball, T. G., Marshall, J. P., & Negretti, M. A. (1999). Internet resources for older adults with sexual concerns. *Journal of Sex Education and Therapy, 24*(3), 183-188.

Harry, B. (1997). Leaning forward or bending over backwards: Cultural reciprocity in working with families. *Journal of Early Intervention, 21,* 62-72.

Harry, J. (1989). Sexual identity issues. In ADAMHA, *Report of the Secretary's Task Force on Youth Suicide* (DHHS Publication No. ADM 89-1622, Vol. 2, pp. 131-142). Washington, DC: U.S. Government Printing Office.

Harry, J. (1991). Sexual identity issues. In L. Davidson & M. Linnoila (Eds.), *Risk factors for youth suicide* (pp. 115-122). New York: Hemisphere.

Hartup, W. W. (1992). Friendships and their developmental significance. In H. McGurk (Ed.), *Childhood social development: Contemporary perspectives* (pp. 175-205). Hove, UK: Lawrence Erlbaum.

Hausman, A., Pierce, G., & Briggs, L. (1996). Evaluation of comprehensive violence prevention education: Effects on student behavior. *Journal of Adolescent Health, 19,* 104-110.

Hawkins, J. D., Catalano, R. F., & Miller, J. Y. (1992). Risk and protective factors for alcohol and other drug problems in adolescence and early adulthood: Implications for substance abuse prevention. *Psychological Bulletin, 112*(1), 64-105.

Hawkins, J. D., Catalano, R. F., & Morrison, D. M. (1989, August). *Seattle social development project: Cumulative effects of intervention in grades 1-4.* Paper presented at the meeting of the Society for Research on Child Development, Kansas City, MO.

Hawkins, J. D., Lishner, D. M., Catalano, R. F., & Howard, M. O. (1985). Childhood predictors of adolescent substance abuse: Toward an empirically grounded theory. *Journal of Children in Contemporary Society, 18*(1-2), 11-48.

Hayes, C. L., & Anderson, D. (1993). Psycho-social and economic adjustment of midlife women after divorce: A national study. *Journal of Women and Aging, 4,* 83-99.

Hayes, C. L., & Deren, J. M. (Eds.). (1990). *Pre-retirement planning for women: Program design and research.* New York: Springer-Verlag.

Heath, S. B., & McLaughlin, M. W. (1993). *Identity and inner-city youth: Beyond ethnicity and gender.* New York: Teachers College Press.

Heinberg, L. J. (1996). Theories of body image disturbance: Perceptual, developmental and sociocultural factors. In J. K. Thompson (Ed.), *Body image, eating disorders, and obesity* (pp. 27-47). Washington, DC: American Psychological Association.

Helms, J. E., & Cook, D. (1999). *Using race and culture in counseling and psychotherapy: Theory and process.* Boston: Allyn & Bacon.

Helsen, M., Vollebergh, W., & Meeus, W. (2000). Social support from parents and friends and emotional problems in adolescence. *Journal of Youth and Adolescence, 29,* 319-335.

Henderson, N., & Milstein, M. M. (1996). *Resiliency in schools: Making it happen for students and educators.* Thousand Oaks, CA: Corwin.

Hendin, H. (1987). Youth suicide: A psychosocial perspective. *Suicide and Life-Threatening Behavior, 17,* 151-165.

Hendin, H. (1991). Psychodynamics of suicide, with particular reference to the young. *American Journal of Psychiatry, 148*(9), 1150-1158.

Heppner, M. J., Good, G. E., Hillenbrand-Gunn, T. L., Hawkins, A. K., Hacquard, L. L., Nichols, R. K., DeBord, K. A., & Brock, K. J. (1995). Examining sex differences in altering attitudes about rape: A test of the Elaboration Likelihood Model. *Journal of Counseling and Development, 73,* 640-647.

Heppner, M. J., Humphrey, C. F., Hillenbrand-Gunn, T. L., & DeBord, K. A. (1995). The differential effects of rape prevention programming on attitudes, behaviors, and knowledge. *Journal of Counseling Psychology, 42,* 508-518.

Heppner, M. J., Neville, H. A., Smith, K., Kivlighan, D. M., & Gershuny, B.S. (1999). Examining immediate and long-term efficacy of rape prevention programming with racially diverse college men. *Journal of Counseling Psychology, 46,* 16-26.

Herman, J. L. (1992). *Trauma and recovery.* New York: Basic Books.

Hermans, H. J. M. (1987). Self as an organized system of valuations: Toward a dialogue with the person. *Journal of Counseling Psychology, 34,* 10-19.

Hermans, H. J. M. (1988). On the integration of ideographic and nomothetic research method in the study of personal meaning. *Journal of Personality, 56,* 785-812.

Hermans, H. J. M. (1989). The meaning of life as an organized process. *Psychotherapy, 26,* 11-22.

Hermans, H. J. M. (1992). Unhappy self-esteem: A meaningful exception to the rule. *Journal of Psychology, 126,* 555-570.

Hermans, H. J. M. (1995). From assessment to change: The personal meaning of clinical problems in the context of the self narrative. In R. A. Neimeyer & M. J. Mahoney (Eds.), *Constructivism in psychotherapy* (pp. 247-272). Washington, DC: American Psychological Association.

Hermans, H. J. M. (1996). The personal meaning of values: Continuity-discontinuity of value experience. *Polish Psychological Bulletin, 27,* 301-317.

Hermans, H. J. M. (1997). Dissociation as disorganized self-narrative: Tension between splitting and integration. *Journal of Psychotherapy Integration, 7,* 213-223.

Hermans, H. J. M., Fiddelaers, R., de Groot, R., & Nauta, J. F. (1990). Self-confrontation for assessment and intervention in counseling. *Journal of Counseling and Development, 69,* 156-162.

Hermans, H. J. M., & Hermans-Jansen, E. (1995). *Self-narratives: The construction of meaning in psychotherapy.* New York: Guilford.

Hermans, H. J. M., Hermans-Jansen, E., & Van Gilst, W. (1987). The *fugit amour* experience in the process of valuation: A self-confrontation with an unreachable other. *British Journal of Psychology, 78,* 465-481.

Hermans, H. J. M., & Oles, P. K. (1996). Value crisis: Affective organization of personal meanings. *Journal of Research in Personality, 30,* 457-482.

Hermans, H. J. M., & Oles, P. K. (1999). Midlife crisis in men: Affective organization of personal meanings. *Human Relations, 52,* 1403-1426.

Hersch, L. (1995). Adapting to health care reform and managed care: Three strategies for survival and growth. *Professional Psychology: Research and Practice, 26,* 16-26.

Hershberger, S. L., & D'Augelli, A. R. (1995). The impact of victimization on the mental health and suicidality of lesbian, gay, and bisexual youths. *Developmental Psychology, 31*(1), 65-74.

Herz, F. (1989). The postdivorce family. In B. Carter & M. McGoldrick (Eds.), *The changing family life cycle.* Boston: Allyn & Bacon.

Herzberg, D. S., Hammen, C., Burge, D., Daley, S. E., Davila, J., & Lindberg, N. (1998). Social competence as a predictor of chronic interpersonal stress. *Personal Relationships, 5,* 207-218.

Hetherington, E. M., Law, T. C., & O'Connor, T. G. (1993). Divorce: Challenges, changes and new chances. In F. Walsh (Ed.), *Normal family processes* (2nd ed., pp. 208-234). New York: Guilford.

Hibbard, J. H., & Pope, C. R. (1991). Effect of domestic and occupational roles on morbidity and mortality. *Social Science and Medicine, 32,* 805-811.

Higgins, N. C. (1986). Occupational stress and working women: The effectiveness of two stress reduction programs. *Journal of Vocational Behavior, 29,* 66-78.

Hill, A. J., Oliver, S., & Rogers, P. J. (1992). Eating in the adult world: The rise of dieting in childhood and adolescence. *British Journal of Clinical Psychology, 31,* 95-105.

Hillenbrand-Gunn, T. L. (1995). *An examination of rape preventive interventions.* Unpublished master's thesis, University of Missouri-Columbia.

Hillman, J. L. (2000). *Clinical perspectives on elderly sexuality.* New York: Plenum.

Hively, R. (Ed.). (1990). *The lurking evil: Racial and ethnic conflict on the college campus.* Washington DC: American Association of State Colleges and Universities.

Hobfoll, S. E. (1989). A new attempt at conceptualizing stress. *American Psychologist, 44,* 513-524.

Hodges, E. L., Cochrane, C. E., & Brewerton, T. D. (1998). Family characteristics of binge-eating disorder patients. *International Journal of Eating Disorders, 23,* 145-151.

Hoff, L. A. (1989). *People in crisis: Understanding and helping* (3rd ed.). Redwood City, CA: Addison-Wesley.

Hoffman, L. W. (1996). Progress and problems in the study of adolescence. *Developmental Psychology, 32,* 777-780.

Hofstede, G. (1980). *Culture's consequences.* Beverly Hills, CA: Sage.

Holden, E. W., & Black, M. M. (1999). Theory and concepts of prevention science as applied to clinical psychology. *Clinical Psychology Review, 19,* 391-401.

Holland, A., & Andre, T. (1994). The relationship of self-esteem to selected personal and environmental resources of adolescents. *Adolescence, 29,* 345-360.

Holmes, T. H., & Rahe, R. H. (1967). The social readjustment rating scale. *Journal of Psychosomatic Research, 11,* 213-218.

Holzworth-Munroe, A., & Stuart, G. L. (1994). Typologies of male batterers. Three subtypes and the differences among them. *Psychological Bulletin, 116,* 476-497.

Home, A. M. (1998). Predicting role conflict, overload, and contagion in adult women university students with families and jobs. *Adult Education Quarterly, 48,* 85-97.

Hooyman, N., & Kiyak, H. (1988). *Social gerontology: A multidisciplinary perspective.* Boston: Allyn & Bacon.

Hooyman, N., & Kiyak, H. (1993). *Social gerontology: A multidisciplinary perspective* (3rd ed.). Needham Heights, MA: Allyn & Bacon.

Hovey, J. D., & King, C. A. (1996). Acculturative stress, depression and suicidal ideation among immigrant and second generation Latino adolescents. *Journal of American Academy of Child and Adolescent Psychiatry, 35,* 1183-1192.

Howard, G. S. (1991). Culture tales: A narrative approach to thinking, cross-cultural psychology and psychotherapy. *American Psychologist, 46,* 187-197.

Howard, K. A., Flora, J., & Griffin, M. (1999). Violence-prevention programs in schools: State of the science and implications for future research. *Applied and Preventive Psychology, 8,* 197-215.

Howard, S., Dryden, J., & Johnson, B. (1999). Childhood resilience: Review and critique of literature. *Oxford Review of Education, 25,* 307-323.

Howard-Pitney, B., LaFromboise, T. D., Basil, M., September, B., & Johnson, M. (1992). Psychological and social indicators of suicide ideation and suicide attempts in Zuni adolescents. *Journal of Consulting and Clinical Psychology, 60*(3), 473-476.

Hoyert, D. L., Kochanek, K. D., & Murphy, S. L. (1999). Deaths: Final data for 1997. *National Vital Statistics Report, 47*(19). (DHHS Publication No. PHS 99-1120). Hyattsville, MD: National Center for Health Statistics.

Huesmann, L., Eron, L., Lefkowitz, M., & Walder, L. (1984). Stability of aggression over time and generations. *Developmental Psychology, 20,* 1120-1134.

Hughes, D. L., & Galinsky, E. (1994). Gender, job and family conditions, and the psychological symptoms. *Psychology of Women Quarterly, 18,* 251-270.

Hughes, D., Galinsky, E., & Morris, A. (1992). The effects of job characteristics on marital quality: Specifying linking mechanisms. *Journal of Marriage and the Family, 54,* 31-42.

Humphreys, K., & Rappaport, J. (1993). From the community mental health movement to the war on drugs: A study in the definition of social problems. *American Psychologist, 48,* 892-901.

Hundley, M. E. (1993). *Awaken to good mourning.* Plano, TX: Awaken.

Hutchinson, M. G. (1994). Imagining ourselves whole: A feminist approach to treating body image disorders. In P. Fallon, M. A. Katzman, & S. C. Wooley (Eds.), *Feminist perspectives on eating disorders* (pp. 152-168). New York: Guilford.

Huyck, M. H. (1989). Midlife parental imperatives. In R. A. Kalish (Ed.), *Midlife loss: Coping strategies* (pp. 115-148). Newbury Park. CA: Sage.

Ikenberry, S. (1988, November). Our students know less than they should of the struggle for civil rights in our country. *Chronicle of Higher Education,* p. B5.

Irving, L. M. (2000). Promoting size acceptance in elementary school children: The EDAP puppet program. *Eating Disorders: The Journal of Treatment and Prevention, 8,* 221-232.

Isaacs, M. A. (1988). The visitation schedule and child adjustment: A three-year study. *Family Process, 27,* 251-256.

Isaacson, L. E., & Brown, D. (2000). *Career information, career counseling, and career development* (6th ed.). Boston: Allyn & Bacon.

Ivey, A. E., & Rigazio-DiGilio, S. A. (1991). Toward a developmental practice of mental health counseling: Strategies for training, practice, and political unity. *Journal of Mental Health Counseling, 13,* 21-36.

Jacob, T., Moser, R. P., Windle, M., Loeber, R., & Stouthamer-Loeber, M. (2000). A new measure of parenting practices involving preadolescent- and adolescent-aged children. *Behavior Modification, 24,* 611-634.

Jacobs, R. H. (1997). *Be an outrageous older woman.* New York: HarperCollins.

Jacobson, N., & Gottman, J. (1998). *When men batter women: New insights into ending abusive relationships.* New York: Simon & Schuster.

James, W. (1890). *The principles of psychology: Vol. 1.* London: Macmillan.

Jemmott, J. B., III, Jemmott, L. S., & Fong, G. T. (1992). Reductions in HIV risk-associated sexual behaviors among Black male adolescents: Effects of an AIDS prevention intervention. *American Journal of Public Health, 82,* 372-377.

Jendrek, M. P. (1993). Grandparents who parent their grandchildren: Effects on life-style. *Journal of Marriage and the Family, 55,* 609-621.

Johnson, D. W., Johnson, R., Dudley, B., & Acikgoz, K. (1994). Effects of conflict resolution training on elementary school students. *Journal of Social Psychology, 134,* 803-817.

Johnston, J. R., & Campbell, L. E. G. (1988). *Impasses of divorce.* New York: Free Press.

Johnston, L. D., O'Malley, P. M., & Bachman, J. G. (1998). *National survey results on drug use from monitoring the future study, 1975-1997: Vol. 1. Secondary school students.* Rockville, MD: National Institute on Drug Abuse.

Jorgensen, R. S., & Dusek, J. B. (1990). Adolescent adjustment and coping strategies. *Journal of Personality, 58,* 503-513.

Josephs, R. A., Markus, H. R., & Tafarodi, R. W. (1992). Gender and self-esteem. *Journal of Personality and Social Psychology, 63,* 391-402.

Josselson, R. (1994a). Identity and relatedness in the life cycle. In H. A. Bosma, T. L. G. Graafsma, H. D. Grotevant, & D. J. De Levita (Eds.), *Identity and development: An interdisciplinary approach* (pp. 81-102). Thousand Oaks, CA: Sage.

Josselson, R. (1994b). The theory of identity development and the question of intervention. In S. L. Archer (Ed.), *Interventions for adolescent identity development* (pp. 12-25). Thousand Oaks, CA: Sage.

Julien, R. M. (1998). *A primer of drug action* (8th ed.). New York: Freeman.

Juntunen, C. L., Cavett, A. M., Clow, R. B., & Suzen, D. (2000, April 14). *A qualitative study of career concerns among welfare recipients.* Paper presented at the Great Lakes Regional Conference of Division 17 of the American Psychological Association, Muncie, IN.

Kaitz, M., Chriki, M., Bear-Scharf, L., Nir, T., & Eidelman, A. I. (2000). Effectiveness of primiparae at soothing their newborn infants. *Journal of Genetic Psychology, 161,* 203-215.

Kalish, R. A. (Ed.). (1989). *Midlife loss: Coping strategies.* Newbury Park, CA: Sage.

Kalish, R. A., & Huyck, M. H. (1989). The T generation. In R. A. Kalish (Ed.), *Midlife loss: Coping strategies* (pp. 301-315). Newbury Park, CA: Sage.

Kann, L., Kinchen, S. A., Williams, B. I., Ross, J. G., Lowry, R., Hill, C. V., Grunbaum, J. A., Blumson, D. S., Collins, J. L., & Kolbe, J. L. (1998). Youth risk behavior surveillance: National alternative high school youth risk behavior survey, United States, 1997. *Morbidity and Mortality Weekly Report, 47,* 1-89.

Karambayya, R., & Reilly, A. H. (1992). Dual earner couples: Attitudes and actions in restructuring work for family. *Journal of Organizational Behavior, 13,* 585-601.

Karasek, R. A. (1979). Job demands, job decision latitude, and mental strain: Implications for job redesign. *Administrative Science Quarterly, 24,* 285-308.

Karkow, B., Germain, A., Tandberg, D., Koss, M., Schrader, R., Hollifield, M., Cheng, D., & Edmond, T. (2000). Sleep breathing and sleep movement disorders masquerading as insomnia in sexual-assault survivors. *Comprehensive Psychiatry, 41,* 49-56.

Kaslow, N. J., & Eicher, V. W. (1988). Body image therapy: A combined creative arts therapy and verbal psychotherapy approach. *The Arts in Psychotherapy, 15,* 177-188.

Kaszniak, A. W. (1996). Techniques and instruments for assessment of the elderly. In S. H. Zarit & B. G. Knight (Eds.), *A guide to psychotherapy and aging: Effective clinical interventions in a life-stage context* (pp. 163-219). Washington, DC: American Psychological Association.

Kater, K. J. (1998). *Healthy body images: Teaching kids to eat, and love their bodies too!* (Curriculum available from Eating Disorders Awareness and Prevention, 603 Stewart Street, Suite 803, Seattle, WA 98101).

Kater, K. J., Rohwer, J., & Levine, M. P. (2000). An elementary school project for developing healthy body image and reducing risk factors for unhealthy and disordered eating. *Eating Disorders: The Journal of Treatment and Prevention, 8*, 3-16.

Katz, P. (1995). The psychotherapeutic treatment of suicidal adolescents. In R. C. Marohn & S. C. Sherman (Eds.), *Adolescent psychiatry: Developmental and clinical studies* (Vol. 20, pp. 325-341). Hillsdale, NJ: Analytic Press.

Katzman, M. A., Weiss, L., & Wolchik, S. A. (1986). Speak, don't eat! Teaching women to express their feelings. *Women and Therapy, 5*, 143-157.

Keating, P. (1996). You can afford the lifestyle you want. *Money, 25*(10), 94-98.

Keel, P. K., Fulkerson, J. A., & Leon, G. R. (1997). Disordered eating in pre- and early adolescent girls and boys. *Journal of Youth and Adolescence, 26*, 203-216.

Keith, P. M., & Schafer, R. B. (1991). *Relationships and well-being over the life stages.* New York: Praeger.

Keller, J., & McDade, K. (2000). Attitudes of low-income parents toward seeking help with parenting: Implications for practice. *Child Welfare, 79*, 285-312.

Kelly, J. B. (2000). Children's adjustment in conflicted marriage and divorce: A decade review of research. *Journal of the American Academy of Child & Adolescent Psychiatry, 39*, 963-973.

Kelly, M. L., Power, T. G., & Winbush, D. D. (1992). Determinants of disciplinary practices in low-income Black mothers. *Child Development, 63*, 573-582.

Kenny, M. E. (1996). Promoting optimal adolescent development from a developmental and contextual framework. *Counseling Psychologist, 24*, 475-481.

Kett, J. F. (1977). *Rites of passage: Adolescence in America, 1790 to the present.* New York: Basic Books.

Keys, C. L. M., & Ryff, C. D. (1999). Psychological well-being in midlife. In S. L. Willis & J. D. Reid (Eds.), *Life in the middle: Psychological and social development in middle age* (pp. 161-180). San Diego, CA: Academic Press.

Khuri, L. (2001). *Anxiety and safety in the intergroup dialogue classroom.* Manuscript submitted for publication.

Killen, J. D., Robinson, T. N., Telch, M. J., & Saylor, K. E. (1989). The Stanford Adolescent Heart Health Program. *Health Education Quarterly, 16*, 263-283.

Killen, J. D., Taylor, C. B., Hayward, C., Haydel, K. F., Wilson, D. M., Hammer, L., Kraemer, H., Blair-Greiner, A., & Strachowski, D. (1996). Weight concerns influence the development of eating disorders: A 4-year prospective study. *Journal of Counseling and Clinical Psychology, 64*, 936-940.

Killen, J. D., Taylor, C. B., Hayward, C., Wilson, D. M., Haydel, K. F., Hammer, L. D., Simmonds, B., Robinson, T. N., Litt, I., Varady, A., & Kraemer, H. (1994). Pursuit of thinness and onset of eating disorder symptoms in a community sample of adolescent girls: A three-year prospective analysis. *International Journal of Eating Disorders, 16*, 227-238.

Killen, M., & Nucci, L. P. (1995). Morality, autonomy, and social conflict. In M. Killen & D. Hart (Eds.), *Morality in everyday life: Developmental perspectives* (pp. 52-86). Cambridge, UK: Cambridge University Press.

Kilpatrick, D. G., Resick, P. A., & Veronen, L. J. (1981). Longitudinal effects of a rape experience. *Journal of Social Issues, 37*, 105-122.

Kilpatrick, D. G., & Veronen, L. J. (1984, February). *Treatment of fear and anxiety in victims of rape* (Final report, grant #MH29602). Washington, DC: National Institute of Mental Health.

Kilpatrick, D. G., Veronen, L. J., & Resick, P. A. (1979). The aftermath of rape: Recent empirical findings. *American Journal of Orthopsychiatry, 49,* 658-669.

Kilpatrick, D. G., Veronen, L. J., Saunders, B. E., Best, C. L., Amick-McMullen, A., & Paduhovich, J. (1987, March). *The psychological impact of rape: A study of randomly surveyed crime victims* (Final report, grant #84-IJ-CX-0039). Washington, DC: National Institute of Mental Health.

Kimm, S. Y., Gergen, P. J., Malloy, M., Dresser, C., & Carroll, M. (1990). Dieting patterns of U.S. children: Implications for disease prevention. *Preventive Medicine, 19,* 432-442.

King, A. C., Rejeski, W. J., & Buchner, D. M. (1998). Physical activity interventions targeting older adults: A critical review and recommendations. *American Journal of Preventive Medicine, 15*(4), 316-333.

King, A. C., Winett, R. A., & Lovett, S. B. (1986). Enhancing coping behaviors in at-risk populations: The effects of time-management instruction and social support in women from dual-earner families. *Behavior Therapy, 17,* 57-66.

Kirby, D. (2000). School-based interventions to prevent unprotected sex and HIV among adolescents. In J. Peterson & R. DiClemente (Eds.), *Handbook of HIV prevention* (pp. 83-101). New York: Kluwer Academic/Plenum.

Kirchmeyer, C. (1993). Nonwork-to-work spillover: A more balanced view of the experiences and coping of professional women and men. *Sex Roles, 28,* 531-552.

Kivett, V. (1993). Racial comparisons of the grandmother role: Implications for strengthening the family support system of older Black women. *Family Relations, 42,* 165-172.

Kleist, D. M., & White, L. J. (1997). The values of counseling: A disparity between a philosophy of prevention in counseling and counselor practice and training. *Counseling and Values, 41,* 128-140.

Klomparens, K., & Beck, J. (1998). *Setting expectations and resolving conflict: Michigan State University.* Retrieved July 23, 1999 from the World Wide Web: http://www.msu.edu/user/gradschl/conflict/proposal.htm

Knight, B. G., Teri, L., Wohlford, P., & Santos, J. (Eds.). (1995). *Mental health services for older adults: Implications for training and practice in geropsychology.* Washington, DC: American Psychological Association.

Kohlberg, L. (1971). From "is" to "ought": How to commit naturalistic fallacy and get away with it in the study of moral development. In T. Mischel (Ed.), *Cognitive development and genetic epistemology* (pp. 151-238). New York: Academic Press.

Kopp, R. G., & Ruzicka, M. F. (1993). Women's multiple roles and psychological well-being. *Psychological Reports, 72,* 1351-1354.

Korbin, F. E., & Hendershot, G. E. (1977). Do family ties reduce mortality? Evidence from the United States, 1966-1968. *Journal of Marriage and Family, 39,* 737-745.

Koss, M. P., Gidycz, C. A., & Wisniewski, N. (1987). The scope of rape: Incidence and prevalence of sexual aggression and victimization in a national sample of higher education students. *Journal of Consulting and Clinical Psychology, 55,* 162-170.

Koss, M. P., Goodman, L. A., Browne, A., Fitzgerald, L. F., Keita, G. P., & Russo, N. F. (1994). *No safe haven.* Washington, DC: American Psychological Association.

Kosterman, R., Hawkins, J. D., Spoth, R., Haggerty, K. P., & Zhu, K. (1997). Preparing for the drug free years: Effects of a preventive parent-training intervention on observed family interactions. *Journal of Community Psychology, 25,* 337-352.

Kot, L. A., & Shoemaker, H. M. (1999). Children of divorce: An investigation of the developmental effects from infancy through adulthood. *Journal of Divorce & Remarriage, 31,* 161-178.

Kragie, E. R., Gerstein, M., & Lichtman, M. (1989). Do Americans plan for retirement? Some recent trends. *Career Development Quarterly, 37,* 232-239.

Krantzler, M. (1981). *Creative marriage.* New York: McGraw-Hill.

Kubler-Ross, E. (1969). *On death and dying.* New York: Macmillan.

Kubzansky, L. D., Berkman, L. F., & Seeman, T. E. (2000). Social conditions and distress in elderly persons: Findings from the MacArthur studies of successful aging. *Journal of Gerontology: Series B: Psychological Sciences and Social Sciences, 55B,* P238-P246.

Kulik, L. (2000). Women face unemployment: A comparative analysis of age groups. *Journal of Career Development, 27,* 15-33.

Kumpfer, K. L. (1996, January). *Principles of effective family-focused parent programs.* Paper presented at NIDA's Family Intervention Research Symposium, Gaithersburg, MD.

Kumpfer, K. L., & Alvarado, R. (1998, November). Effective family strengthening interventions. *Juvenile Justice Bulletin,* pp. 1-15.

Labi, N. (1998, April 6). The hunter and the choirboy. *Time,* pp. 28-37.

Lamb, M. E. (1987). The emergent American father. In M. Lamb (Ed.), *The father's role: Cross-cultural perspectives* (pp. 3-25). Hillsdale, NJ: Lawrence Erlbaum.

Landrum-Brown, J., & Khuri, L. (1998). *Program on intergroup relations: University of Illinois at Urbana-Champaign.* Retrieved July 23, 1999 from the World Wide Web: http://www.intergrouprelations.uiuc.edu

Lapan, R. T. (1999, May). *Framework for a community career system program evaluation model.* Paper presented at the meeting of the Society for Vocational Psychology, Milwaukee, WI.

Larrivee, B. (1996). *Moving into balance: Creating your personal pathway.* Santa Monica, CA: Shoreline.

Lauer, J. C., & Lauer, R. H. (1986). 'Til death do us part: How couples stay together. New York: Haworth.

Lazarus, R. S., & Folkman, S. (1984). *Stress, appraisal and coping.* New York: Springer-Verlag-Verlag.

Lebow, J. L., & Gurman, A. S. (1995). Research assessing couple and family therapy. *Annual Review of Psychology, 46,* 27-47.

Lee, C. C., & Brydges, J. L. (1998). Challenging interpersonal violence. In C. C. Lee & G. R. Walz (Eds.), *Social action* (pp. 67-82). Alexandria, VA: American Counseling Association.

Leenaars, A. (1999, April). *Are adolescents' suicides psychologically different from those of adults?* Paper presented at the 32nd Annual Conference of the American Association of Suicidology, Houston, TX.

Lent, R. W., Brown, S. D., & Hackett, G. (1994). Toward a unified Social Cognitive Theory of career/academic interest, choice, and performance [Monograph]. *Journal of Vocational Behavior, 45,* 79-122.

Lerner, R. M. (1983). The history of philosophy and the philosophy of history in developmental psychology: A view of the issues. In R. M. Lerner (Ed.), *Developmental psychology: Historical and philosophical perspectives* (pp. 3-26). Hillsdale, NJ: Lawrence Erlbaum.

Lerner, R. M. (1995). *America's youth in crisis.* Thousand Oaks, CA: Sage.

Lerner, R. M. (1996). Relative plasticity, integration, temporality, and diversity in human development: A developmental contextual perspective about theory, process, and method. *Developmental Psychology, 32,* 781-786.

Lerner, R. M., & Barton, C. E. (2000). Adolescents as agents in the promotion of their positive development: The role of youth actions in effective programs. In W. J. Perrig & A. Grob (Eds.), *Control of human behavior, mental processes, and consciousness* (pp. 457-475). Mahwah, NJ: Lawrence Erlbaum.

Lester, D. (1997). The effectiveness of suicide prevention centers: A review. *Suicide and Life-Threatening Behavior, 27*(3), 304-310.

Levine, A., & Cureton, J. S. (1998). *When hope and fear collide: A portrait of today's college student.* San Francisco: Jossey-Bass.

Levine, R. A. (1977). Child rearing as cultural adaptation. In P. H. Leiderman, S. T. Tulkein, & A. Rosenfeld (Eds.), *Culture and infancy: Variations in the human experience* (pp. 15-27). New York: Academic Press.

Levinson, D. J. (1978). *The seasons of a man's life.* New York: Knopf.

Levy, A. J., & Wall, J. C. (2000). Children who have witnessed community homicide: Incorporating risk and resilience in clinical work. *Families in Society, 81,* 402-411.

Lewinsohn, P. M., Rohde, P., & Seeley, J. R. (1995). Adolescent psychopathology III: The clinical consequences of comorbidity. *Journal of the American Academy of Child and Adolescent Psychiatry, 34,* 510-519.

Lewinsohn, P. M., Rohde, P., & Seeley, J. R. (1996). Adolescent suicidal ideation and attempts: Prevalence, risk factors, and clinical implications. *Clinical Psychology: Science and Practice, 3*(1), 25-46.

Lewis, J. A., Sperry, L., & Carlson, J. (1993). *Health counseling.* Pacific Grove, CA: Brooks/Cole.

Lewit, E. M., Terman, D. L., & Behrman, R. E. (1997). *Children and poverty: Analysis and recommendations.* Retrieved from the World Wide Web: http://www.futureofchildren.org/cap/index.htm.

Lind, E. A., Huo, Y. J., & Tyler, T. R. (1994). And justice for all: Ethnicity, gender, and preferences for dispute resolution procedures. *Law and Human Behavior, 18,* 269-290.

Lock, R. D. (1992). *Taking charge of your career direction: Career planning guide* (Book 1). Boston: Brooks/Cole.

Loeber, R., & Stouthamer-Loeber, M. (1986). Family factors as correlates and predictors of juvenile conduct problems and delinquency. In M. Tonry & N. Morris (Eds.), *Crime and justice: An annual review of research* (Vol. 7, pp. 29-150). Chicago: University of Chicago Press.

Loeber, R., & Stouthamer-Loeber, M. (1998). Development of juvenile aggression and violence: Some common misconceptions and controversies. *American Psychologist, 53,* 242-259.

Loevinger, J. (1976). *Ego development.* San Francisco: Jossey-Bass.

Logan, J., & Spitze, G. (1996). *Family ties: Enduring relations between parents and their grown children.* Philadelphia: Temple University Press.

Lonsway, K. A., Klaw, E. L., Berg, D. R., Waldo, C. R., Kothari, C., Mazurek, C. J., & Hegeman, K. E. (1998). Beyond "no means no": Outcomes of an intensive program to train peer facilitators for campus acquaintance rape education. *Journal of Interpersonal Violence, 13,* 73-92.

Lopata, H. Z. (1993). The interweave of public and private: Women's challenge to American society. *Journal of Marriage and the Family, 55,* 176-190.

Loprest, P. (1999). *Families who left welfare: Who are they and how are they doing?* Washington, DC: Urban Institute. Retrieved November 30, 2000 from the World Wide Web: http://newfederalism.urban.org/html/discussion99-02.html

Lovitts, B. E. (1996). *Leaving the ivory tower: A sociological analysis of the causes of departure from doctoral study.* Doctoral dissertation, University of Maryland.

Ludwig, M. R., & Brownell, K. D. (1999). Lesbians, bisexual women, and body image: An investigation of gender roles and social group affiliation. *International Journal of Eating Disorders, 25,* 89-97.

Luthar, S. S., & Zigler, E. (1991). Vulnerability and competence: A review of research on resilience in childhood. *American Journal of Orthopsychiatry, 61,* 6-22.

Lyddon, W. J., Schreiber, R., & Alford, D. J. (2000). *Attachment and working models of emotion.* Poster session presented at the 7th International Congress on Constructivism in Psychotherapy, Geneva, Switzerland.

Maccoby, E. F., & Mnookin, R. H. (1992). *Dividing the child: Dilemmas of custody.* Cambridge, MA: Harvard University Press

Machida, S., & Holloway, D. D. (1991). The relationship between divorced mothers' perceived control over child rearing and children's post-divorce development. *Family Relations, 40,* 272-278.

Machung, A. (1991). Talking career, thinking job: Gender differences in career and family expectations for Berkeley seniors. *Feminist Studies, 15,* 35-58.

MacMillan, H. L., MacMillan, J. H., Offord, D. R., Griffith, L., & MacMillan, A. (1993). Primary prevention of child physical abuse and neglect: A critical review. Part 1. *Journal of Child Psychology and Psychiatry and Allied Disciplines, 35,* 835-856.

Mahalik, J. R. (1999). Incorporating a gender role strain perspective in assessing and treating men's cognitive distortions. *Professional Psychology, 30,* 333-340.

Mahalik, J. R., Cournoyer, R., DeFranc, W., Cherry, M., & Napolitano, J. (1998). Men's gender role conflict and use of psychological defenses. *Journal of Counseling Psychology, 45,* 247-255.

Mahler, M. S., Pine, F., & Bergman, A. (1975). *The psychological birth of the human infant.* New York: Basic Books.

Mair, M. (1988). Psychology as storytelling. *International Journal of Personal Construct Psychology, 1,* 125-138.

Malouff, J. M., & Schutte, N. S. (1998). *Games to enhance social and emotional skills: Sixty-six games that teach children, adolescents, and adults skills crucial to success in life.* Springfield, IL: Charles C Thomas.

Mann, T., Nolen-Hoeksema, S., Huang, K., Burgard, D., Wright, A., & Hanson, K. (1997). Are two interventions worse than none? Joint primary and secondary prevention of eating disorders in college females. *Health Psychology, 16,* 215-225.

Marcia, J. E. (1980). Identity in adolescence. In J. Adelson (Ed.), *Handbook of adolescent psychology* (pp. 159-187). New York: John Wiley.

Marcia, J. E. (1994). The empirical study of identity. In H. A. Bosma, T. L. G. Graafsma, H. D. Grotevant, & D. J. de Levita (Eds.), *Identity and development: An interdisciplinary approach* (pp. 67-80). Thousand Oaks, CA: Sage.

Marks, S. R. (1977). Multiple roles and role strain: Some notes on human energy, time, and commitment. *American Sociological Review, 39,* 567-578.

Marsh, H. W. (1989). Age and sex effects in multiple dimensions of self-concept: Preadolescence to early adulthood. *Journal of Educational Psychology, 81,* 417-430.

Marshall, N. L., & Barnett, R. C. (1991). Race, class and multiple role strains and gains among women employed in the service sector. *Women & Health, 17,* 1-19.

Marshall, N. L., & Barnett, R. C. (1994). Family-friendly workplaces, work-family interface, and worker health. In G. P. Keita & J. J. Hurrell (Eds.), *Job stress in a changing workforce: Investigating gender, diversity, and family issues* (pp. 253-264). Washington, DC: American Psychological Association.

Martin, A. D., & Hetrick, E. S. (1988). The stigmatization of the gay and lesbian adolescent. *Journal of Homosexuality, 15,* 163-184.

Martin, J., Chenoweth, L., & Engelbrecht, J. (2000). An emerging trend: Culturally responsive parenting education. *Journal of Family and Consumer Sciences, 92*(3), 11-12.

Martinez, E. A. (1993). Parenting young children in Mexican American/Chicano families. In H. McAdoo (Ed.), *Family ethnicity: Strength in diversity* (pp. 184-198). Newbury Park, CA: Sage.

Marttunen, M. J., Aro, H. M., Henriksson, M. M., & Lonqvist, J. K. (1994). Psychosocial stressors more common in adolescent suicides with alcohol abuse compared with depressive adolescent suicides. *Journal of the American Academy of Child and Adolescent Psychiatry, 33,* 490-497.

Maslow, A. H. (1987). *Motivation and personality* (3rd ed.). New York: Harper.

Masten, A. S., & Braswell, L. (1991). Developmental psychopathology: An integrative framework. In P. R. Martin (Ed.), *Handbook of behavior therapy and psychological science: An integrative approach* (pp. 35-56). New York: Pergamon.

Masten, A. S., & Coatsworth, J. D. (1995). Competence, resilience, and psychopathology. In D. Cicchetti & D. J. Cohen (Eds.), *Developmental psychopathology: Vol. 2. Risk, disorder, and adaptation* (pp. 715-752). New York: John Wiley.

Masten, A. S., & Coatsworth, J. D. (1998). The development of competencies in favorable and unfavorable environments: Lessons from research on successful children. *American Psychologist, 53,* 205-220.

Masunaga, H. (1998). Adult learning theory and Elderhostel. *Gerontology and Geriatrics Education, 19*(2), 3-16.

Matras, J. (1990). Role transitions in middle and later life. In J. Matras (Ed.), *Dependency, obligations, and entitlements* (pp. 230-258). Englewood Cliffs, NJ: Prentice Hall.

Mattessich, P., & Hill, R. (1987). Life cycle and family development. In M. Sussman & S. Steinmetz (Eds.), *Handbook of marriage and family* (pp. 437-469). New York: Plenum.

Mazza, J. J. (1997). School-based suicide prevention programs: Are they effective? *School Psychology Review, 26*(3), 382-396.

McAdams, D. P. (1985). *Power, intimacy, and the life story.* Homewood, IL: Dorsey.

McAdams, D. P. (1993). *The stories we live by: Personal myths and the making of the self.* New York: Guilford.

McAdoo, H. P. (1988). *Black families* (2nd ed.). Newbury Park, CA: Sage.

McCauley, J., Kern, D. E., Kolodner, K., Dill, L., Schroeder, A. F., DeChant, H. K., Ryden, J., Derogatis, L. R., & Bass, E. B. (1997). Clinical characteristics of women with history of childhood abuse: Unhealed wounds. *Journal of the American Medical Association, 277,* 1362-1368.

McClosky, L. A., Figueredo, A. J., & Koss, M. P. (1995). The effects of systemic family violence on children's mental health. *Child Development, 66,* 1239-1261.

McConnell, J. H. (1994). Lesbian and gay male identities as paradigms. In S. L. Archer (Ed.), *Interventions for adolescent identity development* (pp. 103-118). Thousand Oaks, CA: Sage.

McCracken, R. S., & Weitzman, L. M. (1997). Relationship of personal agency, problem-solving appraisal, and traditionality of career choice to women's attitudes toward multiple role planning. *Journal of Counseling Psychology, 44,* 149-159.

McCrae, R. R., & Costa, P. T. (1986). Personality, coping, and coping effectiveness in an adult sample. *Journal of Personality, 54,* 385-405.

McCroskey, J., & Einbinder, S. D. (1998). *Universities and communities: Remaking professional and interprofessional education for the next century.* Westport, CT: Praeger.

McGee, J., & Wells, K. (1982). Gender typing and androgyny in later life. *Human Development, 25,* 116-139.

McGee, L., & Newcomb, M. D. (1992). General deviance syndrome: Expanded hierarchical evaluations at four ages from early adolescence to adulthood. *Journal of Consulting & Clinical Psychology, 60,* 766-776.

McGinnis, J. M., & Foege, W. H. (1993). Actual causes of death in the United States. *Journal of the American Medical Association, 270,* 2207-2212.

McGoldrick, M., Pearce, J. K., & Giordano, J. (Eds.). (1982). *Ethnicity and family therapy.* New York: Guilford.

McKain, W. C. (1972). A new look at older marriages. *Family Coordinator, 21,* 61-69.

McKinney, J. P., Schiamberg, L. B., & Shelton, L. G. (Eds.) (1998). *Teaching about adolescence: An ecological approach.* New York: Garland.

McLaughlin, M., Cormier, L., & Cormier, W. (1983). Relation between coping strategies and distress, stress, and marital adjustment of multiple-role women. *Journal of Counseling Psychology, 35,* 187-193.

Mead, G. H. (1934). *Mind, self, and society.* Chicago: University of Chicago Press.

Mechanic, D., & Hansell, S. (1989). Divorce, family conflict and adolescents' well being. *Journal of Health and Social Behavior, 30,* 105-116.

Merleau-Ponty, M. (1962). *Phenomenology of perception* (C. Smith, Trans.) London: Routledge. (Original work published 1945)

Mertensmeyer, C., & Fine, M. (2000). ParentLink: A model of integration and support for parents. *Family Relations, 49,* 257-265.

Michael, Y. L., Colditz, G. A., Coakley, E., & Kawachi, I. (1999). Health behaviors, social networks, and healthy aging: Cross-sectional evidence from the nurses' health study. *Quality of Life Research: An International Journal of Quality of Life Aspects of Treatment, Care, and Recovery, 8,* 711-722.

Miller, J. B. (1994). Women's psychological development: Connections, disconnections, and violations. In M. M. Berger (Ed.), *Women beyond Freud: New concepts of feminine psychology* (pp. 79-97). New York: Brunner/Mazel.

Miller, T. R., & Spicer, R. S. (1998). How safe are our schools? *American Journal of Public Health, 88,* 413-418.

Mindel, C. H., Haberstein, R. W., & Wright, R. (1988). *Ethnic families in America: Patterns and variations.* New York: Elsevier.

Mirowsky, J., & Ross, C. E. (1980). Minority status, ethnic culture, and distress: A comparison of Blacks, Whites, Mexicans and Mexican Americans. *American Journal of Sociology, 86,* 479-495.

Moen, P., Dempster-McCain, D., & Williams, R. M. (1992). Successful aging: A life-course perspective on women's multiple roles and health. *American Journal of Sociology, 97,* 1612-1638.

Moore, A. R., & O'Keefe, S. T. (1999). Drug-induced impairment in the elderly. *Drugs and Aging, 15*(1), 15-28.

Morelli, P. (1981). *Comparison of the psychological recovery of Black and White victims of rape.* ERIC Document Reproduction Service No. ED208322.

Morgan, C. S. (1992). College students' perceptions of barriers to women in science and engineering. *Youth & Society, 24,* 228-236.

Morrison, G. M., Furlong, M. J., & Morrison, R. L. (1997). The safe school: Moving beyond crime prevention to school empowerment. In A. P. Goldstein & J. Close (Eds.), *School violence intervention: A practical handbook* (pp. 236-264). New York: Guilford.

Morton, S. B. (1998). Lesbian divorce. *American Journal of Orthopsychiatry, 68,* 410-419.

Moscicki, E. K. (1995). Epidemiology of suicidal behavior. *Suicide and Life-Threatening Behavior, 25*(1), 22-35.

Multon, K. D., Brown, S. D., & Lent, R. W. (1991). Relation of self-efficacy beliefs to academic outcomes: A meta-analytic investigation. *Journal of Counseling Psychology, 38,* 30-38.

Muran, E., & DiGiuseppe, R. (2000). Rape trauma. In F. M. Dattilio & A. Freeman (Eds.), *Cognitive-behavioral strategies in crisis intervention* (2nd ed., pp. 150-165). New York: Guilford.

Mutchler, J. E., Burr, J. A., & Massagli, M. P. (1997). Pathways to labor force exit: Work transitions and work instability. *Journal of Gerontology, 52B,* S4-S12.

Muth, J. L., & Cash, T. F. (1997). Body image attitudes: What difference does gender make? *Journal of Applied and Social Psychology, 27,* 1438-1452.

Mutran, E. (1985). Intergenerational family support among Blacks and Whites: Response to culture or to socioeconomic differences. *Journal of Gerontology, 40*(3), 382-389.

Myers, D. G. (1999). *Social psychology* (6th ed.). Boston: McGraw-Hill.

Myers, H. F., Alvy, K. T., Arrington, A., Richardson, M. A., Marigna, M., Robbin, H., Main, M., & Newcomb, M. D. (1992). The impact of a parent training program on inner-city African-American families. *Journal of Community Psychology, 20,* 132-147.

National Association of Student Personnel Administrators. (1994, August). *Complying with the final regulations: The student right to know and Campus Security Act.* Washington, DC: Author.

National Center for Educational Statistics. (1998). *Violence and discipline problems in U.S. public schools: 1996-97.* Pittsburgh, PA: Government Printing Office.

National Center for Health Statistics. (1999). *Latest final mortality statistics available: 1999.* Washington, DC: U.S. Department of Health and Human Services. Retrieved July 1999 from the World Wide Web: http://www.cdc.gov/nchs/releases/99facts/99sheets/97mortal.htm

National Institute on Aging. (1998). *Exercise: A guide from the National Institute on Aging* [Brochure]. Bethesda, MD: Author.

National Lesbian and Gay Health Foundation. (1987). *National lesbian health care survey: Mental health implications.* Unpublished report. Atlanta, GA: Author.

Neimeyer, G. J. (1993). *Constructivist assessment.* Newbury Park, CA: Sage.

Nerad, M., & Miller, D. S. (1996). Increasing student retention in graduate and professional programs. *New Directions for Institutional Research: Assessing Graduate and Professional Education, 92,* 61-67.

Neumark-Sztainer, D., Martin, S. L., & Story, M. (2000). School-based programs for obesity prevention: What do adolescents recommend? *American Journal of Health Promotion, 14,* 232-235.

Nevill, D. D., & Super, D. E. (1986). *The Salience Inventory: Theory, application, and research.* Palo Alto, CA: Consulting Psychologists Press.

Neville, H. A., & Heppner, M. J. (1999). Contextualizing rape: Reviewing sequelae and proposing a culturally inclusive ecological model of sexual assault. *Applied & Preventive Psychology, 8,* 41-62.

Neville, H. A., Heppner, M. J., & Spanierman, L. B. (in press). Sexual violence against African American women: General and cultural factors influencing treatment and prevention strategies. In B. C. Wallace & R. Carter (Eds.), *Understanding and dealing with personal and social violence: A handbook for psychologists and educators.* Newbury Park, CA: Sage.

Neville, H. A., & Pugh, A. A. O. (1996). General and culture-specific factors influencing African American women's reporting patterns and perceived support following sexual assault: An exploratory investigation. *Violence Against Women, 3,* 361-381.

Newcomb, M. D. (1992). Substance abuse and control in the United States: Ethical and legal issues. *Social Science and Medicine, 35,* 471-479.

Newcomb, M. D. (1996a). Adolescence: Pathologizing a normal process. *The Counseling Psychologist, 24,* 482-490.

Newcomb, M. D. (1996b). Pseudomaturity among adolescents: Construct validation, sex differences, and associations in adulthood. *Journal of Drug Issues, 26,* 477-504.

Newcomb, M. D., & Bentler, P. M. (1989). Substance use and abuse among children and teenagers. *American Psychologist, 44,* 242-248.

Newcomb, M. D., Wyatt, G. E., Romero, G. J., Tucker, M. B., Wayment, H. A., Vargas, J. H., Solis, B., & Mitchell-Kernan, C. (1998). Acculturation, sexual risk taking, and HIV health promotion among Latinas. *Journal of Counseling Psychology, 45,* 454-467.

Newman, B. K. (1995). Career change for those over 40: Critical issues and insights. *Career Development Quarterly, 44,* 64-66.

Newman, B. M., & Newman, P. R. (1991). *Development through life* (5th ed.). Pacific Grove, CA: Brooks/Cole.

Newman, B. M., & Newman, P. R. (1998). *Development through life: A psychosocial approach.* Belmont, CA: Wadsworth.

Nolen-Hoeksema, S. (1998). *Abnormal psychology.* New York: McGraw-Hill.

Norval, G. D., & Weaver, C. N. (1981). The contribution of marital happiness to global happiness. *Journal of Marriage and Family, 39,* 737-745.

Novaco, R. W. (1975). *Anger control: The development and evaluation of an experimental treatment.* Lexington, MA: Lexington Books.

Nugent, F. (2000). *Introduction to the profession of counseling* (3rd ed.). Upper Saddle River, NJ: Prentice Hall.

O'Dea, J. (1995). *Everybody's different: A self-esteem program for young adolescents.* Sydney, Australia: University of Sydney Press.

O'Dea, J. (1999). Improving the body image, eating attitudes, and behaviors of young male and female adolescents: A new educational approach that focuses on self-esteem. *International Journal of Eating Disorder, 28,* 43-57.

O'Donnell, C. R. (1995). Firearm deaths among children and youth. *American Psychologist, 50*(9), 771-776.

Oetinger, G. (1996). Positive fantasy and motivation. In P. M. Gollwitzer & J. A. Bargh (Eds.), *The psychology of action: Linking cognition and motivation to behavior* (pp. 236-259). New York: Guilford.

Oettinger, G. (in press). Free fantasies about the future and the emergence of developmental goals. In J. Brandstadter & R. M. Lerner (Eds.), *Action and self-development: Theory and research through the life-span*. Thousand Oaks, CA: Sage.

Offer, D., & Shonert-Reichl, K. A. (1992). Debunking the myths of adolescence: Findings from recent research. *Journal of the American Academy of Child and Adolescent Psychiatry, 31,* 1003-1014.

Ogbu, J. U. (1985). A cultural ecology of competence among inner-city Blacks. In M. B. Spencer, G. K. Brookins, & W. R. Allen (Eds.), *Beginnings: The social and affective development of Black children*. Hillsdale, NJ: Lawrence Erlbaum.

Okagaki, L., & Johnson-Divecha, D. (1993). Development of parental beliefs. In I. Luster & L. Okagaki (Eds.), *Parenting: An ecological perspective* (pp. 35-67). Hillsdale, NJ: Lawrence Erlbaum.

Olds, D. (1997). The prenatal early infancy project: Preventing child abuse and neglect in the context of promoting maternal and child health. In D. A. Wolfe, R. J. McMahon, & R. D. Peters (Eds.), *Child abuse: New directions in prevention and treatment across the lifespan* (pp. 130-154). Thousand Oaks, CA: Sage.

Oles, P. K. (1994). Konstrukcja Kwestionariusza do badania Kryzysu Polowy Zycia: Zalonzenia a fakty empiryczne [Construction of the Mid-life Crisis Questionnaire: Assumptions and empirical facts]. *Przegkad Psychologiczny [Psychological Review], 37,* 159-166.

Oles, P. K. (1995) *Kryzys "polowy zycia" u mezczyzn. Psychologiczne badania empiryczne.* ["Mid-life" crisis in men. Psychological empirical research]. Lublin: RW KUL.

O'Neil, J. M. (1990). Assessing men's gender role conflict. In D. Moore & F. Leafgren (Eds.), *Men in conflict: Problem-solving strategies and interventions*. Alexandria, VA: Association for Counseling and Development Press.

Orpinas, P., Parcel. G. S., McAlister, A., & Frankowski, R. (1995). Violence prevention in middle schools: A pilot evaluation. *Journal of Adolescent Health, 17,* 360-371.

Osipow, S. H., Cohen, W., Jenkins, J., & Dostal, J. (1979). Clinical versus counseling psychology: Is there a difference? *Professional Psychology, 10,* 148-153.

Oyserman, D., Gant, L., & Ager, J. (1995). A socially contextualized model of African American identity: Possible selves and school persistence. *Journal of Personality and Social Psychology, 69,* 1216-1232.

Paa, H. K., & Larson, L. M. (1998). Predicting level of restrained eating behavior in adult women. *International Journal of Eating Disorders, 24,* 91-94.

Pabst, M. (1996). EDAP prevention puppet project. *EDAP Matters: Newsletter of Eating Disorders and Prevention, 1,* 5.

Palmer, R. L., Oppenheimer, R., & Marshall, P. D. (1988). Eating-disordered patients remember their parents: A study using the parental bonding instrument. *International Journal of Eating Disorders, 7,* 101-106.

Palmore, E. B. (1988) *The Facts On Aging Quiz*. New York: Springer-Verlag.

Pargament, K. I. (1997). *The psychology of religion and coping: Theory, research, practice*. New York: Guilford.

Parker, J. G., & Asher, S. R. (1993). Friendship and friendship quality in middle childhood: Links with peer group acceptance and feelings of loneliness and social dissatisfaction. *Developmental Psychology, 29,* 611-621.

Parker, R. A., & Aldwin, C. M. (1994). Desiring careers but loving families: Period, cohort and gender effects in career and family orientation. In G. P. Keita & J. J. Hurrell (Eds.), *Job stress in a changing workforce: Investigating gender, diversity, and family issues* (pp. 23-38). Washington, DC: American Psychological Association.

Parkes, C. M. (1972). *Bereavement: Studies of grief in adult life.* New York: International University Press.

Pascarella, E. T., & Tereznini, P. T. (1977). Patterns of student-faculty informal interaction beyond the classroom and voluntary attrition. *Journal of Higher Education, 48,* 540-552.

Pascarella, E. T., & Tereznini, P. T. (1980). Predicting freshman persistence, involuntary dropout decisions from a theoretical model. *Journal of Higher Education, 51,* 60-75.

Patterson, G. R. (1980). Children who steal. In T. Hirschi & M. Gottfredson (Eds.), *Understanding crime: Vol. 18. Current theory and research* (pp. 411-455). London: Sage.

Pearlin, L., Mullan, J., Semple, S., & Skaff, M. (1990). Caregiving and the stress process: An overview of concepts and their measures. *The Gerontologist, 30*(5), 583-594.

Pedro-Carroll, J. L., & Alpert-Gillis, L. J. (1997). Preventive interventions for children of divorce: A developmental model for 5- and 6-year-old children. *Journal of Primary Prevention, 18,* 5-23.

Pedro-Carroll, J. L., & Cowen, E. L. (1985). The children of divorce intervention project: An investigation of the efficacy of a school-based prevention program. *Journal of Consulting and Clinical Psychology, 53,* 603-611.

Pedro-Carroll, J. L., Cowen, E. L., Hightower, A. D., & Guare, J. C. (1986). Preventive intervention with latency-aged children of divorce: A replication study. *American Journal of Community Psychology, 14,* 277-290.

Perry, C. L. (1999). *Creating health behavior change: How to develop community-wide programs for youth.* Thousand Oaks, CA: Sage.

Perry, C. L., Sellers, D. E., Johnson, C., Pedersen, S., Bachman, K. J., Parcel, G. S., Stone, E. J., Luepker, R. V., Wu, M., Nader, P. R., & Cook, K. (1997). The Child and Adolescent Trial for Cardiovascular Health (CATCH): Intervention, implementation, and feasibility for elementary schools in the United States. *Health Education & Behavior, 24,* 716-735.

Perry, C. L., Williams, C. L., Velben-Mortenson, S., Toomey, T. L., Komro, K. A., Anstine, P. I. S., McGovern, P. G., Finnegan, J. R., Forster, J. L., Wagennaar, A. C., & Wolfson, M. (1996). Project Northland: Outcomes of a communitywide alcohol use prevention program during early adolescence. *American Journal of Public Health, 86,* 956-965.

Perry, W. (1968). *Forms of intellectual and ethical development in college students.* New York: Holt, Rinehart & Winston.

Peters, J. F. (1994). Gender socialization of adolescents in the home: Research and discussion. *Adolescents, 29,* 913-934.

Peters, K. D., Kochanek, K. D., & Murphy, S. L. (1998). Deaths: Final data for 1996. *National Vital Statistics Report, 47*(9). (DHHS Publication No. PHS 99-1120). Hyattsville, MD: National Center for Health Statistics.

Peterson, J. A., & Payne, B. (1975). *Love in the later years.* New York: Association Press.

Petty, R. E., & Cacioppo, J. T. (1981). *Attitudes and persuasion: Classic and contemporary approaches.* Dubuque, IA: Brown.

Petty, R. E., & Cacioppo, J. T. (1986). *Communication and persuasion: Central and peripheral routes to attitude change.* New York: Springer-Verlag.

Phelps, L., Johnston, L. S., & Augustyniak, K. (1999). Prevention of eating disorders: Identification of predictor variables. *Eating Disorders: Journal of Treatment and Prevention, 7,* 99-108.

Phelps, L., Sapia, J., Nathanson, D., & Nelson, L. (2000). An empirically supported eating disorder prevention program. *Psychology in the Schools, 37,* 443-452.

Philips, D. D. (1974). The influence of suggestion on suicide: Substantive and theoretical implications of the Werther effect. *American Sociological Review, 39,* 340-354.

Phillips, S. D., & Imhoff, A. R. (1997). Women and career development: A decade of research. *Annual Review of Psychology, 48,* 31-59.

Phinney, J. (1990). Ethnic identity in adolescents and adults: A review of the literature. *Psychological Bulletin, 108,* 499-514.

Phinney, J., & Rosenthal, D. A. (1992). Ethnic identity in adolescence: Process, context, and outcome. In G. R. Adams, T. P. Gullotta, & R. Montemayor (Eds.), *Adolescent identity formation* (pp. 145-172). Newbury Park, CA: Sage.

Piaget, J. (1926). *The language and thought of the child.* New York: Meridian.

Piechowski, L. D. (1992). Mental health and multiple roles. *Families in Society: The Journal of Contemporary Human Services, 73,* 131-139.

Pinhas, L., Toner, B. B., Ali, A., Garfinkel, P. E., & Stuckless, N. (1999). The effects of the ideal of female beauty on mood and body satisfaction. *International Journal of Eating Disorders, 25,* 223-226.

Pipher, M. (1994). *Reviving Ophelia: Saving the selves of adolescent girls.* New York: Putnam.

Poland, S., & Lieberman, R. (2000, November). *Best practices in suicide intervention.* Paper presented at professional development seminar series at California State University at Northridge Counseling Services.

Polkinghorne, D. P. (1988). *Narrative psychology.* Albany: State University of New York Press.

Polkinghorne, D. P. (1991). Narrative and self-concept. *Journal of Narrative and Life History, 1,* 135-154.

Pollack, W. (1998). *Real boys: Rescuing our sons from the myths of boyhood.* New York: Random House.

Popkin, M. H. (1993). *Active parenting program.* Atlanta, GA: Active Parenting, Inc.

Potter, L. B., Powell, K. E., & Kachur, S. P. (1995). Suicide prevention from a public health perspective. *Suicide and Life-Threatening Behavior, 25*(1), 82-91.

Powell, J. D., & Carter, A. L. (1996, February). *My family/My self: Examining the past for a better present.* Paper presented at the Big Ten Counseling Center Conference, State College, PA.

Price, R. H., Cioci, M., Penner, W., & Trautlein, B. (1993). Webs of influence: School and community programs that enhance adolescent health and education. *Teachers College Record, 94,* 487-521.

Program on Intergroup Relations. (1999). *The program on intergroup relations, conflict, and community: University of Michigan at Ann Arbor.* Retrieved March 29, 2001 from the World Wide Web: http://www.umich.edu/~igrc

Pruchno, R. (1995). The role of the family in clinical geropsychology. In B. G. Knight, L. Teri, P. Wohlford, & J. Santos (Eds.), *Mental health services for older adults: Im-*

plications for training and practice in geropsychology (pp. 85-92). Washington, DC: American Psychological Association.

Pruett, C. L., Calsyn, R. J., & Jensen, F. M. (1993). Social support received by children in stepmother, stepfather, and intact families. *Journal of Divorce and Remarriage, 19,* 165-179.

Pryor, J. (1999). Waiting until they leave home: The experiences of young adults whose parents separate. *Journal of Divorce & Remarriage, 32,* 47-61.

Purcell, P. J. (2000). Older workers: Employment and retirement trends. *Monthly Labor Review, 123,* 19-30. Retrieved December 28, 2000 from the World Wide Web: http://www.bls.gov/opub/mlr/2000/10/art3abs.htm

Quintana, S. M., & Lapsley, D. K. (1987). Adolescent autonomy and ego identity: A structural equations approach to the continuity of adaptation. *Journal of Adolescent Research, 2,* 393-410.

Raiffa, H. (1968). *Decision analysis.* Reading, MA: Addison-Wesley.

Rak, C. F., & Patterson, L. E. (1996). Promoting resilience in children at risk. *Journal of Counseling and Development, 74,* 368-373.

Rapoport, R., & Rapoport, R. N. (1969). The dual-career family. *Human Relations, 22,* 3-30.

Rapoport, R., & Rapoport, R. N. (1972). The dual-career family: A variant pattern and social change. In C. Safilios-Rothschild (Ed.), *Toward a sociology of women.* Lexington, MA: Xerox.

Raudenbush, B., & Zellner, D. A. (1997). Nobody's satisfied: Effects of abnormal eating behaviors and actual and perceived weight status on body image satisfaction in males and females. *Journal of Social and Clinical Psychology, 16,* 95-110.

Rauste-von Wright, M. (1989). Body image satisfaction in adolescent girls and boys: A longitudinal study. *Journal of Youth and Adolescence, 18,* 71-83.

Raveis, V. H. (2000). Facilitating older spouses' adjustment to widowhood: A preventive intervention program. *Social Work in Health Care, 29,* 13-32.

Reed-Victor, E., & Pelco, L. E. (1999). Helping homeless students build resilience: What the school community can do. *Journal for a Just and Caring Education, 5,* 51-71.

Reese, L. E., Vera, E. M., Simon, T. R., & Ikeda, R. M. (2000). The role of families and caregivers as risk and protective factors in preventing youth violence. *Clinical Child and Family Psychology Review, 3,* 61-77.

Reeves, J. B., & Darville, R. L. (1994). Social contact patterns and satisfaction with retirement of women in dual-career/earner families. *International Journal of Aging & Human Development, 39,* 163-175.

Regan, M. C., & Roland, H. E. (1985). Rearranging family and career priorities: Professional women and men of the eighties. *Journal of Marriage and the Family, 46,* 985-992.

Reid, J., & Hardy, M. (1999). Multiple roles and well-being among midlife women: Testing role strain and role enhancement theories. *Journals of Gerontology, 54B,* 329-338.

Reifman, A., Biernat, M., & Lang, E. L. (1991). Stress, social support and health in married professional women with small children. *Psychology of Women Quarterly, 15,* 431-445.

Reis, J., & Riley, W. (1997). *Alcohol 101* [CD-ROM]. Urbana-Champaign, IL: University of Illinois Board of Trustees and The Century Council.

Reiss, D., & Price, R. H. (1995). National research agenda for prevention research: The National Institute of Mental Health Report. *American Psychologist, 51,* 1109-1115.

Remafedi, G., French, S., Story, M., Resnick, M. D., & Blum, R. (1998). The relationship between suicide risk and sexual orientation: Results of a population-based study. *American Journal of Public Health, 88*(1), 57-60.

Renshaw, P. D., & Brown, P. J. (1993). Loneliness in middle childhood: Concurrent and longitudinal predictors. *Child Development, 64,* 1271-1284.

Resick, P. A. (1993). The psychological impact of rape. *Journal of Interpersonal Violence, 8,* 223-255

Resick, P. A., & Schnicke, M. K. (1993). *Cognitive processing therapy for sexual assault victims: A treatment manual.* Newbury Park, CA: Sage.

Resnick, H. S., Kilpatrick, D. G., Dansky, B. S., Saunders, B. E., & Best, C. L. (1993). Prevalence of civilian trauma and posttraumatic stress disorder in a representative national sample of women. *Journal of Consulting and Clinical Psychology, 61,* 984-991.

Resnick, M. D., Bearman, E. S., Biota. R. W., Bauman. K. E., Harris, K. M., Jones, J., Tabor, J., Beuhring, T., Sieving, R. E., Shew, M., Ireland, M., Bearinger, L. H., & Udry, J. R. (1997). Protecting adolescents from harm. Findings from the National Longitudinal Study of Adolescent Health. *Journal of the American Medical Association, 278,* 823-832.

Rice, K. G. (1990). Attachment in adolescence: A narrative and meta-analytic review. *Journal of Youth and Adolescence, 19,* 511-538.

Richards, D. A., Lovell, K., & Marks, I. M. (1994). Post-traumatic stress disorder: Evaluation of a behavioral treatment program. *Journal of Traumatic Stress, 7,* 669-680.

Riddick, C. C., & Stewart, D. G. (1994). Life satisfaction and leisure importance. *Journal of Leisure Research, 26,* 75-87.

Rieves, L., & Cash, T. F. (1996). Social developmental factors and women's body image attitudes. *Journal of Social Behavior and Personality, 11,* 63-78.

Rim, Y. (1989). Self-confrontation and coping styles. *Personality and Individual Differences, 10,* 1011-1014.

Rios-Ellis, B., & Figueroa, M. (1998). HIV/AIDS. In A. Henderson & S. Champlin (Eds.), *Promoting teen health: Linking schools, health organizations, and the community* (pp. 117-131). Thousand Oaks, CA: Sage.

Ritchie, M. H., & Partin, R. L. (1994). Parent education and consultation activities of school counselors. *The School Counselor, 41,* 165-170.

Rivkin, I. D., & Taylor, S. E. (1998). *The effects of mental simulation on coping with controllable stressful events.* Unpublished manuscript.

Robbins, S. B., Lee, R. M., & Wan, T. T. H. (1994). Goal continuity as a mediator of early retirement adjustment: Testing a multidimensional model. *Journal of Counseling Psychology, 41,* 18-26.

Roberts, R. E. (1999, April). *Ethnicity and risk of adolescent suicidal behaviors: A review and commentary.* Paper presented at the 32nd Annual Meeting of the American Association of Suicidology, Houston, TX.

Rogers, C. (1942). *Counseling and psychotherapy.* Boston: Houghton Mifflin.

Rolfes, S. R., DeBruyne, L. K., & Whitney, E. N. (1998). *Life span nutrition: Conception through life* (2nd ed.). Belmont, CA: Wadsworth.

Romano, J. L., & Hage, S. M. (2000). Prevention and counseling psychology: Revitalizing commitments for the 21st century. *The Counseling Psychologist, 28,* 733-763.

Roof, W. C. (1999). *Spiritual marketplace.* Princeton, NJ: Princeton University Press.

Rosen, J. C., Orosan, P., & Reiter, J. (1995). Cognitive behavior therapy for negative body image in obese women. *Behavior Therapy, 26,* 25-42.

Rosen, J. C., Orosan-Weine, P., & Tang, T. (1997). Critical experiences in the development of body image. *Eating Disorders, 5,* 191-204.

Rosen, J. C., Reiter, J., & Orosan, P. (1995). Cognitive-behavioral body image therapy for body dysmorphic disorder. *Journal of Consulting and Clinical Psychology, 63,* 263-269.

Rosenbaum, M. (1993). The changing body image of the adolescent girl. In M. Sugar (Ed.), *Female adolescent development* (2nd ed., pp. 62-80). New York: Brunner/Mazel.

Rosenberg, J. I. (1999). Suicide prevention: An integrated training model using affective and action-based interventions. *Professional Psychology: Research and Practice, 30*(1), 83-87.

Rosenberg, P., Biggar, R., & Goedert, J. (1994). Declining age at HIV infection in the U.S. *New England Journal of Medicine, 330,* 789-790.

Rosenberg, S. D., Rosenberg, H. J., & Farrell, M. P. (1999). The midlife crisis revisited. In S. L. Willis & J. D. Reid (Eds.), *Life in the middle: Psychological and social development in middle age* (pp. 47-73). San Diego, CA: Academic Press.

Rosow, I. (1976). Status and role change through the life span. In R. E. Binstock & E. Shanas (Eds.), *Handbook of aging and the social sciences* (pp. 457-482). New York: Van Nostrand Reinhold.

Rothbaum, B. O. (1997). A controlled study of eye movement desensitization and reprocessing in the treatment of posttraumatic stress disordered sexual assault victims. *Bulletin of the Meninger Clinic, 61,* 1-18.

Rothbaum, B. O., Foa, E. B., Riggs, D., Murdock, T., & Walsh, W. (1992). A prospective examination of post-traumatic stress disorder in rape victims. *Journal of Traumatic Stress, 5,* 455-475.

Rothbaum, B. O., Meadows, E. A., Resick, P., & Foy, D. W. (2000). Cognitive-behavioral therapy. In E. B. Foa, T. M. Keane, & M. Friedman (Eds.), *Effective treatments for PTSD: Practice guidelines from International Society for Traumatic Stress* (pp. 320-325). New York: Guilford.

Rotheram-Borus, M. J., & Wyche, K. F. (1994). Ethnic differences in identity development in the United States. In S. L. Archer (Ed.), *Interventions for adolescent identity development* (pp. 62-83). Thousand Oaks, CA: Sage.

Rothschild, J. M., Bates, D. W., & Leape, L. L. (2000). Preventable medical injuries in older patients. *Archives of Internal Medicine, 160*(18), 2717-2728.

Rowe, J. W., & Kahn, R. L. (1997). Successful aging. *The Gerontologist, 37*(4), 433-440.

Rowe, J. W., & Kahn, R. L. (1998). *Successful aging.* New York: Dell.

Rundall, T. G., & Bruvold, W. H. (1988). A meta-analysis of school-based smoking and alcohol use prevention programs. *Health Education Quarterly, 5,* 317-334.

Rutter, M. (1979). Protective factors in children's responses to stress and disadvantage. In M. W. Kent & J. E. Rolf (Eds.), *Primary prevention of psychopathology* (Vol. 3, pp. 49-74). Hanover, NH: University Press of New England.

Rutter, M. (1987). Psychological resilience and protective mechanisms. *American Journal of Orthopsychiatry, 57,* 316-331.

Sallis, J. F. (1993). Promoting healthful diet and physical activity. In S. G. Millstein, A. C. Petersen, & E. O. Nightingale (Eds.), *Promoting the health of adolescents: New directions for the twenty-first century* (pp. 209-241). New York: Oxford University Press.

Salter, A. C. (1995). *Transforming trauma.* Thousand Oaks, CA: Sage.

Sampler, J. (1980). Where do counseling psychologists work? What do they do? What should they do? In J. M. Whiteley (Ed.), *The history of counseling psychology* (pp. 143-167). Monterey, CA: Brooks/Cole.

San Miguel, S. K., Morrison, G. M., & Weissglass, T. (1995). The relationship of sources of support and service needs: Resilience patterns in low income Latino/Hispanic families. In H. I. McCubbin, E. A. Thompson, A. I. Thompson, & J. E. Fromer (Eds.), *Resiliency in ethnic minority families: Vol. 1. Native and immigrant American families* (pp. 385-399). Madison: University of Wisconsin System.

Sanders, D. R., & Riester, A. E. (1996). School-based counseling groups for children of divorce: Effects on the self-concepts of 5th grade children. *Journal of Child & Adolescent Group Therapy, 6,* 27-43.

Sandler, I., Wolchik, S., Braver, S., & Fogas, B. (1991). Stability and quality of life events and psychological symptomatology in children of divorce. *American Journal of Community Psychology, 19,* 501-520.

Santrock, J. W. (1986). *Life-span development* (2nd ed.). Dubuque, IA: William C. Brown.

Sarbin, T. E. (Ed.). (1986). *Narrative psychology: The storied nature of human conduct.* New York: Praeger.

Savickas, M. L. (1995). Career transitions: Introduction to the special issue. *Career Development Quarterly, 44,* 3-4.

Saywitz, K. J., Mannarino, A. P., Berliner, L., & Cohen, J. A. (2000). Treatment for sexually abused children and adolescents. *American Psychologist, 55,* 1040-1049.

Scarano, G. M., & Kalodner-Martin, C. R. (1994). A description of a continuum of eating disorders among adolescents. *American Journal of Health Promotion, 5,* 100-106.

Scarr, S. (1984). *Mother care/other care.* New York: Warner Books.

Scheer, S. D., Unger, D. G., & Brown, M. B. (1996). Adolescents becoming adults: Attributes for adulthood. *Adolescence, 31,* 127-131.

Scheibe, K. E. (1986). Self narratives and adventure. In T. R. Sarbin (Ed.), *Narrative psychology: The storied nature of human conduct* (pp. 129-151). New York: Praeger.

Scheidt, R. J., Humpherys, D. R., & Yorgason, J. B. (1999). Successful aging: What's not to like? *Journals of Applied Gerontology, 18,* 277-282.

Schinke, S. P., Botvin, G. J., Trimble, J. E., Orlandi, M. A., Gilchrist, L. D., & Locklear, V. S. (1988). Preventing substance abuse among American-Indian adolescents: A bicultural competence skills approach. *Journal of Counseling Psychology, 35,* 87-90.

Schinke, S. P., & Gilchrist, L. D. (1985). Preventing substance abuse with children and adolescents. *Journal of Consulting and Clinical Psychology, 53,* 596-602.

Schlegel, A., & Barry, H. (1991). *Adolescence: An anthropological inquiry.* New York: Free Press.

Schlossberg, N. K. (1984). *Counseling adults in transition.* New York: Springer-Verlag.

Schneer, J. A., & Reitman, F. (1990). Effects of employment gaps on the careers of MBAs: More damaging for men than for women? *Academy of Management Journal, 33,* 391-406.

Schneider, B. H., & Younger, A. J. (1996). Adolescent-parent attachment and adolescents' relations with their peers. *Youth & Society, 28,* 95-108.

Schneidman, E. S. (1986). Some essentials of suicide and some implications for response. In A. Roy (Ed.), *Suicide.* Baltimore, MD: Williams & Wilkins.

Schneidman, E. S. (1993). Some controversies in suicidology: Toward a mentalistic discipline. *Suicide and Life-Threatening Behavior, 23*(4), 292-298.

Schooler, C., & Flora, J. A. (1996). Pervasive media violence. *Annual Review of Public Health, 17,* 275-298.

Schwartz, D. J., Phares, V., Tantleff-Dunn, S., & Thompson, K. J. (1999). Body image, psychological functioning, and parental feedback regarding physical appearance. *International Journal of Eating Disorders, 25,* 339-343.

Sciarra, D. T. (1999). Multiculturalism in counseling. Itasca, IL: F. E. Peacock.

Scott, J. P. (1997). Family relationships of midlife and older women. In J. M. Coyle (Ed.), *Handbook on women and aging* (pp. 367-384). Westport, CT: Greenwood.

Scrutton, S. (1995). *Bereavement and grief.* London: Edward Arnold.

Seid, R. P. (1994). Too "close to the bone": The historical context for women's obsession with slenderness. In P. Fallon, M. A. Katzman, & S. C. Wooley (Eds.), *Feminist perspectives on eating disorders* (pp. 3-16). New York: Guilford.

Seitz, V., & Provence, S. (1990). Caregiver-focused models of early intervention. In S. J. Meisels & J. P. Shonkoff (Eds.), *Handbook of early childhood intervention* (pp. 400-427). New York: Cambridge University Press.

Sellers, D., McGrew, S., & McKinley, J. (1994). Does the promotion and distribution of condoms increase teen sexual activity? Evidence from an HIV prevention program for Latino youth. *American Journal of Public Health, 82,* 1952-1958.

Sells, C. W., & Blum, R. W. (1996). Morbidity and mortality among U.S. adolescents: An overview of data and trends. *American Journal of Public Health, 86,* 513-519.

Selman, R. L. (1980). *The growth of interpersonal understanding: Developmental and clinical analysis.* New York: Academic Press.

Sexton, T. L., & Griffin, B. L. (1997). *Constructivist thinking in counseling practice, research, and training.* New York: Teachers College Press.

Shafer, J. B. P., & Galinsky, M. D. (1989). *Models of group therapy* (2nd ed.). Englewood Cliffs, NJ: Prentice Hall.

Shaffer, D. (1988). The epidemiology of teen suicide: An examination of risk factors. *Journal of Clinical Psychiatry, 49,* 36-41.

Shaffer, D., Garland, A., Gould, M., Fisher, P., & Trautman, P. (1988). Preventing teenage suicide: A critical review. *Journal of the American Academy of Child and Adolescent Psychiatry, 27,* 675-687.

Shaffer, D., Garland, A., Vieland, V., Underwood, M., & Busner, C. (1991). The impact of curriculum-based suicide prevention programs for teenagers. *Journal of the American Academy of Child and Adolescent Psychiatry, 30*(4), 588-596.

Shaffer, D., Gould, M. S., Fisher, P., Trautment, P., Moreau, D., Kleinman, M., & Flory, M. (1996). Psychiatric diagnosis in child and adolescent suicide. *Archives of General Psychiatry, 53,* 339-348.

Shamoo, T. K., & Patros, P. G. (1990). *Helping your child cope with depression and suicidal thoughts.* New York: Lexington Books.

Shanahan, M. J., Valsiner, J., & Gottlieb, G. (1997). Developmental concepts across disciplines. In J. Tudge, M. J. Shanahan, & J. Valsiner (Eds.), *Comparisons in human development: Understanding time and context.* Cambridge, UK: Cambridge University Press.

Shanas, E. (1979). The family as a social support system in old age. *The Gerontologist, 19*, 169-174.

Sharpe, T. M., Killen, J. D., Bryson, S. W., Shisslak, C. M., Estes, L. S., Gray, N., Crago, M., & Taylor, C. B. (1998). Attachment style and weight concerns in preadolescent and adolescent girls. *International Journal of Eating Disorders, 23*, 39-44.

Shaw, D. S. (1991). The effects of divorce on children's adjustment. *Behavior Modification, 15*, 456-485.

Shelov, S. P. (Ed.). (1993). *Caring for your baby and young child.* New York: Bantam.

Sherman, L. (1992). *Policing domestic violence: Experiments and dilemmas.* New York: Free Press.

Sherman, L. W., & Berk, R. (1984). The specific deterrent effects of arrest for domestic assault. *American Sociological Review, 49*, 261-272.

Shibutani, T. (1986). *Social processes: An introduction to sociology.* Berkeley: University of California Press.

Sickmund, M., Snyder, H. N., & Poe-Yamagata, E. (1997). *Juvenile offenders and victims: 1997 update on violence.* Washington, DC: Office of Juvenile Justice and Delinquency Prevention.

Siever, M. D. (1994). Sexual orientation and gender as factors in socioculturally acquired vulnerability to body dissatisfaction and eating disorders. *Journal of Counseling and Consulting Psychology, 62*, 252-260.

Silverman, M. M., & Felner, R. D. (1995). The place of suicide prevention in the spectrum of intervention: Definitions of critical terms and constructs. *Suicide and Life-Threatening Behavior, 25*(1), 70-81.

Silverstein, L. B., & Auerbach, C. F. (1999). Deconstructing the essential father. *American Psychologist, 54*, 397-407.

Silverstone, B., & Hyman, H. K. (1998). *Growing older together: A couple's guide to understanding and coping with the challenges of later life.* New York: Pantheon.

Simeonsson, N. W., & Gray, J. N. (1994). Healthy children: Primary prevention of disease. In R. J. Simeonsson (Ed.), *Risk, resilience and prevention: Promoting the well-being of all children* (p. 102). Baltimore: Brookes.

Simeonsson, R. J. (1994). Promoting children's health, education, and well-being. In R. J. Simeonsson (Ed.), *Risk, resilience and prevention: Promoting the well-being of all children* (pp. 3-12). Baltimore: Brookes.

Simeonsson, R. J., & Bailey, D. B. (1990). Family dimensions in early intervention. In S. J. Meisels & J. B. Shonkoff (Eds.), *Handbook of early childhood intervention* (pp. 428-444). New York: Cambridge University Press.

Slaton, K. D., Lyddon, W. J., & Dale, M. A. (1999, August). *Parental bonding and women's body image satisfaction.* Poster session presented at the annual meeting of the American Psychological Association, Boston, MA.

Slavkin, M. L. (2000). The building healthy families model: Psychoeducational practice with children of divorce. *Journal of Divorce & Remarriage, 32*, 1-17.

Sloboda, Z., & David, S. L. (1997). *Preventing drug use among children and adolescents.* Bethesda, MD: National Institutes of Health.

Smith, D. E., Wesson, D. R., & Calhoun, S. R. (1997). *Rohypnol (Flunitrazepam) fact sheet.* Retrieved July 23, 1999 from the World Wide Web: http://www.lec.org/DrugSearch/Documents/Rohypnol.html

Smith, D. J., & Rutter, M. (1995). Introduction. In M. Rutter & D. J. Smith (Eds.), *Psychosocial disorders in young people: Time trends and their causes.* New York: John Wiley.

Smith, H., & Smith, S. (1999). *The retirement sourcebook*. Chicago: Roxbury Park.

Smith, M. U., & Katner, H. P. (1995). Quasi-experimental evaluation of three AIDS prevention activities for maintaining knowledge, improving attitudes, and changing risk behaviors of high school seniors. *AIDS Education and Prevention, 7,* 391-402.

Smith, S. D. (1997). The retirement transition and the later life family unit. *Public Health Nursing, 44*(1), 67-82.

Smolak, L. (1999). Elementary school curricula for the primary prevention of eating problems. In N. Piran, M. P. Levine, & C. Steiner-Adair (Eds.), *Preventing eating disorders: A handbook of interventions and special challenges* (pp. 87-104). Philadelphia: Brunner/Mazel.

Solberg, V. S., Close, W. M., & Stark, R. (1999). *African American college success: A confirmatory investigation.* Manuscript submitted for publication.

Solberg, V. S., Gusavac, N., Hamann, T., Felch, J., Johnson, J., Lamborn, S., & Torres, J. (1998). The adaptive success identity plan (ASIP): A career intervention for college students [Monograph]. *Career Development Quarterly, 47,* 48-95.

Solberg, V. S., Hale, B., Villarreal, P., & Kavanagh, J. (1993). Development of the college stress inventory for use with Hispanic populations: A confirmatory analytic approach. *Hispanic Journal of Behavioral Sciences, 15,* 490-497.

Solomon, R., & Liefeld, C. P. (1998). Effectiveness of a family support center approach to adolescent mothers: Repeat pregnancy and school drop-out rates. *Family Relations: Interdisciplinary Journal of Applied Family Studies, 47,* 139-144.

Spade, J. Z., & Reese, C. A. (1991). We've come a long way, maybe: College students' plans for work and family. *Sex Roles, 24,* 309-321.

Special Senate Committee Report on Aging. (1991). Washington, DC: Administration on Aging. Retrieved from the World Wide Web: http://www.aoa.dhhs.gov

Spirito, A., Brown, L., Overholser, J., & Fritz, G. (1989). Attempted suicide in adolescence: Review and critique of the literature. *Clinical Psychology Review, 9,* 335-363.

Spitze, G., & Logan, J. (1992). Helping as a component of parent-adult child relations. *Research on Aging, 14*(3), 291-312.

Spivack, G., & Shure, M. B. (1989). Interpersonal cognitive problem solving (ICPS): A competence-building primary prevention program. *Prevention in Human Services, 6,* 151-178.

Spock, B. (1946). *Baby and child care.* New York: Pocket Books.

Spokane, A. R. (1991). *Career intervention.* Englewood Cliffs, NJ: Prentice Hall.

Spoth, R., Reyes, M. L., Redmond, C., & Shin, C. (1999). Assessing a public health approach to delay onset and progression of adolescent substance use: Latent transition and log-linear analyses of longitudinal family preventive intervention outcomes. *Journal of Consulting and Clinical Psychology, 67,* 609-630.

Srebnik, D. S., & Saltzberg, E. A. (1994). Feminist cognitive-behavioral therapy for negative body image. *Women & Therapy, 15,* 117-133.

Sroufe, L. A., & Fleeson, J. (1986). Attachment and the construction of relationships. In W. W. Hartup & Z. Rubin (Eds.), *Relationships and development* (pp. 151-172). Hillsdale, NJ: Lawrence Erlbaum.

Stafford, M. E. (1999). Counseling and psychotherapy with children. In D. Capuzzi & D. R. Gross (Eds.), *Counseling and psychotherapy: Theories and interventions* (2nd ed., pp. 413-433). Upper Saddle River, NJ: Prentice Hall.

Stanfield, J. B. (1998). Couples coping with dual careers: A description of flexible and rigid coping styles. *Social Science Journal, 35,* 53-64.

Stanford, E. P., Peddecord, K. M., & Lockery, S. A. (1990). Variations among the elderly in Black, Hispanic, and White families. In T. H. Brubaker (Ed.), *Family relationships in later life* (2nd ed., pp. 229-241). Newbury Park, CA: Sage.

Staudinger, U. M. (1999, August). *Life review: A social-cognitive process facilitating insight into life.* Paper presented at the annual meeting of the American Psychological Association, Boston, MA.

Steele, J. R., & Brown, J. D. (1995). Adolescent room culture: Studying the media in the context of everyday life. *Journal of Youth and Adolescence, 24*(5), 551-576.

Steffy, B. D., & Ashbaugh, D. (1986). Dual-career planning, marital satisfaction and job stress among women in dual-career marriages. *Journal of Business & Psychology, 1,* 114-123.

Steiger, H., Liquornik, K., Chapman, J., & Hussain, N. (1991). Personality and family disturbances in eating-disorder patients: Comparison of "restricters" and "bingers" to normal controls. *International Journal of Eating Disorders, 10,* 501-512.

Steinberg, L. (1990). Autonomy, conflict, and harmony in the family relationship. In S. Feldman & G. Elliot (Eds.), *At the threshold: The developing adolescent* (pp. 255-276). Cambridge, MA: Harvard University Press.

Steinem, G. (1999, August/September). Supremacy crimes. *Ms., 9*(5), 44-47.

Stern, M., & Alvarez, A. (1992). Pregnant and parenting adolescents: A comparative analysis of coping response and psychosocial adjustment. *Journal of Adolescent Research, 7,* 469-493.

Stern, M., Norman, S. L., & Zevon, M. A. (1991). Career development of adolescent cancer patients: A comparative analysis. *Journal of Counseling Psychology, 38,* 431-439.

Stern, M., & Zevon, M. A. (1990). Stress, coping, and family environment: The adolescent's response to naturally occurring stressors. *Journal of Adolescent Research, 5,* 290-305.

Stevenson, M. R., & Black, K. N. (1995). *How divorce affects offspring: A research approach.* Dubuque, IA: Brown & Benchmark.

Stinnett, N., Collins, J. E., & Montgomery, J. E. (1970). Marital need satisfaction of older husbands and wives. *Journal of Marriage and Family, 32,* 428-434.

Stoller, E., & Pugliesi, K. (1989). Other roles of caregivers: Competing responsibilities or supportive services? *Journal of Gerontology, 44,* S231-S238.

Stoltz-Loike, M. (1997). Creating personal and spiritual balance: Another dimension in career development. In D. P. Bloch & L. J. Richmond (Eds.), *Connections between spirit and work in career development* (pp. 139-162). Palo Alto, CA: Consulting Psychologists Press.

Stone, G. L., & Archer, J. (1990). College and university counseling centers in the 1990s: Challenges and limits. *Counseling Psychologist, 18,* 539-607.

Stormer, S. M., & Thompson, J. K. (1996). Explanations of body image disturbance: A test of maturational status, negative verbal commentary, social comparison, and sociocultural hypotheses. *International Journal of Eating Disorders, 19,* 193-202.

Strand, P. S., & Wahler, R. G. (1996). Predicting maladaptive parenting: Role of maternal object relations. *Journal of Clinical Child Psychology, 25,* 43-51.

Strand, P. S., White, R., & Touster, L. (1998). Formal characteristics of narratives as predictors of maladaptive parenting. *Journal of Child and Family Studies, 7,* 171-186.

Straus, M. A. (1990). Ordinary violence, child abuse, and wife beating: What do they have in common? In M. A. Straus & R. J. Gelles (Eds.), *Physical violence in American families* (pp. 403-424). New Brunswick, NJ: Transaction Books.

Straus, M. A., & Smith, C. (1990). Family patterns and primary prevention of family violence. In M. A. Straus & R. J. Gelles (Eds.), *Physical violence in American families* (pp. 507-526). New Brunswick, NJ: Transaction Books.

Strober, M., & Humphrey, L. L. (1987). Familial contributions to the etiology and course of anorexia nervosa and bulimia. *Journal of Consulting and Clinical Psychology, 55,* 654-659.

Strom, R., & Strom, S. (1988). Preparing grandparents for a new role. *Journal of Applied Gerontology, 6*(4), 476-486.

Strom, R., & Strom, S. (1993). Grandparents raising grandchildren: Goals and support groups. *Educational Gerontology, 19,* 705-715.

Strom, R., Strom, S., & Collinsworth, P. (1990). Improving grandparent success. *Journal of Applied Gerontology, 9*(4), 480-491.

Sue, W. S., & Sue, D. (1999). *Counseling the culturally different: Theory and practice* (3rd ed.). New York: John Wiley.

Sullivan, S. E. (1992). Is there time for everything? Attitudes related to women's sequencing of career and family. *Career Development Quarterly, 40,* 234-243.

Super, D. E. (1957). *The psychology of careers.* New York: Harper & Row.

Super, D. E. (1969). Vocational development theory: Persons, positions, and processes. *The Counseling Psychologist, 1*(1), 2-9.

Super, D. E. (1980). A life-span, life-space approach to career development. *Journal of Vocational Behavior, 16,* 282-298.

Super, D. E. (1984). Transition: From vocational guidance to counseling psychology. In J. M. Whiteley (Ed.), *The history of counseling psychology* (pp. 16-24). Monterey, CA: Brooks/Cole.

Super, D. E. (1990). A life-span, life-space approach to career development. In D. Brown & L. Brooks (Eds.), *Career choice and development: Applying contemporary theories to practice* (pp. 197-261). San Francisco: Jossey-Bass.

Super, D. E. (1994). A life-span, life-space approach to career development. In M. L. Savickas & R. W. Lent (Eds.), *Convergence in career development theories* (pp. 63-74). Palo Alto, CA: Consulting Psychologists Press.

Surgeon General's Report on Physical Activity and Health. (1996). Hyattsville, MD: U.S. Department of Health and Human Services. Retrieved July 1999 from the World Wide Web: http://www.cdc.gov/nccdphp/sgr/sgr.htm

Takanishi, R. (2000). Preparing adolescents for social change: Designing generic social interventions. In L. Crockett & R. K. Silbereisen (Eds.), *Negotiating adolescence in times of social change* (pp. 248-293). New York: Cambridge University Press.

Tangri, S. S., & Jenkins, S. R. (1986). Stability and change in role innovation and life plans. *Sex Roles, 14,* 647-662.

Taylor, S. E., Pham, L. B., Rivkin, I. D., & Armor, D. A. (1998). Harnessing the imagination: Mental simulation, self-regulation, and coping. *American Psychologist, 53,* 429-439.

Teens Against Gang Violence. (1999). Retrieved March 11, 2001 from the World Wide Web: http://www.tagv.org

Teen Choice Awards. (1999). Los Angeles: Fox Network.

Teri, L., McCurry, S. M., & Logsdon, R. G. (1997). Memory, thinking, and aging: What we know about what we know. *Western Journal of Medicine, 167*(4), 269-275.

Tetrick, L. E., Miles, R. L., Marcil, L., & Van Dosen, C. M. (1994). Child-care difficulties and the impact on concentration, stress, and productivity among single and nonsingle mothers and fathers. In G. P. Keita & J. J. Hurrell (Eds.), *Job stress in a changing workforce: Investigating gender, diversity, and family issues* (pp. 229-239). Washington, DC: American Psychological Association.

Thompson, J. K., Heinberg, L. J., Altabe, M., & Tantleff-Dunn, S. (1999). *Exacting beauty: Theory, assessment, and treatment of body image disturbance.* Washington, DC: American Psychological Association.

Thompson, J. K. (Ed.). (1996). *Body image, eating disorders, and obesity: An integrative guide for assessment and treatment.* Washington, DC: American Psychological Association.

Thompson, L., & Walker, A. J. (1989). Women and men in marriage, work, and parenthood. *Journal of Marriage and the Family, 51,* 845-872.

Tinsley, D. J., & Schwendener-Holt, M. J. (1992). Retirement and leisure. In S. D. Brown & R. W. Lent (Eds.), *Handbook of counseling psychology* (2nd ed., pp. 627-662). New York: John Wiley.

Tinsley, H. E. A., & Tinsley, D. J. (1982). A holistic model of leisure counseling. *Journal of Leisure Research, 14,* 100-116.

Tinto, V. (1987). *Leaving college: Rethinking the causes and cures of student attrition.* Chicago: University of Chicago Press.

Tipton, R. M. (1983). Clinical and counseling psychology: A study of roles and functions. *Professional Psychology: Research and Practice, 14,* 837-846.

Tobler, N. (1986). Meta-analysis of 143 adolescent drug prevention programs: Quantitative outcome results of program participants compared to control or comparison group. *Journal of Drug Issues, 4,* 537-567.

Torres, J. B., & Solberg, V. S. (1999). *Role of self-efficacy, stress, and family support on Latino college student outcomes and well-being.* Manuscript submitted for publication.

Traupmann, J., & Hatfield, E. (1981). Love and its effect on mental and physical health. In R. W. Fogel, E. Hatfield, S. B. Kiesler, & E. Shanas (Eds.), *Aging: Stability and change in the family* (pp. 253-274). New York: Academic Press.

Traupmann, J., Hatfield, E., & Wexler, P. (1981). Equity and sexual satisfaction in dating couples. *Archives of Sexual Behavior, 22,* 33-40.

Travis, L. D. (2000). Adolescentology: Youth, their needs, and the professions at the turn of the century. In C. Violato & E. Oddone-Paolucci (Eds.), *The changing family and child development* (pp. 38-47). Aldershot, UK: Ashgate.

Trocki, K. F., & Orioli, E. M. (1994). Gender differences in stress symptoms, stress-producing contexts, and coping strategies. In G. P. Keita & J. J. Hurrell (Eds.), *Job stress in a changing workforce: Investigating gender, diversity, and family issues* (pp. 7-22). Washington, DC: American Psychological Association.

Troiden, R. R. (1989). The formation of homosexual identities. In G. Herdt (Ed.), *Gay and lesbian youth* (pp. 43-73). Binghamton, NY: Harrington Park.

Troll, L. (1971). The family of later life: A decade review. *Journal of Marriage and Family, 33,* 263-290.

Troll, L. (1983). Grandparents: The family watchdogs. In T. Brubaker (Ed.), *Family relationships in later life* (pp. 63-74). Beverly Hills, CA: Sage.

Tschann, J. M., Johnston, J. R., Kline, M., & Wallerstein, J. S. (1990). Conflict, loss, change and parent-child relationships: Predicting children's adjustment during divorce. *Journal of Divorce, 13,* 1-22.

Turner, S. L., Hamilton, H., Jacobs, M., Angood, L. M., & Dwyer, D. H. (1997). The influence of fashion magazines on the body image satisfaction of college women: An exploratory analysis. *Adolescence, 32,* 603-614.

Turner, S., Norman, E., & Zunz, S. (1995). Enhancing resiliency in girls and boys: A case for gender specific adolescent prevention programming. *Journal of Primary Prevention, 16,* 25-38.

Upcraft, M. L., & Schuh, J. H. (1996). *Assessment in student affairs: A guide for practitioners.* San Francisco: Jossey-Bass.

U.S. Bureau of the Census. (1992a). *Marital status and living arrangements, March 1990* (Current Population Reports, Series P-20). Washington, DC: Government Printing Office.

U.S. Bureau of the Census. (1992b). *Statistical abstract of the United States: The national data book* (112th ed.). Washington DC: Government Printing Office.

U. S. Bureau of the Census. (1993). *We . . . the American elderly.* Washington, DC: Government Printing Office.

U.S. Bureau of the Census. (1994). *The elderly population.* Washington, DC: Author. Retrieved from the World Wide Web: http://www.census.gov/population/www/pop-profile/elderpop.html

U.S. Bureau of the Census. (1996). *65+ in the United States.* (Current Population Reports, Special Studies, P23-190). Washington, DC: Government Printing Office.

U.S. Bureau of the Census. (1998, March). *Unpublished tables: Marital status and living arrangements.* Retrieved December 27, 2000 from the World Wide Web: http://www.census.gov/population/www/socdemo/ms-la.html

U.S. Bureau of the Census. (1999). *Statistical abstract of the United States: 1999* (119th ed). Washington, DC: Government Printing Office.

U.S. Bureau of Labor Statistics. (1993). *Employment and earnings.* Washington DC: U.S. Department of Labor.

U.S. Department of Education. (1996). National Center for Education Statistics. *Digest of Education,* 96-133. Washington DC: Government Printing Office.

U.S. Department of Health and Human Services. (1991). *Healthy People 2000: National health promotion and disease prevention objective—full report, with commentary.* Washington, DC: Government Printing Office.

U.S. Department of Health and Human Services. (1996). *Physical activity and health: A report of the surgeon general.* Atlanta, GA: Centers for Disease Control and Prevention, National Center for Chronic Disease Prevention and Health Promotion.

U.S. Department of Health and Human Services. (1998). *Healthy people 2010 objectives: Draft for public comment.* Washington, DC: Government Printing Office.

U.S. Department of Health and Human Services. (2000). *Healthy people 2010: Understanding and improving health.* Retrieved December 1, 2000 from the World Wide Web: http://www.health.gov/healthypeople/Document/Tableofcontents.htm

U.S. Department of Justice, Bureau of Justice Statistics. (1994). *National crime victimization survey: Guns and crime.* Rockville, MD: Author.

U.S. Department of Justice. (1996). *Crime in the U.S., 1995.* Washington, DC: Government Printing Office.

U.S. Department of Labor. (1999). *Facts on employment.* Washington, DC: Author.

U.S. Public Health Service. (1999). *The surgeon general's call to action to prevent suicide.* Washington, DC: Government Printing Office.

Ullman, S. E. (in press). Rape avoidance: Individual self-protection strategies for women and their implications for research and practice. In P. A. Schwewe (Ed.),

Preventing violence in relationships: Developmentally appropriate interventions across the lifespan. Washington DC: American Psychological Association.

Valde, G. A. (1996). Identity closure: A fifth identity status. *Journal of Genetic Psychology, 15,* 245-254.

Van Dusen, R. A., & Sheldon, E. B. (1976). The changing status of American women. *American Psychologist, 31,* 106-116.

Vera, E. M. , Shin, R. Q., Montgomery, G., Mildner, C., Speight, S. L., & London, L. (2000, August). *Resiliency and conflict resolution styles of urban adolescents.* Poster presentation at the annual meeting of the American Psychological Association, Washington, D.C.

Vernon, A. (1993). *Developmental assessment and intervention with children and adolescents.* Alexandria, VA: American Counseling Association.

Visher, E. B., & Visher, J. S. (1979). *Stepfamilies: Myths and realities.* New York: Carol.

Voydanoff, P. (1988). Work and family: A review and expanded conceptualization. *Journal of Social Behavior & Personality, 3,* 1-22.

Vygotsky, L. S. (1978). *Mind in society: The development of higher psychological processes.* Cambridge, MA: Harvard University Press.

Wagenaar, A., & Perry, C. L. (1994). Community strategies for the reduction of youth drinking: Theory and application. *Journal of Research on Adolescence, 4,* 319-345.

Wagner, B. M. (1997). Family risk factors for child and adolescent suicidal behavior. *Psychological Bulletin, 121*(2), 246-298.

Walco, G. A., & Varni, J. W. (1991). Cognitive-behavioral interventions for children with chronic illnesses. In P. C. Kendall (Ed.), *Child and adolescent therapy: Cognitive-behavioral procedures,* (pp. 209-244). New York: Guilford.

Waldron, I., & Jacobs, J. A. (1989). Effects of multiple roles on women's health: Evidence from a national longitudinal study. *Women & Health, 15,* 3-19.

Walker, L. E. (1994). *Abused women and survivor therapy.* Washington, DC: American Psychological Association.

Walker, L. E. (1999). Psychology and domestic violence around the world. *American Psychologist, 54,* 21-29.

Wallace, J. D., Calhoun, A. D., Powell, K. E., O'Neil, J., & James, S. P. (1996). *Homicide and suicide among Native Americans, 1979-1992* (Violence Surveillance Summary Series, No. 2). Atlanta, GA: Centers for Disease Control and Prevention, National Center for Injury Prevention and Control.

Wallace, J. I., Buchner, D. M., Grothaus, L., Leveille, S., Tyll, L., LaCroix, A. Z., & Wagner, E. H. (1998). Implementation and effectiveness of a community-based health promotion program for older adults. *Journals of Gerontology, 53A* (4), M301-M306.

Waller, G., Slade, P., & Calam, R. (1990). Family adaptability and cohesion: Relation to eating attitudes and disorders. *International Journal of Eating Disorders, 9,* 225-228.

Wallerstein, J. S., & Blakeslee, S. (1989). *Second chances: Men, women and children a decade after divorce.* New York: Ticknor & Fields.

Wallerstein, J. S., & Kelly, J. B. (1980). *Surviving the breakup: How children actually cope with divorce.* New York: Basic Books.

Walsh, F., Jacob, L., & Simons, V. (1995). Facilitating healthy divorce processes: Therapy and mediation approaches. In N. Jacobson & A. Gurman (Eds.), *Clinical handbook of couple therapy* (pp. 340-365). New York: Guilford.

Walsh, M. E., Howard, K., & Buckley, M. A. (1999). School counselors in school-community partnerships: Opportunities and challenges. *Professional School Counseling, 2,* 349-356.

Walster, E., Walster, G. W., & Berscheid, E. (1978). *Equity: Theory and research.* Boston: Allyn & Bacon.

Wandersman, A., & Nation, M. (1998). Neighborhoods and mental health: Psychological contributions to understanding toxicity resilience and interventions. *American Psychologist, 53,* 647-656.

Waters, E. B., & Goodman, J. (1990). *Empowering older adults: Practical strategies for counselors.* San Francisco: Jossey-Bass.

Watkins, C. E., Lopez, F. G., Campbell, V. L., & Himmell, C. D. (1986). Contemporary counseling psychology: Results of a national survey. *Journal of Counseling Psychology, 33,* 301-309.

Watts-Jones, D. (1990). Toward a stress scale for African-American women. *Psychology of Women Quarterly, 14,* 271-275.

Webb, N. B. (1993). Helping bereaved children: A handbook for practitioners. In N. B. Webb (Ed.), *The child and death.* New York: Guilford.

Wechsler, H. (1996). Alcohol and the American college campus: A report from the Harvard School of Public Health. *Change, 28,* 20.

Weiss, R. S. (1990). *Staying the course.* New York: Free Press.

Weissberg, R. P., Caplan, M., & Harwood, R. L. (1991). Promoting competent young people in competence-enhancing environments: A systems-based perspective on primary prevention. *Journal of Consulting and Clinical Psychology, 59,* 830-841.

Weitzman, L. M. (1994). Multiple-role realism: A theoretical framework for the process of planning to combine career and family roles. *Applied & Preventive Psychology, 3,* 15-25.

Wells, J. D., Hobfoll, S. E., & Lavin, J. (1997). Resource loss, resource gain, and communal coping during pregnancy among women with multiple roles. *Psychology of Women Quarterly, 21,* 645-662.

Werner, E. E. (1990). Protective factors and individual resilience. In S. J. Meisels & J. P. Shonkoff (Eds.), *Handbook of early childhood intervention* (pp. 97-116). New York: Cambridge University Press.

Werner, E. E., & Smith, R. S. (1982). *Vulnerable but invincible: A longitudinal study of resilient children and youth.* New York: McGraw-Hill.

Werner, E. E., & Smith, R. S. (1992). *Overcoming the odds: High risk children from birth to adulthood.* Ithaca, NY: Cornell University Press.

Whiston, S. C., & Sexton, T. L. (1998). A review of school counseling outcome research: Implications for practice. *Journal of Counseling & Development, 76,* 412-424.

Whitbourne, S. K. (1996). Psychological perspectives on the normal aging process. In L. L. Carstensen, B. A. Edelstein, & L. Dornbrand (Eds.), *The practical handbook of clinical gerontology* (pp. 3-35). Thousand Oaks, CA: Sage.

Whitbourne, S. K., & Connolly, L. A. (1999). The developing self in midlife. In S. L. Willis & J. D. Reid (Eds.), *Life in the middle: Psychological and social development in middle age* (pp. 25-46). San Diego, CA: Academic Press.

Whitbourne, S. K., & Ebmeyer, J. B. (1990). *Identity and intimacy in marriage: A study of couples.* New York: Springer-Verlag.

White, J., & Mullis, F. (1998). A systems approach to school counselor consultation. *Education, 119,* 242-252.

White, L., & Edwards, J. N. (1990). Emptying the nest and parental well-being: An analysis of national panel data. *American Sociological Review, 55*, 235-242.

White, M., & Epston, D. (1990). *Narrative means to therapeutic ends.* New York: Norton.

Whitley, J. M. (1980). *The history of counseling psychology.* Monterey, CA: Brooks/ Cole.

Wiehe, V. R. (1998). *Understanding family violence: Treating and preventing partner, child, sibling, and elder abuse.* Thousand Oaks, CA: Sage.

Wiersma, U. A. (1994). A taxonomy of behavioral strategies for coping with work-home role conflict. *Human Relations, 47*, 211-221.

Wilcox-Matthew, L., & Minor, C. W. (1989). The dual career couple: Concerns, benefits, and counseling implications. *Journal of Counseling & Development, 68*, 194-198.

Wiley, M. G. (1991). Gender, work, and stress: The potential impact of role-identity salience and commitment. *Sociological Quarterly, 32*, 495-510.

Williams, J. E., & Holmes, K. A. (1982). In judgment of victims: The social context of rape. *Journal of Sociology and Social Welfare, 9*, 154-169.

Williams, K. J., & Alliger, G. M. (1994). Role stressors, mood spillover, and perceptions of work-family conflict in employed parents. *Academy of Management Journal, 37*, 837-868.

Williams, T. (1986). *The impact of television: A natural experiment in three communities.* New York: Academic Press.

Willis, S. L., & Reid, J. D. (Eds.). (1999). *Life in the middle: Psychological and social development in middle age.* San Diego, CA: Academic Press.

Wolfe, D. A., & Wekerle, C. (1993). Treatment strategies for child physical abuse and neglect: A critical progress report. *Clinical Psychology Review, 13*, 473-500.

Wolfe, D. A., Wekerle, C., Reitzel-Jaffe, D., Grasley, C., Pittman, A. L., & Maceachran, A. (1997). Interrupting the cycle of violence: Empowering youth to promote healthy relationships. In D. A. Wolfe, R. J. McMahon, & R. D. Peters (Eds.), *Child abuse: New directions in prevention and treatment across the lifespan* (pp. 102-129). Thousand Oaks, CA: Sage.

Wood, K. C., Becker, J. A., & Thompson, J. K. (1996). Body image dissatisfaction in preadolescent children. *Journal of Applied Developmental Psychology, 17*, 85-100.

Worthington, E. L., Jr. (1989). Religious faith across the life span: Implications for counseling and research. *The Counseling Psychologist, 17*, 555-612.

Wurtele, S. K., & Miller-Perrin, C. L. (1992). *Preventing child sexual abuse: Sharing the responsibility.* Lincoln: University of Nebraska Press.

Wyatt, G. E. (1992). The sociocultural context of African American and White American women's rape. *Journal of Social Issues, 48*, 77-92.

Wyman, P. A., Cowen, E. L., Hightower, A. D., & Pedro-Carroll, J. L. (1985). Perceived competence, self-esteem, and anxiety in latency-aged children of divorce. *Journal of Clinical Child Psychology, 14*, 20-26.

Yalom, I. D. (1995). *The theory and practice of group psychotherapy* (4th ed.). New York: Basic Books.

Yauman, B. E. (1991). School-based group counseling for children of divorce: A review of the literature. *Elementary School Guidance & Counseling, 26*, 130-138.

Yolles, R. M., & Yolles, M. (2001). *Getting started in retirement planning: Comprehensive coverage.* New York: John Wiley.

Zarit, S. H., & Knight, B. G. (Eds.). (1996). *A guide to psychotherapy and aging: Effective clinical interventions in a life-stage context.* Washington, DC: American Psychological Association.

Zarit, S. H., & Zarit, J. M. (1998). *Mental disorders in older adults: Fundamentals of assessment and treatment.* New York: Guilford.

Zeiss, A. M., & Zeiss, R. A. (1999). Sexual dysfunction: Using an interdisciplinary team to combine cognitive-behavioral and medical approaches. In M. Diffy (Ed.), *Handbook of counseling and psychotherapy with older adults* (pp. 294-313). New York: John Wiley.

Zucker, R. A., & Gomberg, E. S. L. (1986). Etiology of alcoholism reconsidered: The case for a biopsychosocial process. *American Psychologist, 41,* 783-793.

Zunker, V. G. (1998). *Career counseling: Applied concepts of life planning* (5th ed.). Washington, DC: Brooks/Cole.

Zunker, V. G., & Norris, D. S. (1998). *Using assessment results for career development* (5th ed.). Belmont, CA: Brooks/Cole.

INDEX

ABOUT THE CONTRIBUTORS

José M. Abreu is Assistant Professor of Counseling Psychology at the University of Southern California and teaches a variety of undergraduate and graduate courses. He received his PhD from the University of California at Santa Barbara in 1995. He is author or coauthor of 10 refereed journal articles and 2 book chapters. His research and teaching interests are in the area of multicultural counseling.

Karissa K. Adams is a doctoral student in counseling psychology at the University of North Dakota. She received her M.A. from the University of North Dakota in 1999. She is a student member of the Association for the Advancement of Behavior Therapy and the American Psychological Association, Divisions 17 and 38.

Darlys J. Alford is Associate Professor of Psychology at the University of Southern Mississippi, Gulf Coast campus, and teaches undergraduate courses in psychology. She is a licensed professional counselor in a private practice group with Dr. William J. Lyddon. This is their fourth book chapter collaboration. She received her master's degree in clinical psychology from California State University at Fresno in 1978 and her PhD in social psychology from the University of California at Santa Barbara in 1991.

Donald R. Atkinson is Professor of Education in the combined Counseling/Clinical/School Psychology Program at the University of California at Santa Barbara. He received his PhD from the University of Wisconsin in 1970. He is a Fellow in the American Psychological Society and the American Psychological Association, Divisions 17 and 45. He is coauthor of *Counseling American Minorities: A Cross-Cultural Perspective* (now in its 5th edition), *Counseling Non-Ethnic American Minorities,* and *Counseling Diverse Populations* (now in its 2nd edition). He is also author or coauthor of over 130 journal articles, most of which report the results of research on cultural variables in counseling.

Stephanie San Miguel Bauman is Assistant Professor of Counseling Psychology at Washington State University. She also coordinates the EdM in Counseling Program at the WSU Tri-Cities campus and is working on a project about the role of school counselors in school reform. She received her PhD from the University of California at Santa Barbara in 1995. Her research interests include risk and resiliency factors for children of color, children with disabilities, and their families. She has published in the areas of social support and Latino adolescents and families, learning disabilities and social skills, and multicultural counseling.

Monica Bigler is a doctoral student in counseling psychology in the Department of Psychology at the University of Florida, where she also serves as the coordinator of the Peer Counseling Program. She has worked as a teacher for children with mental disabilities as well as a counselor and administrative assistant in various social settings, including a home for the elderly and CARITAS Switzerland, an international human service organization. She has conducted workshops on career-related issues and academic enhancement.

Wendy Close is a doctoral student in urban education (counseling psychology emphasis) at the University of Wisconsin at Milwaukee. She was the original coordinator of the mental health component of the Achieving Success Identity Pathways curriculum in a low-income high school setting. Her research interests and subject of her dissertation involves the integration of Self-Determination Theory and Social Cognitive Theory as it relates to promoting academic and mental health outcomes of diverse low-income youths.

Merith Cosden is Professor and Director of Training for the combined Counseling/Clinical/School Psychology Program at the University of California at Santa Barbara. She received her PhD in clinical psychology from the University of New Mexico in 1980 with a focus on child clinical psychology and learning disabilities. Most of her recent work has been conducted in collaboration with community-based service agencies, including the courts, probation department, substance abuse treatment providers, and a clinic serving children and families who have experienced abuse or neglect. Her research addresses the multiple risk and protective factors that affect the psychological well-being of children and families. She is author or coauthor of over 50 articles and chapters.

Carolyn Zerbe Enns is Associate Professor of Psychology at Cornell College in Mt. Vernon, Iowa. She received her PhD in counseling psychology from the University of California at Santa Barbara in 1987. She is a Fellow of the American Psychological Association, Division 35 (Psychology of Women). In 1998, she received the Woman of the Year Award by the APA Section for the Advancement of Women (Counseling Psychology). She is author of *Feminist Theories and Feminist Psychotherapies: Origins, Themes, and Variations* (1997) and approximately 25 articles and chapters, most of which focus on feminist therapy and feminist pedagogy.

Michael D. Gaubatz is Assistant Professor of Counseling at the University of Texas at San Antonio. He received his PhD in counseling psychology from Loyola University Chicago in 1998. His research interests include child and adolescent psychotherapy, the social and cultural construction of "mental health" in psychotherapy interventions, and professional fitness review and remediation in counseling and psychotherapy training programs.

Maria Gutierrez is Adjunct Professor at the University of Missouri at Columbia. She teaches play therapy and counseling children and supervises graduate students in administering psychological assessments through the Assessment and Consultation Clinic in the Department of Educational and Counseling Psychology. She is a licensed psychologist and has a private practice in which she specializes in working with children and families. She received her PhD from the University of California at Santa Barbara in 1996.

Marybeth Hallett is Assistant Director and a staff psychologist at the University of Illinois Counseling Center in Urbana-Champaign. She received her PhD in 1994 from the University of Texas at Austin and completed her predoctoral clinical internship at the University of Missouri at Columbia. She is a member of the American Psychological Association, the American Group Psychotherapy Association, and the Association of Women in Psychology. Her primary research interests have been women's career development and dual-career relationships. Her primary clinical interest is the practice of group psychotherapy.

Mary J. Heppner is Associate Professor in the Department of Educational and Counseling Psychology at the University of Missouri and Associate Director of the Career Center on campus. Her areas of research interest are rape prevention interventions, adult career development, and multicultural training issues. She has authored over 60 research articles on these topics and recently coauthored *Career Counseling: Process, Issues and Techniques*. She was recently awarded the Kemper Fellowship for Outstanding Teaching and the American Psychological Association, Division 17, Early Scientist Practitioner Award.

Sue C. Jacobs is Associate Professor and Director of the Counseling Psychology Program in the Department of Counseling at the University of North Dakota in Grand Forks. She received her PhD from the University of Southern

Mississippi in 1989 and did her postdoctoral work at what is now the Mind/Body Medical Institute at Harvard University. She has presented and authored or coauthored articles or chapters on issues related to aging, older adults, women's health, and behavioral medicine. She is active in several professional associations, including the Counseling Health Psychology Section of the American Psychological Association, Division 17, and the Association for the Advancement of Behavior Therapy.

Cindy L. Juntunen is Associate Professor and Chair of the Department of Counseling at the University of North Dakota. She is currently directing an action research project designed to increase career aspirations and enhance work satisfaction for people moving from welfare to self-sufficiency. She received her PhD from the University of California at Santa Barbara in 1994. Her research interests include vocational psychology, supervision, and social action. She has published in the areas of career development for women and Native Americans, school-to-work, and supervision.

Lori R. Kogan is a doctoral student in the Counseling Psychology Program at Colorado State University. She received her M.S. in experimental psychology from Colorado State University in 1997. Her research interests include health psychology and women's issues, and she is involved in both research and clinical work with adults and older individuals. She has provided therapy to a geriatric population for the past year and is author of several journal articles.

Gregory S. Lambeth is a licensed clinical psychologist employed by the University of Illinois Counseling Center. He holds adjunct faculty appointments in the College of Veterinary Medicine and in the Educational Psychology Department. He also consults with the Graduate College, where he conducts dissertation completion workshops and provides individual consultation to graduate students who have difficulty completing their theses. He has also been involved with providing services for students who have cognitive and psychiatric disabilities.

Susana M. Lowe is a researcher and program coordinator at the Asian and Pacific Islander American Health Forum, a national nonprofit policy and advocacy organization. She received her PhD from the University of California at Santa Barbara in the Counseling/Clinical/School Psychology Program and was formerly an Assistant Professor in the Counseling, Developmental, and Educational Psychology Department at Boston College. She is on the editorial board of *Journal of Multicultural Counseling and Development* and on the executive board of the Asian American Psychological Association. She has published and presented in the areas of Asian American mental health, cultural competency, intersections of diversity, and interpersonal coping with discrimination.

William J. Lyddon is Associate Professor of Psychology and Director of Training of the Counseling Psychology Doctoral Program at the University of Southern Mississippi. He received his PhD from the University of California at Santa Barbara in 1989. He has served on the editorial boards of several scholarly journals and is currently assistant editor for *Journal of Cognitive Psychotherapy,* consulting editor for *Counseling Psychology Quarterly,* and an executive board member of the International Association of Cognitive Psychotherapy. He has authored or coauthored 10 book chapters and over 60 journal articles, mostly on the topics of adult attachment, cognitive and constructivist counseling, and conceptual and philosophical issues in counseling.

Jackqueline Mascher is a second-year doctoral student in the Counseling Psychology Program at Boston College. She completed an MEd in counseling and human services and an MEd in social restoration at Lehigh University. She is a student affiliate of the American Psychological Association, Divisions 35, 44, and 45, and has published and presented in areas that address intersections of diversity as well as issues of power and privilege.

Linda G. Matthews is Assistant Professor of Counselor Education and Counseling Psychology at Arizona State University. She received her PhD in counseling psychology from the University of California at Santa Barbara. In addition to her interest in factors impacting career development and satisfaction, she has maintained a research interest in examining traditional and alternative help-seeking behavior among racial and ethnic minority populations. Currently, she is investigating issues of spirituality and religion as they relate to identity development, resilience, and other psychological processes among racial and ethnic minority populations.

A. J. Metz is a doctoral student in urban education (counseling psychology emphasis) at the University of Wisconsin at Milwaukee. She coordinated and administered the Achieving Success Identity Pathways curriculum during a 2-year period.

Helen A. Neville is Associate Professor in the Department of Educational and Counseling Psychology and the Black Studies Program at the University of Missouri at Columbia. She graduated from the Counseling Psychology Program at the University of California at Santa Barbara in 1992. Her research interests focus on general and cultural factors influencing the stress and coping processes of racial and ethnic minority populations, including African American rape survivors and African American students attending predominantly White universities, evaluating the effectiveness of diversity related programs, and multicultural education.

Michael D. Newcomb is Professor of Counseling Psychology and Chairperson of the Division of Counseling Psychology at the University of Southern California. He is also Research Psychologist and Codirector of the Substance Abuse Research Center in the Psychology Department at the University of California at Los Angeles. He received his PhD in clinical psychology from UCLA and is a licensed clinical psychologist in the state of California. He is principal investigator on several grants from the National Institute on Drug Abuse. His research interests include etiology and consequences of adolescent drug abuse; structural equation modeling, methodology, and multivariate analysis; human sexuality; health psychology; attitudes and affect related to nuclear war; etiology and consequences of childhood trauma; and cohabitation, marriage, and divorce. He has published over 200 articles and chapters, two books on drug problems, and one book on sexual abuse and development of women.

Joan I. Rosenberg is Assistant Professor in the Division of Counseling Psychology at the University of Southern California. She received her PhD from the University of Missouri at Columbia in 1986. She is Chair of the Supervision Interest Group for the American Psychological Association, Division 17, and serves on the Education and Training Board and Foundation Board of the California Psychological Association. She has been a practicing clinician for over 20 years. Her research interests focus primarily on clinical training and supervision and the integration of cognitive psychology principles and technology on clinical training.

Karen D. Slaton is an intern at Tulane University School of Medicine in New Orleans. She is completing her PhD in counseling psychology at the University of Southern Mississippi. Her research interests include body image disturbance and disordered eating, psychological interventions for cardiac patients, and women's issues in counseling.

V. Scott Solberg is Associate Professor at the University of Wisconsin at Milwaukee. He received his PhD from the University of California at Santa Barbara in 1989. He is the founder and director of Achieving Success Identity Pathways, a psychoeducational curriculum that improves the academic and mental health outcomes of precollege and college youths. He is an active member of the Society for Vocational Psychology, a section in Division 17 (Counseling Psychology) of the American Psychological Association. His research interests involve improving the academic, occupational, and life outcomes of diverse and low-income populations.

Diane J. Tinsley is a research psychologist in the Psychology Department at the University of Florida and Professor in the WLRA International Centre of Excellence at Waugeningen Agricultural University in the Netherlands. She received her PhD in psychology from the University of Minnesota. She is a Diplomate of the American Board of Vocational Experts and a Fellow of the American Psychological Association. She has served on the editorial boards of four prominent psychology journals and as a manuscript reviewer for several other psychology journals. She has authored over 30 publications and has conducted workshops and presented numerous papers dealing with leisure psychology, retirement, counseling psychology, student services, psychological measurement, and assessment. She is the 1990 recipient of the Outstanding Publication Award of the Commission on Assessment of the American College Personnel Association.

Tammi Vacha-Haase is Assistant Professor in the Psychology Department and Associate Director of Training for the Counseling Psychology Doctoral Program at Colorado State University. She received her PhD in counseling psychology from Texas A&M in 1995. She maintains a limited clinical practice, where she provides therapeutic treatment for adults experiencing developmental transitions. Research interests include professional issues, graduate training, and assessment/evaluation.

Elizabeth Vera is Associate Professor in the Department of Leadership, Foundations, and Counseling Psychology and the Director of Training of the Counseling Psychology Doctoral Program at Loyola University Chicago. She received her PhD from Ohio State University in 1993. Her research and scholarly interests include prevention and resiliency promotion, ethnic identity development, multicultural training, and process/outcome variables in multicultural counseling.

Krislea E. Wegner is a doctoral student in the Counseling Psychology Program at the University of North Dakota. She received her MS in clinical psychology from North Dakota State University in 1999. She is involved in both research and clinical work with children and families and provides therapy in a human service center, primarily focusing on children and families. Her research interests include eating disorders, health psychology, and supervision.

Elizabeth Nutt Williams is Assistant Professor of Psychology at St. Mary's College of Maryland. She teaches counseling-related courses as well as courses in the Women's Studies program. She received her PhD in counseling psychology in 1997 from the University of Maryland. Her primary research interests lie in women's career development, feminist and multicultural approaches to counseling, and the process of psychotherapy. She has also helped develop a qualitative research strategy called Consensual Qualitative Research (CQR).